Educating Deaf Learners

Perspectives on Deafness

Series Editors
Marc Marschark
Patricia Elizabeth Spencer

The Gestural Origin of Language
David F. Armstrong and Sherman E. Wilcox

Teaching Deaf Learners: Psychological and Developmental Foundations
Harry Knoors and Marc Marschark

The People of the Eye: Deaf Ethnicity and Ancestry
Harlan Lane, Richard C. Pillard, and Ulf Hedberg

A Lens on Deaf Identities
Irene W. Leigh

Deaf Cognition: Foundations and Outcomes
Edited by Marc Marschark and Peter C. Hauser

Sign Language Interpreting and Interpreter Education: Directions for Research and Practice
Edited by Marc Marschark, Rico Peterson, and Elizabeth A. Winston

Bilingualism and Bilingual Deaf Education
Edited by Marc Marschark, Gladys Tang, and Harry Knoors

Early Literacy Development in Deaf Children
Connie Mayer and Beverly J. Trezek

The World of Deaf Infants: A Longitudinal Study
Kathryn P. Meadow-Orlans, Patricia Elizabeth Spencer, and Lynn Sanford Koester

Advances in the Sign Language Development of Deaf Children
Edited by Brenda Schick, Marc Marschark, and Patricia Elizabeth Spencer

Advances in the Spoken Language Development of Deaf and Hard-of-Hearing Children
Edited by Patricia Elizabeth Spencer and Marc Marschark

Educating Deaf Learners

Creating a Global Evidence Base

EDITED BY

Harry Knoors
Marc Marschark

OXFORD
UNIVERSITY PRESS

OXFORD
UNIVERSITY PRESS

Oxford University Press is a department of the University of Oxford. It furthers the University's objective of excellence in research, scholarship, and education by publishing worldwide.

Oxford New York
Auckland Cape Town Dar es Salaam Hong Kong Karachi
Kuala Lumpur Madrid Melbourne Mexico City Nairobi
New Delhi Shanghai Taipei Toronto

With offices in
Argentina Austria Brazil Chile Czech Republic France Greece
Guatemala Hungary Italy Japan Poland Portugal Singapore
South Korea Switzerland Thailand Turkey Ukraine Vietnam

Published in the United States of America by
Oxford University Press
198 Madison Avenue, New York, NY 10016

Library of Congress Cataloging-in-Publication Data
Educating deaf learners : creating a global evidence base / edited by Harry Knoors and Marc Marschark.
pages cm. — (Perspectives on deafness)
Includes bibliographical references and index.
ISBN 978–0–19–021519–4
1. Deaf—Education. I. Knoors, Harry, editor. II. Marschark, Marc, editor.
HV2430.E3798 2015
371.91′2—dc23
2014046013

9 8 7 6 5 4 3 2 1
Printed in the United States of America
on acid-free paper

Contents

Preface

A funny thing happened on the way to the 21st century. In a variety of domains, there were new calls for data to support decision making and for evidence-based practice. As this shift began in the education of deaf and hard-of-hearing children, perhaps more slowly or somewhat later than in other fields, it coincided with advances in technology and medicine that were nothing short of revolutionary for deaf children, their parents, and their teachers. But as Tom Waits, an American singer-songwriter, wrote, "The large print giveth, and the small print taketh away." Deaf infants with severe or multiple disabilities at birth were surviving and even thriving as never before, although this meant that teachers were faced with even greater individual differences in deaf learners than they had encountered before (not always successfully). Advances in child development, psychology, and linguistics were giving new insights into the cognitive and language development of deaf children, although individual differences both among those children and the perspectives of various stakeholders often added to controversies surrounding language and instructional methods in deaf education. Heightened visibility and empowerment within the Deaf community led to some deaf (and hearing) individuals pushing for a greater role in determining the structure and philosophy of deaf education, although perhaps too often on the basis of "moral reasoning" rather than empirical evidence of what works, for which children, in what contexts. And so, we have come back to new calls for data to support decision making and for evidence-based practice.

Various countries have approached the above paradigm shift in different ways. In the United States, for example, the 1975 Education of All Handicapped Children Act (PL 94-142) and subsequent amendments mandated the development of Individualized Education Programs (IEPs) for each child requiring special educational programming. These were designed to provide evidence-based practice at the level of the individual, including consideration of communication needs (e.g., language level and the child's and family's preferred modes of communication); potential for using residual hearing with or without amplification; and social, emotional, and cultural needs (e.g., opportunities for interactions and communication with peers). Perhaps most importantly, the law gave parents a greater role in educational decision making for their deaf children, even if many still do not understand their rights fully or encounter barriers in IEP planning and in receiving IEP services. In 2004, Ireland passed the Education for Persons with Special Educational Needs Act, which required that all special education be evidence based. While a laudable goal, the complexities of bringing Irish deaf education in line with the international evidence base, together with the ill health of the Celtic Tiger, have made implementation of the law challenging. Finally, the 2006 United Nations Convention on the Rights of Persons with Disabilities called for not only recognition, promotion, and facilitating the learning of sign language, but also promotion of the linguistic identity of the Deaf community. Yet what is one to do, then, with the Convention's call for ensuring that the education of children, including those who are deaf, is delivered in "the most appropriate languages and modes and means of communication for the individual" (Article 24, Section 3.c.)? What one is to do is not to claim that this must be interpreted as either sign language or spoken language for all, but to defer again to individualized, evidence-based practice and ensure that each deaf child receives language instruction (and instruction in a language) that best fits his or her strengths and needs. That is, we need to recognize that a one-size-fits-all approach is neither effective nor moral.

Whether failures to carry through on initiatives and declarations like those just mentioned are seen as the result of ignorance, circumstances, or willful oppression is a matter of perspective. There can be no doubt that regardless of one's worldview, the goal in any enlightened society is to provide deaf children—indeed all children—with the skills and tools they need to succeed socially, economically, and personally. This certainly is no panacea, given the exponential changes we are experiencing in our 21st-century world as a result of globalization and "informatization." The extent to which this can be achieved in any particular family, community, or nation, however, will vary widely. The best we can do as stakeholders in deaf education is to obtain information through research and practice, package it in a form that can be used by those on the front lines of education (whether in parenting, teaching, or policymaking), and assist in bridging the gap from abstract principles to daily implementation. Given the size of the challenge and the relatively small size of the group we are working for and with (deaf learners), a collaborative, global effort is needed.

We emphasize later that this effort does not require starting from scratch. There is a wealth of knowledge already available about how deaf children learn, appropriate methods of instruction for various content and contexts, and likely outcomes given the differing characteristics of deaf learners. What we need to do is to better organize, understand, and share what we have, find and fill gaps in our knowledge and/or methods of implementation, and communicate better that there are no easy or uniform answers to educating a population as diverse and complex as deaf children. We have no doubt that when we get to the mountains, there will be a way through. We hope that this volume will help to find that way.

Harry Knoors
Marc Marschark
Sint-Michielsgestel, The Netherlands
Rochester, New York, USA
September 2014

Contributors

Shirin D. Antia
University of Arizona
College of Education
Tucson, Arizona USA

Sue Archbold
The Ear Foundation
Nottingham, United Kingdom

Evelien Broekhof
Developmental and Educational Psychology
Leiden University
Leiden, The Netherlands

Marieke Bruin
Faculty of Arts and Education
Department of Education and Sports Science
University of Stavanger
Stavanger, Norway

Maria Cristina Caselli
Institute of Cognitive Sciences and Technologies
National Research Council
Rome, Italy

Stephanie W. Cawthon
Department of Educational Psychology
The University of Texas at Austin
Austin, Texas USA

Kathryn Crowe
Research Institute for Professional Practice, Learning, and Education
Charles Sturt University
Sydney, Australia

Annet de Klerk
Royal Dutch Kentalis
Kentalis Talent
Vught, The Netherlands

Leo De Raeve
Independent Information and Research Center on Cochlear Implants
Zonhoven, Belgium

Meinou de Vries
Dutch Foundation for the Deaf and Hard-of-Hearing Child
Amsterdam, The Netherlands

Evelien Dirks
Dutch Foundation for the Deaf and Hard-of-Hearing Child
Amsterdam, The Netherlands

Susan R. Easterbrooks
Department of Educational Psychology and Special Education
Georgia State University
Atlanta, Georgia USA

Johannes Fellinger
Hospital of St. John of God
Institut fuer Sinnes-und Sprachneurologie
Linz, Austria

Connie Fortgens
Royal Auris Group
Gouda, The Netherlands

Chantal Gervedink Nijhuis
Royal Dutch Kentalis
Kentalis Academy
Sint-Michielsgestel,
The Netherlands

Rosalind Herman
Language and Communication Science Division
City University
Northampton Square
London, United Kingdom

Daan Hermans
Royal Dutch Kentalis
Kentalis Academy
Sint-Michielsgestel,
The Netherlands and
Behavioural Science Institute
Radboud University Nijmegen
Nijmegen, The Netherlands

Manfred Hintermair
University of Education
Heidelberg, Germany

Daniel Holzinger
Hospital of St. John of God
Institut fuer Sinnes- und Sprachneurologie
Linz, Austria

Jet Isarin
Royal Dutch Kentalis
Kentalis Academy
Sint-Michielsgestel,
The Netherlands

Lizet Ketelaar
Leiden University
Department of Developmental Psychology
Leiden, The Netherlands

Harry Knoors
Royal Dutch Kentalis
Kentalis Academy
Sint-Michielsgestel,
The Netherlands and
Behavioural Science Institute
Radboud University Nijmegen
Nijmegen, The Netherlands

Scholastica Lam
Centre for Sign Linguistics and Deaf Studies
Chinese University of Hong Kong
Shatin, Hong Kong

Greg Leigh
RIDBC Renwick Centre
Parramatta, Australia

Michella Maiorana-Basas
Department of Counseling, Educational Psychology, and Special Education
Michigan State University
East Lansing, Michigan USA

Marc Marschark
Center for Education Research Partnerships
National Technical Institute for the Deaf
Rochester Institute of Technology
Rochester, New York USA

Gary Morgan
Deafness, Cognition and Language Research Centre
Language and Communication Science
City University London
London, United Kingdom

Anouk P. Netten
Department of Otorhinolaryngology, Head, and Neck Surgery
Leiden University Medical Center
Leiden, The Netherlands

Daniela Onofrio
Institute of Cognitive Sciences and Technologies
National Research Council
Rome, Italy

Claudia M. Pagliaro
Professions in Deafness
School of Education
University of North Carolina—Greensboro
Greensboro, North Carolina USA

Carolien Rieffe
Developmental Psychology
Leiden University
Leiden, The Netherlands

Pasquale Rinaldi
Institute of Cognitive Sciences and Technologies
National Research Council
Rome, Italy

Eliane Segers
Behavioural Science Institute
Radboud University Nijmegen
Nijmegen, The Netherlands

Ruth Swanwick
School of Education
University of Leeds
Leeds, United Kingdom

Gladys Tang
Centre for Sign Linguistics and Deaf Studies
Chinese University of Hong Kong
Shatin, Hong Kong

Arie Terpstra
Royal Dutch Kentalis
Kentalis Academy
Sint-Michielsgestel, The Netherlands

Corrie Tijsseling
Department of Pedagogical and Educational Sciences
Faculty of Social and Behavioral Sciences
Utrecht University
Utrecht, The Netherlands

Elena Tomasuolo
Institute of Cognitive Sciences and Technologies
National Research Council
Rome, Italy

Lian van Berkel-van Hoof
Radboud University Nijmegen
Behavioural Science Institute
Nijmegen, The Netherlands

Annelies van der Eijk
Royal Dutch Kentalis
Dr. P.C.M. Bosschool
Arnhem, The Netherlands

Guida Veiga
Departamento de Desporto e Saúde
Pavilhão Gimnodesportivo da Universidade de Évora
Évora, Portugal

Ludo Verhoeven
Behavioural Science Institute
Radboud University Nijmegen
Nijmegen, The Netherlands

Brigitte Vugs
Royal Dutch Kentalis
Kentalis Academy
Sint-Michielsgestel, The Netherlands

Loes Wauters
Royal Dutch Kentalis
Kentalis Academy
Sint-Michielsgestel, The Netherlands

Karin Wiefferink
Dutch Foundation for the Deaf and Hard-of-Hearing Child
Amsterdam, The Netherlands

Nina Wolters
Royal Dutch Kentalis
Kentalis Academy
Sint-Michielsgestel, The Netherlands

Chris Kun-Man Yiu
Centre for Sign Linguistics and Deaf Studies
Chinese University of Hong Kong
Shatin, Hong Kong

Anat Zaidman-Zait
Department of School Counseling and Special Education
Constantiner School of Education
Tel-Aviv University
Tel Aviv, Israel

1

Educating Deaf Students in a Global Context

Harry Knoors and Marc Marschark

EDUCATING DEAF STUDENTS: CREATING A GLOBAL EVIDENCE BASE

Formal education of deaf students had its origins in the late 18th century in France, where Abbé de l'Épée started the Paris-based Institute National des Sourds-Muets in 1760, soon followed by Samuel Heinicke's founding of a school for the deaf in Leipzig, Germany, in 1778. Only a few years later schools for the deaf were established in the United Kingdom (1783, London), the United States (1817, Hartford, Connecticut), the Netherlands (1790, Groningen), and many more Western countries. Thus, institutionalized deaf education has existed for over 250 years. Given this long history (for an overview, see e.g., Lane, 1984; Lang, 2011), why is it then that there is a need for a book about the creation of a global evidence base in deaf education, as the title of this volume suggests?

From the first moment of the establishment of schools for the deaf, the field of deaf education has been divided by radically different views with respect to communication and language. Should deaf students be allowed to sign or must they learn to speak? This apparently very simple and simplistic question, phrased in black-and-white terms, has caused many teachers and researchers to put their energies into an endless and, by now we know, not very fruitful, normative and ideological debate about the way parents, teachers, and deaf students should communicate with each other (Knoors & Marschark, 2012). To their detriment, many more teachers, parents, and deaf students themselves have felt torn between these rather extreme ideological opinions. This 200-year "war of methods" (Lang, 2011; Tellings, 1995)—and the time and resources (economic and human) spent fighting it—is one of the main reasons why scholars reviewing research in deaf education in recent years unfortunately had to conclude that the evidence base for many practices in deaf education is weak (Easterbrooks & Stephenson, 2006; Luckner & Cooke, 2010; Luckner, Sebald, Cooney, Young, & Muir, 2005/2006; Spencer & Marschark, 2010).

This is not to say that there is no research evidence at all to support current methods of educating deaf learners. Part of the problem is that the research evidence that is available often is not used in deaf education, either because it is not known or fully understood by practitioners or because it is not implemented (Knoors & Marschark, 2014; Swanwick & Marschark, 2010; see also Easterbrooks & Maiorana-Basas, Chapter 7 in this volume). The gap between research and practice thus is considerable, leading Knoors and Marschark (2014, p. vii), in their review of the research literature about teaching deaf learners, to conclude that "more research could and should be done to support teaching practices with deaf students. But there is already an impressive stock of studies inside and outside of fields related to deaf education that could and should influence teaching deaf and hard-of-hearing learners."

One thing the available research does make clear: Deaf students are not hearing students who cannot hear. The learning profiles of deaf and hearing learners differ, sometimes in subtle ways, sometimes in not so subtle ways. Perhaps most centrally, deaf students differ from hearing students in their access to and proficiency in the language of instruction. Many deaf students function as bimodal bilinguals, using in their daily lives both spoken and signed language, albeit with considerable interindividual (and intraindividual) variation in their language proficiencies (Marschark, Tang, & Knoors, 2014). Differences also are well documented in language-related domains such as reading and writing (Easterbrooks & Beal-Alvarez, 2013). But differences between learning profiles of deaf and hearing students also extend to other domains that affect formal and informal learning. In the cognitive domain, visual perception, attention, working memory, and metacognition are but a few of the cognitive processes in which deaf students generally have been found to function differently compared to their hearing peers (Hermans, Vugs, Van Berkel, & Knoors, Chapter 11 in this volume; Marschark & Hauser, 2008; Marschark & Knoors, 2012; Morgan; Chapter 12 in this volume). And, finally, learning-related differences also are found in social and emotional functioning (Hintermair, Chapter 13; Wolters & Isarin, Chapter 14; Fellinger & Holzinger, Chapter 17; Rieffe, Netten, Broekhof, & Veiga, Chapter 16; Wiefferink, de Vries, & Ketelaar, Chapter 20; all in this volume).

Contrary to what some expected, early cochlear implantation may have changed the nature or expression of some of the above differences, but it did not diminish them. Cochlear implantation has not changed deaf learners into hearing learners, but it has increased the individual differences among deaf learners and, hence, the challenges of deaf education. Therefore, if we want to educate deaf students effectively and efficiently, we can learn a lot from the existing evidence base in general education, but we also have to understand and accommodate the specific educational needs of deaf students. Educating deaf students is not simply educating hearing ones who cannot hear, either when they are in special schools for the deaf or in regular schools. Inclusive education cannot fully match the needs of deaf students in mainstream classrooms without adapting instruction to their specific strengths and needs.

As several chapters in this volume demonstrate, designing specific educational interventions for deaf students, and studying their effectiveness, requires considerable effort. Such interventions have to be constructed for a relatively small group of students and require solid expertise in teaching deaf students. International cooperation in creating global, reliable evidence is an important way forward if we want to be successful in designing and implementing effective and sustainable interventions within an acceptable level of personal and financial resources. This is all the more important because the world in which we live, study, and work is changing rapidly and exponentially and will do so in the foreseeable future. These changes have consequences for both hearing and deaf students and the ways we educate them. But given the differences between deaf and hearing learners, the ways in which we may enable deaf students to meet societal demands differ to some extent from those that seem appropriate for their hearing peers.

THE TIMES THEY ARE A-CHANGIN'

Bob Dylan already sensed it in 1964, "The times they are a-changin." But compared to the world we are living in 50 years later, Dylan had seen nothing yet. Of course, change is always occurring. But the changes we, deaf and hearing people alike, are witnessing in today's 21st-century world are bigger and happen faster than ever before. They seem exponential. Change is not only limited to our physical environments, for example, through urbanization and climate change, or to our demography (because of mortality, fertility, and migration). Change also is apparent in our connections, communications, and relations with each other. Much of these latter changes are driven by technology.

Technological developments in the domain of transport have made it possible for us to visit people around the globe, often in no more than 24 to 36 hours, no matter how far they live from us. Developments in transport have hugely enhanced the mobility of people, bringing into contact people from very diverse cultural and linguistic backgrounds. At the same time, information technology has made it possible for us to be far more connected to people than ever before, without physically visiting them, a development that has had a profound impact on deaf individuals in particular (Lang, 2000). Although the global growth in telecommunication capacity has been less than in computer computation capacity, with an estimated annual growth rate of 28%, the former is still impressive (Hilbert & López, 2011). Through telephone, email, social networking, and video chat connections such as Skype or FaceTime, we are able to communicate in speech, sign language, or script whenever we want and wherever we and our communication partners are. Interaction and communication are no longer constrained by time and space. Although the growth in global computing capacity seems to be slowing down a bit, there is no sign at all that there is a delay in the increasing speed of information processing. This speed is mainly determined by the processing capacity of microchips, and it thus seems that in the telecommunications domain, Moore's law still counts. Every two years, the capacity of microchips doubles (Moore, 1965/1998), fueling exponential growth in transmission of information. Such growth has real potential for how, when, and where we educate our children and opens new possibilities for educating deaf children and others with special needs—that is, if we know how, when, and where to use them.

More and more people are witnessing and being subjected to these changes, becoming part of them as agents and/or patients. The world population continues to rise, although rather unevenly in different parts of our globe. Currently the world population stands at 7.2 billion people (United Nations, 2013) and is expected to rise to 8.1 billion in 2025, with a further increase to 9.6 billion in 2050 and 10.9 billion in 2100. The expected additional 3.7 billion extra people in 2100 will live predominantly in developing countries, while the population in more developed countries is expected to be fairly stable. Much of the growth is due to declining mortality rates, since fertility rates are expected to slow down in developing countries and have been rather low in many developed countries for some time (Bloom & Canning, 2004; Lam & Leibbrandt, 2013). The global population of children under four years of age has been quite stable since 1990. It is noteworthy, however, that as infant mortality decreases, deaf children with multiple disabilities—who would not have lived in the past—create additional challenges for deaf education as well as for parents and medical professionals (Van Dijk, Nelson, Postma, & Van Dijk, 2010).

These and other fast and far-reaching changes in our world have a tremendous impact on people, hearing and deaf. Ways of living and our living environments are influenced, to quite a considerable degree, not only by local developments but sometimes even more so by global factors. The rest of the world has entered the lives of people in even the smallest villages, and the reverse, as many people, including those living in hamlets and villages in remote areas, now travel the world physically and virtually.

The Spanish sociologist Manual Castells (2010, p. 395) has described the promise of the 21st century, the Information Age as he called it, as "the unleashing of unprecedented productive capacity by the power of the mind. I think, therefore I produce." According to Castells, "the generation of wealth, the exercise of power, and the creation of cultural codes came to depend on the technological capacity of societies and individuals, with information technologies as the core of this capacity" (p. 372). It is in and for this 21st century of globalization and informatization that deaf students have to be educated.

GLOBALIZATION AND INFORMATIZATION

The trend toward an increasingly interconnected world with global developments that affect all its inhabitants wherever they live is called globalization (Stromquist & Monkman, 2014). According to Gibson-Graham (2006, p. 120), globalization is "a set of processes by which the world is rapidly being integrated into one economic space via increased international trade, the internationalization of production and financial markets, the internationalization of a commodity culture promoted by an increasingly networked global telecommunication system."

Kluver (2000, p. 427) defined informatization as "the process primarily by which information technologies, such as the world-wide web and other communication technologies, have transformed economic and social relations to such an extent that cultural and economic barriers are minimized." He sees informatization as "the process whereby information and communication technologies shape cultural and civic discourse. This would include not just computers and the internet, but other related technologies that have as their primary characteristic the transfer of information, including more traditional media technologies, such as film, satellite television, and telecommunications. As societies and economies re-orient themselves around technologies, there are inevitable consequences" (p. 427). Globalization is driven by technology, because it is technology that rules the integration of local and national economies into a global one.

The magnitude of the impact of globalization and informatization can hardly be overestimated. Friedman (1999, p. 18) stated that "globalization is not the only thing influencing events in the world today, but to the extent that there is a North Star and a worldwide shaping force, it is this system." Humberto Eco (in Kluver, 2000) made a distinction between globalization as a fact and globalization as a value. Globalization as a fact refers to the foundations of the new economy to be found in economic ties, realities, and institutions. Globalization as a value points to the drive in many people to strive for even further integration of economies, but also of cultures and social connections (see also Tijsseling, Chapter 3 in this volume). Or, in the words of Carnoy (1999, p. 19), "the essence of globalization is not contained strictly in trade and investment figures, [. . .] but in a new way of thinking about economic and social space and time." This reconceptualization of space and time has been referred to as the "space of flows" (Castells, 2010).

And with it comes increasing diversity, locally, regionally, and nationally. The extent to which traditional institutions, including educational institutions, can accommodate such diversity is not always clear.

Globalization is believed to have both positive and negative effects. On the positive side, Kluver (2000) offers the empowerment of individuals and societies to engage in international discourse, enterprise, and society. Globalization offers people access to a greater flow of information. However, the combination of globalization and informatization may also be experienced negatively, because it threatens the centuries-old heritage of locally grounded traditions, cultural integrity, and local autonomy. The tension between global developments and local forces may widen the gap not only between rich and poor countries, but also between well-educated and less well-educated people. It creates new challenges for those existing institutions and ideas and new desires and goals for people who have been underserved, including those who are deaf or have other disabilities and, in turn, those who now must try to accommodate them.

Castells (2010), although appreciative about the potential of the Information Age, warned in this context for the extraordinary gap between the current technological overdevelopment and the parallel social underdevelopment. In his view social exclusion is a real risk for many in today's and tomorrow's society. Safety nets are vanishing quickly and people can only cope in society if they constantly update their skills and can compete with others for jobs. "Thus, processes of social exclusion do not only affect the 'truly disadvantaged,' but those individuals and social categories who build their lives on a constant struggle to escape falling down to the stigmatized underworld of downgraded labor and socially disabled people" (Castells, 2010, p. 381).

Frey and Osborne (2013) tried to quantify what all the recent technological progress means for the future of employment. Once, computers were seen as mainly threatening routine, low-skilled jobs, because routine tasks where transferred from people to computers. But this is no longer the case. Big Data has made pattern recognition increasingly a task for computers, and thus a range of more complex if noncognitive tasks are being computerized, too. At the same time, advanced robots are changing the nature of work in many industries and institutions. The calculations made by Frey and Osborne point to an estimated 47% of all U.S. jobs being seriously at risk of being taken over by computers and robots within one or two decades from now. This will threaten most workers in transport, logistics, offices, administrative support, and industrial production. Frey and Osborne (2013, p. 45) concluded that "as technology races ahead, low-skill workers will reallocate to tasks that are non-susceptible to computerisation—*i.e.,* tasks requiring creative and social intelligence. For workers to win the race, however, they will have to acquire creative and social skills."

EDUCATION IN THE 21ST CENTURY: CONSEQUENCES OF GLOBALIZATION AND INFORMATIZATION

Education is a vital part of our lives. As alluded to above, the fast changes in this 21st-century world affect education too, and deaf education is no exception. Given the ecological nature of learning, this impact should not surprise us, for learning may be seen as "a multidimensional process that results in a relatively enduring change in a person or persons, and consequently how that person or persons will perceive the world and reciprocally respond to its affordances physically, psychologically, and socially. The process of learning has as its foundation the systematic, dynamic, and interactive relation between the nature of the learners and the object of the learning as ecologically situated in a given time and place as well as over time" (Alexander, Schallert, & Reynolds, 2009, p. 186). Thus, if place and time (and thus societal context) change, education will change, since it is situated in place and time.

Globalization and informatization influence education both directly and indirectly, and in more than one way (Carnoy, 1999). First of all, increasingly, the quality of education is compared internationally, resulting in pressure on educational authorities to make changes in curriculum, teacher training, legislation, or other aspects of educational policy if quality turns out to be less than in other countries. Second, because of the impact of globalization and information on requirements for employment, education is influenced too, because students have to be taught, formally and informally, to enable them to fulfill the requirements of 21st-century jobs. And third, the actual process of teaching and learning is changing, because of the use of information and communication technology as well as advances in didactics, psychology, and allied fields. In seeking a more diverse workforce, one goal is a more egalitarian society, one that reduces the gap between rich and poor. At the same time, greater employment for those who are disadvantaged or disabled also will reduce the need for social welfare expenditures.

International Comparisons of Education

More and more countries participate in international comparisons of educational systems and outcomes, leading to results in the form of ranking of countries that influence educational policies and invoke educational reforms. Economic competition fuels this tendency. Clear examples of this trend are studies carried out by the Organization of Economic and Social Development (OECD) or, for special education, by the European Agency for Development in Special Needs Education. So far, these international comparisons have not been carried out for deaf education, at least not formally. However, we already can witness requests by educational authorities (e.g., in Ireland, the United States, and Norway) to assess the quality of their schools (special and mainstream) with deaf students and benchmark this with a literature-based international "standard."

According to Stephen Ball (cited in Paine & Zeichner, 2012), trends resulting from international education comparisons reflect not so much a convergence toward a single set of policies, but rather a shift toward a shared paradigm. Growing pressure for accountability, focus on teacher performance and teacher knowledge, and emphasis on the value of teacher education are but a few elements in this paradigm, but ones that influence educational practices considerably. Teaching and teachers are increasingly assessed in an international context by influential international agencies such as the World Bank or the OECD. Their reports are often considered authoritative (Paine & Zeichner, 2012). Influential international comparisons tend to focus first of all on education outcomes. The OECD-operated Programme for International Student Assessment (PISA) aims "to evaluate educational systems worldwide by testing skills and knowledge of 15-year-old students." The initiative includes currently 70 economies, and the project PISA for Development has started to extend the program to developing countries as well (OECD, 2014a).

Trends in International Mathematics and Science Study (TIMSS) and Progress in International Reading Literacy Study (PIRLS) are programs operated on behalf of the International Association for the Evaluation of Educational Achievement by Boston College in the United States. For 20 years, achievements in mathematics have been assessed internationally in four-year cycles in the fourth grade. Reading comprehension in the fourth grade has been measured internationally in five-year cycles over the past 15 years. More than 60 countries participated in TIMMS 2011 and more than 50 in PIRLS 2011.

Not only educational achievements are compared internationally. By implementing a program focusing on Innovative Learning Environments, the OECD tries to assess the level of innovation in education around the world. The same organization carries out the Teaching and Learning International Survey (TALIS), focusing on training and functioning of teachers. In the words of the OECD (2014b), the objective of TALIS is to be found in our knowledge "that effective teaching and teachers are key to producing high-performing students. So how can countries prepare teachers to face the diverse challenges in today's schools? The OECD Teaching and Learning International Survey (TALIS) helps answer this question." In 2008, 24 countries worldwide participated in TALIS; TALIS 2013 included 33 countries.

Paine and Zeichner (2012) pointed out that national educational organizations increasingly tend to be influenced by the global competition based on international rankings. These influences can be seen in the definition of education goals, the ways quality is measured, and how teachers are trained. They warn of an imbalance in considering global and local factors influencing education: "Teaching is, we argue, inevitably a situated practice, and even though teaching today is situated within a global context of (often) shared pressures, discourses, and even metrics, teaching is also profoundly shaped by its more local (i.e., both national and subnational) contexts in structural and ideational ways" (Paine & Zeichner, 2012, pp. 572–573). When dealing with a small population, like that of deaf learners, we believe that a broader view is important. By seeking to avoid limiting our vision to the ways in which deaf education has been conducted in our own countries, we also can avoid overgeneralizations and take advantage of the innovations of others. For that, we need the global evidence base that this volume is all about.

Education, Skills, and Future Employment

Globalization and informatization are influencing education through goal setting and through curriculum design. Employment and participation in our 21st century requires, to a certain extent, different skills than those taught in most recent decades. These new, 21st-century skills have become globalized too.

In a report about social exclusion in the future, the Dutch National Education Council stated that globalization will have a profound impact on the demands people have to fulfill in their work. Knowledge of English, of other foreign languages, and of other cultures will be increasingly important. The national and international labor market furthermore requires of future workers thorough literacy and numeracy skills, social competencies, skills in handling various information sources, an international orientation, resilience, and above all flexibility. The Education Council pointed out that students with disabilities and students from less affluent backgrounds run a serious risk of being severely socially disadvantaged (Onderwijsraad, 2011): unemployed because of severe limitations in skills, necessary for the current and future labor market. The changing labor market operates in a networked society, a society in which knowing how to interact and communicate with people from many different cultures becomes increasingly important. If nations chose to operate a knowledge economy, as many Western countries do, an international orientation is simply vital. This includes not only the classic curricular topics like literacy and numeracy, but also cognitive skills and competencies like planning, judging, and reflecting, and noncognitive skills such as interaction, communication, and interpersonal negotiating skills. Employees have to be able to build their own social networks, to adjust to job changes, and to maintain a balance between work and private life. This requires a considerable degree of self-reliance and flexibility, characteristics not always found in deaf learners (see Knoors & Marschark, 2014, Chapters 6 and 7).

According to *The Economist* (2014), governments have only a few options to support their citizens in functioning adequately in this 21st century. The most important of these options is education. The requirements of the Industrial Revolution in the 18th and 19th centuries resulted in the establishment of institutionalized education with schools as its key pillar. Living and working in the Informatization Age requires schools to change fundamentally, placing more emphasis on creativity and on critical thinking, less on rote learning. Integration of massive, open online courses (MOOCs) and games that simulate skills needed for work will be needed. And, in the view of *The Economist*, there will have to be a reallocation of (financial) resources from primary, secondary, and tertiary education to preschool and adult education. More emphasis on preschool is needed because social and cognitive skills learned early in life determine to a large extent future potential. Meanwhile, adults need continuous education to maintain their skills and expertise, something that might be enhanced by encouraging adults to take up studies later in life.

At the same time, existing curricula need to be redesigned (Dede, 2010; Voogt & Pelgrum, 2005; see De Klerk, Fortgens, & van der Eijk, Chapter 25 in this volume), paralleled by the development of new teaching methods and assessment procedures (Voogt & Pareja Roblin, 2012). There is general agreement that students need to acquire competencies such as collaboration, communication, digital literacy, citizenship, problem solving, critical thinking, creativity, and productivity to live a good life and to contribute to society (Voogt, Erstad, Dede, & Mishra, 2013). Not all of these competencies are unique and novel (Mishra & Kereluik, 2011), but schools tend to be less familiar with teaching students creativity, productivity, and digital literacy than the traditional reading, writing, and arithmetic. When teachers and schools have to go to great lengths to educate deaf or other students who arrive in the classroom underprepared in those traditional, core content areas, there may be little room left for going beyond immediate needs. Creativity, however, is an area that has been growing in importance as a key 21st-century thinking skill (Robinson, 2011; Wegerif & Dawes, 2004). According to Robinson (2011), the development of creativity through education is desperately needed if we are to survive in the, in his words, revolutionary 21st century with its unprecedented changes in population, climate, and technology.

Mishra and Kereluik (2011) identified three key areas that need to be addressed in a 21st-century curriculum. First is foundational knowledge: What do students need to know? This includes core content knowledge of various subjects (e.g., language, literacy, STEM content), digital literacy (also called information literacy), and knowledge across disciplines, requiring synthesis, a historically challenging skill among deaf learners (Marschark & Wauters, 2011). Second, and also challenging for deaf learners, meta-knowledge should be part of the curriculum: How do students (learn to) act on the basis of their foundation knowledge? This requires teaching skills such as problem solving, critical thinking, communication, collaboration, creativity, and innovation. Finally, humanistic knowledge needs to be part of the curriculum: What values do students develop and apply to their actions? This form of knowledge relates to reflection on learners and learning and on the social contexts of learning.

Multimedia-Enhanced, Computer-Assisted Education

Globalization and informatization are also influencing the actual teaching and learning process. Driving forces behind this are the need for students to become digitally literate, the availability of technological means for fast, short- and long-distance transmission of vast amounts of rich information, and pressure for more efficient use of financial resources.

To start with the latter, according to Voogt, Erstad, Dede, and Mishra (2013, p. 409), "Societies can no longer afford a labour-intensive model of education that uses expensive human resources inefficiently. This is not a temporary financial dislocation due to an economic downturn, but a permanent sea change that has already happened in every other service sector of our economy." This fuels developments like flipping the classroom, where students study curricular content outside school by watching videoclips, going to school mainly to ask questions for clarification, discuss specific topics, and perhaps do "homework" in a setting where they can get immediate collaboration with and assistance from teachers and peers. Sharing lesson plans, teaching materials, and didactic suggestions for free by teachers on the Web may be seen in this light. Increasing the availability of free, open content is seen as a breakthrough development in the next two to three years by trend-watchers specializing in the role of technology in education. And the stunning increase in development, accessibility, and attendance of MOOCs offered by an increasing number of often very prestigious universities around the globe may also lead to learning more while spending less.

Students, both hearing and deaf, have to become digitally literate, meaning that they achieve competence in both simple and advanced information and communication technology skills, ranging from using software to search, comprehend, and control information (simple) to the evaluation, analysis, and interpretation of digital genres and media forms (advanced). This is a requirement, not an option, according to the UNESCO (Anderson, 2010), because the digital universe we are living in is exploding. In 2011, this universe was 10 times the size it was in 2006. In the terms used by UNESCO, we are witnessing a fourth information-related revolution. Information technology allows learning to move beyond the walls of the classroom. As noted earlier, because information transmission is increasing and now potentially independent of time and space, learning can be disconnected from time and space. Through technology, a student in Berlin may learn from videoclips and webinars broadcasted in the middle of his night by a university at the other end of the world. Distance learning using online resources and tapping into Web-based communities of practice makes learning much easier for those who live in rural areas far from schools and universities; for those who live in densely populated, incredibly busy urban areas where schools and universities are harder to reach in a reasonable time because of traffic congestion; and for individuals who are homebound, either by virtue of disability or other factors.

In teaching and instructing hearing and deaf students in the same classroom, teachers may resort to an increasing amount of (software) programs presenting information in multiple media, making use of various information carriers and hardware devices such as smartphones, tablet computers, and laptop or stand-alone computers (Caselli, Rinaldi, Onofrio, & Tomasuelo, Chapter 19 in this volume; Knoors & Marchark, 2014; Segers & Verhoeven, Chapter 21 in this volume). Social contacts between students, hearing and deaf alike, are enhanced by social networking (Blom, Marschark, Vervloed, & Knoors, 2014). To teach students effectively using information technology, teachers need to apply to a certain extent specific didactic skills. The Technological Pedagogical Content Knowledge framework for teacher knowledge has received a significant level of research and scholarly attention and is seen as very helpful in this respect (Mishra & Koehler, 2006; see also Gervedink Nijhuis & Terpstra, Chapter 23 in this volume). Organizations such as the New Media Consortium in the United States and Kennisnet in the Netherlands chart the landscape of emerging technologies for learning, teaching, and research. The New Media Consortium publishes so-called Horizon reports for various levels of education. Among the trends foreseen by these and other organizations are an increase in mobile learning and use of cloud computing (in the short term), the use of learning analytics to enable personalized and adaptive learning (in the mid-term, between one and three years), growth of open content (in the mid-term), and three-dimensional printing of learning materials (in the long term, between three and five years from now) (see, e.g., Johnson, Adams Becker, Estrada, & Freeman, 2014).

DEAF STUDENTS AND DEAF EDUCATION

Where does this all leave deaf students? Are they ready for living, learning, and working in the 21st-century global society? Will they be able to build their social and knowledge networks, necessary as future employees? Are they competent in information technologies that rule their world? Do they have the skills to engage in international discourse, enterprise, and society? Or will they find themselves socially excluded and socially disabled because of a lack of relevant skills and competencies?

One might argue that the chances for deaf students to achieve academically and socially well have never before been so good. Access for such students to communication in spoken and sign language has improved considerably (Archbold, Chapter 2; De Raeve, Chapter 24; Tijsseling, Chapter 3, all in this volume). Investments in specific teaching methods and curricula have improved deaf education overall (Easterbrooks & Maiorana-Basa, Chapter 7; de Klerk et al., Chapter 25; Pagliaro, Chapter 8, all in this volume), and there is an impressive stock of studies inside and outside fields related to deaf education, studies that could and should be used by those teaching deaf students (Knoors & Marchark, 2014). But, on the other hand, the challenges for those educating deaf students to prepare them for a successful life in this era have never been so big. These challenges differ to varying degrees, as emphasized earlier, from those experienced by teachers of hearing students. So, if we want to avoid deaf students' running the risk of social exclusion because education fails to teach them the skills they need today and tomorrow, we need to take action.

Rapid changes in the characteristics of deaf students fuel the variation in students and in their educational needs (see Archbold, Chapter 2 in this volume; Marschark & Knoors, Chapter 27 in this volume). This implies that actions may not come in one size, since one size fits none. Changes in the societal context, as described in this chapter, add considerably to the complexity. And the relatively small number of deaf learners as a proportion of the total number of students certainly does not make things easier. According to the World Health Organization (WHO, 2013), in 2011 over 5% of the world's population suffered from a disabling hearing loss, implying a loss of 40 dB or more in the better ear for adults and 30 dB or more for children (see Goldberg & Richburg, 2004; Moeller, Tomblin, Yoshinaga-Itano, Connor, & Jerger, 2007). In all, 360 million people were affected by hearing loss, 32 million of them being children. Distribution of this percentage across various continents and countries differed considerably, ranging from 2.7% to 4.4% in Western countries (United States, Western Europe, Australia, New Zealand); from 4.4% to 6.1% in Latin America, Africa, and most Asian countries; and from 6.1% to 7.6% in Russia and India (see Leigh, Newall, & Newall, 2010). Differences in the prevalence of congenital and early acquired hearing loss in children are even more pronounced, varying from 0.5 % of all children in high-income Western countries (in countries such as the Netherlands and Flanders even less, between 0.1% and 0.2%) to 1.6% in central and eastern Europe, 1.6% in Latin America and the Caribbean, 1.9% in sub-Saharan Africa, and 2.4% in South Asia (India) (WHO, 2012). Of course the connection with family income and level of health care is apparent. Nevertheless, even in developing countries, deaf children constitute a small minority; deafness is a low-incidence disability.

In other words, if we want our actions to result in meeting the challenges of deaf education in this 21st century and if we want to use resources to accomplish this goal efficiently, we simply cannot act only on our own—not as an individual special or mainstream school, not as an institute or university, not as a country. We have to collaborate internationally if we want to educate deaf students to be successful as global citizens, competent in globally and locally important skills. We must acknowledge that global education policies will influence the teaching of not only hearing learners, but also of deaf learners.

Luckily, the field of deaf education has a long history of international exchange of knowledge, given the International Congresses on Education of the Deaf that have been organized every five years since 1878, the international conferences on sign language and sign language acquisition, and the international conferences about pediatric cochlear implantation more recently. All of these conferences—and volumes like this one—show the value that many teachers and other professionals active in this field attach to international sharing of experiences and knowledge.

Intensifying this international collaboration, needed to meet today's and tomorrow's challenges in deaf education, may be achieved by starting focused, international discussions among researchers and practitioners, by extending collaboration to the development of innovative education practices, and by carrying out multicenter, collaborative research projects. International discussions, in this case through focusing on core aspects of educating deaf students and its (international) evidence base, may be seen as a first but important step in better collaboration. This volume gives evidence of that important first step by bringing together relevant, qualitatively good research and practices carried out and disseminated by excellent scholars and practitioners, building on reviews published by, for example, Spencer and Marschark (2010) and Knoors and Marschark (2014).

THIS VOLUME

In recent years, we have witnessed a gradual shift from debates about the best way to communicate with deaf students to the much more important question how deaf students learn—including children and adolescents, those with moderate to profound hearing losses, and those with and without cochlear implants. Of particular interest are conditions that support deaf learners to reach their full cognitive potentials (or not). In what ways is "deaf learning" similar to "hearing learning" and in what ways are they different (now that research has made it permissible to suggest that they are)? In what ways might learning by deaf students be promoted by teaching differently than is the case for hearing students? In this context, learning is seen as the result of interactions among student characteristics, well-being, and instruction, and education is recognized as being ecological by nature.

Reviews of the evidence for many practices in education of deaf students fueled this shift in attention, because these reviews clearly showed that the evidence base for deaf education left much to be desired (Easterbrooks & Stephenson, 2006; Knoors & Marschark, 2014; Luckner et al., 2005/2006; Spencer & Marschark, 2010). Strengthening attention to these issues is required given the flaws that have been identified, the changes in the characteristics of deaf students, and the even bigger changes in the world in which deaf learners have to study and work.

This volume allows international experts in all areas relevant to deaf education to "speak for themselves" and add to the discussion. The chapters thus add both depth and breadth to the knowledge already available as well as describing cutting-edge research currently being conducted and contributing to the growth of a global evidence base for deaf education. The topics these contributors discuss follow from or are closely related to the core issues identified by various scholars as being crucial for the successful teaching of deaf students. These are topics necessary for parents, teachers, and other professionals to construct effective education for deaf learners: from language development, literacy and numeracy, and cognitive and social development to multimedia-enhanced, computer-assisted learning and the effects of teaching and learning educational contexts.

The chapters that follow go into deaf education and achievement (Antia, Chapter 23); characteristics of deaf students (Archbold, Chapter 2; Tijsseling, Chapter 3); the interplay between child characteristics and early environmental factors (Bruin, Chapter 5); well-being and social-emotional functioning as important aspects of learning (Fellinger & Holzinger, Chapter 17; Hintermair; Rieffe et al., Chapter 16; Wiefferink et al., Chapter 20; Wolters & Isarin, Chapter 14; Zaidman-Zait, Chapter 15); the roles of technology in deaf education (Segers & Verhoeven, Chapter 21; Caselli et al., Chapter 19); language and communication (Tang, Yiu, & Lam, Chapter 6); language assessment (Cawthon, Chapter 10; Herman, Chapter 9); literacy and numeracy (Dirks & Wauters, Chapter 18; Easterbrooks & Maiorana-Basas, Chapter 7; Pagliaro, Chapter 8); cognitive functioning (Hermans et al., Chapter 11; Morgan, Chapter 12); and evidence-based ways in which teachers may learn to enhance the learning process and the academic outcomes of their deaf students (de Klerk et al., Chapter 25; De Raeve, Chapter 24; Gervedink Nijhuis & Terpstra, Chapter 22; Swanwick, Chapter 26). The chapters are organized into five sections: (a) changing student characteristics, (b) language, literacy, and numeracy, (c) social and cognitive aspects, (d) technology for learning and development, and (e) education in context. The volume concludes with a chapter taking a broad view of the current state of the art in deaf education, considering apparent gaps and how to fill them, and suggesting broad outlines for a near-term research agenda.

The central argument of this volume is the need to recognize that in many ways, deaf children are not hearing children who cannot hear. Education for deaf learners has gone through significant changes over the past three decades, and change will certainly be the buzzword in the foreseeable future. The rapid growth of information and communication technology and progress in educational, psychological, and allied research fields have many scholars questioning aspects of traditional schooling. At the same time, inclusive education has changed the landscape of special education and thus of deaf education in many if not all countries. And yet, deaf children continue to lag significantly behind hearing peers in academic achievement. As a consequence of technological innovations (e.g., digital hearing aids and early bilateral cochlear implants), the needs of many deaf learners have changed considerably. Parents and professionals, however, are just now coming to recognize that there are cognitive, experiential, and social-emotional differences between deaf and hearing students likely to affect academic outcomes. Understanding such differences and determining ways in which to accommodate them must become a top priority in educating deaf learners. One constant factor remains in the midst of all this turbulence—although perhaps with a role that might change: the teacher.

The scholars contributing to this edited volume are international experts in their fields. They summarize their work (research and/or development); sketch the background and context of their work, including relevant research by others; and address the implications and future directions for teachers, teaching, and learning. Through the participation of this diverse set of scholars coming together to focus on a specific topic, the volume takes a broad view of learning and academic achievement, considering "the whole child." Such a view is consistent with European psychology and education while contrasting with the more reductionist, modular North American psychological traditions in education. In adopting this broad perspective, the complexities and commonalities in the social, emotional, cognitive, and linguistic mosaic of which the deaf child is a part can better be captured. Only through such a holistic consideration of children developing within the context of communicative-social-educational settings can we truly understand their academic potential. Finally, we hope this volume will provide a research agenda and a benchmark for the teaching of the increasingly diverse population of deaf learners today while charting a course for the future.

REFERENCES

Alexander, P. A., Schallert, D. L., & Reynolds, R. E. (2009). What is learning anyway? A topographical perspective considered. *Educational Psychologist, 44*(3), 176–192.

Anderson, J. (2010). *ICT transforming education. A regional guide.* Bangkok: UNESCO.

Ball, S. J. (1999). *Global trends in educational reform and the struggle for the soul of the teacher!* Paper presented at the British Educational Research Association annual conference, University of Sussex at Brighton, September 2–5. In L. Paine & K. Zeichner (2012). The local and the global in reforming teaching and teacher education. *Comparative Education Review, 56*(4), 569–583.

Blom, H., Marschark, M., Vervloed, M. P., & Knoors, H. (2014). Finding friends online: Online activities by deaf students and their well-being. *PloS One, 9*(2), e88351.

Bloom, D. E., & Canning, D. (2004). *Global demographic change: Dimensions and economic significance.* (No. w10817). Cambridge, MA: National Bureau of Economic Research.

Carnoy, M. (1999). *Globalization and educational reform: What planners need to know*. Paris: UNESCO.

Castells, M. (2010). *End of Millennium. The information age: Economy, society and culture* (2nd ed.). Chichester: John Wiley and Sons.

Dede, C. (2010). Comparing frameworks for 21st-century skills. In J. Bellanca & R. Brandt (Eds.), *21st-century skills* (pp. 51–76). Bloomington, IN: Solution Tree Press.

Easterbrooks, S. R., & Beal-Alvarez, J. (2013). *Literacy instruction for students who are deaf and hard of hearing.* New York: Oxford University Press.

Easterbrooks, S. R., & Stephenson, B. (2006). An examination of twenty literacy, science, and mathematics practices used to educate students who are deaf or hard of hearing. *American Annals of the Deaf, 151*, 385–399.

The Economist (2014, Jan. 18). *Coming to an office near you.* Retrieved July 3, 2014, from www.economist.com.

Frey, C. B., & Osborne, M. A. (2013). *The future of employment: How susceptible are jobs to computerisation?* OMS Working Paper, Oxford University. Retrieved July 3, 2014, from www.futuretech.ox.ac.uk.

Friedman, T. (1999). *The Lexus and the olive tree: understanding globalization.* New York: Farrar, Straus, Giroux.

Gibson-Graham, J. K. (2006). *"The" end of capitalism (as we knew it): A feminist critique of political economy; with a new introduction.* University of Minnesota Press.

Goldberg, L. R. & Richburg, C. M. (2004). Minimal hearing impairment: Major myths with more than minimal implications. *Communication Disorders Quarterly, 25*, 152–160.

Hilbert, M., & López, P. (2011). The world's technological capacity to store, communicate, and compute information. *Science, 332*(6025), 60–65.

Johnson, L., Adams Becker, S., Estrada, V., & Freeman, A. (2014). *NMC Horizon Report: 2014 K-12 Edition*. Austin, TX: The New Media Consortium.

Kluver, R. (2000). Globalization, informatization, and intercultural communication. *American Communication Journal, 3*, 3. Retrieved July 3, 2014, from www.academia.edu.

Knoors, H., & Marschark, M. (2012). Language planning for the 21st century: Revisiting bilingual language policy for deaf children. *Journal of Deaf Studies and Deaf Education, 17*(3), 291–305.
Knoors, H., & Marschark, M. (2014). *Teaching deaf learners. Psychological and developmental foundations.* New York: Oxford University Press.
Lam, D., & Leibbrandt, M. (2013). *Global demographic trends and their implications for employment.* Background research paper submitted to the High Level Panel on the Post-2015 Development Agenda.
Lane, H. (1984). *When the mind hears: A history of the deaf.* New York: Random House Publishers.
Lang, H. G. (2000). *A phone of our own.* Washington, DC: Gallaudet University Press.
Lang, H. G. (2011). Perspectives on the history of deaf education. In M. Marschark & P. Spencer (Eds.), *The Oxford handbook of deaf studies, language, and education* (Vol. 1, 2nd ed., pp. 7–17). New York: Oxford University Press.
Leigh, G., Newall, J. P., & Newall, A. T. (2010). Newborn screening and earlier intervention with deaf children: Issues for the developing world. In M. Marschark & P. Spencer (Eds.), *The Oxford handbook of deaf studies, language, and education* (Vol. 2, pp. 345–359). New York: Oxford University Press.
Luckner, J. L., & Cooke, C. (2010). A summary of the vocabulary research with students who are deaf or hard of hearing. *American Annals of the Deaf, 155*(1), 38–67.
Luckner, J. L., Sebald, A. M., Cooney, J., Young III, J., & Muir, S. G. (2005/2006). An examination of the evidence-based literacy research in deaf education. *American Annals of the Deaf, 150*, 443–456.
Marschark, M., & Hauser, P. C. (Eds.). (2008). *Deaf cognition: foundations and outcomes.* New York: Oxford University Press.
Marschark, M., & Knoors, H. (2012). Educating deaf children: Language, cognition, and learning. *Deafness and Education International, 14*, 137–161.
Marschark, M., Tang, G., & Knoors, H. (Eds.). (2014). *Bilingualism and bilingual deaf education.* New York: Oxford University Press.
Marschark, M., & Wauters, L. (2011). Cognitive functioning in deaf adults and children. In M. Marschark & P. E. Spencer (Eds.), *The Oxford handbook of deaf studies, language, and education* (Vol. 1, 2nd ed., pp. 486–499). New York: Oxford University Press.
Mishra, P., & Kereluik, K. (2011, March). What 21st-century learning? A review and a synthesis. In *Society for Information Technology & Teacher Education International Conference* (Vol. 2011, No. 1, pp. 3301–3312).
Mishra, P., & Koehler, M. (2006). Technological pedagogical content knowledge: A framework for teacher knowledge. *The Teachers College Record, 108*(6), 1017–1054.
Moeller, M. P., Tomblin, J. B., Yoshinaga-Itano, C., Connor, C., & Jerger, S. (2007) Current state of knowledge: Language and literacy of children with hearing impairment. *Ear & Hearing, 28*, 740–753.
Moore, G. E. (1965/1998). Cramming more components onto integrated circuits. *Proceedings of the IEEE 86*, 1, 82–85. Reprinted from G. E. Moore, "Cramming More Components onto Integrated Circuits," *Electronics*, 114–117, April 19, 1965.
Onderwijsraad. (2011). *Maatschappelijke achterstanden van de toekomst* [Social deprivation in the future]. Den Haag: Sdu.

Organization of Economic and Social Development. (2014a). *About Pisa.* Retrieved July 10, 2014, from www.oecd.org/pisa/aboutpisa.

Organization of Economic and Social Development. (2014b). *TALIS. Teaching and Learning International Survey.* Brochure, retrieved July 10, 2014, from www.oecd.org/edu/school/TALIS.

Paine, L., & Zeichner, K. (2012). The local and the global in reforming teaching and teacher education. *Comparative Education Review, 56*(4), 569–583.

Robinson, K. (2011). *Out of our minds: Learning to be creative.* Chichester: John Wiley & Sons.

Spencer, P. E., & Marschark, M. (2010). *Evidence-based practice in educating deaf and hard-of- hearing students.* New York: Oxford University Press.

Stromquist, N. P., & Monkman, K. (2014). Defining globalization and assessing its implications for knowledge and education, revisited. In N. P. Stromquist & K. Monkman (Eds.), *Globalization and education: Interpretation and contestation across cultures* (pp. 1–20). Lanham: Rowman & Littlefield.

Swanwick, R., & Marschark, M. (2010). Enhancing education for deaf children: Research into practice and back again. *Deafness and Education International, 12*, 217–235

Tellings, A. (1995). *The two hundred years' war in deaf education.* PhD dissertation. Katholieke Universiteit Nijmegen.

United Nations, Department of Economic and Social Affairs, Population Division. (2013). *World population prospects: the 2012 revision, key findings and advance tables.* Working Paper No. ESA/P/WP.227.

Van Dijk, R., Nelson, C., Postma, A., & Van Dijk, J. (2010). Assessment and intervention of deaf children with multiple disabilities. In M. Marschark & P. E. Spencer (Eds.), *The Oxford handbook of deaf studies, language, and education* (Vol. 2, pp. 172–191). New York: Oxford University Press.

Voogt, J., Erstad, O., Dede, C., & Mishra, P. (2013). Challenges to learning and schooling in the digital networked world of the 21st century. *Journal of Computer Assisted Learning, 29*, 403–413.

Voogt, J. & Pelgrum, H. (2005). ICT and curriculum change. *Human Technology, 1*(2), 157–175.

Voogt, J., & Roblin, N. P. (2012). A comparative analysis of international frameworks for 21st century competences: Implications for national curriculum policies. *Journal of Curriculum Studies, 44*(3), 299–321.

Wegerif, R., & Dawes, L. (2004). *Thinking and learning with ICT: Raising achievement in primary classrooms.* London: RoutledgeFalmer.

World Health Organization. (2012). *WHO global estimates on prevalence of hearing loss. Mortality and burden of diseases and prevention of blindness and deafness.* WHO report, Geneva.

World Health Organization. (2013). *Multi-country assessment of national capacity to provide hearing care.* WHO report, Geneva.

Part 1

A Changing World for Deaf Learners

2

Being a Deaf Student

Changes in Characteristics and Needs

Sue Archbold

INTRODUCTION

This chapter considers the changing characteristics and needs of deaf students. What do we mean by a "deaf student" in today's changing world? This chapter considers the term and the impact of today's developments on what it means to be deaf and a student. It considers first the impact of hearing loss on educational issues and choices and attempts to ameliorate these, and goes on to consider the impact of changing political and educational policies and the new communication and hearing technologies, particularly cochlear implantation, on these issues. Most importantly, it considers what we are learning from deaf students today of their changing needs, and how we may best meet them.

WHAT IS A DEAF STUDENT?

It has been said that one can be culturally deaf, educationally deaf, and/or audiologically deaf; to make these distinctions can be helpful in thinking about deaf students and their needs. Today's world is a rapidly changing one, socially, politically, and technologically. The challenges of communication have been at the heart of considering the needs of deaf students, and today the opportunities for communication are greater than ever before. The need for effective communication is also greater than ever before; a hundred years ago, the majority of the population worked in jobs that demanded physical skills, while today the demands for employment are for those with good communication skills and often of English. English is the language in which knowledge is transmitted globally: many international companies have their meetings in English, even when based in non–English-speaking countries.

So what about the deaf student in this changing world? The technological changes have made the audiological definitions rather arbitrary: However, in many countries deaf students were, and still are, defined by their level of hearing loss. The term "deaf and hard of hearing" came about, with separate schools for each category. For example, in the Netherlands, children with profound losses were typically educated in schools for the deaf, and children with severe hearing losses in schools for hard-of-hearing children (Wolters, 2013). In the United Kingdom the terms "deaf" and "hard-of-hearing" are not used: Hearing loss is defined as being mild, moderate, severe, or profound. Educational services are provided for deaf pupils, whatever their level of deafness, with potentially greater opportunity to be flexible according to need. For example, a profoundly deaf pupil may in fact need less support in school than a moderately deaf pupil of lesser ability, and to define their educational needs on the basis of audiological functioning may not be appropriate. The impact of technology such as cochlear implantation has changed the functioning of many deaf students dramatically, enabling those who are profoundly deaf to function as those who are much less deaf. As we shall see, there is also increasing awareness of the educational impact and significance of mild or moderate hearing losses, and of unilateral losses. In this world of changing opportunities and challenges, the definition of a student as deaf needs to be all-encompassing, and in this chapter, the deaf student is defined one who has a hearing loss that requires changes in teaching strategies for the student to maximize his or her potential.

INCIDENCE

It is difficult to ascertain exact figures of deaf children in many countries. In England, for example, the incidence of childhood deafness is reported to be as follows (Consortium for Research into Deaf Education Report, 2013):

0–4 years	1.3/1,000
0–16 years	3.4/1,000
16–19 years	0.9/1,000

In the Netherlands it is reported by Wolters (2013) that 3% of children in school have a hearing loss of 30 dB or more. About 30% of deaf children may have another difficulty, the most common being a learning difficulty. This again makes the impact of deafness, and the attempt to categorize the deaf student by hearing loss, more complex.

EFFECT OF DEAFNESS ON CHILDREN'S DEVELOPMENT

Although hearing is important in hearing environmental sounds and thus monitoring one's environment, the major impact of deafness from birth is the difficulty in learning and using spoken language, the language used by society in general (Marschark & Spencer, 2006). Over 95% of deaf children are born to hearing families where the home language is spoken not signed (Mitchell & Karchmer, 2004). Spoken language is usually acquired through the channel of hearing through interaction with caregivers using the language of the home in the first months and years of life. When a child is deaf from birth or early in life, this process is disrupted—the child has difficulty not only in acquiring speech but in acquiring language, essential to participation in everyday communication and in education and later employment. Conrad's classic study showed that half of deaf children leaving school at age 16 had speech that was difficult to understand, and they had a median reading age of nine years (Conrad, 1979). Gregory, Bishop, and Sheldon (1995) painted a depressing picture of families under stress, where deaf young people, unable to hear the conversation of the family, are not fully participating in society or family life:

> You can't have a normal conversation.... he doesn't say he misses anything, but he wouldn't know if he missed anything.

There is also an increasing realization of the linguistic and educational impact of a mild or moderate hearing loss, and of a unilateral hearing loss. Children with these hearing losses may not be immediately apparent, but they are likely to have delayed language development and to be disadvantaged in the classroom, where learning often takes place in background noise and in group conversations (Bess, Dodd-Murphy, & Parker, 1998; Cone, Wake, Tobin, Poulaki, & Rickards, 2010; Lieu, 2004). A mild/moderate hearing loss has an impact on the development of language and reading skills (Moeller, Tomblin, Connor, & Jerger, 2007). Hearing in one ear only makes localization of sound and listening in noise difficult: Both skills are essential to follow the conversation and learning in a busy classroom (Most, 2004). Lieu, Tye-Murray, Karzon, and Piccirillo (2010) also found that school-age children with a unilateral hearing loss have lower oral language scores than their hearing peers. These hearing losses have a further impact on the development of the more subtle aspects of language such as pragmatic skills, without access to the suprasegmental aspects of speech (Most & Peled, 2007). These skills are more challenging to assess than collecting data on vocabulary development for example, but they are important educationally in the development of higher-order literacy skills: the ability to understand challenging texts and to "read between the lines." They are also important socially: Wolters, Knoors, Cillessen, and Verhoeven (2011) report that pragmatic skills are linked to popularity in the classroom, and peer-to-peer communication is also linked to educational success.

There are also those who have a "ski-slope" hearing loss—that is, they can hear the low- but not the high-frequency sounds of speech. For these children, the educational impact of their deafness may also not be immediately apparent, but there are important speech sounds that will not be audible to them. The consonants of speech tend to be quieter and of higher frequency, and therefore not easily audible by these children. But the consonants give speech much of its meaning and clarity and provide many of the grammatical features of language, such as (in English) tense changes and plurality.

Finally, we have not mentioned those who have conductive hearing losses; a conductive hearing loss is often fluctuating, and by its nature makes access to the spoken curriculum in a mainstream class challenging. Students with a conductive hearing loss may not be classified as being deaf and not be easily apparent in the classroom; although evidence is equivocal, it is considered that the effect of their hearing loss may have an impact educationally, particularly if it occurs in association with other factors (Casby, 2001). A conductive hearing loss arising from ongoing otitis media is likely to have a fluctuating nature, making it challenging for student, educator, and audiologist, as its impact may change from day to day and differing teaching and learning strategies be required at different times. A conductive loss arising from atresia (absence of the external ear canal) has been shown to have an impact on academic performance (Kesser, Krook, & Gray, 2013).

IMPACT OF DEAFNESS ON EDUCATIONAL DECISIONS AND MANAGEMENT

Educators of the deaf have strived for many years to overcome the educational effects of deafness but often with little effect, with deaf students still underperforming compared with hearing children. The arguments as to how best to overcome the impact of deafness, including whether to use visual means, such as sign language, sign and speech, lip-reading, or written support, or to use technology and the auditory channels have continued, and deaf education has been the subject of much controversy. Arguments about where deaf students should go to school centered around whether they should attend mainstream or special schools, or resource centers in mainstream schools, and how to be supported in whatever setting they attended. These decisions have often been influenced by political trends; for example, the worldwide trend toward inclusive education for all those with disabilities favored mainstream provision.

However, the arguments about educational practice and the relative merits of these decisions have rarely been supported with evidence (Archbold & Mayer, 2012). Deaf children and young people represent challenges for researchers; they are a particularly heterogeneous population with many variables to account for, including etiology, age at diagnosis and amplification, cognitive ability, socioeconomic status, parental support, communication preference, and educational history.

The advent of technology such as cochlear implantation has added yet more variables: age at implantation, type of implant, preimplant hearing levels, processing strategy, and programming/management of the system. The idea of creating homogeneous groups so that traditional research methodologies can be used to obtain robust evidence may be attractive, but it does not in practice represent the population that educators work with, and it is unlikely to produce research that will influence educational policy and practice in a meaningful way (Archbold, 2010; Archbold & Mayer, 2012; Leigh, 2008). Defining the characteristics of deaf students, and their needs, is inherently messy and complex; any attempt to simplify this group to carry out what might be considered robust research does not recognize their complexities or the number of variables to be taken into account in what is a low-incidence population.

The context in which we are considering the characteristics of deaf students is also changing. The worldwide move toward accountability and evidence-based practice in health and education systems has changed the organization and priorities of educational systems. In the United Kingdom, for example, the practice of creating "school league tables" in which educational results are compared to illustrate which school provides the best results for its pupils may not be supportive of the inclusion of those who are deaf, or with any disability, into their mainstream schools. Greater mainstream education may also mean that teachers of the deaf supporting deaf pupils in mainstream classes do not have the access to the specialist knowledge and expertise available in special schools (Archbold & Mayer, 2012; De Raeve, Baerts, Colleye, & Croux, 2012). Greater financial accountability means that educational services are required to prioritize their activities. Thus, those with lesser hearing losses or with unilateral or conductive hearing losses may well not receive the attention they need to reach their academic potential, as the needs of those with greater losses may be more apparent.

While deaf students have long been recognized as a heterogeneous group, in this changing context, the rapid growth of technology, both communication and hearing technologies, has had a huge impact on their characteristics and made this group of students even more complex to manage and to research.

TECHNOLOGICAL CHANGES: WHAT ARE THEY?

> The widespread implementation of newborn hearing screening and advances in amplification technologies (including cochlear implants) have fundamentally changed the educational landscape for deaf learners. (Mayer & Leigh, 2010, p. 175)

The growing evidence that the earlier intervention took place, the better the linguistic outcomes for deaf children led to the development of newborn hearing screening programs around the world, supported by the technology that could implement it almost immediately after birth (De Raeve, 2006; Yoshinago-Itano, 2004). The insights into the development of the auditory system in utero, and the impact of hearing on the development of communication skills and language at an earlier stage than previously thought, supported the provision of early amplification following identification and diagnosis. In England, for example, the average age of fitting of hearing aids was reduced to three months, from three years, following the rollout of newborn hearing screening in 2005. In Flanders, where newborn hearing screening was implemented in 1998, the average age of implantation was reduced almost immediately to below the age of 18 months (De Raeve, 2010). In many developed countries, cochlear implantation now takes place in the first year of life, and in both ears (Boons, Brokx, Frijns, Peeraer, Philips, & Vermeulen, 2012b).

Compared with the long years of arguments about managing the linguistic and educational needs of deaf students, the growth of technological advances has been fast. This is in line with the technological changes we see in everyday life. Technologies we now take for granted, such as the Internet and mobile phones, have been available only recently. The growth in hearing technologies has been similarly rapid. Hearing aids benefit from digital technology, from miniaturization making them suitable for babies and more acceptable to adolescents, from better microphones with directional capabilities, and from flexible programming to provide better fit for differing hearing losses and for different listening conditions, such as in noise.

The development in hearing technologies with the greatest educational impact of all has been cochlear implantation, where surgically implanted receivers transmit the electronic signal to the auditory nerve directly, providing useful hearing to those who are profoundly deaf for the first time. Although the concept of cochlear implants has been around for many years, it was only in the 1980s that they were developed into functional use, and it was in the 1990s that pediatric cochlear implantation became widely available; for a historical review see Archbold (2010). Despite initial cautions, the outcomes have surpassed expectations, although debate continues about the factors that influence these outcomes. "Performance of these students [teenagers with cochlear implants] far exceeds expectations for children in previous generations with severe-profound sensori-neural hearing losses (SNHL) who used conventional hearing aids before the advent of [cochlear implant] technology" (Geers, Strube, Tobey, Pisoni, & Moog, 2011, p. 85S). Cochlear implantation has become routinely provided for profoundly deaf children, and over 160,000 children now have implants worldwide, at the time of writing. It has been shown to be safe, reliable, and effective, and it is now reasonable for language and educational attainments for profoundly deaf children to be assessed in comparison to their hearing peers. Also, the recognition of the importance of binaural hearing has led to the common practice of bilateral implantation (Boons et al, 2013; De Raeve, Archbold, & Diller, 2013).

There have been significant developments in other auditory implants as well. We have bone-anchored hearing implants, suitable for those with conductive losses, problems with the ear canal or pinna, and single-sided deafness. Soft-bands, which provide the benefits of the technology without surgery, can be used early in life, providing the child with useful hearing. Electroacoustic implants provide a hearing aid and cochlear implant in one system for those with useful low-frequency hearing. Middle ear implants and brain stem implants are available for those who cannot benefit from cochlear implants, having a badly damaged or no auditory nerve. As with all types of technology today, the hearing technologies continue to expand and develop as we write.

In addition to hearing aids and auditory implants, assistive listening devices such as radio hearing aids, sometimes called FM systems, and wireless systems are developing rapidly and are having an impact on hearing loss and its management. They help to overcome the difficulties of listening in the classroom, or outside, caused by background noise, reverberation (echo), and distance from the speaker. Thanks to miniaturization and flexibility, they are increasingly being used in infants and are increasingly acceptable to deaf adolescents, who previously would have rejected them on looks alone.

Medical and surgical advances have meant that today more deaf students are presenting with very complex needs, changing the characteristics of the group. Children who previously may not have survived as infants because of their complex medical needs are now doing so, thanks to medical advances. They are presenting as deaf students, but with more complex needs than seen in the past, and in greater numbers, changing the demands on educational services and the characteristics of the group (Mulla, Harrigan, Gregory, & Archbold, 2013).

IMPACT OF THE TECHNOLOGICAL CHANGES FOR DEAF LEARNERS

These technological developments have been rapid, compared with the history of deaf education, and their impact on the characteristics and needs of deaf students is not yet entirely clear. Marschark and Spencer wrote in 2006 (p. 17):

> Spoken language development of deaf children may be more possible today than ever before. [. . .] we are now presented with the

> opportunity to learn from earlier mistakes and misunderstandings and to synthesize the best ideas of the past with the technological, programming and social advances of today. [. . .] we may finally be able to fulfill the promise of effective support for speech and spoken language with hearing loss.

What do we know about the impact of these changes? Early identification followed by early amplification has been shown to improve auditory abilities and language outcomes (Ching, Dillon, Day, & Crowe, 2008; Philips, Corthals, & De Raeve, 2009). With regard to newborn hearing screening and its impact, the comprehensive Longterm Outcomes from Childhood Hearing Impairment study in Australia, where all those diagnosed with childhood hearing loss have been followed up rigorously, illustrates the benefit of early amplification as a positive predictor of spoken language outcomes (Ching, 2014). However, as always, the picture is not straightforward as to the factors leading to improved language and educational attainments for deaf students. Other predictive factors, such as maternal education and parental involvement, are emerging as significant (Boons et al., 2012a; Ching, 2014).

The impact of cochlear implantation on the developing language skills of profoundly deaf children has been studied closely over the years, with a great deal of evidence emerging, albeit some of it mixed. However, age at implantation has consistently emerged as a factor in producing better outcomes. Early implantation has been established as a predictor in producing language growth comparable to hearing peers (Dettman, Pinder, Briggs, Dowell, & Leigh, 2007; Nicholas & Geers, 2007; Tait, De Raeve, & Nikolopoulos, 2007). Studies now use assessments normed on hearing children, a practice that was uncommon prior to implantation; this is significant in considering the changing characteristics of deaf students today. Dettman and colleagues (2007) looked at 19 infants implanted below age of one (mean age at implant 0.88) and found that language growth was significantly greater in these infants than in a matched group implanted between 12 and 24 months. Their growth rates matched the growth rates of normally hearing infants. Nicholas and Geers (2007) used the Pre-School Language Scales with 76 children aged 3.5 and 4.5 years of age, implanted below the age of three. They found that those implanted between 12 and 16 months were more likely to achieve age-appropriate spoken language. Ching and colleagues (2008) reported that children implanted below the age of 12 months developed normal language skills at a rate comparable to hearing children. Tait and colleagues (2007) compared the preverbal communication skills of children implanted before the age of one with normally hearing children. They found that normally hearing children progressed faster, but the difference was not significant. Over half the school-entry children with cochlear implants studied by Geers, Moog, and Biedenstein (2009) had age-appropriate vocabulary scores.

However, the picture in this, and other studies, is more complex than might first appear: The children with cochlear implants had difficulties in other language skills such as morphology, syntax, and narrative skills (Boons, De Raeve, Langereis, Peeraer, Wouters, & van Wierengen, 2013). Other studies show that deaf children with hearing aids and with cochlear implants have challenges in developing the more subtle skills of language—particularly pragmatic skills, which are important for the later development of higher-order literacy skills: the ability to "read between the lines," for example, in more advanced texts. These subtle skills are also important for social acceptance in the classroom, and for communication with peers, where adolescents need more complex language skills to communicate effectively with their peers (Dammeyer, 2012; Wolters, 2013). Delay in these skills has an important educational and social impact on these deaf learners, which may not be immediately apparent. It would appear that when children are older, there is more room for individual variation, and it should not be assumed that the mastery of age-appropriate early skills guarantees age-appropriate later skills.

Being able to make oneself understood has been a major issue for deaf learners, affecting their ability to communicate in the classroom. Early auditory stimulation provides not only the pathway for the acquisition of spoken language but also the auditory stimulation to produce the speech signals appropriate for the home spoken language (Tobey, Geers, Sundarrajan, & Shin, 2011). Early childhood hearing loss disrupts this process, making intelligible speech unlikely. Modern hearing technologies have changed this: More profoundly deaf children are acquiring spoken language that is intelligible to others using cochlear implants (Nikolopoulos, Archbold, Wever, & Lloyd, 2008; Tobey et al., 2011) now that they have access to the full range of speech sounds. Intelligible spoken communication is important for the deaf learner: Communication in the classroom between student and teacher and student and peer relies on this, and it has been shown to be a vital part of acceptance in the learning environment, wherever it is (Wolters, 2013). Fellinger, Holzinger, Sattel, Luacht, and Goldberg (2009), considering mental health issues in deaf young people, found they were unrelated to hearing loss, but the ability to make oneself understood was significant.

Music is also an important part of development for anyone, but particularly for adolescents because it is part of the culture of their peer group and of their communication. Changing technologies have improved deaf students' access to music. For example, in a study by Gfeller, Driscoll, See Smith, and Scherperle (2013), over two thirds of a group using cochlear implants considered music to be important or very important to them, which has not been the case in the past.

We have mentioned other auditory implants, such as bone-anchored hearing systems. Their increasing use in children is now being monitored much more closely, with encouraging results (Dashi, Sheehan, & McDermott, 2012; Mulla, Wright, & Archbold, 2013). Mulla and colleagues (2013), in an interview study of parents, found that parents considered the most common benefits to be the reduction of isolation and improvements in self-esteem and identity. They observed that the bone-anchored system had improved their child's ability to interact. However, they also reported a lack of information available, and several parents reported having to "fight" for access to this technology. The children in this study included those with unilateral losses or conductive losses and with problems with the ear canal and pinna; these groups of deaf learners were considered to have little technology to help them until recently.

In summary, the technological changes leading to earlier diagnosis, intervention, and amplification have provided deaf learners with increased access through hearing to spoken language, with many implications for their educational management. However, outcomes in all domains are characterized by variability, and a range of factors is considered important. Early studies tended to look only at a limited range of factors, but now others, such as maternal education, gender, cognition, and parental interaction, are increasingly recognized.

EDUCATIONAL PLACEMENT AND MANAGEMENT

What are the implications of this changing technology on educational decisions? Deaf children are increasingly being educated in mainstream schools, with a particular shift for those with cochlear implants (Archbold, Nikolopoulos, Lutman, & O'Donoghue, 2002; De Raeve et al., 2012; Moog, Geers, Gustus, & Brenner, 2011; Uziel, Sillon, & Vieu, 2007). Although this is in line with the political shift in thinking and the promotion of inclusive education, the move toward mainstream education has been strongly influenced by cochlear implantation and by the increasing effectiveness of other technologies such as FM systems. However, for deaf learners in mainstream schools, life may not be straightforward. Young people, their parents, and their teachers described the challenges of handling increasingly complex language and concepts, poor acoustic conditions, greater number of teachers and teaching styles, and the increased use of group work in high school (Royal National Institute for the Deaf [RNID], 2008; Wheeler, Archbold, Gregory, & Skipp, 2007). These can combine to make access to the curriculum and classroom language challenging. Also, the excellent levels of speech intelligibility typically achieved by those implanted early may mask the young person's language delay or difficulty in the more subtle communication skills required in the classroom, particularly at the high school level.

When we observe more closely the functioning of these deaf students in the classroom, some of these challenges become apparent (Dammeyer, 2013). For example, when Damen, Langereis, Snik, Chute, and Mylanus (2007) analyzed the performance of children with cochlear implants in mainstream classrooms using the Assessment of Mainstream Performance (Chute & Nevins, 2006) and the Screening Instrument for Targeting Educational Risk (SIFTER; Anderson, 1989), they found a wide variation in functioning. Some of those using cochlear implants had difficulty with the more subtle areas of communication that are important in the classroom. The most important variables affecting outcomes in this study were age at implantation and duration of deafness. Mukari, Ling, and Ghani (2007) also used the SIFTER and found that children with implants were rated poorly in the communication assessments. They concluded that children with implants continue to need specialist support in mainstream classes, and that linguistic delay may be one of the causes, despite the levels of hearing provided by the implant. However, we need to be cautious, as the technology is changing rapidly, and some of these studies are assessing children with older technology who were implanted at an older age than is common now.

Although there are concerns that deaf young people in mainstream schools would be socially isolated, on the whole this does not appear to be the case. Antia, Jones, Luckner, Kreimeyer, and Reed (2011) found that deaf children educated with hearing children had social skills in the same range; the significant factors were successful intervention by professionals, appropriate language support, and inclusion in activities. Others have stressed the importance of parents and educators to make sure that deaf learners have the opportunity for positive peer interaction to succeed in the classroom (e.g., Wolters, 2013). In the past, intervention has focused on access to the curriculum, perhaps at the expense of the broader context in which successful learning takes place.

Deaf students with mild or moderate hearing losses are much less well studied in the classroom than those with implants, despite similar levels of functional hearing, but they face the same challenges (e.g., Most, 2004). Similarly, those with unilateral hearing losses have issues in the mainstream classroom and are at a disadvantage compared to their hearing peers. Lieu, Tye-Murray, Karzon, and Piccirillo (2010) recommend that hearing-related accommodations should be provided for those with unilateral loss, and parents and educators should be aware of the implications of unilateral hearing losses. Hearing and communication technologies today are well equipped to ameliorate the effects of the range of hearing losses experienced by deaf students, but often parents and educators are unaware of these technologies. As reported, bone-anchored hearing systems can provide useful hearing to those with unilateral hearing loss and mild or moderate losses, but often there is little awareness of the benefits they can bring (Mulla et al., 2013).

Current technological developments can improve the mainstream learning environment significantly for those with hearing losses. With the introduction of improved acoustic treatments and of more acceptable sound field and FM systems, deaf learners with hearing losses can access the curriculum and the conversation of their peers more easily. While hearing technologies have changed dramatically in the past 20 years, communication technologies have changed dramatically too, affecting the educational needs of deaf students. Electronic captioning, speech-to-text services, texting and emailing, and Skype, which provides visual communication, have all changed the landscape of communication for deaf people, and consequently the expectations and opportunities for deaf students. Technologies such as whiteboards and electronic boards, bringing the Internet with its visual resources directly into the classroom, have the potential to have a positive impact on the learning environment for deaf students. Classroom use of laptops, tablets, and iPads brings communication and visual resources directly to the desks of all students, which may benefit deaf students too.

COMMUNICATION DECISIONS

In addition to where deaf students should be educated, the other major educational decision to be made relates to communication mode. Often confusion arises as to whether we are talking about communication mode or language. A rich communication input early in life is crucial to the development of language. For parents, this is likely to be in the language of their home and therefore a spoken one. Oral communication has often been linked with improved outcomes from implantation (Boons et al., 2012; Geers, 2006; Geers et al., 2011; Spencer & Oleson, 2008; Wiefferink, De Raeve, Spaai, Vermeij, & Uilenburg, 2008). Those using spoken language were found to have higher levels of language and literacy at high school (Geers et al., 2011). Dettman, Wall, Constantinescu, and Dowell (2013), using speech perception and vocabulary assessments, showed that an oral/aural approach made a significant difference after implantation. They compared auditory verbal, aural oral, and bilingual bicultural early intervention programs. The results of other studies are less clear-cut. A recent study by Yanbay, Hickson, Scarinci, Constantinescu, and Dettman (2014) showed no difference when comparing differing communication approaches (auditory oral, auditory verbal therapy [AVT], and sign and speech); early implantation and family involvement were the two major predictors of language outcomes rather than communication mode. Once more, care needs to be taken in drawing conclusions: Results may depend on what we are testing—and when.

When discussing choice of communication for deaf children, it is often suggested that communication choice is a "once and for all" decision. However, communication may change over time and different communication modes may be used in different situations. However, children with cochlear implants do change their communication mode after implantation, particularly if implanted early (Tait et al., 2007; Watson, Archbold, & Nikolopoulos, 2006). Parents report that the increase in oral communication, even for children who had initially used signed or gestural support, was driven by the change in access to audition provided by the implant and was led by the child's changing needs and own choice. Those implanted younger were more likely to change their communication mode from sign to oral; the majority of those implanted at age one moved from signed communication to oral within six months of implantation in the study by Tait and colleagues (2007). Parents describe this as a communication journey (Wheeler & Archbold, 2009). While the goal of cochlear implantation for parents was the development of spoken language, parents were also pragmatic about the communication that was crucial to family life, where the language of the home was a spoken one. Prior to implantation they wanted the most effective form of communication, which, for hearing families, who make up 95% of parents of deaf children, was likely to be a spoken language, with or without some signed or gestural support. Following implantation parents reported a reduction of signed support or gesture as spoken language developed through the increasing access to audition provided by an effective implant system. Later, parents and young people showed interest in the use of some signed support or sign language (e.g., BSL) itself, once spoken language had been established. Thus, while cochlear implantation offers an increased opportunity for the development of oral communication, parents recognize that different approaches may be appropriate at different times, and this might include the use of signed support. The concept that parents have to make a "once and for all" decision about communication mode, shortly after diagnosis, may have been changed by cochlear implantation. While cochlear implantation may have brought about new opportunities for spoken language, the decision may not be as clear-cut as once was predicted. Similarly, Mayer (2012) comments

> [. . .] there continue to be learners for whom the auditory channel must be supported by visual input (speech reading or signed support) for language to be acquired. Or they may need this visual support at certain stages of their development (eg before [cochlear implantation] or in poor listening conditions [. . .]

However, these were older studies, and now, with bilateral implantation taking place routinely in many countries in the first year of life, the crucial early rich language input is likely to be using the language of the home, and is likely to be a spoken one. The provision of useful hearing, whether through an implant or hearing aids, is likely to take place prior to the development of sign language skills, and increasingly studies are showing the value of early spoken language input (e.g., Ching, 2014).

Obtaining appropriate provision and flexibility in educational services has long been a source of tension between parents and local teachers (Sach & Whynes, 2005; Sorkin & Zwolan, 2004). Sach and Whynes reported that parents felt they had to "fight" for the provisions they felt appropriate for their child, and Sorkin and Zwolan found that 30% of parents described being unable to obtain the educational provision they wished for their child.

EDUCATIONAL ATTAINMENTS

Although few long-term studies with large numbers have yet been undertaken assessing the educational attainments following screening and early fitting of amplification, early reports, focusing largely on reading outcomes, are encouraging (Archbold, Harris, O'Donoghue, Nikolopoulos, White, & Richmond, 2008; Geers & Hayes, 2011; van der Kant, Vermeulen, De Raeve, & Schrueder, 2010; Vermeulen, Van, Schreuder, Knoors, & Snik, 2007), with age at implantation being a significant factor (e.g., Archbold et al., 2008). A review of reading studies by Marschark, Rhoten, and Fabich (2007) reported improved reading skills in those with implants, but skills were still not on a par with their hearing peers.

However, it is still uncertain whether the early encouraging results continue as deaf learners move into adolescence, with the more demanding and subtle skills required to achieve age-appropriate reading levels (e.g., inferencing), as discussed above. Geers and Hayes (2011) reported on a group that, when assessed at age 8/9 years, had reading levels within normal levels; however, when retested at ages 15/16, although speech perception scores improved over the long term and average language scores improved at a faster than normal rate, there was wide variability in reading scores. Harris and Terlektsi (2010), comparing the reading skills of a group of 12- to 16-year-olds with implants to those with hearing aids, found that the reading ages of all groups were several years below that of their hearing peers.

Despite reports of age-appropriate language development in children who were implanted early (Ching et al., 2008; Dettman et al., 2007), reports of progress in educational attainments in the longer term are more cautious. Thoutenhoofd (2006), in his study of deaf children in Scotland, showed that those with implants had better educational attainments, particularly in mathematics, than those with hearing aids but scored more poorly than their hearing peers. Stacey, Fortnum, Barton, and Summerfield (2006), in an investigation of a large group of cochlear implant users in the United Kingdom, found pediatric cochlear implantation to be associated with reported improvements in some aspects of educational achievements and quality of life, provided that children receive implants before five years of age. In a further study, Geers and Hayes (2011) also reported that there were significant delays in spelling and written expression in their group of 112 adolescents compared with hearing peers. However, many of these studies are based on children implanted later than now is the case, and with older technology, and thus the results may not be representative of today's expectations.

In the comprehensive benchmarking report of outcomes by the National Sensory Impairment Programme (2013) in England, using the national educational measures, there is evidence at the early stages of education of the beneficial effect of cochlear implantation. It is also interesting to note that profoundly deaf children outperform those with severe hearing losses, and those with profound and severe losses outperform those with moderate losses. The possible reasons for this interesting finding are not explored; perhaps educational support is targeted at those with greater hearing losses, as educational services are required to prioritize? The comprehensive Consortium for Research into Deaf Education data for England for 2013 found the following (summarized at www.batod.org.uk):

- There are around 38,000 deaf children in England, a reported increase of 9% in two years.
- 76% of school-aged deaf children attend mainstream schools (where there are no special provisions).
- 21% of deaf children are recorded as having an additional special educational need. The most common appears to be moderate learning difficulties.
- Around 8% of deaf children have at least one cochlear implant.
- 79% of deaf children communicate using spoken English only. 12% speak another spoken language, either on its own or in combination with another language. 9% use sign language in some form, either on its own or alongside another language.
- There are at least 1,117 teachers employed as teachers of the deaf in employment in educational services or resource provisions. Although the reported number of deaf children has increased, the reported number of teachers of the deaf in employment has declined by 3% to 4% in two years.
- There are at least 1,325 other specialist support staff working with deaf children in England, a 4% increase since the prior year.

It is interesting to note that the number of support staff increased, while the number of qualified teachers of the deaf decreased, leading to a corresponding decrease in skills and experience. Large-scale, long-term studies of the educational outcomes of deaf children are needed to enable us to answer some of the questions posed in this chapter. The educational support of children with complex needs, a not insubstantial group of deaf children, is another underresearched area. Parents report huge difficulty in finding educational placements to provide support for their child's complex needs and for their hearing loss, along with the necessary skills and expertise required to manage the hearing technology they need (Mulla et al., 2013).

WHAT DEAF LEARNERS TELL US: "BEING DEAF DIFFERENTLY"

Although we can assess the benefits of the technology on educational decisions for deaf students, what do we know of the impact on the learners themselves? What do they tell us? Have the concerns that the impact of modern technology would create more mental health issues been confirmed?

These fears do not appear to be well founded. Deaf adolescents tell us that they view themselves in more flexible ways than in the past (Moog et al., 2011; Wheeler et al., 2007) and that it is possible to be both deaf AND hearing. With modern technologies this is almost the case; profoundly deaf children who have been implanted early can experience almost total deafness and almost "normal" levels of hearing. Although we have changed dramatically the impact of hearing loss, providing much more useful hearing than in the past, we have not "cured" deafness, but we have changed its implications. Young people talk about "being deaf differently" today. They recognize that they are deaf, as they are dependent on technology to hear, but most do not relate to Deaf culture as viewed in the past (Gfeller et al., 2013; Moog et al., 2011; Wheeler et al., 2007).

Their dependency on technology brings additional issues. In the study by Wheeler and colleagues (2007, p. 308), over a third of the young people worried about the technology they use, being concerned about its breaking down, particularly the internal part: "I'm fine with being deaf but it's like one of your organs failing . . . the fact that at some time you will have to have an operation to replace it." Many showed a lack of understanding of the technology they use daily to access the curriculum and social life, although they were aware of its importance to them.

What do these young people want? When interviewed, young people with cochlear implants reported that listening in groups and noise in school was extremely challenging and resulted in missing important parts of the lessons or instructions (RNID, 2008). One young person, who scored highly on clinical tests of hearing, commented

> I need one person at a time, not all at the same time . . . Whoosh it goes over my head. Group work is the biggest pain you could ever possibly imagine. Small group is all right but big group or class discussions they are the worst. (Mainstream student, 14)

In a study of 90 deaf young people with implants for more than 15 years (Archbold, 2013), a common theme was that they wished to take control of the technology for themselves. This is a generation confident and competent with technology, and the hearing technologies they use do not confound them.

SUMMARY

The comparatively rapid changes that have taken place over the past two decades have had a huge impact on the experiences and opportunities of deaf learners, and in ways that were not entirely expected. Knoors and Marschark (2012) comment on the unexpected perspective given by hearing screening and cochlear implantation on the development of deaf children. These changes have been driven by scientists and surgeons, but their impact is revealed in the classroom, with a profound and ongoing effect on the practice of deaf education.

Deaf learners are now an even more diverse group than before, with changing characteristics and needs. The term may no longer be possible to define, and we need research exploring the experiences of the young deaf learners, enabling them to describe their characteristics and needs for themselves. A major issue is that, for many, their characteristics may not be apparent. In the words of one deaf student

> My university is not deaf aware enough. They think that because I can speak I can understand everything. If I was a signer, my needs would be obvious! (Archbold, 2013)

Where there are political imperatives to prioritize spending on education, the needs of deaf students today may be neglected. For example, Lieu and colleagues (2010) advised that the practice of withholding hearing-related accommodations from those with unilateral loss should not continue: Parents and educators should be aware of the implications of a unilateral loss. Deaf learners with intelligible speech and the ability to converse easily and with confidence may have their subtle language needs overlooked (Archbold, 2010).

To summarize, the characteristics of deaf learners have changed rapidly in recent years:

- They are a more diverse group.
- They have a more flexible view of themselves.
- They show an increased use of spoken language.

- They show more flexibility in changes in use of communication mode over time and in differing situations.
- They have more subtle linguistic and communication needs, which may not be readily apparent.
- They increasingly attend mainstream schools.
- They are concerned about the functioning of their technology.
- They are dependent on technology and often do not have sufficient understanding of it to "own" it.
- They are increasingly supported by those who may not be qualified to do so, or may not be knowledgeable about deafness or the technology used today.

This more diverse group may not be best served by being called "deaf students"; their needs are too variable and flexible for one term to define them. Perhaps we should be using the term "students who have a hearing loss." Hearing loss and its impact may be varied, and defining students and attempting to define their needs audiologically, or educationally, or culturally may not be helpful. The changing technologies have changed the characteristics of the group, and in doing so have changed their needs, making them more difficult to define, with implications for those who have responsibility for planning and providing their educational services. This impact has occurred in a comparatively short time compared with the long history of deaf education. We need to remember that the outcomes reported here are for students identified later than is now the case, and who are using older technology than now the case, and are likely to be conservative.

Although outcomes from the technological interventions have been better than predicted, robust predictors of outcomes are as yet largely unknown, other than early age at fitting of hearing aid or implant, and the absence of other difficulties. Nor is it yet known what type of educational provision best supports children with hearing loss in the long term. For example, children with implants are not performing like hearing children, but neither are they performing like deaf children in the past. This diversity and variation are challenging for teachers and may have added to the challenges in training teachers of the deaf and in planning educational systems.

Research is required and is best carried out by bringing together researchers, teachers, parents, and children and young people. Research on pupils with hearing loss will then be based on real-world issues and will also benefit from the research developments in other fields such as that of cognition and neuroscience. This will enable us to focus further on how these children best learn, rather than on their functioning and on outcome results per se. Thus, changes in practice and management of individual children will be based on robust evidence, supporting deaf educators in moving on from the controversies of the past. Further research bringing together different disciplines may enable us to bring together the best ideas and practice of the past with the exciting developments of today. This may enable deaf education to maximize the benefits for deaf children and capitalize on the greatest opportunities that today's technologies bring. The changing needs of students who are deaf require educational services that provide

- Flexibility in educational provision over time;
- Effective, trained support in mainstream education;
- The skills to monitor subtle changes in progress over time, and identify difficulties that may impede progress, whether residing in the child, the environment, or the technology;
- The provision of appropriate education for those whose main difficulty is no longer deafness but may be an additional learning disability;
- Appropriate support in the secondary or high school, with its increased demands;
- The management of complex, changing technology in a busy educational environment;
- Expertise from other professionals; and
- Peer group support for the psychosocial needs of the increasing numbers of those in mainstream schools.

> The challenge to respond flexibly to an emerging new era of deaf children is one that must be accepted if the diverse needs of all deaf learners are to be accommodated. (Mayer & Leigh, 2010, p. 184)

REFERENCES

Anderson, K. (1989). *Screening instrument for targeting educational risk (SIFTER)*. Tampa, FL: Educational Audiology Association.

Antia, S. D., Jones, P., Luckner, J., Kreimeyer, K. H., & Reed, S. (2011). *Exceptional Children, 77*, 4.

Archbold, S. (2010). *Deaf education: changed by cochlear implantation?* PhD dissertation. Radboud University Nijmegen.

Archbold, S. (2013). *Moving into higher education and the world of work*. Paper presented at the International Federation of Otorhinological Societies, Seoul, June 2013.

Archbold, S., Harris, M., O'Donoghue. G., Nikolopoulos, T., White, A., & Richmond, H. L. (2008). Reading abilities after cochlear implantation: the effect of age at implantation on outcomes at 5 and 7 years after implantation. *International Journal of Pediatric Otorhinolaryngology, 72*, 1471–1478.

Archbold S., & Mayer, C. (2012). Deaf education: the impact of cochlear implantation. *Deafness and Education International, 14*, 1–14.

Archbold, S. M., Nikolopoulos, T. P., Lutman, M. E., & O'Donoghue, G. M. (2002). The educational settings of profoundly deaf children with cochlear implants compared with age-matched peers with hearing aids: implications for management. *International Journal of Audiology*, *41*(3), 157–161.

Bess, F. H., Murphy, J. D., & Parker, R. A. (1998). Children with minimal sensori-neural hearing loss: prevalence, educational performance and functional status. *Ear & Hearing*, *19*, 339–354.

Boons, T., Brokx, J., Dhooge, I., Frijns, J., Peeraer,L., Vermuelen, A., Wouters, J., & van Wieringen, A. (2012a). Predictors of spoken language development following paediatric cochlear implantation. *Ear & Hearing 33*,5, 617–639.

Boons, T., Brokx, J., Frijns, J., Peeraer, L., Philiips, B., & Vermeulen A. (2012b). Effect of paediatric bilateral cochlear implantation on language development. *Archivers of Pediatric & Adolescent Medicine*, *166*, 28–34.

Boons, T., De Raeve, L., Langereis, M., Peeraer L., Wouters, J., & van Wieringen, A. (2013). Expressive vocabulary, morphology, syntax and narrative skills in profoundly deaf children after early cochlear implantation. *Research in Developmental Disabilities*, *34*(6), 2008–2022.

Casby, M. W. (2001). Otitis media and language development: A meta-analysis. *American Journal of Speech-Language Pathology*, *10*, 65–80.

Ching, T. Y. C. (2014). *Outcomes of children with hearing loss: implications for management*. Paper presented at HEAL, Como, June 6, 2014.

Ching, T. Y. C., Dillon, H., Day, J., & Crowe, K. (2008). The NAL Study on Longitudinal Outcomes of Hearing-Impaired Children: interim findings on language of early and later-identified children at 6 months after hearing aid fitting. In R. C. Seewald & J. M. Bamford (Eds.), *A sound foundation through early amplification: Proceedings of the fourth international conference*. Stäfa, Switzerland: Phonak AG.

Chute, P. M., & Nevins, M. (2006). *School professionals working with children with cochlear implants*. San Diego, CA: Plural Publishing.

Cone, B. K., Wake, M., Tobin, S., Poulakis, Z., & Rickards, F. W. (2010). Slight, mild sensori- neural hearing loss in children: audiometric, clinical and risk factor profiles. *Ear & Hearing*, *31*(2), 202–212.

Conrad, R. (1979). *A deaf school child*. London: Harper Row.

Consortium for Research into Deaf Education. (2013). *CRIDE report*. Downloadable from www.batod.org.uk

Damen, G. W., Langereis, M. C., Snik, A. F., Chute, P. M., & Mylanus, E. A. (2007). Classroom performance and language development of CI students placed in mainstream elementary school. *Otology & Neurotology*, *28*, 463–472.

Dammeyer, J. (2013). A longitudinal study of pragmatic language development in three children with cochlear implants. *Deafness and Education International*, *14*, 217–232.

Dashi, J., Sheehan, P., & McDemott A. L. (2012). Bone Anchored Hearing Aids in Children: An update. *Int Jnl Pediatric Otorynolaryngology*, *76*, 5, 618–622.

De Raeve, L. (2006). Making the case for early hearing detection and intervention in Flanders, Belgium. *Volta Voices*, *13*, 14–17.

De Raeve, L. (2010). A longitudinal study on auditory perception and speech intelligibility in deaf children implanted younger than 18 months in comparison to those implanted at later ages. *Otology and Neurotology*, *31*, 1261–1267.

De Raeve, L., Archbold, S., & Diller, G. (2013). Maximising the benefits for bilateral implantation, in therapy, at home and school. *Deafness and Education International*, *15*(1), 52–68.

De Raeve, L., Baerts, J., Colleye, E., & Croux, E. (2012). Changing schools for the deaf: updating the educational setting for deaf children in the 21st century, a big challenge. *Deafness and Education International, 14*(1), 48–59.

Dettman, S. J., Pinder, D., Briggs, R. J., Dowell, R. C., & Leigh, J. R. (2007). Communication development in children who receive the cochlear implant younger than 12 months: risks versus benefits. *Ear & Hearing, 28,* 11S–18S.

Dettman, S., Wall, E., Constantinescu, G., & Dowell R. (2013). Communication outcomes for groups of children using cochlear implants enrolled in auditory-verbal, aural-oral and bilingual bicultural early intervention programmes. *Otology & Neurotology, 34,* 451.

Fellinger, J., Holzinger, D., Sattel, H., Luacht, M., & Goldberg, D. (2009). Correlates of mental health disorders among children with hearing impairment. *Developmental Medicine & Child Neurology, 51*(8), 635–641.

Geers, A. (2006). Factors influencing spoken language outcomes in children following early cochlear implantation. *Advances in Oto-rhino-laryngology, 64,* 50–65.

Geers, A. E., & Hayes, H. (2011). Reading, writing and phonological processing skills of adolescents with 10 or more years of cochlear implant experience. *Ear and Hearing, 32*(1), 49S–59S.

Geers A., Moog, J., & Biedenstein, J. (2009). Spoken language scores of children using cochlear implants compared to hearing age-mates at school entry. *Journal of Deaf Studies and Deaf Education, 14,* 371–385.

Geers, A. E., Strube, M., Tobey, E. A., Pisoni, D., & Moog, J. S. (2011). Epilogue: Factors contributing to long-term outcomes of cochlear implantation in early childhood. *Ear and Hearing, 32*(1), 84S–92S.

Gfeller, K., Driscoll, V., See Smith, R., & Scherperle, C. (2013). The musical experiences and attitudes of a first cohort of prelingually deaf adolescents and young adult cochlear implant recipients. *Seminars of Hearing, 33*(4), 346–360.

Gregory, S., Bishop, J., & Sheldon, L. (1995). *Deaf young people and their families.* Cambridge, UK: Cambridge University Press.

Harris, M., & Terlektsi, E. (2010). Reading and spelling abilities of deaf adolescents with cochlear implants and hearing aids. *Journal of Deaf Studies and Deaf Education, 16*(1), 24–34.

Kesser, B. W., Krook, K., & Gray, L. C. (2013). Impact of unilateral conductive hearing loss due to aural atresia on academic performance in children. *The Laryngoscope, 123*(9), 2270–2275.

Knoors, H., & Marschark, M. (2012). Language planning for 21st century: Bilingual language policy for deaf children. *Journal of Deaf Studies and Deaf Education, 17*(3), 291–305.

Leigh, G. (2008). Changing parameters in deafness and deaf education. In M. Marschark & P. C. Hauser (Eds.), *Deaf cognition: Foundations and outcomes* (pp. 24–51). New York: Oxford University Press.

Lieu, J. E. (2004). Speech language and educational consequences of unilateral hearing loss in children. *Archives of Otology and Head & Neck Surgery, 130,* 524–530.

Lieu, J. E. C., Tye-Murray, N., Karzon, R. K., & Piccirillo, J. S. (2010). Unilateral hearing loss is associated with worse speech and language scores in children. *Pediatrics, 125*(6), 1348–1355.

Marschark, M., Rhoten, C., & Fabich, M., (2007). Effects of cochlear implants on children's reading and academic achievement. *Journal of Deaf Studies and Deaf Education, 12*, 269–282.

Marschark, M., & Spencer, P. (2006). Historical and theoretical perspectives. In P. Spencer & M. Marschark (Eds.), *Advances in spoken language in deaf and hard of hearing children* (pp. 3–21). New York: Oxford University Press.

Mayer, C. (2012, March). A role for total communication in 2012? *BATOD Magazine*, 8–9.

Mayer, C., & Leigh, G. (2010). The changing context for sign bilingual education programs: Issues in language and the development of literacy. *International Journal of Bilingualism and Bilingual Education, 13*(2), 175–186.

Mitchell, R. E., & Karchmer, M.A. (2004). Chasing the mythical ten percent: Parental hearing status of deaf and hard of hearing students in the United States. *Sign Language Studies, 4*(2), 138–163.

Moeller, M. P., Tomblin, B., Connor, C. M., & Jerger, S. (2007). Current state of knowledge, language and literacy of children with hearing impairment. *Ear & Hearing, 28*, 740–753.

Moog, J. S., Geers, A. E., Gustus, C. H., & Brenner, C. (2011). Psychological adjustment in adolescents who have used cochlear implants since pre-school. *Ear and Hearing, 32*(1), 75S–83S.

Most, T. (2004). The effects of degree and type of hearing loss on children's performance in class. *Deafness and Education International, 6*, 154–166.

Most, T., & Peled, M., (2007). Perception of suprasegmental features of speech by children with cochlear implants and children with hearing aids. *Journal of Deaf Studies and Deaf Education, 12*(3), 350–361.

Mukari, S., Ling, L., & Ghani, H. (2007). Educational performance of pediatric cochlear implant recipients in mainstream classes, *International Journal of Pediatric Otorhinolaryngology, 71*, 231–240.

Mulla, I., Harrigan, S., Gregory, S., & Archbold, S., (2013). Children with complex needs and cochlear implants: The parents' perspective. *Deafness and Education international, 12*(4), S38–S41.

Mulla, I., Wright, N., & Archbold, S. (2013). The views and experiences of families of bone- anchored hearing aid use with children: a study by interview. *Deafness and Education International, 15*(2), 70–90.

National Sensory Impairment Programme. (2013). *Outcomes benchmarking report: Summary version academic year 2011—2012*. Available at www.natsip.org.uk

Nicholas, J. G., & Geers, A. E. (2007). Will they catch up? The role of age at cochlear implantation in the spoken language development of children with severe to profound hearing loss. *Journal of Speech, Language and Hearing Research, 50*, 1048–1062.

Nikolopoulos, T. P., Archbold, S. M., Wever, C. C., & Lloyd, H. (2008). Speech production in deaf implanted children with additional disabilities: a comparison with age-equivalent implanted children without such disorders. *International Journal of Pediatric Otology, 72*, 1823–1828.

Philips, B., Corthals, P., & De Raeve, L., (2009). Impact of newborn hearing screening comparing outcomes in pediatric cochlear implant users. *Laryngoscope, 119*, 974–979.

Royal National Institute for the Deaf (RNID). (2008). *Supporting pupils with cochlear implants in secondary schools*. Available at www.earfoundation.org.uk

Sach, T. H., & Whynes, D. K. (2005). Paediatric cochlear implantation: The views of parents. *International Journal of Audiology, 44*(7), 400–407.

Sorkin, D. L., & Zwolan, T. A. (2004). Trends in educational services for children with cochlear implants. *International Congress Series, 1273*, 417–421.

Spencer, L., & Olesen, J. J. (2008). Early listening and speaking skills predict later reading proficiency in pediatric cochlear implant users. *Ear & Hearing, 29*, 270–280.

Stacey, P., Fortnum, H., Barton, G., & Summerfield, A. (2006). Hearing-impaired children in the United Kingdom, I: Auditory performance, communication skills, educational achievements, quality of life, and cochlear implantation. *Ear and Hearing, 27*(2), 161–186.

Tait, M., De Raeve, L., & Nikolopoulos, T. P. (2007). Deaf children with cochlear implants before the age of 1 year: comparison of preverbal communication with normally hearing children. *International Journal of Pediatric Otorhinolaryngology, 71*, 1605–1611.

Thoutenhoofd, E. (2006). Cochlear implanted pupils in Scottish schools: 4 year school attainment data (2000–2004). *Journal of Deaf Studies and Deaf Education, 11*(2), 171–188.

Tobey, E. A., Geers, A. E., Sundarrajan, M., & Shin, S. (2011). Factors influencing speech production in elementary and high school-aged cochlear implant users. *Ear & Hearing, 31*(Suppl. 1), 27S–38S.

Uziel, A. S., Sillon, M., Vieu, A., Artieres, F., Piron, J. P., Daures, J. P., & Mondain, M. . (2007). Ten-year follow-up of a consecutive series of children with multichannel cochlear implants. *Otology & Neurotology, 28*, 615–628.

Van der Kant, A., Vermeulen, A., De Raeve, L., & Schreuder, R. (2010). Reading comprehension of Flemish deaf children in Belgium: sources of variability in reading comprehension after cochlear implantation. *Deafness and Education International, 12*(2), 77–98.

Vermeulen, A. M., Van, B. W., Schreuder, R., Knoors, H., & Snik, A. (2007). Reading comprehension of deaf children with cochlear implants. *Journal of Deaf Studies and Deaf Education, 12*, 283–302.

Watson, L. M, Archbold, S. M., & Nikolopoulos, T. P. (2006). Children's communication mode five years after cochlear implantation: changes over time according to age at implant. *Cochlear Implants International, 7*(2), 77–91.

Wheeler, A., & Archbold, S. (2009). Children with cochlear implants: the communication journey. *Cochlear Implants International, 10*(1), 41–62.

Wheeler, A., Archbold, S., Gregory, S., & Skipp, A. (2007). Cochlear implants: The young peoples' perspective. *Journal of Deaf Studies and Deaf Education, 12*(3), 303–316.

Wiefferink, K., De Raeve, L., Spaai, G., Vermeij, B., & Uilenburg, N. (2008). Influence of linguistic environment on children's language development: Flemish versus Dutch Children. *Deafness and Education International, 10*(4), 226–243.

Wolters, N. (2013). *Social participation of deaf youth in school.* PhE thesis. Radboud University Nijmegen.

Wolters, N., Knoors, H., Cillessen, A. C. N., & Verhoeven, L. (2011). Predicting acceptance and popularity in early adolescence as a function of hearing status, gender, and educational setting. *Research in Developmental Disabilities*, 32, 2553–2565.

Yoshinago-Itano, C. (2004). From screening to early identification and intervention: Discovering predictors to successful outcomes for children with significant hearing loss. In D. Power & G. Leigh (Eds.), *Educating deaf students: Global perspectives* (pp. 69–84). Washington, DC: Gallaudet University Press.

3

When You're Not Average, Be(come) Excellent

Barriers and Opportunities for Deaf Students

Corrie Tijsseling

The field of deaf education has seen important changes in recent decades. In the Netherlands, this type of education started in the 18th century and took place in institutions with boarding schools, segregating deaf pupils from society. From 1864 on, the dominant language method in the education of deaf students in the Netherlands was the oral method, which taught students to speak and to read speech. In the second half of the 20th century, insights from audiology made it possible to differentiate subgroups of deaf students who were categorized according to the degree, the type, and the onset of their hearing loss, as well as their results in the understanding and development of spoken language; these groups frequently were educated separately. Technological devices such as hearing aids were welcomed to contribute to the development of spoken language.

In the same period, however, there was also a growing interest in the language that deaf students developed and used among themselves: sign language. Once this language was scientifically recognized as a full language (Stokoe, 1963), comparable to spoken language but in a different modality, educators of the deaf started to wonder whether including signs as part of language instruction might be beneficial for those pupils who were known as "oral failures." A paradigm shift thus took place: While signing was once considered detrimental for the development of spoken language, it was now investigated how sign language could contribute to language development. Together with the recognition of sign language as a full language, the culture of the Deaf community was recognized (Padden & Humphries, 1988; Woodward, 1972). In the education of deaf students, attention was given to Deaf culture, both in the curriculum and by hiring deaf staff, who functioned as role models for students. From the 1990s on, all Dutch schools for the deaf provided bilingual and bicultural education, in the belief that this type of education offered deaf students the best developmental opportunities (Tijsseling, 2014).

The educational landscape is now changing again, drastically, due to technological and ideological developments. First, the development of digital hearing aids and cochlear implants increased the access to and the development of spoken language in many deaf children. Second, the idea of inclusive education gained ground in the Netherlands, with schools for the deaf investigating possible arrangements for inclusive education for deaf students (De Klerk, Hermans, Knoors, & Wauters, 2009). In 2005, the Dutch government evaluated the Dutch educational system with its two strands, mainstream education and special education, and concluded that action was called for (see De Klerk, Fortgens, & Van der Eijk, Chapter 25 in this volume). Special education is expensive while educational outcomes often are substandard, with a system that is characterized by bureaucracy and inefficiency (Bekkers, Noordegraaf, Waslander, & De Wit, 2011). The *Evaluatie en Adviescommissie Passend Onderwijs* (Evaluation and Advisory Committee for Appropriate Education)) considers qualification, allocation, and socialization as the three main functions of education, not only for general students but also for disabled students, and thus recommends educational integration (Bekkers et al., 2011).

The Dutch government therefore launched a new policy named *Passend Onderwijs* (Appropriate Education). Starting in August 2014, mainstream schools must offer appropriate education for students with special needs. Students who are deaf may be placed individually in mainstream schools, in co-enrollment programs, or in a special school for the deaf. Since the 1980s, deaf and hard-of-hearing students have been educated in mainstream schools, with the expertise that has been developed in schools for the deaf being transferred to mainstream education. Professionals in deaf education inform, advise, and assist mainstream teachers in a cooperative manner. With the new policy of Appropriate Education, the present number of 30% deaf students in mainstream education may rise (Knoors, personal communication, March 18, 2014). Such a major change in the education of deaf pupils, both on ideological and practical levels, leads to an important question: What is good education for deaf pupils? Ideally, education should be barrier-free and offer opportunities. But what are barriers for deaf students, and how can they make the best use of opportunities?

DIFFERENCE AND DIVERSITY

Before exploring the question on what good education is for deaf students, we must identify "the deaf student." Who is he or she? What are her or his characteristics? Consequently, what are important issues concerning his or her education? For this, the development of the current definitions of deaf students will be described, followed by a critical analysis of these definitions. In this chapter, all forms of education are considered—that is, the education of students in primary and secondary education and those in higher education.

The present fields of child development and special education originate from the field of child study that emerged at the end of the 19th century, the experimental approach in science that aimed to find regularities in the development of children by distinguishing between "normal" and "abnormal" children (Dekker, Kruithof, Simon, & Vanobbergen, 2012; Depaepe, 1998; Drenth, 2008; Drenth & Myers, 2011; Lohmann & Mayer, 2009; Turmel, 2004). In the present day, the labels of "normal" and "abnormal" are negatively valued. However, for a proper historical account of these concepts it is necessary to use them, but with quotation marks. In the Netherlands, this field of study was named *pedologie*: the study of the "normal" and "abnormal" child as a basis for the diagnosis and treatment of the abnormal child (Rietveld-van Wingerden & Groenendijk, 2006). Over the decades, scientific knowledge on child development expanded, with the development of the "normal" child considered as the optimal development. Children who could not hear, see, or think like "normal" children were considered to have deficits and in need of treatment. The motivation was to offer the "abnormal" child the best possible opportunities for "normal" development. As a result, however, this approach assumed that the "normal" child was the best possible standard for optimal development of all children.

Regarding the functioning of the auditory sense, the distinction between "normal" and "abnormal" was translated as respectively as "hearing" and "deaf." As mentioned before, medical insights made it possible to differentiate within the group of children labeled "deaf," categorizing them according to the type, onset, and degree of hearing loss; subgroups ranged from mild, moderate, and severe hearing loss to profoundly deaf. The medical understanding of disability, focusing on the body and the impairment, was in the 1970s replaced by a social-constructivist approach (Verstraete, 2012). In this social model, disability was not about physical limitation but about social limitation, with society erecting barriers to the participation of disabled people (Van Trigt, 2013). Regarding deaf people, the distinction was made between the medical condition of deafness and the cultural affiliation ("Deaf"). In the latter perspective, Deaf people form a cultural and linguistic minority, with sign language as their native language, and the accompanying Deaf culture (Padden & Humphries, 1988). Over the years, the concept of deaf/Deaf has become a way for the deaf community to decide who is "in" and who is "out," by labeling those using speech and hearing aids as "deaf" and those preferring sign language as "Deaf." However, the exact processes and effects of this labeling on identity formation and language choices in deaf students have so far not been studied yet.

Deaf studies offers important insights into social and cultural constructions of deaf/Deaf while also revealing power relations. However, the role of the sensory experience seems somewhat ignored in this field. Sensory studies, which is a merger of fields such as anthropology, art history, aesthetics, religion, architecture, and disability, might reveal new insights (www.sensorystudies.org). Research into the history of the senses also offers us new perspectives on (the history of) disability with regard to the role and value of the senses in society. Examples are a study on the social position of blind people in the Netherlands (Van Trigt, 2013) and a study on the role and value of voice in society, exploring the implications of this for deaf people (Rée, 1999). Concerning deafness and Deaf people, it would, for example, be interesting to investigate why Deaf adults use hearing aids or cochlear implants while at the same time claiming to be members of the Deaf community. What motivates them to at least partly use the auditory sense, instead of fully relying on the visual sense? It makes one wonder about the role of the sensory experience in the identity construction of deaf/Deaf people. More importantly, how does the complex relation between the sensory experience and the identity construction work out for deaf students, who are in the process of their identity development while being educated in a mainstream setting and using hearing aids or cochlear implants?

Another problem in identifying deaf students is the categorization of deaf students according to the type, onset, and degree of their hearing loss. While the natural state of a student may be profoundly deaf, the use of a hearing aid or cochlear implant transforms him or her into someone with a mild to moderate hearing loss. Most, if not all, deaf students use technological devices for hearing and understanding spoken language, and eventually use visual input (speech-reading and signs) to process language. Thus, they have to find a balance between their natural state and their "technological" state: between the auditory-verbal language mode and the visual-gestural language mode, and between their membership of the larger society and the Deaf community. The aforementioned medical and social dichotomies of hearing/deaf and deaf/Deaf suggest that the construction of identity in deaf students is actually about making a choice between the one and the other identity, rather than finding a balance between the many aspects of personal identity that all people are confronted with. Also, what does it mean to grow up from early in life with both a natural state and a technological state, being able to hear with hearing aids or cochlear implants and being deaf when the devices are switched off? Moreover, what challenges do deaf students experience regarding identity development in mainstream education, eventually influencing their learning processes?

When approaching deaf students from a sensory perspective, the distinction between deaf as a hearing loss and Deaf as a cultural affiliation is problematic. Indeed, the fact that one does not hear does plays a role in the development of language, but the choice for one or more language modalities (speech and/or sign) is related to parental choices and to being acquainted to languages and their modalities, and is also affected by social expectations and personal desires regarding belonging to the larger (hearing) society and/or the Deaf community. That this can work out differently on an individual level is obvious: Each person is unique and responds differently when confronted with the number of entangled factors and experiences that contribute to making choices in life. In this chapter, deaf students are identified as all students who have a hearing loss and thus have to deal with the intertwining of sensory functioning and social status, an intertwining that has effects on learning processes. No matter the type, onset, or degree of their hearing loss, they all have to deal with this intertwining.

Functional diversity, a concept that evolved from the discourse on ethnic diversity (Bell & Hartmann, 2007), might be an even more appropriate approach in considering these students because this dynamic and constructive paradigm takes into account the diversity of physiological and psychosocial functioning, with regard to both individual and environmental factors (Patston, 2007). However, as this is a new concept that is only recently explored, the choice in this chapter is to use the term "deaf students" for all students with hearing loss. As this chapter is about younger students who thus are in the process of developing their identity, only their sensory disposition will be mentioned by using "deaf" rather than ascribing them an identity by labeling them as "Deaf." In addition, the term "general students" will be used—that is, the majority of students, those enrolled in general education settings who once were labeled "normal."

When considering the question of providing good education for deaf students in mainstream settings, it is important to acknowledge their functional diversity, even when they use hearing aids or cochlear implants, because hearing with technological devices is different from "normal" hearing. Regardless of their abilities in hearing and speech, deaf students always differ from general students because their auditory sense functions differently, with consequences for their embodiment and epistemology. Embodiment is the dynamic interaction of brain, body, and environment that is influenced by the features of the body and the characteristics of the environment (Berthouze & Tijsseling, 2006). Epistemology is the knowledge that we gather about the world through our experiences and interpretations of the world (Honderich, 2005). For those who can hear, sound is the predominant sense of their embodiment and fundamental to their epistemology, with the result that they cannot imagine a life without sound. For those who cannot hear (or hear well enough), sight is the basis of embodiment and epistemology, with sound having no (or less) meaning.

General education is constructed around general students. In the Netherlands, primary education became compulsory in 1900, and in 1903 the Dutch government decided that all atypical students should be removed from general education as they were considered a problem for the teaching activities of teachers and the learning processes of typical students (Tijsseling, 2014). The concept of inclusive education, as expressed in the Salamanca Statement (UNESCO, 1994), shows an almost opposite perspective on students with special needs. It is not the student who has to adapt to general education, but it is about reforming schools and improving pedagogies, with schools responding positively to diversity and individual differences, now being perceived as opportunities and enrichments rather than problems (Ainscow & Cesar, 2006; Florian & Rouse, 2009). The new policy of the Dutch government on Appropriate Education raises questions concerning functionally diverse students, in this case deaf students. Can deaf students develop optimally in an educational system that is historically constructed around general students, not only on the academic level but also on social, cultural, and personal levels? These are questions that relate to the intentions, goals, and values of education. Biesta (2012) offered parameters that can help us discuss the question what good education is, by pointing out three functions of education: qualification, socialization, and individuation. The question of what good education is for deaf students will be explored along these three functions, with an analysis of the intentions, goals, and values of education regarding each function. Finally, this chapter reflects on barriers and opportunities for deaf students.

QUALIFICATION

The qualifying function of education comprises the teaching of knowledge, skills, and understanding to students so they can make decisions on "what to do." It is both the most important function of education and the reason for the existence of education, based on the premise that well-educated citizens contribute to societies. Regarding inclusive education, the intention is to give disabled students, in this case deaf students, the same qualification opportunities as general students (Ainscow & César, 2006). This intention expresses the value of equality, which is considered important in democratic societies where all people are considered equal, regardless of gender, religion, political opinions, sexual orientation, or any other characteristic. The goal is to obtain the best possible qualification for all students, and by measuring learning outcomes we can evaluate whether goals are met.

Qualification is an aspect of education that is highlighted in current educational research and policy regarding regular education, with a number of ranking lists and standardized tests that aim to inform in a quantified manner what methods work best to make the most students reach the highest levels for the several aspects of the curriculum. However, a debate is evolving about this current trend in regular education to consider education only in terms of input and output (Biesta, 2012). There is a growing concern that education is becoming "teaching to the test" (Besturenraad, 2012). Smeyers (2008) states that education is a social activity so educational research should thus use various modes of explanation, as social life cannot be explained by statistics only. We must also look into interpretations and meanings: What do people feel? What are their experiences? What do they say about their reasons, desires, and intentions? Qualitative research could shed light on these aspects by studying common features in different cases in order to describe relations between social categories. According to Smeyers, educational research does not give us a fixed and universal knowledge of the social world but contributes to the improvement of our practical knowledge of ongoing social life. Biesta (2010) concluded that experimental research is useful for educational practitioners as it informs them about evidence from previous situations, giving them suggestions for designing and/or altering teaching methods and strategies.

Biesta (2010) considered it important to reflect on the intentions, goals, and values of education because any educational activity has a normative stance: A certain outcome is desired, and this desired outcome is related to what is considered important in social life. However, whereas philosophy of education plays a significant role in the history of general education by questioning the intentions, goals, and values of education, the history of the education of the deaf in the Netherlands shows that this discipline is relatively unknown in this type of education (Tijsseling, 2014). Therefore, the reader is invited to join in this philosophical journey that aims to discuss the question of good education for deaf students in terms of intentions, goals, and values.

What is considered important in the present social world? While literacy and numeracy for a long time were mainly reserved for the elite, with the common people working with their hands, the technological and digital character of modern Western societies requires all citizens to have a high level of literacy and numeracy. Education thus focuses on the development of literacy and numeracy in students, with educational research seeking for the best teaching methods and materials. However, while the promotion of literacy in all students contributes to the emancipation of all citizens, it also creates social expectancies regarding literacy. Research shows that students in vocational education have a lower self-esteem; when they compare themselves to academic students and social values about education, their conclusion is that they "fail" (Van den Bulk, 2011). With the educational system being constructed around the general student, having developed scientific knowledge on teaching methods and materials for general students so they can reach the best possible results, but with vocational students valuing themselves as "failures," the question rises of what this means for deaf students.

After all, literacy of deaf students in particular is a much-studied topic, as lack of access to an effective language is the main developmental risk for most deaf students. Effective language means that the language modality of a child matches the language modality of the environment. That is, hearing students who grow up in hearing families or deaf students who grow up in Deaf families have access to an effective language. Most deaf students, however, grow up in hearing families, and even when parents opt for a bilingual upbringing, the language environment of the family will remain less natural and spontaneous. In turn, deaf students who grow up in a Deaf family encounter the same mismatch in education as non–Dutch-hearing students whose home language is not Dutch, because spoken Dutch and Dutch culture are fundamental to the educational system. Beyond this mismatch, deaf students are confronted with a limited access to spoken language.

With the current focus on qualification in general education, expressed in scores and results, the risk is that deaf students experience a social pressure with feelings of failure, much like vocational education students experience. In the Netherlands, the results of secondary schools concerning their educational quality, expressed in the number and levels of graduated students, are since 1997 published annually in a national newspaper, with the result that schools have developed a strict selection procedure for new students based on their grades (Abels, 2014; Schoolprestaties, 2014). With the new policy of the Dutch government regarding inclusive education, it can be questioned how general schools, which aim to have the best students possible so they can reach the highest scores, will deal with functionally diverse students. Regardless of the best intentions of schools and teachers, there is a tension between the policy of the "best scores" and the policy to include atypical students, in this case deaf students. Again, this illustrates the importance of defining "good education" as the educational policy in the Netherlands presents schools with a possible conflict of interests.

This does not mean that deaf students cannot attain average or high academic results. On the contrary, they can, as anyone involved in the education of deaf students or working with d/Deaf professionals will attest. The question is, however, how do they do that? Research on the learning processes of deaf students gives us important insights (Knoors & Marschark, 2014). Research into the motivations and strategies of successful deaf students adds to this as it gives us insights in the assets of deaf students rather than the risks (see Antia, Chapter 23 in this volume). Family support, parental commitment, and a refusal to attribute one's problems to deafness encourage deaf students to benefit optimally from general education by developing traits such as assertiveness, independence, and persistence (Antia, Chapter 23 in this volume).

However, the focus again should not be only on the student but also on (a reform of) the general educational system itself. A recent evaluative study (Steenkamp, 2013) showed that disabled students in Dutch universities are not satisfied with their education: Universities do not provide enough adapted materials and stress that students finish their education in a set time. Disabled students do not feel understood and state that their educational needs are not met (Steenkamp, 2013), which impedes their education. Lundie (2009) suggests that the medicalization of disability adjustments and attempts to "normalize" the disabled student through compensatory approaches demotivate students, as the individual's self-concept is formed in negotiation with feedback from others. He considered it necessary to value an individual's skills over the value of medical "expert" advice. Further, it is necessary to negotiate need rather than assuming that all disabled students aspire to the same goals by the same means as nondisabled students. In relation to this, educational institutions should encourage students and should provide a curriculum that motivates them to meet their ends.

Terzi (2005) discussed the reconceptualization of disability by presenting the capability approach: The question is not what the disabilities of students are but what enables them. Universal Design, access for anyone in all situations, is essential for successful inclusive education (McQuire, Scott, & Shaw, 2006; Michael & Trezek, 2006). From this concept and its principles Universal Design for Learning evolved, designing and developing educational programs for all types of students (Hall, Meyer, & Rose, 2012; Rose & Meyer, 2002). Computer programs for deaf students, for example, need to be developed while taking in account that visual perception is different in deaf students than in others (see Caselli, Rinaldi, Onofrio, & Tomasuolo, Chapter 19 in this volume). When such programs offer a choice between directions in written language or sign language, they would be in line with the principle of Universal Design for Learning, giving access to educational content for any student in all situations, with the student having control over, and responsibility for, his or her learning processes.

Considering qualification, it can be said that inclusive education promotes educational opportunities for deaf students. However, the main barrier is the combination of the fact that their language development already is at a risk because they more often than not are confronted with a mismatch regarding language modality, and the fact that literacy and numeracy are the most important educational goals in present-day society. Further, a lot is known about the developmental risks and learning difficulties of deaf students, but less is known about the assets and learning strategies of successful deaf students. To create opportunities, a reconceptualization of deaf students is needed, focusing on their capabilities and what enables them, rather than what disables them. Expecting deaf students to adapt to the general system is contrary to the principles of inclusive education and may be detrimental to their educational results and/or self-esteem. On the other hand, segregating deaf students into sign language environments is merely an avoidance of the problem rather than a solution to the problem, as someday these students will have to function independently in this digital and technological society. Such approaches, which expect deaf students to adapt to the general educational system and/or to focus on their visual language modality only, turn a blind eye to the diversity of deaf students today and their capacities. After all, there is more than one path to educational success.

SOCIALIZATION

The second function of education is socialization: the many ways in which we become, through education, part of specific social, cultural, and political "orders." Education can deliberately seek this, by transferring norms and values to pupils and discussing these with them, such as respect for diversity and equality, or by transferring specific cultural or religious traditions. Regarding inclusive education, the intention is to socialize disabled students for a life in a society to which they make a contribution. The goal is to educate them to fit into society and to experience social well-being. This intention and goal are related to the value of democratic societies to include all, while respecting diversity. However, Bourdieu and Passeron (1990) showed how education reproduces and maintains social structures of class, production, and power. Indeed, educational researchers have pointed out how mismatches in culture, language, and communication style between students from ethnic minorities and (professionals in) the educational system contribute to the underachievement of these students. Ogbu (2008) proposed an oppositional theory, explaining how minority students react to cultural dominance. While "voluntary minorities" such as refugees seek assimilation into the dominant culture, "involuntary minorities," such as those from a lineage that started with slaves, form a resistance to the dominant culture. For the latter, educational success is associated with assimilation; as a result, successful students from minorities may be rejected by their ethnic peers.

An interesting finding is that resistance also occurs with disabled students. Davis and Watson (2002) built on their body of reflexive ethnographic research in their discussion on resistance among disabled children with all forms of functional diversity, with resistance being understood as a response to oppressive cultures, structures, and individuals. In their research, disabled students were not considered as passive, vulnerable, or incompetent, nor as victims, but as agents—that is, acting persons who respond to actions of others. It was found that attitudes, prejudices, and presuppositions on the part of teachers and peers regarding disabled students contributed to resistance by disabled students. The dominant status given by teachers to the disability in explaining events and problems ("you do not understand this because you cannot see/hear/comprehend") and the objectification of disabled students (ignoring their opinions, experiences, and even presence) by teachers fuel this resistance. One might wonder, when pondering the oppositional theory of Ogbu (2008), the findings of Davis and Watson (2002), and the observation that the labels of deaf/Deaf are used in the Deaf community to decide who is "in" and who is "out" whether opposition and resistance occur among deaf students. It would be interesting to study whether the human desire to belong to social groups influences students' educational aspirations. Similarly, perhaps, the assumption that proficiency in speech, reading, and writing reflects assimilation by the dominant "hearing" world or the assumption that using sign language reflects an exclusive choice for the Deaf community has some influence on the determination of deaf students to choose and learn languages.

Not only do teachers play an important role in the learning processes of students, but in educational settings they are also pivotal in their socialization process, functioning as examples and role models (Florian, 2012; see Leigh & Crowe, Chapter 4 in this volume). However, inclusive education proves to be a challenge to teachers as they are confronted with increasing cultural, linguistic, and developmental diversity and often are not hands-on experts (Avramidis, Bayliss, & Burden, 2000; Avramidis & Norvich, 2002; Cook, 2001; Hastings & Oakford, 2003). Florian (2012) studied how inclusion is incorporated in the professional development of teachers and suggests that more attention should be given to theoretical and practical implications of inclusion in the training of teachers so they can take responsibility for everyone while respecting student diversity.

Cochran-Smith and Dudley-Marling (2012) discussed the gap between general and special teacher education, with issues dividing the two fields. With experts from both fields working together in the education of deaf students in inclusive settings (such as co-enrollment programs, see De Klerk et al., 2009; Tang, Yiu, & Lam, Chapter 6 in this volume), a shared meaning of theoretical and practical issues of inclusion is necessary. The first issue dividing the fields according to Cochran-Smith and Dudley-Marling is that special teacher educators work from a medical model, whereas general teacher educators work from a social justice perspective (Cochran-Smith & Dudley-Marling, 2012).

Second, different meanings are attached to the "dis" in disability, with special teachers' training focusing on what students cannot do well and general teachers' training focusing on social constructivist views on learning. The third and final issue is the curriculum, where the training of special education teachers includes how to create access to the curriculum for disabled students, whereas the training of general education teachers includes transforming the curriculum in fundamental ways and challenging "normal" structures of schooling that continue the oppression of marginalized social groups. Cochran-Smith and Dudley-Marling recommended finding collaborative spaces for the preparation of tomorrow's teachers, those who will guide the socialization process of students with all forms of diversity in a diverse society.

Studies show that while inclusive education leads to better learning outcomes for disabled children, problems are found concerning their social development and social adjustment (Kroesbergen, Sontag, Van Steensel, Leseman, & Van der Ven, 2010; Quintero, DiGenarro Reed, McIntyre, & Dusek, 2011; Wolters, 2013). Socialization is becoming part of social orders, and education plays an important role in this process. This role can be positive, promoting socialization, or negative, emphasizing differences and defining who is "in" and who is "out." Inclusive education strives to include all students and to tackle problems that risk exclusion. An important difference between students from ethnic minorities and "disabled" students, in this case deaf students, is the home environment. Where in the case of ethnic minorities solutions can be sought in creating a balance between the ethnic background of their family and the culture and language in education, disabled students also differ from their families. In the case of deaf students, this also means that they differ from their family concerning language, as 90% to 95% of deaf students have hearing parents. Therefore, their home culture and language are similar to the dominant language and culture in the educational system. For which social and cultural orders should deaf students be socialized, and how? These are difficult questions. Where in the case of ethnic minorities a distinction could be made between home and school, with parents socializing the child for their culture and eventually teaching their language and the school socializing students for society, teaching them the language and culture of society, boundaries between home and school are blurred for deaf students.

VERTICAL AND HORIZONTAL IDENTITIES

Solomon (2012) offered an interesting approach to socialization by distinguishing what he referred to as vertical and horizontal identities. Vertical identities are identities in which children share at least some traits with their parents and in which attributes and values are passed down from parents to the child across generations. An example of a vertical identity is ethnicity. Horizontal identities are identities in which traits are shared with peer groups, as well as the accompanying attributes and values. Examples of horizontal identities are a gay identity or a physical disability. Deaf students thus have to deal with both a vertical identity (i.e., Dutch deaf students share Dutch culture and language with their parents, in addition to social class and family history) and a horizontal identity (they share "being deaf" with their deaf peers). In special education, deaf students may form peer groups and share a language and culture: sign language and Deaf culture. In addition to this development of their horizontal identity, their vertical identity is developed in their education and home environment. However, while inclusive education offers opportunities for the development of a (stronger) vertical identity, it may form a barrier to the development of the horizontal identity of deaf students, due to the lack of deaf peers.

A disparity between vertical and horizontal identity leads to higher levels of depression in adolescence, whereas growing up with both identities (i.e., sharing traits both with parents and peers) leads to the internalization of more self-affirming conceptions of "normal" (Solomon, 2012). As mentioned before, studies show that disabled students in inclusive education experience problems with social development and social adjustment. Strengthening horizontal identities could perhaps decrease these problems by allowing the formation of groups of students who share the same functional diversity, rather than placing them individually in different schools. Deaf students form a special group, and with identity in this day and age already being multifaceted, they also have to deal with the labels of deaf/Deaf, and a natural state and a technological state. Most deaf students will use a hearing aid or cochlear implant both at home and in school, where spoken language is used. Once they switch off their devices, sign language is the only fully accessible form of communication. Instrumentally, they may not "need" sign language but socially, any language implies belonging to a group and its culture. How can deaf students in inclusive education develop not only their vertical but also their horizontal identity? An opportunity for this is to add the national sign language to the curriculum, taught by a professionally trained teacher, in addition to the forming of peer groups in inclusive settings, with an additional contingent of deaf students in the same school.

By forming peer groups and offering sign language as part of the curriculum, the goals and values of inclusive education are met: Social well-being is promoted and diversity is respected. However, some may counter this by stating that some deaf students with hearing aids or cochlear implants do not need sign language, as studies show that these devices are beneficial for their development of spoken language. With sign language having mainly an instrumental value in the education of deaf students—that is, a means to an end rather than an intrinsic value

(Tijsseling, 2014)—it is no surprise that the discussion on sign language in the education of deaf students is revived (Knoors & Marschark, 2012). The risk of basing discussions about language development and language method on an instrumental approach only is that descriptive statements can become normative statements. This is known as the ethical "is-ought" problem: Descriptive statements ("is") become normative statements ("ought"), but as these statements have a different nature, this is inappropriate (Honderich, 2005). Scientific research only describes (what is) but never prescribes (what ought to be done), with research offering information that may serve as a basis for decision making. In democratic societies, all parties are involved in the debate about decisions: parents, teachers, students, researchers, and the wider audience (Rawls, 1999; Taylor, 1989).

However, as Knoors and Marschark (2012) mention, some deaf students themselves seem to refrain from sign language and prefer spoken language. This should be taken into account, as it raises questions about (influences on) the socialization of deaf students. Do deaf students prefer spoken language for instrumental reasons—that is, they understand the language well enough and feel comfortable with it? Or is their preference primarily for social reasons—that is, they do not want to be different from their parents, siblings, family, and social environment? O'Neill, Arndt, and Marschark (2014) found that only 18% of deaf 17- to 25-year-olds in Scotland preferred to use British Sign Language. It would be interesting to study influences on the motivation for language preferences of deaf students, and relate the findings to issues such as dominant/minority cultures and the social status of spoken/sign languages.

Inclusive education seems to contribute to socialization in general society only, but with a tendency to normalization. Also, it cannot be expected that deaf students who are educated individually in inclusive education will develop sign language on their own or seek peers on their own. After all, socializing happens in social groups, and thus to promote optimal social well-being in deaf students, a situation should be created that does justice to all aspects of the identity of deaf students: their vertical and horizontal identity as well as their natural and technological state. Such a situation reflects respect for diversity, a value in democratic societies.

INDIVIDUATION

Becoming an autonomous person who makes independent choices is implied in the third function of education, individuation, which is about developing ways of being that create a certain independence of existing social orders, social structures, and social expectations. In a democratic society, the intention of education is to promote processes of becoming a citizen by contributing to the autonomous and independent thinking and acting of students. The goal is to help students to become citizens, full and active members of their society. The values in this respect are personal freedom and moral rights. Whereas socialization aims to make students acquainted with cultural and social orders, individuation is about enabling the student to make personal and informed choices in life, independent from social orders, structures, and expectations.

Feinberg (1992) stressed the right of children to an open future—that is, a right to have the future options kept open until the child is a fully formed, self-determining adult capable of deciding among them. The right to an open future is in line with the ultimate goal of education in a democratic society: to promote processes of becoming a subject that contribute to the autonomous and independent thinking and acting of those who are educated. For deaf students, this would mean that both society and the Deaf community should be options, including their languages. For this, it is necessary that they have opportunities to explore both options. Again, there is a risk that "is" leads to "ought," with on the one hand people claiming that deaf students belong to the "hearing world" because technological devices make them "almost hearing" and on the other hand people claiming that deaf students belong to the Deaf community because the natural state of these students is deaf. However, no social group has a moral right to determine or define the identity of minors, but all social groups have a moral duty to respect the right of minors to an open future.

However, professionals unintentionally and unknowingly direct students toward socially accepted forms of thinking and acting. Michalko (2002) showed how the pertinent strategy of teachers and therapists in special education to normalize disabled students estranges these students from themselves. He used the example of a sighted therapist who continuously denies and corrects the meanings that a blind student gives to objects in her world, with as a result that the student becomes estranged from her own experiences while attempting to become acquainted with the experiences of sighted people. Michalko evaluates how the different epistemology of disabled students is consequently ignored and replaced by the epistemology of the majority of people. With individuation being the process of becoming an autonomous person who thinks independently, developing one's own epistemology is important.

Michalko (2008) acknowledged that the feeling of "two-ness"—that is, being different but living in a "normal" world—and the desire to belong tempt disabled people to act in as ordinary a way as possible. This may even be truer for students, as their identity is still under construction. Moreover, adolescence is already a troublesome period for all people and even more for deaf students (see Zaidman-Zait, Chapter 15 in this volume). Deaf students might at a given moment reject all that is related to "being deaf" in their desire to belong to their hearing peers in inclusive settings. Other deaf students, however, may reject all that is related to the "hearing world" because this belonging did not turn out as they expected it to. In the Netherlands, at least some young deaf adults who belong to the first group of children who received a cochlear implant 20 years ago no longer use it and have a strong preference for Dutch Sign Language. We should study the motivations behind these choices as they might shed light on social constructions of disability, deaf, and belonging. For adolescent deaf students, teachers and other professionals must take up the challenge to keep the future open for them until their maturity by consistently referring to all social orders, including offering access to their cultures and languages. Such a challenge can be compared to teaching mathematics or adequate social behavior to adolescents: They may not want to meet the challenge but will benefit from doing so once they are adults.

Individuation is about becoming an individual, and in present-day society individual traits such as assertiveness, independency, and taking initiative are valued and aimed for in education. Deaf students actually have to be more assertive than general students as it is in their best interest to express their educational needs—for example, to let the teacher know that he or she has to speak up, face the class when speaking, and/or write down difficult words. They also have to make their fellow students aware of their communicative needs. These are quite difficult tasks to adolescents, but even more so for pupils in primary education, which relate to some recurring observations about deaf students, such as learned helplessness, external locus of control, and lack of perseverance (Tijsseling, 2006). Learned helplessness seems to result from an unbalanced form of educational support: Too little or too much support creates feelings of uncertainty and helplessness in deaf students. External locus of control refers to a student's belief that external factors and persons such as fate, coincidence, parents, or teachers define her or his life. Such psychological characteristics do not contribute to autonomy and independence; they actually form a barrier for deaf students in their educational process. Regarding individuation, it is thus important to identify psychological traits that may form a barrier. An educational climate that expresses respect for diversity would create opportunities to enhance assertiveness and independence in deaf students.

Another barrier is the seemingly overlooked aspect of physical and psychological effort. Having to look and listen all day, having to think and consider all day, and trying to grasp meanings and understand differences between the meanings that oneself and others give to the same phenomena are tiring for all students. For deaf students, however, it is often simply exhausting. Hands-on experts such as Noon (2013) and Williams (2013) described the impact of deafness and the tiring effect of it. A search for research articles on fatigue in deaf students, however, turned up only a few results. Hornsby, Werfel, Camarata, and Bess (2013) concluded in their preliminary findings that students with hearing loss are significantly more fatigued than students without hearing loss. Hicks and Tharpe (2002) also suggested that students with hearing loss expend more effort in listening. Regarding fatigue in deaf students and sign language, no studies have been found. There is little research into the effort that deaf students expend and their fatigue, or to the effects of this on learning processes or learning outcomes. Fatigue mostly is mentioned for deaf adults in work life, but it can be expected, especially in inclusive education, that deaf students expend more energy to learning processes than general students. So, another recommendation is to study the practical implications of "being deaf," as well as the psychological and social aspects of it.

It is thus a challenge for professionals in inclusive educational settings not to reduce students to their hearing loss but to help them to make their different sensory experiences a resource instead of a risk factor. Students need to explore the social orders in society as well as their different sensory experience, and the embodiment and epistemology that results from it, to find ways to function optimally. At the same time, they have to acknowledge that they differ from general students. After all, autonomy and independence result from a clear and defined identity, and to create such an identity, the student needs to know her or his strengths and weaknesses. Education that values the open future of deaf students while promoting their autonomy and independence offers opportunities for them to fully explore who they are, how they relate to others, what they consider important, and what is meaningful to them.

BARRIERS AND OPPORTUNITIES FOR DEAF STUDENTS

The question about good education for deaf students (i.e., education with the fewest barriers and the best opportunities) has been discussed by analyzing the intentions, goals, and values underlying the three functions of education:

1. *Qualification*: Simply inserting deaf students into an educational system represents a barrier because this system is designed for general students. Equality and equal chances for all can only be met when the educational system is redesigned. When educational institutions first respect diversity and second practice Universal Design, opportunities are created for deaf students.
2. *Socialization*: In inclusive educational settings, socialization should not only consider the dominant culture and language but also respect cultural, linguistic, ethnic, and functional

diversity. Exploring both their vertical and horizontal identities offers deaf students opportunities to attain social well-being.

3. *Individuation*: Education must value the open future of each and every student, giving extra attention to deaf students whose pathways to autonomy and independence not only differ from that of general students but also have more pitfalls.

We hope that these ideas, thoughts, and discussions about good education for deaf students will provide some food for thought. To conclude, good education for deaf students is an education that does not aim for deaf students to become average but focuses on finding and promoting their own pathways, strategies, and capacities in learning. In other words: Good education of deaf students is education that enables them to become excellent in finding and mastering a balance between their natural and technological states, between their horizontal and vertical identities, and between spoken language and sign language and their accompanying cultures.

ACKNOWLEDGMENTS

The author wishes to thank Dr. Stijn Sieckelinck for his careful reading of the text and his helpful comments.

REFERENCES

Abels, R. (2014). Goede resultaten maken nog geen goede school. *Trouw*. Retrieved April 11, 2014, from http://www.trouw.nl/tr/nl/4556/Onderwijs/article/detail/3575766/2014/01/11/Goede-resultaten-maken-nog-geen-goede-school.dhtml

Ainscow, M., & César, M. (2006). Inclusive education ten years after Salamanca: setting the agenda. *European Journal of Psychology of Education, 11*(3), 231–238.

Avramidis, E., Bayliss, P., & Burden, R. (2000). Students teachers attitudes towards the inclusion of children with special educational needs in the ordinary school. *Teaching and Teacher Education, 16*, 277–293.

Avramidis, E. & Norvich, B. (2002). Teachers' attitudes towards integration/inclusion: a review of the literature. *European Journal of Special Needs Education, 17*, 129–147.

Bekkers, V., Noordegraaf, M., Waslander, S., & De Wit, B. (2011). *Passend Onderwijs—passend beleid? Drie visies op beleidsvorming rondom Passend onderwijs*. ECPO: evaluatie en adviescommissie passend onderwijs.

Bell, J. M., & Hartmann, D. (2007). Diversity in everyday discourse: the cultural ambiguities and consequences of "happy talk." *American Sociological Review, 72*, 895–914.

Berthouze, L., & Tijsseling, A. (2006). A neural model for context-dependent sequence learning. *Neural Processing Letters, 23*(1), 27–45.

Besturenraad tegen 'Cito-isering' van het onderwijs. (2012). Besturenraad, centrum voor christelijk onderwijs. Retrieved April 11, 2014, from http://www.besturenraad.nl/content/besturenraad-tegen-cito-isering-van-het-onderwijs

Biesta, G. G. J. (2010). Why 'what works' still won't work: from evidence-based education to value-based education. *Studies in Philosophy and Education, 29*, 491–503.

Biesta, G. G. J. (2012). *Good education in an age of measurement: ethics, politics, democracy*. Boulder, CO: Paradigm Publishers.

Bourdieu, P., & Passeron, J.P. (1990). *Reproduction in education, society and culture* (2nd ed.). London: Sage.

Cochran-Smith, M., & Dudley-Marling, C. (2012). Diversity in teacher education and special education: the issues that divide. *Journal of Teacher Education, 63*(4), 237–244.

Cook, B. G. (2001). A comparison of teachers' attitudes toward their included students with mild and severe disabilities. *Journal of Special Education, 34*, 203–213.

Davis, J., & Watson, N. (2002). Countering stereotypes of disability: disabled children and resistance. In M. Corker & T. Shakespeare (Eds.) *Disability/Postmodernity. Embodying disability theory* (pp. 159–174). London/New York: Continuum.

Dekker, J., Kruithof, B., Simon, F., & Vanobbergen, B. (2012). Discoveries of childhood in history: an introduction. *Paedagogica Historica: International Journal of the History of Education, 48*(1), 1–9.

De Klerk, A., Hermans, D., Knoors, H., & Wauters, L. (2009). Passend onderwijs in de Twinschool. Dove, slechthorende en horende leerlingen samen naar school. *Van Horen Zeggen, 50*(1), 10–17.

Depaepe, M. (1998). *De pedagogisering achterna: aanzet tot een genealogie van de pedagogische mentaliteit in de voorbije 250 jaar*. Leuven: Acco.

Feinberg, J. (1992). *Freedom and fulfillment. Philosophical essays*. Princeton, NJ: Princeton University Press.

Florian, L. (2012). Preparing teachers to work in inclusive classrooms: key lessons for the professional development of teacher educators from Scotland's Inclusive Practice Project. *Journal of Teacher Education, 63*(4), 275–285.

Florian, L., & Rouse, M. (2009). The inclusive practice project in Scotland: teacher education for inclusive education. *Teaching and Teacher Education, 25*, 594–601.

Hall, T. E., Meyer, A., & Rose, D. (2012). *Universal Design for learning in the classroom: practical applications*. New York: Guilford Publications.

Hastings, R. P., & Oakford, S. (2003). Student teachers' attitudes towards the inclusion of children with special needs. *Educational Psychology, 23*, 87–94.

Hicks, C. B., & Tharpe, A. M. (2002). Listening effort and fatigue in school-age children with and without hearing loss. *Journal of Speech, Language & Hearing Research, 45*(3), 573–584.

Honderich, T. (2005). *The Oxford companion to philosophy*. New York: Oxford University Press.

Hornsby, B. W., Werfel, K., Camarata, S., & Bess, F. H. (2013). Subjective fatigue in children with hearing loss: some preliminary findings. *American Journal of Audiology*. Retrieved April 11, 2014, from http://www.ncbi.nlm.nih.gov/pubmed/?term=Subjective+Fatigue+in+Children+with+Hearing+Loss%3A+Some+Preliminary+Findings

Knoors, H., & Marschark, M. (2012). Language planning for the 21st century: revisiting bilingual language policy for deaf children. *Journal of Deaf Studies and Deaf Education*, *17*(3), 291–305.

Knoors, H., & Marschark, M. (2014). *Teaching deaf learners. Psychological and developmental foundations*. New York: Oxford University Press.

Kroesbergen, E. H., Sontag, L., Van Steensel, R. C. M., Leseman, P. P. M., & Van der Ven, S. H. G. (2010). Plaatsing van leerlingen met een beperking in het reguliere onderwijs: de ontwikkeling van schoolvaardigheden, competentiebeleving en probleemgedrag. *Pedagogische Studiën*, *87*, 350–366.

Lohmann, I., & Mayer, C. (2009). Lessons from the history of education for a "century of the child at risk". *Paedagogica Historica: International Journal of the History of Education*, *45*(1-2), 1–16.

Lundie, D. (2009). A theory of motivation and ontological enhancement: the role of disability policy in student empowerment and institutional change. *Educational Philosophy and Theory*, *41*(5), 539–552.

McGuire, J., Scott, S., & Shaw, S. (2006). Universal design and its applications in educational environments. *Remedial and Special Education*, *27*, 166–175.

Michael, M. G., & Trezek, B. J., (2006). Universal design and multiple literacies: creating access and ownership for students with disabilities. *Theory into Practice*, *45*(4), 311–318.

Michalko, R. (2002). Estranged-familiarity. In M. Corker & T. Shakespeare (Eds.), *Disability/Postmodernity. Embodying disability theory* (pp. 175–183). London/New York: Continuum.

Michalko, R. (2008). Double trouble: disability and disability studies in education. In S. L. Gabel & S. Danforth (Eds.), *Disability & the politics of education* (pp. 401–415). New York: Peter Lang.

Noon, I. (2013). *The impact of concentration fatigue on deaf children should be factored in.* Retrieved April 11, 2014, from: http://limpingchicken.com/2013/06/28/ian-noon-concentration-fatigue/

Ogbu, J. U. (2008). *Minority status, oppositional culture & schooling*. New York: Routledge.

O'Neill, R., Arndt, J., & Marschark, M. (2014). *Report from the Achievement and Opportunities for Deaf Students in the United Kingdom: From Research to Practice Project*, final project report to the Nuffield Foundation.

Padden, C., & Humphries, T. (1988). *Deaf in America: Voices from a culture.* Cambridge, MA: Harvard University Press.

Patston, P. (2007). Constructive functional diversity: a new paradigm beyond disability and impairment. *Disability and Rehabilitation*, *29*, 1625–1633.

Quintero, N., DiGennaro Reed, F. D., McIntyre, L. L., & Dusek, J. (2011). Preliminary assessment of friendship, problem behavior, and social adjustment in children with disabilities in an inclusive education setting. *Journal of Developmental and Physical Disabilities*, 23(6), 477–489.

Rawls, J. (1999). *A theory of justice* (Rev. ed.). New York: Oxford University Press.

Rée, J. (1999). *I see a voice: deafness, language and the senses: A philosophical history*. London: HarperCollins.

Rietveld-van Wingerden, M. & Groenendijk, L. F. (2006). Jan Waterink (1890–1966). Pedoloog uit overtuiging. In J. D. van der Ploeg (Ed.), *Kopstukken van de orthopedagogiek* (pp. 20–38). Rotterdam: Lemniscaat.

Rose, D., & Meyer, A. (2002). Teaching every student in the digital age: universal design for learning. Retrieved April 11, 2014, from http://www.cast.org/teachingeverystudent/ideas/tes/

Schoolprestaties. (2014). Retrieved April 11, 2014, from http://schoolprestaties.trouw.nl/

Smeyers, P. (2008). Qualitative and quantitative research methods: old wine in new bottles? On understanding and interpreting educational phenomena. *Paedagogica Historica, 44*(6), 691–705.

Solomon, A. (2012). *Far from the tree. Parents, children, and the search for identity.* New York: Scribner.

Steenkamp, F. E. M. (2013). *"Studeren met een handicap". De tiende gebruikerstoets, De oordelen van studenten met een functiebeperking over hun studie en instelling.* Leiden: Centrum Hoger Onderwijs Informatie.

Stokoe, W.C. (1963). Sign language structure. *Annual Review of Anthropology, 9,* 365–390.

Taylor, C. (1989). *Sources of the self: the making of the modern identity.* Cambridge: Cambridge University Press.

Terzi, L. (2005). Beyond the dilemma of difference: the capability approach to disability and special educational needs. *Journal of Philosophy of Education, 39*(3), 443–459.

Tijsseling, C. (2006). *Anders doof zijn. een nieuw perspectief op dove kinderen.* Twello: Van Tricht.

Tijsseling, C. (2014). *"School, waar?" Een onderzoek naar doveninstituten met een verschillende levensbeschouwelijke grondslag, 1790–1990.* Forthcoming doctoral dissertation, Utrecht University, Utrecht.

Turmel, A. (2004). Towards a historical sociology of developmental thinking: the case of generation. *Paedagogica Historica: International Journal of the History of Education, 40*(4), 419–433.

UNESCO. (1994). *The Salamanca Statement and Framework for Action on Special Needs Education.* Paris: UNESCO.

Van den Bulk, L. (2011). *Later kan ik altijd nog worden wat ik wil: statusbeleving, eigenwaarde en toekomstbeeld van leerlingen in het voortgezet onderwijs, met de nadruk op de relatieve positie van vmbo-leerlingen.* Antwerpen: Garant.

Van Drenth, A. (2008). Caring power and disabled children: the rise of educational élan in Europe, in particular Belgium and the Netherlands. In S. L. Gabel & S. Danforth (Eds.), *Disability and the politics of education: an international reader* (pp. 433–449). New York: Peter Lang.

Van Drenth, A., & Myers, K. (2011). Normalising childhood: policies and interventions concerning special children in the United States and Europe (1900–1960). *Paedagogica Historica: International Journal of the History of Education, 47*(6), 719–727.

Van Trigt, P. (2013). The imperfection of narrative: sensory history and the inclusion of blind people in Dutch society in the twentieth century. In S. Barsch, A. Klein, & P. Verstraete (Eds.), *The imperfect historian: disability histories in Europe* (pp. 59–72). Frankfurt am Main: Peter Lang Publishers.

Verstraete, P. (2012). *In the shadow of disability. Reconnecting history, identity and politics.* Opladen/Berlin/Toronto: Barbara Budrich Publishers.

Williams, K. C. (2013). *Why is hearing impairment exhausting?* Retrieved April 11, 2014, from http://hearingourselvesthink.wordpress.com/2013/07/02/why-is-hearing-impairment-exhausting/

Wolters, N. (2013). *Social participation of deaf youth in school: predictors and consequences of acceptance and popularity of deaf early adolescents before and after a major school transition.* Unpublished doctoral dissertation, Nijmegen: Radboud University.

Woodward, J. (1972). Implications for sociolinguistic research among the deaf. *Sign Language Studies, 1*(1), 1–7.

4

Responding to Cultural and Linguistic Diversity Among Deaf and Hard-of-Hearing Learners

Greg Leigh and Kathryn Crowe

For as long as there have been formal approaches to teaching deaf children, issues pertaining to language use and the teaching of language and literacy have been at the very center of teachers' thinking and practical endeavors (Lack, 1955; Paul & Quigley, 1990). As important as these issues are, however, they cannot be considered in isolation. Language use and the teaching of (or about) language are both inextricably bound to cultural contexts. Indeed, language and the way it is used may be seen to be determined by culture, and, to a certain extent, culture may be seen to be determined by language (Crozet & Liddicoat, 2000). Given this relationship, there is clearly a great deal to be considered in regard to how best to teach deaf and hard-of-hearing (DHH) learners across the wide range of cultural and linguistic backgrounds from which they may come.

Since the declaration of the UNESCO World Conference on Cultural Policies in 1982, culture has come to be regarded as "the whole complex of distinctive spiritual, material, intellectual and emotional features that characterize a society or social group. It includes not only the arts and letters, but also modes of life, the fundamental rights of the human being, value systems, traditions and beliefs" (UNESCO, 1982, p. 1). By this definition, the cultural context for DHH learners is potentially a complex one. In addition to diversity among learners that relates to factors such as race, country or region of family origin, religious beliefs, and sexual orientation, there is the range of issues that pertain specifically to Deaf[1] people as a cultural and linguistic entity in their own right. Issues related to Deaf culture and identity have been widely discussed in the literature and have been a significant consideration in the education of DHH learners for some time (Power & Leigh, 2011). As a consequence, there is a substantial literature and resource base addressing those issues from the perspective of professional awareness and preparation and also as a curriculum area for Deaf learners themselves (De Klerk, Fortgens, & Van der Eijck, Chapter 25 in this volume; National Deaf Studies Working Group, 2009). As complex and important as those issues are, however, teachers and other providers of services to DHH learners must be aware of the impact of *all sources* of cultural and linguistic diversity among DHH learners.

This chapter considers the issues associated with cultural and linguistic diversity that affect teaching and the delivery of other services to DHH learners and their families. This is not an exhaustive discussion but rather serves to highlight the complexities of the cultural and linguistic milieu for these learners and the potential for some groups to be disadvantaged or disenfranchised if these issues are not appropriately addressed.

CULTURAL AND LINGUISTIC DIVERSITY: AN INTERNATIONAL PERSPECTIVE

Regardless of hearing status, the greatest contributor to cultural and linguistic diversity among learners around the world is transnational or transregional migration. Migration is associated with a range of factors, including international trade and investment, national economic development policies, military alliances, and the movement of refugees and asylum seekers occasioned by war and civil unrest. In many countries, these factors add to a cultural and linguistic diversity that already exists because of the interface of nonindigenous and indigenous societies. The United States of America, Canada, Australia, and New Zealand are all examples of this type of multifaceted cultural and linguistic diversity (Li, 2008). In each of these countries colonization and the long-term effects of immigration have resulted in the presence of numerous culturally and linguistically diverse minorities, including substantial indigenous minorities. Notably, these countries are also in regions that continue to account for the highest rates of net migration in the world. According to the United Nations (2006), the world's highest rate of annual net migration gain during the period from 2000 to 2005 was in the North American region (4.2 migrants per 1,000 population), followed by Oceania (3.2 per 1,000). In contrast, Europe had an overall rate of just 1.5 per 1,000, and Asia had a rate of –0.3 per 1,000 (i.e., more migrants leaving than arriving).

Taking several factors into account, there may be even greater cultural and linguistic diversity among DHH people. Perhaps the most obvious factor is the potential for some DHH learners to be part of the Deaf community and to identify as being culturally Deaf (Padden & Humphries, 2005) and thus to be primarily users of a sign language rather than the majority spoken language. Also, hearing loss is likely to be more common among population subgroups that are already culturally and linguistically diverse relative to the majority population—namely, indigenous peoples and recent migrants, particularly refugees.

Taking the example of the four Pacific Rim countries that have already been considered (i.e., USA, Canada, Australia, and New Zealand), it is apparent that there is a significantly higher incidence of hearing loss among the indigenous populations of all four nations. This is partly due to the fact that indigenous children in those countries experience otitis media (middle ear disease) more frequently than their nonindigenous peers (Morris & Leach, 2009). Taking Australia as an example, the prevalence of hearing loss among indigenous (Aboriginal or Torres Strait Islander) children under 14 years of age is almost four times that among nonindigenous children (Australian Institute of Health and Welfare, 2013). The high incidence of hearing loss within indigenous populations presents particular challenges for managing the interface between these culturally diverse groups and educational service delivery systems, as well as health and other human services.

With respect to issue of hearing loss among migrants, it is significant that recent migration to many developed countries includes the settlement of large numbers of refugees from regions in the developing world where the incidence of permanent childhood hearing loss is significantly higher (Leigh, Newall, & Newall, 2010). According to Smith, Bale, and White (2005), the expected rate of permanent childhood hearing impairment in the developed world is in the range of 2 to 4 per 1,000 births, whereas Olusanya and Newton (2007) have conservatively speculated that the incidence in the developing world is likely to be at least 6 per 1,000. Clearly, this creates the possibility that there will be higher proportions of children with hearing loss in translocated families and their respective cultural and linguistic communities. Here again, the higher incidence of hearing loss among these already culturally and linguistically diverse groups presents particular issues for educational service delivery.

In countries like those on the Pacific Rim that have high rates of net migration and diverse indigenous communities, governments have typically legislated or put policy approaches in place that seek to ensure that public programs and services are responsive to the needs of their culturally and linguistically diverse populations. The Canadian Multiculturalism Act (Government of Canada, 1988), for example, commits the government of that country to "foster the recognition and appreciation of the diverse cultures" and "preserve and enhance the use of languages other than English and French" (Section 3[1], p. 3). Similarly in Australia, the national Multicultural Policy (Australian Government, 2011) requires that "government services are responsive to the needs of Australians from culturally and linguistically diverse backgrounds" (p. 5). Given these types of legislative and policy initiatives, it follows that such countries also have policies in place to ensure (or at least to seek) equality of access and opportunity to *educational services* for their citizens who come from culturally and linguistically diverse backgrounds. Such policy initiatives, whether they are at national, provincial, or local levels, provide imperatives for responding to the diversity that exists among learners from culturally or linguistically diverse backgrounds—including DHH students.

Given the potential complexity of the cultural milieu for DHH learners, it is appropriate to consider how their specific needs are, or may be, accommodated under such frameworks and what additional or alternative considerations are required to meet their needs. In the remainder of this chapter we consider those issues as they relate to DHH learners in three sections: (a) cultural diversity and deaf learners, (b) linguistic diversity and deaf learners, and (c) some conclusions and general implications for good educational practice.

CULTURAL DIVERSITY AND DEAF LEARNERS

Cultural identification is not just a matter of ethnicity or race; it is a complex amalgam of many factors and influences. It includes "everything that you do that enables you to identify with people like you and distinguishes you from people who differ from you" (Lindsey, Robins, & Terrell, 2003, p. 41). In this regard, the possible cultural identities of DHH people are many and varied. For example, one learner might identify strongly with a country's dominant culture but be culturally Deaf, whereas another may identify as a person who is hard of hearing and be ethnically and culturally most closely affiliated with the Chinese community. Clearly, the possible cultural permutations of identities for DHH learners in otherwise culturally diverse societies are far too numerous to consider individually. The real issues at play here are not the specifics of cultural differences but rather the need for all those involved in education to be aware of the *potential* for cultural diversity and to be competent in dealing with that diversity.

According to Edgar, Patton, and Day-Vines (2002), "the extent to which educators, students, and the total educational environment reflect cultural competence significantly affects the nature and type of schooling, conditions for learning, and learning outcomes" (p. 235). The key concept here is the notion of *cultural competence,* which Denboba (2013) has defined as "a set of values, behaviors, attitudes, and practices . . . which enable them (professionals in education, health and related areas) to work effectively cross culturally" (p. 4). Denboba (2013) argued that cultural competence involves professionals (a) having the knowledge that is necessary for working (with learners) in multicultural or cross-cultural situations and (b) examining their own attitudes and values in regard to people from culturally and linguistically diverse backgrounds. Each of these two areas warrants consideration in regard to working with DHH learners from culturally diverse backgrounds.

Knowing About and Working with Cultural Diversity

In many countries—particularly the Pacific Rim countries—there was a time when public policies and practices in regard to cultural diversity were aimed exclusively at assimilation into the mainstream culture. In some cases such policies were extreme. In Australia, for example, the commitment to cultural assimilation throughout the first half of the 20th century culminated in policies such as the removal of Aboriginal children from their families so they could be raised by non-Aboriginal families—a practice and period now widely referred to as "The Stolen Generations" (Human Rights and Equal Opportunity Commission, 1997). In education, policies were less extreme but were no less specific in regard to their intention of having learners from culturally diverse backgrounds assimilate both culturally and linguistically into the Anglocentric mainstream. Schools and other educational services were party to a process of excluding or at least minimizing any reference to home cultures or other social identities in the name of assimilation.

Public policies in these countries now typically seek to ensure that cultural diversity is maintained and responded to fairly and equitably. In Australia, the Multicultural Education Policy of the state of New South Wales (Department of Education and Communities, 2005) is an example of a policy that seeks to maintain and foster cultural diversity. Among a host of specific provisions, that policy requires services, schools, and colleges to

- "ensure inclusive teaching practices which recognize and value the backgrounds and cultures of all students and promote an open and tolerant attitude towards different cultures" (Section 1.3);
- "provide specific teaching and learning programs to support the particular learning needs of students from culturally and linguistically diverse backgrounds" (Section 1.5); and
- "promote positive community relations through effective communication with parents and community members from diverse cultural and linguistic backgrounds and by encouraging their participation" (Section 1.6).

These few extracts illustrate several important considerations in regard to what may be considered to be support for the cultural diversity among learners. The first is that responding to cultural diversity is a highly individualized process. It must be so because effective responses can only be relative to a particular learner's own cultural identity. The second issue relates to the fact that educational responses to diversity among learners cannot be in isolation from the family context.

Supporting Cultural Identity (an Individual Approach)

Multicultural polices such as that in New South Wales are based on the notion of retaining learners' cultural identities. This implies that the cultural identities of those students are patent—both to the learners and to those who are teaching or otherwise engaging with them. In many cases (e.g., indigenous peoples and members of ethnic or racial minorities) this may be true, but for other learners, identities will be far less patent, much more complex, and potentially still very much in formation. In these cases, supporting diversity is not just about recognizing the cultures and backgrounds of learners but may be a matter of supporting their processes for acknowledging and understanding their developing cultural identities. This would appear to apply particularly in the case of DHH learners.

The development and maintenance of cultural identity has roots in the recognition and understanding of both personal (individual) and shared (group) experiences. Ohna (2003) described this notion eloquently: "Because identity is developed dialogically, in conjunction with other people, it will be influenced by those I want to be like (affiliation). But identity will also be created in opposition to what is not recognized by others" (p. 8). This means that, for DHH learners, their identity—whether it is related to their race, ethnicity, gender, sexual orientation, or hearing status—is likely to be still in formation rather than being something that is brought intact to the experience of formal education. Forming or acknowledging their social or cultural identity will be a process of managing different and possibly incompatible views about themselves into an understanding of who they are (Ohna, 2003). For teachers and others in education, this poses a challenge in regard to how best to support learners as they develop more sophisticated understandings of cultural identity—their own and those of others in their communities—in a highly individualized way.

Such an individualized approach to supporting cultural diversity contrasts with some curriculum approaches where the formation of a particular cultural identity may be seen as an aim rather than a process. In some schools (e.g., see Grosjean, 2010), *biculturalism* is seen as an educational objective—typically expressed as the aim for learners to be both bilingual and bicultural. In this context the aim of bilingualism is clear. It relates to what will be the reality for most d/Deaf learners who use a sign language; that is, that they will also learn to use the spoken (and/or written) language of their community. The aim of biculturalism, however, is less clear and is potentially inconsistent with an individualized social justice approach to supporting diversity.

Ohna (2003) argued that, in this context, biculturalism is a potentially misleading concept because it presupposes two discrete cultural alternatives rather than recognizing the range of alternative ways of constructing a life as a DHH person. It also potentially complicates the discernment of identity related to the wide range of other dimensions around which individual identities may be formed. Rather than seeing identity as a choice between alternatives, a socially just approach would suggest that learners should be assisted to understand their identities, whatever they may be, for what they are rather than as a matter of just two alternatives (see Tijsseling, Chapter 3 in this volume). For teachers, this means providing opportunities to view themselves from multiple perspectives, and it demands that they constantly consider how they teach, not just what they teach.

In the context of a framework for a socially just education (Adams, Bell, & Griffin, 2007) this suggests a particular focus on acknowledging and supporting individual experience though reflection and analysis, while making connections to the complex nature of both shared and individual social and cultural experiences. In such a learning context there can be no *one view* of cultural identity; rather, there should be a concept of personal identity that expands and evolves and accommodates multiple perspectives (Adams et al., 2007; Welch, 2000).

Supporting Family Engagement

The issue of a learner's cultural identity cannot be seen in isolation from the cultural identity and cultural values of the family. Once again, the potential permutations of family cultural and social identities among DHH learners are too numerous to consider individually. In any case, generalizations about issues specific to particular groups or backgrounds are of limited value, if not misleading. For example, despite the stereotypes, not all parents from a Chinese background will hold the same views about the importance of homework, and not all Deaf parents will hold the same views about cochlear implants or the role of natural sign languages in their child's education. It is neither appropriate nor productive to approach relationships with families from culturally diverse backgrounds based on any normative expectations or assumptions about their behavior or perspectives. It is possible, however, to identify a number of areas where families from culturally different backgrounds *may* have attitudes, beliefs, and patterns of engagement that are different from those of the majority of the community—either collectively or individually. For anyone working with learners from culturally diverse backgrounds, it is important to ensure that those areas are carefully and sensitively explored, *without assumptions*, to ensure that the particular family's values are taken into consideration when designing and implementing learning experiences for a particular learner. Such issues include the following:

- **Willingness to engage with professionals (seeking help).** People from different cultural backgrounds may differ in their willingness to seek assistance from professionals (Mizuno & Ishikuma, 1999; Mojaverian, Hashimoto, & Kim, 2013). Similarly, cultural groups may differ with regard to the type of support or assistance they seek when dealing with stressful issues. Taylor and colleagues (2004), for example, found that, for several Asian and Asian American cultural groups, the use of implicit social support (i.e., emotional support that can be obtained from social networks without seeking assistance or disclosing issues) was more beneficial than explicitly seeking support. They concluded that "the decision to seek or not to seek social support is guided by the norms and concerns of a given culture" (p. 362) and noted "the importance of considering culture in order to understand why and how people seek the advice and comfort of others when facing stressors" (p. 361).

Clearly, whatever they may be, patterns of reliance on, rejection of, or deferral to support systems need to be carefully and sensitively explored and understood as a basis for engagement with families—particularly in regard to the provision of the types of counseling and support that are central to involvement in early intervention and education programs.

- **Cultural beliefs about hearing loss.** From some cultural perspectives, the stigma attached to the presence of any disability, including hearing loss, may prevent parents from engaging with professional services specific to that disability, or from accepting the use of visible (potentially stigmatizing) interventions such as hearing aids or cochlear implants (Olusanya, Luxon, & Wirz, 2004). Similarly, if professional services are seen as an intrusion into areas that are typically handled through respected traditional activities and rituals, "families may be reluctant to make use of professional services and devices" (Louw & Avenant, 2002, p. 147). Alternatively, if cultural perspectives lead to disability being seen as a source of shame, then engagement with any support—professional or personal—may be compromised. Or, if disability of any kind is seen as karma, as it may be in some cultures or religions, then a family may react with a sense of resignation or helplessness that is equally an impediment to seeking professional assistance or support (Akamatsu & Cole, 2000).
- **Systems of community and kinship support.** The extent to which family or community members other than the child's parents take responsibility for the raising or care of a child may vary significantly across different cultural groups. As noted by Dunst and Trivette (1990), the perception of need for, or appropriateness of, extrafamilial support may differ widely across cultural groups, with some groups not seeing the need for such engagement at all. Also, the person who is the primary source of interaction with the early intervention or educational

professional (the mother or other extended family member) may not be the primary decision maker and may not have the familial responsibility for making the types of decisions that are required in the context of early intervention or early learning programs (Stewart & Kluwin, 2001).

- **Response to systems and authority.** Culturally deferential responses to authority or professional status (e.g., teachers or health care professionals) may mean that parents feel unempowered to work directly with their child's needs themselves (Akamatsu & Cole, 2000). Alternatively, it may be that families—particularly families from refugee or asylum seeker backgrounds—may be fearful of social systems and structures because of persecution or oppression in their own country, or because they are uncertain about their status in their new country (Stewart & Kluwin, 2001).

This list is not exhaustive, but it does underscore the need for awareness of such possibilities and the need to employ culturally sensitive practices in working with families. In particular it highlights the importance of undertaking the research needed to fully understand the culture-specific meanings of families' actions *and* of seeking to employ alternative strategies for engagement as required. In addition to strategies that may appear obvious (e.g., the use of interpreters), alternative strategies for engagement with families may include working with cultural advisers or even alternative service deliverers who are from the same cultural or linguistic groups as the family. The latter is a particularly pertinent possibility where the delivery of services such as early intervention and parent education is concerned and is well supported by research. Sue, Fujino, Hu, Takeuchi, and Zane (1991) investigated engagement with therapeutic interventions by several cultural minorities in the United Sates. They found that client–therapist cultural matches were associated with lower rates of dropout from therapy and significantly longer periods of engagement and satisfaction with those professional services.

Professional Attitudes and Values

Examination of personal attitudes and beliefs relative to other cultures is the second critical aspect of cultural competence (Denboba, 2013). In regard to educational services, Power and Leigh (2011) noted that the values that underpin a professional's attitude toward a learner's cultural identity will influence the way in which services are provided to that learner. This raises questions about the cultural perspective, attitudes, and values of the educational professionals who design learning experiences for any group of learners and whether they reflect all or only some constructions of reality as it exists for those learners.

In most countries, the vast majority of teachers and other educational professionals belong to the dominant culture and are educated within that culture. In Australia, for example, even though 44% of the population were born overseas or have at least one parent who was (Australian Government, 2011), just 14% of primary (elementary) school teachers and 19% of high school teachers were born outside of Australia, and less than 2% of Australian teachers are indigenous (McKenzie, 2008). In most countries, the mismatch between the social and cultural backgrounds of teachers and students is even more apparent where DHH learners are concerned, with only a small minority of teachers being DHH themselves (Knoors, Tang, & Marschark, 2014). Clearly, under these circumstances, cultural awareness—much less cultural competence—cannot be assumed and must be actively sought as an outcome of professional education or continuing professional development by teachers who work with learners from culturally diverse backgrounds.

In the case of DHH learners, the group status of the vast majority of teachers raises obvious questions about how they may construe life as a DHH person and whether (and how) their perspectives will shape the nature of the educational experiences they provide. Teachers and associated professionals must examine and clarify their own attitudes and beliefs about DHH learners, including those from other cultural backgrounds. This includes examining their own cultural, ethnic, or racial background *and* exploring their conscious or unconscious preferences for people (in this case, learners) from particular backgrounds. Informally, such a process requires careful and considered reflection. More formally, the process can be assisted greatly by the use of an instrument such as the Implicit Social Attitudes Association Tests (Project Implicit, 2007). These tests are designed to probe attitudes toward a range of characteristics, including race, gender, religion, and sexual orientation. Such a level of examination is necessary to ensure that professionals understand their own comfort level and willingness to accept cultures different from their own.

In addition to this broad examination of personal values and attitudes, teachers and other professionals should examine (a) their beliefs and attitudes about the various potential therapeutic, educational, and medical interventions (e.g., cochlear implants) used with DHH children (Power & Leigh, 2011); (b) their comfort with and commitment to social justice and inclusion (Adams et al., 2007); (c) the esteem in which they hold different languages, including sign languages, as vehicles for social and educational engagement (Leigh, 2001; Power & Leigh, 2011), and (d) their ability to engage with children and families in a manner that displays cultural empathy and a willingness to see the world from someone else's point of view (Chi-Ying Chung & Bemak, 2002).

If left unexamined or taken for granted, values and attitudes across these areas may give rise to what has been called the hidden curriculum—the unplanned and typically unrecognized teaching and learning of beliefs, norms, and cultural mores that reflect the cultural or ideological perspective of teachers or other professionals (Power & Leigh, 2011; Seddon, 1983). Lovat and Smith (2003) argued that "many of the messages of the hidden curriculum are concerned with power, authority, access and participation: these are messages that continually shape learners' developing views of the world . . . their creating of reality" (p. 36). In light of this possibility, considering one's own values and attitudes would appear to be particularly important for professionals working with DHH infants, in situations where the learners may be the children's parents and the families as much as the children themselves.

The vast majority of parents come to the experience of having a DHH child with no experience relating to deafness whatsoever. In most early intervention or early learning programs, professionals will be the primary source of parents' information related to the options for their child's development. Power and Leigh (2011) noted that, in this situation, the messages conveyed in the statements and actions of professionals will carry particular salience for families and will become potent learning experiences in their own right. Taking the example of helping parents to decide which form of communication to use with their child, they argued that if "an influential and respected professional is enthusiastic about a particular form of communication . . . is incapable of using an alternative mode of communication comfortably, or is uncomfortable in the presence of people from a different linguistic or cultural perspective on deafness, an effective hidden curriculum will have been constructed" (p. 35). Through such powerful demonstrations parents will almost inevitably "learn" that one approach is preferable to another. In such situations, the learning outcomes are not confined to the planned content or activities but rather are carried through the attitudes and actions of professionals. It is only through self-awareness and a thorough examination of personal attitudes that professionals can avoid these unintended learning outcomes.

LINGUISTIC DIVERSITY AND DEAF LEARNERS

According to Nagy and Meyerhoff (2008), most countries are multilingual, albeit with widely different patterns of usage and relative status of those multiple languages. Data from the four Pacific Rim countries already discussed support this claim. According to the 2007 census data, 20% of people in the United States spoke a language other than English at home. Of them, more than 60% (i.e., approximately 12% of the population) used Spanish (Shin & Kominski, 2010). In Australia, 23% of people reported that they used one or more of 260 languages other than

English at home, with the most prevalent languages (Mandarin, Italian, and Arabic) being used by less than 2% of the population (Australian Bureau of Statistics, 2012). In Canada, 24% of the population reported that they use one or more of 200 immigrant languages at home (i.e., a language other than English, French, or an Aboriginal language) (Statistics Canada, 2102). In New Zealand, more than 160 languages are reported to be used (The Royal Society of New Zealand, 2013), with the most frequently used language after English being te reo Māori, which is used by just 3.5% of the population.

Thus, many DHH learners will grow up in environments where they are exposed to two or more languages (Knoors & Marschark, 2012; Romaine, 2013). Data for this specific group, however, are much less available. The most readily accessible source of such information is in the United States, where the Annual Surveys of Deaf and Hard-of-Hearing Children and Youth collect information about the languages used by children at home and at school. In the most recent survey, 82% of children used English at home, 22% used Spanish, and 6% used American Sign Language (Gallaudet Research Institute, 2011).

Mahon and colleagues (2011) studied 147 children attending a cochlear implant center in England. They reported that 28% of the children were from families that used English as an additional language to one of 15 different home languages, such as Urdu, Bengali, Punjabi, and Tamil. In an Australian study, Crowe, McLeod, and Ching (2012) studied a population-based cohort of 3-year-old DHH children ($n = 406$) and found a prevalence of linguistic diversity similar to that in the wider Australian population. Notably, however, they found that although 25% of parents used a language other than English at home, only 17% of children used a language other than English with their families. Children were more likely to use a language other than English at home if they communicated exclusively through speech (Crowe, McKinnon, McLeod, & Ching, 2013).

Clearly, such diversity of language usage is likely to create issues for a population of learners who are already likely to encounter difficulties in acquiring and using spoken language. This is not a recent phenomenon. In 1921 Hurd discussed the difficulties encountered by children from linguistically diverse background attending the Rhode Island School for the Deaf. He attributed the poor speech and (majority) language development of those students to their language models at home (Hurd, 1921 cited in Fischgrund, 1982). Since Hurd, others have also recognized that multilingual children with hearing loss form a complex group about which little is known (Mahon, 2009; Secada, 1984; Waltzman, McConkey Robbins, Green, & Cohen, 2003). There is little research describing the language and subsequent educational outcomes of DHH children who are multilingual (Crowe & McLeod, 2014) or the decision-making processes associated with their use of particular languages as learners (Crowe, Fordham, McLeod, & Ching, 2014).

Linguistic Diversity and Decision Making

Language choices and decisions about how and when to use those languages are particularly complex issues for the families of DHH children from culturally and linguistically diverse backgrounds. This is perhaps most evident in regard to their involvement in early intervention and early education programs, where they are faced not only with the need to make decisions about their children's use of their home language and/or the majority community language, but also with decisions about the use of a spoken and/or a sign language.

Caregivers of all children who are being raised in multilingual environments make decisions about the languages their children will learn and use at home, at school, and in the broader community. Such decisions constitute a *family language policy*—a deliberate choice of "a particular language use pattern and particular literacy practices within home domains and among family members" (Curdt-Christiansen, 2009, p. 352). Several factors may influence the nature and the success of a family language policy, including caregivers' language proficiency, family structure, level of caregiver education and acculturation, family cohesiveness, the nature of emotional relationships within the family, and the opportunities for linguistic enrichment outside the home (Clyne, 2005; Schwartz, 2010). The creation of a family language policy, whether explicit or implicit, relates to the "ideas, value, beliefs, attitudes, prejudices, myths, religious structures, and other cultural 'baggage' that speakers bring to their dealings with language from their culture" (Schiffman, 2006, p. 112). Notwithstanding the commonly held desire for preservation of home language ability, caregivers across numerous studies have consistently expressed the desire for their children to also be competent users of the language of the wider community as the basis for opportunities for social, educational, and vocational success (Bird, Lamond, & Holden, 2012; Curdt-Christiansen, 2009; Ó hlfearnáina, 2007; Steinberg, Bain, Li, Delgado, & Ruperto, 2003). Family language planning is a dynamic process as caregivers react to the emerging competence of their children in each language by constantly reevaluating the effect of their own language practices (Schwartz & Moin, 2012; Tannenbaum, 2011).

Family language policy planning is no less of a phenomenon for families of DHH children. However, in this case, the issue of language planning exists both for families from culturally and linguistically diverse backgrounds *and* for families who are part of the majority culture but face the issues associated with their child's possible use of a signed language and their relationship with the Deaf community. Early intervention and early education programs tend to encourage the parents of DHH children—explicitly or implicitly—to make such language policy decisions early in their child's development. These decisions have consequences that go far beyond the immediate context of early intervention and will have an impact on their children's future lives in terms of their linguistic, cognitive, social, emotional, and vocational experiences (Crowe, Fordham, et al., 2014).

How and when parents make decisions about language use with their DHH children is a relatively unexplored area, as is the process by which educators and clinicians inform and advise parents about their choices (Crowe, Fordham, et al., 2014; Crowe, McLeod, McKinnon, & Ching, 2014; Guiberson, 2005). What *is* known is that parents make deliberate choices (i.e., family language polices) about how and when they will use different languages with their children. Guiberson (2013) examined decision-making processes about language and communication for 71 Spanish caregivers of DHH children. He found that 38% of the DHH children used two spoken languages and that the majority of parents, regardless of whether their children were bilingual, believed that multilingualism was associated with better education and job opportunities and that DHH children were able to learn two or more spoken languages. However, although many parents indicated their belief that multilingualism was both possible and beneficial for DHH children, few children were actually multilingual (Guiberson, 2013).

Crowe, McLeod and colleagues (2014) investigated the factors associated with communication and language decisions made by 177 parents of 157 DHH Australian children. For the 17 parents who used a spoken a language other than English at home, the most important influences on their language policy decision making were a desire to ensure that their child would be able to (a) communicate with the immediate and extended family, (b) participate in the Australian culture, and (c) access education services provided in English. Frequently, parents indicated that their choice to use English only, in preference to another spoken language, was influenced by their belief that using English was associated with better literacy, academic, and vocational outcomes for their children, and also by their desire for their children to form and maintain friendships.

One consistently reported influence on parents' decision making about language and communication mode for their children is the advice that they receive from professionals (e.g., Decker, Vallotton, & Johnson, 2012). Guiberson (2013) postulated that professional advice about language choice may be related to a professional's own sociolinguistic context: "Professional practice in a multilingual country, in which multilingualism is both common and valued, may shape professionals' attitudes about bilingualism, and this likely influences professionals' support of spoken language bilingual options for children who are deaf and hard of hearing" (p. 107). This attitude is in sharp contrast to the *monolingual mindset* that is common in many Western countries, where multilingualism is seen from a majority language perspective and may be perceived as having a potentially negative impact

(Clyne, 2005; O'Neill, 2013). McConkey Robbins, Green, and Waltzman, (2004) and Waltzman, McConkey Robbins, Green, and Cohen (2003) both reported that the multilingual parents of American children with cochlear implants in their studies were typically advised by professionals to speak only English with their children. Steinberg, Bain, Li, Delgado, and Ruperto (2003) reported that Spanish-speaking parents in the United States were advised to use English, combined with sign, with their children. However, in a study of caregivers in highly multilingual areas of Spain, Guiberson (2013) reported that 50% of caregivers were encouraged by someone to raise their child using more than one spoken language, and only 36% were discouraged from doing so.

Clearly, the potential impact of national, community, educational, and family language demography, policies, and practices need to be considered when engaging with DHH children in educational contexts. Whether language policies and practices relate to the modes of communication that are used, or the use of one or more spoken languages, there are important implications for the education and development of DHH children and their identity and roles in their family, school, and communities. The practices of professionals in these situations are highly significant and need to be considered—particularly in contexts where families would otherwise place a high value on multilingual outcomes for their children. Macrory (2006) has argued that, for some families, their child's development of more than one language may be seen as just as important as developing a single language for a child from monolingual backgrounds. Here again it is important for professionals to engage in a thorough examination of their personal attitudes and beliefs so that there are no unintended systematic barriers to parents' pursuing such an aim with their children.

Linguistic Diversity and Educational Practice

Multilingual environments complicate the processes of language development—both spoken and/or signed—for DHH children, their families, and the professionals who work with them. The task of assisting children to develop language in those environments is made more complex still by the fact that professionals working with leaners from multilingual backgrounds rarely share the ability to use the home language of the children and families they are supporting. Nevertheless, if multilingual outcomes are to be the aim for any DHH learners, then, according to Macrory (2006), a number of areas need to be addressed. First is the need to gain a clear picture of the learners' language contexts and the opportunities they have for understanding and using each of their languages. Secondly, professionals must understand both multilingual language development and the expected developmental patterns of languages other than English, as an indication of how the learners are progressing in their language development. Finally, professionals need to work in partnership with families, communities, and other professionals to develop practices that support DHH children (Macrory, 2006).

In regard to the first consideration—understanding language contexts—there can be no substitute for the investment of time in the task of understanding the home language environment, language needs, and aspirations of families. Sensitive and culturally competent observation is the basis for such understanding. In addition to these processes, professionals can build a more formal profile of children's different language environments and parental language skills by using instruments such as the Language Experience and Proficiency Questionnaire (LEAP-Q) developed by Marian, Blumenfeld, and Kaushanskaya (2007) or questionnaires of the type designed by Bird and colleagues (2005). Instruments such as these are designed to provide an understanding of a learner's language environment by exploring his or her use of language in a variety of household, community, and educational activities.

When it comes to the second point (i.e., understanding multilingual language development and tracking learners' progress in development of those languages), the task for professionals who do not themselves know or use the languages concerned is significantly more challenging. Clearly, it is impossible for every professional to know the typical developmental pathway of every language that may be used. However, numerous resources can provide detailed information about the structure and features of other languages, as well as providing information about typical acquisition. In terms of speech development, for example, the International Guide to Speech Acquisition (McLeod, 2007) provides information about the features of a variety of languages (i.e., their phonetic and phonological structure as well as typical and atypical acquisition). Similarly, resources such as those provided by the Minnesota Speech-Language-Hearing Association (2014) can provide information about a range of languages and the cultural contexts for their development. Professionals must be aware that when children acquire more than one language simultaneously, the development of each language may differ from the pattern expected for either language developing independently. Development in each of the languages needs to be actively monitored as a basis for support and, where required, intervention.

McLeod (2012) reviewed a wide variety of sources to compile a list of instruments to assess children's articulation and phonology across an array of spoken languages. The instruments that she identified, however, could typically be used only by professionals who know the target language. In contrast, the Intelligibility in Context Scale is a parent-report measure that allows professionals to describe children's speech intelligibility *in any language* in the seven contexts that relate to the International Classification of Functioning, Health, and

Disability for Children and Youth (World Health Organization, 2007). The Intelligibility in Context Scale has been translated into more than 50 languages, has been validated in English (see McLeod, Harrison, & McCormack, 2012a, 2012b), and is available to download free of charge (McLeod et al., 2012b). Where DHH children are learning their home language as their first language, this instrument provides professionals with the ability to assess the developing intelligibility of their speech in that language.

In regard to language skills more broadly, instruments have been created for assessing learners' developing skills in many, but certainly not all, of the world's languages. Once again, for the most part, those instruments can only be used by professionals who are themselves users of the target language. As an alternative, however, some instruments for assessing language abilities can be completed by scoring parental or caregiver reports of children's developmental progress in their own language. The MacArthur-Bates Communicative Development Inventory, for example, is a parent-report instrument for assessing young children's communicative development that has been adapted for use in more than 60 languages. Similarly, developmental checklists such as the Student Oral Language Observation Matrix (SOLOM; Montebello Unified School District Instructional Division, 1978) can be used to evaluate learners' comprehension, fluency, vocabulary, pronunciation, and grammar in any language. Although it was designed for use by teachers, the SOLOM can also be completed by parents to document and monitor children's proficiency in their home language.

In addition to these parent and caregiver reports, there are several other strategies that educators and related professionals can use to better understand the patterns of childhood development in a child's home language *and* to gather specific information about the child's development of that language. The International Expert Panel on Multilingual Children's Speech (2012) recommended that assessment of skills in languages not spoken by a professional can be supported through "appropriate resourcing, research, and relevant partnerships (e.g., with people around the world, including SLPs, linguists, cultural support workers, interpreters, educators, and community groups)" (pp. 2–3). The concept of *partnerships* is particularly pertinent because, increasingly, these can be facilitated using telepractice (Douglas, 2012). In this case, telepractice would involve the use telecommunications technologies, including videoconferencing, and the skills of a remotely located professional (i.e., in this case a professional who both speaks and is capable of assessing language skills in the child's home language). The use of telepractice and international resources (both personal and material) makes family support and programming of intervention for children from multilingual backgrounds more feasible (Douglas, 2012). Given the increasing ease and availability of international collaboration using videoconferencing, for example, it is entirely possible for a professional working with a Turkish-speaking child in Australia to discuss developmental milestones and relevant interventions with professionals working in Turkey or for a professional in Turkey to be directly engaged to undertake relevant assessments or interventions with the child in Turkish.

These considerations are but a few of the possible responses to supporting multilingual developmental outcomes for DHH children. Providing linguistically appropriate services for DHH children who are in multilingual environments requires significant planning and commitment. Apart for assembling multilingual resources and assessments of the type described in this section, effective educational responses demand clear and explicit language policies and planning in all educational contexts (Clyne, 2005). In particular, acquisition and maintenance of multiple languages by DHH learners will involve significant investment in investigating the individual needs of learners and their families; reexamination of approaches to supporting children's language development; the use of interpreters or other language models; consultation and collaboration with other professionals such as linguists, speech-language pathologists, and sociologists (Macrory, 2006); and, potentially, partnerships with professionals who have skills in the target language. Such considerations are important from the earliest stages of children's development, as is support for families' decision making about language use for their children and family.

SUMMARY AND CONCLUSIONS

Given the high levels of cultural and linguistic diversity in many countries, there is no reason to suspect that any less diversity exists among DHH populations. Indeed, taking several factors into account and considering a number of investigations into the linguistic diversity among young DHH learners, there is likely to be even greater cultural and linguistic diversity among that group. From an educational perspective—particularly from a monocultural or monolingual mindset—accommodating such diversity could be viewed as challenging. However, cultural and linguistic diversity can and should be accommodated through an approach to education that is based in social justice, one that acknowledges the wide range of possible social and cultural identities of DHH learners and their families and that seeks to foster their acquisition and use of whichever languages accord with those identities or backgrounds.

A culturally inclusive approach to planning and implementing developmental interventions and learning experiences for learners from diverse backgrounds requires that professionals be culturally competent. Professionals must know about and be sensitive to the range of issues likely to arise in multicultural or cross-cultural teaching and learning contexts and must examine their own personal attitudes, values, and beliefs toward people from other cultures and linguistic backgrounds—in this case, DHH learners. We discussed each of these processes, highlighting their importance and pointing to available resources for approaching these tasks.

The requirements of professionals outlined in this chapter *are* potentially challenging and could be seen to place considerable burdens on teachers, therapists, and associated professionals. Systems should be in place to assist professionals to meet those expectations. Both preservice and in-service professional education should reflect the need for the development of the types of knowledge and attitudes identified in this chapter. The issues associated with a cultural perspective on being Deaf have been well included in programs of preparation and professional standards for teachers of the deaf. Such input should be extended to include speech-language pathologists, auditory-verbal therapists, and associated professionals. Such awareness should be considered as a key part of professional preparation. However, hearing status is not the only driver of cultural differences among DHH learners, and development of the knowledge, sensitivity, and self-awareness necessary to be culturally competent across of wide range of cultural and linguistic differences should be a priority for all professional educational programs.

The principles discussed in this chapter—inclusiveness and individualization—are nothing more than would be expected as good practice in education more broadly. Professionals should respond to diversity—in this case cultural and linguistic diversity—with an individualized approach that seeks to thoroughly understand learners' personal circumstances and learning needs in their specific context, as a basis for designing inclusive learning experiences that are fair, equitable and, most of all, effective.

NOTE

[1] In this chapter "Deaf" is used exclusively in reference to the Deaf community or to people who identify as members of that cultural and linguistic community.

REFERENCES

Adams, A., Bell, L. A., & Griffin, P. (Eds.) (2007). *Teaching for diversity and social justice*. New York: Routledge.

Akamatsu, C. T., & Cole, E. (2000). Immigrant and refugee children who are deaf: Crisis equals danger plus opportunity. In K. Christensen (Ed.), *Deaf plus: A multicultural perspective* (pp. 93–120). San Diego, CA: Dawn Sign Press.

Australian Bureau of Statistics. (2012). *2011 Census QuickStats*. Retrieved March 28, 2014, from http://www.censusdata.abs.gov.au/census_services/getproduct/census/2011/quickstat/0?opendocument&navpos=220

Australian Government. (2011). *The people of Australia: Australia's multicultural policy*. Canberra, Australia: Department of Immigration and Border Protection.
Australian Institute of Health and Welfare. (2013). *Aboriginal and Torres Strait Islander health performance framework 2012: Detail analyses*. Canberra, Australia: Australian Institute of Health and Welfare.
Bird, E. K.-R., Cleave, P., Trudeau, N., Thordardottir, E., Sutton, A., & Thorpe, A. (2005). The language abilities of bilingual children with Down Syndrome. *American Journal of Speech-Language Pathology, 14*(3), 187–199.
Bird, E. K.-R., Lamond, E., & Holden, J. (2012). Survey of bilingualism in autism spectrum disorders. *International Journal of Language and Communication Disorders, 47*(1), 52–64.
Chi-Ying Chung, R., & Bemak, F. (2002). The relationship of culture and empathy in cross-cultural counseling. *Journal of Counseling and Development, 80*(2), 154–159.
Clyne, M. (2005). *Australia's language potential*. Sydney, Australia: UNSW Press.
Crowe, K., Fordham, L. A., McLeod, S., & Ching, T. Y. C. (2014). "Part of our world": Influences on caregiver decisions about communication choices for children with hearing loss. *Deafness and Education International, 16*(2), 61–85.
Crowe, K., McKinnon, D. H., McLeod, S., & Ching, T. Y. C. (2013). Multilingual children with hearing loss: Factors contributing to language use at home and in early education. *Child Language Teaching and Therapy, 29*(1), 103–121.
Crowe, K., & McLeod, S. (2014). A systematic review of cross-linguistic and multilingual speech and language outcomes for children with hearing loss. *International Journal of Bilingual Education and Bilingualism, 17*(3), 287–309.
Crowe, K., McLeod, S., & Ching, T. Y. C. (2012). The cultural and linguistic diversity of 3-year-old children with hearing loss. *Journal of Deaf Studies and Deaf Education, 17*(4), 421–438.
Crowe, K., McLeod, S., McKinnon, D. H., & Ching, T. Y. C. (2014). Speech, sign, or multilingualism for children with hearing loss: Quantitative insights into caregivers' decision-making. *Language, Speech, and Hearing Services in Schools, 45*, 234–247.
Crozet, C., & Liddicoat, A. (2000). Teaching culture as an integrated part of language: Implications for the aims, approaches and pedagogies of language teaching. In A. Liddicoat & C. Crozet (Eds.), *Teaching languages, teaching cultures* (pp. 1–18). Melbourne, Australia: Applied Linguistics Association of Australia.
Curdt-Christiansen, X. (2009). Invisible and visible language planning: Ideological factors in the family language policy of Chinese immigrant families in Quebec. *Language Policy, 8*(4), 351–375.
Decker, K. B., Vallotton, C. D., & Johnson, H. A. (2012). Parents' communication decision for children with hearing loss: Sources of information and influence. *American Annals of the Deaf, 157*(4), 326–339.
Denboba, D., (2013). *Funding opportunity announcement: HRSA-13-206*. U.S. Department of Health and Human Services, Health Resources and Services Administration. National Center for Family/Professional Partnerships. Retrieved March 28, 2014, from https://grants3.hrsa.gov/2010/Web2External/Interface/FundingCycle/ExternalView.aspx?&fCycleID=d3982daf-56e1-4bd4-b978-5fd3c375dba3&txtAction=View+Details&submitAction=Go&ViewMode=EU

Department of Education and Communities. (2005). *Multicultural Education Policy*. Sydney, Australia: Government of New South Wales. Retrieved March 28, 2014, from: *https://www.det.nsw.edu.au/policies/student_serv/equity/comm_rela/PD20050234.shtml*

Douglas, M. (2012). The Center for Hearing and Speech: Bilingual support services through videoconferencing technology. *Volta Review, 112*(3), 345–356.

Dunst, C. J., & Trivette, C. M. (1990). Assessment of social support in early intervention programs. In S. J. Meisels & J. P. Shonkoff (Eds.), *Handbook of early childhood intervention* (pp. 326–349). New York: Cambridge University Press.

Edgar, E., Patton, J. M., & Day-Vines, N. (2002). Democratic dispositions and cultural competency: Ingredients for school renewal. *Remedial and Special Education, 23*(4), 231–241.

Fischgrund, J. E. (1982). Language intervention for hearing-impaired children from linguistically and culturally diverse backgrounds. *Topics in Language Disorders, 2*(3), 57–66.

Gallaudet Research Institute. (2011). *Regional and national summary report of data from the 2009-10 annual survey of deaf and hard of hearing children and youth* Washington, DC: Gallaudet Research Institute, Gallaudet University.

Government of Canada. (1988). *Canadian multiculturalism act*. Ottawa, Canada: Minister of Justice, Government of Canada.

Grosjean, F. (2010). Bilingualism, biculturalism, and deafness. *International Journal of Bilingual Education and Bilingualism, 13*(2), 133–145.

Guiberson, M. (2005). Children with cochlear implants from bilingual families: Considerations for intervention and a case study. *Volta Review, 105*(1), 29–39.

Guiberson, M. (2013). Survey of Spanish parents of children who are deaf or hard of hearing: Decision making factors associated with communication modality and bilingualism. *American Journal of Audiology, 22*(1), 105–119.

Human Rights and Equal Opportunity Commission. (1997). *Bringing them home: Report of the National Inquiry into the Separation of Aboriginal and Torres Strait Islander Children from their Families*. Sydney, Australia: Author.

International Expert Panel on Multilingual Children's Speech. (2012). *Multilingual children with speech sound disorders: Position paper.* Bathurst, Australia: Research Institute for Professional Practice, Learning & Education (RIPPLE), Charles Sturt University.

Knoors, H., & Marschark, M. (2012). Language planning for the 21st century: Revisiting bilingual language policy for deaf children. *Journal of Deaf Studies and Deaf Education, 17*(3), 291–305.

Knoors, H., Tang, G., & Marschark, M. (2014). Bilingualism and bilingual deaf education: Time to take stock. In M. Marschark, G. Tang, & H. Knoors (Eds.), *Bilingualism and bilingual deaf education* (pp. 1–20). New York: Oxford University Press.

Lack, A. (1955). *The teaching of language to deaf children.* London, UK: Oxford University Press.

Leigh, G. R. (2001). Curriculum considerations. In R. G. Beattie (Ed.), *Ethics in deaf education: The first six years* (pp. 143–166). San Diego, CA: Academic Press.

Leigh, G., Newall, J. P., & Newall, A. T. (2010). Newborn screening and earlier intervention with deaf children: Issues for the developing world.

In M. Marschark & P. E. Spencer (Eds.), *The Oxford handbook of deaf studies, language, and education* (Vol. 2, pp. 345–359). New York: Oxford University Press.

Li, W. (2008). Changing Asian immigration and settlement in the Pacific Rim. *New Zealand Population Review, 33/34*, 69–93.

Lindsey, R. B., Robins, K. N., & Terrell, R. D. (2003). *Cultural proficiency: A manual for school leaders* (2nd ed.). Thousand Oaks, CA: Corwin Press.

Louw, B., & Avenant, C. (2002). Culture as context for intervention: Developing a culturally congruent early intervention program. *International Pediatrics, 17*(3), 145–150.

Lovat, T. J., & Smith, D. L. (2003). *Curriculum: Action on reflection* (4th ed.). Tuggerah, Australia: Social Science Press.

Macrory, G. (2006). Bilingual language development: what do early years practitioners need to know? *Early Years, 26*(2), 159–169.

Mahon, M. (2009). Interactions between a deaf child for whom English is an additional language and his specialist teacher in the first year at school: Combining words and gestures. *Clinical Linguistics and Phonetics, 23*(8), 611–629.

Mahon, M., Vickers, D., McCarthy, K., Barker, R., Merritt, R., Szagun, G., . . . & Rajput, K. (2011). Cochlear-implanted children from homes where English is an additional language: Findings from a recent audit in one London centre. *Cochlear Implants International, 12*(2), 105–113.

Marian, V., Blumenfeld, H. K., & Kaushanskaya, M. (2007). The Language Experience and Proficiency Questionnaire (LEAP-Q): Assessing language profiles in bilinguals and multilinguals. *Journal of Speech, Language, and Hearing Research, 50*(4), 940–967.

McConkey Robbins, A., Green, J. E., & Waltzman, S. B. (2004). Bilingual oral language proficiency in children with cochlear implants. *Archives of Otolaryngology: Head and Neck Surgery, 130*(5), 644–647.

McKenzie, P. (2008). Staff in Australia's schools. *Research Developments*, 19, Article 4. Retrieved March 28, 2014, from http://research.acer.edu.au/resdev/vol19/iss19/4

McLeod, S. (2007). *The international guide to speech acquisition*. New York: Thomson Delmar Learning.

McLeod, S. (2012). *Multilingual speech assessments*. Bathurst, NSW, Australia: Charles Sturt University. Retrieved March 28, 2014, from http://www.csu.edu.au/research/multilingual-speech/speech-assessments

McLeod, S., Harrison, L. J., & McCormack, J. (2012a). The Intelligibility in Context Scale: Validity and reliability of a subjective rating measure. *Journal of Speech, Language, and Hearing Research, 55*(2), 648–656.

McLeod, S., Harrison, L. J., & McCormack, J. (2012b). *Intelligibility in Context Scale*. Bathurst, NSW, Australia: Charles Sturt University. Retrieved March 28, 2014, from http://www.csu.edu.au/research/multilingual-speech/ics

Minnesota Speech-Language-Hearing Association. (2014). *Talk with me manual—revised*. Retrieved February 23, 2014, from http://msha.net/displaycommon.cfm?an=1&subarticlenbr=86

Mizuno, H., & Ishikuma, T. (1999). Help-seeking preferences and help-seeking behaviors: An overview of studies. *Japanese Journal of Educational Psychology. 47*, 530–539.

Mojaverian, T., Hashimoto, T., & Kim, H. S. (2013). Cultural differences in professional help seeking: A comparison of Japan and the U.S. *Frontiers in Psychology, 3*(615), 1–8.

Montebello Unified School District Instructional Division. (1978). *Student Oral Language Observation Matrix (SOLOM)*. Montebello, CA: Author.

Morris, P. S., & Leach A. J. (2009). Acute and chronic otitis media. *Pediatric Clinics of North America, 56*(6), 1383–1399.

Nagy, N., & Meyerhoff, M. (2008). Introduction: Social lives in language. In N. Nagy & M. Meyerhoff (Eds.), *Social lives in language: Sociolinguistics and multilingual speech communities* (pp. 1–16). Amsterdam, The Netherlands: John Benjamin's Publishing Company.

National Deaf Studies Working Group. (2009). *Deaf studies curriculum: Foundation stage to key stage four for deaf children*. Coleford, UK: Forest Books.

Ó hlfearnáina, T. (2007). Raising children to be bilingual in the Gaeltacht: Language preference and practice. *International Journal of Bilingual Education and Bilingualism, 10*(4), 510–528.

Ohna, S. E. (2003). Education of deaf children and the politics of recognition. *Journal of Deaf Studies and Deaf Education, 8*(1), 5–10.

Olusanya, B. O., & Newton, V. E. (2007). Global burden of childhood hearing impairment and disease control priorities. *The Lancet, 369*, 1314–1317.

Olusanya, B. O., Luxon, L. M., & Wirz, S. L. (2004). Benefits and challenges of newborn hearing screening for developing countries. *International Journal of Pediatric Otorhinolaryngology*, 68, 287–305.

O'Neill, F. (2013). Making sense of being between languages and cultures: A performance narrative inquiry approach. *Language and Intercultural Communication, 13*(4), 386–399.

Padden, C., & Humphries, T. (2005). *Inside Deaf culture*. Cambridge, MA: Harvard University Press.

Paul, P. V., & Quigley, S. P. (1990). *Education and deafness*. New York: Longman.

Power, D. J., & Leigh, G. (2011) Curriculum: Cultural and communicative contexts In M. Marschark & P. Spencer (Eds.), *The Oxford handbook of deaf studies, language and education* (Vol. 1, 2nd ed., pp. 32–46). New York: Oxford University Press.

Project Implicit. (2007). *The Implicit Association Test*. Retrieved February 2, 2014, from https://implicit.harvard.edu/implicit/

Romaine, S. (2013). The bilingual and multilingual community. In T. K. Bhatia & W. C. Ritchie (Eds.), *The handbook of bilingualism and multilingualism* (2nd ed., pp. 445–465). Malden, MA: Blackwell.

Schiffman, H. (2006). Language policy and linguistic culture. In T. Ricento (Ed.), *An introduction to language policy: Theory and method* (pp. 111–125). Oxford, UK: Blackwell Publishing.

Schwartz, M. (2010). Family language policy: Core issues of an emerging field. *Applied Linguistics Review, 1*(270), 171–192.

Schwartz, M., & Moin, V. (2012). Parents' assessment of their preschool children's bilingual development in the context of family language policy. *Journal of Multilingual and Multicultural Development, 33*(1), 35–55.

Secada, W. G. (1984). The language of instruction for hearing impaired students from non-English-speaking homes: A framework for considering alternatives. In G. L. Delgado (Ed.), *The Hispanic deaf: Issues and challenges for bilingual special education* (pp. 80–93). Washington, DC: Gallaudet College Press.

Seddon, T. (1983). The hidden curriculum: An overview. *Curriculum Perspectives, 3*, 1–6.

Shin, H. B., & Kominski, R. A. (2010). *Language use in the United States: 2007. American Community Survey Reports* (pp. 1–16). Washington, DC: US Census Bureau.

Smith, R. J., Bale, J. F, & White, K. R. (2005). Sensorineural hearing loss in children. *The Lancet, 365*, 879–890.

Statistics Canada. (2012). *Linguistic characteristics of Canadians: Language, 2011 census of population*. Ottawa, Canada: Statistics Canada.

Steinberg, A. G., Bain, L., Li, Y., Delgado, G., & Ruperto, V. (2003). Decisions Hispanic families make after the identification of deafness. *Journal of Deaf Studies and Deaf Education, 8*(3), 291–314.

Stewart, D., & Kluwin, T. N. (2001). *Teaching deaf and hard of hearing students: Content, strategies and curriculum.* Boston, MA: Allyn & Bacon.

Sue, S., Fujino, D., Hu, L., Takeuchi, D., & Zane, N. (1991).Community mental health services for ethnic minority groups: A test of the cultural responsiveness hypothesis. *Journal of Consulting and Clinical Psychology, 59*(4), 533–540.

Tannenbaum, M. (2011). Family language policy as a form of coping or defence mechanism. *Journal of Multilingual and Multicultural Development, 33*(1), 57–66.

Taylor, S. E., Sherman, D. K., Kim, H. S., Jarcho, J., Takagi, K., & Dunagan, M. S. (2004). Culture and social support: Who seeks it and why? *Journal of Personality and Social Psychology, 87*, 354–362.

The Royal Society of New Zealand. (2013). *Languages in Aotearoa New Zealand.* http://assets.royalsociety.org.nz/media/Languages-in-Aotearoa-New-Zealand.pdf

UNESCO. (1982). *Final report of the World Conference on Cultural Policies, Mexico City, 26 July–6 August, 1982.* Paris, France: United Nations Educational, Scientific, and Cultural Organization: Author. Retrieved March 28, 2014, from http://unesdoc.unesco.org/images/0005/000525/052505eo.pdf

United Nations. (2006). *International migration 2006*. New York: United Nations Department of Economic and Social Affairs. Retrieved March 28, 2014, from http://www.un.org/esa/population/publications/2006Migration_Chart/Migration2006.pdf

Waltzman, S. B., McConkey Robbins, A., Green, J. E., & Cohen, N. L. (2003). Second oral language capabilities in children with cochlear implants. *Otology and Neurotology, 24*(5), 757–763.

Welch, O. M. (2000), Building a multicultural curriculum: Issues and dilemmas. In K. Christiansen (Ed.), *Deaf Plus: A multicultural perspective*. San Diego, CA: Dawn Sign Press.

World Health Organization. (2007). *International classification of functioning, disability and health: Children and youth version*. Geneva, Switzerland: World Health Organization.

5

Research on Language Development

Discourses on Learning and Messages to Family Support After Cochlear Implantation

Marieke Bruin

> *O! this learning, what a thing it is.*
>
> —W. Shakespeare, *The Taming of the Shrew*[1]

Learning is an everyday concept, but when scrutinizing its content, a myriad of perspectives comes to the fore. The concept is tricky, generating different perspectives and considerable disagreement on how learning is described and where it is situated (Bråten, 2002). Each perspective represents its own particular view on how to facilitate learning. In the field of educational research there are various ways of viewing learning, communicating divergent understandings along with their subsequent recommendations toward different practice fields.

The way that learning is understood is important because it affects how support for learning is designed (Wenger, 1998). Thus, underlying understandings of learning are central to the design of family support after cochlear implantation (CI). According to Wenger, "what we think about learning influences where we recognize learning" (1998, p. 9), and therefore it directs both people's perspectives and actions. A similar argument is offered by Alexander, Schallert, and Reynolds (2009), who emphasize that understandings of learning, whether expressed or not, shape everyday decisions, thus significantly affecting people's lives.

The central matter of interest of this chapter is the concept of learning and how different understandings of it are significant for the design of family support after CI. The focus is on different understandings of learning in research on language development after CI, and in research on language development regarding the broader, more generic, context of children who are deaf and hard of hearing (DHH). The purpose is to explore how various understandings of learning are expressed in this body of research and to bring into conversation how understandings of learning are fundamental to the way that family support after CI is designed. In this context, questions of language modality will not be addressed; therefore, throughout the chapter the general term *language development* will be used. However, all the studies analyzed in this chapter center on spoken language development. It remains an open question whether a focus on sign language development would result in similar answers, but that is not the topic of discussion here.

In the case of children with CIs, the issue of language learning is the primary focus after implantation. Research states that the parents' choice of CI for their child is motivated by their desire to increase the child's opportunities for understanding and developing spoken language, thus enabling interaction based on oral communication (American Speech-Language Hearing Association, 2003; Archbold, Sach, O'Neill, Lutman, & Gregory, 2006; Kluwin & Stewart, 2000). However, how that goal is best achieved is still a matter of debate (Archbold & Wheeler, 2010). Research on language learning after CI shows considerable variability in children's development. Even though efforts to explain differences in development have resulted in the identification of several factors (e.g., see Kronenberger et al., 2013), a significant amount of variance remains unexplained (Pisoni, Conway, Kronenberger, Henning, & Anaya, 2010). However, an extensive literature review on outcomes after CI concludes that the child's family is a specific key factor influencing the child's language learning after implantation (Thoutenhoofd et al., 2005).

ROLE OF THE FAMILY IN THE CHILD'S LANGUAGE LEARNING

The family is essential to a child's development (Knoors & Marschark, 2014). From a sociological perspective, the family is the area for a child's primary socialization, the first stage in which a child learns to become a member of society (Berger & Luckmann, 1966). Here, conditions for learning are situated in the family's everyday life; learning is participation in the family practice. In the family context, through the process of primary socialization, young children learn their first language without formal instruction (Rogoff et al., 2003).

Similarly, family involvement is significant for the language development of children who are deaf and hard of hearing (Calderon, 2000; Moeller, 2000; Quittner, Cruz, Barker, Tobey, Eisenberg, & Niparko, 2013); hence, family support services after CI are essential (Archbold & Wheeler, 2010; DesJardin & Eisenberg, 2007; Hintermair, 2006; Kushalnagar et al., 2007). It is suggested that language development may be influenced by the challenges parents face in scaffolding their child's environment to facilitate learning and communication (Cruz, Quittner, Marker, & DesJardin, 2013; DesJardin & Eisenberg, 2007; Quittner et al., 2010; Spencer, Erting, & Marschark, 2000). Therefore, interventions should be targeted toward the family to provide maximum support for language development (e.g., see Cruz et al., 2013; DesJardin, Ambrose, & Eisenberg 2009; DesJardin & Eisenberg, 2007). Even though family support after CI is considered crucial, the topic is underresearched and parental views are considered sparse (Archbold & Wheeler, 2010; Thoutenhoofd et al., 2005). Therefore, this chapter directs a particular interest toward research concerning language development where the empirical field includes parents of children with CIs, as well as on studies concerning parental views on family support after CI.

TWO WAYS OF UNDERSTANDING LEARNING

Hodkinson, Biesta, and James (2008) refer to the major debate raging at the end of the 1990s about contrasting ways of understanding learning, which they describe as "the cognitive versus situated learning debate" (p. 29). Since then the debate has continued, although some theorists strive to bridge the cognitive and situated positions (Hodkinson et al., 2008). Contemporary learning theories describe the inherent complexities of learning, indicating various dimensions intrinsic to the process and concurring that a comprehensive understanding involves both individual and social dimensions (Alexander et al., 2009; Bråten, 2002; Illeris, 2009; Jarvis, 2006, 2010; Sfard, 2009). An individual perspective on learning focuses on what happens in the singular mind of the learner, reflecting cognitive learning theories (Piaget, 1952). A social perspective on learning focuses on learning through social interaction and communication, reflecting situated, sociocultural learning theories (Rogoff, 2003; Wenger, 1998). Illeris (2009) holds that the process of learning implies the integration of both individual and social dimensions. Notwithstanding this integration,

> Many learning theories deal only with one of these processes, which of course does not mean that they are wrong or worthless, as both processes can be studied separately. However, it does mean that they do not cover the whole field of learning. [. . .] it seems evident that both processes must be actively involved if any learning is to take place. (Illeris, 2009, p. 9)

As noted by Illeris, both the individual and the social processes can be studied separately. However, when studied on its own, each process alone does not cover the entire process of learning. Moreover, "it must be clear that the situation or process has not been fully covered, and an open question will remain as to what happens in the areas that are not discussed" (Illeris, 2009, p. 18).

This chapter roughly distinguishes between individual and social perspectives on learning as an analytical lens for identifying different understandings, being sensitive to the fact that such a rough division does not adequately reflect the infinite complexity of the concept of learning. The following section describes how these two perspectives, individual and social, are conceptualized in this chapter.

Learning Understood as an Individual Process

Traditionally in Western society, learning is viewed as an individual process, as "assembly-line instruction" (Rogoff, Paradise, Arauz, Correa-Chávez, & Angelillo, 2003, p. 176). It is based on the idea that learning occurs through transmission of knowledge. As such, the image of learning "immediately conjures up images of classrooms, training sessions, teachers, textbooks, homework and exercises" (Wenger, 1998, p. 8). Individual perspectives on learning are based on cognitive theories (Piaget, 1952), which are centered on the individual learner's mind and the accumulation of knowledge. "Modern cognitivism holds that individual brains, acting as solitary units from birth, possessed of representational structures and transformation rules, and receiving 'input' from the exterior, can account for the way in which we learn" (Winch, 1998, p. 46). In this view learning is decontextualized, separated from ordinary everyday activities; it has a beginning and an end and is the result of teaching in formally structured settings. The process of learning is confined to the individual mind of the learner. As noted by Hodkinson and colleagues (2008), individual understandings of learning that are primarily concerned with cognition run the risk of downplaying the physical, practical, and emotional dimensions of learning and are as such not understood as "embodied and social" (p. 31).

Learning Understood as a Social Process

Wenger (1998) challenges the predominance of individual understandings, stating explicitly that in his efforts to think differently about learning he does not aim to cover the whole field of learning. He makes a case for rethinking learning as a fundamentally social phenomenon, where learning takes place through active participation in the practices of social communities. Participation is viewed as "the transformative potential" (p. 56) of active membership in social communities of practice, where participants shape each other's experiences of meaning (Wenger, 1998). The family is an example of a social community constituting a community of practice. According to Wenger, communities of practice are quite familiar to all people, because they are an integral part of people's daily lives (e.g., the local soccer team, a neighborhood, a group of colleagues), although they rarely come into focus explicitly.

Most communities of practice do not have a name and do not issue membership cards, although we tend to know quite well who belongs to our communities of practice and why (Wenger, 1998). In this view learning is contextualized; it involves participation in communities of practice, situated in everyday life contexts. The process of learning is of a social, interactional nature.

WHY DO UNDERSTANDINGS OF LEARNING MATTER?

The processes of learning involve both social and individual dimensions. However, at times one understanding may dominate the other. Following Illeris (2009), whenever learning is viewed as predominantly individual or social, an open question must remain to what happens in the areas that are not discussed. The way we understand learning, says Wenger, requires urgent attention because a key implication for attempts to design support for learning is that "we must become reflective with regard to our own discourses of learning and to their effects on the ways we design for learning" (1998, p. 9). In other words, in designing follow-up systems supporting families in the child's language learning after CI, it is essential to reflect on how learning is understood, and to reflect on how these understandings may affect the ways in which family support is constructed. In connection to the provision of family support services, the following question becomes relevant: How do understandings of learning come forward in research on language development after CI? The next section will explore how learning is expressed in research focusing on language development after CI. As follows from the text, this body of research views learning to a large degree as a predominantly individual process.

RESEARCH ON LANGUAGE DEVELOPMENT AFTER PEDIATRIC COCHLEAR IMPLANTATION

There is a vast body of studies reporting on language development after CI. In this research, both the social and medical research paradigms come into play, differing in their emphasis (Thoutenhoofd et al., 2005). From a historical perspective, because CI is a surgical procedure, the research on language development after CI is inevitably influenced by values of traditional research set in the medical domain, characterized by recognized levels of evidence. Furthermore, the demands made on the research have been that CI should prove its efficacy and justify its implementation (Thoutenhoofd et al., 2005). This has resulted in "a comparatively large amount of research in a comparatively short space of time" (p. 264). Undoubtedly the fact that CI has had to legitimize its existence has caused many studies to investigate factors related to speech perception and speech production, measuring language development quantitatively. This might in turn contribute to the predominantly individual perspective on learning in studies on language development after CI. Learning is understood as decontextualized, taking place in structured training sessions, generating keywords such as "spoken language outcomes," "rehabilitation and treatment of deafness," and "auditory skills." For example, one of the topics currently addressed is *word learning processes* (e.g., see Lund & Schuele, 2014; Walker & McGregor, 2013). Walker and McGregor (2013) explored the word learning abilities in children with cochlear implants. They compared the responses of 24 children with CIs, 24 age-matched hearing children, and 23 vocabulary-matched hearing children in a word learning experiment, concluding that "children with CIs demonstrated deficits in word learning" (p. 375), showing "slower vocabulary growth" (p. 386). The underlying assumption is that the learner is the owner of the indicated skills, in this case skills that are lacking. Skills are measured in a clinical test, out of context. The concept of *word learning* reflects a focus on the cognitive processes in the mind of the learner. The approach reflects a perspective on learning as decontextualized and individual.

Likewise, in an article entitled *Effects of a Word-Learning Training on Children with Cochlear Implants* by Lund and Schuele (2013), the individual and decontextualized approach to learning is present in the title: The word *training* emphasizes that learning is a result of structured teaching and practice, and the word *effects* indicates measurements. Learning is conceptualized as accumulating basic units of knowledge (Sfard, 1998). Expressions such as "deficient word-learning abilities" (p. 68) and "receptive and expressive performance" (p. 81) represent a perspective of knowledge and skills as residing in the individual learner. "The language of 'knowledge acquisition' and 'concept development' makes us think about the human mind as a container to be filled with certain materials and about the learner as becoming an owner of these materials" (Sfard, 1998, p. 5). Lund and Schuele recommend that "Professionals can begin to explore the possibility that systematic training can improve the overall lexical learning process" (2013, p. 80). In this view learning is understood as a predominantly individual process.

An interesting example with regard to different understandings of learning is a study by Holt, Beer, Kronenberger, Pisoni, and Lalonde (2012) that evaluated family environments of children with CIs and examined relationships between the family environment and language development after CI. They concluded that family environment may cause some of the variability in CI outcomes and suggested that families can be helped "to create robust language-learning environments that can maximize their child's potential with a cochlear implant" (p. 848). On the one hand, the acknowledgment that learning depends on a relationship between the learner and his or her social environment represents a social perspective. On the other hand, the language used in the text expresses to a large degree a view of learning based on a predominantly individual perspective. The learner is described as a singular individual; no remarks are made toward learning as a result of mutual meaning making in communication or the learner becoming a part of the family's community of practice. The article concludes that

> families with higher levels of self-reported control had children with smaller vocabularies. Families reporting a higher emphasis on achievement had children with fewer executive function and working memory problems. Finally, families reporting a higher emphasis on organization had children with fewer problems related to inhibition. (Holt et al., 2012, p. 848)

The quotations express a view of knowledge as something that resides as a measurable amount, in accumulated form, in the mind of the child, as such representing a view of learning as individual. However, this is one of the few studies in the field of CI that emphasize that affordances for the child's spoken language development are to be found within the child's family environment. The article concludes that the study holds exciting promise for its potential application to intervention:

> Because family dynamics are fluid and can be changed with explicit communication education and therapy, there is a real possibility that families that function in ways that do not maximize the likelihood of success with a cochlear implant could learn to function in ways more conducive to a child's likely success. (Holt et al., 2012, p. 861)

The use of a word such as *therapy* can be interpreted as reflecting a view of learning as an individual process, where knowledge is transmitted in decontextualized settings.

Notwithstanding the fact that families are important for the child's learning, within the vast body of research on pediatric CI the parental view is hardly ever present (Archbold & Wheeler, 2010). In their review, Archbold and Wheeler (2010) explored research on parental views concerning the decision-making process, outcomes from CI, and educational implications. Since then, only a handful of studies have discussed parental views on family support after CI; three of them are presented in the following section. Understandings of learning influence how learning is facilitated, and as such they have an impact on the construction of family support. Therefore, it is relevant to ask how parents view the support they receive and how they view learning. As follows from the text, the parents' narratives largely reflect perspectives that view learning as a predominantly individual process.

In a qualitative study on parental experiences, Hardonk and colleagues (2011) analyzed the parents' perspectives on "early care trajectories" (p. 305) after Universal Neonatal Hearing Screening in Flanders (the Dutch-speaking part of Belgium). Sixteen families participated in the study. At the time of the interview the children were between five and seven years of age. In the study the child's learning is viewed as a predominantly individual process, by both the support system and the researchers. This is reflected in the researchers' choice of words and in the parents' descriptions of their encounters with the support system. The child's development in relation to his or her CI is aligned with "rehabilitation care" and "rehabilitation therapy" (p. 319), understanding learning as a result of structured teaching and training sessions, out of context, where "the intensity of therapy is measured in relation to the functional (developmental) dimension of the care trajectory" (Hardonk et al., p. 319). The authors write that their analysis shows that "therapy is often reduced at the moment when satisfactory oral language development is reached" (p. 319). Through this particular manner of description, oral language development is described as the result of decontextualized training sessions, having a beginning and an end, inherent in the nature of therapy sessions. In relation to CIs, an interesting factor in connection with training sessions is "the perception of the burden of therapy by the child and/or the family" (p. 319). The quotation from Jonas's mother reflects the family's encounter with a support system that views learning predominantly as an individual process, with devastating consequences for the child:

> After a while my child couldn't take any more, he really became aggressive because it was too much. They kept demanding intellectual effort from him, but playing and relaxing was never part of the schedule. (Hardonk et al., 2011, p. 319)

In another example, Sien's father is concerned by the burden that is placed on his daughter by the therapy: "She already spends six hours at school, behind a desk. Three hours in extra therapy plus the extra school support would have been just too much" (Hardonk et al., 2011, p. 319). In the realm of the support system that the family encounters, and through the way the parents describe the encounter, a predominant view of learning as an individual process emerges, with no reference to opportunities for learning that are present in communication through social interaction and informal learning through participation in everyday family life.

Huttunen and Välimaa (2011) explored experiences of Finnish parents of children with CIs and their views on follow-up. The authors state that it is "essential to know parents' expectations and experiences after paediatric implantation to be able to counsel and support them in obtaining maximal habilitation outcomes" (p. 186). The expressions used are concurrent with an individual perspective on learning. From the text, it appears that *habilitation* refers to structured training sessions where knowledge is transferred, and *obtaining maximal outcomes* reflects an understanding of knowledge as an accumulative commodity in the mind of the learner. The parental perspectives on follow-up in relation to their child's language learning are connected to "speech and language therapy" (p. 191), and five years after implantation the parents were asked how support services could be improved. In some cases, "the parents hoped for more speech and language therapy services" (Huttunen & Välimaa, 2011, p. 191). The study does not mention support to help parents enhance their child's opportunities for language learning through everyday family interaction and communication, which would represent a more social perspective on learning.

In Bruin (2014, manuscript in progress), Norwegian parents of children with CIs were asked about the support they receive in relation to their child's language learning. The following data are based on 27 written parental responses to an online questionnaire with 23 open-ended questions. The data were constructed as part of a research project on parental perspectives on follow-up after CI. Within the larger project, the aim of the data construction was to gather information to explore the parents' experiences with follow-up after CI (see also Bruin & Nevøy, 2014), with a focus on parental perspectives on the child's learning and participation in the family's community of practice. When asked about the focus of the family support, the parents describe their child's language learning as an individual process:

> The focus in the follow-up is on pronunciation, concepts, understanding, grammar, etc., together with a playful way of learning. For our daughter it works well, she works a lot herself and well, in order to become good at speaking. (mother of Rosemary, age 6)

Oscar's parents wrote that they feel secure when preparing effective strategies for "good spoken language development in combination with regular assessment of progression of speech and speech understanding." They said they have become more aware of what to do and are therefore able to "work more goal-oriented"; the "evidence from the assessments that there is a progression happening" gives them a sense of security (parents of Oscar, age 4). Concepts like "training to listen," "assessment," "acquisition of speech," "listening skills," "learning sounds," "speech understanding," "profits," "gains," and "to drill the right pronunciation" all reflect a view of learning as an individual process, a result of decontextualized and structured training sessions. The expressions are used by all 27 parents in a range of contexts.

> We are still lacking some repetition of words, the ones he doesn't pronounce rightly (lacking first letters or syllable in certain words) + new words and subjects! (mother of Fredric, age 5)

The parents display ways of thinking about learning as individual acquisition, gaining "basic units that can be accumulated" (Sfard, 1998, p. 6). "The focus in follow-up until now has been language-building, concepts, pronunciation, listening" (mother of Marcus, age 9).

In summary, in the three studies on parental views, language development is described from a predominantly individual perspective on learning. The parents' perspective on learning is apparent from the way they describe their encounters with the support system. More generally, studies on language development after CI typically take, to a large degree, a predominantly individual perspective on learning. The aforementioned studies describe learning as instrumental, taking place in the singular mind of the learner and being the result of structured training and therapy. No generalizations regarding support services can be made from the limited number of studies available. However, the studies on parents' views do yield thought-provoking examples of underlying understandings of learning, especially when considering that the understandings of learning and the way parents describe their experiences are tied to the realm of family support after CI. With a few exceptions—in particular the work of DesJardin and collegues (2005, 2007, 2009, 2011) and Cruz and colleagues (2013), which will be discussed in the next section—research on language development after CI displays a narrow focus, viewing the process of learning from a predominantly individual perspective. In most studies that explicitly cover the area of CI, the actual content and quality of social interaction and communication within the family's community of practice seem barely addressed as dimensions relevant to the language learning process.

Do any studies take a broader, more social perspective on learning or emphasize social interaction as a central dimension in the child's language development? To find them, the net has to be cast more widely, covering not only studies in the area of CI but also the broader, more generic field of children who are deaf and hard of hearing.

SOCIAL PERSPECTIVES ON LEARNING IN RESEARCH ON LANGUAGE DEVELOPMENT OF CHILDREN WHO ARE DEAF AND HARD OF HEARING

The current section presents studies on language development regarding children who are deaf and hard of hearing. Although children with CIs may be part of the empirical field in these studies, they are not discussed explicitly, with the exception of the work of DesJardin and colleagues and Cruz and colleagues. As follows from the text, in the quest for social perspectives on learning it becomes apparent that these are to be found in the more extensive category of research on children who are deaf and hard of hearing.

In 2006, Brown and Nott referred to the change in the Western approach of childhood development, which they regarded as particularly useful in understanding and promoting language development in DHH children. The change referred to is the shift toward the influence of the work of Vygotsky, with a main focus on the principle that early development and learning best take place within the context of the child's cultural group, usually the family (Brown & Nott, 2006). According to the authors, a similar trend took place within theories of child language development in the 1970s and 1980s, when emerging views of child language development pointed to the importance of the parents as tutors and to the family and its activities as the primary learning context in early childhood. Interactionist perspectives on children's language learning emphasize that young children learn their language through everyday life experiences and especially in the context of their family (Chapman, 2000), and for both DHH and hearing children, factors related to their parents have been associated with language development (Cruz, Quittner, Marker, & Desjardin, 2013). This orientation toward the child-in-context perspective has led to the philosophy of *family-centered practice* (Brown & Nott, 2006; Dunst, Trivette, & Deal, 1988). From this viewpoint the focus is on promoting an environment that provides an optimal context for the child's learning, rather than direct intervention with the child. The principle of family-centered practice is in concert with a sociocultural perspective, which views learning as situated in social interaction where people interact with mediating, cultural tools (Rogoff, 2003; Säljö, 2000; Vygotsky, 1962).

Reviewing the literature on general language development, Brown and Nott (2006) identified four features of parent–child interaction that promote communication development and that would be important in dyads in which young DHH children are developing spoken language. The first feature the authors identified was *joint attention,* which is said to scaffold the child's early language development (e.g., see Bruner, 1978). The second feature was *responsiveness* (e.g., see Bornstein, Tamis-LeMonda, & Haynes, 1999), defined as a verbal sensitivity where "positive and meaningful changes in the mother's verbal behavior are seen in response to a child's vocal and exploratory behavior" (Brown & Nott, 2006, p. 148). The third feature was *child-directed speech,* described as speech adapted to the language level of the listener (e.g., see Owens, 2001). This includes, for example, using a slower rate of speech, shorter sentences, higher intonation, and so forth. The fourth feature was *everyday life experiences,* which are said to provide a context for language learning (e.g., see Hart & Risley, 1995). Brown and Nott also refer to the work of Dunst and colleagues (Dunst et al., 2001; Dunst, Hamby, Trivette, Raab, & Bruder, 2000), stating that their research has improved the understanding of the learning opportunities afforded by everyday life experiences and how this affects practices for children with disabilities. Brown and Nott present the four features as facilitative practices for parents interacting with their DHH children, enabling scaffolding of the child's language development. These four features reflect a social understanding of learning.

A 1999 study found evidence of maternal sensitivity predicting language development in children who are deaf and hard of hearing (Pressmann, Pipp-Siegel, Yoshinaga-Itano, & Deas, 1999). Since then, however, only a handful of studies on children with CIs have emphasized the impact of maternal facilitative language features on language development (e.g., see DesJardin, 2005; DesJardin, Ambrose, & Eisenberg, 2009, 2011; DesJardin & Eisenberg, 2007). Cruz and colleagues (2013) found that regardless of child and family characteristics, facilitative language features provide an enriched language environment and enhanced improvements in expressive language for children with CIs.

Similarly, a recent German study reports a parent intervention program, the Muenster Parental Programme, designed to teach parents skills in enhancing responsiveness in communication with their DHH child (Reichmuth, Embacher, Matulat, am Zehnhoff-Dinnesen, & Glanemann, 2013). The aim of the program is to empower parents to communicate with their children using a highly responsive style, focusing on everyday parent–child interaction from the child's first year of life. In a connected study, the parent program was shown to enhance parental responsiveness and increase the infants' vocalization after three months (Glanemann, Reichmuth, Matulat, & am Zehnhoff-Dinnesen, 2013).

James, Wadnerkar-Kamble, and Lam-Cassettari (2013) conducted a study designed to test the centrality of parental responsiveness in the scaffolding of early speech and language development. The authors built on work by Goldstein and Schwade (2008) that highlights "the role of parental contingency in the development of pre-linguistic speech skills" (James et al., 2013, p. 667) and on Vygotsky's theories on scaffolding in general child development (Vygotsky, 1978). The study's approach to learning emphasizes informal, unstructured learning in everyday communication. It acknowledges the "social construction of speech-language that we think is built as co-endeavor between parent and child" (p. 677) and recognizes mutual participation in social interaction and meaning making as a central dimension for learning.

These studies emphasize the value of facilitative language features enabling parent–child communication and therefore the child's language learning. They focus on the broad generic category of children who are deaf and hard of hearing, with the exception of the studies by DesJardin and Cruz and their colleagues, who focus explicitly on CI. The studies display perspectives on learning based on social aspects of the learning process, emphasizing social interaction and communication within the family's community of practice, enhancing opportunities for language learning in the family's everyday life. Learning is viewed as contextualized, situated in the family life in which the child takes part.

In summary, research on language development after CI largely views learning from a predominantly individual perspective, whereas more social understandings are to be found in the wide-ranging category of "deaf and hard-of-hearing children." The next section will continue with a discussion that problematizes the predominant views on learning present in research that focuses on language development after CI. These views implicitly may convey unintended messages to the areas of family support. According to Foucault, to problematize is "an endeavor to know how and to what extent it might be possible to think differently, instead of legitimizing what is already known" (Foucault, 1985, p. 9). Problematizing understandings of learning may provide opportunities to think differently and open up new areas of inquiries.

IMPLICATIONS OF PREDOMINANTLY INDIVIDUAL PERSPECTIVES ON LEARNING IN THE RESEARCH ON COCHLEAR IMPLANTATION

According to Jackson (2011), within deaf education there seems to be a general turn toward more family-centered support and away from the special education paradigm, where "the historical trend of centered-based, impairment-focused services has gradually shifted to acknowledge the importance of building the capacity of family members and existing support systems within the child and family ecosystem and natural environments" (Jackson, 2011, p. 343). Nonetheless, research on language development after CI largely views learning as a predominantly individual process and echoes as such the child-centered diagnostic values and norms connected with the special education paradigm. It needs to be discussed whether this is a problem. By virtue of its very nature, research is never neutral and as such is free to choose its ontological stances. However, in an implicit manner the research on CI sends out divergent signals about the nature of learning.

A risk develops when the predominantly individual perspective that is present in research on language development after CI were interpreted by practitioners as though the studies were covering the process of learning in its entirety. A predominant view on learning as an individual process may lead to an interpretation that language development after CI primarily depends on speech therapy, training, and structured teaching. It will downplay the importance of social dimensions for learning and thus the innate power of the family as a community of practice. In other words, a problem arises when the remaining "open question" as to "what happens in the areas that are not discussed" (Illeris, 2009, p. 18), is in fact not discussed at all.

One of the main messages of contemporary learning theories is that a comprehensive view of learning implies the integration of both individual *and* social dimensions. In other words, given the interactional complexity of learning, viewing learning predominantly as individual would be reductionist. Research on language development after CI communicates dominant understandings of learning toward the practice field and hence toward the construction and development of family support systems. If the language development of the child with CIs is reduced—by research, by practitioners, and consequently by parents—to a predominantly individual process, what implications would that have? The research may convey to parents and practitioners that language development after CI largely depends on therapy, training, and structured teaching sessions in decontextualized settings. There are several dimensions to this notion that illustrate why a hegemonic perception such as this could be problematic, in particular within the family context.

Emphasizing the individual dimension in language learning after CI downplays the important social dimensions of learning. It undermines the innate power of the family as a community of practice to facilitate the child's language learning through actively enhancing the opportunities for learning that are present in the family's everyday life. Thoutenhoofd and colleagues (2005, p. 254) found that "intensive rehabilitation can be a strain on family resources." Hardonk and colleagues (2011, p. 319) mention the "burden of therapy." Bosteels, Van Hove, and Vandenbroeck (2012) describe parenting of DHH children as a process being reduced to language development, through following a path of intensive rehabilitation. They quote Jolien's mother, who says, "you end up being a therapist, you're no longer a mother or father" (p. 992). Quittner and colleagues (2010) emphasize that strategies such as parental use of facilitative language practices may reduce the stress associated with being both a parent and a language teacher, therefore enhancing the child's learning opportunities. Families would be well served by knowing that therapy and structural training are only several of numerous alternatives when it comes to learning. The knowledge that there is much that parents can actively do in everyday family life to stimulate their child's language learning, for instance based on facilitative language features, may ease some of the burden and stress.

Another reason why a hegemonic understanding of learning as a predominantly individual process may be problematic is connected to the view of the child as a person. Sfard (1998) addresses in this context the question of norms and values: If knowledge is conceived of as a commodity, this is likely to influence how it establishes people's identities and defines their social positions. In other words, describing children largely by the skills they lack, as emphasized by the need for therapy and training sessions, might have negative impacts on the child. Bosteels and colleagues (2012) point to the argument made by Landsman (2002), who explains the problem of conflicting forces influencing the parenting of children with disabilities. Parents are torn between loving the child and hoping to erase the disability; they are torn between a profound paradox of saying to the child "I love you as you are" and "I would do anything to change you" (Landsman, 2002, p. 1949). Foucault (1977) speaks of a *normalizing judgment*, individualizing persons by measuring gaps, determining levels, and fixing that which is considered special. The acquisition of language can be measured, and measurements will reflect certain "degrees of normality," establishing over individuals "a visibility through which one differentiates them and judges them" (Foucault, 1977, p. 184). A perspective where learning is viewed predominantly as individual and decontextualized acquisition might lead to learners being "perceived as objects" (Foucault, 1977, p. 185), which might be particularly unfortunate within the family context. In particular within the realm of family support, a more contextualized, social approach to learning will enable a view of the child as more than an individual in need of fixing, thereby acknowledging the learner as an active participant in and contributor to the family's community of practice.

In short, the main issue is which understandings of learning lie at the basis of the construction of family support services. The perspectives that are brought to the endeavors of designing support for learning "are important because they shape both what we perceive and what we do" (Wenger, 1998, p. 225). Hence, these perspectives require careful reflection.

The focus on learning through social interaction in general and the family's community of practice in particular brings to the fore a task for practitioners who are guiding families: helping parents to enhance learning opportunities for their child within the informal context of the family's everyday life. The family's innate power to create opportunities for learning resides in Wenger's concept of *building social infrastructures that foster learning* (1998). Families need guidance on how to build social infrastructures. They need to learn how they can scaffold their child's social environment in order to enhance the child's opportunities for learning and participation in the family's community of practice.

There is a body of research confirming the role of family involvement in the child's language development after CI. As noted by Brown and Nott (2006), there is also a body of research on general language development confirming the importance of the parents and the family as the primary learning context in early childhood. This implies there is a central role for family support systems to teach parents how to facilitate language interaction. The crucial question however, as prompted by Brown and Nott (2006), is to what degree family support services are able to teach parents of children with CIs these facilitative features of parent–child interaction.

UNDERSTANDINGS OF LEARNING IN THE CONTEXT OF FAMILY LIFE

In summary, learning can be viewed as both an individual and a social process, but a comprehensive understanding of learning requires the acknowledgment of both dimensions. Exploring the literature brings to the fore a predominantly individual perspective on learning in the research on language development after CI. The chapter problematizes such a reduced understanding and discusses how it may convey messages to family support services that language learning after CI largely depends on therapy and structured, decontextualized training. Such a predominant understanding may downplay the family's innate power to facilitate language learning through opportunities that are present in the family's everyday life. The purpose has been to create awareness that the understanding of learning affects the way that learning is recognized, and hence it will have consequences for how support for learning is designed and how family support is constructed. An approach to learning that disregards "what happens in the areas that are not discussed" (Illeris, 2009, p. 18) may lead practitioners and parents to believe that the process of learning were covered in its entirety; social dimensions crucial to the process of learning may become overlooked while researchers' focus on measurable variables will influence what is conveyed as principal dimensions in the design of family support.

In the area of language development after CI, the child as a learner is more than a single individual, lacking certain skills that need fixing. When learning enters areas outside the institutionalized realm of schooling, and into the context of family life, there is a need for rethinking the concept of learning. The purpose of designing support for the child's learning in the family context requires reflection on how learning is understood. In concert with the sociological notion of primary socialization, Brown and Nott (2006, p. 160) state that the most critical issue in follow-up after CI should be "the understanding that a child's first language is the tool for the enculturalization of that child into the family group." The child is a partaker in the family's community of practice, learning to participate and participating to learn.

In 2007, Harry Knoors wrote that there is a need to establish a research agenda that systematically fills in gaps in current knowledge about learning processes in DHH children, with a particular focus on the conditions in the child's environment (Knoors, 2007). Two years later, DesJardin, Ambrose, and Eisenberg (2009) wrote about the importance of providing hands-on training in facilitative language techniques for parents of children with CIs. Following this, Cruz and colleagues (2013) emphasize the need to teach parents how to use facilitative language features in everyday life and family contexts. Families' changing needs in this technological era of CI require more research on family perspectives to ensure that—in order to meet those needs—support services can adjust accordingly (Archbold & Wheeler, 2010).

In conclusion, research on language development after CI must expand its focus to include the family's community of practice as an important arena for the child's language learning. Likewise, family support services must not base their knowledge exclusively on research on language development after CI but extend their focus to studies displaying social perspectives on learning as they are present in the broader category of children who are deaf and hard of hearing. Moving the focus to the child's environment and directing it toward participation has implications for what it takes to understand and support learning (Wenger, 1998). For the child, it means that learning involves engaging in and contributing to the family's community of practice; for the family, it means that learning involves refining their practice (Wenger, 1998). There is an important role for support systems to help families refine these practices to facilitate the child's learning processes and enhance opportunities for learning in the family's everyday life. Correspondingly, future research needs to explore how support systems can help families make this happen and to investigate the nature of the interaction between families and their support systems.

Understanding learning in the context of family life implies becoming aware of more contextualized forms of learning. Comprehensive understandings of learning encompass the process of learning as individual *and* as social. Therefore, in the on-going process of providing family support after CI, becoming reflective to how learning is understood is vital.

> Learning cannot be designed. Ultimately, it belongs to the realm of experience and practice. It follows the negotiation of meaning; it moves on its own terms. It slips through the cracks; it creates its own cracks. Learning happens, design or no design. And yet there are few more urgent tasks than to design social infrastructures that foster learning [. . .] Those who can understand the informal yet structured, experiential yet social, character of learning—and can translate their insight into designs in the service of learning—will be the architects of our tomorrow. (Wenger, 1998, p. 225)

NOTE

1 From Sfard (1998).

REFERENCES

Alexander, P. A., Schallert, D. L., & Reynolds, R. R. (2009). What is learning anyway? A topographical perspective considered. *Educational Psychologist, 44*(3), 176–192.

American Speech-Language Hearing Association. (2003). Technical report: Cochlear implants. *American Speech-Language Hearing Association, 1*(Suppl. 24), 1–35.

Archbold, S., Sach, T., O'Neill, C., Lutman, M., & Gregory, S. (2006). Deciding to have a cochlear implant and subsequent after-care: parental perspectives. *Deafness & Education International, 8*(4), 190–206.

Archbold, S., & Wheeler, A. (2010). Cochlear implants: Family and young people's perspectives. In M. Marschark & P. E. Spencer (Eds.), *The Oxford handbook of deaf studies. Language, and education* (Vol. 2, pp. 226–240). Oxford: Oxford University Press.

Berger, P., & Luckmann, T. (1966). *The social construction of reality: A treatise in the sociology of knowledge*. New York: Doubleday.

Bornstein, M. H., Tamis-LeMonda, C. S., & Haynes, O. M. (1999). First words in the second year: Continuity, stability, and models of concurrent and predictive correspondence in vocabulary and verbal responsiveness across age and context. *Infant Behavior and Development, 22*(1), 65–85.

Bosteels, S., Van Hove, G., & Vandenbroeck, M. (2012). The roller-coaster of experiences: Becoming the parent of a deaf child. *Disability & Society, 27*(7), 983–996.

Brown, P. M., & Nott, P. (2006). Family-centered practice in early intervention for oral language development: Philosophy, methods, and results. In P. E. Spencer & M. Marschark (Eds.), *Advances in the spoken language development of deaf and hard-of-hearing children* (pp. 136–165). New York: Oxford University Press.

Bruin, M. (2014). *Parental narratives on educational follow-up of children who use cochlear implants. A study on parent support of children with additional educational needs* (Doctoral dissertation). University of Stavanger, Faculty of Arts and Education, Stavanger, Norway. Manuscript in preparation.

Bruin, M., & Nevøy, A. (2014). Exploring the discourse on communication modality after cochlear implantation—A Foucauldian analysis of parents' narratives. *Journal of Deaf Studies and Deaf Education, 19*(3), 385–399.

Bruner, J. (1978). From communication to language: A psychological perspective. In I. Markova (Ed.), *The social context of language* (pp. 255–287). New York: Wiley.

Bråten, I. (2002). Ulike perspektiver på læring [Different perspectives on learning]. In I. Bråten (Ed.), *Læring i sosialt, kognitivt og sosialt-kognitiv perspektiv [Learning in a social, a cognitive and social-cognitive perspective]*. Oslo: Cappelen Akademisk Forlag.

Calderon, R. (2000). Parental involvement in deaf children's education programs as a predictor of child's language, early reading, and social-emotional development. *Journal of Deaf Studies and Deaf Education, 5*(2), 140–155.

Chapman, R. S. (2000). Children's language learning: An interactionist perspective. *Journal of Child Psychology and Psychiatry, 41*(1), 33–54.
Cruz, I., Quittner, A. L., Marker, C., & Desjardin, J. L. (2013). Identification of effective strategies to promote language in deaf children with cochlear implants. *Child Development, 84*(2), 543–559.
DesJardin, J. L. (2005). Maternal perceptions of self-efficacy and involvement in the auditory development of young children with prelingual deafness. *Journal of Early Intervention, 27*(3), 193.
DesJardin, J. L., Ambrose, S. E., & Eisenberg, L. S. (2009). Literacy skills in children with cochlear implants: The importance of early oral language and joint storybook reading. *Journal of Deaf Studies and Deaf Education, 14*(1), 22–43.
DesJardin, J. L., Ambrose, S. E., & Eisenberg, L. S. (2011). Maternal involvement in the home literacy environment: Supporting literacy skills in children with cochlear implants. *Communication Disorders Quarterly, 32*(3), 135–150.
DesJardin, J. L., & Eisenberg, L. S. (2007). Maternal contributions: Supporting language development in young children with cochlear implants. *Ear and Hearing, 28*(4), 456–469.
Dunst, C. J., Bruder, M. B., Trivette, C., Hamby, D., Raab, M., & McLean, M. (2001). Characteristics and consequences of everyday natural learning opportunities. *Topics in Early Childhood Special Education, 21*(2), 68–92.
Dunst, C. J., Hamby, D., Trivette, C. M., Raab, M., & Bruder, M. B. (2000). Everyday family and community life and children's naturally occurring learning opportunities. *Journal of Early Intervention, 23*(3), 151–164.
Dunst, C. J., Trivette, C., & Deal, A. (1988). *Enabling and empowering families: Principles and guidelines for practice*. Cambridge, MA: Brookline Books.
Foucault, M. (1977). *Discipline and punish*. London: Tavistock.
Foucault, M. (1985). *The use of pleasure: The history of sexuality*. Harmondsworth: Penguin.
Glanemann, R., Reichmuth, K., Matulat, P., & am Zehnhoff-Dinnesen, A. (2013). Muenster Parental Programme empowers parents in communication with their infant with hearing loss. *International Journal of Otorhinolaryngology, 77*, 2023–2029.
Goldstein, M. H., & Schwade, J. A. (2008). Social feedback to infants' babbling facilitates rapid phonological learning. *Psychological Science, 19*, 515–523.
Hardonk, S., Desnerck, G., Loots, G., Van Hove, G., Van Kerschaver, E., Sigurjónsdóttir, H. B., . . . & Louckx, F. (2011). Congenitally deaf children's care trajectories in the context of universal neonatal hearing screening: A qualitative study of the parental experiences. *Journal of Deaf Studies and Deaf Education, 16*(3), 305–324.
Hart, B., & Risley, T. R. (1995). *Meaningful differences in the everyday experience of young American children*. Baltimore, MD: P. H. Brookes.
Hintermair, M. (2006). Parental resources, parental stress, and socioemotional development of deaf and hard of hearing children. *Journal of Deaf Studies and Deaf Education, 11*(4), 493.
Hodkinson, P., Biesta, G., & James, D. (2008). Understanding learning culturally: Overcoming the dualism between social and individual views of learning. *Vocations and Learning, 1*, 27–47.
Holt, R. F., Beer, J., Kronenberger, W. G., Pisoni, D. B., & Lalonde, K. (2012). Contribution of family environment to pediatric cochlear implant users'

speech and language outcomes: Some preliminary findings. *Journal of Speech, Language and Hearing Research*, *55*, 848–864.

Huttunen, K., & Välimaa, T. (2011). Perceptions of parents and speech and language therapists on the effects of paediatric cochlear implantation and habilitation and education following it. *International Journal of Language & Communication Disorders*, *47*(2), 184–196.

Illeris, K. (2009). A comprehensive understanding of human learning. In K. Illeris (Ed.), *Contemporary theories of learning. Learning theorists… in their own words* (pp. 7–20). New York: Routledge.

Jackson, C. W. (2011). Family supports and resources for parents of children who are deaf or hard of hearing. *American Annals of the Deaf*, *156*(4), 343–362.

James, D., Wadnerkar-Kamble, M. B., & Lam-Cassettari, C. (2013). Video feedback intervention: A case series in the context of childhood hearing impairment. *International Journal of Language & Communication Disorders*, *48*(6), 666–678.

Jarvis, P. (2006). *Towards a comprehensive theory of human learning. Lifelong learning and the learning society* (Vol. 1). London, UK: Routledge.

Jarvis, P. (2010). *Adult education and lifelong learning. Theory and practice*. Oxon, UK: Routledge.

Kluwin, T., & Stewart, D. (2000). Cochlear implants for younger children: A preliminary description of the parental decision process and outcomes. *American Annals of the Deaf*, *145*(1), 26–32.

Knoors, H. (2007). Educational responses to varying objectives of parents of deaf children: A Dutch perspective. *Journal of Deaf Studies and Deaf Education*, *12*(2), 243–253.

Knoors, H., & Marschark, M. (2014). *Teaching deaf learners. Psychological and developmental foundations*. New York: Oxford University Press.

Kronenberger, W., Pisoni, D. B., Harris, M. S., Hoen, H. M., Xu, H., & Myamoto, R. T. (2013). Profiles of verbal working memory growth predict speech and language development in children with cochlear implants. *Journal of Speech, Language, and Hearing Research*, *56*, 805–825.

Kushalnagar, P., Krull, K., Hannay, J., Mehta, P., Caudle, S., & Oghalai, J. (2007). Intelligence, parental depression, and behavior adaptability in deaf children being considered for cochlear implantation. *Journal of Deaf Studies and Deaf Education*, *12*(3), 335–349.

Landsman, G. (2002). Emplotting children's lives: Developmental delay vs. disability. *Social Science & Medicine*, *56*(9), 1947–1960.

Lund, E., & Schuele, C. M. (2014). Effects of a word-learning training on children with cochlear implants. *Journal of Deaf Studies and Deaf Education*, *19*(1), 68–84.

Moeller, M. P. (2000). Early intervention and language development in children who are deaf and hard of hearing. *Pediatrics*, *106*(e43).

Owens, R. E. (2001). *Language development*. Needham Heights, MA: Allyn and Bacon.

Piaget, J. (1952). *The origins of intelligence in children*. New York: International Universities Press.

Pisoni, D. B., Conway, C. M., Kronenberger, W., Henning, S., & Anaya, E. (2010). Executive function, cognitive control, and sequence learning in deaf children with cochlear implants. In M. Marschark & P. E. Spencer (Eds.), *The Oxford handbook of deaf studies, language, and education* (Vol. 2, pp. 439–457). New York: Oxford University Press.

Pressmann, L., Pipp-Siegel, S., Yoshinaga-Itano, C., & Deas, A. (1999). Maternal sensitivity predicts language gain in preschool children who are deaf and hard of hearing. *Journal of Deaf Studies and Deaf Education*, *4*(4), 294–304.

Quittner, A. L., Barker, D. H., Cruz, I., Snell, C., Grimley, M. E., & Botteri, M. (2010). Parenting stress among parents of deaf and hearing children: Associations with language delays and behavior problems. *Parenting: Science and Practice*, *10*, 136–155.

Quittner, A. L., Cruz, I., Barker, D. H., Tobey, E., Eisenberg, L. S., & Niparko, J. K. (2013). Effects of maternal sensitivity and cognitive and linguistic stimulation on cochlear implant users' language development over four years. *Journal of Pediatrics*, *162*(2), 343–348.

Reichmuth, K., Embacher, A. J., Matulat, P., am Zehnhoff-Dinnesen, A., & Glanemann, R. (2013). Responsive parenting intervention after identification of hearing loss by universal newborn hearing screening: The concept of the Muenster Parental Programme. *International Journal of Pediatric Otorhinolaryngology*, *77*, 2030–2039.

Rogoff, B. (2003). *The cultural nature of human development*. New York: Oxford University Press.

Rogoff, B., Paradise, R., Arauz, R. M., Correa-Chávez, M., & Angelillo, C. (2003). Firsthand learning through intent participation. *Annual Review of Psychology*, *54*, 175–203.

Sfard, A. (1998). On two metaphors for learning and the dangers of choosing just one. *Educational Researcher*, *27*(2), 4–13.

Sfard, A. (2009). *Moving between discourses: From learning-as-acquisition to learning-as-participation*. Paper presented at the 2009 Physics Education Research Conference, Ann Arbor, MI. Paper retrieved from http://scitation.aip.org/content/aip/proceeding/aipcp/10.1063/1.3266753

Spencer, P. E., Erting, C. J., & Marschark, M. (2000). *The deaf child in the family and at school. Essays in honor of Kathryn P. Meadow-Orlans*. Hove: Psychology Press, Taylor & Francis Group.

Säljö, R. (2000). *Lärande i praktiken: ett sociokulturellt perspektiv [Learning in practice: a sociocultural perspective]*. Stockholm: Prisma.

Thoutenhoofd, E., Archbold, S., Gregory, S., Lutman, M., Nikolopoulos, T. P., & Sach, T. (2005). *Paediatric cochlear implantation. Evaluating outcomes*. London & Philadelphia: Whurr Publishers.

Vygotsky, L. (1962). *Thought and language*. Cambridge, MA: MIT Press.

Vygotsky, L. (1978). *Mind in society: The development of higher psychological processes*. London: Harvard University Press.

Walker, E. A., & McGregor, K. K. (2013). Word learning processes in children with cochlear implants. *Journal of Speech, Language, and Hearing Research*, *56*, 375–387.

Wenger, E. (1998). *Communities of practice. Learning, meaning, and identity*. New York: Cambridge University Press.

Winch, C. (1998). *The philosophy of human learning*. London: Routledge.

Part 2

Language, Literacy, and Numeracy

6

Awareness of Hong Kong Sign Language and Manually Coded Chinese by Deaf Students Learning in a Sign Bilingual and Co-enrollment Setting

A Hong Kong Case Study

Gladys Tang, Chris Kun-Man Yiu,
and Scholastica Lam

INTRODUCTION

As a consequence of the promotion of inclusive deaf education in recent years, signed language support is no longer confined to deaf schools in many countries and may be brought into mainstream settings attended by deaf students. It is usually rendered by Deaf teachers/paraprofessionals, hearing itinerant teachers for the deaf, or sign interpreters (Humphries & Allen, 2008; McKee, 2005). To some extent, such signed language support indirectly promotes bimodal bilingualism of these deaf students although it is usually not the primary goal but deaf students' "rights to access to information."

The inertia of promoting bimodal bilingualism for deaf students seems to stand against the accumulative research findings of bilingualism over the past decades. In spoken languages, results suggest a cognitive advantage rather than disadvantage. Constant code switching between languages, for instance, reflects the bilingual language user's linguistic sophistication rather than confusion. It may also lead to a heightened metalinguistic awareness of the similarities and differences between two linguistic systems (Bialystok, 2001; Bialystok & Barac, 2012; Bialystok, Peets, & Moreno, 2014; Grosjean, & Li, 2013). On the sign bilingual front, research on bimodal bilingualism features code blending to be more prominent than code switching. The facility of using both the oral and manual articulators simultaneously is one reason; another more important reason is the possibility of accessing two grammatical systems simultaneously during linguistic processing (Donati & Branchini, 2013; Emmorey, Borinstein, & Thompson, 2005; Fung & Tang, submitted; Lillo-Martin, Quadros, Koulidobrova, & Chen Pichler, 2010; van den Bogaerde & Baker, 2005). Co-activation of two lexicons is also observed among bimodal bilinguals, adults and children alike (Ormel & Giezen, 2014). Taken as a whole, this body of research underscores the possibility of cross-linguistic or cross-modal transfer of knowledge of two linguistic systems in bimodal bilinguals, both in terms of language acquisition and language processing.

In recent years, deaf school education where the philosophy of sign bilingualism found its origin in the early 80s is being replaced gradually by inclusive education. However, as said, the adoption of natural signed language in regular school settings is not automatic. The increasing popularity of cochlear implantation seems to make signed language look superfluous or an unfounded threat to deaf students' oral language development when they are educated in regular school settings. Even for research on the effectiveness of signed language on supporting deaf students' education, there are constant debates about the choice between natural signed language or manually coded spoken language (Schiavetti, Whitehead, & Metz, 2004). In fact, it is common to find different forms of signing in sign bilingual classrooms, namely natural signed languages and other codes of communication such as manually coded spoken language (i.e., sign-supported speech), cued speech, fingerspelling, and the like. Learning under such conditions, deaf students need to glean classroom contents as well as linguistic input from the naturalistic and artificial forms of signing in the learning environment. This raises an empirical question of whether they are conscious of the distinctions between the variety of signing around them.

Apparently, what influences the decision to adopt either natural signed language or manually coded spoken language in teaching and learning can be boiled down to factors like the ideology of deaf education, educational settings, signing skills of the teachers of the deaf, as well as the educators' attitudes toward the utility of adopting natural signed language or manually coded spoken language as a medium of instruction, over and above their concern over whether these forms of signing support deaf students' academic attainment or literacy development. All these considerations aside, whether deaf students themselves mark a distinction and how they perceive the utility of the two forms of signing are left unexplored.

In this chapter, we report on a study that investigated the extent to which severely and profoundly deaf students educated in a sign bilingual and co-enrollment environment in Hong Kong developed an awareness that there are two different forms of signing—Hong Kong Sign Language (HKSL) and manually coded Chinese (MCC)—in their learning environment. We examined the strategies these deaf students adopted to mark a characteristic distinction between the two forms of signing which intriguingly occur in the same visual modality. We also attempted to explore how they perceived the utilities of these signing varieties in supporting teaching and learning. In this chapter, MCC is defined as a form of artificial signing that is usually adopted to accompany speech; hence, it reflects, either in full or in part, the grammar of either Cantonese or written Chinese. In the Hong Kong context, written Chinese is pronounced via a Cantonese sound system. Although deaf students educated in such an environment are constantly exposed to input from HKSL, MCC, and Cantonese,[1] the language contact situation plus the possibility of cross-modal, cross-linguistic transfer also implies that there may be occasions for the use of MCC. Are deaf students cognizant of the existence of the two different forms of signing in their sign bilingual learning environment? We argue that acquiring such awareness is crucial because it enables us to examine the extent of metalinguistic awareness that these bimodal bilingual deaf children normally demonstrate, on the assumption that they also engage themselves in switching between HKSL and MCC in the learning environment. More importantly still, as language learners, they need to attune to those data that necessitate HKSL acquisition, and this process also requires that they can differentiate HKSL from MCC the latter of which is based on the grammar of Chinese. In bilingual acquisition research, language differentiation at the phonological level may come as early as the first few months after birth. Cross-linguistic influence during the development of the two grammars occurs at a subsequent stage.

We will first provide a brief discussion on bilingualism and metalinguistic awareness, then a description of the forms of signing observed in the sign bilingual and co-enrollment environment in Hong Kong. Next, we will report on the methodology of the current study and results based on three tasks. Lastly, we will offer some implications for future research.

BILINGUALISM AND METALINGUISTIC AWARENESS

According to Bialystok (2001), the term "metalinguistic" may be used as a qualifier for three distinct constructs: *knowledge, ability, and awareness. Metalinguistic knowledge* refers to knowledge *about*, not *of*, language. In the study of linguistics, knowledge of language refers to one's intuitions about linguistic representations reflecting word order, morphological structure, thematic relations, and linguistic constraints, and the like. *Metalinguistic ability* refers to the capacity for using knowledge about language for certain tasks, as opposed to the capacity for using language in daily interactions. According to Bialystok, metalinguistic ability is an additional capacity, independent of the basic mechanisms that drive language acquisition and use. Accumulating intelligence, multilingualism, and education are factors underlying the growth of such a capacity. Last, *metalinguistic awareness* is associated with the attention given to the mental representations of linguistic structures in real-time processing. It is a cognitive process, as the user's attention actively focuses on the domain of knowledge that reflects properties of linguistic structures, sometimes independently of its meaning.

Do bilingual children demonstrate stronger metalinguistic awareness than their monolingual counterparts? Earlier studies by Tunmer and Myhill (1984) observed that fluent bilinguals demonstrated increased metalinguistic abilities, laying the foundation for literacy acquisition and academic achievement. Galambos and Hakuta's (1988) longitudinal studies found that bilingual children from ages 4;6 to 8;0 were better than monolinguals at judging grammaticality in syntactic tasks, but only the older bilinguals were better at determining ambiguity in sentences. In Galambos and Goldin-Meadow (1990), they compared Spanish-English bilinguals with English and Spanish monolinguals at ages from 4;5 to 8;0 and found that bilinguals displayed a faster transition from content-based to form-based judgments when attempting to detect and correct ungrammaticality, although less of an effect was found with explaining grammatical anomalies.

Recent research by Bialystok and Barac (2012) and Bialystok, Peets, and Moreno (2014) argued for a bilingual advantage in the domain of metalinguistic performance that requires a higher level of executive control. In their studies, they compared the performance of a series of English metalinguistic tasks by Anglophone children in French immersion programs with that of the English monolingual children in regular programs. Whereas the monolingual and bilingual children showed no obvious differences in judgments of grammaticality (i.e., judgments of correct or incorrect sentences), demonstrating their equivalent knowledge of linguistic structures, bilinguals performed better than monolinguals in metalinguistic tasks that demanded a higher level of executive control and selective attention. One such task required them to judge the grammaticality of linguistic structures that were semantically anomalous. They confirmed that improvement in the executive control of bilingual children was a function of increased experiences in using the two languages in the immersion environment. In Bialystok and colleagues' (2014) study, the monolingual and bilingual children at grade two did not show significant differences in judging semantically anomalous sentences; but such a difference eventually emerged at grade five, with bilingual children performing significantly better than the bilingual children at grade two, and also better than monolingual children at equivalent grades. This study points to the significance of duration of exposure to both languages.

Research findings of other studies also suggested that skills for inhibitory control can be transferred to other general cognitive domains. Costa, Hernández, and Sebastián-Gallés (2008) found that bilinguals' constantly exercising inhibitory control over one language while the other one is adopted in processing has a positive impact on their executive control even in other general cognitive tasks that deal with attention networks—alerting (i.e., achieving and maintaining an alert state), orienting (i.e., selecting information from sensory input), and executive control (i.e., monitoring and resolving conflict). In their study, bilinguals were faster in responding to task demands and more efficient in alerts and networks of executive control. For instance, compared with monolinguals, they were faster in responding to alerting cues and were less affected by tasks that required attentional demands for resolving incongruent information.

In the deaf education context, Singleton, Morgan, DiGello, Wiles, and Rivers (2004) argued for advantage of improved metalinguistic awareness among bimodal bilinguals. According to them, it is common for deaf bimodal bilinguals to engage in a cognitive mapping process in which they attempt to align the form-meaning mapping of linguistic units of a natural signed language with their spoken language counterparts, either in speech or in print. Since this metalinguistic mapping process is cognitively challenging, these researchers called for effective pedagogical strategies to support this development because of its obvious relationship with literacy development. Metalinguistic awareness at the discourse level, according to Rathmann, Mann, and Morgan (2007), may be observed where deaf children learn how to combine narrative skills with linguistic skills in the construction of a coherent narrative structure. They argued that development of those metacognitive skills such as how to represent perspective shift, reason, and motives behind the characters in signed language narratives supports the corresponding development of a similar set of skills in written language narratives.

In sum, findings of the potential positive effects of bilingualism on the linguistic and cognitive development of young children are encouraging. However, the context of sign bilingual education is more complex than any ordinary bilingual classroom involving two spoken languages, like those French immersion programs in Canada or Spanish immersion programs in America. As mentioned above, in a sign bilingual classroom, deaf children are exposed to spoken language and at the same time to different forms of signing. The question is how deaf children mediate between the myriad of linguistic input from spoken language, natural signed language, and other forms of signing reflecting properties of the spoken language. Whether or how deaf learners perceive these forms of artificial signing as sources of linguistic input remains an open question.

NATURAL SIGNED LANGUAGE AND VISUAL COMMUNICATION SYSTEMS

With 95% of deaf children born to hearing families without any knowledge of a natural signed language, Knoors and Marschark (2012) argued that this phenomenon poses a huge challenge to supporting the signed language acquisition of deaf children in the home environment. The inadequacy of nonnative input by parents who are adult second language learners of signed language themselves and the inadequacy of spoken language input due to deaf students' hearing impairment make some education researchers query if this situation warrants optimal input for signed language acquisition or literacy development of deaf and hard-of-hearing (DHH) children (Mayer & Akamatsu, 2000; Mayer & Leigh, 2010). The situation is further complicated by the global trend of mainstreaming school-age deaf students with support of advanced hearing technology like cochlear implantation, which may potentially subdue the demand for natural signed language to support the children's overall development (Cripps & Supalla, 2012; Humphries et al., 2012).

Regardless of education settings, supporters for manually coded spoken language argue for a facilitative effect when deaf students are taught using this medium, for it lays a more solid foundation, so to speak, for the acquisition of spoken language and literacy skills, in English for example (Akamatsu, Stewart, & Mayer, 2002; Mayer & Leigh, 2010). Therefore, natural signed languages in different parts of the world have been "competing" with manually coded spoken language, the latter of which is often embedded in simultaneous communication in deaf education. The extensive use of manually coded English by hearing teachers of the deaf in the midst of promoting use of natural signed language in the classroom was documented in Woodward and Allen (1988), and it still is a common phenomenon today.

Where the spoken language of the larger community is alphabetic and phonetic, such as English, manually coding this spoken language has led to the creation of varieties like Signed Exact English or Pidgin Sign English, some of which incorporate bound grammatical morphemes like "-ing" or "-ed" or alphabetically driven initialized signs into the signing system. In the Chinese context, MCC is generally character or word based. In Mainland China, there are also attempts to create signs that are based on the alphabetic "pinyin" system, and this form of signing is more or less the designated "language" second to speech in educating deaf students. In some extreme cases, natural signed language in the playground is perceived as "nonstandard" and thus avoided (Lin, Gerner de García, & Chen-Pichler, 2009; Yang, 2011). From a linguistic perspective, deaf children accessing education in this kind of classroom condition are undergoing monolingual rather than bilingual education with input that Supalla and McKee (2002) would characterize as "impoverished," In the American context, they argued that manually coded English is just an artificial signing system to supplement speech for deaf students' comprehension. The language acquisition task still rests upon how much linguistic information they can access through the spoken language using hearing devices.

If language acquisition is contingent upon positive evidence based on naturalistic input, whether manually coded spoken language is a potential source of positive evidence for acquiring a spoken language by deaf students is questionable, especially during the initial stages of their language development. In fact, recent attempts in the wake of emergence of sign linguistic research are to promote use of natural signed language to support deaf children's overall language development (Plaza-Pust, 2014; Plaza-Pust & López, 2008; Tang, Lam, & Yiu, 2014), development of literacy skills in spoken language (Wilbur, 2000), mathematics skills (Chamberlain & Mayberry, 2000), and cognitive development (Schick, de Villiers, de Villiers, & Hoffmeister, 2007). Goldin-Meadow and Mayberry (2001) also pointed out that exposure to an artificial visual communication system does not bolster language acquisition.

Is it easy to adapt a spoken language to a sign representation in the visual modality? Linguistic research to date has revealed certain distinguishable grammatical processing characteristics between signed language and spoken language (Brentari, 2011; Emmorey, 2007; Klima & Bellugi, 1979). The size of the articulators is one reason why signs take longer to articulate than spoken words. Depending on the language pair, there may also be a lack of direct correspondence in terms of syllable–morpheme mapping between sign and speech. Therefore, adaptations from sign to speech and vice versa are bound to result in the change of the prosody of language articulation. For instance, except for compounds, lexical signs in HKSL are generally monosyllabic and monomorphemic, but there is a significant proportion of signs such as agreeing verbs or classifier verbs that are analyzable at the phrasal level and polymorphemic. Therefore, simultaneously aligning syllables and morphemes between sign and speech in the Chinese context should pose a big challenge in processing terms.

In the general literature, such discrepancies may lead to consequences such as longer duration in sign articulation or sign omission, especially of the functional categories of the language (Supalla, 1991; Supalla & Mckee, 2002; Wilbur & Pertersen, 1998). From the perspective of language acquisition, acquisition of functional categories offers deaf students knowledge of subtle linguistic principles to build the grammatical system. Therefore, failure to induce the acquisition of functional categories of the spoken language may lead to consequences of not achieving full mastery of linguistic knowledge, affecting the subsequent development of spoken language literacy. Interestingly, Supalla (1991) observes that deaf students exposed to manually coded English long enough still tend to modify it to fit a more natural language representation in the visual modality. In other words, deaf students need to make extra efforts to "nativize" an artificial visual communication system in order to cope with the demands of language acquisition or processing constraints. To date, use of simultaneous communication in deaf education remains controversial (see Marschark & Lee, 2014), probably due to a lack of research on the linguistic nature of this mode of communication, which we suspect can vary quite extensively among users.

HONG KONG SIGN LANGUAGE AND MANUALLY CODED CHINESE: A HONG KONG SITUATION

In Hong Kong, HKSL is the natural language variety used by members of the Deaf community; Cantonese, a dialect of Chinese, is the spoken language and also the language of speech and language therapy. However, written Chinese, which follows the grammar of Mandarin Chinese, is pronounced via the Cantonese sound system. In language acquisition terms, Cantonese is the first language of most typically developing children, and written Chinese is their second language. However, the dialectal differences between the two grammatical systems are marred by pronouncing written Chinese using the Cantonese sound system.

Deaf education in Hong Kong is primarily auditory-oral in both deaf school and regular school settings. In recent years, mainstream education for the deaf with hearing devices to promote speech is the norm, leaving little room for HKSL development in deaf education. The predominance of oralism in Hong Kong's deaf education also means that there have been no government efforts to manually codify Cantonese/written Chinese, giving HKSL more room to explore its existence.

The impact of MCC on deaf education is far greater in Mainland China than in Hong Kong. Note that HKSL and Chinese Sign Language share typological lineage to some extent (Sze, Lo, Lo, & Chu, 2013; Woodward & Allen, 1988). However, in Mainland China, the policy of teaching "pinyin" in basic education for the general mass indirectly encourages educators for the deaf to also use this alphabetic system to create artificial signs or simply fingerspell the Chinese characters in "pinyin" (Lin et al., 2009; Yang, 2011). In Hong Kong, Cantonese romanization is not taught to students, nor has Mandarin pinyin until recently. These factors have implications for the form of MCC that deaf students in Hong Kong are exposed to. In this chapter, we grouped the signing input of both Cantonese and written Chinese under the general terminology of "manually coded Chinese," as their grammatical differences are not the focus of the current study. In the Hong Kong context, it is a kind of contact signing adopted by Deaf people in interactions with hearing people, or by teachers for the deaf when teaching in the deaf school. It may be accompanied with mouthing and/or vocalization (i.e., speech) to various degrees. Also, this form of contact signing seldom contains lexical signs for function words, fingerspelling, or alphabetically initialized signs (Tang & Sze, to appear).

As said previously, there is no direct one-to-one mapping between syllable and morpheme between HKSL and Cantonese/written Chinese. The discrepancy is pronounced because (a) Cantonese/written Chinese is rich in bisyllabic compounds while most lexical signs in HKSL are monosyllabic and (b) Chinese is regarded as inflectionally poor while HKSL is rich, as shown by the agreeing verbs or classifier verbs of HKSL. Hence, the discrepancy in linguistic organization between the two languages results in processing adaptations when Cantonese and written Chinese are represented orally as well as manually to the deaf students simultaneously. Examples are the lengthening of sign duration or repeating the movement of a sign to fit the prosody of bisyllabic words in Cantonese. In addition, in fast signing or producing longer stretches of signing discourse, signs for functional categories in Chinese are either non-existent or omitted if they exist, In (1) below, we leave out the tone markers for ease of reading. In this example, the HKSL lexical signs are adopted in MCC, but a lot of function words in Cantonese (i.e., emboldened) are left unsigned. Obviously in HKSL, the entire description will be encoded by a series of classifier predicates.

(1) MCC:		WATER			TUBE	BOIL	ONE^HUNDRED,
CAN:	**Dong di**	seoi	**hai**	**go**	si^gun	bou-**dou**	jat baak dou
Gloss:	when CL	water	LocV	CL	test-tube	boil-reach	one hundred degree
MCC:			WILL	CHANGE	STEAM		
CAN:	**si,**	**zau**	will	bin-sing	seoi^zing^hei	**ga la.**	
Gloss:	time,	FOCUS	will	change	water^steam^gas	sentence final particles	

"When the water in the test tube boils to 100°C, it will turn into steam."

INVESTIGATING DEAF STUDENTS' LANGUAGE AWARENESS: METHODS

In the current study, we asked (a) whether and how deaf students studying in a sign bilingual and co-enrollment environment differentiated between HKSL and MCC, (b) when they became aware of the two signing modes, (c) how they subscribed to the two signing modes themselves, and (d) whether there was an interaction between this awareness and their knowledge of HKSL, Cantonese and written Chinese. For the hearing and the Deaf teachers, we asked how they perceived the functions of HKSL and MCC in teaching or in interacting with deaf students.

The sign bilingual and co-enrollment program (SLCO program) admits six deaf students each year into a class of twelve to twenty hearing students co-taught by a hearing teacher and a Deaf teacher. The Deaf teacher uses primarily HKSL; the hearing teacher adopts Cantonese in teaching the whole class. He/she may switch to HKSL or sometimes MCC, when (a) interacting with the deaf students, (b) communicating with the deaf teacher, and (c) there is a need to convey messages to the whole class spontaneously. hearing students included. Certainly for some hearing teachers, their level of HKSL proficiency is also a factor accounting for the use of MCC, as they only started to learn HKSL when they joined the program. Sometimes these teachers also adopt MCC in certain pedagogical contexts, which we will describe below.

The current study involved 18 deaf students who were studying from Primary 4 to Secondary 1 at the time of the experiment. They were recruited based on three criteria: (a) they were exposed to HKSL consistently in a school environment from KG-3 onward, (b) they had severe to profound hearing loss (i.e., average loss in 500 Hz, 1 KHz, and 2 KHz higher than 70 dB in their better ears), and (c) they had no other disabilities. Their ages ranged from 9;8 to 15:0 (average age: 11; 11). Twelve of them were implanted at an average age of 2;4, and six began to wear hearing aids at age 1;5. Among them, four were born to Deaf parents, and they studied at three different grades. Two of them had a Mainland Chinese background, with exposure to Chinese Sign Language through either one parent or both. The rest of the deaf students were born to hearing parents.

There were two sets of procedures used in the current study, one for the students and one for the Deaf and hearing teachers. For the students, we invited them to complete an online language differentiation task and a questionnaire survey on language awareness. A week later, we invited them back for a focus group discussion led by a Deaf researcher assisted by a hearing researcher. For the hearing and Deaf teachers, we invited them to arrange a focus group discussion among themselves. Except for the language differentiation task, the data were qualitative in nature, so we deemed it necessary to triangulate the observations obtained from the deaf students and the Deaf as well as hearing teachers.

Elicitation Procedures for Deaf Students

Task 1: Language Differentiation

This task examined the students' abilities to differentiate between HKSL and MCC. The 32 stimuli were distributed over three categories: (a) signing that followed the grammar of HKSL with appropriate mouth gestures, (b) signing that followed the Chinese grammar with mouthing, and (c) signing that followed the Chinese grammar without mouthing. A native Deaf signer was recruited to produce the stimuli according to the three renditions stated. We decided to control for mouthing and mouth gestures in the stimuli in order to examine whether deaf students used them as cues for differentiating between MCC and HKSL. The sentences in MCC with mouthing represent the signing mode used by many oral deaf adults in Hong Kong, by teachers for the deaf at deaf school settings, and sometimes by native deaf signers when interacting with hearing people. We included a category of MCC without mouthing because we wanted to know how the students responded to this form of signing if mouthing was removed—that is, if the cue was absent. In HK, MCC without mouthing is observed sometimes among sign interpreters or deaf people when interacting with hearing people.

Five grammatical components—negation, modal, wh-question, classifier predicate, and verb agreement—commonly observed in HKSL were used to construct the stimuli, and we matched these components by translating the HKSL sentences into Chinese sentences. The first three components involved syntactic word order and the last two morphosyntax of HKSL. We included an additional component when constructing the stimuli, which involved longer signing discourses of more than one sentence. We assumed that expanding the number of sentences in a signing discourse would enable the students to access the cues involved in encoding some subtle properties of HKSL, such as the spread of nonmanuals, more readily.

Accompanied by a Deaf researcher, the deaf students had to categorize the stimuli into either (a) MCC or (b) HKSL. If they felt they could not make a judgment about the status of the stimuli, they clicked the category of "not sure." The video instructions for the task were in HKSL.

Task 2: Students' Self-Reports on Language Awareness

In this task, we examined the extent to which the students were aware that the grammars of HKSL, Cantonese, and written Chinese were different. The students' self-reflections could be compared with their abilities for language differentiation between HKSL and MCC as demonstrated in Task 1. It was an online survey and the questions were signed in HKSL. Accompanied by a Deaf researcher, the students were invited to watch the questions and choices all signed in HKSL. They then indicated their choices by clicking a button.

Task 3: Post Hoc Focus Group Discussions

Few studies have attempted to invite deaf students to articulate their awareness of the linguistic differences in modes of communication or the strategies they adopt in differentiating between the signing modes.

Age and metacognitive abilities are the two major concerns as they may have an effect on the reliability of the observations. Therefore, in the focus group discussions, we modified Gutiérrez's (2011) technique by engaging the students in a series of "language-related episodes" in which they were encouraged to scaffold their comments about the forms of signing among themselves. By directing their attention to the language issues in the metatalk, we could collect the qualitative data based on their metalinguistic awareness of the languages or forms of signing. According to Gutiérrez, metatalk as a form of overt metalinguistic activity is part and parcel of language learning. To warrant more detailed analysis of each of the participants, the students from each level were divided into two small groups, with two or three members per group. The Deaf researcher served as a facilitator during the discussion. The sessions were videotaped and transcribed for subsequent analysis. The Deaf researcher initiated the discussion with the following questions: (i) "Do you know the differences between MCC and natural HKSL?" (ii) "How do the two forms of signing differ from each other?" and (iii) "How do you come to know the differences?" To facilitate the discussions, they were invited to watch four pairs of test sentences selected from Task 1.

Elicitation Procedures for Deaf and Hearing Teachers

A focus group discussion was also conducted among the Deaf and hearing teachers of the SLCO program to document their attitude towards the use of HKSL and MCC in teaching. Specifically, we wanted to identify which pedagogical processes would invite the use of HKSL or MCC effectively. We decided not to incorporate a researcher to lead the discussion because the presence of an outsider might skew their views. A teacher who coordinated the discussion would make a record of the discussion, especially the possible relationships between the pedagogical processes and the respective forms of signing, with rationales behind their choices.

RESULTS

Language Differentiation by Deaf Students

Our first research question was whether the deaf students in the SLCO program were able to distinguish natural signing from MCC. Table 6.1 summarizes the scores of the Deaf students based on the forms of signing adopted in the experiment. In this analysis, we used a score of at least 75% as an index of achievement and calculated the number of students who successfully displayed a clear awareness of the differences between the three forms of signing.

Table 6.1 shows that 13 out of 18 deaf students managed to differentiate between the three forms of signing fairly accurately. Most students

Table 6.1 Deaf Students' Performance on Language Differentiation

Subjects	HKSL (Total = 16 items)	MCC (with mouthing) (Total = 8 items)	MCC (without mouthing) (Total = 8 items)
Subjects scoring at least 75% for all 3 tasks			
C1-1-CTY	100%	100%	100%
C1-2-HST	75%	88%	88%
C1-3-LKY	94%	75%	88%
C1-4-SMC	100%	100%	100%
C2-1-CYF	100%	88%	88%
C2-2-SMY	100%	100%	88%
C2-3-TWK	100%	100%	88%
C2-5-WCY	88%	100%	88%
C2-6-WSY	100%	100%	100%
C3-1-CKY	100%	75%	88%
C4-2-CWK	100%	100%	75%
C4-3-CWL	100%	100%	88%
C4-5-GTC	100%	100%	88%
Mean	96.63%	94.23%	89.42%
Subjects scoring less than 75% for any of the 3 tasks			
C1-5-TKH	94%	100%	63%
C3-2-CKW	69%	88%	63%
C3-5-OTN	56%	63%	38%
C3-6-TSM	88%	100%	0%
C4-1-CNW	94%	88%	50%
Mean	80.00%	87.50%	42.50%
Overall Means	92.01%	92.36%	76.39%

in this group, having been immersed in the SLCO environment for at least four years, have developed some degree of awareness that differences exist between natural signing and the signing that manually codes spoken language. In other words, they performed equally well in distinguishing the three forms of signing, although there was a slight dip with MCC without mouthing.

The remaining five deaf students, who achieved a score lower than 75% in any one form of signing, had relative ease in differentiating HKSL and MCC with mouthing only. However, difficulty arose in judging MCC without mouthing. One-way ANOVA (i.e., two groups of students times three forms of signing) confirmed that there was no interactive effect but a significant main effect with judging HKSL and MCC without mouthing between the two groups of students. As both

Table 6.2 ANOVA Results Between the Two Groups of Subjects

Forms of Signing	Results
MCC with mouthing	$F(1,16) = 1.266, p = 0.227$
MCC without mouthing	$F(1,16) = 38.970, p = 0.000$**
HKSL	$F(1,16) = 8.892, p = 0.009$**

** Significant at the 0.01 level.

groups of students performed quite well on MCC with mouthing, no significant difference was found between them (Table 6.2).

A set of pairwise T-tests was conducted to compare the students' performance on the three forms of signing independently. For the 13 stronger students (group 1), a significant difference was found between HKSL and MCC without mouthing only, while no significant differences were found either between HKSL and MCC with mouthing or between MCC with and without mouthing (Table 6.3). It seems that this group of students had no problem distinguishing HKSL and MCC, thus achieving a very high score with these two categories. However, when mouthing was removed from the stimuli, some students just associated the signing with HKSL, leading to poor performance and a significance difference when compared with HKSL.

With the five students (group 2 in Table 6.3) whose scores for the language differentiation task were under 75% with some forms of signing, results of the pairwise T-tests showed that a significant difference was found only between MCC with and without mouthing, while no significant difference was found either between MCC with mouthing and HKSL or between MCC without mouthing and HKSL (see Table 6.3). In other words, they could only distinguish HKSL and MCC with mouthing, leading to no differences in their performance on these two forms of signing. The percentage scores of Table 6.1 showed that they performed better in differentiating HKSL and MCC with mouthing, but their ability to differentiate MCC without mouthing from HKSL was rather low.

Table 6.3 Pairwise T-tests on the Three Forms of Signing and Two Groups of Students

Pairs of Signing		Group 1 (≥75%)	Group 2 (<75%)
MCC with mouthing	MCC without mouthing	$t(12) = 1.594, p = 0.137$	$t(4) = 3.207, p = 0.033$*
MCC with mouthing	HKSL	$t(12) = -0.811, p = 0.433$	$t(4) = 1.809, p = 0.145$
MCC without mouthing	HKSL	$t(12) = -2.739, p = 0.018$*	$t(4) = -2.683, p = 0.055$

* Significant at the 0.05 level.

Taken together, it seems that a prominent cue for distinguishing HKSL from MCC lies in the students' awareness of the distinction between mouth gestures with HKSL and mouthing with MCC, the latter of which is reminiscent of speech. When mouthing was removed as a cue in MCC and deaf students were forced to rely on their grammatical knowledge of HKSL to mark the distinction, difficulty arose for both groups of deaf students, and even more so with those students whose scores were lower than 75% for one or more of the categories. Therefore, proficiency in HKSL seems to be an important factor determining their performance. When their HKSL proficiency improves, they became better at differentiating HKSL from MCC without mouthing.

Next, we reorganized the scores of the students according to (a) the grammatical components embedded in a single sentence (i.e., morphosyntax and syntactic word order) and (b) longer signing discourses with more than one sentence. The percentages within each category represent a composite score based on the three forms of signing, HKSL and MCC with and without mouthing. Our assumption with grouping the stimuli in this manner was that the linguistic contrasts in terms of the morphosyntax and syntactic word order between HKSL and Chinese might be due to the students' growing grammatical competence in these languages. In this analysis, again, we grouped the data using 75% as a threshold for analysis. The results are summarized in Table 6.4.

Results of paired samples T-tests in Table 6.5 show no significant differences between any forms of signing for the students in group 2 whose scores of the language differentiation task were under 75%. It seems that without a sufficient level of competence of the grammars of HKSL and Chinese, specifically Cantonese, these students had difficulty in making appropriate distinctions, especially when the stimuli involved more advanced morphosyntactic constructions such as those in HKSL. Embedding the grammar in a longer signing discourse had little effect on their performance. For the students in group 1, significant differences were found between morphosyntax and syntactic word order and between morphosyntax and longer signing discourse but not between syntactic word order and longer signing discourse. The mean percentage scores for syntactic word order and longer signing discourse showed comparable performance, but a gap was found with morphosyntax in their performance, suggesting that this grammatical component demanded more advanced knowledge of both grammars of HKSL and Chinese to mark appropriate distinctions.

Taken together, the analysis suggested that the ability to differentiate between the forms of signing was contingent upon whether the students had attained a sufficient level of grammatical knowledge of the respective components in HKSL and Chinese to make a judgment. Their ongoing development of the morphosyntax of HKSL was suggestive of

Table 6.4 Language Differentiation Based on Grammar and Longer Signing Discourse

	Sentence Level		
Subject	Morphosyntax (Total = 12 items)	Syntactic word order (Total = 12 items)	Longer signing discourse (Total = 8 items)
Subjects scoring at least 75% for all 3 tasks			
C1-1-CTY	100%	100%	100%
C1-3-LKY	75%	100%	88%
C1-4-SMC	100%	100%	100%
C1-5-TKH	75%	92%	100%
C2-1-CYF	92%	92%	100%
C2-2-SMY	92%	100%	100%
C2-3-TWK	92%	100%	100%
C2-5-WCY	92%	100%	75%
C2-6-WSY	100%	100%	100%
C3-1-CKY	83%	100%	88%
C4-1-CNW	75%	92%	75%
C4-2-CWK	92%	92%	100%
C4-3-CWL	92%	100%	100%
C4-5-GTC	92%	100%	100%
Mean	89.29%	97.62%	94.64%
Subjects scoring less than 75% for any of the 3 tasks			
C1-2-HST	67%	83%	100%
C3-2-CKW	67%	75%	75%
C3-5-OTN	50%	67%	38%
C3-6-TSM	75%	58%	75%
Mean	64.58%	70.83%	71.88%
Overall Mean	83.08%	91.6%	89.58%

such an effect. Even the group of deaf students whose scores were at least 75% still faced difficulty in differentiating signing involving the morphosyntax of HKSL. Nevertheless, as most of these students had been in the program since kindergarten, increasing immersion experiences in a sign bilingual environment positively impacted their HKSL development and at the same time allowed them plenty of opportunities to appreciate the differences between HKSL and MCC as well as oral languages.

Did their language awareness correlate with their proficiency of the target languages? To address this issue, we conducted a correlation analysis using the following scores: (a) language differentiation, (b) Cantonese narratives, (c) written Chinese narratives, and (d) HKSL narratives. The narratives were based on the Frog Story (Mayer, 1969) and

Table 6.5 Results of Pairwise T-tests Between Grammatical Components and Longer Signing Discourse

Variable 1	Variable 2	Group 1 (≥75%)	Group 2 (<75%)
Morphosyntax	Syntactic word order	$t(13) = -3.894, p = 0.002$**	$t(3) = -0.792, p = 0.486$
Morphosyntax	Longer signing discourse	$t(13) = -2.188, p = 0.048$*	$t(3) = -0.753, p = 0.506$
Syntactic word order	Longer signing discourse	$t(13) = 1.114, p = 0.286$	$t(3) = -0.096, p = 0.929$

* Significant at the 0.05 level.
** Significant at the 0.01 level.

scored by native users of the target languages based on criteria such as contents, language, and coherence. The correlation analyses revealed a significant relationship between the students' performance on HKSL narratives and language differentiation; however, no significant relationship was found between language differentiation and Cantonese or written Chinese narratives (Table 6.6). In other words, the students seemed to be using their knowledge of HKSL as a reference against which they differentiated the different forms of signing. Further investigation is needed to examine whether a relationship exists between language differentiation and written Chinese and Cantonese proficiency.

In summary, immersed in a sign bilingual environment with sustained HKSL and oral/written Chinese input for five to seven years, these students had developed an awareness about characteristic distinctions associated with the signing of natural HKSL and MCC. The data suggest that they initially ascribed mouthing to signing based on spoken language and mouth gestures to HKSL. They seemed to be adopting this distinction as a general rule of thumb in differentiating the forms of signing they were exposed to in the learning environment.

Table 6.6 Correlations Between Language Differentiation and Cantonese, Written Chinese, and HKSL Narratives

	Cantonese Narratives	Written Chinese Narratives	HKSL Narratives
Language differentiation	$r = 0.410, p = 0.091$	$r = 0.359, p = 0.144$	$r = 0.641, p = 0.004$**
Cantonese narratives	—	$r = 0.695, p = 0.001$**	$r = 0.070, p = 0.782$
Written Chinese narratives	—	—	$r = 0.134, p = 0.595$

* Significant at the 0.05 level.
** Significant at the 0.01 level.

This may explain why when mouthing was removed in the stimuli, the students had difficulty making consistent judgments about which grammar the signing was based on. This ability for language differentiation was associated with their developing competence in HKSL.

Students' Self-Reports on Language Awareness

Table 6.7 summarizes the students' self-reflections upon whether they perceived differences in the grammars of Cantonese, written Chinese, and HKSL.

In Table 6.7, a great majority of the deaf students agreed that the grammar of HKSL was different from that of Cantonese or written Chinese (see Q1 and Q2). On the other hand, 10 students (55.56%) thought the

Table 6.7 Language Awareness

		Choice of Responses (Total = 18)		
No.	Questions	Different	Same	Not sure
1	Do you think the grammars of natural signing (i.e., HKSL) and speech (i.e., Cantonese) are different?	88.89% (16)	11.11% (2)	0%
2	Do you think the grammars of natural signing (i.e., HKSL) and written Chinese are different?	72.22% (13)	22.22% (4)	5.56% (1)
3	Do you think the grammars of speech (i.e., Cantonese) and written Chinese are different?	44.44% (8)	55.56% (10)	0%
4	Do you think the grammars of natural s igning (i.e., HKSL) and "sign & speak at the same time" (i.e., manually coded Chinese) are different?	83.33% (15)	11.11% (2)	5.56% (1)
		I can	I cannot	Not sure
5	When you see someone sign (naturally), can you tell whether his/her signing follows the grammar of HKSL?	83.33% (15)	11.11% (2)	5.56% (1)
6	When you see someone "signs & speaks at the same time," can you tell whether his/her signing follows the Chinese grammar?	55.56% (10)	38.89% (7)	5.56% (1)
		Always	Sometimes	No
7	Do you watch the Deaf teacher's signing in class?	38.89% (7)	61.11% (11)	0%
8	Do you listen to the hearing teacher in class?	22.22% (4)	61.11% (11)	16.67% (3)

two spoken language grammars were the same, and only eight (44.4%) thought they were different (see Q3). Hence, their awareness about the grammatical differences between Cantonese and written Chinese was rather weak. This was in stark contrast to their awareness about the grammatical differences between HKSL and MCC, as 15 students (83.3%) agreed that they were different (see Q4).

The students' responses to Q5 and Q6 partially corroborated their high scores in the language differentiation task. When asked whether they could judge someone's signing as following the grammar of HKSL, 15 of the 18 students (83.33%) were quite positive (see Q5). This result suggested that they could readily perceive the grammar of HKSL if someone was signing naturally. When the signing was accompanied with speech, as in MCC with mouthing, only 10 students (55.56%) replied that they could judge the signing as following the grammar of Cantonese/written Chinese (see Q6); seven of them (38.89%) claimed they could not; one (5.56%) responded "not sure." In other words, judging whether the signing followed the grammar of HKSL was easier than whether it followed the grammar of Chinese. It is possible that studying in this environment where both forms of signing co-occur, deaf students would initially rely on mouth gesture or mouthing to distinguish categorically HKSL from MCC.

Table 6.7 also summarizes how frequently the students access the lesson contents through signing or speech. Regardless of their hearing levels or speech perception abilities, relying on the signing of the Deaf teachers in class was a common strategy of all students: Seven of them (38.89%) chose "Always" and 11 (61.11%) chose "Sometimes" (see Q7). Paying attention to the speech of the hearing teachers was also quite common: 11 of them (61.11%) chose "Always" and four of them (22.22%) chose "Sometimes." Three students (16.67%) said they did not pay attention to the speech of the hearing teacher in class at all (see Q8). Their level of hearing loss ranged between 105 and 120 dB and their speech perception scores between 0% (two students) and 60.8% (one student). Obviously, classroom learning to these deaf students was primarily through the signing mode. On the other hand, four students (22.22%) said they "always" paid attention to the speech of the hearing teachers. These students had a lesser degree of hearing loss (between 72 and108 dB) and relatively better speech perception abilities (between 93.33% and 100%). Interestingly, two of the students said they also "always" watched the signing of the Deaf teachers, and the other two said they did so "sometimes." Eight students (44.44%) chose the option "Sometimes" for Q7 and Q8, suggesting that they paid attention to the instruction of both the Deaf teacher and the hearing teacher in class.

Apparently, with a Deaf teacher and a hearing teacher in a sign bilingual classroom, the students became flexible enough to capitalize on the linguistic resources of both Cantonese and HKSL to access the lesson contents. The choice is not random but is systematically mediated by the deaf students themselves to achieve comprehension, subject to their speech perception abilities and familiarity with HKSL. For these students, consistent engagement in classroom discourses in both HKSL and Cantonese enabled them to access comprehensible input for language acquisition.

Focus Group Discussions: Deaf Students

To further verify the findings of the language differentiation task and language awareness survey, we conducted a focus group discussion with the deaf students. We will present the results according to two major themes that we picked up from the discussions: (i) how the deaf students differentiated HKSL from MCC, and (ii) what their views were regarding the roles of HKSL and MCC in the development of Chinese.

From the metatalk, almost all deaf students were able to provide some accurate metalinguistic descriptions about the properties of HKSL and MCC, although the depth of their linguistic characterizations varied according to their grade levels. A summary of the grammatical properties as described by the deaf students during the discussions can be found in Table 6.8.

Most deaf students talked about the differences in syntactic word order, facial expressions, and mouthing and mouth gestures. They generally associated mouthing and Chinese word order with MCC, and facial expression or mouth gesture with HKSL. Two examples of metatalk are provided below; they are quite elaborate in terms of the depth of metalinguistic descriptions:

Table 6.8 Grammatical Properties Described by the Deaf Students

Properties	MCC	HKSL
Lexical items	One sign for one word in Chinese	One sign for a few words in Chinese
Morphosyntax	NA	Use of classifier predicates, verb agreement
Syntax	Chinese word order	Syntactic position of function words (e.g., negators)
Prosody	Choppy, a lot of pauses, slow, protracted	Fluent, short, dynamic
Discourse	Presentation of information in a serial manner	Role shift to express multiple events serially or simultaneously
Mouthing	Yes	Little or none
Facial expression	Expressionless	Rich
Head or body movement	No	Yes

(2) THE_THIRD_VIDEO NATURAL_SIGNING. *"IX_1 ELDER_BROTHER EAT ICE_CREAM SWEET NOT"*, IX [i.e., the sign NOT] PLACE_IN_FRONT NOT BUT PLACE_AT_THE_END. WHAT, MANUALLY_CODE_CHINESE, *"IX_1 ELDER_BROTHER EAT NOT EAT ICE_CREAM"*, PLACE_IN_MIDDLE

"The third video is natural signing. In the sentence `My brother does not eat ice cream and sweets,' the sign `not' is not placed in front, but at the end (of the sentence). How about manually coded Chinese? In the question `Does elder brother eat ice cream?' the sign `not' is placed between the two verbs."

(C1-5-TKH, S1, profound, deaf child of hearing parents)

(3) BECAUSE FIRST HAVE SIGN_AND_SPEAK_AT_THE_SAME_TIME CAN_SEE THE_OTHER WHAT, MOUTH_CLOSE, NATURAL SIGNING

"You could see mouthing during signing in the first video. As for the other, the mouth is closed, and it is natural signing."

(C2-2-SMY, P6, moderate to severe, deaf child of deaf parents)

The form of the lexical items, signing prosody, and head or body movements were also considered as cues for differentiating the different forms of signing. Some students noticed that one Chinese character was often represented by one sign in MCC, but a few Chinese characters might be represented by one sign in HKSL. They also managed to point out that the prosody of MCC and HKSL was different. While MCC looked quite "choppy," lacked rhythm, and contained a lot of pauses, HKSL was "smooth" in rhythm and "fluent" (i.e., seamless). Deaf students at the junior levels primarily commented on the lack of correspondence between the number of signs in HKSL and the number of characters in MCC, as shown by the comments made by C4-5-GTC and C3-1-CKY below:

(4) SEE SEEM NATURAL_SIGNING WHAT TWO WORD THREE WORD GO_TOGETHER CHANGE ONE SIGN FINISH BUT IX_3 BUT THE_OTHER IX_3 MANUALLY_CODED_CHINESE ALWAYS ONE CHARACTER SIGN ELDER_BROTHER ELDER_BROTHER, NOT EAT

"It seems to me that natural signing may cover two or three Chinese characters in one sign; however, in manually coded Chinese, each character is expressed by one sign, like repeating the sign ELDER_BROTHER twice for `elder brother' in Chinese and signing two signs NOT and EAT to express `not eating'."

(C4-5-GTC, P4, profound, deaf child of deaf parents)

Some students noticed that there was head or body movement in the longer signing discourses in HKSL but it was not observed in MCC. They also pointed out that HKSL represented "events in the form of conversations." What the children meant was the use of role shift where signers assumed the roles of different participants in the conversation. See (5):

(5) BODY_SHIFT_TO_ONE_SIDE BODY_SHIFT_TO_OTHER_SIDE MEANING TWO_PERSON_GO_TOGETHER SEEM TWO_PERSON_GO_TOGETHER IMAGINE PERSON_ONE PERSON_TWO TALK_TO_EACH_OTHER

> "The body shifting to one side and then to another means there is a conversation going on between two participants."
>
> (C1-3-LKY, S1, profound, deaf child of hearing parents)

When asked about how they became aware of the cues for differentiating between the different forms of signing, only those deaf students who managed to differentiate HKSL and MCC accurately were able to articulate this awareness in concrete terms. Two students at Secondary 1 indicated quite firmly that they had intuitions for differentiating between the different forms of signing. The Secondary 1 and Primary 5 students claimed that their frequent contact with both forms of signing could be the reason why they knew how to characterize them differently. Some younger ones from Primary 4 and 5 were less clear about the reasons, but they reported that their teachers had clarified the two forms of signing to them explicitly. Three students at the junior level expressed that they did not know how they managed to distinguish one form of signing from the other, but they just did.

As a whole, these deaf students have developed various levels of metalinguistic awareness about certain characteristic distinctions between HKSL and MCC. Their awareness varied on a continuum of explicitness. Students at the senior levels could afford more explicit metalinguistic statements about HKSL and MCC, while the junior ones focused more on the signing forms at the lexical level or implicit intuitions.

According to the students, both HKSL and Cantonese were the two major languages they adopted to access the lesson contents in class, although they recognized that they could communicate with their Deaf or hearing teachers using other visual modes of communication, such as MCC. Twelve of the 18 students (66.66%) said they interacted with their hearing teachers in Cantonese. The remaining six who did not choose Cantonese commented that they would use MCC and/or written Chinese. When asked about the modes of communication that they thought would facilitate spontaneous access to lesson contents, almost all students chose both HKSL and spoken language, the latter of which could be Cantonese and written Chinese. Only a few students voted for MCC, in addition to HKSL. In sum, these students appreciated the flexibility in terms of access to linguistic resources and lesson contents as provided by the sign bilingual and co-enrollment environment.

Although these students acknowledged the importance of HKSL in classroom instruction, they also accepted MCC as a tool that indirectly demonstrating the linguistic differences between HKSL and Cantonese/written, despite the fact that a majority of students held an ambivalent attitude toward this artificial communication system. During the metatalk, the deaf students brought up some evaluative judgments about the two forms of signing. Many of them commented that HKSL was "dynamic," "smooth," and "seamless," thus facilitating faster and more effective comprehension of information. On the other hand, 16 of the 18 deaf students had rather negative comments about MCC. According to them, it was "unclear," "incomprehensible," "boring," and "not dynamic enough." One deaf student (C2-2-SMY) claimed that "Clever students learnt Chinese idioms via natural signing, only stupid students learn Chinese idioms first using MCC and later using natural signing." Only four students gave either neutral or positive comments on MCC, such as supporting the learning of Chinese and reading skills, or filling the gaps in speech.

One specific pedagogical function that some deaf students consistently alluded to was using MCC to understand certain formal properties of Chinese. Scanning their comments, we suspect that it was the growing proficiency of both HKSL and Chinese but not speech perception abilities that created an effect on their preferred choice of communication codes. As their proficiency in HKSL and Chinese improved, all Secondary 1 students asserted that natural signing was useful for explaining the meaning of the Chinese characters and idioms. It had the advantage of showing which Chinese characters were adopted in a word or an idiom, and how the characters appeared in a sequence. In other words, MCC was used only to artificially represent the characters of words or idioms in sequence, which did not necessarily bear any significant relationship to the words' actual meanings.

In sum, the comments made by the deaf students during the metatalk were quite informative. While they appreciated the efficiency of HKSL in facilitating effective comprehension of the lesson contents, they agreed that MCC could be used to help them understand the character sequence of Chinese words and idioms, although they did not seem to appreciate the effectivenss of this type of signing.

Focus Group Discussions: Deaf and Hearing Teachers

To address the issue concerning the relationship between the forms of signing and pedagogical processes in the classroom, we invited the Deaf and hearing teachers to organize two focus group discussions among themselves. One meeting was held among two hearing and two Deaf teachers of the secondary SLCO program, and the other one was held among three hearing teachers and seven Deaf teachers of the primary SLCO program. The hearing teachers had worked in the SLCO environment from two to six years and had acquired good signing skills. The Deaf teachers had taught in the program for one to six years. They had received basic training in sign linguistics and deaf education after joining the program. From their discussions, all teachers agreed that HKSL had to be the primary language of instruction to support the students' comprehension of lesson contents, especially the complex concepts involved in Mathematics and General Studies. HKSL was the major language of management talk in class, such as giving instructions to students and explaining classroom routines and task arrangements. It was also used in spontaneous classroom interactions such as comprehension checks or clarification requests. The teachers also stated their preference for using HKSL to deliver the lesson contents in class. According to them, deaf students found it easier to comprehend the contents if explained in HKSL. Both the Deaf and the hearing teachers commented that HKSL was effective in explaining new or abstract concepts such as "reflection or refraction in physics." Some hearing teachers added that when they had to interpret for the Deaf teachers or students, they preferred HKSL because of efficiency of information delivery. HKSL was also used to support some pedagogical processes involving audiovisual resources because of the lack of subtitles with some video programs. In the last situation, they agreed that HKSL-Cantonese interpretation by the hearing teachers was necessary.

Besides HKSL, both the Deaf and the hearing teachers commented that MCC could be adopted as an auxiliary code to fulfill some specific pedagogical goals. Like the students, they cited the teaching of Chinese lexical items and specific grammatical components as examples. The teaching of jargons in Mathematics (e.g., 畢氏定理 "Pythagorean theorem"), Chinese two- and three-syllable compounds (e.g., 清香 "fragrant," 三文治 "sandwich"), and four-character idioms (e.g., 樂於助人 "be happy to help people") lend themselves to the alternate use of HKSL and MCC. According to the teachers, HKSL was excellent for clarifying the meaning of the abstract concepts involved. When comprehension of the concepts was achieved, they would then sign the word according to the character sequence to facilitate character/word recognition, although the meaning of the signs combined did not necessarily yield a direct correspondence with the meaning of the words. Obviously, signing under this condition did not serve any communicative purpose but functioned as a mnemonic to assist the deaf students in remembering the character sequence of words. Also, according to the teachers, MCC with mouthing was also adopted to help deaf students remember the mouth movements or to distinguish different Chinese words or characters that shared a similar HKSL sign "HAPPY," such as "開心"<open-heart>, "快樂" <quick-happy>, and "高興" <high-charged>. In this regard, the use of MCC became a source for training of mouth movement, to facilitate speech reading.

At the grammatical level, the teachers reported that MCC was adopted to highlight the morphological process of reduplication in Chinese (e.g., 綠油油 <green-oil-oil> "lush greenery," where the character "油" [oil] is reduplicated). Again, MCC would serve as a mnemonic to heighten the students' awareness about the specific morpheme for and the sequence of morphemes in reduplication in Chinese. Using MCC to draw deaf students' attention to word order differences between HKSL and Chinese was also considered quite effective. The Deaf teachers said that HKSL was most effective when explaining the meaning of Chinese and English sentences, and presenting the examples in MCC helped deaf students see the contrasts in word order between HKSL and Chinese. This explanation from the teachers corroborated the deaf students' comments. Both Deaf and hearing teachers agreed it was important to draw the deaf students' attention to the linguistic differences between HKSL and Chinese, and MCC performed the pedagogical function of presenting the Chinese data metalinguistically in the signing mode, but it was certainly not adopted for explanation, which would be the job of HKSL.

DISCUSSION

These results above suggest that deaf students studying in a sign bilingual and co-enrollment school setting can develop metalinguistic awareness about the characteristic distinctions between HKSL and MCC. In addition to an enriched linguistic exposure to different languages and different forms of signing, this environment encourages both deaf and hearing students to constantly engage themselves in code switching or code blending between HKSL and Cantonese/written Chinese, and, on some occasions, code switching between HKSL and MCC. When HKSL and MCC are placed in tandem to fulfill the requirements of certain pedagogical processes, it seems that both the teachers and the deaf students are conscious of the roles each variety of signing plays in promoting learning. In other words, this learning context provides ample opportunities for the deaf students, and probably the hearing students, to formulate and verify hypotheses about the characteristic distinctions of the languages, or the different forms of signing that occur in the school environment. We suggest that these learning experiences in turn enhance the deaf students' development of metalinguistic awareness about the languages they are exposed to. Moreover, the fact that they can differentiate between HKSL and MCC also implies that such ability facilitates their access to appropriate naturalistic input for the acquisition of HKSL. We hypothesize that this constant comparison of linguistic structures at the metalinguistic level may also ultimately support the acquisition of Chinese as well as the related literacy skills in the long run.

What enhances the use of HKSL in learning and social interactions in the school environment? Singleton and Morgan (2006) summarized a number of studies in which they described the differences in deaf–deaf as well as hearing–deaf interactions in the home and classroom contexts. They argued that the presence of a Deaf teacher in the classroom is beneficial to deaf students' classroom learning because Deaf teachers know how to use Deaf-sensitive strategies like eye gaze to engage deaf students' attention in classroom interactions. They further argued that joint attention is a prerequisite for effective information exchange, especially in the signing modality. In the sign bilingual and co-enrollment setting in Hong Kong, the fact that HKSL is one of the languages of instruction in addition to Cantonese is made possible by the presence of Deaf teachers. It is possible that joint attention between the Deaf teacher and students in the classroom enables access to lesson contents as well as naturalistic input in HKSL. Linguistically, Deaf teachers serve the important function of providing naturalistic input in HKSL for both deaf and hearing students. Pedagogically, the division of labor in terms of the language of instruction, primarily HKSL by a Deaf teacher and Cantonese by a hearing teacher, allows deaf and sometimes hearing students to access information flexibly in the classroom. Moreover, being Deaf role models themselves, Deaf teachers also support the deaf students to learn how to negotiate with the hearing world from a Deaf perspective.

Immersed in such a learning environment, deaf students become adept at constantly switching their communication codes subject to the domains of conversations and the hearing status of the participants. One such domain that may potentially induce constant attention to code choice is classroom instruction. The self-reports and metatalk have affirmed a functional role of HKSL in classroom learning through discussions in HKSL. This language, according to the deaf students, supports effective comprehension of spontaneous classroom interactions, abstract subject knowledge, and metalinguistic discussions.

While most deaf students endorsed HKSL as a primary language of instructions, a few also opted for MCC, in addition to HKSL and Cantonese. These students came from a group that exhibits better speech perception abilities, thus enabling them to accept a wider range of signing options in the classroom. As it stands, the crux of the matter is to identify which pedagogical functions necessitate the use of HKSL or MCC to support learning. Such a process of identifying a specific language or signing option to fulfill particular pedagogical functions certainly underscores the continuously negotiated decisions on code choice between the students and the teachers in the classroom. Clearly, both the students and the teachers regard HKSL as most important for effective classroom communication, especially for presentation, clarification, and feedback. However, to highlight the properties of Chinese metalinguistically, such as word order syntax or the character sequences of Chinese words and idioms, the deaf students as well as the Deaf and hearing teachers agreed to adopt MCC as a supplement to HKSL and Cantonese.

Another theme that the teachers identified during the focus group discussion was the factors that underlie the sociolinguistic context of language use. One such factor is the level of HKSL proficiency of the participants in the classroom. According to the hearing teachers, they would adopt HKSL in small group discussions involving deaf students as far as possible, especially when they perceived that the hearing students had better HKSL skills. Some hearing teachers acknowledged that their dominant language was Cantonese while HKSL was just their second language that they started to develop when joining the program; therefore, their falling back on MCC when interacting with deaf students is understandable. Indeed, the hearing teachers were aware of this artifact of language use. Another context determining the use of MCC was when the hearing teacher needed to convey messages to the whole class of hearing and deaf students spontaneously in the presence of the Deaf teacher. Under such circumstances, the Deaf teacher would be cued to pick up the messages through the MCC of the hearing teacher.

Both the teachers and students said they were cognizant of the specific functions of HKSL and MCC in class. They had reached a consensus that HKSL was for clarification of meanings, abstract concepts, grammatical or cross-linguistic descriptions, and the like, while MCC was usually restricted to metalinguistic demonstrations such as word forms or word orders. Some of these strategies are similar to those adopted in the study by Berke (2013), in which certain shared reading techniques adopted by Deaf parents also involved the raising of metalinguistic skills to maximize the deaf child's exposure to English in print through American Sign Language (ASL). They included word definition, explanations about the differences in spelling between two similar-looking words, or the differences between ASL and English, as well as translation through ASL.

In sum, the deaf students' performance in the language differentiation task, their self-reflections about the linguistic differences between the two forms of signing, and their tendency of tuning themselves to the Deaf and hearing teachers' language of instruction so readily revealed their highly proficient skills of linguistic adaptations. Evidentially, over time, they became aware of which teacher was responsible for which language, as well as the linguistic differences between a signed language and a spoken language, even when the latter is represented in the same signing modality. This language awareness should potentially pave the way for their access to appropriate linguistic input for bilingual acquisition, and more importantly, subject knowledge when learning in a sign bilingual classroom.

CONCLUSION

Deaf students studying in a sign bilingual and co-enrollment program team-taught by a Deaf and a hearing teacher displayed a growing metalinguistic awareness and capacity for distinguishing HKSL from MCC, and this performance correlated with the students' HKSL proficiency. They initially used mouth gesture and mouthing to categorize the two forms of signing. From the students' self-reports, they could achieve a sufficient level of understanding of the characteristic distinctions between HKSL and MCC by Primary 4, after four to five years of immersion in a sign bilingual and co-enrollment learning environment. We suggest that intrinsic to this environment is the Deaf teacher, whose presence offers the students the flexibility of accessing linguistic input and lesson contents in class through HKSL, in addition to Cantonese by the hearing teacher who can also sign. Because research on language use in a sign bilingual classroom having a Deaf teacher and a hearing teacher is limited, more fine-grained analysis of the linguistic resources embedded in this kind of classroom interactions would shed light on bilingual acquisition in a classroom condition.

The study also revealed that immersing deaf students in a linguistically rich environment potentially enhances their growth of metalinguistic awareness of the ontological differences between HKSL and MCC. The results offer a different angle in our awareness of the functions of HKSL and MCC in classroom learning. The evidence justifies the use of a natural sign language to meet the constantly shifting demands for information access in classroom learning. Although the students' attitudes toward MCC for effective communication were less than positive, the evidence does not reject the use of MCC altogether.

Instead, this visual communication system was perceived by the teachers and the students alike as a tool for fulfilling some specific pedagogical functions, which potentially heightened the students' metalinguistic awareness of the linguistic differences between HKSL and Chinese.

The current study represents the first attempt to investigate deaf students' awareness of HKSL and Chinese when both languages are transmitted in the signing modality. The results are preliminary, and future research is certainly necessary. In future, grammaticality judgments that are commonly adopted to measure the metalinguistic knowledge of monolingual or bilingual children are necessary, especially in light of the proposal of cognitive advantage that bilingual children demonstrate in various studies involving spoken language. It is important to examine whether deaf students studying in a sign bilingual environment with input from HKSL and Cantonese/written Chinese also demonstrate this advantage. It is also important to further identify the pedagogical processes in which HKSL or MCC may play a part. Although the debate between adopting a natural signed language or a manually coded spoken language in educating deaf students will continue for some time among educators for the deaf, the results of the current study contribute to the tenet that deaf students have the ability to differentiate the two forms of signing to support their language acquisition and classroom learning, so long as the two signing varieties are placed alongside each other with clearly spelt out functional roles. We argue that this facility is made possible through collaborative teaching between a Deaf teacher and a hearing teacher, and collaborative learning between deaf and hearing students in a co-enrollment classroom.

ACKNOWLEDGMENTS

We acknowledge the generous donations of The Hong Kong Jockey Club Charities Trust, the Lee Hysan Foundation, and the Fu Tak Iam Foundation for the unprecedented establishment of the sign bilingualism and co-enrollment approach toward educating deaf and hearing students in Hong Kong. Thanks are due also to the deaf and hearing colleagues of the Centre for Sign Linguistics and Deaf Studies who participated in the research project. The statistical support from David Lam is deeply appreciated.

NOTE

1 In fact, deaf students in Hong Kong are also exposed to English as well. However, in this chapter, we only focus on the Chinese-related spoken languages.

REFERENCES

Akamatsu, C. T., Stewart, D. A., & Mayer, C. (2002). Is it time to look beyond teachers' signing behavior? *Sign Language Studies*, *2*(3), 230–254.

Berke, M. (2013). Reading books with young Deaf students: Strategies for mediating between American Sign Language and English. *Journal of Deaf Studies and Deaf Education*, *18*(3), 299–311.

Bialystok, E. (2001). *Bilingualism in development: Language, literacy and cognition*. Cambridge, UK: Cambridge University Press.

Bialystok, E., & Barac, R. (2012). Emerging bilingualism: Dissociating advantages for metalinguistic awareness and executive control. *Cognition*, *112*, 67–73.

Bialystok, E., Peets, K-F., & Moreno, S. (2014). Producing bilinguals through immersion education: development of metalinguistic awareness. *Applied Psycholinguistics*, *35*, 177–191.

Brentari, D. (2011) Sign language phonology. In J. Goldsmith, J. Riggle, & A. Yu (Eds.), *A handbook of phonological theory* (2nd ed., pp. 691–721). New York/London: Blackwell.

Chamberlain, C., & Mayberry, R. I. (2000). Theorizing about the relationship between ASL and reading. In C. Chamberlain, J. P. Morford, & R. I. Mayberry (Eds.), *Language acquisition by eye* (pp. 221–260). Mahwah, NJ: Lawrence Erlbaum and Associates.

Costa, A., Hernández, M., & Sebastián-Gallés, N. (2008). Bilingualism aids conflict resolution: Evidence from the ANT task. *Cognition*, *106*(1), 59–86.

Cripps, J. H., & Supalla, S. (2012). The power of spoken language in schools and deaf students who sign. *International Journal of Humanities and Social Science*, *2*(16), 86–102.

Donati, C., & Branchini, C. (2013). Challenging linearization: Simultaneous mixing in the production of bimodal bilinguals. In T. Biberauer & I. Roberts (Eds.), *Challenges to linearization*. Berlin/New York: Mouton de Gruyter.

Emmorey, K. (2007). The psycholinguistics of signed and spoken language: how biology affects processing. In G. Gaskell (Ed.), *The Oxford handbook of psycholinguistics* (pp. 703–721), Oxford, UK: Oxford University Press.

Emmorey, K., Borinstein, H. B., & Thompson, R. (2005). Bimodal bilingualism: code-blending between spoken English and American Sign Language. In J. Cohen, K. T. McAlister, K. Rolstad, & J. MacSwan (Eds.), *Proceedings of the 4th International Symposium on Bilingualism* (pp. 663–673). Somerville, MA: Cascadilla Press.

Fung, H.-M. C., & Tang, G. (submitted). Code-blending of functional heads in Hong Kong Sign Language and Cantonese: A case study. *Bilingualism, Language and Cognition*.

Galambos, S. J., & Goldin-Meadow, S. (1990). The effects of learning two languages on levels of metalinguistic awareness. *Cognition*, *34*(1), 1–56.

Galambos, S. J., & Hakuta, K. (1988). Subject-specific and task-specific characteristics of metalinguistic awareness in bilingual children. *Applied Psycholinguistics*, *9*, 141–162.

Goldin-Meadow, S., & Mayberry, R. I. (2001). How do profoundly deaf students learn to read?. *Learning Disabilities Research & Practice*, *16*(4), 222–229.

Grosjean, F., & Li, P. (2013). *The psycholinguistics of bilingualism.* Oxford: John Wiley & Sons.

Gutiérrez, X. (2011). Knowledge representations underlying covert metalinguistic activity: a working hypothesis. *Language Awareness, 20*(3), 239–254.

Humphries, T., & Allen, B. (2008). Re-organizing teacher preparation in Deaf Education. *Sign Language Studies, 8*(2), 160–180.

Humphries, T., Kushalnagar, P., Mathur, G., Napoli, D. J., Padden, C., Rathmann, C., & Smith, S. R. (2012). Language acquisition for deaf students: Reducing the harms of zero tolerance to the use of alternative approaches. *Harm Reduction Journal, 9*(1), 1–9.

Klima, E. S., & Bellugi, U. (1979). *The signs of language.* Cambridge, MA: Harvard University Press.

Knoors, H., & Marschark, M. (2012). Language planning for the 21st century: revisiting bilingual language policy for deaf students. *Journal of Deaf Studies and Deaf Education, 17*(3), 291–305.

Lillo-Martin, D., Quadros, R. M. de, Koulidobrova, H., & Chen Pichler, D. (2010). Bimodal bilingual cross-language influence in unexpected domains. In J. Costa, A. Castro, M. Lobo, & F. Pratas (Eds.), *Language acquisition and development: Proceedings of GALA 2009* (pp. 264–275). Cambridge: Cambridge Scholars Publishing.

Lin, C. M. C., Gerner de García, B., & Chen-Pichler, D. (2009). Standardizing Chinese Sign Language for use in post-secondary education. *Current Issues in Language Planning, 10*(3), 327–337.

Marschark, M., & Lee, C. M. (2014). Navigating two languages in the classroom: Goals, evidence, and outcomes. In M. Marschark, G. Tang, & H. Knoors, H. (Eds.), *Bilingualism and bilingual education* (pp. 213–241). New York: Oxford University Press.

Mayer, C., & Akamatsu, C. T. (2000). Deaf students creating written texts: Contributions of American Sign Language and signed forms of English. *American Annals of the Deaf, 145*(5), 394–403.

Mayer, C., & Leigh, G. (2010). The changing context for sign bilingual education programs: Issues in language and the development of literacy. *International Journal of Bilingual Education and Bilingualism, 13*(2), 175–186.

Mayer, M. (1969). *Frog, where are you?* New York: Dial Press.

McKee, R. L. (2005). `As one deaf person to another': Deaf paraprofessionals in mainstream schools. *Deaf Worlds*, 21(1), 1–48.

Ormel, E., & Giezen, M. (2014). Bimodal bilingual cross-language interaction: Pieces of the puzzle. In M. Marschark, G. Tang, & H. Knoors (Eds.), *Bilingualism and bilingual education* (pp. 74–101). New York: Oxford University Press.

Plaza-Pust, C. (2014). Language development and language interaction in sign bilingual language acquisition. In M. Marschark, G. Tang, & H. Knoors (Eds.), *Bilingualism and bilingual education* (pp. 23–53). New York: Oxford University Press.

Plaza-Pust, C., & López, E. M. (2008). Sign bilingualism: Language development, interaction and maintenance in sign language contact situation. In C. Plaza-Pust & E. Morales-López (Eds.), *Sign bilingualism* (pp. 333–379). Amsterdam: Benjamins.

Rathmann, C., Mann, W., & Morgan, G. (2007). Narrative structure and narrative development in deaf children. *Deafness & Education International*, *9*(4), 187–196.

Schiavetti, N., Whitehead, R. L., & Metz, D. E. (2004). The effects of simultaneous communication on production and perception of speech. *Journal of Deaf Studies and Deaf Education*, *9*(3), 286–304.

Schick, B., de Villiers, P., de Villiers, J., & Hoffmeister, R. (2007). Language and theory of mind: A study of deaf students. *Child Development*, 78(2), 376–396.

Singleton, J., & Morgan, D. D. (2006). Natural signed language acquisition within the social context of the classroom. In B. Schick, M. Marschark, & P. E. Spencer (Eds.), *Advances in the sign language development of deaf students* (pp. 344–375). New York: Oxford University Press.

Singleton, J. L., Morgan, D., DiGello, E., Wiles, J., & Rivers, R. (2004). Vocabulary use by low, moderate, and high ASL-proficient writers compared to hearing ESL and monolingual speakers. *Journal of Deaf Studies and Deaf Education*, *9*(1), 86–103.

Supalla, S. (1991). Manually coded English: The modality question in signed language development. In P. Siple & S. D. Fischer (Eds.), *Theoretical issues in sign language research* (pp. 85–109). Chicago, IL: University of Chicago Press.

Supalla, S., & McKee, C. 2002. The role of manually coded English in the language development of deaf students. In R. Meier, K. Cormier, & D. Quinto-Pozos (Eds.), *Modality and structure in signed and spoken languages* (pp. 143–166). Cambridge: Cambridge University Press.

Sze, F., Lo, C., Lo, L., & Chu, K. (2013). Historical development of Hong Kong Sign Language. *Sign Language Studies*, *13*(2), 155–185.

Tang, G., Lam, S., & Yiu, C. (2014). Language development of deaf students in a sign bilingual and co-enrollment setting. In M. Marschark, G. Tang, & H. Knoors (Eds.), *Bilingualism and bilingual education* (pp. 313–341). New York: Oxford University Press.

Tang, G., & Sze, F. (to appear). Hong Kong Sign Language. In W. Behr, Y-G. Gu, Z. Handel, C.-T. J. Huang, & R. Sybesma (Eds.), *Encyclopedia of Chinese and linguistics*. Leiden: Brill.

Tunmer, W. E., & Myhill, M. E. (1984). Metalinguistic awareness and bilingualism. In W. Turner, C.Pratt, & M. Herriman (Eds.), *Metalinguistic awareness in children* (pp. 169–187). Heidelberg: Springer Berlin.

Van den Bogaerde, B., & Baker, A. (2005). Code mixing in mother–child interaction in deaf families. *Sign Language & Linguistics*, *8*(1-2), 1–2.

Wilbur, R. B. (2000). The use of ASL to support the development of English and literacy. *Journal of Deaf Studies and Deaf Education*, *5*(1), 81–104.

Wilbur, R. B., & Pertersen, L. (1998). Modality interactions of speech and signing in simultaneous communication. *Journal of Speech, Language & Hearing Research*, *41*, 200–212.

Woodward, J., & Allen, T. (1988). Classroom use of artificial sign systems by teachers. *Sign Language Studies*, *61*, 405–418.

Yang, J. H. (2011). Social situations and the education of deaf students in China. In G. Mathur & D. J. Napoli (Eds.), *Deaf around the world: The impact of language* (pp. 339–351). New York: Oxford University Press.

7

Literacy and Deaf and Hard-of-Hearing Students

Research and Practice

Susan R. Easterbrooks and
Michella Maiorana-Basas

Literacy outcomes in students who are deaf or hard of hearing (DHH) vary considerably based on age of identification and intervention (Svirsky, Tech, & Neuberger, 2004; Szagun & Stumper, 2012; Yoshinaga-Itano, Sedey, Coulter, & Mehl, 1998), aspects of hearing loss (Colletti, Wilkinson, & Colleti, 2013; Liu, Farrell, MacNeil, Stone, & Barfield, 2008), type of amplification (Connor & Zwolan, 2004), maternal education (Quittner, Cruz, Barker, Tobey, Eisenberg, & Niparko, 2013), existence of additional compromising factors such as secondary disabilities (Robertson, 2013; Zazove, Meador, Reed, & Gorenflo, 2013), and the availability of good instruction (Van Staden, 2013). Historically a chasm has existed between research findings and implementation of evidence-based practices in classrooms in a way that would enhance good instruction (Cook, Cook, & Landrum, 2013). Researchers have often overlooked providing advice on valid and reliable instructional practices in favor of promoting one or another belief system. In addition, research has tended to be conducted in pursuit of an empirical question for which no follow-through was intended. Until recently journals have been replete with messages to which classroom teachers could rightly ask, "So what?" Children with hearing loss don't read as well as children who hear. So what? What is the teacher to do, specifically? Children with better memory skills read better than children with poor memory? So what? What is the teacher to do about it in his or her classroom on Monday morning? Classroom-relevant research is the kind of research we need.

The term "literacy" has been described from many perspectives, including visual literacy (Elkins, 2010; Petitto, 2012), science, technology, and math literacy (STEM Education Coalition, 2013; http://www.stemedcoalition.org/policies), and digital literacy (Gui & Argentin, 2011), among others. To be clear, this chapter focuses on print literacy, or the ability to read and comprehend the intended message in, for example, a book, story, newspaper, recipe, blog, job application, or other document. We do not address DHH students' acquisition of writing skills and strategies (see Antia, Jones, Reed, & Kreimeyer, 2009; Wolbers, Dostal, & Bowers, 2012). Nor do we engage in the newer debate regarding whether older students learn better from text or from sign language (Borgna, Convertino, Marschark, Morrison, & Rizzolo, 2011; Marschark et al., 2006) and its ensuing debate of the nature of visual literacy. Rather, we focus on the challenges children face in learning to read and the challenges their teachers face in teaching them to do so. First, we describe how our debates in the scientific literature have focused on practically anything and everything that took us away from helping teachers understand and engage in the most effective practices to produce positive outcomes in the children under their guidance, in particular as it relates to the acquisition of print literacy. Next, we summarize the evidence on good instruction and discuss what *should* be the relation between research and practice. Finally, we make some suggestions for doing a better job of pairing researchers with practitioners so that fewer research projects end up warranting dismissal by teachers with a "So what!"

WHERE WE STRAYED FROM THE "RIGHT KIND" OF RESEARCH

The translation of research results into effective classroom practice, more recently referred to as *implementation science* (Cook & Odom, 2013), has been diverted over the years by one education war after another from the goal of providing teachers with effective and efficient strategies, techniques, methods, and materials by which to teach their students. In fact, new methods seem to have come along at least every 10 years (Knoors & Marschark, 2014), causing many teachers to feel as if they were the proverbial ball in a fast-moving ping pong match. In the 1940s and 1950s, journal articles batted the idea back and forth of whether or not language (a precursor to literacy) should be taught in a structured manner (e.g., Fitzgerald, 1949) or a manner more reflective of natural mother–child interactions (e.g., Groht, 1958). Organizations and their associated journals tended to form camps around the separate perspectives, and teachers were compelled to align with one position or another. The 1960s and 1970s saw us in the midst of the so-called reading wars (Chall, 1996) between those favoring top-down, whole-language approaches (Goodman, 1967, 1986; Smith, 1973) and those in support of a bottom-up, phonics-based approach (Fleisch, 1955). Schools aligned with one or another position and teachers were expected to teach from that frame of reference. Then in the United States, we spent the 1970s into the 1990s arguing whether mainstream education (Afzali-Nomani, 1995) or separate school education (Cohen, 1995; Lane, 1992; Moores, 1995) was more effective and whether or not one should provide a child with a cochlear implant (Luetke-Stahlman, 1995). The relative merits of cochlear implantation are still under discussion in the literature (Niparko et al., 2010). These bifurcations in perspective tore schools apart, and teachers had little say as to how they influenced the classroom, as these decisions were managed at the level of the medical profession and general education policymakers (PL 94-142; IDEA). While those arguments continued, the period from the 1980s into the turn of the century saw further diversion of research away from efforts to support learning in classrooms as a result of the debate over bilingual/bicultural instruction for DHH children (Johnson, Liddell, & Erting, 1989) and its relationship to the broader argument of whether sign language should follow the indigenous grammatical structure of the sign language of a country or the grammatical structure of its spoken language (Gee & Goodhart, 1985; Luetke-Stahlman, 1988; Paul & Drasgow, 1998). With the turn of the century and the publication of the National Reading Panel's report (National Institute of Child Health and Human Development, 2000) highlighting their conceptualization of the six most important factors in literacy acquisition in hearing children (phonological awareness, alphabetics, vocabulary, fluency, text comprehension, and motivation), arguments appeared in the literature on DHH children (Johnson & Goswami, 2010; Musselman, 2000) regarding (a) whether one or the other of these components was important in literacy acquisition (Schirmer & McGough, 2005) and (b) whether or not DHH children's learning was qualitatively or quantitatively different (Allen et al., 2009; Corina, Lawyer, Hauser, & Hirshorn, 2013; Paul & Lee, 2009; Paul, Wang, Trezek, & Luckner, 2009) from that of hearing children. Simultaneously we saw literature reviews and meta-analyses examining whether there existed a sufficient evidence base in deaf education (Luckner, Sebald, Cooney, Young, & Muir, 2005/2006), including what was and was not an available intervention related to phonological awareness (Tucci, Trussell, & Easterbrooks, 2014), vocabulary (Luckner & Cooke, 2010), fluency (Luckner & Urbach, 2012), and text comprehension (Luckner & Handley, 2008). These, along with summaries of the existing evidence for a handful of commonly used practices (Easterbrooks & Stephenson, 2006, 2012), further pointed out that the half-century of reading and language wars had achieved one resounding effect: We still didn't know much about what happened in deaf education classrooms and between children and their teachers during literacy instruction (Spencer & Marschark, 2010). We still do not have sufficient research on good literacy instruction for DHH children, and although literacy outcomes may be improving for some students (Easterbrooks & Beal-Alvarez, 2013), they are still insufficient for many children (Qi & Mitchell, 2012). Furthermore, children in developing nations fare worse than those in developed nations. The 32 million children worldwide with hearing loss are unequally distributed across the world, and the prevalence of hearing loss and illiteracy in children increases linearly as parents' illiteracy rates increase (WHO, 2012). This circumstance is untenable and as yet poorly addressed. Still, we have opinions about everything: what language we should teach, where DHH children should be educated (assuming they are fortunate enough to live in an area where educational services are provided), how the teacher should be trained (assuming the teacher receives training) (Van Staden, 2013), what type of technology should be in a classroom (and whether it should be in the classroom, in the home, or both), what topics and standards should be covered on any given day, what standards of cleanliness should be required in a building, and what type of behavior management is most effective. With all these arguments to which teachers must provide a response and about which they must provide documentation, we as researchers have failed to tell them one thing: how to implement our findings with their pupils in a reasonable, effective, efficient, and affordable manner. We have failed to answer their question of "So what?"

EMERGING UNDERSTANDINGS IN LITERACY ACQUISITION AND LEARNING

The fact is that the educational research community went off track in providing real support for classroom teachers, which can be seen worldwide with students not performing at levels commensurate with their hearing peers even where bilingual instruction and proper listening technologies are readily available (Hendar, 2009; Qi & Mitchell, 2012; Rydberg, Gellerstedt, & Danermark, 2009). In developed countries, where many children have access to cochlear implant technologies along with early identification and intervention (Connor, Craig, Raudenbush, Heavner, & Zwolan, 2006), great strides have been made in literacy outcomes for some segments of the population. As stated earlier, however, access to cochlear implants and sufficient interventions vary greatly around the world (Corvera & Corvera, 1991; Jeyaraman, 2013; McPherson & Brouillette, 2004), and even children who have ready access make different progress one from another (Archbold, Harris, O'Donoghue, Nikolopoulos, White, & Richmond, 2008; Marschark, Sarchet, Rhoten, & Zupan, 2010; Pisoni, Conway, Kronenberger, Henning, & Anaya, 2010; Stinson & Kluwin, 2011). The problem in developing nations is even more serious, as many children lack basic access to language (Musengi, Ndofirepi, & Shumba, 2013), to technology (McPherson & Brouillette, 2004), and in many cases to good instruction (Van Staden, 2013). Two factors are crystal clear. First, if we expect children to learn to read, they must have a *language*. For some, that is spoken language (Geers, 2002, 2003; Musselman & Szanto, 1998); for others, that is a signed language (Padden & Ramsey, 2000;

Singleton, Supalla, Litchfield, & Schley, 1998). Next, it is quite clear that children need *teachers*. They need well-trained, experienced, caring, and committed teachers. When children receive quality instruction from well-prepared teachers, academic outcomes improve (Stronge, 2010; Van Staden, 2013). Assuming that children have access to good teachers and good language, then, what are the knowledge and skill sets that good literacy teachers need to understand and use?

Alphabetics, Word Recognition, and Decoding

Good literacy teachers (whether parent, educator, or other practitioner) know that DHH children need instruction in how to manage the alphabetic system of the language with which they are going to read (Bergeron, Lederberg, Easterbrooks, Miller, & Connor, 2009). Children need multiple skill sets surrounding the printed code of language in order to be good readers, which include sufficient skills both in decoding (Bergeron, Lederberg, & Easterbrooks, 2009) and knowledge of sight words (Ehri, 2014; Kelly, 1993; Phillips & Feng, 2012). Knowledge of alphabetics is important, but how we get there is quite controversial.

Children who begin school with alphabetic knowledge are more likely to become successful readers (Adams, 1990; Stevenson & Newman, 1986) than those who do not. Studies of children's letter–sound correspondence skills demonstrate a clear relationship with word recognition (Aghababian, Nazir, Lancon, & Tardy, 2001; Trezek & Malmgren, 2005), and DHH children's letter–sound knowledge appears to correlate strongly with phonological awareness and other literacy skills both concurrently and across time (Easterbrooks, Lederberg, Miller, Bergeron, & Connor, 2008; Ehri, 2014). A meta-analysis of relevant studies by Mayberry, del Giudice, and Lieberman (2011) found that deaf readers' phonological awareness and use explained 11% of the variance in their reading proficiency, whereas language abilities more broadly explained 35%. Thus ensued another argument in the literature regarding whether or not the phonological code was necessary (Paul et al., 2009). Rather than engaging in arguments in the literature that one piece of the puzzle is more important than another, a more productive view would be to embrace the fact that reading requires multiple skill sets and that these sets may vary by child. Phonology is important, but lack thereof may not be a deal-breaker for all learners in the reading experience (Belanger, Mayberry, & Rayner, 2013); Ehri (2014) pointed out that grapheme–phoneme relationships may better explain vocabulary acquisition and mastery than phonemic awareness. Teachers may use different approaches to letter–sound acquisition (Tucci et al., 2014), such as fingerspelling (Emmory & Petrich, 2012; Haptonstall-Nykaza & Schick, 2007), semantic icons (Beal-Alvarez, Lederberg, & Easterbrooks, 2012; Miller, Lederberg, & Easterbrooks, 2013), visual phonics (Bergeron et al., 2009;

Guardino, Syverud, Joyner, Nichols, & King, 2011; Trezek, Wang, Woods, Gampp, & Paul, 2007), or morphographemics (Harris, Schumkaer, & Deshler, 2011; Perfetti & Stafura, 2014) as alternatives to letter–sound understanding. Morphographemic knowledge allows the reader to decode words in orthographic chunks (Belanger, Slattery, Mayberry, & Rayner, 2012; Carlson, Jenkins, Li, & Brownell, 2013), requiring sufficient perceptual span (Belanger, Mayberry, & Rayner, 2013). Although evidence suggests that speech-reading ability may be a predictor of reading achievement (Kyle & Harris, 2006, 2010), there is no research describing either the availability or the effectiveness of any speech-reading intervention that might serve to support the development of letter–sound correspondences (Tucci et al., 2014). We know the factors that cause good learning outcomes (Easterbrooks & Beal-Alvarez, 2013), but the field has a long way to go in developing interventions that spring from these factors.

Word recognition and decoding require both the ability to deconstruct and reconstruct a word (e.g., via segmenting, blending, elision, or structural analysis) and to recognize a word by sight. Sight words are problematic because the majority of words on many lists, such as the Dolch list (Dolch, 1948; Otto & Chester, 1972), tend to be of the category of vocabulary referred to as *function words*. Lexical-functional grammar (Chomsky, 1995; Kaplan & Bresnan, 1995) provides a structure for understanding how we use words broadly. Words are either lexical (e.g., nouns and verbs), and therefore contain meaning in and of themselves, or functional (i.e., they have the function in a sentence of connecting lexical elements to one another). and therefore contain no meaning in and of themselves (e.g., a, the, of, is, do, shall, never, only). Sight word lists tend to contain function words and therefore ask children to remember them "by sight" without necessarily imparting meaning. Many of the function words are described in the research on morphosyntax (e.g., accusative first- and second-person singular, copular "be," accusative third-person number/gender, locative pronominals, auxiliary "be," and prenominal determiners) as being particularly difficult for DHH students to master (Cannon & Kirby, 2013). Programs such as the Bridging materials (Ausbrooks-Rusher, Schimmel, & Edwards, 2012) are attractive to teachers because they contextualize the function words for developing readers (*put out the fire*, where "the" has meaning only in relation to "fire") often within the context of secondary word meanings (e.g., *put out the fire*, where "put" does not refer to picking up and setting down an object, and where "out" does not refer to a location opposite of "in" but rather to a state or condition). Brannon (1968) found that DHH readers tended to overuse nouns and articles and underuse prepositions, quantifiers, and indefinites, most of which fall into the *function* category. To teach sight words, the skilled teacher understands that sight/function words are grammatically complex, and children need to read them in a meaningful context (Ehri, 2014; Perfetti & Stafura, 2014).

Vocabulary

Good literacy teachers know that DHH children need instruction in discerning the meaning of words if they are to decode successfully. Otherwise they may become great decoders and good word callers but not necessarily understand the meaning of the word they are reading (Valencia & Buly, 2004). Vocabulary is delayed in young DHH students, and this delay can remain with them through college (McEvoy, Marschark, & Nelson, 1999; Sarchet, Marschark, Borgna, Convertino, Sapere, & Dirmyer, 2014). Vocabulary delays result from learning vocabulary later than hearing children and from a degraded signal, whether signed or spoken. However, early use and size of vocabulary predicts later reading ability in both hearing (Perfetti & Hart, 2002; Perfetti & Stafura, 2014) and DHH children (Verhoeven, van Leeuwe, & Vermeer, 2011), making early vocabulary acquisition a critical element in the reading instruction of all young readers, especially those who are DHH. Not only is the quantity of the lexicon important but also the quality (Perfetti, 2007). In particular the DHH child's productive vocabulary (i.e., the words he or she uses in a decontextualized, conversational manner) is highly predictive of later reading success (Kyle & Harris, 2010, 2011).

Vocabulary knowledge is related to a variety of reading elements in DHH students (Hermans, Knoors, Ormel, & Verhoeven, 2008; Wauters, Van Bon, Tellings, & Van Leeuwe, 2006). DHH children need both breadth (i.e., quantity) and depth (i.e., quality) in their lexicons. *Breadth of vocabulary* refers to the range of concrete and abstract words a student uses, including such parts of speech as nouns, verbs, adjectives, adverbs, prepositional phrases, question forms, negation, connectors, and so forth. To have a *depth of vocabulary* requires an understanding of various multiple and obscure meanings of quotidian language, including figurative uses.

DHH children have fewer experiences with words and do not overlearn their meanings through conversations with others. This is due, in large part, to the fact that they do not have ready access to incidental language learning that is such a key component of normal child language and second language acquisition; DHH children do not listen "out of the corner of their ears" or the corner of the eyes (Saffran, Newport, Aslin, Tunick, & Barrueco, 1997). To date, there is very little information in the evidence base regarding incidental language learning in DHH children and not a single incidental language intervention. How one might foster this should become a research agenda item for future practitioners.

Known practices for vocabulary acquisition include the semantically based "knowledge model" (Paul, 1996), morphologically based models, and pragmatically based models. The knowledge model suggests that integrated strategies (e.g., semantic maps, word maps, and semantic features analysis), repetition, and meaningful use in natural, contextual situations support learning vocabulary in depth. Morphologically based models suggest that we can expand vocabulary knowledge through derivational morphemes and roots and provide better understanding of segment words containing multiple morphemes (Gaustad & Kelly, 2004). Young readers need to develop automaticity in decoding of multimorphemic words, but this tends to be a problem for DHH students (Van Hoogmoed, Verhoeven, Schreuder, & Knoors, 2011, 2013). The pragmatic language abilities of DHH students are predictive of their reading success no matter whether that language is signed or spoken (Thagard, Hilsmier, & Easterbrooks, 2011) and no matter the degree of loss. Pragmatically based instruction is poorly understood and poorly researched, and there are no pragmatically based literacy interventions with an evidence base.

Consistent with Paivio's (1986) dual-coding model, DHH children need multiple ways of encoding words into meaning. When Wauters, Tellings, van Bon, and Mak (2008) increased the modalities through which children experienced the meaning of words (e.g., hearing, seeing, smelling, touching), children's facility with words became more automatic. Strategies such as chaining and visually representing words take advantage of this multimodal benefit. Chaining (Seal, Nussbaum, Scott, Waddy-Smith, Clingempeel, & Belzner, 2005) is the process of linking print to signs, fingerspelling, and the spoken form. Sandwiching (Easterbrooks & Estes, 2007) refers to a set of techniques for helping children learn to relate new information to old, thus learning new information within the context of the old. The *concept or vocabulary sandwich* is used to develop word meaning and follows a *known–unknown–known* pattern. This is often accompanied by a child-friendly definition. For example, if the child encounters an unknown word in print, the teacher would read the sentence and then sandwich the meaning (e.g., Child reads, "The wall was unscalable." Teacher explains, It means he couldn't climb it. The wall was not climbable. The wall was unscalable. Not climbable.). The *thinking sandwich* is used to promote the child's discernment of information, whether academic or linguistic, and follows the *unknown–known–unknown* information pattern (e.g., Teacher points to and reads, "This is a striped [unknown] fish. It has lines [known] on it. Here are two pictures. Can you show me another striped [unknown] fish?).

Whichever strategy they use, good teachers know that they must use multiple modalities and multiple examples to provide the richness of input necessary to promote sufficient uptake. For example, Van Staden

(2013) compared results of a multimodal, multimedia intervention with DHH children to a control group receiving business-as-usual instruction at an institution in South Africa. When this package intervention was presented over time, Van Staden (2013) noted large effect sizes. This high-intensity intervention included a package of word walls, chaining, sandwiching, instruction from skilled signers, multiform representation, fingerspelling, repetition, categorization, automatic recall of sight words, games, Big Books, reciprocal reading, visualization and mental imagery, summarizing, and retelling, among other strategies, demonstrating that multiple approaches to the problem may form an effective literacy instructional practice.

Text Comprehension, Grammar, and Fluency

Good literacy teachers know that teaching children to comprehend text requires a multipronged attack. This "attack" includes knowledge of grammar, including morphographemic representations and knowledge of sentence parsing, which involves fluent representation of meaning, as well as metacognitive strategies, such as inference (Perfetti & Stafura, 2014), for unlocking meaning. New readers benefit from direct instruction in the grammar they will read because good readers using spoken communication parse sentence meaning via inflection and the speech envelope (also called chunking or phrasing) and good readers using signed communication render print via the hands through the use of various chunking skills that represent the visual envelope of a meaningful chunk or phrase (Easterbrooks & Huston, 2008). Therefore, new readers benefit from direct instruction in the grammar they will read. In the United States, kindergarten-aged children (i.e., five-year-olds who will turn six during the school year) are expected to learn to read the following high-frequency words by sight: the, of, to, you, she, my, is, are, do, and does (CCSS.ELA-Literacy. RF.K.3c http://www.corestandards.org/ELA-Literacy/RF/K), but until they understand what a phrase containing these words means (e.g., *do the laundry* means *wash the laundry*), they will struggle with the grammatical purpose of sight words (e.g., determiners, partitives, prepositions, pronouns, "be" verbs, and the auxiliary use of "do") as meaningful words around which phrases are formed. Function words, addressed earlier, are mentioned again here as they pertain to direct instruction in grammar. Sentence-level fluency has been associated with 60% to 80% of the variance in reading among struggling readers (O'Connor, Swanson, & Geraghty, 2010), and fluent readers become fluent by learning to parse sentences into phrases. It is the function words of a language (in this example, English) that influence how we carve words out into phrase units (e.g., a piece *of the pie*, what *do you want*), and children who are better sentence parsers are better readers (Daane, Campbell, Grigg, Goodman, & Oranje, 2005). The ability to parse English and represent it via the visual envelope also correlates with DHH children's reading levels (see Easterbrooks & Huston, 2008, for a discussion of signed fluency).

Morphological skill is another grammatical predictor of vocabulary knowledge and assists children in reading and spelling words (McBride-Chang, Wagner, Muse, Chow, & Shu, 2005; Nagy, Beringer, Abbott, Vaughan, & Vermeulen, 2003). Inflectional morphology ability in second grade predicts fourth-grade reading (Berninger, Abbott, Nagy, & Carlisle, 2010) in hearing children and is also a predictor for deaf readers (Nunes, Bryant, & Evans, 2010). Students who apply derivational and inflectional morphographic skills to decoding are using a meaning-oriented decoding strategy that gives them clues to the grammar of the sentence (Arnbak & Elbro, 2000; Reichle & Perfetti, 2003). Inflectional morphemes such as plurals and prepositions are also standards under the Common Core in the United States (http://www.corestandards.org/ELA-Literacy/L/K; CCSS. ELA-Literacy. L.K.1c and CCSS. ELA-Literacy, L.K. 1e). Kindergarten-aged children are also expected to understand and read derivational morphology (CCSS. ELA-Literacy.L.K.4b: Use the most frequently occurring inflections and affixes, such as *-ed, -s, re-, un-, pre-, -ful, -less*) as a clue to the meaning of an unknown word). Clearly the morphosyntax (grammar) of the language plays a large role in a child's reading acquisition, and it is via fluency that we tie semantic meaning (vocabulary) to grammar, including function words and morphology.

One area of investigation seeking to make the point that spoken or signed fluency is the glue between grammar and meaning centers around the use of signed renderings of stories and/or repeated readings. Researchers have used these practices with both speaking and signing DHH children with varying success. Struggling readers have made gains in fluency and comprehension through repeated readings (Therrien, 2004). The use of electronic books and signed books influences reading outcomes in DHH students (Beal-Alvarez & Huston, 2014; Guardino, Cannon, & Eberst, 2014) but are more effective when used in conjunction with a teacher-mediator (Cannon, Fredrick, & Easterbrooks, 2010). More information is needed regarding the intersection between the teacher-mediator and the signed, electronic version of reading materials.

EMERGING RESEARCH

Perhaps as a result of all the education wars and the fact that the evidence base is so lean, the Institute of Education Sciences funded a multiyear project (#R24C120001) to address in a comprehensive and systematic way the basic questions of what works in literacy and for which DHH children. The Center on Literacy and Deafness project (http://clad.gsu.edu) aims to identify child-by-instructional factors that affect reading growth in this population and to develop individualized interventions specifically designed for struggling DHH readers in kindergarten through grade 2. One goal of the study is to identify malleable child and instructional characteristics associated with literacy gains across the school year in children with moderate to profound hearing loss who are in grades K through 2 in a variety of school settings. Potential child factors include phonological, decoding, language, and cognitive abilities. Another goal is to develop complementary supplemental interventions specifically developed to fit the needs of students in kindergarten through grade 2 who have moderate to profound hearing loss and reading and/or language delays. A third goal is to engage in small-scale cluster randomized controlled field trials to investigate the promise of the interventions designed. The project is gathering thousands of hours of videos of classroom instruction and will be available for primary and secondary analysis. Early results from a small set of the sample, gathered from a variety of schools and programs, revealed that up to 70% of the participants in the classes studied used sign language of some nature and up to 70% of the participants used spoken language; thus, there was a notable overlap in who used spoken and signed modes, suggesting that tomorrow's teacher will need to take a centrist perspective on communication and placement arguments because most children are somewhere in the middle. Thus, to provide effective literacy instruction to all students with hearing loss, the typical teacher must be skilled in providing effective interventions along all continuums.

EMERGING PARADIGMS IN RESEARCH AND PRACTICE

Implementation Science

The research is clear that implementation of evidence-based practices yields positive outcomes in learners (Cook, Smith, & Tankersley, 2011; Slavin, 2008). While the first decade and a half of the 21st century finds us better at identifying what constitutes *evidence*, we have been less successful at ensuring that evidence-based practices are actually implemented, the result of which is a wide chasm between research and practice (Donovan & Cross, 2002). The response to this chasm, the clarion call for the next 15 to 20 years, is the emergence of the field of *implementation science*. Implementation science is "the scientific study of methods to promote the systematic uptake of research findings and other evidence-based practices into routine practice" (Eccles & Mittman, 2006, p. 1). The idea of uptake into routine practice is key, because implementation of research into everyday practice requires a certain degree of buy-in from teachers and administrators. Cook and Odom (2013) identified several aspects to consider when supporting uptake of a practice, including quality of implementation (i.e., the fidelity with which teachers implement the practices as researched), reach (i.e., what percentage of the target population is using the innovation), and maintenance (i.e., whether the teacher has routinely integrated the strategy into his or her repertoire). Stephenson, Dostal, and Wolbers (2013) used the Levels of Use (Hall, Dirksen, & George, 2006) tool in their research on written language and discovered that it takes two or three years for teachers to become comfortable with an instructional innovation when they receive ongoing support for implementation.

The Radical Middle

In the fall of 2010, the National Leadership Consortium in Sensory Disabilities (NLCSD; http://www.salus.edu/nlcsd/index.html), with funding from the U.S. Office of Special Education Programs (Cooperative Agreement #H325V090001), undertook an unprecedented collaboration to prepare two national cohorts of PhD-level professionals from a consortium of universities across the United States. Among their primary goals was the development of a research-based enrichment program to develop an inclusive online community of Fellows from the field of DHH education with the lofty goal of creating a community of practice steeped in the tradition of collaboration and with recognition that all points of view can contribute to the solution of a problem. This group of young professionals exceeded the expectations of the consortium by establishing a grassroots effort to promulgate research from "the radical middle." Working and studying within a collaborative, technology-based, dispersed environment, this group of young professionals realized that researchers have spent far too many decades arguing the ends of the continuums (e.g., spoken to signed language; separate schooling to full inclusion; phonics to whole language). Focusing research and practice on the ends of the continuums has diverted researchers' attention from the true task at hand, which is this: identifying evidence-based classroom literacy interventions that meet the needs of *all* readers with hearing losses. Rather than focusing on the problem from the radical ends, the NLCSD DHH Fellows formed a community of practice that advocates focusing on the radical middle.

The radical middle is an idea that was conceived from discussions of the current tensions around the philosophical bifurcation in the field of deaf education. Several NLCSD Fellows representing different educational, cultural, and linguistic philosophies discussed the idea over a period of time and came to the conclusion that the current polarization in the field was a potential barrier to progress, especially in regard to literacy and language outcomes of DHH students. The mission of the radical middle philosophy is to encourage scholars from a wide range of educational, cultural, and linguistic perspectives to develop collaborative research agendas and efforts toward a common goal of effecting positive academic change for all DHH children. In developing the concept of the radical middle, the Fellows queried respected scholars in the field about this notion and were met with additional bifurcation. Some scholars stated "We solved this problem years ago," while others felt that support of their preferred end of a continuum warranted continued separate study. However, in conversations with teachers and parents of DHH children and members of the Deaf community, it was clear that consumers were frustrated with the controversy and dogma they faced during their most vulnerable times. In fact, parents reported that they were quite frustrated with early intervention professionals, both educational and medical, who pushed and pulled them from philosophy to philosophy and overwhelmed them with diverse information (Matthijs et al., 2012). When professionals attempt to comfort parents by downplaying the severity of a hearing loss diagnosis, some parents may feel distrustful after receiving the conclusive results. This experience causes those parents to be skeptical and lose confidence in audiological services (Young & Tattersall, 2005). When parents do not feel that professionals (e.g., teachers, audiologist) are being open and honest with them, it directly affects their degree of trust in those professionals. Parents shared that they would rather be told something that was difficult to accept than be told something that was not completely true. In addition, parents also felt distrust if they perceived that they were not being included in decisions and that circumstances were being predetermined (Tattersall & Young, 2006).

Advocating for the ends of the continuum has caused parents to look at the field with suspicion and distrust. Researching from the radical middle might provide essential information long needed by centrist teachers in today's classrooms.

RESEARCH AGENDA

In addition to skepticism from families, there exists a "culture of collective indignation against researchers for excluding practitioners from the design, conduct, analysis, and interpretation of traditional research" (Smith, Schmidt, & Edelen-Smith, 2013, p. 150) that is sufficient to be a contributing factor in the problems we face in translating research to practice. Researchers blame practitioners for lack of rigor in their classrooms and action research. Practitioners blame researchers for their lack of relevance in research addressed and frequently come to the inevitable "so what" when reading research findings. Smith, Schmidt, and Edelen-Smith (2013) provide a compelling discussion for reframing the research agenda to address not only the rigor of evidence-based practices but also the relevance of practice-based evidence to move forward in meeting the needs of DHH learners and their families (for a discussion of the interplay between evidence-based practices and practice-based evidence, see Smith et al., 2013). The radical middle proposes adopting a more centrist/holistic approach to how scholars design research and disseminate knowledge among academics, educators, and families of DHH children. It is about expanding our community of practice and refocusing both on evidence-based practices and practice-based evidence, sharing information rather than diffusing time, resources, and energy in arguing a stance, and finding balance and common ground. This perspective has been argued by others since the inception of efforts to identify evidence-based practices (Knoors & Marschark, 2014; Swanwick, Chapter 26 in this volume; Swanwick & Marschark, 2010). It is time to reach across the aisle and address the bottom-line issue of what a parent or teacher can do *this very day* to improve literacy outcomes for the actual learners in his or her purview and not some idealized version thereof.

What does the radical middle look like relative to the development of print literacy? Researchers and practitioners need to come together around a group of children and discuss these questions. How do we make sure that a student is processing connected text meaningfully, no matter what language he or she uses? What can we agree on that all children would need in order to read a particular passage, even if this means we must develop multiple tracks for the intervention? For example, renewed models of collaboration and implementation of research (Gutierrez & Penuel, 2014) as well as video-coaching (Wauters & de Klerk, 2014) may prove beneficial in implementing research into practice. Assuming we are teaching the range of children suggested by emerging Center on Literacy and Deafness data, what would need to transpire to meet the needs of all of the students? Research should be in the service of children's learning, conducted with an eye to effective interventions, and from both the evidence-based practices and practice-based evidence perspectives. Researchers have much to share with practitioners, such as an understanding of the importance of fidelity of implementation, and practitioners have much to share with researchers, such as a deep understanding of the relevance of a line of research. We propose that researching from the radical middle and in the context of an extended community of practice should be the next wave of effort.

SUMMARY

The research on language and literacy acquisition prior to the 21st century can be characterized as "the wars of diversion" that have sidetracked education researchers from their prime directive of influencing outcomes in the classroom. Somewhere around the turn of the century we woke up and noticed that there were almost no evidence-based practices available for classroom teachers in most areas, but most importantly in the area of literacy acquisition. Further, researchers who demanded rigor and practitioners who demanded relevance have not seen eye to eye, and there is a huge chasm between research and practice. Summarizing the evidence base, this chapter pointed to areas where research efforts are most needed. These include questions such as: What interventions are most effective for increasing depth of vocabulary knowledge, multiple meanings of words, incorporation of morphographemic strategies to reading decoding, the role of fingerspelling in reading, and the promotion of decontextualized language mastery and productive vocabulary? What is necessary for mastery of essential function words in addition to lexical items that support the language facility needed to promote fluent parsing of phrases (chunks) of sentences that promote the relationship between grammar and meaning? We propose that the new wave of researchers must work in communities of practice that respect both the researcher's and the practitioner's knowledge and should be framed not on arguments at the ends of a continuum but from the radical middle and with centrist-oriented teachers and their students at heart.

When designing educational interventions, we must know: Do teachers see this as relevant to what they need? Is the intervention effective, efficient, reasonable, and affordable? If you can answer those questions, teachers may take seriously what you are doing and not dismiss your efforts with a "So what?"

ACKNOWLEDGMENTS

Some of the research reported was supported by the Institute of Education Sciences, U.S. Department of Education, through Grant #R24C120001. Some of the information reported was development by Fellows from the National Leadership Consortium on Sensory Disabilities, a project of the Office of Special Education Programs, U.S. Department of Education, through Cooperative Agreement #H325V090001.

REFERENCES

Adams, M. A. (October 1990). Beginning reading instruction in the United States. *ERIC Digest*. ERIC Clearinghouse on Reading and Communication Skills.

Afzali-Nomani, E. (1995). Educational conditions related to successful full inclusion programs involving deaf/heard of hearing children. *American Annals of the Deaf, 140*(5), 396–401.

Aghababian, V., Nazir, T. A., Lancon, C., & Tardy, M. (2001). From "logographic" to normal reading: The case of a deaf beginning reader. *Brain and Language, 78*, 212–223.

Allen, T. F., Clark, M. D., del Giudice, A., Koo, D., Lieberman, A., Mayberry, R., & Miller, P. (2009). Phonology and reading: A response to Wang, Trezek, Luckner, & Paul. (2009). *American Annals of the Deaf, 154*(4), 338–345.

Antia, S. D., Jones, P. B., Reed, S., & Kreimeyer, K. H. (2009). Academic status and progress of deaf and hard-of-hearing students in general education classrooms. *Journal of Deaf Studies and Deaf Education, 14*(3), 293–311.
Arnbak, E., & Elbro, C. (2000). The effects of morphological awareness training on the reading and spelling skills of young dyslexics. *Scandinavian Journal of Educational Research, 44*, 229–251.
Archbold, S., Harris, M., O'Donoghue, G., Nikolopoulos, T., White, A. & Lloyd Richmond, H. (2008). Reading abilities after cochlear implantation: the effect of age at implantation on outcomes at five and seven years after implantation. *International Journal of Pediatric Otorhinolaryngology, 72*(10), 1471–1478.
Ausbrooks-Rusher, M., Schimmel, C., & Edwards, S. (2012). Utilizing Fairview as a bilingual response to intervention (RTI): Comprehensive curriculum review with supporting data. *Theory and Practice in Language Studies, 2*(7), 1317–1329.
Beal-Alvarez, J. S., & Huston, S. G. (2014). Emerging evidence for instructional practice: Repeated viewings of sign language models. *Communication Disorders Quarterly, 35*, 93–102.
Beal-Alvarez, J., Lederberg, A., & Easterbrooks, S. (2012). Grapheme phoneme acquisition of deaf preschoolers. *Journal of Deaf Studies and Deaf Education, 17*(1), 39–60. doi: 10.1177/1525740113514437
Belanger, N. N., Mayberry, R. I., & Rayner, K. (2013). Orthographic and phonological preview benefits: Parafoveal processing in skilled and less-skilled deaf readers. *Quarterly Journal of Experimental Psychology*, doi:10.1080/17470218.2013.780085
Belanger, N. N., Slattery, T. J., Mayberry, R. I., & Rayner, K. (2012). Skilled deaf readers have an enhanced perceptual span in reading. *Psychological Science, 23*(7), 816–823.
Bergeron, J. P., Lederberg, A., Easterbrooks, S., Miller, E., & Connor, C. (2009). Building the alphabetic principle in deaf emergent readers. *Volta Review, 109*(2), 91–114.
Berninger, V. W., Abbott, R. D., Nagy, W., & Carlisle, J. (2010). Growth in phonological, orthographic, and morphological awareness in grades 1 to 6. *Journal of Psycholinguistic Research, 39*, 141–163.
Borgna, G., Convertino, C., Marschark, M., Morrison, C., & Rizzolo, K. (2011). Enhancing deaf students' learning from sign language and text: Metacognition, modality, and the effectiveness of content scaffolding. *Journal of Deaf Studies and Deaf Education, 16*, 79–100.
Brannon, J. B. (1968). Linguistic word classes in the spoken language of normal, hard-of-hearing, and deaf children. *Journal of Speech, Language, and Hearing Research, 11*, 279–287.
Cannon, J. E., Fredrick, L., & Easterbrooks, S. (2010). Vocabulary instruction through books read in American Sign Language for English language learners with hearing loss. *Communication Disorders Quarterly, 31*, 98–112.
Cannon, J. E., & Kirby, S. (2013). Grammar structures and deaf and hard of hearing students: A review of past performance and a report of new findings. *American Annals of the Deaf, 158*(3), 292–310.
Carlson, E., Li, T., Jenkins, F., & Brownell, M. T. (2013). Literacy development for young children with disabilities: The interactions of phonemic awareness, vocabulary, decoding, and reading comprehension. *Journal of Educational Research, 106*, 120–131.

Chall, J. S. (1996). *Learning to read: The great debate*. Fort Worth, TX: Harcourt Brace College Publishers.

Chomsky, N. (1995). *The minimalist program.* Cambridge, MA: MIT Press.

Cohen, O. P. (1995). The adverse implications of full inclusion for deaf students. *ERIC*, EBSCO*host* (accessed Dec. 30, 2013).

Colletti, L., Wilkinson, E. P., & Colletti, V. (2013). Auditory brainstem implantation after unsuccessful cochlear implantation of children with clinical diagnosis of cochlear nerve deficiency. *Annals of Otology, Rhinology & Laryngology, 122*(10), 605–612.

Connor, C. M., Craig, H. K., Raudenbush, S. W., Heavner, K., & Zwolan, T. A. (2006). The age at which young children receive cochlear implants and their vocabulary and speech-production growth: Is there an added value for early implantation? *Ear and Hearing, 27*, 628–644.

Connor, C. M., & Zwolan, T. (2004). Examining multiple sources of influence on reading comprehension skills of children who use cochlear implants. *Journal of Speech, Language, and Hearing Research, 47*, 509–526.

Cook, B. G., Cook, L., & Landrum, T. J. (2013). Moving research into practice: Can we make dissemination stick? *Exceptional Children, 79*(2), 163–180.

Cook, B. G., & Odom, S. L. (2013). Evidence-based practices and implementation science in special education. *Exceptional Children, 79*(2), 135–144.

Cook, B. G., Smith, G. J., & Tankersley, M. (2011). Evidence-based practices in education. In K. R. Harris, S. Graham, & T. Urdan (Eds.), *APA educational psychology handbook* (Vol. 1, pp. 495–528). Washington, DC: American Psychological Association.

Corina, D. P., Lawyer, L. A., Hauser, P., & Hirshorn, E. (2013). Lexical processing in deaf readers: An fMRI investigation of reading proficiency. *PLoS One, 8*(1), 1–10.

Corvera, G., & Corvera, J. (1991). Ethical and economical considerations on cochlear implants in developing countries. *Revue De Laryngologie Otologie Rhinologie, 112*(5), 413–414.

Daane, M. C., Campbell, J. R., Grigg, W. S., Goodman, M. J., & Oranje, A. (2005). Fourth-grade students reading aloud: NAEP 2002 special study of oral reading (NCES 2006-469). U.S. Department of Education. Institute of Education Sciences, National Center for Education Statistics. Washington, DC: Government Printing Office.

Dolch, E. W. (1948). *Problems in reading.* Champaign, IL: The Garrard Press.

Donovan, M. S, & Cross, C. T. (Eds.) (2002). *Minority students in special and gifted education.* Washington, DC: National Academies Press.

Easterbrooks, S. R., & Beal-Alvarez, J. (2013). *Literacy instruction for students who are deaf and hard of hearing.* New York: Oxford University Press.

Easterbrooks, S. R., & Estes, E. (2007). *Helping deaf and hard of hearing children to use spoken language.* Thousand Oaks, CA: Corwin Press

Easterbrooks, S., & Huston, S. (2008). Visual reading fluency in signing deaf children. *Journal of Deaf Studies and Deaf Education, 13*(1), 37–54.

Easterbrooks, S. R., Lederberg, A. R., Miller, E. M., Bergeron, J. P., & Connor, C. M. (2008). Emergent literacy skills during early childhood in children with hearing loss: Strengths and weaknesses. *Volta Review, 108*(2), 91–114.

Easterbrooks, S. R., & Stephenson, B. (2006). An examination of twenty literacy, science, and mathematics practices used to educate students who are deaf or hard of hearing. *American Annals of the Deaf, 151*, 385–399.

Easterbrooks, S. R., & Stephenson, B. H. (2012). Clues from research: Effective instructional strategies leading to positive outcomes for students who are deaf or hard of hearing. *Odyssey Magazine, 13*, 44–49.

Eccles, M. P., & Mittman, B. S, (2006). Welcome to *Implementation Science. Implementation Science, 1*(1), 1–3. Retrieved from http://www.implementationscience.com/content/1/1/1

Ehri, L. (2014). Orthographic mapping in the acquisition of sight word reading, spelling memory, and vocabulary learning. *Scientific Studies of Reading, 18*(1), 5–21.

Elkins, J. (2010). Introduction: The concept of visual literacy, and its limitations. In J. Elkins (Ed.), *Visual literacy* (pp. 1–10) New York: Routledge.

Emmorey, K., & Petrich, J. A. F. (2012). Processing orthographic structure: Associations between print and fingerspelling. *Journal of Deaf Studies and Deaf Education, 17*(2), 194–204.

Fitzgerald, E. (1949). *Straight language for the deaf. A system of instruction for deaf children*. Washington, DC: AG Bell Association for the Deaf.

Fleisch, R. (1955). *Why Johnny can't read and what you can do about it.* New York: Harper Collins Publishers.

Gaustad, M. J., & Kelly, R. R. (2004). The relationship between reading achievement and morphological word analysis in deaf and hearing students matched for reading level. *Journal of Deaf Studies and Deaf Education, 9*(3), 269–285.

Gee, J. P., & Goodhart, W. (1985). Nativization, linguistic theory, and deaf language acquisition. *Sign Language Studies, 49*, 291–342.

Geers, A. E. (2002). Factors affecting the development of speech, language, and literacy in children with cochlear implants. *Language, Speech, and Hearing Services in Schools, 33*, 172–183.

Geers, A. E. (2003). Predictors of reading skill development in children with early cochlear implantations. *Ear & Hearing, 24*, 59–68.

Goodman, K. S. (1967). Reading: A psycholinguistic guessing game. *Journal of the Reading Specialist, 6*, 126–135.

Goodman, K. S. (1986). *What's whole in whole language?* Portsmouth, NH: Heinemann.

Groht, M. A. (1958). *Natural language for deaf children.* Washington, DC: AG Bell Association for the Deaf.

Guardino, C., Cannon, J. E., & Eberst, K. (2014). Building the evidence-base of effective reading strategies with deaf English-language learners. *Communication Disorders Quarterly, 35*(1), 59–73.

Guardino, C., Syverud, S., Joyner, A., Nichols, H., & King, S. (2011). Further evidence of the effectiveness of phonological instruction with oral-deaf readers. *American Annals of the Deaf, 155*(5), 562–568.

Gui, M. & Argentin, G. (2011). Digital skills of internet natives: Different forms of digital literacy in a random sample of northern Italian high school students. *New Media & Society*. 13(6), 963–980.

Gutierrez, K. D., & Penuel, W. R. (2014). Relevance to practice as a criterion for rigor. *Educational Researcher, 43*(1), 19–23.

Hall, G. E., Dirksen, D. J., & George, A. A. (2006). *Measuring implementation in schools: Levels of Use.* Austin, TX: SEDL.

Haptonstall-Nykaza, T. S., & Schick, B. (2007). The transition from fingerspelling to English print: Facilitating English decoding. *Journal of Deaf Studies and Deaf Education, 12*(2), 172–183.

Harris, M., Schumaker, J., & Deshler, D. (2011). The effects of strategic morphological analysis instruction on the vocabulary performance of secondary students with and without disabilities. *Learning Disabilities, 34*(1), 17–33.

Hendar, O. (2009). *Goal fulfillment in school for the deaf and hearing impaired.* Härnösand, Sweden: The National Agency for Special Needs Education and Schools.

Hermans, D., Knoors, H., Ormel, E., & Verhoeven, L. (2008). Modeling reading vocabulary learning in deaf children in bilingual education programs. *Journal of Deaf Studies and Deaf Education, 13*, 155–174.

Jeyaraman, J. (2013). Practices in habilitation of pediatric recipients of cochlear implants in India: A survey. *Cochlear Implants International, 14*(1), 7–21.

Johnson, C., & Goswami, U. (2010). Phonological awareness, vocabulary, and reading in deaf children with cochlear implants. *Journal of Speech, Language, and Hearing Research, 53*, 237–261.

Johnson, R. E., Liddell, S., & Erting, C. (1989). *Unlocking the curriculum: Principles for achieving access in deaf education*. Washington, DC: Gallaudet Research Institute.

Kaplan, R. M., & Bresnan, J. (1995). Lexical-functional grammar: A formal system for grammatical representation. In J. T. Maxwell, R. M. Kaplan, M. Dalrymple, & A. E. Zaenen (Eds.), *Formal issues in lexical-functional grammar* (pp. 29–130). Stanford, CA: CSLI Publications.

Kelly, L. P. (1993). Recall of English function words and inflections by skilled and average deaf readers. *American Annals of the Deaf, 138*(3), 288–296. doi: 10.1353/aad.2012.0481

Knoors, H., & Marschark, M. (2014). *Teaching deaf learners: Psychological and developmental foundations*. New York: Oxford University Press.

Kyle, F., & Harris, M. (2006). Concurrent correlates and predictors of reading and spelling achievement in deaf and hearing school children. *Journal of Deaf Studies and Deaf Education, 11*, 273–288.

Kyle, F., & Harris, M. (2010). Predictors of reading development in deaf children: A 3-year longitudinal study. *Journal of Experimental Child Psychology, 107*(3), 229–243.

Kyle, F., & Harris, M. (2011). Longitudinal patterns of emerging literacy in beginning deaf and hearing readers. *Journal of Deaf Studies and Deaf Education, 16*(3), 289–304.

Lane, H. (1992). *The mask of benevolence. Disabling the deaf community*. San Diego, CA: Dawn Sign Press.

Liu, C., Farrell, J., MacNeil, J. R., Stone, S., & Barfield, W. (2008). Evaluating loss to follow-up in newborn hearing screening in Massachusetts. *Pediatrics, 121*(2), 335–343.

Luckner, J. L. & Cooke, C. (2010). A summary of the vocabulary research with students who are deaf or hard of hearing. *American Annals of the Deaf, 155*(1), 38–67.

Luckner, J. L., & Handley, C. M. (2008). A summary of the reading comprehension research undertaken with students who are deaf or hard of hearing. *American Annals of the Deaf, 153*, 6–36.

Luckner, J. L., Sebald, A. M., Cooney, J., Young III, J. & Muir S. G. (2005/2006). An examination of the evidence-based literacy research in deaf education. *American Annals of the Deaf, 150*, 443–456.

Luckner, J. L., & Urbach, J. E. (2012). Reading fluency and students who are deaf or hard of hearing: Synthesis of the research. *Communication Disorders Quarterly, 33*(4), 230–241.

Luetke-Stahlman, B. (1988). The benefit of oral English-only as compared with signed input to hearing-impaired students. *Volta Review, 90*(7), 349–61.

Luetke-Stahlman, B. (1995). On deciding to implant. Issues in the use of cochlear implants with prelingually deaf children. *American Annals of the Deaf, 140*(1), 4–5.

Marschark, M., Leigh, G., Sapere, P., Brunham, D., Convertino, C., Stinson, M., . . . & Noble, W. (2006). Benefits of sign language interpreting and text alternatives for deaf students' classroom learning. *Journal of Deaf Studies and Deaf Education, 11*(4), 421–437.

Marschark, M., Sarchet, T., Rhoten, C., & Zupan, M. (2010). Will cochlear implants close the reading achievement gap for deaf students? In M. Marschark & P. Spencer (Eds.), *Oxford handbook of deaf studies, language, and education* (Vol. 2, pp. 127–143). New York: Oxford University Press.

Matthijs, L., Loots, G., Mouvet, K., Van Herreweghe, M., Hardonk, S., Van Hove, G., . . . & Leigh, G. (2012). First information parents receive after UNHS detection of their baby's hearing loss. *Journal of Deaf Studies and Deaf Education*, doi: 10.1093/deafed/ens020

Mayberry, R. I., Del Giudice, A. A., & Lieberman, A. M. (2011). Reading achievement in relation to phonological coding and awareness in deaf readers: A meta-analysis. *Journal of Deaf Studies and Deaf Education, 16*, 164–188.

McBride-Chang, C., Wagner, R. K., Muse, A., Chow, B., & Shu, H. (2005). The role of morphological awareness in children's vocabulary acquisition in English. *Applied Psycholinguistics*, 26(3), 415–535.

McEvoy, C., Marschark, M., & Nelson, D. L. (1999). Comparing the mental lexicons of deaf and hearing individuals. *Journal of Educational Psychology, 91*, 1–9.

McPherson, B., & Brouillette, R. (2004). A fair hearing for all: Providing appropriate amplification in developing countries. *Communication Disorders Quarterly, 25*(4), 219–223.

Miller, E. M., Lederberg, A. R., & Easterbrooks, S. R. (2013). Phonological awareness: Explicit instruction of young deaf and hard-of-hearing children. *Journal of Deaf Studies and Deaf Education*. *18*(2), 206–227.

Moores, D. F. (1995). Inclusion and segregation: Separate and unequal. *American Annals of the Deaf, 140*(4), 309–310.

Musengi, M., Ndofirepi, A., & Shumba, A. (2013). Rethinking education of deaf children in Zimbabwe: Challenges and opportunities for teacher education. *Journal of Deaf Studies and Deaf Education, 18*(1), 62–74.

Musselman, C. (2000). How do children who can't hear learn to read an alphabetic script? *Journal of Deaf Studies and Deaf Education, 5*, 9–31.

Musselman, C., & Szanto, G. (1998). The written language of deaf adolescents: Patterns of performance. *Journal of Deaf Studies and Deaf Education, 3*, 245–257.

Nagy, W., Berninger, V., Abbott, R., Vaughan, K., & Vermeulen, K. (2003). Relationship of morphology and other language skills in at-risk second-grade readers and at-risk fourth-grade writers. *Journal of Educational Psychology, 95*, 730–742.

National Institute of Child Health and Human Development. (2000). *Report of the National Reading Panel. Teaching children to read: An evidence-based assessment of the scientific research literature on reading and its implications for reading instruction* (NIH Publication No. 00-4769). Washington, DC: U.S. Government Printing Office.

Niparko, J. K., Tobey, E. A., Thal, D. J., Eisenberg, L. S., Wang, N. Y., Quittner, A. L., & Fink, N. E. (2010). Spoken language development in children following cochlear implantation. *Journal of the American Medical Association, 303*(15), 1498–1506.

Nunes, T., Bryant, P., & Evans, D. (2010). Morphological knowledge and learning new words. *Revista Portuguesa de Pedagogia & Psychologica, Special joint volume*, 67–74.

O'Connor, R. E., Swanson, H. L., & Geraghty, C. (2010). Improvement in reading rate under independent and difficult text levels: Influences on word and comprehension skills. *Journal of Educational Psychology, 102*(1), 1–19.

Otto, W., & Chester, R. (1972). Sight words for beginning readers. *Journal of Educational Research, 65*(10), 435–443.

Padden, C., & Ramsey, C. (2000). American Sign Language and reading ability in deaf children. In C. Chamberlain, J. Morford, & R. Mayberry (Eds.), *Language acquisition by eye* (pp. 165–189). Mahwah, NJ: Lawrence Erlbaum Associates.

Paivio, A. (1986). *Mental representations: A dual coding approach*. New York: Oxford University Press.

Paul, P. (1996). Reading vocabulary knowledge and deafness. *Journal of Deaf Studies and Deaf Education, 1*(3), 3–15.

Paul, P., & Drasgow, E. (1998). The great ASL-MCE debate: A rejoinder. *The CAEDHH Journal/La Revue ACESM, 24*(1), 5–15.

Paul, P., & Lee, C. (2009). The qualitative similarity hypothesis. *American Annals of the Deaf, 5*, 456–462.

Paul, P. V., Wang, Y., Trezek, B. J., & Luckner, J. L. (2009). Phonology is necessary, but not sufficient: A rejoinder. *American Annals of the Deaf, 154*(4), 346–56.

Perfetti, C. A. (2007). Reading ability: Lexical quality to comprehension. *Scientific Studies of Reading, 11*, 357–383.

Perfetti, C. A., & Hart, I. (2002). The lexical quality hypothesis. In I. Verhoeven, C., Elbro & P. Reitsma (Eds.), *Precursors of functional literacy* (pp. 189–213). Amsterdam: John Benjamins.

Perfetti, C. A., & Stafura, J. (2014). Word knowledge in a theory of reading comprehension. *Scientific Studies of Reading*, 18(1), 22–37.

Petitto, L. A. (2012). Revolutions in the science of learning: A new view from a new center—visual language and visual learning. *Odyssey: New Directions in Deaf Education*, 13, 70–75.

Phillips, W. E., & Feng, J. (2012). *Methods for sight word recognition in kindergarten: Traditional flashcard method vs. multisensory approach*. Presented at the Annual Conference of the Georgia Educational Research Association, Savannah, GA, October 18–20, 2012.

Pisoni, D. B., Conway, C. M., Kronenberger, W., Henning, S., & Anaya, E. (2010). Executive function, cognitive control, and sequence learning in deaf children with cochlear implants. In M. Marschark & P. Spencer (Eds.), *Oxford handbook of deaf studies, language, and education* (Vol. 2, pp. 439–457). New York: Oxford University Press.

Qi, S., & Mitchell, R. E. (2012). Large-scaled academic achievement testing of deaf and hard-of-hearing students: Past, present, and future. *Journal of Deaf Studies and Deaf Education, 17*, 1–18.

Quittner, A. L., Cruz, I., Barker, D. H., Tobey, E., Eisenberg, L. S., & Niparko, J. K., (2013). Effects of maternal sensitivity and cognitive and linguistic stimulation on cochlear implant users' language development over four years. *Journal of Pediatrics, 162*(2), 343–348.

Reichle, E. D., & Perfetti, C. A. (2003). Morphology in word identification: A word experience model that accounts for morpheme frequency effects. *Scientific Studies of Reading, 7*, 219–237.

Robertson, J. (2013). Children with cochlear implants and autism—challenges and outcomes: The experience of the National Cochlear Implant Programme, Ireland. *Cochlear Implants International: An Interdisciplinary Journal, 14*, S11–S14.

Rydberg, E., Gellerstedt, L. C., & Danermark, B. (2009). Toward an equal level of educational attainment between deaf and hearing people in Sweden? *Journal of Deaf Studies and Deaf Education, 14*, 312–323.

Saffran, J., Newport, E., Aslin, R., Tunick, R., & Barrueco, S. (1997). Incidental language learning: listening (and learning) out of the corner of your ear. *Psychological Science, 8*, 101–105.

Sarchet, T., Marschark, M., Borgna, G., Convertino, C., Sapere, P. & Dirmyer, R. (2014). Vocabulary knowledge and meta-knowledge in deaf and hearing students. *Journal of Postsecondary Education and Disability. 27*, 161–178.

Schirmer, B. R., & McGough, S. M. (2005). Teaching reading to children who are deaf: Do the conclusions of the National Reading Panel apply? *Review of Educational Research, 75*(1), 83–117.

Seal, B., Nussbaum, D., Scott, S., Waddy-Smith, B., Clingempeel, K., & Belzner, K. (2005, November). *Evidence for sign-spoken language relationships in children with cochlear implants.* Presented at the American Speech, Language, and Hearing Society Annual Conference, San Diego, CA.

Singleton, J. L., Supalla, S., Litchfield, S., & Schley, S. (1998). From sign to word: Considering modality constraints in ASL/English bilingual education. *Topics in Language Disorders, 18*(4), 16–29.

Slavin, R. E. (2008). What works? Issues in synthesizing educational program evaluations. *Educational Researcher, 37*, 5–14.

Smith, F. (1973). *Psycholinguistics and reading*. Stamford, CT: Thomson Learning.

Smith, G. J., Schmidt, M. M., Edelen-Smith, P. J., & Cook, B. G. (2013). Pasteur's quadrant as the bridge linking rigor and relevance. *Exceptional Children, 79*(2), 147–161.

Spencer, P., & Marschark, M. (2010). *Evidence-based practices in educating deaf and hard-of-hearing students.* New York: Oxford University Press.

STEM Education Coalition. (2013, June). *The case for STEM education as a national priority: Good jobs and American competitiveness.* http://www.stemedcoalition.org/wp-content/uploads/2013/10/Fact-Sheet-STEM-Education-Good-Jobs-and-American-Competitiveness-June-2013.pdf (retrieved Dec. 30, 2013).

Stephenson, B., Dostal, H. & Wolbers, K. (2013, February). *Year 3: Impact of professional development on classroom implementation of Strategic and Interactive Writing Instruction (SIWI).* Presented at the meeting of ACE-D/HH, Santa Fe, NM.

Stevenson, H. W., & Newman, R. S. (1986). Long-term prediction of achievement and attitudes in mathematics and reading. *Child Development, 57*, 646–659.

Stinson, M. S., & Kluwin, T. N. (2011). Educational consequences of alternative school placements. In M. Marschark & P. Spencer (Eds.), *Oxford handbook of deaf studies, language, and education* (Vol. 1, 2nd ed., pp. 47–52). New York: Oxford University Press.

Stronge, J. H. (2010). Effective teachers = student achievement: What the research says. *Eye on Education, ERIC*, EBSCO*host* (accessed Dec. 30, 2013).

Svirsky, M. A., Teoh, S., & Neuburger, H. (2004). Development of language and speech perception in congenitally, profoundly deaf children as a function of age at cochlear implantation. *Audiology & Neurotology, 9*(4), 224–233.

Swanwick, R., & Marschark, M. (2010). Enhancing education for deaf children: Research into practice and back again. *Deafness and Education International, 12*, 217–235.

Szagun, G., & Stumper, B. (2012). Age or experience? The influence of age at implantation and social and linguistic environment on language development in children with cochlear implants. *Journal of Speech, Language, and Hearing Research, 55*, 1640–1654.

Tattersall, H., & Young, A. (2006). Deaf children identified through newborn hearing screening: parents' experiences of the diagnostic process. *Child: Care, Health and Development 32*(1), 33–45.

Thagard, E. K., Hilsmier, A. S., & Easterbrooks, S. R. (2011). Pragmatic language in deaf and hard of hearing students: Correlation with success in general education. *American Annals of the Deaf, 155*(5), 516–534.

Therrien, W. J. (2004). Fluency and comprehension gains as a result of repeated readings: A meta-analysis. *Remedial and Special Education, 25*, 252–261.

Trezek, B. J., & Malmgren, K. W. (2005). The efficacy of utilizing a phonics treatment package with middle school deaf and hard-of-hearing students. *Journal of Deaf Studies and Deaf Education, 10*(3), 256–271.

Trezek, B. J., Wang, Y., Woods, D., Gamp, T., & Paul, P. (2007). Using visual phonics to supplement beginning reading instruction for students who are deaf or hard of hearing. *Journal of Deaf Studies and Deaf Education, 12*(3), 373–384.

Tucci, S., Trussell, J., & Easterbrooks, S. R. (2014). A review of the evidence on strategies for teaching children who are DHH grapheme-phoneme correspondence. *Communication Disorders Quarterly*, doi: 10.1177/1525740114523776

Valencia, S. W., & Buly, M. R. (2004). Behind test scores: What struggling readers really need to know. *The Reading Teacher, 56*, 520–531.

Van Hoogmoed, A., Knoors, H., Schreuder, R., & Verhoeven, L. (2013). Complex word reading in Dutch deaf children and adults. *Research in Developmental Disabilities, 34*(3), 1083–1089.

Van Hoogmoed, A., Verhoeven. L., Schreuder, R. & Knoors, H. (2011). Morphological processing in deaf readers. *Applied Psycholinguistics 32*(3), 619–634.

Van Staden, A. (2013). An evaluation of an intervention using sign language and multi-sensory coding to support word learning and reading comprehension of deaf signing children. *Child Language Teaching and Therapy, 29*(3), 305–318.

Verhoeven, L., van Leeuwe, J., & Vermeer, A. (2011). Vocabulary growth and reading development across the elementary school years. *Scientific Studies of Reading, 13*, 205–223.

Wauters, L., & de Klerk, A. (2014). Improving reading instruction to deaf and hard-of-hearing students. In M. Marschark, G. Tang, & H. Knoors (Eds.), *Bilingualism and bilingual deaf education* (Vol. 1, pp. 242–271). New York: Oxford University Press.

Wauters, L. N., Tellings, A. E., van Bon, W. H., & Mak, W. M. (2008). Mode of acquisition as a factor in deaf children's reading comprehension. *Journal of Deaf Studies and Deaf Education, 13*(2), 175–192.

Wauters, L. N., Van Bon, W. H. J., Tellings, A. E. J. M., & Van Leeuwe, J. (2006). In search of factors in deaf and hearing children's reading comprehension. *American Annals of the Deaf, 151*, 371–380.

Wolbers, K., Dostal, H., & Bowers, L. (2012). "I was born full deaf." Written language outcomes after one year of Strategic and Interactive Writing Instruction (SIWI). *Journal of Deaf Studies and Deaf Education, 17*(1), 19–38.

World Health Organization. (2012). *WHO global estimates on prevalence of hearing loss: Mortality and burden of diseases and prevention of blindness and deafness.* Retrieved Dec. 31, 2013, from http://www.who.int/pbd/deafness/WHO_GE_HL.pdf

Yoshinaga-Itano, C., Sedey, A. L., Coulter, D. K., & Mehl, A. L. (1998). Language of early- and later-identified children with hearing loss. *Pediatrics, 102*(5), 1161–1171.

Young, A., & Tattersall, H. (2005). Parents' of deaf children evaluative accounts of the process and practice of universal newborn hearing screening. *Journal of Deaf Studies and Deaf Education, 10*(2), 134–145.

Zazove, P., Meador, H. E., Reed, B. D., & Gorenflo, D. W. (2013). Deaf persons' English reading levels and associations with epidemiological, educational, and cultural factors. *Journal of Health Communication, 18*(7), 760–772.

8

Developing Numeracy in Individuals Who Are Deaf and Hard of Hearing

Claudia M. Pagliaro

Think about your day today. Did you use an alarm clock this morning so you could get up in time for work or school? How did you know the time for which to set the alarm? Think of the process you went through, perhaps working backward, knowing you had to arrive at the office or to class by a certain hour. You might have figured in how long it would take you to drive, walk, or ride the bus to your destination. You considered how long you needed to get ready—an aggregate of how long it would take for you to shower, wash/dry your hair, dress, do your makeup or shave, and so forth. You may have also factored in some breakfast or a stop for coffee, perhaps a phone call. As you thought about all of these events, you adjusted and recalculated before finally setting the alarm clock with a numerical representation of the hour and minutes.

What you did is solve a multistep mathematics problem, using numerous operations and estimations, approximations, and inferences to solve an unknown (i.e., what time to get up)—an unknown that has meaning and purpose to you. Perhaps it was a more difficult problem than those given in school, but you do it every day, day in and day out, most likely with little effort, all because you know mathematics. There is *no way* you could have done it without mathematics, and you can do it because you are "numerate." In other words, you have an understanding of concepts related to number and measurement (time), how they function, their internal relationships, and how to manipulate them toward a goal. You have functional numeracy.

This chapter will further define numeracy, discuss trajectories of typical mathematics development, highlight some factors that must be considered in the mathematics development of deaf and hard-of-hearing (DHH) learners, and conclude with suggestions for classroom instruction and assessment.

NUMERACY

First named in the United Kingdom in 1959, numeracy was not fully defined until 1982 by members of the Committee of Inquiry into the Teaching of Mathematics in Schools in Great Britain (New South Wales Department of Education and Communities, 1999–2011). Numeracy is the ability to understand, reason with, manipulate, and apply mathematical concepts, symbols, and techniques accurately, appropriately, and efficiently in a particular context toward a goal. Like literacy, which is not simply knowing letters or words by themselves but also using them to read and write so as to communicate, numeracy is not just knowing numbers and shapes, but also understanding when and how to use them so as to solve an unknown. A numerate person, then, is one who can understand information presented in mathematical terms and notation and who, given a particular set of circumstances, can actively and efficiently draw upon that understanding to make sense of the world. The numerate person decides what mathematics to use, when, and how, and then critically evaluates the merit of the end result. Also like literacy, which includes reading and writing and their components (e.g., fluency, comprehension, spelling), numeracy encompasses multiple areas, including number and operations, geometry and spatial sense, measurement, and probability and data interpretation, along with critical thinking skills within each area that include executive functions such as organization, planning, and problem solving.

There are also various levels of numeracy, just as there are in literacy. Those who have a basic level of numeracy understand the rudimentary concepts of numbers, shapes, patterns, and measurements and can logically use the basic operations involved to problem solve. Understanding more sophisticated, higher-order mathematical concepts and skills across these areas, as well as the relationships between them, and having the ability to manipulate them (within set rules) to solve more sophisticated problems (of mathematical and authentic nature) show an advanced level of numeracy. Higher numeric proficiency provides for greater professional opportunities as well as personal benefits.

Regardless of where we live, our lives and successes and our understanding of each other and the world we live in are determined by our level of numeracy—much more, arguably, than our level of literacy. Although it may be difficult (especially given the popularity of texting and blogging), we can have a fairly successful day without reading or writing, depending perhaps on others who can tell us what is happening in the world or what the weather is outside, but we will not be able to truly understand their *communication* (not just the words) if we do not know that a "high of 17 degrees Fahrenheit" means that we better put on a coat and bring our mittens because "it's going to be cold out there!" Consider the following paragraph taken from the Internet during the aftermath of one of the most horrific natural disasters of the decade thus far. Words related to mathematical concepts of number, categorization, and measurement and related executive functioning skills such as comparison, organization, and problem solving have been italicized. These are the words that require some level of numeracy to understand. Twenty-four of the 52 words—almost half—are mathematics related.

> The Philippines, a *nation* of *more than 7,000* islands, faces *enormous* devastation *in* the *aftermath* of Typhoon Haiyan that produced *record strength* winds *along with high* storm surges. *Approximately 10 million* people *across 40 provinces* have been affected with *as many as 600,000* people displaced and the death *toll continuing* to *rise*. (American Red Cross, 2013)

Numeracy helps us to understand, interpret, and contribute to the world, but how (and why) does a person become numerate?

DEVELOPMENT OF NUMERACY

Human beings are naturally curious about their surroundings. Whether through direct experience, communication, or personal inner contemplation, from infancy through adulthood, people seek to explain the unknown, make sense of their environment, and enhance their own existence. It is this basic desire that instigates and propels someone to gain numeracy. Thus, the *need for* mathematics contributes greatly to a person's level of numeracy; in turn, a person's level of numeracy determines his or her ability to use mathematics to further his or her experiences and successes in meeting those needs.

Decades of research in the fields of mathematics education, cognitive science, and developmental psychology have provided insight into the development of numeracy. Research has shown that beginning in the first year of life, humans seem to have the ability to compare and discriminate between objects and symbols and have a basic understanding of quantities and amounts of "more" and "less" (Brannon, Abbott, & Lutz, 2004; Clearfield & Mix 2001). Then, as the child grows in experiences, increases and controls attention, and develops memory retention and language capacities (Cross, Woods, & Schweingruber, 2009), he or she begins to expand, enhance, and refine his or her understanding of mathematical concepts in number as well as in other areas such as geometry and measurement (Cross et al., 2009; Deak, Ray, & Pick, 2002; Geary, 1994; Gelman & Gallistel, 1978; Sarama & Clements, 2009).

As concepts become more complex, adults in the environment (e.g., parents, teachers, or any person more knowledgeable than the child) become critical factors in numeracy development (National Institute of Child Health and Human Development, Early Child Care Research Network, 1999). Through daily interactions, they mediate learning by focusing the child on the concept, asking questions, making comparisons, and offering explanations. They model systematic exploration for the child and guide him or her to make connections with previous experiences and preexisting knowledge. The frequency and quality of the mediation to which a child has been exposed will directly relate to the level of mathematics ability and understanding that he or she acquires (Anderson, 1997, 1998). Children who are exposed to high-quality mediation in the home perform at a higher cognitive level (Klein, 1991, 2000).

In mathematics education, this developmental progression over time from "informal ideas to increasingly complex understandings" (Wilson, Mojica, & Confrey, 2013, p. 104) is illustrated by learning trajectories. These trajectories show a progression or likely sequence of increasingly sophisticated mathematics—that is, concepts and skills that support and/or depend on one another. On the trajectory, these concepts and skills act as markers or steps of development (Confrey & Maloney, 2010; Consortium for Policy Research in Education, 2011; Wilson et al., 2013).

An example of a learning trajectory for early mathematics is provided in Table 8.1. Constructed by Kritzer and Pagliaro (2013) from several evidence-based sources, including the National Council of Teachers of Mathematics (2000), the Child Development Tracker from PBS Parents (n.d.), and the work of Sarama and Clements (2009), the trajectory suggests the development of foundational numeracy in the major concept areas. As illustrated, there is suggested a particular order or sequence of development of concepts and skills within each area. For instance, a child will first learn to rote count to 3, then 5, then 10, before rote counting to 20. Likewise, in the area of geometry, a child will be able to match identical shapes before matching similar shapes of different sizes or orientations. Within a concept area, however, it is possible—and probable—that a child will be on one level in a particular concept or skill and at a higher level (more complex) or a lower level (less complex) in another *if* that higher concept or skill is not dependent upon the understanding of the lower one. For example, in the area of number, a child may indeed be able to rote count to 20 without being able to count objects to 10 or even 5, as counting objects requires a different understanding of "five"—that is, its association or relationship as a label for a particular object in a set versus its placement in a sequence of number words or signs. However, a child will not be able to count objects to 20 if he or she can only rote count to 5, as the knowledge of the sequence of numbers found in rote counting is embedded in or is in support of the ability to count objects. Thus, knowledge of the sequence of numbers is not dependent on that related to counting objects; however, counting

Table 8.1 Early Mathematics Development Trajectory

	Number	Geometry & Spatial Sense	Measurement	Operations & Problem Solving	Patterns, Reasoning, & Algebra
2 years	• Understands and distinguishes 1 and 2 from many • Rote counts to at least 3 (may be incorrect beyond 3)	• Orders by size • Completes simple 3–4 piece puzzles	• Explores objects by filling and emptying containers • Begin to understand and describe same and different	• Can nonverbally determine that one item added to another makes "two"	• Learning order of day • Begin to notice patterns • Begin to use terms for "today", "tomorrow" "yesterday" • Show interest in pattern or sequence (e.g., stringing beads) • Begins to logically sort and classify
3 years	• Understands and distinguishes 1, 2, & 3 from many; • Rote count to 5, possibly 10; • Counts objects to 5; • Demonstrates one-to-one correspondence up to 3; • Uses "more" to identify larger of two collections (if difference is obvious)	• Completes 4–10 piece puzzle • Understands that wholes can be separated into parts (e.g., a pizza) • Match shapes with same size and orientation • Experiments with spatial labels, may not be correct • Identifies basic shapes (circle, square, possibly triangle)	• Develop sense of time for regular events (knows basic sequence of day) • Develops early time concepts (morning, afternoon, night, later, soon)—sometimes confuses yesterday, today, and tomorrow • Recognizes differences between measurable concepts	• Using context and objects, begin to nonverbally solve problems involving sums up to "five"; • Intuitively recognize that if you change the size of part of a collection you also change the whole	• Can identify repeating unity and begin to extend a simple pattern • Sort arbitrarily ("because I like it") • Match perceptually by characteristics that are observable (e.g., match socks that are the same)

(*continued*)

Table 8.1 Continued

	Number	Geometry & Spatial Sense	Measurement	Operations & Problem Solving	Patterns, Reasoning, & Algebra
4 years Pre-K	• Rote count to 10 (correctly); • Counts 5–10 objects; • Subitizes to 4; • Recognizes that last number counted represents the total; • Understands that numbers later in counting sequence are larger (up to 10) • Recognizes/reads numerals 0–9	• Completes puzzle with up to 15 pieces • Match shapes with different size and orientation • Recognize and name simple shapes and some variations (circle, square, triangle, rectangle)—does not yet make a distinction between sides and corners; • Build, copy and describe 2 dimensional shapes • Begin to use/ understand words representing physical relations or positions (over, under, left, right, etc.) in particular—those that remain regardless of perspective • Uses simple map to find a hidden object	• Figure out that different size containers hold more or less • Develop language to describe attributes (big, small, long, tall, short, heavy, light, fast, slow) • Can describe how things are "same" or "different" • Can compare a single attribute across several objects (e.g., sizes of pieces of cake) • Can order objects from smallest to largest and describe the relationship among them • Can recite days of week • Knows time associated with specific events • Can compare length or area of two specific objects using direct comparison	• Using objects, can mentally determine sums up to "five" and their subtraction counterparts	• Understand a sequence of events when explained (e.g., first, next, last) • Can complete an adult-imposed classification task—sticking with one observable feature (e.g., sort by color, shape, size)

5 years K	• Rote count to 20; • Counts 10–20 items; • Subitizes up to 5; • Names number before and after up to 30; • Counts backwards from 10; • Skip counts to 100 by 10s • Makes reasonable estimates up to 20; Understands terms related to estimation (about, closer to, between, etc.); • Understands that numbers later in counting sequence are larger (up to 100); • Can use mental number line to determine relative proximity up to 9; • Can copy or write numerals 0–9 and connect them to quantitative value	• Continues to recognize simple shapes that vary in size and orientation (more complex variations than previous level) • Copies shape from memory after seeing model briefly • Matches shapes with objects that have same shape or size (congruence) • Identifies more complex shapes by name (e.g., hexagon) and distinguishes sides from corners; • Completes increasingly complex puzzles (smaller pieces, more numerous)	• Strong sense of time—know when familiar events take place • Know days, months, and seasons • Beginning to learn to tell time • Begin to understand conservation (number remains the same unless items are added or removed) • Compare length of two objects by representing length with one unit (e.g. string)—then comparing two strings • May begin to measure length of an object using same-size units laid end-to-end	• Can nonverbally and mentally determine sums up to "five" and their subtraction counterparts (labels all arrangements up to 5, then 10—e.g., 1&4, 2&3) • Can use informal knowledge to estimate the sums of addition word problems • Begin to use concrete counting strategies to solve addition story problems • Can use various addition strategies to mentally determine sums up to "nine" • Understands "part-whole" relationship of addition; can solve part-part-whole story problem with missing whole and sums up to "10"	• Can sort and classify by more than one feature and articulate why items are grouped the way they are (features may not be directly observable—e.g., function, number) • Begin to understand growing pattern involved with counting ("one" is added to get to the next number) • Begins to use letters to represent the core of a repeating pattern • Can use deductive reasoning to solve a simple problem (e.g., figures out who is missing by looking at children present) • Can sequence events chronologically

(*continued*)

Table 8.1 Continued

	Number	Geometry & Spatial Sense	Measurement	Operations & Problem Solving	Patterns, Reasoning, & Algebra
		• Understands and uses words to represent physical relations/ positions, including spatial labels that change based on perspective (e.g., left, right) • Creates a simple map		• Can group objects into 5's or 10's • Recognizes that position of a digit in a number affects its value • *Can read multidigit numerals up to "19" • *Can use informal strategies to solve fair-sharing problems	• Begin to construct algebra sense—can use problem solving strategies to solve a problem (e.g., draw a picture, draw and adjust, work backwards)
6 years 1st	• Can count to "200" by rote; • Counts 20 items; • Can name number before/after up to 99; • Counts backwards from 20; • Beginning to count by 5's to 100; • Beginning to count by 2s to 20; • Can make reasonable estimates up to 100;	• Identifies and counts sides of shapes; beginning to count angles • Can use class names to classify and sort shapes • Can accurately visualize two-dimensional shapes and draw them from memory	• Understands that unless more is added or removed, the number of objects in a collection remains the same even if the appearance changes • Can measure using same size unit laid end to end	• Begin to count-on to solve a problem (e.g., to solve 3+2, counts on from 3) • Labels arrangements up to 20 (e.g., 4 groups of 5) • Can break a larger unit (e.g., 100) into smaller units and combine smaller units to make larger units	• Understands even and odd numbers • Begin to understand that the "equals" sign can be interpreted as "the same as" • Begin to understand the "other name for a number" concept (e.g., 12 = 12 + 0; 11 + 1, etc.)

• Can use mental number line to determine relative proximity with two-digit numbers; • Can identify written number words 1–9 and use them to represent number of items in a collection; • Can describe parallels between ordinal terms (e.g., 1st, 2nd, 3rd) and cardinal terms	• Can define congruence and match shapes to show congruence • Can create new shapes by combining shapes • Can give and follow directions for moving in physical space and on a map	• Can make informal comparisons and estimates	• Can read multi-digit numerals up to 99 • Can accurately write multi-digit numbers up to 999 • Can solve fair sharing problems where up to 20 items are divided among 3 to 5 people • Begins to compar e simple fractions (1/2, 1/4,. 1/3) • Can solve repeated addition problems using objects, mentally, or through use of verbal counting	• Can sort and classify on the basis of more than one characteristic and/or consider an implicit relationship

(Pagliaro & Kritzer, 2013, pp. 15–18; Kritzer & Pagliaro, 2011)

Mathematics Development Grid adapted from: http://www.pbs.org/parents/childdevelopmenttracker.html

NCTM Standards, 2010; Sarama & Clements, 2009

objects *is* dependent on the knowledge related to rote counting. This same logic applies to a child's development across concept areas as well. On the other hand, there are certain concepts/skills that do develop around the same time, especially those in support of one another. For example, again in number, at approximately the same developmental time that a child is learning one-to-one correspondence, he or she is also learning to count objects, a task whereby a unique label is assigned to a unique object (mimicking one-to-one correspondence).

Other examples of higher-order learning trajectories can be found in studies by Confrey and colleagues (Confrey & Maloney, 2010; Confrey, Maloney, Nguyen, Mojica, & Myers, 2009; Mojeca & Confrey, 2009; Wilson et al., 2013), who do extensive work with the equipartitioning and rational number reasoning trajectories, and those by Carpenter and colleagues (Carpenter, Fennema, & Franke, 1996; Carpenter, Fennema, Franke, Levi, & Empson, 1999) on Cognitively Guided Instruction (CGI). Confrey, Nguyen, Lee, Panorkou, Corley, and Maloney (2012) have also created a wonderful, though somewhat daunting, graphic interpretation of learning trajectories embedded in the Common Core Standards for Mathematics (http://www.corestandards.org/math), now adopted by most states in the United States for all K–12 mathematics education. The graphic can be accessed on the Internet at www.turnonccmath.net and includes learning trajectories for K–8 (Confrey, Nguyen, & Maloney, 2011) for various concept areas in mathematics such as numbers and operations, geometry, and ratio and proportions.

It is important to note that although learning trajectories, including those mentioned as examples here, may provide approximate age or grade levels, mathematics learning is *developmental* and the trajectories show what is probable or can be expected, and not a fixed arrangement of requisite stages (Confrey & Maloney, 2010; Wilson et al. 2013). Individual learners may not follow the same path of concept and skill development exactly as the trajectory suggests (Sztajn, Confrey, Wilson, & Edgington, 2012) because learning is closely tied to experience and culture (Consortium for Policy Research in Education, 2011; Kleemans, Peeters, Segers, & Verhoeven, 2011; Mojica & Confrey, 2009; Sarama & Clements, 2009). This is especially significant when considering the DHH learner.

MATHEMATICS DEVELOPMENT AND THE DEAF OR HARD-OF-HEARING LEARNER

Regardless of their communication preference or their parents' hearing status, DHH learners, by the simple fact that they access the world differently, are unique learners, and this distinctiveness must be taken into consideration in regard to their mathematics development. As in the Indian parable of the blind men who were asked to describe an elephant (each one describing it completely differently based on th elephant he experienced with his hands), the DHH learn tions and conceptual understanding will reflect the inform gathered. Thus, a DHH child's input and resulting cogniti tion will be different from that of those who hear (Marschar 2008, 2012)—not better or worse necessarily, but different. Even within the deaf community, no two DHH learners will necessarily be the same because their experiences vary widely, given the environments, audiological levels, etiologies, ages of onset, language/communication, and any disabilities (not deafness) that might be present.

Pagliaro and Kritzer (2013) used the trajectory included in Table 8.1 in a recent study to better understand young DHH children's knowledge of early mathematics concepts and skills. In doing so, they found areas in which the DHH children seemed to excel and others in which they exhibited great difficulty. For example, understanding of number is said to be most important for preschool hearing children (Cross et al., 2009; Gersten, Clarke, Jordan, Newman-Gonchar, Haymond, & Wilkins, 2012). However, Pagliaro and Kritzer (2013) found that DHH children of this age show greatest understanding in concepts related to geometry and space, not number, and were weakest in the understanding of concepts associated with measurement and problem solving (an area affiliated with number and operations). Zarfety, Nunes, and Bryant (2004) also showed a propensity toward spatial sense in young DHH learners. Their study found that 3–4-year-old DHH children outperformed hearing children of the same age in their ability to represent a specific set given to them in a spatial presentation. It may be, then, that for DHH learners, the geometry concepts and skills are developed sooner and/or more quickly than those of other areas, perhaps influenced by their visual access to information. It is the mediator's (i.e., educator, parent) task, then, to recognize this difference and capitalize on this relatively strong area when teaching concepts and skills in weaker areas.

In another study based on the problem-solving trajectory used in the CGI investigations (Carpenter et al., 1996, 1999), Pagliaro and Ansell (2012) analyzed the success and solution strategies of American DHH students in grades K–3. While the CGI studies showed that hearing students' solution strategies generally proceeded from modeling to counting to fact-based, counting strategies permeated those used by signing DHH children regardless of age, suggesting that counting strategies for such learners may surface prior to traditional modeling strategies or that perhaps early counting strategies may include modeling, given the cardinal nature of number signs 1 through 5 in American Sign Language.

Differences in interactions with others will also affect the DHH learner's conceptual organization in mathematics (Marschark & Hauser, 2008, 2012). Results from several analyses (Kritzer, 2008, 2009b;

Kritzer & Pagliaro, 2012; Pagliaro & Kritzer, 2010) suggest a relationship between parent mediation and preschool DHH children's mathematics abilities. Kritzer (2008, 2009b) and Pagliaro and Kritzer (2010) performed three separate analyses on this topic with various data from six preschool DHH children, aged four to six years. Although all tested below average on the Test of Early Mathematics Ability-3 (TEMA-3; Ginsburg & Baroody, 2003) compared to normative age-equivalency scores (Kritzer, 2009a), three of these children scored one standard deviation above the mean score of the sample, thus displaying relatively high mathematics ability, and three scored one standard deviation below the mean sample score, performing at a relatively low mathematics ability. Data were gathered during an all-day observation of each family in which parent–child interactions were recorded and coded in relation to mathematics concepts and skills and to mediation behaviors. In each of these analyses, children whose parents engaged them in meaningful, cognitively challenging conversations exhibited a greater understanding of early mathematics concepts and skills than did those whose parents did not.

In one analysis, Kritzer (2009b) found that the children who tested in the relatively high mathematics ability group were exposed more frequently to mathematics concepts throughout the day than were their lower-ability counterparts. Parents of these children made reference to numbers, time and sequencing, and categorization six times more often. In addition, these parents elevated the importance of these concepts by encouraging their children to use them to gather information, perform needed tasks, and problem solve.

Likewise, in a second analysis of the data that focused specifically on a prescribed problem-solving activity in which parents were asked to play a categorization game with their child (Kritzer, 2008), parents of those children who exhibited relatively high mathematics ability not only performed the activity as directed but also extended the activity to include tangent, higher-order problem solving and enhanced thinking skills. For example, instead of simply requesting that their children choose an item for a particular category, they asked them to consider the total number of items in that category. They also made connections within the activity with the use of labels (words or signs) that indicated a sequence or transfer of events in time, such as using "now" or "before." Parents of children with relatively low mathematics ability, for the most part, relegated the activity to a much lower cognitive level (lower still than the required categorization), one of labeling attributes, with very little use of specific mathematics-related language.

Finally, Pagliaro and Kritzer (2010) performed an extended analysis of the data collected on these six children and their families, employing a multiple case study design to investigate the overall mediation behaviors (not necessarily related to mathematics) employed by adults during interactions with their children. The coded mediation behaviors, marked by Feuerstein and Rand (1997) as critical for informal learning in young children, included those that focus the child on the environment, offer explanations, extend thinking and learning through questioning, recognize abilities, and inhibit impulsivity. As in the previous two analyses that centered on mathematics-related activities and topics, results showed a clear difference between the two groups of parents. Parents of children with high mathematics ability employed not only more mediation behaviors but also more sophisticated ones than did those of children with low mathematics ability. These behaviors included responding to the child's initiation or question with a question and/or an explanation, event, or action; asking questions; offering explanations; and providing directives. In addition, these parents became models for their children, who adopted those same behaviors as their own, in effect having "learned how to learn" from their parents. Further, these children combined these behaviors into "networks," increasing their access to information and their ability to understand concepts.

Of course, common communication and language proficiency in both adults and children is critical to successful mediation, but it does not guarantee it. Deaf parents with DHH children who have language skills that mirror typical development of any child with normal linguistic capabilities and full access to a complete language may still struggle with mathematics, as do some hearing children with hearing parents. In the Kritzer (2008, 2009b) and Pagliaro and Kritzer (2010) analyses mentioned above, although the three randomly selected children in the group with relatively high mathematics ability happened to all have at least one deaf parent and the three randomly selected children in the group with relatively low mathematics ability happened to all have hearing parents, it is important to reiterate that all six children scored below the normed average on the TEMA-3. Thus, it is not just "having or not having language" that determines conceptual development and organization, but also the quality of the interaction performed with that language. When adults know how to mediate a child's thinking to support mathematical development, children respond.

A third factor that must be considered in the mathematics development of the DHH learner is prior knowledge or the depth of understanding of previously "learned" concepts and skills. Research studies over the past four decades (see Fuentes, 2011; Pagliaro, 2006, 2010) have shown that DHH students' understanding of mathematics, even at preschool ages, is significantly behind in overall achievement (Allen, 1995; Foisack, Pagliaro, & Kelly, 2013; Leybaert & Van Cutsem, 2002; Traxler, 2000) and in specific areas of numeracy such as number (Austin, 1975, as cited in Zarfaty et al., 2004; Kritzer, 2009a; Nunes & Moreno, 1998), geometry (Kemp, 2004; Mason, 1995), measurement (Austin, 1975, as cited in Zarfaty et al., 2004; Pagliaro & Kritzer, 2013), fractions

(Titus, 1995), and problem solving (Luckner & McNeill, 1994; Nunes, 2004; Pagliaro & Kritzer, 2013). With some exceptions where DHH students have performed similar to or better than hearing students (e.g., Leybaert & Van Custem, 2002; Zafarty et al., 2004), most point to the DHH learner's mathematics development as "delayed." Depending on the concept or skill, these delays or gaps may be indicative of a weak understanding of related lower-level concepts and skills or may be the cause of deficiencies in higher-level concepts and skills. One explanation for these "weak spots" may relate to curriculum and pedagogical practices.

More than a few studies (e.g., Kelly, Lang, & Pagliaro, 2003; Pagliaro, 1998b; Pagliaro & Ansell, 2002; Pagliaro & Kritzer, 2005; Swanwick, Oddy, & Roper, 2005) have described the formal mathematics instruction of the DHH learner to be procedure oriented, focusing students on algorithms and formulas, keywords, and practice exercises for short-term success (teaching to the inevitable upcoming test, or as a way of moving through the curriculum quickly), instead of on a deeper conceptual understanding of the mathematics that is at the foundation of algorithms and formulas, of higher-order thinking, and of true problem solving. Such a rote and routine-based pedagogy may stem from the symbiotic web of inadequate teacher preparation in mathematics education, little understanding of mathematics development, and low expectations of students, as well as a standard course of instruction and assessment that does not take into account the cognitive organization and experiences of the DHH learner (Fuentes, 2011; Marschark & Hauser, 2012; Pagliaro, 2006).

Over the years, research has marked the preparation of deaf education teachers in mathematics as insufficient (Fridriksson & Stewart, 1988; Kelly, Lang, & Pagliaro, 2003; Pagliaro, 1998a; Pagliaro & Kritzer, 2010; Swanwick et al., 2005). While some progress has been made toward better training, mainly due to legislation such as in the United States that mandates teachers be "highly qualified" (No Child Left Behind, 2002), few deaf education teacher preparation programs require more than one methods course in mathematics education for elementary-level certification (the formative years for mathematics understanding), and even fewer offer a course in mathematics education for the DHH learner. The result is teachers who may not be knowledgeable or comfortable in teaching mathematics or who misunderstand its trajectory of development. This ignorance, and perhaps anxiety with mathematics, may cause teachers to incorrectly alter the intellectual content of his or her lessons and thus inhibit student learning (Swanwick et al., 2005). Consequently their students may develop deficiencies ("weak spots") in their conceptual understanding, restricting their access to higher-order concepts. Teachers, then, may see the failure of their students not as a reflection of their own (or their colleagues') instructional decisions or of an inappropriate curriculum, but rather as a result of factors surrounding the students' deafness, thereby lowering their expectations of the DHH learner's ability to be successful in mathematics. Two studies in which teachers explicitly expressed their choice to limit their presentation of certain mathematics topics and problems support this conjecture (Pagliaro & Ansell, 2000; Pagliaro & Kritzer, 2005).

Pagliaro and Kritzer (2005) received survey responses from 290 K–12 teachers of the deaf across the United States regarding their mathematics instruction (content and pedagogy), specifically in relation to discrete mathematics topics and practices. When these educators were asked why they did not include a particular topic or skill in their teaching, the majority stated that they believed that it was too advanced for their students. Similarly, as part of a larger investigation, early elementary deaf education teachers from five schools for the deaf in the United States were interviewed by Pagliaro and Ansell (2000) regarding their thoughts on various arithmetic story problems in relation to their DHH students. Teachers attributed problem difficulty to a variety of factors, including students' paucity of formal and informal experiences with story problems, their struggles in understanding the related mathematics concepts and language, and the complexity of solution strategies needed to solve the problem. For example, teachers indicated that a start-unknown problem (such as, "Sofia had some crackers. Eric gave her 4 more crackers. Now Sofia has 11 crackers. How many crackers did Sofia have in the beginning?") would be difficult because a student would have to "think backward" to solve it, implying that the DHH student could not do this (see also Ansell & Pagliaro, 2006). Although these story problems are considered suitable for their grade levels, and they admitted that their students needed more practice with them, many teachers said they would not include such problems in their instruction.

Of course, not all teachers involved in the previous studies were incorrect in their perceptions of their students' abilities; the suggested topics and problems may indeed have been at an inappropriate developmental level for the students with whom they worked. However, it stands to reason that erroneous expectations (too low or too high) and a lack of understanding of the trajectory of mathematics development, including how the DHH learner's experiences and cognitive organization might affect this development, may lead teachers to make instructional decisions, such as teaching procedures in lieu of concepts, that can cause further "weak spots" and poorer performance as the student moves from grade to grade. Subsequent teachers then lower their expectations of the student and the damaging cycle repeats, hindering the DHH learner's numeracy development. As such, professional development in trajectory-based instruction that takes into account the uniqueness of the DHH individual as well as mediation techniques may be a successful approach.

TRAJECTORY-BASED INSTRUCTION

Notwithstanding differences in individual development, learning trajectories can be useful tools that provide teachers with conceptual frameworks for mathematics instruction and learning (Clements, Sarama, Spitler, Lange, & Wolfe, 2011). Learning trajectories help teachers to identify concepts mastered by each individual student and to plan subsequent instruction that targets related concepts and skills in order to advance the student to a higher level of mathematical understanding and thinking (Duncan & Hmelo-Silver, 2009). Individualized construction of knowledge is the emphasis.

Wilson and colleagues (2013) showed the benefit of elementary teachers having knowledge of learning trajectories. After participating in professional development sessions focused on a trajectory of rational number reasoning, teachers were clearer and more precise in their descriptions of students' understanding and were able to frame their students' work in the context of development. Evaluating and comparing each student to the trajectory, teachers were able to explain an individual's level of understanding and make predictions about his or her mathematical thinking. This study added support to previous trajectory-based investigations such as the CGI studies (Carpenter & Fennema, 1992) that indicate a relationship between the teacher's knowledge of trajectories, improved instruction, and student achievement.

Specific to the DHH learner, although focused on the home environment, Kritzer and Pagliaro (2012, 2013) provided parents of young DHH children with an intervention that included learning trajectories on early mathematics development in each of five concept areas (number; geometry; measurement; patterns, logic, and algebra; and problem solving), information on mediation in general, and specific suggestions on how to mediate their children's learning within natural, daily events (e.g., meals, bedtime routines and play). The intervention was presented across three phases in two different formats—once in a hybrid fashion including face-to-face workshops conducted with families every other month, and twice fully online with modules provided to families approximately every four weeks. Although the intervention's core components remained the same throughout, the intervention was modified and improved according to parents' feedback after each phase. Data were analyzed both quantitatively and qualitatively for change in the use of mathematics vocabulary by children and parents, change in mathematics understanding by children as measured by the TEMA-3 and the Early Mathematics Performance Diagnostic (EMPD; Kritzer & Pagliaro, 2013), and change in mediation behavior by parents. In each phase, results showed a dramatic increase in the use of mathematics vocabulary by both parents and children over the course of the intervention, with the last phase yielding a mean increase of 85% for parents and greater than 200% for children (Kritzer & Pagliaro, 2012, 2013). All children whose families fully participated in the intervention increased their performance on the TEMA-3 and the EMPD measures. More than half made statistically significant gains on the TEMA-3 according to test documentation, with five of the 12 children increasing by one grade level or more in less than one year's time (three gaining two grade levels and one gaining between one and two grade levels). Likewise, EMPD results from phases 2 and 3 (statistics for phase 1 are invalid as the measure was redesigned during this time) showed that participating children increased their understanding within each of the concept areas by a greater margin than did those children whose families did not participate in the intervention, performing better across concept areas by more than 55% (Kritzer & Pagliaro, 2013; Pagliaro & Kritzer, 2014).

As expected, qualitative analyses showed a positive effect of the intervention on parent mediation as well. In all phases, mediation by parents who followed the intervention fully became more intentional and meaningful, incorporating a purpose or goal that went beyond simple mathematics. Children were encouraged to use higher-order thinking skills, to reason logically, to estimate, to problem solve, and to formulate a supported opinion. The mathematical concepts and skills became a natural, useful part of daily activities and events, a tool by which to gain information, as opposed to a forced, artificial, and arbitrary task (e.g., counting to determine how many forks were needed for dinner that night vs. counting for the sake of counting). Parents also included more variety in their mediation, involving mathematics concepts related to measurement, geometry, and patterns, as well as number.

Although more study is warranted, the research mentioned above gives support to the likely relationship between knowledge of mathematics development, mediation, and achievement in mathematics.

ASSESSMENT

While trajectories provide a guideline or map of how students are likely to progress, they do not provide information on the depth of a student's understanding; thus, formative assessment is a critical component of trajectory-based instruction (Sztajn et al., 2012). Further, given a DHH learner's experiences and possible schematic differences, it is imperative that teachers elicit evidence beyond an evaluation of correct/incorrect answers, rather valuing students' work and explanations as a lens to their thinking and learning. A CRA assessment, for example, can provide the teacher with such evidence.

A CRA assessment (Allsopp, Kyger, & Lovin, 2007) is a strategy whereby the student's understanding is evaluated at three levels—concrete (C), representational or pictorial (R), and abstract or symbolic (A). Understanding at the concrete level means that the student can demonstrate the concept with manipulatives or authentic objects. At the representational level, students illustrate a concept or equation using pictures or drawings, tally marks, or some form of symbolic likeness. At the abstract level, students can use and manipulate numerals and other mathematical symbols to denote the concept or skill. Success at all three levels connotes a clear, in-depth understanding of the concept or skill. Students who struggle with mathematics or with a particular mathematics concept or skill, however, may not be able to demonstrate that particular concept or skill at all three levels, thus indicating a shallow or incomplete understanding and a potential "trouble spot" for related higher-level concepts.

For example, students (DHH and hearing) can usually demonstrate multiplication of fractions at the abstract level, having been taught the procedure to "multiply the numerators to get the numerator in the answer and multiply the denominators to get the denominator in the answer." However, many would be hard pressed to show proficiency at the concrete and/or representational level, indicating a procedural understanding only. Not having the conceptual understanding of multiplication of fractions that can be shown at the concrete and representational levels, the student may be confused as to why the product is a smaller fraction than either of the multiplicands, especially when multiplication of whole numbers "makes things greater!" This confusion and incomplete comprehension will restrict the student in his or her application or future use of the concept and limit his or her level of numeracy. Subsequent instruction, then, might focus on explaining the concept at the concrete and pictorial levels, thereby building in the student a deeper, comprehensive, *conceptual* understanding.

Conversely, some elementary students are very adept at counting out manipulatives to form two separate groups, then putting the groups together and counting the total number of manipulatives in the now larger group. These students may also be able to do the task as represented in pictures. If the child, as determined according to the trajectory of foundational mathematics, also has an understanding of cardinality (that the last number counted in a set represents the whole set), then the teacher may conclude that it is appropriate to provide the student with the abstract labels (numerals) for each of the separate sets (the addends), the operation (addition), and the sum.

Learning trajectories along with formative assessments, like the CRA assessment, guide the teacher in making instructional decisions that repair, expand, or advance an individual's mathematics understanding. The definition of numeracy, however, includes a goal or purpose to the mathematics, and that the desire to learn mathematics is based in need. Thus, the most important part of mathematics instruction, especially for DHH learners who may have varied experiences, may be linking mathematics to meaning.

Recall the example given at the start of this chapter. No doubt you can think of hundreds more examples now where you use mathematics every day, perhaps even in some tasks that you literally could not live without (e.g., taking medications). Mathematics has such significance in life, yet most of the time instruction does not connect mathematics concepts and skills to their *value*. Mathematics is often taught out of context and isolated from the rest of the curriculum, boring students and making mathematics a chore. Connecting mathematics instruction to the student's life (*not* the teacher's) provides "the goal" for numeracy that propels interest in learning. Students are actively engaged in mathematics, as well as critical thinking and executive functions. They are invested in increasing their own numeracy, learning the concepts and skills because they *need* them, as tools to accomplish a task in which they are interested and also from which they benefit.

With "meaningful mathematics," knowledge of learning trajectories, rich data from formative assessments, and recognition of the DHH learner's distinctiveness, teachers can design instruction that advances the level of numeracy in their students and helps them to "live *mathematically* ever after."

REFERENCES

Allen, T. E. (1995). Demographics and national achievement levels for deaf and hard of hearing students: Implications for mathematics reform. In C. H. Dietz (Ed.), *Moving toward the standards: A national action plan for mathematics education reform for the deaf* (pp. 41–49). Washington, DC: Pre-College Programs, Gallaudet University.

Allsopp, D., Kyger, M., & Lovin, L. (2007). *Teaching mathematics meaningfully: Solutions for reaching struggling learners.* Baltimore, MD: Paul H. Brookes Publishers.

American Red Cross. (2013, Nov. 12). *Global Red Cross response effort underway in wake of typhoon.* Retrieved from http://www.redcross.org/news/article/Red-Cross-Sends-Support-to-Philippines-for-Typhoon-Response?

Anderson, A. (1997). Families and mathematics: A study of parent–child interactions. *Journal for Research in Mathematics Education, 28*(4), 484–511.

Anderson, A. (1998). Parents as partners: Supporting children's mathematics learning prior to school. *Teaching Children Mathematics, 4*, 331–337.

Ansell, E., & Pagliaro, C. M. (2006). The relative difficulty of signed arithmetic story problems for primary level deaf and hard-of-hearing students. *Journal of Deaf Studies and Deaf Education, 11*(2), 153–170.

Brannon, E., Abbott, S., & Lutz, D. (2004). Number bias for the discrimination of large visual sets in infancy. *Cognition, 93*(2), 59–68.

Carpenter, T., & Fennema, E. (1992). Cognitively guided instruction: Building on the knowledge of students and teachers. *International Journal of Educational Research, 17*(5), 457–470.

Carpenter, T., Fennema, E., & Franke, M. (1996). Cognitively guided instruction: A knowledge base for reform in primary mathematics instruction. *Elementary School Journal*, *97*(1), 3–20.

Carpenter, T., Fennema, E., Franke, M., Levi, L., & Empson, S. (1999). *Children's mathematics: Cognitively guided instruction.* Portsmouth, NH: Heinemann.

Clearfield, M. W., & Mix, K. S. (2001). Amount versus number: Infants' use of area and contour length to discriminate small sets. *Journal of Cognition and Development*, 2(3), 243–260.

Clements, D., Sarama, J., Spitler, M., Lange, A., & Wolfe, C. (2011). Mathematics learned by young children in an intervention based on learning trajectories: A large-scale cluster randomized trial. *Journal for Research in Mathematics Education*, 42 (2), 127–166.

Confrey, J., & Maloney, A. (2010). The construction, refinement, and early validation of the equipartitioning learning trajectory. *International Society of the Learning Sciences, Proceedings of the 9th International Conference of the Learning Sciences*, *1*, 968–975.

Confrey, J. Maloney, A., Nguyen, K., Mojica, G. & Myers, M. (2009). Equipartioning/splitting as a foundation of rational number reasoning using learning trajectories. In M. Tzekaki, M. Kaldrimidou, & C. Sakonidis (Eds.), *Proceedings of the 33rd Conference of the International Group for the Psychology of Mathematics Education.* Thessaloniki, Greece: PME.

Confrey, J., Nguyen, K., Lee, K., Panorkou, N., Corley, A., & Maloney, A., (2012). *Turn-On Common Core Math: Learning Trajectories for the Common Core State Standards for Mathematics.* Retrieved from www.turnonccmath.net

Confrey, J., Nguyen, K., & Maloney, A. (2011). *Hexagon map of learning trajectories for the K-8 Common Core Mathematics Standards.* Retrieved from http://www.turnonccmath.net/p=map

Consortium for Policy Research in Education Research. (2011). *Learning trajectories in mathematics: A foundation for standards, curriculum, assessment, and instruction.* Philadelphia: PA: P. Daro, F. Mosher, & T. Corcoran.

Cross, C., Woods, T., & Schweingruber, H. (2009). *Mathematics learning in early childhood: Paths toward excellence and equity.* Washington, DC: National Academies Press.

Deak, G. G., Ray, S. D., & Pick, A. D. (2002). Matching and naming objects by shape or function: Age and context effects in preschool children. *Developmental Psychology*, *38*(4), 503–518.

Duncan, R., & Hmelo-Silver, C. (2009). Learning progressions: Aligning curriculum, instruction, and assessment. *Journal of Research in Science Teaching*, *46*(6), 606–609.

Feuerstein, R., & Rand, Y. 1997. *Don't accept me as I am: Helping retarded performers excel.* Arlington Heights, IL: Skylight.

Fridriksson,T.,&Stewart,D.S.(1988).Fromtheconcretetotheabstract:Mathematics for deaf children. *American Annals of the Deaf*, *133*(1), 50–55.

Foisack, E., Pagliaro, C. M., & Kelly, R. R. (2013). Matematikprestationer och elever med dövhet eller hörselnedsättning (Mathematics achievement and students with deafness or hearing loss). *EDUCARE*, *1*, 68–92.

Fuentes, M. (2011). Equal opportunities in mathematics: what does research on how young deaf children learn teach us? *Annales Universitatis Paedagogicae Cracoviensis. Studia Psychologica*, *4*, 49–57.

Geary, D. (1994). *Children's mathematical development: Research and practical applications*. Washington, DC: American Psychological Association.

Gelman, R., & Gallistel, C. R. (1978). *The child's understanding of number.* Cambridge, MA: Harvard University Press.

Gersten, R., Clarke, B., Jordan, N., Newman-Gonchar, R., Haymond, K., & Wilkins, C. (2012). Universal screening in mathematics for the primary grades: Beginnings of a research base. *Exceptional Children*, *78*(4), 423–445.

Ginsburg, H. P., & Baroody, A. J. (2003). *Test of early mathematics ability*. Austin, TX: Pro-Ed.

Kelly, R. R., Lang, H. G., & Pagliaro, C. M. (2003). Mathematics word problem solving for deaf students: A survey of perceptions and practices. *Journal of Deaf Studies and Deaf Education*, *8*(2), 104–119.

Kemp, V. (2004). The van Hide levels of geometric though and achievement among deaf undergraduate students. In D. Martin (Ed.), *Advances in cognition, education, and deafness*. Washington, DC: Gallaudet University Press.

Kleemans, T., Peeters, M., Segers, E., & Verhoeven, L. (2011). Child and home predictors of early numeracy skills in kindergarten. *Early Childhood Research Quarterly*, *27*, 471–477.

Klein, P. (1991). Improving the quality of parent interaction with very low birth weight children: A longitudinal study using a mediated learning experience model. *Infant Mental Health Journal*, *12*(4), 321–337.

Klein, P. (2000). A mediational approach to early intervention. In A. Kozulin & Y. Rand (Eds.), *Experience of mediated learning, an impact of Feuerstein's theory in education and psychology* (pp. 240–256). Amsterdam: Pergamon.

Kritzer, K. L. (2008). Family mediation of mathematically based concepts while engaged in a problem-solving activity with their young deaf children. *Journal of Deaf Studies and Deaf Education*, *13*(4), 503–517.

Kritzer, K. L. (2009a). Barely started and already left behind: A descriptive analysis of the mathematics ability demonstrated by young deaf children, *Journal of Deaf Studies and Deaf Education*, *14*(4), 409–421.

Kritzer, K. L. (2009b). Families with young deaf children and the mediation of mathematically based concepts within a naturalistic environment. *American Annals of the Deaf*, *153*(5), 474–483.

Kritzer, K. L. & Pagliaro, C. M. (2012). An intervention for early mathematics success: Building Math Readiness Parents as Partners project, phase 1 outcomes. *Journal of Deaf Studies and Deaf Education*, *17*(4), 30–46.

Kritzer, K., & Pagliaro, C. (2013). *Building math readiness in young deaf/hard-of-hearing children: Parents as partners* (Final Performance Report). Washington, DC: Institute of Education Sciences, U.S. Department of Education.

Leybaert, J., & Van Cutsem, M. (2002). Counting in sign language. *Journal of Experimental Child Psychology*, *81*(4), 482–501.

Luckner, J., & McNeill, J. (1994). Performance of a group or deaf and hard-of-hearing students and a comparison group of hearing students on a series of problem-solving tasks. *American Annals of the Deaf*, *139*(3), 371–377.

Marschark, M., & Hauser, P. (2008). Cognitive underpinnings of learning by deaf and hard-of-hearing students. In M. Marschark & P. C. Hauser (Eds.), *Deaf cognition: Foundations and outcomes* (pp. 3–23). New York: Oxford University Press.

Marschark, M., & Hauser, P. (2012). *How deaf children learn: What parents and teachers need to know*. New York: Oxford University Press.

Mason, M. (1995). Geometric knowledge in a deaf classroom: An exploratory study. *FOCUS on Learning Problems in Mathematics, 17*(3), 57–69.

Mojeca, G., & Confrey, J. (2009) Pre-service elementary teachers' understanding of an equipartitioning learning trajectory. In S. L. Swars, D. W. Stinson, & S. Lemons-Smith (Eds.), *Proceedings of the 31st annual meeting of the North American Chapter of the International Group for the Psychology of Mathematics Education.* Atlanta, GA: Georgia State University.

National Council of Teachers of Mathematics. (2000). *Principles and standards for school mathematics*. Reston, VA; Author.

National Institute of Child Health and Human Development, Early Child Care Research Network. (1999). Child-care and mother–child interaction in the first 3 years of life. *Developmental Psychology, 35*, 1399–1413.

New South Wales Department of Education and Communities. (1999–2011). *Numeracy: What is it?* Retrieved from http://www.curriculumsupport.education.nsw.gov.au/primary/mathematics/numeracy/what/index.htm

No Child Left Behind (NCLB) Act of 2001, Pub. L. No. 107-110, § 115, Stat. 1425 (2002).

Nunes, T. (2004). *Teaching mathematics to deaf children.* London: Whurr Publishers.

Nunes, T., & Moreno, C. (1998). Is hearing impairment a cause of difficulties in learning mathematics? In C. Donlan (Ed.), *The development of mathematical skills: Studies in developmental psychology* (pp. 227–254). Hove, UK: Psychology Press.

Pagliaro, C. M. (1998a). Mathematics preparation and professional development of deaf education teachers. *American Annals of the Deaf, 143*(5), 373–379.

Pagliaro, C. M. (1998b). Mathematics reform in the education of deaf and hard-of-hearing students. *American Annals of the Deaf, 143*(1), 22–28.

Pagliaro, C. M. (2006). Mathematics education and the deaf learner. In D. F. Moores & D. S. Martin (Eds.), *Deaf learners: Developments in curriculum and instruction* (pp. 29–40). Washington, DC: Gallaudet University Press.

Pagliaro, C. M. (2010). Mathematics instruction and learning of deaf/hard-of-hearing students: What do we know? Where do we go? In M. Marschark & P. Spencer (Eds.), *Oxford handbook of deaf studies, Language and Education—Vol. 2* (pp. 156–171). New York: Oxford University Press.

Pagliaro, C. M., & Ansell, E. (2000). *Primary-level deaf education teachers' pedagogical content knowledge related to arithmetic story problems.* Unpublished manuscript, Department of Instruction and Learning, University of Pittsburgh, Pittsburgh, PA.

Pagliaro, C. M., & Ansell, E. (2002). Story problems in the deaf education classroom: Frequency and mode of presentation. *Journal of Deaf Studies and Deaf Education, 7*(2), 107–119.

Pagliaro, C. M., & Ansell, E. (2012). Deaf and hard-of-hearing students' problem-solving strategies with signed arithmetic story problems. *American Annals of the Deaf, 156*(5), 438–458.

Pagliaro, C. M., & Kritzer, K. L. (2005). Discrete mathematics in deaf education: A survey to determine knowledge and use. *American Annals of the Deaf, 150*(3), 251–259.

Pagliaro, C. M., & Kritzer, K. L. (2010). Learning to learn: An analysis of early learning behaviours demonstrated by young deaf/hard-of-hearing children with high/low mathematics ability. *Deafness and Education International, 12*(2), 54–76.

Pagliaro, C. M., & Kritzer, K. L. (2013). The math gap: A description of the mathematics performance of preschool-aged deaf/hard-of-hearing children. *Journal of Deaf Studies and Deaf Education, 18*(2), 139–160.

Pagliaro, C. M., & Kritzer, K. L. (2014). *The Building Math Readiness: Parents as Partners Online Intervention—The Final Chapter* [working title]. Manuscript in preparation.

PBS Parents. (n.d.). *The Child Tracker.* Retrieved from http://www.pbs.org/parents/childdevelopmenttracker.html

Sarama, J., & Clements, D. (2009). *Early childhood mathematics education research: Learning trajectories for young children.* New York: Routledge.

Swanwick, R., Oddy, A., & Roper, T. (2005). Mathematics and deaf children: An exploration of barriers to success. *Deafness and Education International, 7*(1), 1–21.

Sztajn, P., Confrey, J., Wilson, P., & Edgington, C. (2012). Learning trajectory-based instruction: Toward a theory of teaching. *Educational Researcher, 41*(5), 147–156.

Titus. J. (1995). *The concept of fractional number among hearing impaired students.* Presented at the Annual Conference of the American Educational Research Association, San Francisco, CA, April 20–24.

Traxler, C. B. (2000). The Stanford Achievement Test, 9th Edition: National norming and performance standards for deaf and hard-of-hearing students. *Journal of Deaf Studies and Deaf Education, 5*(4), 337–348.

Wilson, P. H., Mojica, G. F., & Confrey, J. (2013). Learning trajectories in teacher education: Supporting teachers' understandings of students' mathematical thinking. *Journal of Mathematical Behavior, 32*, 103–121.

Zarfaty, Y., Nunes, T., & Bryant, P. (2004). The performance of young deaf children in spatial and temporal number tasks. *Journal of Deaf Studies and Deaf Education, 9*(3), 315–326.

9

Language Assessment of Deaf Learners

Rosalind Herman

WHY ASSESS LANGUAGE DEVELOPMENT IN DEAF CHILDREN?

Spoken language has become increasingly attainable for deaf children in recent years. Due to the changing context of deafness (Mayer & Leigh, 2010), it is now possible to identify childhood deafness at a much earlier stage than was previously possible; as a result, newborn hearing screening has become routine practice in many parts of the world (e.g., United Kingdom: Pimperton & Kennedy, 2012; United States: Green, Gaffney, Devine, & Grosse, 2007; Switzerland: Metzger, Pezier, & Veraguth, 2013; Taiwan: Huang, Chiang, & Shiau, 2013; Chile: Krauss, Heider, Sierra, & Ribalta, 2013). Identification of deafness soon after birth provides opportunities for earlier intervention, and a priority for all services is the provision of appropriate amplification. Deaf children now benefit from increasingly sophisticated amplification options, including bilateral cochlear implants and digital hearing aids that offer far better auditory access than was previously possible. There is also widespread recognition of the need for interventions to support families in developing their deaf child's communication, although the precise nature of such interventions, at least in the United Kingdom, is less well defined (Rees, Mahon, Herman, Newton, & Craig, 2014). Despite these advances, deaf children continue to be at risk for language delay, with corresponding consequences for mental health, literacy development, and academic achievement.

Sarant, Holt, Dowell, Rickards, and Blamey (2009), summarizing research over the previous 15 years, reported that many deaf children start school with a language delay of at least one year and have a generally slower rate of language acquisition, averaging approximately half that found in the hearing population. Children with cochlear implants have higher levels of language than have previously been observed among hearing aid wearers (e.g., Boons et al., 2012; Geers, Strube, Tobey, Pisoni, & Moog, 2011). Implantation before the age of one leads to speech intelligibility and language that of parallel hearing children, at least at the early stages of development (Dettman, Pinder, Briggs, Dowell, & Leigh, 2007; Leigh, Dettman, Dowell, & Briggs, 2012). Outcomes for children implanted later are more mixed: although speech perception and production are often good, language delays may persist (Leigh et al., 2012). Although some longitudinal research is emerging in this area, more is needed that follows children with implants into their secondary education to monitor the long-term effects.

One consequence of earlier diagnosis and better amplification is that deaf children are increasingly placed in mainstream schools (Consortium for Research into Deaf Education, 2013; De Raeve et al., 2012; Uziel, Sillon, & Vieu, 2007). Many of these children present with clear speech and competent conversational skills, skills that effectively mask subtler underlying problems with language comprehension (Archbold & Mayer, 2012). Those who do present with good spoken language may be perceived as needing relatively little support. However, minimal or no support that continues into secondary education, despite the substantial increase in curriculum demands, has consequences for poor outcomes. Harris and Terlektsi (2011) looked at reading and spelling in older deaf children (12 to 16 years) with either cochlear implants or digital hearing aids. The children with digital aids were found to perform at a higher level than those with implants. Children with digital aids were more often in specialist education settings, whereas those with implants tended to be in mainstream schools. The authors suggest that it may be the lack of support provided in mainstream schools that accounted for the implanted children's poorer literacy skills. Although Harris and Terlektsi did not focus specifically on language, it is the language deficit that underpins literacy that is widely acknowledged to be at the root of the literacy problem for deaf readers (see Marschark, 2002). Others (Mukari, Ling, & Ghani, 2007) have also stated the importance of providing ongoing support for deaf children with implants, despite the improved access to speech provided by the device. Without regular language monitoring, the need for support cannot be determined.

For children who use sign language to communicate, the visual accessibility of signs has the potential to facilitate language development, subject to sufficient and timely exposure. This is evidenced by deaf children in deaf families where sign language is used, who develop language at the same rate as hearing children acquire spoken language (see Morgan & Woll, 2002; Schick, Marschark, & Spencer, 2006). However, for the majority of deaf children, sign language input from hearing parents who are not themselves fluent signers means that exposure to signing is delayed and from poor language models (Marschark, 2002; Mayberry, 2007; Woolfe, Herman, Roy, & Woll, 2010). Research on deaf signing children with hearing parents has shown that these factors lead to poorer comprehension and morphological skills that vary more widely when compared to native signers (Kyle, 1990; Mayberry, 2007; Newport, 1990). These findings further highlight the importance of language assessment for signing deaf children.

Between 30% and 40% of deaf children are known to have additional disabilities ranging from visual impairments to learning disabilities and autism spectrum disorders (Edwards, 2010). Although many such children are now receiving cochlear implants, these children have poorer outcomes for language development (Cupples et al., 2014; Holt & Kirk, 2005), so careful monitoring is needed.

Some researchers have documented the co-occurrence of language impairments in children who have a hearing loss. Gilbertson and Kamhi (1995) and Norbury, Bishop, and Briscoe (2001) both investigated primary-aged children with mild to moderate sensorineural deafness and found some of their participants to have language impairments. Gilbertson and Kamhi reported this to be the case in half of their sample, whereas Norbury and colleagues found 22% with language impairments (mainly younger participants). These figures are higher than the 7% reported among the hearing population (Tomblin et al., 1997). Other researchers who have include investigated oral deaf children with suspected language impairments Hawker and colleagues (2008) who studied six children with implants whose spoken language outcomes were lower than expected, and Murphy and Dodd (2010) who described in greater detail an older oral deaf child with a language impairment.

There has also been research investigating language impairments in deaf children who sign (Mason et al., 2010; Morgan, Herman, & Woll, 2007; Quinto-Pozos, Forber-Pratt, & Singleton, 2011). Differentiating the language delay that frequently occurs in the majority of signing children in hearing families from language impairment presents particular challenges (Hermans, Knoors, & Verhoeven, 2010), but in some countries the availability of standardized language measures with deaf norms has made this possible (Herman, Holmes, & Woll, 1999; Herman et al., 2004; Woolfe et al., 2010). Mason and colleagues used a cutoff of −1.5 standard deviations on standardized measures of sign language comprehension and production to determine language impairment. On this basis, they estimated the prevalence of language impairment among their sample of signing children to be 6.4%, a figure more comparable to the prevalence noted previously for hearing children (Tomblin et al., 1997).

In cases where language impairment coexists with deafness, language assessment has diagnostic significance in helping professionals, families, and children to better understand the nature of these difficulties and in planning more appropriate interventions (Herman et al., 2014). For example, whereas deaf children with language delay respond to language enrichment programs, children with impaired language require specialist interventions; for many, intervention will need to be long term, although the precise nature of such interventions has not to date been described (Herman et al., 2014). Nonetheless, there is no doubt that detailed assessment findings to profile a child's strengths and needs can inform individualized interventions. Reassessment is then needed to evaluate whether interventions are effective.

We have presented a number of factors that explain deaf children's struggle to acquire language at the same time as their peers. Although recent research on early language acquisition in children implanted in their first year seems promising, it remains to be seen whether such progress is maintained in the longer term, for which regular assessment is needed. Poor communication is associated with increased emotional and behavioral difficulties in childhood and higher rates of mental health problems in adults (Fellinger, Holzinger, & Pollard, 2012). Delayed language is also associated with lower levels of literacy, with consequences for academic achievement and subsequent employment (Marschark et al., 2006). Assessment is needed to monitor development, diagnose language impairment, and design and evaluate interventions. Assessment findings contribute to the decision-making process for educational placement. For these reasons, deaf children's language development must be monitored regularly throughout their education, whether they communicate using spoken or sign language. For bilingual deaf children who use spoken and sign languages, or indeed additional spoken/sign languages, assessment of all languages is necessary.

For all deaf children, the aims of assessment are broadly the same:

- To obtain an accurate sample of the child's communicative repertoire that represents the communicative contexts the child regularly encounters;
- To determine whether language is developmentally age-appropriate;
- If acquisition is not proceeding as expected, to provide a differential diagnosis and profile strengths and development needs to inform intervention;
- To provide a baseline for reevaluation.

Before addressing each of these in turn, we consider the skills required to carry out a valid and accurate language assessment.

CHALLENGES IN ASSESSMENT

When planning a language assessment, a number of decisions must be made:

- Which areas of language should be assessed?
- What assessment methods should be used?
- How should the assessment be conducted and by whom?

Answering these questions requires a specific set of knowledge and skills. In this section, we consider the specialist knowledge and skills needed by professionals to fulfill this role, although we note at the outset that in many cases no single professional will possess all of them. Therefore, in many settings, and in particular with deaf children who sign or who have additional difficulties, assessment will require a team approach (Herman, 1998). Team members include speech and language therapists, teachers of the deaf, deaf staff, mainstream teachers, and other specialists, as well as parents. Each team member makes his or her own contribution to the assessment process. For the remainder of this chapter, we will refer at times to the "language assessment professional" and at others to the "language assessment team."

The communication difficulties encountered by deaf children have been widely documented and span a range of language domains, including phonology, morphology, semantics, syntax, and pragmatics. It is beyond the scope of this chapter to review all of these, and the interested reader is directed to Lederberg, Schick, and Spencer (2013) for a review of the language achievements of deaf children. Some professionals who carry out assessments with deaf children, such as speech and language therapists, have a firm background in the linguistic structure of spoken language and ways in which it may be compromised by different communication disabilities, including deafness. Language assessors also require extensive knowledge of typical patterns of language acquisition in both spoken and sign language (Easterbrooks & Baker, 2002). This knowledge provides an essential backdrop to determining whether observed deficits are due primarily to deafness or may be explained by additional difficulties.

For any individual deaf child, one, several, or all areas of communication may be affected. Although in principle assessment should be comprehensive and detailed, too much time spent on assessment places a burden on staff and children alike and takes time away from the child's education. Therefore, an important first step is identifying priorities for assessment before deciding on the appropriate method. Prioritizing involves taking account of the child's history and current circumstances as well as communication needs of particular concern to the child, parents, or teachers. Knowledge of the individual child, consultation, and information sharing within the assessment team is essential in order to assemble the necessary background information.

Thereafter, the language acquisition professional needs to have a sound understanding of testing principles (Jamieson & Simmons, 2011), familiarity with a range of assessment methods, and a high level of skill in communicating flexibly and effectively during the assessment process. Flexible communication includes using spoken communication, sign language, or sign support, according to each child's communication preference. If testers lack the necessary communication skills, identifying and training staff with the appropriate skills to deliver the assessment is an option.

For language testing with deaf children, testers need to know how to optimize the test environment so the child is not disadvantaged. This includes ensuring that the test environment is quiet and free from distractions, conducive to the needs of a hearing aid or implant user, and that any amplification devices used are fully functional at the outset. Testers also need to provide full visual access to speech reading or signing as needed, achieved by appropriate face-to-face seating and adequate lighting. Testers should be aware of the need to establish eye contact with the deaf child prior to delivering test instructions. In some cases, deaf children may require more explanation of what is needed. Additional practice items can also be helpful in ensuring that children understand the task demands before starting the test proper. Use of gesture, signs, and other cues such as writing may also be helpful in explaining what is involved.

ASSESSMENT METHODS

The assessment approach must be planned with reference to the child's age and the presence of additional difficulties. In most cases, a combination of formal and informal methods is appropriate (Jamieson & Simmons, 2011).

Language sampling is widely used for an informal assessment of language development. In the hands of a skilled language acquisition professional, a language sample can yield much useful information and provide a preliminary screen to guide the selection of further formal measures. It is important to observe children communicating in a range of contexts to establish their preferred mode of communication and the ways they adjust their communication with different conversation partners. This is particularly important for deaf children who use sign language or sign support. We mentioned previously that many are exposed to a range of communication modes from people with different levels of skill in each. As a result, deaf children are often adept at modifying their communication to meet the needs of the person with whom they are communicating. For example, the child may use signing that more closely follows spoken language (e.g., Sign Supported English) when communicating with a hearing person, particularly one who is less fluent in sign, whereas he or she may revert to full sign language structures when among deaf signers (Erting, 1988).

The skills of the communication partner are also important. An oral deaf child observed with someone who has experience of deafness may appear to be a more proficient communicator than when seen with an individual who has minimal experience. Sampling only one of these situations fails to capture the child's full communicative repertoire;

indeed, the information derived may say more about the skills of the conversation partner than the child. Language samples should be drawn from everyday communication situations and include interactions with deaf and hearing adults and children to build a full picture of the child's communication abilities. Analysis of data serves to identify an individual child's strengths and weaknesses and to guide decisions about areas requiring further assessment.

Formal assessment is needed to make comparisons with typical development, for which norm-referenced assessments are generally used. However, few assessments have been developed for deaf children, and hardly any provide deaf norms. As a result, professionals who work with deaf children rely on assessments that have been developed and standardized on children who are not deaf and who have language learning backgrounds that are very different from those of deaf children. Use of such tools can be appropriate for some deaf children, particularly those who use spoken language. Furthermore, since so many are increasingly schooled in mainstream classrooms and are expected to keep up with their hearing peers, comparison with hearing norms is relevant.

For children who use sign to communicate, hearing norms are never valid. Translating spoken language assessments into sign language, or using key word signs when carrying out a test of spoken language, is clearly a violation of the established test procedure; as a result, standard scores cannot be applied. There is a strong case for assessments to be developed specifically for sign language and standardized on deaf children (Singleton & Supalla, 2011). In some cases, a test developed for one sign language can be successfully adapted to another (Haug & Mann, 2008). However, even this entails careful consideration of the differences between the source and destination sign languages and cultures, new norms must be collected (Enns & Herman, 2011), and further work is needed to establish the psychometric qualities of the adapted test (Haug & Mann, 2008).

Developing tests of sign language acquisition also raises questions about the nature of the standardization sample—that is, whether all deaf signers or only native signers should be included. Although native signers form a more homogeneous group, sign language tests are needed for the majority of deaf children who are not native signers. Some researchers have addressed this issue by developing and piloting early versions of a test on native signers but collecting normative data on a wider sample that includes native and nonnative signers (Herman et al., 1999). Others, such as Anderson and Reilly's (2002) adaptation of the MacArthur Communicative Development Inventories (CDI; Fenson et al., 1994) to American Sign Language and Woolfe, Herman, Roy, and Woll's (2010) adaptation of the same measure to British Sign Language (BSL), have argued that measures of sign language development should be based solely on children in deaf families, since their exposure more closely approximates that of hearing children acquiring spoken languages.

There is also the separate issue of accessing sufficient numbers of participants to derive meaningful norms. It is accepted that norms in tests of spoken languages should be based on large numbers of native users, should reflect a significant proportion of the population size, and should capture normal variability. However, the population of deaf children is much smaller (2 to 3 per 1,000 births, Vohr, 2003), so it is impossible to obtain data on such large numbers. Restricting test development to native signers further reduces the population to be sampled, carrying the inherent danger that small samples are more prone to sample bias (Prezbindowski & Lederberg, 2003).

Woolfe and colleagues (2010) initially collected data from deaf parents on their deaf and hearing children's BSL vocabulary acquisition to develop BSL norms on the CDI. Although both deaf and hearing children in deaf families are considered native signers, hearing children are likely to be bilingual from an early age, whereas deaf children tend to be initially monolingual (Herman & Roy, 2000). Indeed, Woolfe and colleagues (2010) observed differences in the trajectories of BSL vocabulary development between their young deaf and hearing native signers; as a result, they presented data only on their deaf participants. They collected repeated datasets from 29 deaf children in all. Although a small number, this represented approximately 30% of the estimated number of deaf children born to deaf parents in the United Kingdom of the designated age group and as such is a much larger proportion of the potential population than is found in any other test standardization.

Considering the age of the child to be assessed, Prezbindowski and Lederberg (2003) reviewed a range of measures suitable for the earliest stages of language acquisition. Since very young deaf children cannot cooperate with formal testing, assessments that rely on observation and parental report are used, including parental diaries and checklists. Parental diaries can offer rich insights into a child's communication but require the parents to provide consistent and accurate information. This can be an issue in some cases, for instance for signing children if hearing parents do not know sufficient sign language themselves.

Parent checklists such as the CDI (Fenson et al., 1994) are more reliable and have been used successfully with deaf children. Mayne and colleagues (2000) collected normative data on the CDI based on 202 deaf children aged 8 to 37 months, and as we noted previously some sign language versions have also been developed (Anderson & Reilly, 2002; Woolfe et al., 2010).

Although parent checklists have their place in the assessment of very young children, they become less accurate for the later stages of acquisition when language is too extensive to report, in which case direct testing methods are preferable (Prezbindowski & Lederberg, 2003).

A wide range of formal assessments examining different language domains is available for use with preschool and school-aged hearing children, some of which are also used with oral deaf children. The interested reader is directed to Jamieson and Simmons (2011) for a review of formal tests that are commonly used.

Before using any language assessment developed for hearing children with an oral deaf child, testers need to review the test items to evaluate their suitability. This includes considering the phonological, morphological, and speech-readability characteristics of the language used. For example, test items that focus on morphological inflections used in English to mark plurals or tenses may lead to low scores in deaf children who are less able to detect acoustically nonsalient phonemes such as /s/. Alternatively, asking a deaf child to select "sock" from an array of toys that also includes "doll" challenges a deaf child's speech perception skills, since both words appear similar when speech-reading. In both of these examples, results may be indicative of difficulties with speech perception rather than language comprehension.

The test response mode also deserves consideration. Some tests require nonverbal responses such as picture selection; others rely on spoken responses. For deaf children with unclear speech, poor intelligibility is likely to contribute to lower test scores. Tester familiarity with the speech patterns of deaf children is therefore important for scoring accuracy.

A final consideration when carrying out a test is where to start and when to finish testing. In most tests, items are organized in order of difficulty and testing often starts at an item prescribed in the test manual and determined by the child's age. The problem for deaf children who have delayed language is that the starting point is often too high and gaps in vocabulary can make it difficult to establish basal scores (Zemann, 1999). Alternative attempts to estimate a starting point for each child may become arbitrary and can lead to further consequences. Starting the test at too low a level runs the risk of fatiguing deaf children, as they are then expected to attempt more test items than other children. Conversely, starting too high can be demotivating for a child who cannot achieve early success (Zemann, 1999).

INTERPRETING ASSESSMENT FINDINGS

Once the tester has completed administering the test, it is important to reflect on the assessment process in light of what has been said previously. When scoring results and applying hearing norms, the assessor must remember that deaf children have very different language experiences from those of hearing children; therefore, the value of hearing norms must be considered on a case-by-case basis. For children who have had a late diagnosis of deafness and/or late provision of effective amplification, standard scores should be interpreted particularly cautiously and explained within the context of the child's circumstances. When interpreting test scores, the tester must therefore review a range of factors related to the child's age at diagnosis of deafness, use of amplification, communication environment, presence of other disabilities, family factors, and so forth.

With respect to signing deaf children, for whom relatively few standardized measures exist, some researchers have presented an approach to evaluating deaf children's test performance when using nonstandardized tools. Herman and colleagues (2014) describe the development of new measures designed to investigate and characterize language impairments in their signing deaf participants. For newly developed tests of sentence repetition and vocabulary, there were no norms available, so a control group was needed to aid interpretation of assessment results. The authors describe how they matched children with suspected language impairments with a group of typically developing deaf children on variables such as age, gender, and parental hearing status. In many cases, the controls attended the same schools as the language-impaired participants, so language exposure was more closely matched. In other words, for this study, comparison of language-impaired deaf signers, almost all of whom were from hearing families, with other children who were also nonnative signers was key. In this way, the performance of language-impaired and non-impaired participants could be compared and the value of the different experimental measures determined, prior to their standardization.

Interpreting test scores initially involves comparison with others who have similar language experiences. Testers must also evaluate the extent to which assessment findings can be generalized to the child's everyday context (Easterbrooks & Baker, 2002). Formal testing is typically carried out under carefully controlled conditions to obtain the best possible picture of a child's language abilities. Yet outside the test situation, the deaf child is rarely in such optimal conditions; therefore, assessment findings may not give a true indication of how the child functions in his or her everyday learning environment.

Young deaf people themselves have described the poor acoustic conditions and difficulties listening in groups that they experience in mainstream schools (Wheeler et al., 2007). Many find it difficult to follow the complex spoken language used in class and require communication support to clarify or repeat what is said. In addition, teachers who lack experience with deaf children expect them to take advantage of incidental learning, where information is gleaned passively through overhearing what is said (Calderon & Greenberg, 2003). Hearing children readily pick up on communication that is not addressed to them and use this to support their learning. However, this is far more challenging for a deaf child, for whom communication needs to be more explicit. Therefore, the assessor's role extends beyond analyzing test scores and includes explaining how a deaf child's language profile affects his or her ability to understand and contribute to classroom learning. Teachers also need to appreciate the significance of the classroom as a language-learning environment for deaf children. With deaf-friendly classroom management, classroom conversations can support effective development of the deaf child's language acquisition. This includes carefully managing classroom discussions, keeping noise and distractions to a minimum, and repeating and rephrasing key concepts and new terms.

CONCLUSIONS AND FUTURE DIRECTIONS

This chapter has presented the case for the regular assessment of deaf children's language from the point of diagnosis and throughout the school years. Assessment is needed to monitor the early stages of language acquisition and to identify children who are failing to acquire age-appropriate language. Assessment is also necessary as the child gets older to ensure that progress is maintained and review the need for support.

Assessment is important in helping to identify deaf children who have language impairments or additional difficulties that affect their learning. In these cases, assessment findings can inform the design of interventions and reassessment serves to evaluate the efficacy of interventions.

Considerable skills and knowledge are required by testers, and particularly in the case of deaf children who sign, language assessment requires additional expertise for which a team approach is recommended.

With advances in earlier diagnosis of deafness and improvements in amplification technology, expectations for deaf children's achievements have been raised (Knoors & Marschark, 2012). The growing use of norm-referenced language assessments forces the comparison of deaf children's achievements more directly with those of hearing children, although there is also the need for skill in interpreting the results of such tests. Interpretation of assessment findings includes their generalizability to the language-learning contexts that deaf children encounter in school.

We have described the assessment of spoken and sign language development using different tests. For children who use both spoken and sign language, there is a need for measures that allow comparisons to be made between these languages. The CDI is one such measure, and work is under way at City University London and the Deafness, Cognition and Language Research Centre at University College London to develop parallel tests for spoken and sign language using the same elicited narrative test format.

There is also a need to look beyond the use of traditional assessments that generate a snapshot of a child's performance at one point in time and focus instead on the nature of the learning process. One potential approach is dynamic assessment. Employing a test–teach–retest paradigm, dynamic assessment focuses on the emerging skills a learner shows when facing a new task and the amount of support required by the assessor for optimal learning (Haywood & Tzuriel, 1992). This approach uses tasks that are slightly above the child's level, thereby enabling the examiner to target skills that are difficult for the test taker. The use of dynamic assessment procedures to detect differences in deaf children's language learning profiles is currently being investigated within a vocabulary context (Mann, Pena, & Morgan, 2014). A combination of traditional and dynamic assessments can provide professionals working with deaf children with further insights about strengths and weaknesses and guide the development of suitable interventions.

Future developments in language assessment will inevitably include the use of new technologies. Haug, Herman, and Woll (2014) describe the development of a Web-based platform to host different sign language adaptations of the same test to be delivered and standardized via the Internet. Current research techniques such as eye gaze tracking may also have a future role in language assessment of younger deaf children and those with additional disabilities.

In the hands of skilled assessors, a range of informal, formal, and dynamic testing methods is available and is increasingly on the agenda to complement existing approaches.

REFERENCES

Anderson, D., & Reilly, J. (2002). The MacArthur Communicative Development Inventory: Normative data for American Sign Language. *Journal of Deaf Studies and Deaf Education*, *7*(2), 83–119.

Archbold, S., & Mayer, C. (2012). Deaf education: The impact of cochlear implantation? *Deafness and Education International*, *14*(1), 2–15.

Boons, T., Brokx, J. P. L., Dhooge, I., Frijns, J. H. M., Peeraer, L., Vermeulen, A., . . . & van Wieringen, A. (2012). Predictors of spoken language development following pediatric cochlear implantation. *Ear & Hearing*, *33*(5), 617–639.

Calderon, R., & Greenberg, M. (2003). Social and emotional development of deaf children. In M. Marschark & P. Spencer (Eds.), *Oxford handbook of deaf studies, language and education* (pp. 177–189). New York: Oxford University Press.

Consortium for Research into Deaf Education. (2013). *CRIDE report on 2012 survey on educational provision for deaf children: UK-wide summary.* Available at http://www.batod.org.uk/content/resources/survey/CRIDE2013.pdf (accessed May 5, 14).

Cupples, L., Ching, T. Y. C., Crowe, K., Seeto, M., Leigh, G., Street, L., . . . & Thomson, J. (2014). Outcomes of 3-year-old children with hearing loss and different types of additional disabilities. *Journal of Deaf Studies and Deaf Education, 19*(1), 20–39.

De Raeve, L., Baerts, J., Colleye, E., & Croux, E. (2012). Changing schools for the deaf: Updating the educational setting for deaf children in the 21st century, a big challenge. *Deafness and Education International, 14*(1), 48–59.

Dettman, S. J., Pinder, D., Briggs, R. J., Dowell, R. C., & Leigh, J. R. (2007). Communication development in children who receive the cochlear implant younger than 12 months: Risks versus benefits. *Ear& Hearing, 28*, 11S–18S.

Easterbrooks, S. R., & Baker, S. (2002). *Language learning in children who are deaf and hard of hearing: Multiple pathways.* Boston, MA: Allyn & Bacon.

Edwards, L. (2010). Learning disabilities in deaf and hard of hearing children. In M. Marschark & P. Spencer (Eds.), *Oxford handbook of deaf studies, language and education* (vol. 2, pp. 425–438). New York: Oxford University Press.

Enns, C., & Herman, R. (2011). Adapting the Assessing British Sign Language Development Receptive Skills Test into American Sign Language. *Journal of Deaf Studies and Deaf Education, 16*, 362–374.

Erting, C. J. (1988). Acquiring linguistic and social identity: Interactions of deaf children with a hearing teacher and a deaf adult. In M. Strong (Ed.), *Language learning and deafness* (pp. 192–219). Cambridge: Cambridge University Press.

Fellinger, J., Holzinger, D., & Pollard, R. (2012). The mental health of deaf people. *Lancet, 379*, 1037–1044.

Fenson, L., Dale, P. S., Reznick, J. S., Bates, E., Thal, D., & Pethick, S. J. (1994). Variability in early communicative development. *Monographs of the Society for Research in Child Development, 59*, 1–173.

Geers, A. E., Strube, M., Tobey, E. A., Pisoni, D., & Moog, J. S. (2011). Epilogue: Factors contributing to long-term outcomes of cochlear implantation in early childhood. *Ear & Hearing, 32*(1), 84S–92S.

Gilbertson, M., & Kamhi, A. G. (1995). Novel word learning in children with hearing impairment. *Journal of Speech & Hearing Research, 38*(3), 630–642.

Green, D. R., Gaffney, M., Devine, O., & Grosse, S. D. (2007). Determining the effect of newborn hearing screening legislation: An analysis of state hearing screening rates. *Public Health Reports,;122*(2), 198–205.

Harris, M., & Terlektsi, E. (2011). Reading and spelling abilities of deaf adolescents with cochlear implants and hearing aids. *Journal of Deaf Studies and Deaf Education, 16*(1), 24–34.

Haug, T., Herman, R. & Woll, B. (2014). Constructing an online test framework using the example of a sign language receptive skills test. *Deafness and Education International.* doi: http:/dx.doi.org/10:1179/1557069X 14Y.0000000035 (accessed April 2, 2014).

Haug, T., & Mann, W. (2008). Developing tests for sign language assessment—A review of common problems and other related issues. *Journal of Deaf Studies and Deaf Education, 13*(1), 138–147.

Hawker, K., Ramirez-Inscoe, J., Bishop, D. V. M., Twomey, T., O'Donoghue, G. M., & Moore, D. R. (2008). Disproportionate language impairment in children using cochlear implants. *Ear & Hearing, 29*(3), 467–471.

Haywood, C., & Tzuriel, D. (1992). *Interactive assessment.*New York: Springer.

Herman, R. (1998). The need for an assessment of deaf children's signing skills. *Deafness & Education, 22*(3), 3–7.

Herman, R., Grove, N., Holmes, S., Morgan, G., Sutherland, H., & Woll, B. (2004). *Assessing BSL development: Production test (narrative skills).* City University London.

Herman, R., Holmes, S., & Woll, B. (1999). *Assessing British Sign Language development: Receptive Skills Test.* Gloucestershire, UK: Forest Bookshop.

Herman, R., Rowley, K., Marshall, C., Mason, K., Atkinson, J., Woll, B. & Morgan, G. (2014). Profiling SLI in deaf children who are sign language users. In D. Quinto-Pozos (Ed.), *Multilingual aspects of signed language communication and disorder* (pp. 45–69). Bristol, UK: Multilingual Matters.

Herman, R., & Roy, P. (2000). The influence of child hearing status and type of exposure to BSL on BSL acquisition. *Proceedings of the 1999 Child Language Seminar, City University, London, 1,* 116–122.

Hermans, D., Knoors, H., & Verhoeven, L. (2010). Assessment of sign language development: The case of deaf children in the Netherlands. *Journal of Deaf Studies and Deaf Education, 15,* 107–119.

Holt, R. F., & Kirk, K. I. (2005). Speech and language development in cognitively delayed children with cochlear implants. *Ear & Hearing, 26,* 132–148.

Huang, H., Chiang, S., & Shiau, Y. (2013). The universal newborn hearing screening program of Taipei City. *International Journal of Pediatric Otorhinolaryngology, 77*(10), 1734–1737.

Jamieson, J. R., & Simmons, N. R. (2011). Formal and informal approaches to the language assessment of deaf children. In M. Marschark & P. Spencer (Eds.), *Oxford handbook of deaf studies, language & education* (vol. 2, pp. 290–309). New York: Oxford University Press.

Knoors, H., & Marschark, M. (2012). Language planning for the 21st century: Revisiting bilingual language policy for deaf children. *Journal of Deaf Studies and Deaf Education, 17*(3), 291–305.

Krauss, K. M., Heider, C. C., Sierra, M. G., & Ribalta, G. L. (2013). Strategies to improve follow-up of the universal newborn hearing screening program. *Revista de Otorinolaringologia y Cirugia de Cabeza y Cuello, 73*(2). doi.org/10.4067/S0718-48162013000200005 (accessed April 2, 2014).

Kyle, J. G. (1990). *BSL development: Final report.* Centre for Deaf Studies, Bristol.

Lederberg, A. R., Schick, B., & Spencer, P. E. (2013). Language and literacy development of deaf and hard-of-hearing children: Successes and challenges. *Developmental Psychology, 49*(1), 15–30.

Leigh, J., Dettman, S., Dowell, R. & Briggs, R. (2012). Communication development in children who receive a cochlear implant by 12 months of age. *Otology & Neurotology, 34*(3), 443–450.

Mann, W., Pena, E., & Morgan, G. (2014). Exploring the use of dynamic assessment with deaf children: Two case studies. *Journal of Communication Disorders.* doi: 10.1016/j.comdis.2014.05.002.

Marschark, M. (2002). Foundations of communication and the emergence of language in deaf children. In G. Morgan & B. Woll (Eds.), *Directions in sign language acquisition—trends in language acquisition research* (pp. 1–28). Amsterdam: John Benjamins Publishing Company.

Marschark, M., Schick, B., & Spencer, P. E. (2006). Understanding sign language development of deaf children. In B. Schick, M. Marschark, & P. E. Spencer (Eds.), *Advances in the sign language development of deaf children* (pp. 3–19). New York: Oxford University Press.

Mason, K., Rowley, K., Marshall, C.R., Atkinson, J., Herman, R., Woll, B., & Morgan, G. (2010). Identifying specific language impairment in British Sign Language: Implications for theory and practice. *British Journal of Developmental Psychology, 28*, 33–49.

Mayberry, R. I. (2007). When timing is everything: Age of first-language acquisition effects on second-language learning. *Applied Psycholinguistics, 28*(3), 537–549.

Mayer, C., & Leigh, G. (2010). The changing context for sign bilingual education programs: Issues in language and the development of literacy. *International Journal of Bilingualism and Bilingual Education, 13*(2), 175–186.

Mayne, A. M., Yoshinaga-Itano, C., Sedey, A. L., & Carey, A. (2000). Expressive vocabulary development of infants and toddlers who are deaf or hard of hearing. *Volta Review, 100*(5), 1–28.

Metzger, D., Pezier, T. F., & Veraguth, D. (2013). Evaluation of Universal Newborn Hearing Screening in Switzerland 2012 and follow-up data for Zurich. *Swiss Medical Weekly, 143*, w13905. doi: 10.4414/smw.2013.13905.

Morgan, G., Herman, R., & Woll, B. (2007). Language impairments in sign language: Breakthroughs and puzzles. *International Journal of Language and Communication Disorders, 42*(1), 97–105.

Morgan, G., & Woll, B. (Eds.). (2002). *Directions in sign language acquisition—trends in language acquisition research.* Amsterdam: John Benjamins Publishing Company.

Mukari, S., Ling, L. & Ghani, H. (2007). Educational performance of pediatric cochlear implant recipients in mainstream classes. *International Journal of Pediatric Otorhinolaryngology, 71*, 231–40.

Murphy, J., & Dodd, B. (2010). A diagnostic challenge: Language difficulties and hearing impairment in a secondary-school student from a non-English-speaking background. *Child Language Teaching and Therapy, 26*, 207–220.

Newport, E. L. (1990). Maturational constraints on language learning. *Cognitive Science, 14*, 11–28.

Norbury, C. F., Bishop, D. V. M., & Briscoe, J. (2001). Production of English finite verb morphology: A comparison of SLI and mild-moderate hearing impairment. *Journal of Speech, Language & Hearing Research, 44*, 165–178.

Pimperton, H., & Kennedy, C. R. (2012). The impact of early identification of permanent childhood hearing impairment on speech and language outcomes. *Archives of Disease in Childhood, 97*, 648–653.

Prezbindowski, A. K., & Lederberg, A. R. (2003). Vocabulary assessment of deaf and hard-of-hearing children from infancy through the preschool years. *Journal of Deaf Studies and Deaf Education, 8*(4), 383–400.

Quinto-Pozos, D., Forber-Pratt, A., & Singleton, J. L. (2011). Do developmental communication disorders exist in the signed modality? Perspectives from professionals. *Language, Speech, and Hearing Services in Schools, 42*, 423–443.

Rees, R., Mahon, M., Herman, R., Newton, C., & Craig, G. (2014). Communication interventions for families of pre-school deaf children in the UK. *Deafness & Education International*, doi: 10.1179/1557069X14Y.0000000043

Reilly, J., & Anderson, D. (2002). The acquisition of non-manual morphology in ASL. In G. Morgan & B. Woll (Eds.), *Current developments in the study of signed language acquisition* (pp. 159–181). Amsterdam: John Benjamins Publishing Company.

Sarant, J. Z., Holt, C. M., Dowell, R. C., Rickards, F. W., & Blamey P. J. (2009). Spoken language development in oral preschool children with permanent childhood deafness. *Journal of Deaf Studies and Deaf Education, 14*(2), 205–217.

Schick, B., Marschark, M., & Spencer, P. E. (Eds.) (2006). *Advances in sign language development in deaf children.* New York: Oxford University Press.

Singleton, J., & Supalla, S. (2011). Assessing children's proficiency in natural signed languages. In M. Marschark & P. Spencer (Eds.), *The Oxford handbook of deaf studies, language and education* (vol. 2, pp. 306–322). New York: Oxford University Press.

Spencer, P. M., & Marschark, M. (2006). *Advances in the spoken language development of deaf and hard of hearing children.* New York: Oxford University Press.

Tomblin, B., Records, N., Buckwater, P. Zhang, X., Smith, E., & O'Brien, M., (1997). Prevalence of specific language impairment in kindergarten children. *Journal of Speech, Language and Hearing Research, 40,* 1245–1260.

Uziel, A. S., Sillon, M., & Vieu, A. (2007). Ten-year follow-up of a consecutive series of children with multichannel cochlear implants. *Otology and Neurotology, 28,* 615–628.

Vohr, B. (2003). Overview: Infants and children with hearing loss—Part I. *Mental Retardation & Developmental Disabilities Research Reviews, 9,* 62–64.

Wheeler, A., Archbold, S., Gregory, S. & Skipp, A. (2007). Cochlear implants: The young peoples' perspective. *Journal of Deaf Studies and Deaf Education, 12*(3), 303–316.

Woolfe, T., Herman, R., Roy, P. & Woll, B. (2010). Early vocabulary development in deaf native signers: A British Sign Language Adaptation of the Communicative Development Inventories. *Journal of Child Psychology and Psychiatry, 51,* 322–331.

Zemann, B. (1999). The applicability of the test of word knowledge of hearing impaired children. *Independent Studies and Capstones.* Paper 515. Program in Audiology and Communication Sciences, Washington University School of Medicine. Available at http://digitalcommons.wustl.edu/pacs_capstones/515 (accessed April 2, 2014).

10

Issues of Access and Validity in Standardized Academic Assessments for Students Who Are Deaf or Hard of Hearing

Stephanie W. Cawthon

Creating evidence-based practice in deaf education typically focuses on methods of instruction, ranging broadly from bilingual education models to interactive writing curricula for preschoolers. There is also a focus on educational structures that surround and support classroom activities, addressing issues about school philosophies, professional credentialing, language modalities, cultural context, and degree of inclusion with hearing peers. In the current climate of determining "what works" and "accountability" for student learning outcomes, a third area of evidence-based practice in deaf education has emerged: assessment and testing (Rieke, Lazarus, Thurlow, & Dominguez, 2012). As with instruction and educational structures, assessment and testing with students who are deaf or hard of hearing (DHH) requires careful consideration of what it means to be effective and successful with this population specifically.

This chapter will discuss the evidence base for accessible standardized academic assessment with DHH students. The focus will be on two key concepts: access and validity. Because the majority of standardized assessments are developed for students who are hearing and have spoken language as their first language, there are sometimes barriers to full access to test content for DHH students (see also Leigh & Crowe, Chapter 4 in this volume). Test developers and test administrators both play a role in decreasing the barriers, and there is an emerging research base on best practices in this area (Fairbairn & Fox, 2009; Kopriva, Emick, Hipolito-Delgado, & Cameron, 2007; Sireci, Scarpati, & Li, 2005). Issues of access and fairness are twinned with the need for test score validity (Messick, 1989; Shaftel, Yang, Glasnapp, & Poggio, 2005). To have a valid score in tests of student achievement is to be able to say, within a degree of certainty, what that score represents (e.g., that a student is proficient in multiplying fractions or knowing the different components of an ecosystem). Furthermore, validity in standardized testing is also concerned with comparability of scores. In other words, the same score on an item from two different students needs to represent similar levels of knowledge. Without confirmation that this is the case, it is impossible to know how to meaningfully interpret both what they mean as far as a measure of student knowledge and what response, such as a change in instructional approach, might be appropriate.

Before delving into specific features of an assessment that may increase access to test item content for DHH students, it is first important to consider the physical context of most standardized assessments. The traditional format for most standardized assessments is using paper and pencil, either with responses written directly into a booklet for hand grading (as in an essay exam) or on an answer sheet for electronic scoring (for multiple-choice items). Within the past decade or so there has been an increase in computer-based assessments, either in standalone computers or using a Web-based system. This chapter will refer to these as "next-generation" assessments.

One of the advantages of the next-generation approach to testing is that it allows for very tight control of how test items are presented while at the same time allowing for greater flexibility in how individual students experience the test (Ketterlin-Geller & Tindal, 2008; Segers & Verhoeven, Chapter 21 in this volume). For example, font size can be individually tailored with little difficulty if a student wishes to have larger or smaller font for ease of text legibility. However, the range of font sizes could be limited to only those that do not disrupt other test item features, such as tables or figures, for which alignment of text to graphic may affect how a student interprets the item content. The degree of control reflects the need to ensure validity, while the flexibility to choose font size reflects the principle of access.

The remainder of this chapter addresses strategies for increasing access to test content while maintaining the validity of test scores, with an eye toward work specifically related to DHH students. Some of the strategies focus on changing how the test is administered, typically referred to as providing test accommodations. Many DHH students are eligible to use accommodations, and there is a range of accommodations that may be effective in improving the fairness of the test for all students (Cawthon & the Online Research Lab, 2006). Other strategies focus on the test items themselves, looking to reduce barriers by altering the way the test item content is presented (Abedi, 2006). Although this process is more intensive, it does prevent some of the ad hoc alteration of the test experience that is inherent in an assessment accommodation approach. Regardless of which approach is taken, there are implications for how test scores are used when there are changes from the original version. This chapter will conclude with a discussion of important considerations to take into account when balancing access and validity of testing for DHH students.

TEST ACCOMMODATIONS

Policies

In the United States, the impetus for test accommodations and related policies came from two sources: civil rights legislation and standards-based educational reforms. Civil rights legislation mandated the full inclusion of individuals with disabilities into society, including education, most commonly in the form of inclusion into classroom instruction. Standards-based reform movements addressed inclusion from a different angle, focusing on what students were learning; if schools were being evaluated based on student achievement, assessments needed to include students with disabilities. Adaptations to classroom instruction paved the way for adaptations to testing, which in turn paved the way for inclusion in large-scale tests of standardized assessments used for "high-stakes" purposes.

High-stakes decisions are those where the test score is used to determine something of consequence about the test taker, such as whether he or she is ready for the next grade level or entrance into a training program. In a clinical context, the score can be used to diagnose a condition or disorder. High-stakes decisions also apply to school systems, such as when a school receives a rating based on its student's proficiency rates. Funding mechanisms can be tied to scores, such as a teacher's bonus pay or restrictions on flexibility in spending for a school or regional administrative body. In short, having an accurate test score has implications that matter a great deal.

Assessment accommodations policies reflect this historical context as well as the need to balance access and validity (Rieke et al., 2012). In the United States, policies for assessment are often determined at a state level, parallel with many other educational decisions such as curriculum and teaching credentialing. Each state has its own jurisdiction, therefore, on how tests are developed, how DHH students are included in large-scale assessments, what accommodations are permitted, and what format (e.g., computer-based assessments) is available for administration and scoring. These multiple approaches to assessment policy provide some variability in examples of how one might approach the challenging balance between access and validity.

Policies on accommodations focus on whether they change the difficulty of the test (Cawthon, 2007). For elementary and secondary education, assessments are frequently broken down into content areas, such as subtests for math (computation, problem solving), language arts (vocabulary, reading comprehension), science (factual, procedural knowledge), and history (events, government). Accommodations policies distinguish between accommodations that are allowed to be used without restriction and those that cannot be used or involve a change in how the score is used. These designations sometimes differ by content area—for example, an accommodation allowed on a science section but not a language arts section of the test. If the accommodation is used without restriction, it is viewed as both giving access and having minimal threat to the validity of the test score. These scores are rarely flagged or noted as different from test scores without accommodations (in fact, it can be challenging to track whether they have been used!). In contrast, other policies refer to an accommodation as "allowed but with restriction," meaning that either the score is flagged or that it will be dropped from any aggregation of scores from that test for reporting purposes. This policy emphasizes the need for access—in other words, that the student needs the accommodation to take the test—but places caution on assumption of validity. Although this approach acknowledges the challenge of this balance, it also raises questions about how scores are used, a subject discussed in the conclusion section of this chapter.

Generally accepted accommodations for DHH students that come without restriction include giving the student additional time (either time and a half or double time, less so for unlimited time); having someone interpret, read aloud, or otherwise paraphrase the directions for a test (in either an oral or signed language modality); and allowing the student to take the test in a separate room, or with frequent breaks, or over the space of several testing periods. These accommodations are seen to remove barriers that are not essential to the test item tasks, directly, and are thus generally not controversial when used in practice. Although implementation can still be a challenge at the local level (e.g., scheduling testing over several days for an individual student when the majority of the students test within a shorter period of time), when it comes to the actual content of the test, very little is changed.

Other accommodations frequently used by DHH students either fall into the gray area of "allowed with restrictions" or, for some subject areas, are not allowed at all. Most of these restricted accommodations center on language and communication, and thus hold special relevance for the DHH population. Key accommodations and applicable research findings are summarized in the next section.

A Focus on Literacy, Language, and Communication

When thinking about issues of access and validity in standardized testing for DHH students, the emphasis is often on literacy, language, and communication. In academic assessment, particularly in a school environment, students must read a test item to answer the question. There are times when reading the test item is the target skill, such as in tests of reading comprehension, and times when reading is an access skill, or a part of how a student engages with the material but not the specific skill of interest on the test. For example, a word problem in science or math may include a significant reading component, representing the test construct in written text, with a list of potential responses also in written form.

Current dialogue about test accessibility focuses on distinguishing between test items where decoding text, specifically, is a target or access skill (Ketterlin-Geller, 2008). When thinking about accommodations and their use, the goal is typically to remove barriers that are associated with reading as an access skill but to maintain test content and format when reading is associated with the target skill. Because many DHH students have different language and literacy proficiency levels than their hearing peers, in some cases reading test items may place these students at a disadvantage in accessing the target construct. In cases where reading is considered more of an access skill than a target skill, accommodations that change the linguistic representation of the item may be considered. More specifically, accommodations used for test directions, such as a sign language interpreter, read aloud, or other type of translation/transliteration into a visual modality, could be used for the test items themselves.

From a conceptual point of view, and from an access point of view, changing the linguistic representation of a test item when reading is an access skill would not seem to pose a threat to the validity of the test item. Questions of interpreter quality and standardization of translations across students aside (more on this later), one would expect to see differences in student performance between standard (i.e., reading the test item) and accommodated (i.e., different linguistic representation) versions of similar tests, but only if the different linguistic representations resulted in different levels of information retrieval and higher-order processing (Marschark, Sapere, Convertino, Mayer, Wauters, & Sarchet, 2009). Furthermore, if sign language reduces the reading as an access skill, one would expect to see improvements and not decreases in students' scores in the interpreted condition. If reading *is* the target skill, from a validity point of view, tests should be accommodated only if the inclusion of an interpreter does not change the difficulty of the test items and result in scores that over- or underrepresent what students know, particularly in comparison with previous tests of student knowledge without the accommodation. Whether or not scores increase in accommodated conditions thus depends on several factors, including the literacy and sign language proficiency of the student, the degree to which a sign language representation results in different levels of information retrieval and processing than reading, and the extent to which English literacy is an access or a target skill in the assessment.

Research findings in this area are inconclusive but point toward some interesting considerations of issues of access and validity in standardized assessments (Qi & Mitchell, 2012). From a user standpoint, students sometimes prefer test administration contexts that more closely align with full communication models; Russell, Kavanaugh, Master, Higgins, & Hoffman, 2009). It is possible that students are more engaged and less stressed about performing up to their potential when the language of the test is the same as the language of instruction. There may also be cultural assumptions embedded in how the test items are presented that are different when created in sign language versus text (Sligar, Cawthon, Morere, & Moxley, in press). When seeking comparability of scores across students, it is important to be aware that test item features may contain culturally sensitive aspects that differentially affect DHH students versus their hearing peers. The issue is whether there are cultural assumptions that do not align with those of the student, thus serving as distractors because the assumptions are unfamiliar to the student or have different meanings than intended by the test item. Finally, questions of student motivation and teacher perception of fairness, while largely unanswered in the research literature on assessment for DHH students, may be worth considering when making decisions about accommodation use in the classroom (Cawthon et al., 2006).

The expectation that test scores rise when students take assessments with the linguistic accommodation is largely unsupported in the research (Cawthon & Leppo, 2013; Marschark et al., 2006). There are two sides to this finding. First, from an access perspective, if there is no harm done in providing accommodations, and the content is still presented in a conceptually rigorous manner, there might not need to be strict controls on the linguistic form of the test item. This finding is in contrast to what is suggested about the differential effects of sign versus text-based modalities in instruction—that there does not appear to be a sign advantage in information retention from students who have the literacy skills to access the material in English form (Marschark et al., 2006; Stinson, Elliot, Kelly, & Liu, 2009). From a validity perspective, there is a bit of a "black box" in that there is little research that directly measures what changes in terms of information retrieval, response time, mental representation of the construct, formulation of strategies to solve the problem, and articulation of response. In other words, the field does not really know what changes and what does not, and whether target constructs remain the same in accommodated and unaccommodated items in terms of what the test is asking students to do. One assumes that changes (or no changes) in scores indicate something meaningful about the presence or absence of accommodations, but the results do not have close enough indicators of changes in what students are showing about what they know under different conditions. From a validity perspective, therefore, not knowing what the changes might be leads toward a more conservative approach of limiting the use of linguistic accommodations (Keiffer, Lesaux, Rivera, & Francis, 2009).

In any implementation, whether in the classroom or for research, a great deal of attention must be paid to the quality of the language-based accommodation. Interpreters need to have a high standard of both technical and linguistic expertise in order to maintain the goals of access and validity in a standardized testing context (Antia, 2007). In their analysis of educational interpreter skills, Schick and colleagues (2006) found that only 40% of the interpreters in the study had adequate skills to provide deaf students with full access. The quality of interpreters in the field varies greatly, due in part to inconsistent guidelines on prerequisites for educational interpreters as well as the challenges of interpreting content that the professional has not seen before the test day (for test security purposes). Creating a high-quality visual language modality testing experience that at the same time reflects the local language use is one of the biggest challenges for large-scale testing with students dispersed often across schools and districts a significant distance apart. Logistics and financial and timing considerations affect how language-based accommodations are implemented for students during standardized testing periods.

Computer-based accommodations are a part of presumed future test delivery for all students. Language-based accommodations can take many forms in a digital format, including pop-up word definitions when a student hovers over a word or embedded sign representations of the test item stem and response options. In the United States, a few states have begun work in implementing video-based assessments for DHH students, and the new national curriculum initiatives have afforded the opportunity to expand these early adopters to a national approach. The next-generation assessments employ computer adaptive techniques as well as customizable assessment delivery formats using a range of access strategies. (For examples of assessment items, see the Guidelines for Accessible Assessment Project at http://www.measuredprogress.org/gaap, the ONPAR assessments at http://onpar.us/, or the Institute for Innovative Assessment at http://iiassessment.wceruw.org/research/.) Many strategies, such as a sign-interpreted test item, a calculator for basic computation, or a glossary for access vocabulary, are being built directly into the assessment platform. This format creates a more proactive, less reactive model of accessibility for students who have traditionally used accommodations. The next section discusses test item features that, in addition to language-based accommodations, work to address issues of access and validity for DHH students.

TEST ITEM FEATURES

Accessible item development is a bottom-up approach to improving access that, from the beginning, aims to develop a test system that embodies both rigor and equity. Much of the foundation for current practices in item development, including those for next-generation assessments, draws from principles of flexible testing and universal design. When it draws from the research literature on how item features interact with student characteristics, accessible item development is essentially overlapping good test construction and takes into account differential approaches that fit a diverse test-taking student population (Kettler, Rodriguez, Bolt, Elliott, Beddow, & Kurtz, 2011). While it may be possible to tweak test item features from an established standard, most of the previous attempts at changing test items were made not holistically from the beginning but after the original "mold" had been established. For example, suppose an original, standard-version science word problem contains extensive passive tense and low-frequency vocabulary terms (words that are not related to the target construct). A revision to this item might take the original structure and change the sentence order and structure to provide the prompt in active tense. The revision might also identify synonyms that students may be more likely to know, especially students with less exposure to English.

The closer the process of focusing on the accessibility of items is to the identification of test item constructs and tasks, the more integrated accessibility considerations can be into the full testing paradigm. In other words, how students access items needs to be addressed at the same time as decisions about what to measure. If test developers know that students with a broad range of proficiency in academic English will be participating in the assessment, test items might start with active-tense, high-frequency vocabulary instead of requiring a revision round to address these elements that may serve as barriers to students accessing target content in the test item.

Policies surrounding item modification, as this process is sometimes called, have shifted dramatically over the past two decades (Elliott & Roach, 2007). As standardization of academic achievement moved from a focus on students in general education to include all students (the mantra "all means all"), testing systems for students with disabilities moved away from individualized, checklist or portfolio demonstrations of student knowledge into alternate or modified formats of the original standardized assessment. In an effort to make the standardized assessments accessible for students who could not meaningfully participate because of a disability, assessment policies expanded to include tests that were shorter, used simpler language prompts, or tested on a more limited range or depth of student knowledge within the target content area (e.g., DePascale, 2010; Kopriva, 2008). While these alternate tests scores were not assumed to be comparable with scores taken using the standard tests, it was clear what was being measured and how the alternate test allowed for inferences about student proficiency.

Next-generation assessments seek to build many of these alternate assessment components into the main testing system framework, focusing on individual item characteristics. For example, multiple-choice responses typically have a question stem and four responses, one correct answer and three distractors. The distractors are designed to capture student responses that use incorrect (but relevant) strategies (vs. choosing a response at random). Because students might, if they are unsure of their response, consider each response option, three distractors may have a higher level of work (cognitive load) than two distractors. The number of distractors can thus play a role in how accessible an item might be, particularly for students who may have dyslexia or attention-deficit/hyperactivity disorder (ADHD). For DHH students who also have fluency issues or ADHD, reducing the number of distractors may be a good strategy to reduce unnecessary cognitive load. Next-generation systems can set these options automatically depending on a student's individual profile without needing to have a completely separate version of the test.

Research on item features and accessibility for DHH students include both linguistic and nonlinguistic components (Cawthon, Carr, Leppo & Kopriva, 2013). Linguistic components often focus on reducing the amount of text that is used as an access skill, either by providing pictures or by simplifying the written text itself. These modifications may be in addition to the use of interpreters who then translate the items into sign language, but this combination has yet to be explored in the research literature. Most nonlinguistic components focus on adding visual components that add function such as organizing information in a table, graph, or other tool. As with accommodations, item features are typically investigated as a set, or as part of a process where more than one change has occurred between the original form and the adapted form (one exception is discussed below). It is not possible to infer from the literature how one specific item feature may increase or decrease access and validity over another (Sireci, Scarpati, & Li, 2005). Measures of how access may have changed rate items in terms of their complexity often cannot provide specific guidance as to potential changes in the validity of the interpretation of the test score. Thinking about item adaptation and access is thus, at this point, a holistic process (Kopriva, 2008).

The linguistic complexity of text in written items is one feature that has been systematically identified as a possible mechanism for increasing access while maintaining test validity (Abedi, 2006, 2011). Linguistic complexity includes the syntactic structure of sentences, vocabulary and its familiarity to the test taker, and ambiguous referents and other potentially confusing aspects of the task setup. The majority of the work in this area has been done when thinking about test accessibility for English language learners, a population with some similarities to but also some important differences than DHH students (Abedi, 2006, 2011; Cawthon, Highley, & Leppo, 2011; Kopriva, 2008). Research has consistently found that low-frequency vocabulary words (that are not related to the target construct) make test items more difficult for students, particularly in math. When developing test items in written form, it is important to ensure that the word problem setup and context do not require the use of words that are unfamiliar to students.

There are cases, however, where simplifying the text may be a disservice to students. When math test items are more complex and include multiple steps, sometimes there is a need for complete explanations of what students are expected to do. If the student is accessing the linguistic context of a test item in his or her first language, or in his or her more proficient language, it may be more relevant to the student to provide a full linguistic representation of the item than to translate a simplified or reduced-complexity version of the original item. In other words, the linguistic accessibility of the item depends, in part, on the student's language proficiency. If the student needs additional language supports to understand the task, it should be a priority to use the native or first language to explain the context of the test item, and in a robust manner that represents the rigor of the test item. In some cases, next-generation assessments offer a more interactive way of representing knowledge (e.g., having students move objects on a computer screen with multiple potential outcomes instead of solving for an equation with a single answer). It appears that these test items are more demanding than the static paper-and-pencil items traditionally used in the field, requiring as full an explanation as possible. In other words, if complex language is needed to represent the cognitive level of the task, that should take priority over reducing the reading level of the test item.

Bringing the conversation full circle, there are some situations in which an item feature such as linguistic complexity may interact with an accommodation (Cawthon, Kaye, Lockhart, & Beretvas, 2012). An interaction in this sense means that the impact of a test item feature changes depending on the presence or absence of an accommodation. This may mean that having an accommodation exacerbates the difficulty of the item due to that item feature, but in most situations, the hope is that accommodations amplify a positive effect of the item feature on student performance. One study examined the degree to which the relationship between the linguistic complexity of a test item and student performance was moderated by the presence of different types of accommodations, including additional time, separate test settings, frequent breaks, and presentation of the test by a familiar staff person (Cawthon et al., 2012). For math, students who had the accommodations showed stronger test performance on the highly linguistically complex items than those who did not. While this study was conducted examining student performance for students with learning disabilities and not DHH students (the sample size was too small), it raises an important consideration when looking at different strategies for increasing accessibility in a next-generation test that may combine accommodations (e.g., sign embedded video) and test item adaptations (e.g., click-and-drag items that rely less on text and more on procedural demonstration of understanding). While these combinations may make determination of access and validity more difficult, they do afford educators with ways to tailor test-taking experiences to meet individual students' needs.

IMPLICATIONS IN A DATA-DRIVEN WORLD

Issues of access and validity now count more than ever in educational assessment. Whether or not a student had equal access to the targeted test item construct is not just an issue of measurement but is an issue of justice when high-stakes decisions are tied to resultant test scores. Only valid interpretations of what a student's test score signifies about his or her knowledge and proficiency in content areas can lead to appropriate and effective evaluation of the learning process. High-stakes measurement is high stakes not only for students but also for schools, school systems, and test developers. This section considers the implications of our discussion on accommodations and test item adaptations within the context of how scores are used in high-stakes decision making in education.

Aggregation and Disaggregation of Scores

Two main assumptions about an inclusive assessment policy are relevant to the discussion in this chapter: (a) that the goal is to include all students to the greatest extent possible with scores that are comparable measures of student knowledge even with potential accommodations or item adaptations and (b) that once these scores are included, scores of subgroups of students can be compared to better understand parities or disparities in student achievement and the school system's effectiveness in supporting diverse student populations. If tests are both accessible and valid at the item and student level, there is a greater chance that they will yield the kind of data that can be used at the subgroup or overall level. The degree to which one can verify the accessibility of target test constructs and the validity of the test scores directly influences the strength of inferences made at these more global levels.

One of the greatest challenges in deaf education is the lack of information about deaf students' performance on large-scale assessments. Unless there are sufficient numbers of DHH students in the test sample *and* the agency is willing to release this information separately, most tests of student proficiency, at best, group DHH students in with all "students with disabilities" (Cawthon, 2007). Without this specific information it is almost impossible to identify, on a broader scale, what types of accommodations work for which DHH students, and why. Recall that the use of accommodations may not be flagged at all if they are considered not to be a threat to the validity of the score.

Aggregation of scores thus takes on special meaning within the field, beyond that of an individual student's progress through school or an evaluation of a teacher's effectiveness. Because hearing loss among youth has a low incidence, these students are often spread across multiple education agencies and educational structures, often with different instructional approaches and student demographics. What the field gains by aggregation of scores, at least within defined contexts with "groups" that are specific to DHH students, is a snapshot of how students are doing on standardized tests of achievement. The critical point here is thus the group, or the unit of analysis. When DHH students are included with all other "students with disabilities" (as is usually the case), one learns very little about DHH students. However, when DHH students are considered separately, as their own group, it is possible to learn a great deal. Yet such disaggregation can only happen at a higher level or at an organizational level that has enough students to make a meaningful inference about what that group looks like in terms of achievement. In some contexts, there are figures that represent real population statistics. For example, a single school or education region, or even countries that do a national assessment of all students, can measure student proficiency for the overall population of DHH students. In other contexts that do not measure student achievement using a common metric, including the United States, there are sampled estimates of student achievement, drawing on a proportion of the entire population to provide estimates (but not exact counts) of student outcomes at the national level. Each approach has its own strengths and weaknesses, often reflecting the size, coherence, and resources of the local region. The extent to which decisions about accommodations affect inclusion of test scores in accountability systems will have an impact on how much the field knows about achievement for DHH students.

Adaptive Testing and Accommodations Provision

One of the issues in the current implementation of accommodations is that it is unclear when students do or do not use them in testing situations. Having accommodations available is not the same thing as using them, and this gray area may be one reason why there have not been conclusive findings about the effect of accommodations on test scores. Some of the next-generation computer-based assessments directly parallel the paper-and-pencil formats, with all students following the same sequence of items, whereas others use an adaptive approach to measurement. When a student answers a question in an adaptive model, the degree of difficulty of the next question depends, in part, on his or her response to the previous question. An adaptive strategy provides students with questions that are closer to their proficiency level, limiting the frustration that students may experience if they have items that are far outside of their knowledge base. Many standardized paper-and-pencil formats, in contrast, provide test questions in a set order (even if different items are randomly assigned to students to increase test security). When there is a concern about grade-level testing because the student has not received instruction in that area, adaptive testing can result in more reliable information because it has the potential to more closely represent what the students actually know. If judgments are to be made about what students know, the interpretation of a test score from an adaptive test may also increase over a standard linear approach.

One of the implications here for next-generation assessments is that actual accommodations use may look very different from student to student. Because of the adaptive nature of the tests, the timing of the accommodations would vary among students even if they are in the same classroom. Also, depending on the item, accommodations may need to be switched on or off at an item level, depending on the threat to validity. Furthermore, it is feasible that students with strong literacy skills will not choose to use the accommodations, as suggested in previous studies (Marschark, Pelz, Convertino, Sapere, Arndt, & Seewagen, 2005). This may be due to the additional time that it might take to view a video of the item in sign language, slowing down students who may not feel that it adds information they do not already glean from the written version of the test item. There is also some evidence (Abedi, 2011) that students who use the accommodations are those with low literacy and low content knowledge skills, but because the testing system typically requires that they be tested on grade level, the impact of a language translation is not as evident (floor effect) as it would be if one could compare their performance on tests that are closer to their proficiency areas. In other words, the "boost" from a test in sign language may be stronger when there is a greater opportunity for growth in performance because the level of the content on the test is closer to their actual proficiency level and not that of their same-age peers. This may be a rationale for teachers to use language-translated tests when assessments are not high stakes, and to see whether students' performance on the tests is commensurate with their documented achievement in the content area via other tasks.

CONCLUSION

DHH learners participate in an assessment framework that is based on a spoken-language, hearing paradigm of learning. An "access" perspective on testing emphasizes the importance of providing opportunities for students to show what they know. A "validity" emphasis strives to maintain equality in rigor and confidence in the "sameness" in the constructs measured. The extent to which accommodations and test modifications level the playing field while still maintaining the intent of testing, which is to reliably measure student knowledge, can often be clouded by scant data and tentative inferences about their effect on student performance. Next-generation assessments have the potential to provide opportunities for individualization of the testing experience, more options for multiple-modality representations of test items, and more accurate tracking of how different students use accommodations during an assessment. In reality, only teachers in classrooms will have an accurate perspective on the effects of these new (and old!) features of the testing environment. For example, teachers can provide critical information about what works in their own classrooms, what students find to be accessible about computer-based testing, and what explanations students need (and in what form) to understand the test item tasks. Collaboration among teachers, test developers, and policymakers is critical for the future success of next-generation assessments for DHH students.

REFERENCES

Abedi, J. (2006). Language issues in item development. In S. Downing & T. Haladyna (Eds.), *Handbook of test development* (pp. 377–399). Rahway, NJ: Erlbaum.

Abedi, J. (2011). Language issues in the design of accessible items. In S. N. Elliott, R. J. Kettler, P. A. Beddow, & A. Kurz (Eds.), *Handbook of accessible achievement tests for all students: bridging the gaps between research, practices, and policy*. New York: Springer Publisher.

Antia, S. (2007). Can deaf and hard of hearing students be successful in general education classrooms? *Teachers College Record*. Retrieved Jan. 2, 2014, from http://www.tcrecord.org.

Cawthon, S. (2007). Hidden benefits and unintended consequences of No Child Left Behind polices for students who are Deaf or hard of hearing. *American Educational Research Journal*, *44*, 460–492.

Cawthon, S., Carr, T., Kopriva, R., & Leppo, R. (2013). Towards accessible assessments: The promises and limitations of test item modifications for students with disabilities and English language learners. *Educational Assessment*, *18*, 73–98.

Cawthon, S., Highley, K., & Leppo, R. (2011). Test item modifications for English language learners: Review of the empirical literature and recommendations for practice. *School Psychology Forum: Research in Practice*, *5*, 28–41.

Cawthon, S., Kaye, A., Lockhart, L., & Beretvas, S. N. (2012). Effects of linguistic complexity and accommodations on estimates of ability for students with learning disabilities. *Journal of School Psychology*, *50*, 293–316.

Cawthon, S., & Leppo, R. (2013). Assessment accommodations on tests of academic achievement for students who are deaf or hard-of-hearing: A qualitative meta-analysis of the research literature. *American Annals of the Deaf*, *157*, 363–376.

Cawthon, S., & the Online Research Lab (2006). Findings from the National Survey on Accommodations and Alternate Assessments for Students who are Deaf or Hard of Hearing. *Journal of Deaf Studies and Deaf Education, 11,* 337–359.

DePascale, C. (2010). Modified tests for modified achievement standards: Examining the comparability of scores to the general test. In P. C. Winter (Ed.), *Evaluating the comparability of scores from educational achievement test variations*. Washington, DC: Council of Chief State School Officers.

Elliott, S. N., & Roach, A. T. (2007). Alternate assessments in students with significant disabilities: Alternative approaches, common technical challenges. *Applied Measurement in Education, 20,* 301–333.

Fairbairn, S., & Fox, J. (2009). Inclusive achievement testing for linguistically and culturally diverse test takers: Essential considerations for test developers and test makers. *Educational Measurement: Issues and Practice, 28,* 10–24.

Keiffer, M. J., Lesaux, N. R., Rivera, M., & Francis, D. J. (2009). Accommodations for English language learners taking large-scale assessments: A meta-analysis on effectiveness and validity. *Review of Educational Research, 79,* 1168–1201.

Ketterlin-Geller, L. R. (2008). Testing students with special needs: A model for understanding the interaction between assessment and student characteristics in a universally designed environment. *Educational Measurement: Issues and Practice, 27,* 3–16.

Ketterlin-Geller, L. R., & Tindal, G. (2008). Embedded technology: Current and future practices for increasing accessibility for all students. *Journal of Special Education Technology, 22,* 1–15.

Kettler, R. J., Rodriguez, M. R., Bolt, D. M., Elliott, S. N., Beddow, P. A., & Kurz, A. (2011). Modified multiple-choice items for alternate assessments: Reliability, difficulty and differential boost. *Applied Measurement in Education, 24,* 1–25.

Kopriva, R. J. (2008). *Improving testing for English language learners: A comprehensive approach to designing, building, implementing, and interpreting better academic assessments*. New York: Routledge Publishers.

Kopriva, R., Emick, J., Hipolito-Delgado, C., & Cameron, C. (2007). Do proper accommodation assignments make a difference? Examining the impact of improved decision-making on scores for English language learners. *Educational Measurement: Issues and Practice, 26,* 11–20.

Marschark, M., Leigh, G., Sapere, P., Burnham, D., Convertino, C., Stinson, M., . . . & Noble, W. (2006). Benefits of sign language interpreting and text alternatives to classroom learning by deaf students. *Journal of Deaf Studies and Deaf Education, 11,* 421–437.

Marschark, M., Pelz, J., Convertino, C., Sapere, P., Arndt, M. E., & Seewagen, R. (2005). Classroom interpreting and visual information processing in mainstream education for deaf students: Live or Memorex®? *American Education Research Journal, 42,* 727–761.

Marschark, M., Sapere, P., Convertino, C., Mayer, C. Wauters, L., & Sarchet, T. (2009). Are deaf students' reading challenges really about reading? *American Annals of the Deaf, 154, 357–370.*

Messick, S. (1989). Validity. In R. L. Linn (Ed.), *Educational measurement* (3rd ed., pp. 13–103).

Qi, S., & Mitchell, R. E. (2012). Large-scale academic achievement testing of deaf and hard-of-hearing students: Past, present, and future. *Journal of Deaf Studies and Deaf Education, 17,* 1–18.

Rieke, R., Lazarus, S. S., Thurlow, M. L., & Dominguez, L. M. (2012). *2012 survey of states: Successes and challenges during a time of change*. Minneapolis: University of Minnesota, National Center on Educational Outcomes.
Russell, M., Kavanaugh, M., Masters, J., Higgins, J., & Hoffmann, T. (2009). Computer-based signing accommodations: Comparing a recorded human with an avatar. *Journal of Applied Testing Technology, 10*, 1–20.
Shaftel, J., Yang, X., Glasnapp, D., & Poggio, J. (2005). Improving assessment validity for students with disabilities in large-scale assessment programs. *Educational Assessment, 10*, 357–375.
Sireci, S. G., Scarpati, S. E., & Li, S. (2005). Test accommodations for students with disabilities: An analysis of the interaction hypothesis. *Review of Educational Research, 75*, 457–490.
Sligar, S., Cawthon, S., Morere, D., & Moxley, A. (in press). Test equity considerations for individuals who are deaf or hard of hearing. *JADARA*.
Stinson, M., Elliot, L, Kelly, R., & Liu, Y. (2009). Deaf and hard-of-hearing students' memory of lectures with speech-to-text and interpreting/note taking services. *Journal of Special Education*. *43*, 52–64.

Part 3

Cognitive, Social, and Emotional Development

11

Deaf Children's Executive Functions

From Research to Practice?

Daan Hermans, Brigitte Vugs,
Lian van Berkel-van Hoof, and Harry Knoors

How do you get what you want? How do you control your behavior and your thoughts in order to achieve your goals in life? Executive functions (EFs) are the set of processes that are involved in the control of oneself and one's cognitive resources in order to achieve a goal, especially in nonroutine situations (Banich, 2009). Executive functioning is one of the most widely invoked constructs in many domains of science, including cognitive science, neuropsychology, and developmental and clinical research (Toplak, West, & Stanovich, 2013). At the same time, it is an ill-defined concept, lacking a precise definition (Kerr & Zelazo, 2004). This complicates not only the scientific study and clinical assessment of EFs but remedial or compensatory interventions on EFs as well.

Almost two decades ago, Monsell (1996) stated that the scientific domain of how specific cognitive processes are controlled and coordinated during the performance of complex cognitive tasks is an "embarrassing zone of almost total ignorance" (p. 93). During the past two decades numerous studies addressing EFs from different scientific perspectives have been published. More detailed theories of EFs have been proposed (Barkley, 1997; Hoffman, Schmeichel & Baddeley, 2012; Stanovich, 2009). Furthermore, the importance of EFs for language development, school achievements, and occupational functioning has been demonstrated (Barkley & Fisher, 2011; Engle, Carullo, & Collings, 1991; Jarvis & Gathercole, 2003; Just & Carpenter, 1992; Swanson, Jerman, & Zheng, 2008; see Pagliaro, Chapter 8 in this volume). New norm-referenced assessment instruments have been developed, enabling clinicians to assess EFs more extensively, such as the BRIEF (Goia, Isquith, Guy, & Kenworthy, 2000), the BDEFS-CA (Barkley, 2012a), the AWMA (Alloway, 2007), the BADS-C (Emslie, Wilson, Burden, Nimmo-Smith, & Wilson, 2003), the D-KEFS (Delis, Kaplin, & Kramer, 2001), and the TEA-Ch (Manly, Robertsen, Anderson, & Nimmo-Smith, 1999), to name but a few. Last and most importantly, research on EFs in deaf children and adolescents has revealed that many of them have delays or deficits in this domain (Hauser, Lukomski, & Hillman, 2008; Hintermair, 2013; Pisoni, Kronenberger, Roman, & Geers, 2011).

The relatively recent findings on delays or deficits in EFs in deaf children and adolescents require a different stance toward the programs used in early intervention and schools for deaf children. More than one change seems to be required. First, EFs are usually not extensively addressed in clinical assessments of the skills of deaf children and adolescents. Clearly, that must change. If our aim is to create an environment that optimally stimulates deaf children's and adolescents' development, their EFs need to be assessed. Second, we need to evaluate to what extent the interventions we provide to deaf children and adolescents are appropriate, given their EF skills—and if our current interventions are not appropriate, how can we adjust them? Third, because recent research studies have shown that EFs can be trained, we need to evaluate how and to what extent we should incorporate training programs on EFs in early intervention and educational programs for deaf children. Thus, the traditionally strong focus in our field on stimulating language development and making information accessible to deaf children no longer seems to suffice. In other words, we may have to realize that our interventions should no longer be solely centralized around language development and access to language.

THE ALGORITHMIC AND REFLECTIVE MIND

The continuing debate regarding many fundamental aspects of EFs in the scientific literature does not help us much in achieving these aims. One of the debates that is highly relevant, at least from our perspective, is the discussion on what different types of EFs assessment instruments actually measure. EFs can be assessed through neuropsychological tests such as the D-KEFS battery (Delis et al., 2001) or through behavior ratings questionnaires such as the BRIEF (Goia et al., 2000).

Quite remarkably, there is often only a weak to moderate association between performance-based measures and behavior ratings of EFs (see for a meta-analysis Toplak et al., 2013). To illustrate, Bennett, Ong, and Ponsford (2005) observed weak to moderate associations (average $r = 0.19$) between performance-based tasks (such as the Zoo Map Test) and the behavior rating questionnaire of the BADS. Toplak and colleagues (2013) interpreted these findings within Stanovich's (2009) tripartite model of cognitive functioning. Stanovich made an important distinction between the algorithmic and reflective mind with respect to conscious, nonautonomous, cognitive functioning. The algorithmic component of the system is concerned with information processing in the brain (input coding, working memory [WM], long-term memory). The reflective component of the system is concerned with an individual's goals, his or her beliefs that are relevant to those goals, and the choice of action given those goals and beliefs. Stanovich (2009) argued that the reflective mind consists of higher-level goal states and epistemic thinking dispositions. Thinking dispositions can be viewed as higher-level regulatory states—for instance, the tendency to think about the future before taking action. Thinking dispositions are informative on what the algorithmic mind is computing and why. These higher-level regulatory states eventually initiate action.

Toplak and colleagues (2013) argued that performance-based measure of EFs tap predominantly into the algorithmic component of the system. The choice of action in performance-based tasks is mainly determined by the test structure or the administrator (Gioia, Isquith, & Kenealy, 2008), and most performance-based tasks are strongly constrained with respect to intentional-level functioning (Toplak et al., 2013). Therefore, performance-based measures of EFs assess usually only the efficiency of the processing system (optimal performance) that is needed for goal pursuit. In other words, the algorithmic mind can be seen as the computational tool that is needed by the reflective mind for efficient goal pursuit. At the level of the reflective mind, issues regarding optimal decision making for efficient goal pursuit come into play. Toplak and colleagues (2013) argued that behavior ratings of EFs tap more into the reflective component of the system and are generally more informative on people's success in goal pursuit in everyday life. But both measures of EFs provide valuable information about an individual's success in achieving goals. Deficits or delays in either performance-based measures of EFs (reflecting predominantly the algorithmic mind) or in rating scales of EFs (reflecting the combined functioning of the algorithmic and the reflective mind) both will affect an individual's success in achieving goals in life.

In this chapter, we use Stanovich's (2009) and Toplak and colleagues' (2013) distinction between the algorithmic and the reflective mind as the theoretical framework for the assessment of EFs and intervention studies on EFs in deaf children and adolescents. Although there are clearly alternative theoretical perspectives (e.g., Barkley, 1997, 2012b), the distinction between the algorithmic and reflective mind captures the vital distinction between children's functioning in highly structured and less structured environments. Performance-based measures of EFs provide valuable information on how individuals perform in highly structured environments, like during language instruction or speech therapy at a primary school. In such instructional settings, children's success in achieving their goals is mainly determined by the functioning of their algorithmic mind as it requires little intentional-level functioning. If deaf children demonstrate weaknesses in processing efficiency (reflected by poor performance in performance-based measures), we should further adapt the environment in early intervention programs and schools (i.e., adapt our interventions). Alternatively, we may try to stimulate deaf children's processing efficiency through specific intervention programs such as Cogmed (Klingberg, 2010) or Braingame Brian (Prins et al., 2010).

In contrast, achieving goals in less structured environments requires more intentional (voluntary) control of one's behavior and thoughts. For instance, children's functioning during independent work in the classroom or during school playtime is to a larger degree determined by the combined functioning of their algorithmic and reflective mind. In such settings, it is necessary for children to regulate their own behavior and thoughts. Rating measures provide valuable information on how people succeed in achieving goals in such less structured environments (Toplak et al., 2013). If children show deficits or delays in rating measures of EFs, interventions should target improvements at both the algorithmic and reflective component of nonautonomous cognitive functioning. Programs such as Tools of the Mind typically aim at improving both components of EFs (Bodrova & Leung, 2000, 2007).

THE ALGORITHMIC MIND: WORKING MEMORY

As we pointed out in the previous section, the algorithmic component of the tripartite system is concerned with information processing. EFs on this level of analysis concern the cognitive functions that exert control during information processing. There is disagreement in the literature on whether the EFs of the algorithmic mind should be conceptualized as a unitary construct or as consisting of several separate functions, such as shifting, inhibition, and updating (Barkley, 2012b; McCabe, Roediger, McDaniel, Balota, & Hambrick, 2010). Miyake, Friedman, Emerson, Witzki, Howerter, and Wager (2000) found evidence that EFs such as shifting, inhibition, and updating are separate functions that also share some commonalities. The diversity among EFs is also supported by studies that have shown that children with specific language impairments, on average, have problems with some (e.g., updating, inhibition) but not all (e.g., shifting) EFs (Henry, Messer, & Nash, 2010).

Interestingly, McCabe and colleagues (2010) recently observed a very strong correlation ($r = 0.97$) between four complex span tasks of WM and four EF tasks in a group of 206 adults. These findings suggest a great deal of communality between WM tasks and neuropsychological tasks assessing specific EFs. Furthermore, current theories of WM often assume that the regulatory functions of WM include a diversity of EFs like allocation, updating, sustained and selective attention, and inhibition (Montgomery, Magimairaj, & Finney, 2010). We will therefore restrict our analysis of the algorithmic mind in this chapter to theories and findings on WM.

The concept of WM is central within most theories of (control of) information processing. WM is viewed to be part of a larger memory system that allows people to perceive, attend to, and retrieve information (Baddeley, 1996, 2000, 2003, 2007). The WM component of this larger memory system is usually described as a capacity-limited system involved in the active maintenance and manipulation of incoming sensory information over brief periods of time (Miyake & Shah, 1999). In other words, sequential processing is central to WM.

Baddeley's Working Memory Model

The vast majority of research on WM has been conducted within Baddeley's model of WM (Baddeley, 1996, 2000, 2003, 2007; Baddeley & Hitch, 1974). Baddeley's WM model consists of four separable yet interactive components. The central executive is responsible for the control and coordination of activities in WM. As the central executive has limited resources, the control of attention is the key. Although there is considerable disagreement on the specific regulatory functions of the central executive in the literature, these functions presumably include allocation, updating, sustained and selective attention, and inhibition (Montgomery et al., 2010). The second and third components are domain-specific storage components responsible for the temporary retention of verbal (phonological loop) and visuospatial (visuospatial sketchpad) input. The processing of verbal and visual information can be seen as relatively independent processes, each with a limited capacity drawing upon different resources (Baddeley, 1992). The relative independence of these processes is also central within Paivio's dual coding theory (Paivio, 1986).

Interestingly, the phonological loop for signs and that for spoken words have an internal structure that is functionally remarkably similar (Wilson & Emmorey, 1997a, 1997b, 1998, 2003). Despite these functional similarities, there are also noticeable differences. For instance, deaf adolescents use visuospatial codes (to a stronger degree) to retain signs in the phonological loop (Wilson & Emmorey, 2001). Such differences do not seem to affect the available WM resources in deaf native signers (Boutla, Supalla, Newport, & Bavelier, 2004).

The fourth component of Baddeley's WM model, the episodic buffer, is a temporary store that integrates verbal, visual, and spatial information of the phonological loop and visuospatial sketchpad and semantic information from long-term memory into a multimodal code. The (active) binding of multisensory information in the episodic buffer is controlled by the central executive (Baddeley, 2007). Most empirical work on the episodic buffer has focused on the binding problem: How does the brain construct coherent representations of the world from incoming multisensory information? For instance, how is the concept of a "dog" jointly activated by incoming auditory (e.g., barking) and visual (e.g., seeing the shape and location of a dog) sensory information? Thus, most studies typically focus upon the question of how linguistic and nonlinguistic input from different sensory systems from the same source in reality is integrated in the brain, and most of them have revealed that multisensory encoding is beneficial for learning (Sham & Seitz, 2008). An extensive discussion on research and theories on this domain is beyond the scope of this chapter, although there are certainly interesting and important issues with respect to, for instance, the integration of visual and auditory information of spoken words in deaf and hearing children (Bergeson, Houston, & Miyamoto, 2010; Schorr, Fox, Wassenhove, & Knudson, 2005; Ting, Bergeson, & Miyamoto, 2012).

Baddeley's Working Memory Model and Dual Coding

How do people process and integrate multisensory information coming simultaneously from different sources in reality? Because many interventions in education and early intervention programs for deaf children use visual compensatory approaches to enhance deaf children's development, understanding more about the mechanisms underlying dual coding is vital. Does bimodal input increase WM capacity, and therefore enhance learning? This is the central issue within theories of multimedia learning that build upon Baddeley's WM model and Paivio's dual coding theory (Mayer, 2001).

On the one hand, the relatively independence of WM for visuospatial and verbal processing suggests that bimodal input may increase overall WM capacity (Baddeley, 1992; Paivio, 1986). On the other hand, because the central executive is involved in the active binding of multisensory information in the episodic buffer (Baddeley, 2007), bimodal input may reduce WM capacity, especially under conditions of high processing load (Mayer, 2001; see Segers & Verhoeven, Chapter 21 in this volume).

There is indeed evidence that multisensory information coming from different external linguistic (spoken words, written words) and extralinguistic (pictures) sources facilitates the temporary storage of information in WM for hearing adults (Goolkasian & Fools, 2005) and deaf adults (Hamilton & Holtzman, 1989). Furthermore, bimodal input facilitates (language) learning in hearing adults (Macedonia, Muller, & Friederici, 2011) and hearing children (Tellier, 2008).

Goolkasian and Fools (2005) found that bimodal presentation of information increases the temporary retention of information in WM. Participants recalled lists of bimodal stimuli (spoken words/pictures, spoken words/written words, pictures/written words) better than lists of unimodal stimuli (spoken words, written words, pictures). However, Goolkasian and Fools (2005) observed two critical findings that qualify this finding. First, the bimodal advantage was not observed when the bimodal input consisted of written words and pictures; in fact, the retention of pictures in WM was hampered when pictures were accompanied by written words. Goolkasian and Fools (2005) argued that the processing of printed words is a special case as they are processed in a complex manner that is split between visual WM and verbal WM. Therefore, the temporary storage of written words in WM partly draws upon the same resources as the temporary storage of pictures. The absence of a facilitatory effect of bimodal input consisting of written words and pictures over unimodal input can explain the occurrence of the split-attention effect observed by Mayer and Moreno (1998). Mayer and Moreno (1998) found that participants performed much worse, for instance on the retention of information, when an animation was accompanied by a written text in comparison to a spoken text. By assuming that processing of written words and processing of animations draw upon the same limited resources, this type of bimodal input may have overloaded the WM system. In other words, the facilitatory effect of bimodal input on WM capacity depends upon the type of bimodal input.

Second, Goolkasian and Fools (2005) found that the beneficial effects of bimodal input over unimodal input strongly decreased or even disappeared under conditions that put more burden on WM capacity (e.g., when the list length was increased). This finding suggests that the beneficial effect of bimodal information processing in relatively simple instructional settings (the use of pictures or signs in vocabulary training in speech therapy) does not necessarily generalize to more complex instructional settings (the use of multimedia in the classroom).[1]

Assessment of Working Memory

The functioning of the domain-specific storage components is usually measured by tasks that require the immediate recall of information, like simple memory span tasks. The functioning of the phonological loop is assessed with verbal stimuli (words, nonwords, digits, or letters), while the functioning of the visuospatial sketchpad is assessed with visual patterns. It is therefore generally assumed that simple span tasks do not require much involvement of the regulatory functions of the central executive. Furthermore, as performance in simple verbal span tasks is strongly related to word learning, the phonological loop has been argued to be an important device in the acquisition of new words (Gathercole, 2006).

The combined functioning of the domain-specific storage component and the central executive component is measured by tasks that require significant processing in addition to storage, like backward span tasks, reading or listening span tasks, or operation span tasks (Montgomery et al., 2010). Performance on WM tasks is strongly related to language comprehension (Engle et al., 1991), reading comprehension (Just & Carpenter, 1992), and mathematics (Jarvis & Gathercole, 2003).

Finally, although the integration of multisensory information in the episodic buffer (and the use of knowledge from long-term memory) in creating episode is a crucial function of WM, there are currently no norm-referenced tests available specifically designed to assess the functioning of the episodic buffer (Nobre et al., 2013). Nevertheless, clinicians occasionally use subtests of the Test of Memory and Learning (the Paired Recall test) and the Clinical Evaluation of Language Fundamentals (the Recalling Sentences test) as an indicator of the functioning of the episodic buffer (Nobre et al., 2013).

The Algorithmic Mind of Deaf Children

Do deaf children and adolescents show delays or deficits on performance-based tasks that assess the functioning of verbal WM? Let's first turn briefly to WM for signs. Studies that have focused on the functioning of the phonological loop have revealed that the immediate serial recall span is shorter for signs in native deaf signers than the immediate serial recall span for spoken words, both for adults (Boutla et al., 2004) and for children (Wilson, Bettger, Niculae, & Klima, 1997). Wilson and colleagues (1997) assessed the combined functioning of the domain-specific storage component and the central executive component for signs in deaf native signers and deaf nonnative signers using a backward digit span task. They also compared the backward digit spans of deaf children for signed stimuli with the backward digit spans of hearing children for spoken stimuli. Quite remarkably, deaf native signers outperformed not only deaf nonnative signers in the backward span task, but hearing children as well. Such findings have not been replicated with adults using a more complex WM task (Wang & Napier, 2013). Although no statistical analyses were reported, hearing children in Wilson and colleagues' (1997) study seemed to outperform deaf nonnative signers. Furthermore, deaf native signers had similar scores on the forward and backward span task for signed digits. Wilson and colleagues (1997) argued that the absence of a difference between the forward and backward spans suggests that deaf native signers may have used visuospatial coding strategies to retain the temporal order of signs in WM.

There is still too little known about WM for signs in deaf children. As sign language is still the instructional language in many (bilingual) education programs for deaf children throughout the world, there is an apparent need for more studies on WM capacity for signs in deaf children.

Let us turn to deaf children's WM for spoken words, from now on referred to as auditory WM. The functioning of auditory WM has become more important as the increase in the number of deaf children who receive (bilateral) cochlear implants at an early age has led to major improvements in the hearing skills and speech abilities of many deaf children (Dettman & Dowell, 2010). As a consequence, an increasing number of deaf children in many countries currently receive instruction in spoken language. During the past decade, Pisoni and colleagues have investigated auditory WM skills in large-scale studies with deaf children with cochlear implants (Pisoni & Cleary, 2003; Pisoni, Conway, Kronenberger, Horn, Karpicke, & Henning, 2008; Pisoni et al., 2011). These studies have revealed that those deaf children, on average, have deficits in tasks that assess the functioning of the phonological loop, the verbal storage component of WM (forward digit span tasks), and in tasks that assess the combined functioning of the verbal storage component and the central executive (backward digit span tasks) in comparison to hearing children. Pisoni and colleagues (2011) also found that the deficits or delays of deaf children with cochlear implants in forward span tasks were larger than the deficits or delay in backward span tasks. Importantly, the deficits or delays in the functioning of the phonological loop decreased over time, whereas the deficits or delays of the functioning of both the phonological loop and the central executive increased over time. Finally, performance on forward span tasks was associated with speech and language outcomes (e.g., spoken word recognition), whereas performance on backward span tasks was associated with higher-order language processing (e.g., vocabulary knowledge, spoken language comprehension, and reading comprehension).

These findings are consistent with the idea that forward and backward span tasks tap into different components of WM (Baddeley, 2003). The deficits of deaf children in forward span tasks reflect their problems to effectively store incoming auditory information in the phonological loop. Deaf children may have difficulties in recovering the salient phonological representations from the speech signal and use these representations for storage (Nittrouer, Caldwell-Tarr, & Lowenstein, 2013). The continuing use of cochlear implants over time may have strongly reduced deaf children's problems in identifying the phonological structure of incoming information, facilitating the temporary storage of this information in the phonological loop and stimulating deaf children's speech and language skills. Nittrouer and colleagues (2013) pointed out that these findings suggest that clinical efforts to reduce auditory WM problems in deaf children should focus on providing phonological training in addition to improving the quality of sensory information available to deaf children. The different developmental paths observed for forward and backward span tasks (digit forward span increase in combination with digit backward span decrease), however, suggest that deaf children also have problems with some of the regulatory functions of the central executive.

It is quite remarkable that relatively few studies to date have addressed auditory WM capacity in deaf children. Furthermore, the studies that have addressed auditory WM in deaf children typically administer tasks in which the processing load is relatively low, such as backward span tasks (Nittrouer et al., 2013; Pisoni & Cleary, 2003; Pisoni et al., 2008, 2011). Tasks that require considerably more processing, like the operation span task, tap more into the functioning of the central executive. In the operation span task, participants have to verify sequentially presented mathematical operations (e.g., 2 + 6 = 8, 8 – 3 = 4) while they have to remember words or letters that follow the presentation of each mathematical operation (e.g., dog, spoon) at the same time. These tasks are, therefore, more likely to detect differences between hearing and deaf children with respect to the functioning of the central executive during information processing. As deficits or delays in WM have important clinical implications (Kronenberger, Pisoni, Henning, Colson, & Hazard, 2011; Nittrouer et al., 2013; Pisoni et al., 2011), future studies on auditory WM on deaf children should include these measures of WM as well. Nevertheless, there is sufficient evidence in the literature to conclude that deaf children have deficits in both the domain-specific storage component and the central executive component of auditory WM. It is important to note here that delays or deficits among deaf children have also been observed for sequential processing of nonverbal materials. Conway, Karpicke, Anaya, Henning, Kronenberger, and Pisoni (2011) found that motor sequencing skills were impaired in deaf children in comparison to hearing children. Furthermore, they found that hearing children outperform deaf children in visual sequence learning. Similarly, Cockcroft and Dhana-Dullabh (2012) found that deaf children of hearing parents showed deficits on the six visuospatial WM tasks of the AWMA.

However, studies on visuospatial WM in deaf children and deaf adults have not always yielded consistent results (Falkman & Hjelmquist; 2006; Marschark, Morrison, Lukomski, Borgna, & Convertino, 2013; Marschark, Sarchet, & Trani, 2014; Remoro Lauro, Crespi, Papagno, & Cecchetto, 2014; Wilson et al., 1997).[2,3] Finally, Mitchell and Quittner (1996) found that sustained and selective attention (regulatory skills related to visual WM performance) were impaired in deaf children, especially at a younger age (see also Quittner et al., 2007). The combined results of these studies suggest that the WM deficits or delays of deaf children are not restricted to auditory WM but manifest themselves in visuospatial WM as well. In other words, deaf children seem to exhibit domain-general problems in sequential processing that may be rooted in the absence of or degraded experiences with sound (Conway, Pisoni, & Kronenberger, 2009).

There is, to our knowledge, little work on the functioning of the episodic component of WM in deaf children either with respect to the integration of verbal and visuospatial information from different sources in reality or with respect to the role of knowledge in long-term memory on the creation of episodes in the episodic buffer. Hamilton and

Holzman (1989) found that deaf participants recalled the temporary order of bimodal stimuli (signs and spoken words) better than the temporary order of unimodal stimuli (signs or spoken words.) This finding shows that bimodal input can indeed increase the temporary retention of information in WM. More empirical work on the functioning of the episodic component is necessary for more than one reason. First, the studies described above have shown that many deaf children have deficits in verbal and visuospatial WM. The use of multimodal input in many interventions (e.g., at school) may enhance deaf children's WM capacity and, therefore, stimulate their development. Alternatively, the use of multimodal input may result in a cognitive overload, which will interfere with their learning at school. We need to identify whether and under what circumstances bimodal input facilitates deaf children's learning. Second, studies by Marschark and colleagues have revealed that deaf students typically have less content knowledge in comparison to hearing students (Marschark, Sapere, Convertino, & Pelz, 2008; Marschark, Sapere, Convertino, & Seewagen, 2005). As knowledge in long-term memory is assumed to facilitate the creation of multimodal episodes, studies on how information from long-term memory interacts with WM are of genuine importance.

THE REFLECTIVE MIND

The reflective component of Stanovich's (2009) tripartite model of cognitive functioning is concerned with the goals of the system, beliefs relevant to those goals, and the choice of action given the system's goals and beliefs (see Fellinger & Holzinger, Chapter 17 in this volume; Rieffe, Netten, Broekhof, & Veiga, Chapter 16 in this volume). Thinking dispositions reflect an individual's goals and epistemic values. They can be viewed as tendencies of pragmatic and epistemic self-regulation at the intentional level (Stanovich, 2009). Thinking dispositions eventually initiate action and are therefore vital in the control of thought and behavior. In other words, intentional (voluntarily) control of one's behavior and thoughts is exerted by the reflective component of Stanovich's model. As the algorithmic component can be viewed as the computational tool that is needed by the reflective component for efficient goal pursuit in life, the combined functioning of the algorithmic and reflective components determines one's success in efficient goal pursuit.

Assessing the Combined Functioning of the Algorithmic and Reflective Mind

Toplak and colleagues (2013) argued that people's success in goal pursuit in life can be assessed by rating measures of EFs, such as the BRIEF (Goia et al., 2000) or the BDEFS-CA (Barkley, 2012a). In other words, rating measures such as the BRIEF are likely to measure the combined functioning of the algorithmic and reflective components of cognitive functioning. These measures have been argued to reflect the integrated, multidimensional priority-based decision making that is central to executive functioning in daily life much more accurately (Goia, Isquith, Retzlaff, & Espy, 2002). Furthermore, a study by Barkley and Murphy (2010) on adults with attention-deficit/hyperactivity disorder (ADHD) has shown that the association between behavior ratings of EFs and ratings of occupational functioning is much stronger than the association between performance-based measures of EFs and ratings of occupational functioning. Behavior rating measures of EFs therefore seem to be an ecologically more valid indicator of people's EFs.

The most frequently used rating measure is the BRIEF (Goia et al., 2000). This instrument consists of 86 items that describe difficulties in everyday activities that map onto eight individual scales (Inhibit, Shift, Emotional Control, Initiate, WM, Plan/Organize, Organization of Materials, and Monitor). The first three individual scales compose the Behavioral Regulation Index, while the last five individual scales compose the Metacognition Index. Those two composite scores can be combined to an overall Global Executive composite. Each of the 86 items is rated on whether or not difficulties have been encountered in the past six months (never, sometimes, often). The original BRIEF rating instrument is suitable for children between five and 18 years old and has a teacher and a parent form. The teacher and parent versions in the BRIEF have separate norms. On most scales, parents report more executive functioning problems than teachers (Smidts & Huizinga, 2009), and the correlation between parents' and teachers' reports is generally moderate. This is likely to be caused by the relatively structured environment at primary and secondary schools in comparison to life outside school. In such structured environments, executive functioning problems are less likely to manifest themselves. The BRIEF-P was developed for younger children (between two and five years old) and also has a teacher/daycare giver and parent version. In 2004 and 2005 two self-report versions appeared, the BRIEF-SR for children between 11 and 18 years and the BRIEF-A for adults. Only this latter questionnaire has been validated for deaf students (Hauser, Lukomski, & Samar, 2013).

The Combined Functioning of the Algorithmic and Reflective Mind of Deaf Children

Studies involving deaf individuals or children have mainly used the BRIEF questionnaire to assess EF in everyday behavior (Hauser et al., 2013; Hintermair, 2013; Oberg & Lukomski, 2011; Pisoni, Conway, Kronenberger, Henning, & Anaya, 2010; Rhine, 2002). These studies have not yielded consistent results on deaf children's and adolescent's EFs.

Rhine (2002) administered the BRIEF parent form to the parents of 62 deaf children (average age of 11 years). She found deficits or delays on three out of eight scales of the BRIEF (Inhibition, Shifting, WM). Pisoni and colleagues (2010) administered the BRIEF parent form to the parents of 19 deaf children with cochlear implants (five to 10 years old) and the parents of 30 hearing children (five to eight years old). They found deficits or delays of deaf children on five out of eight scales (Shifting, Emotional Control, Initiation, Planning and Organization, WM). Oberg and Lukomski (2011) investigated the EF of a group of 22 deaf children (five to 18 years old) using both teachers and parents as informants on deaf children's EF. They found that the average T-scores of deaf children on the eight subscales of the BRIEF fell below the cutoff criterion (T-score = 65, normative mean = 50). Descriptively, however, elevated scores were found on all eight subscales, the two indices, and the composite score of the BRIEF (T-scores ranged from 52.7 to 63.7). To illustrate, the Global Executive composite scores in the parent and teacher form were 60.2 and 63.0 respectively. Unfortunately, Oberg and Lukomski did not report statistics to assess whether the average T-scores of deaf children deviated from the normative mean.

Hintermair (2013) conducted a large-scale study with the BRIEF with deaf children in Germany between five and 18 years old. He administered the teacher form to 214 deaf and hard-of-hearing children. Approximately 70% of the children were enrolled in special schools and 30% of the children were enrolled in mainstream schools. Hintermair found that deaf and hard-of-hearing children in special schools showed executive functioning deficits or delays on all scales of the BRIEF. About 48% of the children in special schools had a Global Executive composite score above 65, which is the cutoff score of significant EF problems. Hintermair reported more positive results for deaf and hard-of-hearing children in mainstream schools; nevertheless, this group showed deficits on six scales of the BRIEF (Shifting, Emotional Control, Initiation, WM, Organization of Materials, and Monitoring), and about 15% had a Global Executive composite score above the cutoff criterion of 65. To account for this difference, Hintermair argued that the two groups differed in a range of characteristics that might be relevant (fewer additional handicaps, parents with higher educational status). Alternatively, teachers in mainstream schools may stimulate (deaf) children's development of EFs more extensively in comparison to teachers in special schools. For instance, the small class sizes in special schools may tempt teachers to use a more individualized approach to teaching (Hermans, Wauters, De Klerk, & Knoors, 2014). Such individualized approaches may be useful to provide deaf children with maximum access to instruction, but it may be less effective for the stimulation of deaf children's EFs. Overall, the results obtained in these studies suggest that many deaf children and adolescents have severe EF deficits or delays, especially on the scales WM and Shifting.

More positive results were found by Hauser and colleagues (2013). They administered the BRIEF-A to 176 deaf and 184 hearing students from the Rochester Institute of Technology. They found that the scores of deaf participants were actually lower than the scores of hearing participants on most of the scales of the BRIEF. It is, however, questionable the extent to which their results can be generalized to the deaf population because they administered the BRIEF solely to university students.

The Algorithmic and Reflective Mind of Deaf Children: Summary

The algorithmic component of Stanovich's (2009) tripartite model of cognitive functioning is concerned with information processing in the brain. The central EF question at this level of analysis is how cognitive processes are controlled and coordinated during the performance of complex cognitive tasks. The reflective component of Stanovich's model is concerned with the goals of the system, beliefs relevant to those goals, and the choice of action given the system's goals and beliefs.

Assessments of the functioning of the algorithmic mind by performance-based measures of EF therefore reflect the efficiency of the processing system that is required for goal pursuit. Central to most theories of control during information processing is the concept of WM. Studies conducted with deaf children and deaf adolescents have revealed that many of them have delays or deficits with sequential processing in auditory (and visual) WM (Cockcroft & Dhana-Dullabh, 2012; Conway, Karpicke et al., 2011; Conway, Pisoni, Anaya, Karpicke, & Henning, 2011; Pisoni et al., 2011). Assessment of the combined functioning of the algorithmic and reflective mind by behavior ratings of EF has revealed that many deaf children and adolescents have severe EF deficits (Hintermair, 2013).

INTERVENTION PROGRAMS AND EXECUTIVE FUNCTION: REMEDIAL AND COMPENSATORY APPROACHES

How do we incorporate these new insights on EF deficits or delays in deaf children in our programs in early intervention and at schools for deaf children? Dehn (2008) and Dawson and Guare (2004) argued that there are basically two approaches to handle executive functioning deficits or delays in schools. First, compensatory interventions aim to reduce the negative consequences of EF deficits or delays on children's development. But how do we modify or fine-tune the current interventions or the educational environment we provide to deaf children and adolescents to their EF skills? Second, remedial interventions aim to improve children's EFs, by teaching the child either to develop a specific EF or to use an already acquired EF (i.e., generalize). Do we need to incorporate remedial training programs on EFs in early intervention and educational programs for deaf children? And which programs are promising in enhancing deaf children's EF skills? In the next sections we will describe several promising compensatory and remedial EF interventions for deaf children. However, as we will see, most of these require firmer scientific justification.

Compensatory Interventions Bypassing Deficits of the Algorithmic Mind

Compensatory interventions aim to reduce the negative consequences of EF deficits or delays on children's development. These interventions generally describe approaches that compensate for children's weaknesses in information processing (compensatory interventions of the algorithmic mind). We will discuss two types of compensatory interventions. The first one focuses on general didactic strategies that teachers can use in the classroom to attune their instruction to the EF skills of children. The second one focuses on the use of bimodal input to enhance deaf children's learning.

Didactic Strategies in the Classroom

Hamilton (2011) provided a detailed and extensive overview of general didactic strategies teachers of deaf children can employ to take their pupils' WM deficits into account. Central to such strategies is the notion that teachers should be alert in detecting signals of cognitive overload in deaf children and subsequently adjust their didactic approach in the classroom. Hamilton (2011) argued that teachers may adapt their language use to prevent overloading the WM of deaf children. For instance, using simple and structured language with familiar or meaningful content will put less burden on WM than complex and unstructured language with unfamiliar or meaningless content. Furthermore, teachers should focus on one classroom activity at a time, as multitasking places a heavy load on WM capacity. Finally, deaf children should have sufficient time to process instruction in the classroom, and teachers may present classroom curriculum more than once to deaf children.

Gathercole, Lamont, and Alloway (2006) suggested that the didactic approach of "errorless learning" may be more suitable than "trial-and-error learning" for children with WM deficits. The concept of errorless learning is based on Skinner's (1953) instructional approach to learning. The reduction of errors in learning can be accomplished by a variety of instructional techniques (e.g., dividing complicated classroom tasks into smaller, less complicated tasks; modeling the classroom task by the teacher; discouraging them from guessing; immediately correcting children's errors; carefully fading prompts that are provided to the child to facilitate learning). Gathercole and colleagues (2006) argued that children with WM deficits have difficulties learning from the errors they make during learning.

Bimodal Coding

Many interventions in education for deaf children use visual compensatory methods to increase deaf children's access to information and, therefore, stimulate their development. In other words, the visual support in interventions is not directly related to deaf children's WM deficits but rather to their limited access to spoken language. For instance, teachers often use Sign Supported Dutch as the language of instruction in special schools in the Netherlands. The use of signs in instruction is assumed to enhance deaf children's comprehension of spoken Dutch and therefore to increase their access to the information provided by the teacher.

Beneficial effects on bimodal input have been observed in several studies. As we described earlier, Hamilton and Holzman (1989) found that deaf participants recalled the temporary order of bimodal stimuli (signs and spoken words) better than the temporary order of unimodal stimuli (signs or spoken words). In a training study, Wauters, Knoors, Vervloed, and Aarnoutse (2001) found deaf children's accuracy at recognizing written words increased when the written words were taught to the children using a multimodal code (spoken words and signs) in comparison to a unimodal code (spoken words). Similarly, Mollink, Knoors, and Hermans (2008) found that hard-of-hearing children learned a new set of spoken words better when those words were accompanied by signs during the training. Mollink and colleagues (2008) also found that the beneficial effect was much larger for strongly iconic signs in comparison to weakly iconic signs. These findings suggest that providing deaf children with bimodal input can be beneficial for deaf children's acquisition of vocabulary. It is unclear the extent to which the benefits in the vocabulary training studies by Wauters and colleagues (2001) and Mollink and colleagues (2008) have arisen from enhanced WM capacity due to bimodal input. This is one of the questions central to a PhD project by Lian van Berkel that has recently started on bimodal input, WM, and vocabulary learning in deaf children and children with a specific language impairment.

The studies by Wauters and colleagues (2001) and Mollink and colleagues (2008) have been conducted in experimental settings that place a relatively low burden on WM capacity. It is unclear the extent to which the beneficial effects of bimodal input, in this case Sign Supported Dutch, generalize to more complicated classroom situations. During instruction in Sign Supported Dutch in the classroom, the sensory information perceived through the eyes and ears has to be processed rapidly. It is conceivable that bimodal input under such conditions will overload the WM system of deaf children, especially those with WM deficits. As pointed out by Hamilton (2011), more research is needed on how bimodal signed and spoken input is processed in situations that go beyond the retention and comprehension of word lists.

Deaf children's learning also may be stimulated by visual support that requires much less sequential processing, such as pictures, flowcharts, and diagrams. Rudner and Rönnberg (2008) argued that visuospatial tools in bimodal input that place less emphasis on sequential processing may indeed reduce memory load and facilitate learning.[4] Visuospatial tools that reduce memory load may also be very useful during activities that put a heavy load on WM capacity, as is often, but not necessarily, the case in hypertext reading (DeStefano & Lefevre, 2007). DeStefano and Lefevre argued that the flexibility and interactivity of hypertexts may increase the cognitive load in comparison to regular texts. Consistent with this assumption, Lee and Tedder (2003) found that especially readers with low WM capacity were disadvantaged in reading hypertexts. The presence of a visually simple graphical overview may help readers with low WM capacity (Chen & Rada, 1996), but this remains to be established empirically.

In other words, providing deaf children with bimodal input seems to be a promising approach to compensate for deaf children's EF deficits as it may enhance overall WM capacity. However, the facilitatory effects of bimodal input for deaf children may be strongly constrained by the specific properties of the bimodal input. It is likely that bimodal input that requires sequential processing in both channels will not facilitate deaf children's comprehension of the bimodal input and will, therefore, not enhance their learning. In other words, many questions need to be answered before we can effectively incorporate bimodal input in our intervention programs.

Remedial Interventions

Remedial EF intervention aim to enhance children's EF skills (Dawson & Guare, 2004; Dehn, 2008). Many of these interventions attempt to improve children's functioning at the algorithmic level of analysis, but some aim to improve children's functioning at both the algorithmic and reflective levels. In the next sections, both types of interventions will be described.

Remedial Interventions on the Algorithmic Mind: Working Memory Enhancement

As we described earlier, Nittrouer and colleagues (2013) pointed out that clinical efforts to reduce deaf children's problems with WM should, in addition to improving the quality of sensory information available to deaf children, be focused on providing auditory training. Problems with the identification of the phonological structure of incoming information will lead to a higher processing load, reducing the overall WM capacity (Pisoni et al., 2011). Deaf children's improved skills in identifying incoming auditory information therefore also should enhance their auditory WM capacity. Conventional auditory training programs (e.g., Sweetow & Palmer, 2005) and computer-based auditory training programs (e.g., Henswaw & Ferguson, 2013) have been found to be effective in improving speech recognition skills. Interestingly, Sweetow and Henderson-Sabes (2006) also observed improvements in auditory WM capacity in their evaluation of the computer-based LACE program with adults with a moderate hearing loss. Although these findings are certainly encouraging, it remains to be seen whether auditory training programs can enhance the capacity of auditory WM capacity in deaf children. Interestingly, enhanced auditory WM skills have not been observed for compensatory programs that aim to improve speech production and speech recognition skills, such as cued speech (Bouton, Bertoncini, Serniclaes, & Cole, 2011).

Vocabulary training also may enhance deaf children's capacity to identify incoming auditory information. The phonological sensitivity hypothesis states that vocabulary growth will enhance the segmental analysis skills of children that facilitate the temporary retention and learning of new words (Gathercole, 2006). Enhanced segmental analysis skills will reduce the processing load in auditory WM. As a consequence, deaf children's auditory WM capacity will increase. However, it remains to be seen whether vocabulary training in deaf children will indeed increase their segmental analysis skills, which, in turn, will enhance their auditory WM capacity.

Finally, verbal WM (e.g., for spoken language and sign language) and visual WM of deaf children may be increased by computer-based training programs such as Cogmed (Klingberg, 2010; Kronenberger et al., 2011) and Braingame Brian (Prins et al., 2010). The effectiveness of such programs is highly controversial (Gathercole, Dunning, & Holmes, 2012; Hulme & Melby-Lervåg, 2012; Klingsberg, 2010; Shipstead, Hicks, & Engle, 2012). Cogmed aims to improve both the storage and processing components of verbal and nonverbal memory. It was originally designed to improve WM for children with ADHD. The program works with a gamelike interface in which exercises are adapted to the child's performance on the previous trial. Furthermore, the child's engagement in the program is supported externally through rewards for successful completion of exercises and supervision by a parent and/or a Cogmed training coach. Proponents of computer-based programs such as Cogmed have argued that particularly children with low WM capacity can benefit a great deal from such intensive training programs (Klingberg, 2010). However, Shipstead and colleagues (2012) argued that many of the claims of Cogmed are not supported by experimental evidence (see also Hulme & Melby-Lervåg, 2012).

Most importantly, recent studies suggest that WM capacity can indeed be enhanced by training programs (e.g., Harrison, Shipstead, Hicks, Hambrick, Redick, & Engle, 2013). Harrison and colleagues found that WM training tasks (especially tasks focusing both on the storage and the central executive components of WM) indeed lead to generally improved performance on WM tasks. However, they also found that such effects did not transfer to tasks assessing fluid intelligence. Dunning, Holmes, and Gathercole (2013) recently observed mixed findings in the first randomized controlled trial evaluation of Cogmed with children with low WM capacity. They administered an adaptive WM training (Cogmed), a nonadaptive WM training (Cogmed developed for evaluation trials, Klingberg et al., 2005) or no training to three groups of children with WM deficits. They found that the adaptive version led to improvements in multiple untrained WM tasks, especially in verbal tasks that assessed the combined functioning of the phonological loop and the central executive. These benefits were sustained one year after the training, suggesting that the training has long-lasting beneficial effects on WM. However, no changes were observed in the performance of children in structured classroom tasks, and the training also did not affect the children's reading or mathematic skills. Dunning and colleagues (2013) argued that their findings may imply that the benefits of WM training programs are restricted to laboratory WM tasks (which is obviously not what WM training programs aim for). Alternatively, the transfer of WM benefits obtained in computer-based programs to everyday activities may just require external guidance (scaffolding and support). Dunning and colleagues (2013) pointed out that it seems that computer-based programs such as Cogmed need to be imbedded in activities that help children to apply their enhanced WM skills to situations in the classroom.

Kronenberger and colleagues (2013) conducted a first pilot study for Cogmed with nine deaf children. Although the children's scores on most WM tasks had significantly improved immediately after the training and one month later, these benefits were not sustained after six months. Quite remarkably, the benefits of the training were sustained for children's performance on a sentence repetition task. However, Kronenberger and colleagues pointed out that this may at least be partly due to practice effects. More studies on the impact of Cogmed or alternative computer-based programs on deaf children's WM capacity are needed.

To conclude, there seem to be different ways to improve deaf children's auditory WM skills. Professionals in the field may try to improve the quality of sensory information available to deaf children, teachers and speech therapists may try to increase deaf children's vocabulary knowledge, and computer-based programs such as Cogmed may be administered at home. These three different efforts, separately or combined, may lead to improvements in deaf children's auditory WM capacity. Computer-based programs such as Cogmed aim to enhance deaf children's verbal WM (e.g., for spoken language and sign language) and visual WM.

Remedial Interventions on the Algorithmic and Reflective Mind: Tools of the Mind

Diamond (2012) reviewed a variety of current interventions that aim to stimulate children's EFs. One of these interventions is the Tools of the Mind curriculum (Bodrova & Leung, 2001, 2007) for preschool and kindergarten children. It is inspired by the cultural-historical approach of Vygotski (1978), who proposed that self-regulation is the primary characteristic of high-level cognitive functions (the ability to think, to reason). He argued that children's learning can become intentional, on purpose, and active only when children can regulate their own thoughts and behavior.

Vygotski (1978) proposed that three conditions are necessary for children to be able to regulate their own behavior. First, the acquisition of any higher cognitive function on an intrapersonal level requires that children have experienced that particular function on an interpersonal level. In other words, self-regulation is necessarily preceded by "other-regulation." In being regulated by someone else (e.g., a parent or a teacher), children learn to internalize the rules dictated to them. In regulating someone else (e.g., a peer or a younger child), children practice the internalized rules by applying them to the someone else's behavior. Experiences with these two forms of other-regulation are necessary for children to develop self-regulation. Second, children have to acquire cultural tools that allow them to regulate their own behavior. An example of such a cultural tool is "self-talk" or "private speech." Children use private speech for the purpose of self-regulation, first in an overt form (out aloud) and subsequently in a covert form (inner speech). Third, children have to be engaged in well-developed, mature make-believe play. Make-believe play allows children to effectively practice multiple aspects of self-regulation.

The Tools of the Mind curriculum contains many Vygotski-inspired activities. In Tools of the Mind, mature pretend play is considered to be the most important tool for children in the development of self-regulation. Unique to the Tools of the Mind curriculum is the active and supportive role of the teacher in children's development of mature pretend play. Teachers consistently make sure that the pretend scenarios are planned, complex, and sustained, that they involve more than one role, and that children become and remain involved in play.

Because the Tools of the mind curriculum aims to stimulate children's self-regulation (voluntarily applying internalized rules to children's own behavior in everyday life), the program eventually aims to lead to EF improvements at the reflective level of analysis. Consistent with this assumption, Bodrova and Leung (2007) pointed out that the major aim of the Tools of the Mind program is to enhance children's critical thinking skills. Nevertheless, the Tools of the Mind curriculum also contains activities that stimulate skills at the algorithmic level of analysis. It can, therefore, be considered an intervention program that aims to enhance children's skills at the algorithmic and reflective levels.

The effectiveness of the Tools of the Mind curriculum has been investigated in several studies (Barnett et al., 2008; Diamond, Barnett, Thomas, & Munro, 2007; Farran, Wilson, & Lipsey, 2013). Even though the Tools of the Mind curriculum eventually targets children's EF development at the reflective level of analysis, the evaluations have mainly used (1) neuropsychological tests assessing children's skills at the algorithmic level of analysis (inhibition tasks, WM tasks, and shifting tasks, (2) tests assessing children's language skills and children's emerging literacy and mathematic skills, (3) teacher ratings of children's (social) behavior in the class, and (4) the classroom climate. Questionnaires that assess children's EF in everyday life, such as the BRIEF, have not been administered in research studies so far. The Tools of the Mind evaluations that have been conducted with hearing children have reported inconsistent results. Diamond and colleagues (2007) found that children using the curriculum outperformed children in a curriculum of similar quality that did not specifically focus on the development of children's EF skills on two inhibition tasks. Barnett and colleagues (2008) found advantages of the Tools of the Mind curriculum on questionnaires that assessed the social development of children and to a lesser degree on questionnaires that focused on the classroom climate. Small or no differences were observed for children's cognitive development. In a randomized controlled trial, Farran and colleagues (2013) found no beneficial effects of the Tools of the Mind curriculum on school achievement, language development, self-regulation (as measured by performance-based test of WM, inhibition, and shifting and sustained attention), or social development. In other words, studies on the impact of Tools of the Mind have not yet shown many beneficial effects on children's development. However, it is questionable whether the appropriate instruments have been used in the evaluations so far. Furthermore, the impact of such programs on children's development may take longer to manifest itself. Finally, more beneficial effects of the program may be observed for children with EF deficits or delays, like many deaf children or children with specific language impairment.

Several months before preparing this chapter, we started an intervention called De Kleine Kapitein (The Little Captain) developed by Sardes, which is based on the Tools of the Mind program. De Kleine Kapitein is a teacher training program for teachers working with children in prekindergarten. Teachers are trained to recognize children's EF deficits in the classroom and subsequently to enhance EF development by setting goals and structurally incorporating EF activities into their daily program. Three special schools participated in the intervention. The experiences of teachers of the deaf were somewhat mixed. On a positive note, teachers in special schools reported that they already have incorporated many Tools of the Mind activities into their daily program. However, teachers reported that it was very difficult to incorporate mature pretend play (the pretend scenarios are planned, complex, and sustained and involve multiple roles) into the classroom. First, deaf children are often delayed in the development of mature pretend play (Brown, Rickards, & Bortoli, 2001). Second, the language delays of the deaf children make it more difficult for the teacher to develop pretend play activities in the classroom. The training program, which was developed for hearing children without language delays, provided our teachers with little help in developing activities in the classroom to enhance deaf children's EF skills through mature role play. The difficulties teachers encountered in providing mature pretend play for deaf children also highlight the need to enhance deaf children's mature pretend play. We are exploring how we can stimulate deaf children's mature role play in the classroom more effectively.

Intervention Programs and Executive Function: Summary

In the previous sections we discussed several remedial or compensatory interventions. We have argued that remedial interventions such as auditory training, vocabulary training, WM training programs such as Cogmed, and a curriculum such as Tools of the Mind may lead to improvements in deaf children's EF skills. Alternatively, professionals may try to bypass deaf children's WM deficits by adjusting their instruction (simple and structured language use with familiar or meaningful content), choosing a more appropriate didactic approach in their teaching (errorless learning), or using bimodal input in their instruction to increase WM capacity. However, because the evidence from the scientific literature is still not conclusive with respect to the effectiveness of most of these interventions, they clearly require more evidence-based support. In addition, it is also unclear the extent to which the effectiveness of remedial and compensatory interventions depends on the (bilingual) language profile and language preference of deaf children.

SUMMARY AND CONCLUSION

How do deaf children and adolescents get what they want? How do they control their behavior and thoughts to achieve their goals in life? Many deaf children and adolescents have noticeable EF deficits or delays that affect their success in goal pursuit in life. These problems seem to manifest themselves at both the algorithmic level of analysis (the processing system that is needed for efficient goal pursuit) and the reflective level of analysis (higher-level regulatory states that initiate action). These findings require a different stance toward the programs that are used in early intervention and at schools for deaf children. First, the current interventions that are provided to deaf children and adolescents need to be attuned to their EF skills to enhance their development. Such approaches (e.g., general didactic approaches, the use of bimodal input) generally reduce the negative impact of children's information processing deficits on their learning at school. Although such compensatory approaches are widely used in early intervention and at schools, there are still many questions regarding their effectiveness. We need more research. Second, it seems that we need to incorporate more remedial interventions that enhance deaf children's and adolescents' EF. Some of these interventions (e.g., auditory training, vocabulary training, WM training programs such as Cogmed) aim to enhance children's deficits in information processing only, whereas other interventions (e.g., Tools of the Mind) aim to enhance EF more broadly. Although such interventions are theoretically very promising in enhancing children's and adolescents' success in goal pursuit in life, more research is needed to establish their effectiveness for deaf children.

NOTES

1 Consistent with this finding are the results from several separate studies conducted in the Netherlands with children with a specific language impairment. The children often have problems with verbal WM (Montgomery et al., 2010) and visuospatial WM (Vugs, Cuperus, Hendriks, & Verhoeven, 2013). Studies on the impact of bimodal input (signs and spoken words) relative to unimodal input (spoken words) on language learning have shown that the use of signs with children with a specific language impairment increases their learning in very simple instructional settings (Bode & Knoors, 2002). However, no beneficial effect of bimodal input (Sign Supported Dutch) over unimodal input (spoken Dutch) was observed in a study on children's comprehension of classroom instruction (Voogt, 2009).

2 It is often assumed that deaf children and students are, because of their hearing loss, visual learners (Marschark et al., 2013). The experimental findings mentioned above suggest that, as far as sequential processing of visual information is concerned, then, if anything, deaf children are disadvantaged in comparison to hearing children. Marschark and colleagues (2013) therefore concluded that deaf children are no more likely to be visual learners than hearing children and suggested that they may be no more likely to be visual learners than verbal learners.

3 Baddeley's WM model focuses predominantly on the retention of information during sequential information processing. Dye and Bavelier (2010) pointed out that deaf children and adolescents may have deficit or delays in information processing in time, but their skills seem to be enhanced with respect to information processing in space. To illustrate, when working tasks place less emphasis on the retention of temporal order of stimuli, the WM capacity of deaf children and deaf adults is comparable or even better than the WM

capacity of hearing children (Alamargot, Lambert, Thebault, & Dansac, 2007; Boutla et al., 2004). However, the retention of serial order information is a central part of and essential to information processing.

4 Bimodal input from two visual sources (pictures and written words) does not show the bimodal advantage over unimodal input (Goolkasian & Fools, 2005), and the retention of information from two visual dynamic sources (animations and written words) has been found to be less poor than the retention of information from two dynamic sources from a different modality (animation and spoken words). It is therefore not surprising that Marschark and colleagues (2006) found no benefit of interpreting and subtitling over only interpreting the contents of a television program. In other words, the combination of information from two dynamic resources is not likely to improve deaf children's understanding of information.

REFERENCES

Alamargot, D., Lambert, E., Thebault, C., & Dansac, C. (2007). Text composition by deaf and hearing middle-school students: The role of working memory. *Reading and Writing*, *20*, 333–360.

Alloway, T. (2007). *The Automated Working Memory Assessment.* London: Pearson Assessment.

Baddeley, A. (1992). Working memory. *Science*, *255*, 556–559.

Baddeley, A. (1996). Exploring the central executive. *Quarterly Journal of Experimental Psychology*, *49*, 5–28.

Baddeley, A. (2000). The episodic buffer: New component of working memory? *Trends in Cognitive Sciences*, *4*, 417–423.

Baddeley, A. (2003). Working memory and language: An overview. *Journal of Communication Disorders*, *36*, 189–208.

Baddeley, A. D. (2007). *Working memory, thought, and action.* New York: Oxford University Press.

Baddeley, A., & Hitch, G. (1974). Working memory. In G. A. Bower (Ed.), *Recent advances in learning and motivation* (Vol. 8, pp. 47–99). New York: Academic Press.

Banich, M. T. (2009). Executive function: the search for an integrated account. *Current Directions in Psychological Science*. *18*, 89–94.

Barkley, R. A. (1997). *ADHD and the nature of self-control.* New York: Guilford Press.

Barkley, R. A. (2012a). *The Barkley Deficits in Executive Functioning Scale—Children and Adolescents.* New York: Guilford.

Barkley, R. A. (2012b). *Executive functions. What they are, how they work and how they evolved.* New York: Guildford Press.

Barkley, R. A., & Fischer, M. (2011). Predicting impairment in major life activities and occupational functioning in hyperactive children as adults: Self-reported executive function (EF) deficits versus EF tests. *Developmental Neuropsychology*, *36*, 137–161.

Barkley, R. A., & Murphy, K. R. (2010). Impairment in occupational functioning and adult ADHD: The predictive utility of executive function (EF) ratings versus EF tests. *Archives of Clinical Neuropsychology*, *25*, 157–173.

Barnett, W. S., Jung, K., Yarosz, D. J., Thomas, J., Hornbeck, A., Stechuk, R., & Burns, S. (2008). Educational effects of the Tools of the Mind curriculum: a randomized trial. *Early Childhood Research Quarterly*, *23*, 299–313.

Bennett, P. C., Ong, B., & Ponsford, J. (2005). Measuring executive dysfunction in an acute rehabilitation setting: Using the Dysexecutive Questionnaire (DEX). *Journal of the International Neuropsychological Society, 11*, 376–385.

Bergeson, T. R., Houston, D. M., & Miyamoto, R. T. (2010). Effects of congenital hearing loss and cochlear implantation on audiovisual speech perception in infants and children. *Restorative Neurology and Neuroscience, 28*, 157–165.

Bode, D., & Knoors, H. (2002). Het effect van het gebruik van gebaren op de woordproductie van kinderen met specifieke taalstoornissen. *Van Horen Zeggen, 43*, 4–9.

Bodrova, E., & Leong, D. J. (2001). *Tools of the mind: A case study of implementing the Vygotskian approach in American early childhood and primary classrooms.* Geneva: International Bureau of Education, UNESCO.

Bodrova, E., & Leong, D. J. (2007). *Tools of the mind: The Vygotskian approach to early childhood education.* Upper Saddle River, NJ: Pearson Education, Inc.

Boutla, M., Supalla, T., Newport, E. L., & Bavelier, D. (2004). Short-term memory span: Insights from sign language. *Nature Neuroscience, 7*(9), 997–1002.

Bouton, S., Bertoncini, J., Serniclaes, W., & Cole, P. (2011). Reading and reading-related skills in children using cochlear implants: Prospects for the influence of cued speech. *Journal of Deaf Studies and Deaf Education, 16*, 458–473

Brown, P. M., Rickards, F. W., & Bortoli, A. M. (2001). Structures underpinning pretend play and word productions in young hearing children with hearing toss. *Journal of Deaf Studies Education, 6*, 15–31.

Chen, C., & Rada, R. (1996). Interacting with hypertext: A meta-analysis of experimental studies. *Human-Computer Interaction, 11*, 125–156.

Cockcroft, K., & Dhana-Dullabh, H. (2012). Deaf children and children with ADHD in the inclusive classroom: working memory matters. *International Journal of Inclusive Education, 17*, 1023–1039.

Conway, C. M., Karpicke, J., Anaya, E. M., Henning, S. C., Kronenberger, W. G., & Pisoni, D. B. (2011). Nonverbal cognition in deaf children following cochlear implantation: Motor sequencing disturbances mediate language delays. *Developmental Neuropsychology, 36*, 237–254.

Conway, C. M., Pisoni, D. B., Anaya, E. M., Karpicke, J., & Henning, S. C. (2011). Implicit sequence learning in deaf children with cochlear implants. *Developmental Science, 14*, 69–82.

Conway, C. M., Pisoni, D. B., & Kronenberger, W. (2009). The importance of sound for cognitive sequencing abilities: the auditory scaffolding hypothesis. *Current Directions in Psychological Science, 18*, 275–279.

Dawson, P., & Guare, R. (Eds.). (2004). *Executive skills in children and adolescents: A practical guide to assessment and intervention.* New York: Guilford.

Delis, D. C., Kaplan, E., & Kramer, J. H. (2001). *Delis-Kaplan Executive Function System (D-KEFS).* San Antonio, TX: Psychological Corporation.

Dehn, M. (2008). *Working memory and academic learning: Assessment and intervention.* Hoboken, NJ: Wiley.

DeStefano, D., & LeFevre, J. A. (2007). Cognitive load in hypertext reading: A review. *Computers in Human Behavior, 23*, 1616–1641.

Dettman, S., & Dowell, R. (2010). Language acquisition and critical periods for children using cochlear implants. The demands of writing and the deaf writer. In M. Marschark & P. E. Spencer (Eds.), *The Oxford handbook of deaf studies, language and education* (Vol. 2, pp. 331–342). New York: Oxford University Press.

Diamond, A. (2012). Activities and programs that improve children's executive functions. *Current Directions in Psychological Science, 21*, 335–341.

Diamond, A., Barnett, W. S., Thomas, J., & Munro, S. (2007). Preschool program improves cognitive control. *Science, 318*, 1387–1388.

Dunning, D. L., Holmes, J., & Gathercole, S. E. (2013). Does working memory training lead to generalized improvements in children with low working memory? A randomized controlled trial. *Developmental Science, 6*, 915–925.

Dye, M. W., & Bavelier, D. (2010). Attentional enhancements and deficits in deaf populations: An integrative review. *Restorative Neurology and Neuroscience, 28*, 181–192.

Emslie, H. C., Wilson, F. C., Burden, V., Nimmo-Smith, I., & Wilson, B. A. (2003). *Behavioural Assessment of the Dysexecutive Syndrome in Children (BADS-C)*. Bury St. Edmunds, UK: Thames Valley Test Company.

Engle, R. W., Carullo, J. J., & Collins, K. W. (1991). Individual differences in working memory for comprehension and following directions. *Journal of Educational Research, 84*, 253–262.

Falkman, K., & Hjelmquist, E. (2006). Do you see what I mean? Shared reference in non-native, early signing deaf children. *Journal of Deaf Studies and Deaf Education, 11*, 410–420.

Farran, D. C., Wilson, S. J., & Lipsey, M. W. (2013). *Effects of a curricular attempt to improve self-regulation and achievement in prekindergarten children*. Presented to the Society of Research in Child Development, April 19, 2013.

Gathercole, S. (2006). Nonword repetition and word learning: The nature of the relationship. *Applied Psycholinguistics, 27*, 513–543.

Gathercole, S. E., Dunning, D. L & Holmes, J. (2012). Cogmed training: Let's be realistic about intervention research. *Journal of Applied Research in Memory and Cognition, 3*, 201–203.

Gathercole, S. E., Lamont, E., & Alloway, T. P. (2006). Working memory in the classroom. In S. Pickering (Ed.), *Working memory and education* (pp. 219–240). Amsterdam: Elsevier Press.

Gioia, G. A., Isquith, P. K., Guy, S. C., & Kenworthy, L. (2000). *Behavior Rating Inventory of Executive Function*. Odessa, FL: Psychological Assessment Resources.

Gioia, G. A., Isquith, P. K., & Kenealy, L. E. (2008). Assessment of behavioral aspects of executive function. In V. Anderson, R. Jacobs, & P. J. Anderson (Eds.), *Executive functions and the frontal lobes* (pp. 179–202). New York: Psychology Press.

Goia, G. A., Isquith, P. K., Retzlaff, P. D., & Espy, K. A. (2002). Confirmatory factor analysis of the Behavior Rating Inventory of Executive Function (BRIEF) in a clinical sample. *Child Neuropsychology, 8*, 249–257

Goolkasian, P., & Foos, P. W. (2005). Bimodal format effects in working memory. *American Journal of Psychology, 118*, 61–78.

Hamilton, H. (2011). Memory skills of deaf learners: Implications and applications. *American Annals of the Deaf, 156*, 402–423.

Hamilton, H., & Holzman, T. G. (1989). Linguistic coding in short-term memory as a function of stimulus type. *Memory and Cognition, 17*, 541–550.

Harrison, T. L., Shipstead, Z., Hicks, K. L., Hambrick, D. Z., Redick, T. S., & Engle, R. W. (2013). Working memory training may increase working memory capacity but not fluid intelligence. *Psychological Science, 24*, 2409–2419.

Hauser, P. C., Lukomski, J., & Hillman, T. (2008). Development of deaf and hard-of-hearing students' executive function. In M. Marschark & P. C. Hauser (Eds.), *Deaf cognition: Foundations and outcomes* (pp. 286–308). New York: Oxford University Press.

Hauser, P. C., Lukomski, J., & Samar, V. (2013). Reliability and validity of the BRIEF-A for assessing deaf college students' executive function. *Journal of Psychoeducational Assessment*, 31, 363–374.

Henshaw, H., & Ferguson, M. A. (2013). Efficacy of individual computer-based auditory training for people with hearing loss: A systematic review of the evidence. *PLoS One, 8*, 628–636.

Hermans, D., Wauters, L., de Klerk, A., & Knoors, H. (2014). Quality of instruction in bilingual schools for deaf children: through the children's eyes and the camera's lens. In M. Marschark, G., Tang, & H. Knoors (Eds.), *Bilingualism and bilingual deaf education* (pp. 396–423). New York: Oxford University Press.

Hintermair, M. (2013). Executive functions and behavioral problems in deaf and hard-of-hearing students at general and special schools. *Journal of Deaf Studies and Deaf Education*, *18*, 344–359.

Hofmann, W., Schmeichel, B. J., & Baddeley, A. D. (2012). Executive functions and self-regulation. *Trends in Cognitive Sciences*, *16*, 174–180.

Hulme, C., & Melby-Lervåg, M. (2012). Current evidence does not support the claims made for CogMed working memory training. *Journal of Applied Research in Memory and Cognition*, *3*, 197–200.

Jarvis, H., & Gathercole, S. (2003). Verbal and non-verbal working memory and achievements on national curriculum tests at 11 and 14 years of age. *Educational and Child Psychology*, *87*, 93–102.

Just, M. A., & Carpenter, P. A. (1992). A capacity theory of comprehension: individual differences in working memory. *Psychological Review*, *99*, 122–149.

Kerr, A., & Zelazo, P. D. (2004). Development of "hot" executive function: The children's gambling task. *Brain and Cognition*, *55*, 148–157.

Klingberg, T. (2010). Training and plasticity of working memory. *Trends in Cognitive Sciences*, *14*, 317–324

Klingberg, T., Fernell, E., Olesen, P. J., Johnson, M., Gustafsson, P., Dahlstrom, K., . . . & Westerberg, H. (2005). Computerised training of working memory in children with ADHD: a randomized controlled trial. *Journal of the American Academy of Child and Adolescent Psychiatry*, *44*, 177–186.

Kronenberger, W. G., Pisoni, D. B., Henning, S. C., Colson, B. G., & Hazzard, L. M. (2011). Working memory training for children with cochlear implants: A pilot study. *Journal of Speech Language and Hearing Research*, *54*, 1182–1196.

Lee, M. J., & Tedder, M. C. (2003). The effects of three different computer texts on readers' recall based on working memory capacity. *Computers in Human Behavior*, *19*, 767–783.

Macedonia, M., Muller, K., & Friederici, A. D. (2011). The impact of iconic gestures on foreign language word learning and its neural substrate. *Human Brain Mapping*, *32*, 982–998.

Manly, T., Robertson, I. H., Anderson, V., & Nimmo-Smith, I. (1999) *The Test of Everyday Attention for Children (TEA-Ch)*. Bury St. Edmunds, UK: Thames Valley Test Company.

Marschark, M., Leigh, G., Sapere, P., Burnham, D., Convertino, C., Stinson, M., . . . & Noble, W. (2006). Benefits of sign language interpreting and text alternatives to classroom learning by deaf students. *Journal of Deaf Studies and Deaf Education, 11*, 421–437.

Marschark, M., Morrison, C., Lukomski, J., Borgna, G., & Convertino, C. (2013). Are deaf students visual learners? *Learning and Individual Differences, 25*, 156–162.

Marschark, M., Sapere, P., Convertino, C. M., & Pelz, J. (2008). Learning via direct and mediated instruction by deaf students. *Journal of Deaf Studies and Deaf Education, 13*, 446–461.

Marschark, M., Sapere, P., Convertino, C., & Seewagen, R. (2005). Access to postsecondary education through sign language interpreting. *Journal of Deaf Studies and Deaf Education, 10*, 38–50.

Marschark, M., Sarchet, T., & Trani A. (2014). *Effects of hearing loss and sign language use on working memory.* Manuscript submitted for publication.

Mayer, R. E. (2001). *Multimedia learning*. New York: Cambridge University Press.

Mayer, R. E., & Moreno, R. (1998). A split-attention effect in multimedia learning: Evidence for dual processing systems in working memory. *Journal of Educational Psychology, 90*, 312–320.

McCabe, D. P., Roediger, H. L., McDaniel, M. A., Balota, D. A., & Hambrick, D. Z. (2010). The relationship between working memory capacity and executive functioning: Evidence for a common executive attention construct. *Neuropsychology, 24*, 222–243.

Mitchell, T. V., & Quittner, A. L. (1996). Multimethod study of attention and behavior problems in hearing-impaired children. *Journal of Clinical Child Psychology, 25*, 83–96.

Miyake, A., Friedman, N. P., Emerson, M. J., Witzki, A. H., Howerter, A., & Wager, T. D. (2000). The unity and diversity of executive functions and their contributions to complex 'frontal lobe' tasks: A latent variable analysis. *Cognitive Psychology, 41*, 49–100.

Miyake, A., & Shah, P. (Eds.). (1999). *Models of working memory*. New York: Cambridge University Press.

Mollink, I., Hermans, D., & Knoors, H. (2008). Vocabulary training of words in hard-of-hearing children. *Deafness and Education International, 10*, 80–92.

Monsell, S. (1996). Control of mental processes. In V. Bruce (Ed.), *Unsolved mysteries of the mind: Tutorial essays in cognition* (pp. 93–148). Hove, UK: Erlbaum.

Montgomery, J. W., Magimairaj, B. M., & Finney, M. C. (2010). Working memory and specific language impairment: an update on the relation and perspectives on assessment and treatment. *American Journal of Speech-Language Pathology, 19*, 78–94.

Nash, G., Henry, L. A., & Messer, D. J. (2010). *Verbal and non-verbal fluency in children with specific language impairment.* Presented at the Child Language Seminar, City University, London, June 2010.

Nittrouer, S., Caldwell-Tarr, A., & Lowenstein, J. H. (2013). Working memory in children with cochlear implants: Problems are in storage, not processing. *International Journal of Pediatric Otorhinolaryngology, 77*, 1886–1898.

Nobre, A. P., Rodrigues, J. C., Sbicigo, J. B., Piccolo, L. R., Zortea, M., Duarte Jr., S., & de Salles, F. F. (2013). Tasks for assessment of the episodic buffer: a systematic review. *Psychology & Neuroscience, 6*, 331–343.

Oberg, E., & Lukomski, J. (2011). Executive functioning and the impact of a hearing loss: Performance-based measures and the Behavior Rating Inventory of Executive Function. *Child Neuropsychology, 17*, 521–545.

Paivio, A. (1986). *Mental representations: A dual coding approach.* Oxford, England: Oxford University Press.

Pisoni, D. B., & Cleary, M. (2003). Measures of working memory span and verbal rehearsal speed in deaf children after cochlear implantation. *Ear and Hearing, 24,* 106–120.

Pisoni, D. B., Conway, C. M., Kronenberger, W., Henning, S., & Anaya, E. (2010). Executive function, cognitive control and sequence learning in deaf children with cochlear implants. In M. Marschark & P. E. Spencer (Eds.), *The Oxford handbook of deaf studies, language, and education* (pp. 439–457). New York: Oxford University Press.

Pisoni, D. B., Conway, C. M., Kronenberger, W., Horn, D. L., Karpicke, J., & Henning, S. (2008). Efficacy and effectiveness of cochlear implants in deaf children. In M. Marschark & P. C. Hauser (Eds.), *Deaf cognition: Foundations and outcomes* (pp. 52–101). New York: Oxford University Press.

Pisoni, D. B., Kronenberger, W. G., Roman, A. S., & Geers, A. E. (2011) Measures of digit span and verbal rehearsal speed in deaf children after more than 10 years of cochlear implantation. *Ear and Hearing, 32,* 60–74.

Prins, P. J. M., Ten Brink, E. L., Dovis, S., Ponsioen, A. J. G. B., Geurts, H., de Groot, H., . . . & Van der Oord, S. (2010). *Braingame Brian: An executive function training program with game-elements for children with cognitive control problems.* University of Amsterdam; Lucertis & Shosho.

Quittner, A. L., Barker, D. H., Snell, C., Cruz, I., McDonald, L. G., Grimely, M. E., . . . & CDACI Investigative Team. (2007). Improvements in visual attention in deaf infants and toddlers after cochlear implantation. *Audiological Medicine, 5,* 242–249.

Rhine, S. (2002). *Assessment of executive function.* Unpublished master's thesis. Gallaudet University, Washington, DC.

Romero Lauro, L. J., Crespi, M., Papagno, C., & Ceccetto, C. (2014). Making sense of an unexpected detrimental effect of sign language use in a visual task. *Journal of Deaf Studies and Deaf Education.* doi: 10.1093/deafed/enu001

Rudner, M., & Rönnberg, J. (2008). Explicit processing demands reveal language modality—specific organization of working memory. *Journal of Deaf Studies and Deaf Education, 13,* 466–484.

Schorr, E. A., Fox, N. A., van Wassenhove, V., & Knudsen, E. I. (2005). Auditory-visual fusion in speech perception in children with cochlear implants. *Proceedings of the National Academy of Sciences USA, 102,* 18748–18750.

Shams, L., & Seitz, A. R. (2008): Benefits of multisensory learning. *Trends in Cognitive Sciences, 12,* 411–417.

Shipstead, Z., Hick, K. L., & Engle, R. W. (2012). Cogmed working memory training: Does the evidence support the claims? *Journal of Applied Research in Memory and Cognition, 3,* 185–193.

Skinner, B. F. (1953). *Science and human behavior.* New York: Macmillan.

Smidts, D. P., & Huizinga, M. (2009). *BRIEF Executieve Functies Gedragsvragenlij st: Handleiding.* Amsterdam: Hogrefe.

Stanovich, K. E. (2009). Distinguishing the reflective, algorithmic, and autonomous minds: It is time for a tri-process theory? In J. St. B. T. Evans & K. Frankish (Eds.), *In two minds: Dual processes and beyond* (pp. 55–88). New York: Oxford University Press.

Swanson, H. L., Jerman, O., & Zheng, X. (2008). Growth in working memory and mathematical problem solving in children at risk and not at risk for serious math difficulties. *Journal of Educational Psychology, 100*, 343–379.

Sweetow, R. W., & Henderson-Sabes, J. (2006). The need for and development of an adaptive Listening And Communication Enhancement (LACE™) program. *Journal of the American Academy of Audiology, 17*, 538–558.

Sweetow, R. W., & Palmer, C. V. (2005). Efficacy of individual auditory training in adults: A systematic review of the evidence. *Journal of the American Academy of Audiology, 16*, 494–504.

Tellier, M. (2008). The effect of gestures on second language memorisation by young children. *Gesture, 8*, 219–235.

Ting, J. Y., Bergeson, T. R., & Miyamoto, R. T. (2012). Effects of simultaneous speech and sign on infants' attention to spoken language. *Laryngoscope, 122*, 2808–2812.

Toplak, M. E., West, R. F., & Stanovich, K. E. (2013). Do performance-based measures and ratings of executive function assess the same construct? *Journal of Child Psychology, 54*, 131–143.

Voogt, M. (2009). *Een gebaar: Zomaar een handbeweging of ook effectief?* Masterscriptie Radboud Universiteit Nijmegen.

Vugs, B., Cuperus, J., Hendriks, M., & Verhoeven, L. (2013). Visuospatial working memory in specific language impairment: A meta-analysis. *Research in Developmental Disabilities, 34*, 2586–2597.

Vygotsky, L. S. (1978). *Mind in society: The development of higher psychological processes.* Cambridge, MA: Harvard University Press.

Wang, J., & Napier, J. (2013). Signed language working memory capacity of signed language interpreters and deaf signers. *Journal of Deaf Studies and Deaf Education, 18*, 271–286.

Wauters, L., Knoors, H., Vervloed, M., & Aarnoutse, C. (2001). Sign facilitation in word recognition. *Journal of Special Education, 35*, 31–40.

Wilson, M., Bettger, J. G., Niculae, I., & Klima, E. S. (1997). Modality of language shapes working memory: Evidence from digit span and spatial span in ASL signers. *Journal of Deaf Studies & Deaf Education, 2*, 150–160.

Wilson, M., & Emmorey, K. (1997a). Working memory for sign language: a window into the architecture of working memory. *Journal of Deaf Studies and Deaf Education, 2*, 123–132.

Wilson, M., & Emmorey, K. (1997b). A visuospatial "phonological loop" in working memory: Evidence from American Sign Language. *Memory & Cognition, 25*, 313–320.

Wilson, M., & Emmorey, K. (1998). A "word length effect" for sign language: Further evidence for the role of language in structuring working memory. *Memory & Cognition, 26*, 584–590.

Wilson, M., & Emmorey, K. (2001). Functional consequences of modality: Spatial coding in working memory for signs. In V. Dively, M. Metzger, S. Taub, & A. Baer (Eds.), *Sign languages: Discoveries from international research* (pp. 91–99). Washington, DC: Gallaudet University Press.

Wilson, M., & Emmorey, K. (2003). The effect of irrelevant visual input on working memory for sign language. *Journal of Deaf Studies and Deaf Education, 8*, 97–103.

12

Social-Cognition for Learning as a Deaf Student

Gary Morgan

This chapter describes research findings on deaf children's understanding of others—an ability termed social-cognition, with one important component called Theory of Mind (ToM). The chapter attempts to link what we know about social-cognitive development and its function for deaf students in a school classroom. With this in mind, it is aimed at teachers, communication support workers, and parents of deaf children. The chapter title is purposely about how social-cognition enables or facilitates academic learning; we will highlight research findings that might be relevant for deaf children's academic progress. In this chapter "learning" refers to the mastery of academic concepts: numeracy, encyclopedic knowledge, and the epistemological skills to appreciate different points of view in science and so forth.

In the United Kingdom 1 in 1,000 children are born each year with a significant hearing loss that affects their language and educational achievement (Davis et al., 1997). The recent survey by the Consortium for Research in Deaf Education (CRIDE, 2012) estimated this equated to 37,400 school-aged children in England. Furthermore, 95% of these children are born to hearing parents with little experience or knowledge of deafness. While intelligence scores are within the normal range for these children (Braden, 1994), they lag behind their hearing peers in educational achievement. Powers and colleagues (1998) reported that only 14% of 16-year-old deaf children achieved the higher grades (GCSE A through C) necessary for advanced studies compared with 44% of hearing children at this age. Powers and colleagues (1998), in a systematic review of educational achievement of deaf children, reported significant delays in language, reading, writing, and mathematics, which they concluded was an indication of pervasive underachievement.

Much research over the same time period has described developmental differences between deaf and hearing children in their social-cognitive skills (see recent review in Meristo, Helmquist, & Morgan, 2012), yet very little research addresses the question of social-cognition and academic learning directly or even what happens with deaf children's interactions in the classroom (e.g., Delana, Gentry, & Andrews, 2007; Singleton & Morgan, 2006). How might academic achievement and social-cognitive development be linked? It is generally accepted that the early home environment, especially early, rich interaction and language, can provide children with good social-cognitive foundations for school learning (see Hintermair, Chapter 13 in this volume; Tang, Yiu, & Lam, Chapter 6 in this volume. The same can be assumed for how deaf children develop social-cognitive skills needed for academic achievement.

This chapter focuses on how deaf children view other people and understand the social consequences of their own and others' behavior and thinking. An increased understanding of this aspect of deaf children's development might help teachers appreciate why deaf children could be different types of academic learners. For example, if a 6-year-old deaf child does not understand other people's thinking, this will affect how well he or she can participate in a classroom discussion about the reasons for different outcomes in a story. Deafness might affect learning in many ways—for example, by affecting the development of language comprehension, by its consequences for different aspects of nonverbal intellectual development (e.g., memory, attention and executive functions), or more widely in terms of the level of parental involvement in a deaf child's education (see Hermans, Vugs, van Berkel-van Hoof, & Knoors, Chapter 11 in this volume). However, a child with delays in understanding the reasons for other people's behavior and mental states will be at a disadvantage for learning in a classroom as well. Social awareness and abilities in understanding others are crucial elements for a deaf child's full inclusion in the mainstream classroom.

The chapter is organized as follows. First a working definition of social-cognition in classroom learners will be outlined. This involves more specifically what ToM and understanding of false belief entail. Many studies have linked language development with ToM and especially children's understanding of explicit false belief tasks (tested with questions and answers), and this will be described in the second section. The third section will describe research on deaf children's performance on ToM tasks. In the same section, a framework based on access to conversation as a trigger for ToM development will be described (Siegal, 1997), followed by a summary of research in this area with deaf child–hearing parent dyads. The chapter concludes with a section on possible intervention and training studies for improving social-cognition in deaf children in their families and classrooms. The purpose of this last section is to stimulate discussion on how educational professionals and groups who work with parents of deaf children can intervene in social-cognition development at various levels.

UNPACKING SOCIAL-COGNITION

Social-cognition revolves around how we learn to understand other people's mental states (e.g., knowledge, beliefs, desires, emotions) and how these states are related to certain patterns in other's behavior. To illustrate one aspect of this domain, appreciating other people's false beliefs, an everyday family interaction, is described here. Picture this scene: You arrive home from work and your six-year-old daughter, Ruby, announces that she has made you a cake. Ruby is wearing an apron and is carrying a dirty bowl. You take this as evidence that there is a cake somewhere that can be eaten. Your one-year-old son, James, is observing this from his high chair and watches you as you proceed to the kitchen. But on opening the oven you are confronted with a very wobbly-looking pile of Play-Doh made of different colors in the rough shape of a cake. You hesitate a second before laughing: Ruby really got you this time, and both of you share the joke. At the same time James is looking at the both of you trying to understand what has happened: Is there a cake after all, why is this all so funny, and what are these two people thinking about as they laugh?

This story describes an example of people using their social-cognition. Specifically, Ruby planted a false belief in your mind: You believed that you were going to eat a real cake. Ruby knew what you were thinking while at the same time she knew that this belief was false—there was no real cake. This ability to reason about other's beliefs is enabled by what psychologists term metarepresentation and is at the heart of the ability to reflect on the reasons for other people's behavior. Metarepresentation allows the child to hold in her mind another person's cognitions or thinking, which in the cake example is in fact different from her own understanding of reality. The child knows there is no real cake but also knows that her father is thinking that there is. Being able to do this allows you to reason about, predict, and explain the behavior of others.

Ruby was able to understand and even predict your surprise at opening the oven and clearly enjoys the confusion the false belief led you to. This is all fine for the six-year-old; however, the interesting question is this: What did James get out of it? This question is over 30 years old in the research literature on social-cognitive or ToM development. To be able to enter into the ToM game, children need to be able to understand the language and pragmatics of the situation ("We made you a cake," but we know it is not a real cake), which entails some appreciation of the rules of conversations; to understand the emotional response (surprise, laughter) and why it had come about; to be able to represent another person's belief (he thinks the cake in the oven is going to be a real cake, but only I know that); and finally to reason about that representation (I know his belief is false). All of these complex developments are required before children can fully understand what has happened in the false belief situation.

The first studies of false belief understanding proposed that these abilities emerged in typically developing children between four and five years of age. What enables this development to happen (i.e., the stimulation or triggers) is still the subject of much debate. One area of research proposes that ToM development is determined by language acquisition. For this reason, many studies have investigated social-cognitive development in deaf children who have different degrees of language development delay. If we imagine that the children in the cake scenario were the deaf offspring of hearing parents, what would we expect of them in terms of understanding false beliefs? Would a six-year-old deaf child playing the cake game have this complex ability to manipulate metarepresentations of the beliefs of adults, and how much would the one-year-old deaf child understand if everyone playing the game around him were hearing and speaking? From many studies of children born deaf to hearing parents it is clear that these kinds of social-cognitive skills develop significantly later than in both deaf children with deaf parents and hearing children of hearing parents (e.g., Courtin & Melot, 2005; Figueras-Costa & Harris, 2005; Schick, deVilliers, deVilliers, & Hoffmeister, 2007; Meristo et al., 2012, Morgan & Kegl, 2006; Wimmer & Perner, 1983). There is, however, continuing debate as to what factors in deaf children's development may be different or deficient that lead to such ToM delays.

While little of the previous research concerns exactly how delays in understanding false belief would affect academic learning in classrooms, we can speculate how the two areas are related. We know that understanding false belief is linked to appreciating other people's emotions, mental states, desires, and intentions, and so a difficulty in reasoning about the mental lives of others would affect how successful a child is in accessing the interpersonal dynamics of the classroom. Equally, understanding the social-cognitive factors that explain other people's behaviors would offer children in the classroom a better grasp of the reasons for specific requests from teachers and other children. This would be important when these requests involved understanding pragmatics—for example, rhetorical questions from teachers, reflecting on why one's own actions and behavior are linked to other people's emotions, and so on. ToM would allow deaf children to navigate between different perspectives on the same situation, discussions of scientific or philosophical points of view, for example, in the question of whether all wars are bad. A well-developed ToM would be extremely important for deaf children's understanding of abstract concepts discussed in the classroom that require some level of metarepresentation of mental states. While ToM might not be necessary for all academic learning, it is an important skill for accessing the classroom dynamics where learning is taking place.

Two related issues in deaf children's language development are important to set out early. First, language itself (via the semantics, syntax, and grammar) will facilitate understanding of complex ToM-related concepts encountered in classrooms for the first time (e.g., appreciating the difference among "remember," "recall," "call to mind," and "rings a bell") as well as understanding sentence structures used in hypothetical language (e.g., "if you were *X*"). In the wider field many theorists have linked the role of language development to the development of ToM in typically developing hearing children (e.g., deVilliers & deVilliers, 2000; Milligan, Astington, & Dack, 2007). Second, there is an issue about how deafness affects access to language in the ambient discourse where abilities in understanding other's talk around you will be important for accessing mental state knowledge. The first issue has been very well documented in deaf children, and results are changing rapidly. However, despite great improvements, language development (especially spoken) is effortful and usually delayed in deaf children with hearing parents (e.g., Quittner et al., 2013, and reviews in Spencer & Marschark, 2006). However, the second issue (access to overheard ToM-related talk of others in the classroom) has received much less attention in the research literature. Hearing children typically experience much everyday discussion and conversation of different points of view just by overhearing older siblings or parents talking (O'Brien, Slaughter, & Peterson, 2011) and enter naturally into what Nelson, Plesa, and Henseler (1998) termed the "community of minds." There is very little research looking at mainstream classroom interaction with deaf children, but we could speculate that even those children with good hearing because of their use of cochlear implants (CIs) will be less able to access this ambient language in noisy classroom environments. CIs, while they work well for face-to-face communication if a child can use spoken language, do not give a child fully functioning hearing for multiple conversations around him or her in a noisy classroom to the same extent as for typically hearing children (Akhtar, 2005).

For full participation in classrooms and for effective learning, deaf children need to be able to better understand social situations involving themselves and other children. When other children act in particular ways in response to the teacher, it is important that deaf children in mainstream classrooms grasp what mental states are driving these actions. For example, a hearing child in a classroom hears the upset cry of a hearing pupil at another desk. The first child looks up and, while still holding his pencil to the paper, works out what has happened: The second child has ripped her drawing. The first child overhears the word "rubber" (eraser) and surmises the second child was upset because while rubbing out her picture the page got ripped. This happens in a split second, and the first child takes this in and then looks down and continues with his work. The deaf peer sitting nearby missed all of this happening. At break time the two hearing children brush past each other and the second child acts as if she is angry about the collision. The first hearing child correctly understands that the motives for this reaction are linked to the previous event with the paper and rubber and is able to regulate his own behavior as a result. The deaf child looks at the angry girl in confusion.

Any deaf child would find this social-cognitive situation quite challenging to resolve; ambient noise and incidental language might be more difficult to process quickly in a noisy classroom, even for a hearing child. A skilled classroom assistant working with a deaf child is going to struggle to explain everything that is happening around a deaf child. We can also think about how much incidental learning happens in the home among parents, siblings, and friends. How much information is relayed to young deaf children about things happening beyond their hearing range?

For typically developing children, teachers and parents explain incidental social situations as learning is taking place. As children read, for example, the teacher may be asking one child to "explain to your friend what you are reading because she doesn't understand the first line." Deaf children might be getting reduced input of this incidental discussion of mental states. Children develop their social cognition through informal overheard and direct conversation and experience of rich accessible social situations, and through their developing language ability (Akhtar, 2005). If even those deaf children with good language skills and some amount of hearing are missing out on some incidental information around them, this will contribute to difficulties in completing the complex picture of how world and social knowledge fit together. There is a part of the ToM difficulty therefore linked to how much young deaf children are active participants in social situations, which is connected to their language and conversational skills and how much they miss from not overhearing information occurring around them.

There are significant academic consequences of social-cognitive delay; for example, access to higher levels of literacy will require high levels of pragmatic comprehension of plot components and ToM abilities. Teachers and educational professionals need to know more about social-cognitive development and how deaf children are at risk for missing this important set of milestones.

SELECTIVE RETROSPECTIVE ON THEORY OF MIND RESEARCH

The first published studies of ToM were those by Wimmer and Perner (1983) and involved typically developing hearing children where, in the standard test scenario, the experimenter introduces the child being tested to two dolls called Sally and Anne. The experimenter uses the Sally doll to hide a marble in a basket in front of Anne's view. Then

Sally is removed from the test situation by telling the child that the doll had to go outside. While Sally is absent the experimenter uses the Anne doll to move a marble from the basket to a closable box. Now the experimenter brings back the Sally doll and the child is asked, "Where will Sally look for her marble?" Wimmer and Perner (1983) argued that the ability to appreciate another person's false belief went through a change during four to five years of age. While younger children answer that Sally will look for her marble in the box (thus failing to appreciate that Sally has a false belief), older children answer correctly that she will look for it in the original location—that is, in the basket.

Following this study, Baron-Cohen, Leslie, and Frith (1985) showed that children with autism and Down syndrome had difficulties with these types of tasks, but when children with Down syndrome got older and achieved a sufficient language level to understand the story, they were able to pass the test (i.e., make the correct predictions). Children with autism, even with sufficient language skills, however, had persistent difficulties in the task. This pinpointed one of the areas of difficulty for children with autism as being in the social-cognition domain. At the same time, linguists were investigating the role of language in the ability to use cognitive metarepresentations to solve false belief problems. For many years philosophers and psychologists have questioned what role language has for thinking (e.g., Carruthers, 2009). One theory argued that children needed to have developed an understanding of the syntax necessary to embed one clause in another (termed sentence complements)—for example, "Sally thought that the marble was in the basket." The theory was that by being able to do this in language, children would be able to manipulate the two clauses in an internal metarepresentation.

Other researchers (e.g., Milligan et al., 2007) have argued that rather than syntax, it is lexical development that triggers children to think about mental states more explicitly. This research highlights the acquisition of vocabulary linked to mental state verbs—"to think, to know, to not know" and so on. But other researchers instead have claimed that the key to understanding the role of language in children's ToM development is to look not at their acquisition of formal properties (e.g., verb semantics, syntax) but instead their experience of language and communication in conversation (Siegal, 1997). This point of view focused on how children come to develop the pragmatic skills necessary to understand conversations and interaction between themselves and others, which was thought to be the trigger for ToM development.

Theory of Mind Development in Deaf Children

As described previously, language and social-cognitive development have been investigated extensively in deaf children over the past two decades. Currently, what childhood deafness means for development is going through rapid and profound changes. The spoken language abilities of deaf children has changed over the past 15 to 20 years, with advances in neonatal screening (Mayer & Leigh, 2010; Watson, Archbold, & Nikolopoulos, 2006), hearing technologies (Davis et al., 1997), and changes to educational provisions (Knoors & Marschark, 2014). In the classroom, language development is important for all types of academic activity (e.g., literacy, discussions, following instructions, interpreting complex situations, planning your own work), and this might be why much effort is placed on deaf children's learning of vocabulary, grammar, and literacy in the early school years. With the increasing popularity of CIs, it is clear that deaf children have greater spoken language development than ever before. However, it is not clear whether this is the same for all other areas of communicative development, especially their pragmatics (Surian, Tedoldi, & Siegal, 2010). More recently, Rinaldi, Baruffaldi, Burdo, and Caselli (2013), looking at a sample of deaf Italian 12- to 36-month-olds, found that despite improvements in spoken language vocabulary as reported on the MacArthur-Bates Child Development Inventory (CDI) vocabulary checklist, the young deaf children still had severe difficulties in the pragmatic aspects of language.

Children in a mainstream classroom who use CIs may cope well one on one or in a quiet room, but as conversation partners, ambient noise, and distances between speakers increase, more complex pragmatic skills may be required for academic learning. Despite improved outcomes for hearing and spoken language for children with Cis, many still have disruptions to their spoken and signed language development, leading to language development delays. In a recent study Woll (2013) looked at a sample of deaf children with hearing parents who had an early diagnosis of deafness. Using the English and British Sign Language versions of the CDI vocabulary checklist, Woll found that in both their spoken English and British Sign Language they were significantly delayed compared to their native signing or speaking peers. In other countries changes to the spoken language outcomes of intervention for young deaf children with CIs is also changing rapidly (e.g., Perez, Valmaseda Balanzategui, & Morgan, 2014). One potential concern for language development delay, especially in pragmatics, is on social-cognitive functions.

When the first studies on deaf children's ToM began to emerge in the 1980s, there was a clear negative affect of deafness on this social-cognitive milestone. A wide range of delays was reported for deaf children of hearing parents from between three and 10 years (for a recent review see Meristo et al., 2012). These findings continued apace throughout the next 20 years, with studies appearing about deaf children in different countries. There were variations in how much delay was reported across these studies, but deaf children clearly had difficulty on false belief tasks. Many of the early studies were less able to control a number of factors important for passing these tasks (e.g., hearing levels, language levels, family background). This made interpreting the overall results difficult. Part of the reason why several different delays were reported across different studies may also have been due to different testing methods, including the use of signing or speaking in the testing situation or the use of sign language interpreters to explain tasks.

The main problem in several early studies was that the groups that were tested were very diverse. For example, some studies included deaf children from deaf parents and hearing parents in the same sample. This led to great variability in performance and suggested that all deaf children, regardless of parental hearing status, were performing similarly on the false belief tests. Woolfe, Want, and Siegal (2002) ruled out the notion that deafness per se was the cause of false belief failure by demonstrating that a group of four- and five-year-old deaf children of deaf parents passed a standard ToM test at age-equivalent levels. Following on from this work, Schick and colleagues (2007) further investigated these issues by comparing groups of children based on parental hearing status and language preferences: the deaf children of deaf parents and the hearing children passed standard false belief tasks at the same ages, but the two groups of deaf children of hearing parents (educated using oral methods or American Sign Language) displayed a three-year delay.

Interestingly, family signing skills may not be the only predictor of children's success on ToM tasks. Meristo and colleagues (2007) compared social-cognitive development of deaf children of deaf parents in different school situations. One group of native signers attended signing schools adopting a bilingual approach to communication in the classroom (teachers could use sign and spoken language fluently), while the other group of native signers was being educated in oral-language-only school situations. Recall that this group of deaf children had been reported to have typical development of social-cognitive skills compared with the deaf children of hearing parents. Strikingly, the children in the oral schools had more difficulty with social-cognitive tasks than their peers in the bilingual signing schools. The argument Meristo and colleagues (2007) put forward was that the bilingual signing schools provided an accessible environment and stimulation that further developed the native signers' social-cognitive skills. While ToM development progressed well in both groups up to the point of starting school, the conditions needed for the further development of these abilities were less available in an oral-language-only school.

Social-Cognition Beyond False Beliefs

Up to this point it has been argued that hearing children of hearing parents pass ToM tasks involving false beliefs during their fourth to fifth year of age, and this means ToM typically develops in this time window. The shortcoming with this idea is that it equates understanding of "false belief" with more basic skills involved in ToM and in wider social-cognition. But appreciation of false beliefs is only one area that children use to understand others. What might be more accurate is that there is a spectrum of abilities in ToM, and these develop in children over a protracted time frame, from basic precursors of understanding others to more advanced levels of mental state reasoning. Wellman and Liu (2004) put forward just this perspective in a five-stage ToM scale that begins with children first acquiring knowledge about the mind by understanding desires ("I like, she likes, wants, doesn't like" and so forth), then diverse beliefs (thinking differs across people), followed by an understanding of knowledge and ignorance (e.g., seeing leads to knowing, not seeing leads to not knowing), and then false ideas/beliefs; finally, children gain an understanding of hidden emotions (e.g., "she is pretending to be sad"). Peterson and Wellman (2009) went on to investigate the ToM scale in 93 children (33 deaf, 60 hearing) aged three to 13 years who were tested on a set of six ToM tasks. The results showed that deaf children were substantially delayed in the chronological age at which they passed the tests compared to hearing children, especially in understanding pretending and false belief, and this was correlated with the deaf children's delays in social pretend play. But the results also confirmed the five-step developmental progression for ToM. Both groups progressed through the same sequence, in the same order, albeit at different ages.

To summarize the ideas up to this point, social-cognition includes a spectrum of abilities linked to understanding other minds and how mental states link to others' behavior. One area of development thought to be crucial is the metarepresentation of mental states through language (i.e., "she thinks that *X*"). Many researchers have argued that some linguistic abilities lie behind children's use of metarepresentations to reason about ToM, and research on deaf children with hearing parents and their ability to pass ToM tasks has been used to confirm this. Understanding others' thinking is an important skill for many areas of children's lives, especially mental health, emotional regulation, understanding of complex language, and pragmatics, and therefore any delays can be problematic. Once a deaf child demonstrates atypical development of social understanding, this can lead to consequences in other areas of his or her development—for example, appreciation of complex mental state dilemmas in narratives and being able to monitor and regulate one's own emotions (e.g., Rieffe, & Meerum Terwogt, 2006; see Rieffe, Netten, Broekhof, & Veiga, Chapter 16 in this volume). If a deaf child has difficulty with social-cognition, this will affect his or her academic learning directly as a barrier to integrating into the shared discourse around ideas in the classroom. More indirectly, the cognitive resources required for understanding others may also divert resources away from the task of academic learning. While different perspectives exist on what aspects of language are important for social-cognition, a main area this chapter has focused on is conversational interaction.

THE IMPORTANCE OF CONVERSATION FOR SOCIAL COGNITION

There have been many attempts to find a causal explanation for deaf children's difficulty with ToM tasks, and these have identified the formal structures of language being delayed in this group's development. We can also think about language not just as a system of words and sentences but as a way people communicate with each other. Through interaction and especially conversation, speakers enter into series of interactive mind-reading activities. This can also happen even when they are not directly involved in these interactions, as in overhearing others' conversations (Siegal, 1997). These skills emerge early in typically developing children, during the first year of life (e.g., Carpenter & Liebal, 2012). During this period, children establish joint attention, and this connectedness to the "conversation" partner is seen as a precursor to later ToM development. Joint attention is something many deaf children with hearing parents have problems achieving (Harris & Chasin, 2005; Lederberg & Mobley, 1990; Lieberman, Hatrak, & Mayberry, 2013; Moeller & Schick, 2006). In preschool, professionals working with deaf children often anecdotally report that three- and four-year-old deaf children of hearing parents have difficulty knowing when to look at adults at the right time when they speak or sign.

Connected to the argument that early conversations play a role in the development of ToM skills is work on the importance of the quality of input to young children from their caregivers. Taumoepeau and Ruffman, (2006) reported that maternal mental state talk to hearing infants correlated with these children's later ToM skills. Parents who were more engaged in mental state talk had children who were more able to solve ToM-type tasks later. From previous research, we also know that the types of conversations hearing parents have with their deaf children are somewhat different from those that typically developing children experience (Janjua, Woll, & Kyle, 2002; Lederberg & Mobley, 1990; Moeller & Schick, 2006). Language addressed to deaf children tends to be simpler and directive, with more naming and questions. This is also found in other parent–child dyads where hearing children have been identified with a disability.

How does this relate to deaf children's social-cognitive development? In a recent study, Morgan and colleagues (2014) analyzed the conversational experience of deaf and hearing children with hearing parents, aged 17 to 35 months. Parents had to describe pictures that elicit mental and emotional state language to their children following Taumoepeau and Ruffman's (2006) methodology. Parents of the deaf children could describe the pictures in their preferred way, whether in sign or speech or a combination of both. We analyzed the content and "connectedness" of the conversations and found that input to the deaf children from their hearing caregivers differed greatly in terms of mental state labels compared with hearing mothers talking to their hearing same-age children. Parents of hearing infants referred to cognitions (i.e., using words such as "think," "know," or "remember") significantly more often than did those of deaf infants. There were no differences between groups in references to desires or emotions. For conversation connectedness, the parents with a hearing child produced significantly more connected turns overall than did the parents with a deaf child. Among parents with a hearing child, turns were significantly more likely to be connected than initiated and more likely to be connected than failed. But for the parents with a deaf child, turns were both more likely to be failed than connected and more likely to be initiated. Parents with a deaf child thus have difficulty maintaining a conversation and initiate turns more. This suggests conversations are more parent-led when a deaf child takes part.

A last finding from the study by Morgan and colleagues (2014) has consequences for how we think about early language intervention with young deaf children and their caregivers. In the hearing child–parent dyads, only 2% to 5% of the interaction concerned references to cognitive and mental states, but this presumably will be sufficient to trigger their typical ToM development. This final point highlights that the amount by which parents adapt their language and conversation style when they talk to their deaf children might not be large.

FUTURE DIRECTIONS FOR INTERVENTIONS ON SOCIAL-COGNITION

From the previous literature review, it should be clear that deaf children of hearing parents are at risks for delays in the development of social-cognition. Deaf children's spoken language skills are improving, but these children's ToM development is still an issue (e.g., Remmel & Peters, 2009). In the school context, deaf children in the classroom are learning some of the pieces of the social puzzle but continue to have difficulty making it all fit together. So how can we try to remedy this?

From studies of false belief understanding, we see that deaf children's development is delayed, but they do catch up rather than displaying permanent impairments as in children with autism. This is an important difference because it opens up the opportunity for focused interventions. However, any early delays can lead to later academic difficulties because the level of social-cognitive problems children face increases exponentially as they enter primary school and on to adolescence in secondary schools. As children get older, the higher-level ToM skills necessary for a child to be socially included in the classroom become more complex.

Many schools are aware of the importance of social-cognition for hearing children and have in place practices to make this area of development a priority. In the United Kingdom, for example, it is now common to hear about social and emotional aspects of learning, and this policy has been shown to be affective at increasing social inclusion (Durlak, Weissberg, Dymnicki, Taylor, & Schellinger, 2011). It is timely that research efforts move from identifying the problem to investigating solutions for deaf schoolchildren. The question is how to intervene based on the research evidence to date to try to close the social-cognition gap for deaf children with hearing parents and their peers. Researchers can systematically evaluate what types of interventions are viable; if, through training, outcomes change, they can ask whether these effects are long-lasting. This final section summarizes research work on interventions for social-cognition in different populations of children. However, before this happens, it is important to note that, in general, moving from results from research to an intervention does not happen directly but instead requires several steps:

1. First, identify the risk factors that seem to be evident from the research. For example, deaf children have a delay in passing false belief tests, and there appears to be a link between this difficulty and their language and communicative development. Furthermore, in some studies deaf children are shown to be involved in qualitatively different types of early interaction with their hearing parents. In this chapter we have identified two risk factors: delays in ToM development and decreased access to conversations.
2. Next, test the reliability of the emerging research findings by replicating these in different contexts and cultures. This is especially important if the initial research was carried out with small numbers of participants, as is often the case with deaf children. The follow-up research should include bigger groups as well as an attempt to include parents and children from wider social backgrounds.
3. When designing the intervention, ask what exactly the work is aiming to achieve (i.e., what is the outcome measure?). In our context, is the training going to attempt to increase deaf children's ability to pass a false belief test, or is it aimed more generally at improving their classroom academic learning? Both of these elements might be related, but they are very different in terms of how easily they can be evaluated.

4. After this planning stage, spend some time trying to understanding how a training study is going to be run before embarking on a bigger and longer intervention project. A training study in this context is a smaller-scale piece of work aimed at implementing some intervention in a small group to test its feasibility before widening this to a full-scale intervention with a larger group of children and parents. For example, is it feasible to train parents to involve more mental state conversation in their early interaction?
5. When developing the intervention, decide on the location and participant details: Where will it take place: in a clinic or in the home? Will it involve the family, school, siblings, and so forth? Each of these options opens up a different set of issues for researchers when collecting evidence of change.
6. Work out the details for each type of intervention being tested: the duration, rate, who does it, how do you measure change, what are the post-intervention evaluations, are randomized controlled trials feasible, and so forth?

Given this list of challenges, it is no surprise that many researchers avoid tackling intervention research. Fortunately, there are many areas of research that have been translated into intervention, especially with children with autism, reading difficulties, and developmental language impairments. Here, some of these studies are reviewed with key points highlighted for designing a future ToM intervention.

The first example of a training study stems from research on the linguistic skills hypothesized to be behind children's development of metarepresentations of mental states. Hale and Tager-Flusberg (2003) carried out this work with 60 typically developing children aged 36 to 58 months who were randomly assigned to three groups who received focused training on understanding social-cognitive problems and different types of language structure. Group 1 had training on false beliefs; group 2 had training on relative clauses (i.e., "Which one did Mary want to buy?"); and group 3 focused on sentence complements (i.e., "Mary said that she would like to buy the blue one"). The researchers first evaluated false beliefs, sentence complements, and relative clauses before training the children. The three groups then received two amounts of training one week apart given by the experimenter. While carrying out this type of training work with deaf children, in a school setting it would be possible for teachers or teaching assistants to do this amount of work with deaf children without disturbing their everyday learning. The training consisted of reenacting false belief scenarios (in a Sally and Anne story) aimed at better understanding these scenarios through feedback. This is also relevant for schools where deaf children are placed, as many preschool children engage in role-playing activities. The two language training groups also reenacted relative clause and sentence complement sentences. Two days after the training the children were tested on three different false belief, sentence complement, and relative clause assessments. The children with sentence complement training and the children with false belief training improved on false belief scores, but the children with relative clause training did not.

The conclusion we can draw from this ToM training study is that even a small amount of training over a short time can make a difference to understanding of ToM in typically developing children. A more recent study with similar outcomes was reported by Gavazzi and Ornaghi (2011). The question for work on deaf children is whether this amount and type of training would be sufficient. Also, it is not clear how the language training would work with deaf children who use a sign language. But the false belief role play is an interesting idea and could be carried out quite easily. During the classroom or assembly time when a conflict is discussed, this could be a good time for children to express what caused a problem and why other children might not have understood these causes. These situations stimulate much discussion on false belief. Children can start to talk about mental states that were incomplete or incorrect—for example, "You thought that, but I thought something different." Professionals working with deaf children might need to make these kind of discussions more explicit by using drawings or role play in the classrooms.

Turning to studies with children with a social-cognition disability, Golan and colleagues (2010) carried out a training study involving children with autism designed to improve their understanding of the links between facial expressions and emotions. Much information used in social-cognition is expressed via the face and thus can be useful to interpret others' behaviors. Individuals with autism generally avoid engaging with other people via facial expressions. Deaf children do not have difficulties with face processing, but some research has suggested they might have problems interpreting emotions correctly (e.g., Rieffe & Meerum Terwogt, 2006). Thus, this intervention study is a relevant methodology to consider for social-cognition in deaf children. The study had 20 children with autism (aged four to seven years) and two matched control groups, one comprising children with autism who received no intervention and the other a typically developing group. The training consisted of children watching computer-animated cartoons called "Transporters," which were about trains that had human faces and their interactions. The children in the training groups watched the video daily for four weeks. Children were tested before and after training on their understanding of emotional vocabulary and emotion recognition. The posttraining evaluation was based on watching videos and naming emotions in novel situations.

Effects were evaluated in novel situations to test whether training had transferred to comprehension of emotion in a wider rather than narrow manner—that is, beyond just the items they had been trained on. The intervention groups did better than the nonintervention groups on the posttraining evaluations, and this transferred to novel situations. Summarizing this study, it was found that in a relatively easy-to-carry-out intervention involving watching videos every day, children with autism improved their emotion comprehension, and this transferred to novel situations. In terms of deaf children with delays in ToM, similar videos could be made with false belief role play. These scenarios could be devised with real-world characters or animations with signing characters, subtitles, signed captioned interpreters, or nonverbal videos.

A last study looks at the results of communication and language training for parents of deaf children. Botting and Morgan (2007) evaluated an already existing family training package delivered face to face and via Web-based materials to parents of deaf children (see http://www.familysignlanguage.org.uk/mainpage.htm.) The research looked at whether training hearing parents on communication skills and British Sign Language vocabulary would lead to improvements in the children's language development, beyond those occurring over time. The study compared pretest and posttest scores on the British Sign Language CDI (Woolfe et al., 2010) in children whose parents had and had not received training. There were 29 deaf children of hearing parents (12 months to five years) and a matched control group who had no training. Both groups were assessed using the CDI at two time points, with access to the communication training in between. Training was through face-to-face courses and access to a website with 300 British Sign Language phrases listed under family-oriented topics. The analyses revealed faster vocabulary development for the children whose parents received training on several of the CDI subsections: overall sign understanding and use of content words and grammatical/syntactic words. While these results are preliminary, they suggest that parents who receive some training can improve communication, and this affects their children's language development.

From these three studies we can see that an intervention aimed at social cognition in deaf children could target language and ToM skills, using a video or play setting, and could be delivered as a parent training component in a course or as Web materials.

Proposals for Three Levels of Theory of Mind Intervention for Deaf Children

Training for deaf children and their parents and teachers in social-cognitive skills can be viewed as a gradual process based on

Wellman and Liu's (2004) stage framework. Here some ideas for intervention are discussed across three time points:

1. A first period of intervention can be aimed at early communication in infancy with family members during the entire first 12 months of the deaf child's life. While this is a crucial period for ToM intervention, there are also major effects of an early diagnosis of deafness on the family happening at this time that will have an impact on feasibility. Training will develop skills involving establishing joint attention, turn-taking, and interaction in direct/indirect conversation about intentions and emotions.
2. The second period of intervention is aimed at early preschool-aged children (12 to 36 months). It focuses on parents' ability to discuss mental states and emotions in conversations, exercises in developing child–parent conversations about knowledge and ignorance, talking with the child using decontextualized language (i.e., not only the here and now but also "what happened yesterday," "when granddad was a boy," and so forth), encouraging conversations about overhearing news and stories, and also developing skills in "book reading." Many of these activities can take place in the context of symbolic play. For example, in a nursery school or kindergarten classroom where there are different learning zones or corners, one area can be dedicated to ToM. If a deaf child has very little expressive language, this may have a negative effect on the complexity of symbolic play because it may impede games where an object is substituted for another—for example, playing with a box as if it is a mountain. Children who have developed a good level of metarepresentations can use their language skills to underpin their manipulations of such symbols (i.e., with linguistic labels such as "imagine if," "let's pretend that," "this is really an *X* but let's make it a *Y*"). Intervention by professionals can work well here: During the play situation they can provide deaf children with labels for objects through this level of hypothetical language and propose how to make one object stand in for another. Another activity involving knowledge and ignorance is based on guessing where an object is hidden; clues from a parent (e.g., "hot" and "cold") help the child find the hidden thing. This game highlights the idea that one person can be thinking something another person does not know and can be played with simple signs or words.
3. Finally, a school intervention aimed at deaf children aged three to five years tackles explicit ToM reasoning. Here the training aims to develop false belief understanding through role play, scenarios where knowledge comes from multiple sources, training on "I do not know situations" where children have

to explore what happens when they do not something about someone, second-order false belief ("I know that she knows that I do not know"), conversations about unusual ToM situations, training on managing and inhibiting one's first response in social situations, and scenarios with moral dilemmas. All of these activities revolve around social-cognition. These activities and interventions can be linked to literacy time in the classroom. Texts that are rich in false beliefs, for example the storybook *The Gruffalo* (Donaldson & Scheffler, 1999), can be chosen for deaf children to read and explain the stories and jokes to adults or other peers. This could be done in small groups or in the whole class using an electronic whiteboard. In other contexts (e.g., class or grade assembly), deaf and hearing children can work together on shared social-cognitive activities. In one of these, for example, each child has a suitcase containing several objects that are important to him or her. The aim is for the other children to get to know more about the child by finding out about the contents. This type of activity encourages children "to put themselves in the shoes of the other child" and to understand more about their tastes and likes and dislikes. Professionals working with deaf children's language development as well as parents might need to work beforehand with the deaf child on the language skills required for these activities. Children can express themselves through their preferred way (speech, signs, pictures, or even telling a close friend, who could then tell the whole group). In all classroom activities (preschool and primary school), it is important that these types of interventions are carried out systematically and regularly so that deaf children can anticipate and predict what is going to happen. If professionals are working on augmenting the child's mental state language, then anything done in the classroom should to be relayed to parents so that they can carry on the activities at home.

FINAL COMMENTS

Several aspects of understanding other people underpin how deaf children learn, as navigating social situations supports inclusion in educational contexts (Chilton & Beazley, 2014). In modern preschools and classrooms, deaf children are achieving greater access to information through hearing and speech, and there is an emphasis on the evaluation of their vocabulary and literacy. However, it is crucial not to neglect the social experiences of these children to avoid exclusion. Interactions in the family and classroom based around complex understanding of mental states and the pragmatics of conversation are still a deficit area for deaf children, and this can be traced back to different early experience of conversations (Surian, Tedoldi, & Siegal, 2010). Interventions with deaf children thus need to start in the home and build up through preschool and primary school. As the demands of communication grow once children enter school, the need to be socially aware and have a fully developed ToM also becomes important for learning. Future research needs to be carried out to evaluate the impact of such interventions and the transfer of any effects onto wider school learning.

ACKNOWLEDGMENTS

This research was funded by the Economic and Social Research Council of Great Britain (Grant 620-28-600 Deafness, Cognition and Language Research Centre). I would like to thank Ros Herman and Mar Perez for their comments during the writing of this chapter.

REFERENCES

Akhtar, N. (2005). The robustness of learning through overhearing. *Developmental Science*, 8, 199–209.

Baron-Cohen, S., Leslie, A. M., & Frith, U. (1985). Does the autistic child have a 'theory of mind'? *Cognition*, 21, 37–46.

Botting, N., & Morgan, G. (2007). *Parent training improves deaf children's language development.* Presented at the British Psychological Society Developmental Section conference, University of Plymouth, August 2007.

Braden, J. (1994). *Deafness, deprivation and I.Q.* London: Plenum Press.

Carpenter, M., & Liebal, K. (2011). Joint attention, communication, and knowing together in infancy. In A. Seemann (Ed.), *Joint attention: New developments in psychology, philosophy of mind, and social neuroscience* (pp. 159–181). Cambridge, MA: MIT Press.

Carruthers, P. (2009). How we know our own minds: The relationship between mindreading and metacognition. *Behavioral and Brain Sciences*, *32*, 121–138.

Chilton, H., & Beazley, S. (2014). Theory of mind: are there wider implications from working with d/Deaf people? *Disability & Society*, *29*, 184–197.

Courtin, C., & Melot, A.-M. (2005). Metacognitive development of deaf children: lessons from the appearance–reality and false belief tasks. *Developmental Science*, *8*, 16–25.

CRIDE. (2012). http://www.ndcs.org.uk/professional_support/national_data/uk_education_.html

Davis, A., Bamford, J., Wilson, I., Ramkalawan, T., Forshaw, M. & Wright, S. (1997). A critical review of the role of neonatal hearing screening in the detection of congenital hearing impairment. *Health Technology Assessment*, *1*, 1–177.

DeLana, M., Gentry, M. A., & Andrews, J. (2007). The efficacy of ASL/English bilingual education: Considering public schools. *American Annals of the Deaf*, *152*(1), 73–87.

deVilliers, J., & deVilliers, P. (2000). Linguistic determinism and the representation of false beliefs. In P. Mitchell & K. Riggs (Eds.). *Children's reasoning and the mind.* Florence, KY: Psychology Press.

Donaldson, J., & Scheffler, A. (1999). *The Gruffalo*. Macmillan Children's Books, London, UK (ISBN 0-333-71093-2).

Durlak, J. A., Weissberg, R. P., Dymnicki, A. B., Taylor, R. D., & Schellinger, K. (2011). The impact of enhancing students' social and emotional learning: A meta-analysis of school-based universal interventions. *Child Development, 822*, 405–432.

Figueras-Costa, D., & Harris, P. L. (2005). Theory of mind development in deaf children: a nonverbal test of false-belief understanding. *Journal of Deaf Studies and Deaf Education, 6*, 92–102.

Golan, O., Ashwin, E., Granader, Y., McClintock, S., Day, K., Leggett, V., & Baron-Cohen, S. (2010). Enhancing emotion recognition in children with autism spectrum conditions: an intervention using animated vehicles with real emotional faces. *Journal of Autism and Developmental Disorders, 40*, 269–279.

Grazzani, I., & Ornaghi, V. (2011). Emotional state talk and emotion understanding: A training study with preschool children, *Journal of Child Language, 38*(5), 1124–1139.

Hale, C. M., & Tager-Flusberg, H. (2003). The influence of language on theory of mind: a training study. *Developmental Science, 6*, 346–359.

Harris, M., & Chasin, J. (2005). Attentional patterns in deaf and hearing infants: the role of auditory cues. *Journal of Child Psychology and Psychiatry, 46*, 1116–1123.

Janjua, F., Woll, B., & Kyle, J. (2002). Effects of parental style of interaction on language development in very young severe and profound deaf children. *International Journal of Pediatric Otorhinolaryngology, 64*, 193–205.

Knoors, H., & Marschark, M. (2014). *Teaching deaf learners: Psychological and developmental foundations*. New York: Oxford University Press.

Lederberg, A., & Mobley, C. (1990). The effect of hearing impairment on the quality of attachment and mother–toddler interaction. *Child Development, 61*, 1596–1604.

Lieberman, A. M., Hatrak, M., & Mayberry, R. I. (2013). Learning to look for language: Development of joint attention in young deaf children. *Language Learning and Development, 10*, 19–35.

Mayer, C., & Leigh, G. (2010). The changing context for sign bilingual education programs: Issues in language and the development of literacy. *International Journal of Bilingual Education and Bilingualism, 13*(2), 175–186.

Meristo, M., Falkman, K. W., Hjelmquist, E., Tedoldi, M., Surian, L., & Siegal, M. (2007). Language access and theory of mind reasoning: evidence from deaf children in bilingual and oralist environments. *Developmental Psychology, 43*, 1156–1169.

Meristo, M., Hjelmquist, E., & Morgan, G. (2012). How access to language affects theory of mind in deaf children. In M. Siegal & L. Surian (Eds.), *Access to language and cognitive development* (pp. 44–61). New York: Oxford University Press.

Milligan, K., Astington, J. W., & Dack, L. A. (2007). Language and theory of mind: meta-analysis of the relation between language ability and false-belief understanding. *Child Development, 78*, 622–646.

Moeller, M. P., & Schick, B. (2006). Relations between maternal input and theory of mind understanding in deaf children. *Child Development, 77*, 751–766.

Morgan, G. & Kegl, J. (2006). Nicaraguan Sign Language and Theory of Mind: The issue of Critical Periods and Abilities. *Journal of Child Psychology and Psychiatry*, 47, 811-819.

Morgan, G., Meristo, M., Mann, W., Hjelmquist, E., & Siegal, M. (2014). Mental state language and quality of conversational experience in deaf and hearing children. *Cognitive Development*, *29*, 41–49.

Nelson, K., Plesa, D., & Henseler, S. (1998). Children's theory of mind: An experiential interpretation. *Human Development*, *41*, 7–29.

O'Brien, K., Slaughter, V., & Peterson, C. (2011). Sibling influences on theory of mind development for children with ASD. *Journal of Child Psychology and Psychiatry*, *52*, 713–719.

Perez, M., Valmaseda Balanzategui, M., & Morgan, G. (2014). Bilingual sign education in Madrid, Spain. In M. Marschark, G. Tang, & H. Knoors (Eds.), *Bilingualism and bilingual deaf education* (pp. 368–395). New York: Oxford University Press.

Peterson, C., & Wellman, H. (2009). From fancy to reason: scaling deaf and hearing children's understanding of theory of mind and pretence. *British Journal of Developmental Psychology*, *27*, 297–310.

Powers, S., Gregory, S., & Thoutenhoofd, E. D. (1998).*The educational achievements of deaf children*. DfEE Research Report RR65. London: DfEE.

Quittner, A., Cruz, I., Barker, D., Tobey, E., Eisenberg, S., & Niparko, J (2013). Effects of maternal sensitivity and cognitive and linguistic stimulation on cochlear implant users' language development over four years. *Journal of Pediatrics*, *162*(2), 343.

Remmel, E., & Peters, K. (2009). Theory of mind and language in children with cochlear implants. *Journal of Deaf Studies and Deaf Education*, *14*, 218–236.

Rieffe, C., & Meerum Terwogt, M. (2006). Anger communication in deaf children. *Cognition and Emotion*, *20*, 1261–1273.

Rinaldi, P., Baruffaldi, F., Burdo, S., & Caselli, M. C. (2013), Linguistic and pragmatic skills in toddlers with cochlear implant. *International Journal of Language & Communication Disorders*, *48*, 715–725.

Schick, B., de Villiers, P., de Villiers, J., & Hoffmeister, R. (2007). Language and theory of mind: a study of deaf children. *Child Development*, *78*, 376–396.

Siegal, M. (1997). *Knowing children: experiments in conversation and cognition* (2nd ed.). Hove, East Sussex, UK: Psychology Press.

Singleton, J. L., & Morgan, D. D. (2006). Natural signed language acquisition within the social context of the classroom. In B. Schick, M. Marschark, & P. E. Spencer (Eds.), *Advances in sign language development by deaf children* (pp. 344–373). New York: Oxford University Press.

Spencer, P. E., & Marschark, M. (Eds.). (2006). *Advances in the spoken language development of deaf and hard-of-hearing children*. New York: Oxford University Press.

Surian, L., Tedoldi, M., & Siegal, M. (2010). Sensitivity to conversational maxims in deaf and hearing children. *Journal of Child Language*, *37*(4), 929–943.

Taumoepeau, M., & Ruffman, T. (2006). Mother and infant talk about mental states relates to desire language and emotion understanding. *Child Development*, *77*, 465–481.

Watson, L. M., Archbold, S. M., & Nikolopoulos, T. P. (2006) Children's communication mode five years after cochlear implantation: changes over time according to age at implant. *Cochlear Implants International*, 7(2), 77–91.

Wellman, H., & Liu, D. (2004). Scaling of theory of mind tasks. *Child Development*, *75*, 523–541.
Wimmer, H., & Perner, J. (1983). Beliefs about beliefs: Representation and constraining function of wrong beliefs in young children's understanding of deception. *Cognition*, *13*, 103–128.
Woll, B. (2013). Sign language and spoken language development in young children: Measuring vocabulary by means of the CDI. In L. Meurant, A. Sinte, M. van Herreweghe, & M. Vermeerbergen (Eds.), *Sign language research, uses and practices: Crossing views on theoretical and applied sign language linguistics*. Berlin: deGruyter Mouton & Ishara Press.
Woolfe, T., Want, S. C. & Siegal, M. (2002). Signposts to development: Theory of mind in deaf children. *Child Development*, 73, 768–778.
Woolfe, T., Herman, R., Roy, P., & Woll, B. (2010). Early vocabulary development in deaf native signers: a British Sign Language adaptation of the communicative development inventories. *Journal of Child Psychology and Psychiatry*, *51*, 322–331.

13

Social Relations of Deaf Learners

Important Resources for Socioemotional Well-Being and Academic Success

Manfred Hintermair

The importance of social relations for the development of human beings in general and for the development and maintenance of health and well-being in particular has drawn the attention of scholars and practitioners across a large number of scientific disciplines for many decades (Rogoff, 2003; Schmidt-Denter, 1996). Studies show that social relationships have short- and long-term effects on health. These effects emerge in childhood and are then refined and differentiated throughout life, which can lead to either cumulative health-related advantages or disadvantages (Umberson & Montez, 2010). There is now a substantial body of evidence that indicates that the extent to which social relationships are strong and supportive is related to the quality of health of individuals (Cohen, Gottlieb, & Underwood, 2000; Economic & Social Research Council, 2013).

Given the essential role of social relations for human development, it is important to study social relationships in deaf and hard-of-hearing (DHH) children, because establishing social relationships is a big challenge for a child with a hearing loss, for whom smooth communication with its environment may be limited (Antia, Kreimeyer, Metz, & Spolsky, 2011; Marschark, 2007). Therefore, poor social relations may have a detrimental impact on the learning processes of DHH children, with consequences for their academic and socioemotional outcomes.

This chapter will present a review of the role of social relations in general, and for DHH children in particular. Suggestions for diagnostic procedures to assess social relations in DHH children will be given, as well as for interventions to facilitate and strengthen social relationships.

SOCIAL RELATIONS AND HUMAN DEVELOPMENT

Gergen (1990) highlights the psychological dimension of social relations and social networks: "The Self is [. . .] nothing more than a node in the chain of relationships. Each person lives in a network of relationships and is defined differently in each of these" (p. 197). This social constructivistic perspective of learning and development gives us at least two issues to examine more closely in order to understand what social relations mean for a child's development: One issue is the psychological meaning that an individual draws from relations with other persons, and the other is that an individual apparently has many different experiences in various social networks during the course of his or her life.

The Psychological Meaning of Social Relationships with Significant Others

When it comes to the question of what makes social relations so important for human development (here addressing the positive and strengthening aspects of social relationships), two essential functions become apparent. The first is the *emotionally stabilizing function* of social relationships. There is strong evidence that social networks give us shelter and provide us with safe passage through all the perils of life. To have the feeling that we are not on our own to cope with all problems in life, and to be sure that there is someone who listens to us or comforts us—all of this acts as a protective emotional shield that gives us security and strength and a feeling of being emotionally involved in the world. The second function of positive social relations, which is equally important, is their *identity-giving function*. People need social relationships with other persons in every phase of their lives as a compass, so to speak, as a niche for reflection and a fallback, as well as a point of orientation to know who they are, who they want to be, and how they want to live (Hintermair, 2009). This need arises from the fact that a central aspect of our identity work is recognition by social affiliation (Keupp, 2005). To summarize, it can be said that the feeling of belonging to social communities represents an important resource for one's own life project (Sen, 2006) and that the quality of one's relations to the people in these communities is of extreme importance.

What makes this issue so important for the development of DHH children is the fact that the quality of social relations is strongly affected by the intensity of communicative interactions between the persons involved. The concepts we develop of the world around us arise from the experiences with a world of meanings, symbols, and social tie-ups in which all people are inevitably integrated. Following the theory of symbolic interactionism (Blumer, 1969), humans act toward physical, social, or abstract objects in their environments on the basis of the meanings they ascribe to things in our world, and these meanings are derived from the social interaction that an individual has with other persons who speak (or sign) with him or her about the things in the world. So the world for a DHH child does not only become real for this child when, say, someone teaches him or her some new words or shows the child new things, but how the person teaches, with which kind of emotion this is done and in which context, seems much more important. A DHH baby bottle-fed in a nice, warm room, by a mother who likes to see her baby and to talk (or sign) to him or her during feeding, will have a different experience compared to one whose mother has little time, is nervous, and hopes the feeding will be over quickly. The quality of interactions within this social relation determines what kind of experience the baby transfers from this event into his or her personal future (Stern, 2004). DHH children are at risk regarding the quality of their social relationships because of the communicative problems that may arise (particularly when the parents are hearing, which applies to 95% of parents with DHH children), and intuitive parenting may be jeopardized. The relations may frequently generate stressful moments that do not promote good child development and overall well-being.

The Diversity of Social Relationships During the Course of Life

An individual is born into a system of social relationships. All the connections within this system become a part, in the course of our life, of our personal social network and accompany us from the cradle to the grave. This social network is not static but is continuously changing (with respect to its size and its constitution, the nearness and the distance of its members, and so forth).

Antonucci (2001) has presented a convoy model of social relations that exemplifies how social relations emerge over the lifespan. The model offers a framework that shows the variety of persons and networks that become variously important in different periods of life. Antonucci compares the social development of human beings to the image of a passing caravan, which initially represents the small relationship system—mostly the nuclear family—in which a child was born. During early childhood new relationships are constantly joining this small convoy—for example, relations with relatives, neighbors, or other caregivers. From the age of about three years, the contact with peers in particular increases. Another boost in peer contacts takes place from age nine onward, while the regular contact with relatives reduces significantly. Between nine and 13 years of age contacts with peers double, indicating the essential importance of friendships and relationships with peers in middle childhood and adolescence. Without going into further detail here, it should be clear that there emerges a picture of a widening social world of the child, which makes him or her increasingly independent of primary bonds.

Focusing on the situation of children and young people, it seems that particularly when addressing critical stages in development and life transitions they require social support from significant others in their networks. This has a great influence on child development in various domains. In hearing children, positive correlations between social relationships and language development, academic achievement, social skills, cognitive and motor skills, social-emotional development, and self-concept have been shown (Nestmann & Wehner, 2008). According to Nestmann and Wehner, social networks of children and youth are cognitively, emotionally, and socially stimulating; they are also helpful in coping with developmental tasks and can make an important contribution to the children's identity work.

SOCIAL RELATIONS OF DEAF AND HARD-OF-HEARING CHILDREN IN EDUCATIONAL SETTINGS

Research focusing on DHH children, adolescents, and adults has provided us over the past decades with much data with respect to the role of social relationships in various domains. In the following we will focus on the social relations of DHH in educational settings (kindergarten, preschool, school), and we will review how these relations function and what their impact is on relevant domains in development. Relations with teachers and peers, communicative participation, and social outcomes as well as academic outcomes will be addressed.

Social relations play an important role for the early years as well as for DHH adults. Regarding the early years, we know from several studies that the emotional availability (which is an indicator of a satisfying relationship) of parents and their DHH child, particularly in the first year of life, is crucial for the child's overall development in later years (Pressman, Pipp-Siegel, Yoshinaga-Itano, & Deas, 1999; Pressman, Pipp-Siegel, Yoshinaga-Itano, Kubicek, & Emde, 2000). Research data show that emotional availability of parents and children in the first two years contributes significantly to the children's verbal development when they are three years old. Parental support is an ongoing important factor for the development of mental health and well-being in DHH children. Van Gent, Goedhart, Knoors, Westenberg, and Treffers (2012), for example, in a study on self-concept and ego development in a group of 68 DHH adolescents, showed among other things that support for signing during childhood and positive parent–child communication were associated with a higher global self-worth. Kushalnagar, Topolski, Edwards, Skalicky, and Patrick (2011) showed a comparable association for adolescent quality of life. With regard to the role of social networks for DHH adults, a study by Gerich and Fellinger (2011) provided data from 107 participants aged 45 to 81 years. These data show that a larger social network is associated with a higher quality of life.

To return to the social relations of DHH children in educational settings, after a review of the available research one has to conclude, with Antia, Kreimeyer, and Reed (2010), that most of the research in this domain was published prior to 2000. If we take into account the far-reaching changes in deaf education since 2000 (e.g., the widespread implementation of universal newborn hearing screening in many countries, resulting in a very early start for intervention for DHH babies and an increasing number of DHH children who receive a cochlear implant very early, and also an increasing number of DHH children who attend a general education classroom), we should doubt whether the results of these early studies fully reflect the reality of DHH children in the 21st century. Today, DHH children are provided with better conditions for communication and language development, and this gives them the opportunity to have better cognitive, emotional, and social development. In the following we focus primarily on more recent studies, the number of which is steadily increasing.

Social Relations of Deaf and Hard-of-Hearing Children and Academic and Social Outcomes

It is well known that DHH children face specific challenges that may have consequences for their development in various domains. Regarding academic success, Qi and Mitchell (2012) emphasized that DHH students' test performance profile using standardized test scores has changed little over the past three decades, and the achievement gaps between DHH students and their hearing peers remain large; however, progress is apparent, particularly in DHH students at general schools (Antia et al., 2010). Hintermair (2014) provided a recent survey on the psychosocial situation of DHH children. With respect to the key concepts of self-concept/self-esteem, quality of life, and socio-emotional problems, a significant number of DHH children still show serious lags in development.

The reasons for discrepancies in academic and social outcomes are manifold; one central issue to discuss with respect to the situation of DHH children at school is classroom participation (Antia et al., 2011; Knoors & Hermans, 2010; Stinson & Antia, 1999). To participate intensively in educational instructional situations, children need to be able to communicate smoothly with their teachers as well as their peers in the classroom, because teacher–student communication and student–student communication are very important vehicles for learning in the classroom. The quality of those interactions is a key factor in driving classroom learning (Stinson & Antia, 1999). This means that instruction has to be accessible for students if we want them to become academically successful. At the same time, classroom participation is important not only for academic learning but also for social and emotional well-being. Students are not only at school to learn academically. Social network research shows how important peers are (in and outside the school) for experiencing friendships and for receiving impulses for identity development (see more in the paragraph on peer relations).

In these respects DHH children may be at risk: If you have problems in fully understanding your teacher and/or your peers at school you may, on the one hand, have problems catching the details of subject matter (as in social studies or in math); on the other hand, you may also be separated from many classroom activities that may have a great influence on learning, and this could finally result in less academic success. Thus, reduced language and communication can be a critical barrier for classroom participation. At the same time, unsatisfactory social relations with teachers and other students in the classroom can also lead to problems in affective functioning concerning loneliness, perceived social competence, or self-esteem.

At first glance DHH students at special schools seem to be disadvantaged less because fluent communication between teachers and students (and between students themselves) is to be expected there. This may apply to countries where an array of communication options in education is offered, including the use of sign language for the instruction of DHH students. However, there are many countries (e.g., Germany) where sign language is not always an educational option for DHH students, not even for those who need it. In general education classrooms too (apparently the preferred educational option for more and more DHH students in the future) where most of the students are hard of hearing and prefer to use spoken language, full classroom participation may be reduced by many factors. For example, barriers can emerge, if teachers are not aware of them, because of the rapid rate (including rapid turn-taking, rapid change of topics, and a high number of speakers) at which communication and learning take place in a classroom with hearing students. This can frequently result in fragmented learning situations for DHH children. If a deaf child learns by the support of a sign language interpreter in the general classroom, the lag time between the spoken message and the interpreted message may be another barrier to full participation. There are always delays in relaying what has been said, so the DHH child is inevitably just a tad behind the others. This makes it difficult for him or her to participate actively in class discussion.

If we look at empirical studies regarding the consequences of communicative participation on academic and social outcomes, we find several studies that confirm the significance of this issue. Braeges, Stinson, and Long (1993) carried out an investigation with 98 deaf junior and senior high school students aged 12 to 21 years from a special school for the deaf and asked them about their experiences with communication ease and their engagement. Student as well as teacher data were collected. The results show that higher ratings for communication ease (by the teachers as well as by the students) were associated with higher academic achievements as measured by the Stanford Achievement Test. Student-rated communication ease and teacher-rated engagement were the two best predictors of the DHH students' academic achievements. The authors concluded that it is very important for teachers to maximize their students' communicative comfort in class because this would enhance engagement and involvement, which in turn contributes to higher academic achievement.

Lang, Stinson, Kavanagh, Liu, and Basile (1999) explored the learning styles of 100 DHH college students and also their teachers' preferred learning styles and correlated them with students' academic achievement and motivation. The results showed that a learning style that emphasizes the participation of the students in instruction was associated significantly (albeit weakly) with course grade, indicating that students with higher scores on the participation learning styles scale receive better grades. Participative learning therefore seems to contribute to higher achievement and greater motivation for the subject matter.

A more recent study, which among other things also investigated the importance of communicative participation for academic achievement, was carried out by Antia, Jones, Reed, and Kreimeyer (2009). They presented data of 197 DHH students with mild to profound hearing loss who all attended general schools. Academic achievements in math, reading, and language/writing were studied annually over a period of five years. Regarding communication participation, the authors used the Classroom Participation Questionnaire (CPQ), an instrument that requests data from the DHH students' perspective. The CPQ comprises four subscale scores: Understanding Teacher, Understanding Students, Positive Affect, and Negative Affect. The results revealed that all academic achievements (standardized test scores and teacher-rated academic competences) were significantly and positively correlated with the participation experienced by the students. This means that good communicative participation may have a significant impact on academic learning at school.

Hintermair and Lepold (2010) used a German version of the CPQ and surveyed 213 DHH students at general schools. To assess academic outcomes they used the students' grades for math and German (this comprises the evaluation of the students' achievements in reading and language/writing); for social outcomes they used the Inventory of Life Quality of Children and Youth (ILC; Mattejat & Remschmidt, 2006), a fast and practical screening instrument for assessing health-related quality of life. The results showed that the CPQ subscale Understanding Teacher had a significantly positive (but rather low) correlation with the students' grades in math and German; for German this also applied to the sum score of communication participation. Regarding the social outcomes, the correlations between all CPQ scores and most of the ILC scores (concerning the domains school, social contact with peers, mental health, and the overall quality of life) showed a strong positive association. The results confirm the importance of classroom participation for students' quality of life (Hintermair, 2011).

Another study that centers on the role of the teacher–student relationship for socioemotional development in DHH preschool children was presented by Hintermair, Krieger, and Mayr (2011). They surveyed the kindergarten teachers of 104 DHH children; 69 of them attended a kindergarten at a special school and 35 attended a regular kindergarten together with hearing children. A modified short version of the Student Teacher Relationship Scale (STRS) in German was used as well as a questionnaire that covers six important domains regarding resilient development (interpersonal skills, self-monitoring, self-assertion, stress regulation, initiating structure, rejoice in exploration). The results revealed that DHH children from special schools showed more conflicting relations with their educators and were more dependent on their educators than DHH children from a regular kindergarten and a normative group of hearing children. Regarding emotional closeness, neither group of DHH children differed, but they showed higher scores than the children from the normative group (cf. comparable results of school-aged DHH students by Hermans, Wauters, de Klerk, & Knoors, 2014). Regarding the social development of the DHH children, there were highly significant interrelations between relationship scales and resilience factors of child development: DHH children who were less dependent and had less conflict with their educators, and at the same time showed much emotional closeness to their educators, had significantly higher scores in five of the six assessed domains of child development. The data also revealed the role of communicative competence: The DHH children with better competencies showed a stronger and more positive relationship with their educators as well as a more positive development in the tested developmental domains.

Wolters, Knoors, Cillessen, and Verhoeven (2012), in two studies with 736 hearing students and 104 DHH students from grades 6 and 7 attending general schools and special schools for the deaf, explored the impact of the peer and teacher relationship on the overall well-being of the DHH adolescents. In the cross-sectional part of the study, when comparing data from the hearing group with the data from the DHH group, the researchers showed that the relationship with the teacher was the sole predictor for well-being when the students were in grade 6, regardless of the educational setting. Looking at the mainstream setting, the data confirmed the importance of the teacher–student relationship, but the role of peers for well-being also emerged. Acceptance by peers and popularity predicted well-being too. After the students entered grade 7 (junior high school), some changes were found: For hearing students and DHH students from special schools, the quality of teacher–student relationships predicted the students' well-being, but this was not the case for the DHH students in mainstream schools: For them, acceptance by peers and popularity predicted well-being the most. In study 2 a subgroup of 39 hearing and 59 DHH students were surveyed longitudinally. Well-being remained stable for the hearing group but not for the DHH group (mainstream and special school). Gender seemed to play a central role here. The well-being of DHH boys in mainstream schools increased from grade 6 to grade 7, but the well-being of DHH girls in mainstream schools decreased. For DHH students at special schools the results were exactly the opposite: Girls in grade 7 had a higher well-being than boys (see also Wolters & Isarin, Chapter 14 in this volume).

To summarize, the available data on social relations of DHH children in educational settings show that extensive communicative participation may contribute to better academic and social outcomes in this group. Furthermore, we see that the role of teacher–student relationships and peer relationships with respect to emotional well-being must be considered with regard to educational contexts as well as to additional demographic factors, in particular the child's gender.

The Importance of Peer Relations for Deaf and Hard-of-Hearing Children

We have already mentioned the role of peers for the development of DHH children, but this topic deserves focus in more detail because of the importance of having good and extensive social relations with other peers for child development. Interactions with peers are necessary to model social competencies for building and prolonging enduring friendships. Peers may contribute to personal orientation and stabilization and to emotional security. Good relations with peers also facilitate trying out new opportunities of social behavior and provide an opportunity to test how these new experiences feel. So peer relations can serve as a bridge for reaching out beyond the family and taking on the new developmental task of learning to design one's own life.

Contacts with peers also support young people in finding their identity, and therefore they are a significant requirement for their identity work. Emerging challenges in adolescence can be mastered better with social, emotional, and informational support from peers. Emotional well-being can be enhanced by those contacts, and opportunities to try out different identities will be offered.

So what does research on peer relationships in DHH children tell us? Antia and colleagues (2011) did an extensive survey of available research on this issue. Although the evidence is not totally clear, some sensitive issues may be highlighted. Regarding the quantity of social interactions with peers, DHH children seem to have less frequent contacts with peers, they spend less time interacting with them, and the interactions they share with peers are briefer compared to those of hearing children. The language proficiency of DHH children seems to be one important factor for this because it influences the communication with peers, in particular the frequency and duration of those interactions. Another relevant issue is that the child's hearing status influences peer relationships: Hearing children prefer to interact with other hearing peers and DHH children prefer to do this with other DHH children. Nevertheless, interactions with hearing peers may have positive effects on the quality of social play in DHH children, so DHH children can learn from interactions with hearing children by modeling social behaviors for designing social relations.

Regarding the quality and success of initiations of social interactions in DHH children, the data available are not unequivocal. Some studies found similar initiation strategies of DHH and hearing children; others found more direct and nonlinguistic strategies in DHH children initiating relations with peers. In terms of the success of initiating interactions, the results of empirical studies are not clear either. In studies where DHH children show less success than hearing children, the explanation for this may be that the nonlinguistic strategies that are often preferred by DHH children may have less power to initiate and sustain an interaction. Data on the quality of social interactions suggest that there are some differences between hearing children and DHH children: DHH children seem to focus more on literal and familiar events, whereas hearing children also relate to abstract or absent events within their relationships with other peers. Antia and colleagues (2011) underlined that because the available studies on peer interaction differ in many respects (children's characteristics, observation contexts, hearing status), it is difficult to clarify the situation regarding the quantity and quality of peer interactions in DHH children.

Taking into account that, as noted above, most of the reported data have been collected prior to 2000, it is interesting to look at data from some more recent studies that address social relations in DHH children. Because the opportunities for developing spoken language have improved considerably in recent years and the quality of language has proved to be an important factor for initiating social interactions with peers, it is interesting to test whether better spoken language competencies may have a positive impact on the communication and relationships of DHH children with their hearing peers.

Bat-Chava and Deigman (2001) conducted a study with 25 parents with cochlear-implanted children aged 6 to 10 years about their children's relations with their peers. All children had been using their cochlear implant for at least two years. The authors focused on communication skills and peer relations before and after the implantation from the parents' perspective. In addition to the qualitative interviews performed with the parents, the competence section of the Child Behavior Check List was used to test the change of the child's competencies over time. The data showed a significant positive correlation between the children's oral communication ability and peer relationships after the implantation, at least according to these parents' judgments. Even though the parents reported progress in peer relations, they also noticed some barriers in their children's relationships with hearing peers. The acceptance and the patience of hearing children needed for successful interactions were reported by nearly half of the parents as an important issue here. If hearing children exhibit patience (i.e., are willing to take additional time and effort), the relations were evaluated as better. Also, familiarity with other hearing children seemed to be an advantage. The longer the children know each other, the better relationships seem to work. Further, despite the success in developing oral language competencies through the cochlear implant, there remained difficulties in speech and hearing that left some DHH children out of social activities and compromised full inclusion. Finally, for a significant number of the cochlear-implanted children, there was a big difference in communicating with one hearing child compared to communicating with a group of hearing children. Nearly a quarter of the parents mentioned without prompting that their children had DHH friends and that these friendships are very important to their child.

Martin, Bat-Chava, Lalwani, and Waltzman (2011), in a study with 10 five- and six-year-old children with a cochlear implant, confirmed some of the results of the study by Bat-Chava and Deigman (2001). They explored the relationship between the duration of cochlear implant use, the ability to initiate and maintain social relations with peers, and self-esteem. There were two different conditions for entry into a social relationship: One situation was an interaction with one hearing child, and the second and more difficult situation was with two hearing children who had just communicated with each other for five minutes. The results revealed that children with a cochlear implant had fewer problems interacting when there was only one hearing child to contact. Longer duration of cochlear implant use and higher self-esteem were associated with better performance on the peer task. Additional data revealed that the children's competencies in socializing with other peers were associated with children's social functioning outside the test situation as reported by their parents: Children who were better at initiating social relations with peers typically had better social competencies.

Yetman and Brice (2002) examined self-concept/self-esteem in inclusion or mainstream educational programs in the United States, looking in particular at the number of DHH children in the programs and the extent to which this affected their self-esteem. It was found that the number of hours weekly that the DHH children were together with hearing children was important: The DHH children who were together with hearing children for the majority of the time had lower global self-esteem and lower levels in various domains (academic, social, and behavioral self-esteem) than the DHH children who spent less time with hearing children. In addition, peer surveys showed that the DHH students were neither preferred nor rejected but were mostly overlooked or ignored. These results might indicate that contact and exchange with other DHH children is an important aspect of good socioemotional development.

Punch and Hyde (2011), in a study on social participation of children and adolescents with cochlear implants, reported data from interviews with 25 parents, 15 teachers, and 11 children with a cochlear implant. The results showed a high commonality between the answers from the three groups. Their views confirmed results from other studies (see above) that despite clear progress in spoken language and social relationships with hearing peers, problems remained when communication challenges had to be handled in groups with more than one hearing person. There were problems reported even for students with very good outcomes in spoken language. Of great importance was the information regarding the adolescents with a cochlear implant. The data indicated that the challenges associated with adolescence may be particularly large, related to the question of what it means to be deaf or hard of hearing. Emerging psychological or mental health problems must be anticipated by parents and professionals. The data further indicated that early access to sign language and social relations with other DHH children and adults may be beneficial for the socioemotional well-being of cochlear implanted children. Opportunities to meet other children with a hearing loss should be offered.

Some promising studies on social relationships in DHH children were presented recently by a group of researchers from the Netherlands. Wauters and Knoors (2008) conducted a study with DHH students in an inclusive setting and surveyed 18 DHH students and 344 hearing students twice with different tasks regarding peer ratings, peer nominations, and sociometric assessments. The results revealed a rather positive picture of social relationships, as the scores on peer acceptance, social status, and friendship relations were similar to the scores of the hearing students. The structure of the interrelations between sociometric measures for the two measurement points was also similar. Differences were observed in social competence and the stability of prosocial behavior. The DHH students scored lower on prosocial behavior and higher on withdrawal behavior than hearing children. Wauters and Knoors concluded that despite the overall positive results, it is important to recognize the differences between hearing students and DHH students in inclusive settings in order to address the DHH children's emotional and academic needs sufficiently.

Wolters, Knoors, Cillessen, and Verhoeven (2011) presented data from a study with 87 DHH and 627 hearing students in sixth grade at general schools and schools for the DHH regarding acceptance and popularity of early DHH adolescents. Their data are of special importance because they showed gender-specific differences in designing social relationships with peers. DHH boys in mainstream educational settings had more problems with being accepted and being popular in comparison with their hearing classmates and the DHH students from the special schools. For DHH mainstreamed girls, the data showed that they were not less accepted, but they did show problems in becoming popular (see also the data from Wolters et al., 2012, discussed earlier).

In summary, the more recent studies on social relations of DHH children reveal some important issues to consider when discussing the role of peer relations for socioemotional well-being. Although opportunities for the development of DHH children today are better than ever before, there remain some barriers to overcome. First, DHH children are different, and therefore each child with his or her special characteristics (e.g., gender, hearing status, language competence) has to be watched carefully to create optimal conditions for his or her socioemotional well-being. Communicative interaction with hearing peers also remains a big challenge for cochlear-implanted children, in particular when there are interactions to manage where more than one child is present. In this regard social relations with other peers who are also DHH or have a cochlear implant seem to be of great importance to strengthen DHH students for their identity work. In particular this needs to be addressed for those DHH children who will be educated in inclusive educational settings, where they are often the only DHH child in the class.

ASSESSMENT OF SOCIAL RELATIONSHIPS IN DEAF AND HARD-OF-HEARING CHILDREN

The data provided have shown that social relations of DHH children with significant others play a central role for their socioemotional and academic development. Therefore, it is important to have diagnostic tools available to assess the quantity as well as the quality of social relationships in DHH children.

In the studies reviewed so far, questionnaires such as the CPQ and the STRS or sociometric measures such as peer nomination and peer ratings were used. These are valuable instruments for empirical research, but they can also be used for individual assessment of a DHH child. So, for example, the information on communicative participation of a DHH child obtained by the CPQ can be helpful, provided the teacher looks at the scores the child has given to the items. The children can answer the question with ratings from 1 to 4 (e.g., I understand my teacher: 1 = almost never, 2 = seldom, 3 = often, 4 = almost always). Regarding the mean scores of the subscales found in the existing studies (Antia, Sabers, & Stinson, 2007; Hintermair & Lepold, 2010), it seems obvious that it is important to look more closely at those items where a child has given a score of 1 or 2. These can be sensitive issues regarding participation that will have to be clarified with the child in a one-to-one interview. In any case, questionnaires or sociometric data are effective for assessment and educational practice only if they are explored further by a dialogue with the child to understand what the reality is behind the scores with respect to the child's participation.

Thus, to have better access to and a deeper understanding of social relations in DHH students, in many cases one should go beyond using a questionnaire. A promising instrument for educational practice to assess social relationships both in quantity and, in particular, in quality is the use of a social network map. This is a tool used to demonstrate and describe human social relations (Freeman, 2006). It accommodates the paradigm shift in recent childhood studies to view children not as passive research objects but as productive social and cultural stakeholders (Mukherji & Albon, 2009). So it is important in educational research and practice to look at the perspectives, experiences, perceptions, and feelings of children about the things in their lives, and let them express these. The communicative participation of DHH children at school or in their extracurricular experiences with peers or with other significant persons will achieve more clarity through the narration of experiences, their interpretation, and visualization.

The social network map is an approach that provides qualitative access to insights into social relationships and has proven, in conjunction with a qualitative interview, to be a useful tool in allowing a more detailed description and in-depth understanding of the processes of both social support and stress. The special strength of the social network map lies in the combination of visualizing social relationships and reflecting them in a dialogue with the subject. For the person who designs the map (e.g., with a DHH child), this method offers much freedom in how to use it. You can explore the experiences of a DHH child in his or her entire living environment, or you can focus on the situation at school and analyze the child's social networks in this domain.

To produce an ego-centered network map, there are several steps to follow (see in detail Hintermair, 2009). First you will need to have a large sheet of paper (Fig. 13.1) with seven concentric circles drawn on it. This serves as the basic chart. You also will need paper flags to identify the people named in the social network and a pencil and an eraser or a few pins and some thread to mark the borders of the sectors on the network map. Second, the concentric circles are divided into sections like a pizza to represent the different areas of the situation concerned (e.g., classroom, school break, extracurricular events). The next step is to use the flags to assign all of the important individuals in the child's social network to a particular sector. The distance of the flags from the "I" circle at the center of the map shows how close or distant

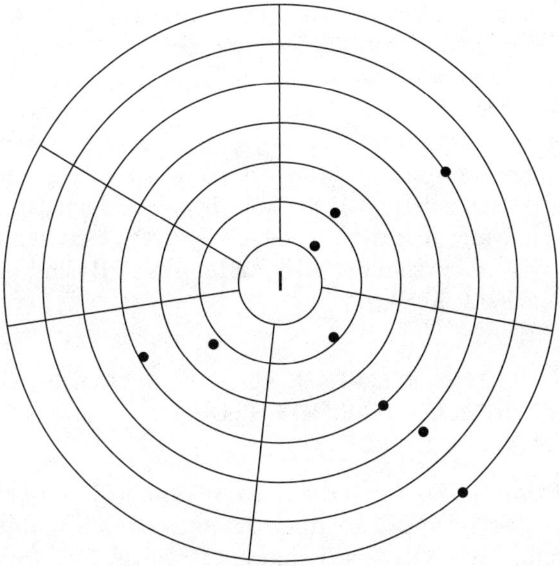

Figure 13.1 Social network map (formalized example).

their relationship is to the child. The closer they are to him or her, the nearer the flag is placed to the "I" in the middle. The network map is very flexible to use and can be adapted to the concrete situation and to the needs of the child in question.

In deaf education the ego-centered network map has been applied with parents of DHH children to assess the social support they receive after the diagnosis of a hearing loss for their child (Hintermair, 2009). In a German pilot study with 11 DHH children from grade 4 and grade 5, Hintermair and Landerer (2011) piloted an adapted version of the network map to test whether it can also be used with young DHH children. The group contained children with various degrees of hearing loss; four children had a cochlear implant. All children preferred spoken language for communication. The adaption included in particular the material the children worked with. The most important adaption was that instead of flags to show the position and distance of a person to the "I," wooden bricks of different sizes (representing adults or children) and different colors (representing different groups of people [e.g., family, school, leisure time]) were used. The "I" brick could be painted by the child at the beginning of the procedure, and at the end of the work the child could take the brick home.

The results show that this adapted form of the network map worked sufficiently. The teacher who conducted the inquiry reported that, all in all, there were no problems creating the network map with the children; all the DHH children said they enjoyed working with the map. Significant correlations emerged between the teachers' evaluation regarding the practicability and the children's intelligence, their communicative competence, and their language ability (both evaluated by their class teacher): DHH children with a higher IQ and better language and communication competencies rated the feasibility of the map higher. Therefore, it seems that the social network map is a method that is associated with the cognitive and language abilities of DHH children. More research is needed to draw a conclusion regarding the benefit of the social network map with DHH children (cf. Piso, Knoors, & Vervloed, 2009).

INTERVENTIONS TO STRENGTHEN POSITIVE RELATIONSHIPS OF DEAF AND HARD-OF-HEARING CHILDREN WITH SIGNIFICANT OTHERS

The results from studies about the social relations of DHH children and their impact on social and academic outcomes seem to confirm the need for educational interventions. Relations between DHH children and their parents, their teachers, and their peers should be strengthened from an early age onward. This applies to DHH children at schools for the deaf as well as to DHH children in an inclusive setting. There are some key points to consider in this regard.

Enhancing Parent–Child Relations

Although this chapter focuses on the social relations of DHH children at school, it is important to note that an effective intervention for this purpose starts in the families the children are born in. The family-centered philosophy provides a promising framework for developing and implementing effective programs for DHH children and their families (Sass-Lehrer, 2012; see also Bruin, Chapter 5 in this volume). Families who are enrolled in a family-centered intervention service learn to develop personal strengths. Together with hearing or DHH professionals they can learn what it means to be DHH and what they can do as parents to provide a supportive interactive family environment for their child. An essential issue here is that DHH children can experience in their families that communication and interaction work from birth. This may help them to build social relationships with other adults, and in particular with other peers, later in life, and they will learn social skills on how to manage social interactions with significant others. Data from longitudinal studies in hearing children showed that various aspects of early child–parent interaction (in particular parents' sensitive and contingent responsiveness) predict competencies in the academic as well as the socioemotional domain when the children are in kindergarten and first grade (for a review see Pianta, Nimetz, & Bennett, 1997).

Enhancing Teacher–Student Relations

The research presented has shown that the quality of social interactions between DHH children and their educators is of the utmost importance for their academic and socioemotional development. Educators who work together with DHH children in kindergarten or at school are primarily responsible for providing a clear communication basis built on the language modality the DHH child prefers. Social relations are based on effective communication geared at understanding each other and understanding the motives, emotions, and thoughts of partners in interaction. No matter whether they want to present a new learning subject or want to clarify the social or emotional problems of a DHH student, teachers must be able to manage this challenge through their communicative skills. The teacher has to provide the students with opportunities to learn socially and academically in the classroom: "They do so by using a sensitive and responsive interaction style, thus allowing students plenty of opportunities to initiate interactions and to participate in classroom discourse" (Knoors & Herman, 2010, p. 66).

When searching for opportunities to enhance teacher–student relationships, Knoors and Marschark (2014) argued that because of the important role of instructional factors in understanding DHH students' social and academic outcomes, it seems useful to analyze the competencies of skilled teachers of the DHH. Skilled teachers have been shown to attain better results with their students (Marschark, Bull, Sapere, & Lee, 2013; Marschark, Sapere, Convertino, & Pelz, 2008). The reason for this may be that they can adjust their methods and materials to match the cognitive styles of DHH learners. This includes also the competencies of teachers to manage the classroom environment so that the students have the opportunity to learn, not only from their teacher but also from peers (see for more information Knoors & Marschark, 2014, Chapter 11).

In this context one may think that teachers who are themselves DHH are better prepared to teach DHH children in this preferred way, because they are more sensitive to the core issues regarding the learning and language processes of a DHH child. However, so far there is no evidence for this assumption. Marschark and colleagues (2008) did not find significant differences between hearing and deaf teachers in achieving learning gain in their students. This confirms the position above that the success of learning depends more on the teacher's skills in instructing DHH students and his or her expert knowledge on what makes DHH learners "tick" than on the teacher's hearing status. Future research should identify the most important features and competencies of skilled teachers, and teacher preparation courses must include the development of those competencies and use the expertise of such competent teachers (cf. Knoors & Marschark, 2014, Chapter 12).

Because many DHH students unfortunately still encounter experiences in their development that are far from optimal, age-appropriate development of social and emotional skills is at risk (Calderon & Greenberg, 2011). So, in addition to a cooperative and interactive learning environment for DHH students, training in social competencies may also be helpful to increase the skills DHH children need to interact successfully with adults as well as with their peers. Knoors and Marschark (2014) refer to some programs with hearing children that focus on social and emotional learning. One interesting work in this regard is by Durlak, Weissberg, Dymnicki, Taylor, and Schellinger (2011), who conducted a meta-analysis of 213 school-based programs. They highlighted two important educational strategies that proved to be effective. One strategy relies on direct instruction of the students in processing, integrating, and applying social-behavioral skills in an appropriate way; the second strategy refers to the challenges for schools to establish a sound atmosphere by creating safe and caring learning environments for their students. The results showed that these strategies led to significant positive effects on social, emotional, and academic outcomes in hearing students.

In DHH students, approaches to foster various socioemotional skills have been discussed by various authors. For example, Most and Aviner (2009) suggested that increasing exposure to socioemotional situations and emotional language at home as well as school can help deaf students to recognize emotional states in others. However, Knoors and Marschark (2014) emphasize that, at present, research evaluating these various alternatives (particularly in deaf students) is lacking.

The PATHS curriculum is still the best-validated program for DHH children. It provides many suggestions for enhancing their social and emotional competence (Greenberg & Kuschè, 1998). PATHS facilitates the development of self-control, emotional awareness, and interpersonal problem-solving skills in both DHH and hearing children. These skills are important for a successful design of relationships with adults or peers.

Because DHH learners are a heterogeneous group, there is a great need to adapt the instruction process at school and the curricula on social competencies to the individual needs of DHH learners. This applies both to DHH learners at schools for the deaf, where the heterogeneity between the children seems to be very high, and to DHH learners at general schools, where the teachers have to take into account the different learning styles of hearing and DHH students (for more information on this see Knoors & Hermans, 2010).

Peer Relations

Positive peer relationships are an additional important issue for the development of DHH students, in particular for their socioemotional and identity development. Therefore, fostering skills for building peer relations should be a subject in the curricula at schools for the deaf as well as at general schools. The aim is either to increase the occurrence of social interactions of DHH youth at schools for the deaf through instruction in specific peer interaction skills, or to increase the quantity and quality of interaction between hearing students and DHH students at general schools (cf. Antia et al., 2011). Antia and colleagues (2011) reviewed the impact of interventions regarding the improvement of social interactions of DHH children with other DHH children or with hearing peers.

One study of interest with DHH students at special schools was carried out by Ducharme and Holborn (1997). They evaluated the efficacy of a social skills training and its generalization with five oral preschool children whose hearing loss ranged from moderate to severe. The interventions were carried out by the preschool teachers who used verbal instructions, modeling, prompting, and verbal praise focusing on the social behaviors desired during children's play activities. The evaluation was conducted within a multiple baseline design. The data revealed that initially the training succeeded only in the training setting in producing high, stable rates of social interaction. However, there were problems in generalizing the acquired social skills to new situations, persons, and challenges outside of the training setting. The authors therefore implemented generalization programming strategies in the original training setting by introducing new teachers, peers, or play activities. This procedure resulted in significantly higher social activities in the generalization session as well. Ducharme and Holborn emphasized that increasing the number of teachers, peers, and play activities in the generalization program resulted in increasing the opportunities for the children to experience the impact of their actions on teachers and peers in a more natural way. This seemed to be the key strategy for promoting generalization of social interaction competencies.

Antia and Kreimeyer (1996) studied enhancement of peer interactions by having teachers plan arts and crafts activities and cooperative games for their DHH and hearing students. During these activities (cf. Ducharme & Holborn, 1997) they modeled and prompted various social behaviors such as greeting, sharing, assisting, inviting, or praising to offer positive models to the students to engage with each other. They controlled for the effects of peer familiarity by introducing hearing children in free-play sessions. These hearing children had not participated in the social interaction training with DHH and hearing children. If social skills intervention is successful, social interactions should be enhanced within the intervention group and positive effects should transfer to situations with children who were not part of the intervention. The data revealed that the social skills intervention increased interactions among DHH children; the increase in particular included nonlinguistic behaviors. However, when looking at the social interactions between DHH and hearing children, no increase was found. It was thus not possible to analyze the impact of familiarity on peer interactions, because the intervention did not result in a significant change in interactions between DHH and hearing children.

Antia and colleagues (2011) concluded from the available studies that positive and enduring results for interventions among DHH students may be obtained when there is careful programming, but not so for programs or interventions with DHH children and hearing children. They assumed that overcoming the communicative barriers between DHH and hearing children seems to be the major challenge when operating programs to increase social interaction. Because short-term interventions seem to dominate the field, this could be a reason why only minor effects on development of social interactions have been documented.

Twenty years ago Paul and Jackson (1993) were already arguing that as well as qualified instruction of DHH students and special programs and interventions for socioemotional development, the inclusion of peers in peer counseling programs would be an important preventive and intervention strategy at school. Peer counselors are young DHH people who are prepared and qualified by special courses for their job to be available as contact persons for other DHH peers who have problems they want to discuss or solve without their teacher. A peer counseling approach assumes that DHH students can often better understand and relate to other DHH individuals (e.g., trying to deal with their hearing loss or supporting them in their search for a deaf identity). Although data from many biographies of DHH persons support the important role of other DHH persons in this respect, documented evidence on the effect of a systematic peer counseling program is rare. Jókay (2004) implemented a peer tutoring program at a German school for the deaf and evaluated its effects. Because the focus in her work was on the training of peer tutors and how they evaluated the training and their work with DHH peers, there were few data on the evaluation of the program by the tutored peers. Jókay interviewed 50 students who were engaged in the peer tutoring program about their experiences. Sixty-four percent of them reported that such a program would be very meaningful for the school; most of them saw problems of the student as the most important reason to contact the peer tutors. A few students valued the organization of projects for the students by the tutors. In these programs students could have fun together as well as could learn new social competencies and behaviors.

Peer counseling seems to be a good option for DHH students who attend a school for the deaf because there is a critical mass of DHH peers on location. However, more and more DHH students around the world attend a general school in the context of inclusion endeavors, often as the only DHH child in a classroom with hearing children. As the research data provided showed, there are considerable challenges for these DHH children in terms of their academic progress as well as their socioemotional situation. This applies even though the early detection of hearing loss through UNHS and early provision with hearing aids or cochlear implants has facilitated the development processes of DHH children (cf. Martin et al., 2011; Punch & Hyde, 2011). For DHH children in inclusive settings, aside from special attention being paid to modifying instruction (and intensive as well as comprehensive counseling of the classroom teacher by an itinerant teacher, cf. Luckner & Ayantoye, 2013) and modifying the classroom environment to increase participation (cf. Antia et al., 2010; Guardino & Antia, 2012), special attention has to be paid to their socioemotional development. Again, this depends on their relationships not only with hearing peers but also with other DHH peers. Some recent data suggest that co-enrollment programs (where a group of several DHH children goes to school together with hearing children) seem to combine the best practices in regular and special education and may protect DHH students from isolation by ensuring that they have DHH peers in the classroom. However, more research is necessary to document more comprehensively the effects of such programs (cf. for recent data see Hermans et al., 2014; Hermans, de Klerk, Wauters, & Knoors, 2014; Hintermair, 2014; Tang, Lam, & Yiu, 2014).

For the majority of the mainstreamed DHH children who are the only DHH child in their class, it is important to provide extracurricular opportunities for them to meet other DHH peers. Gugel, Blochius, and Hintermair (2012), for example, interviewed 11 mainstreamed hard-of-hearing children who were the only DHH children in their class. These youths, aged eight to 16 years, attended a youth club, supervised by hard-of-hearing adults, where, at weekends, they participated in special leisure activities along with other hard-of-hearing peers. The interviewed children had attended the youth club for over two years. The results showed that the contacts with other hard-of-hearing peers were extremely important for their social and emotional well-being. Many of them reported that social relations with their peers enabled them to recognize that being hard-of-hearing was a critical part of their identity. Therefore, providing opportunities for DHH children who are the only DHH child in a hearing classroom to meet other DHH peers seems to be very important for their overall well-being.

CONCLUSIONS

Human beings rely on satisfying social relations throughout their lives, starting at birth, to develop overall well-being. Children with a hearing loss are at risk in this regard because the quantity and quality of social relations depend on efficient communication between interaction partners, which is a big challenge for many DHH children.

The studies discussed in this chapter show that, in an educational context, teacher–student communication and student–student communication are very important for effective learning in the classroom and are highly relevant for the social-emotional development of DHH children. Keeping an eye on the social relations of DHH children, therefore, has been and will remain a major task in deaf education.

Much of the available research on social relations, in particular concerning peer relations, was done prior to the year 2000. We need more recent data that document the quality and quantity of interactions of DHH students who have grown up after 2000. Because the preconditions for communication and language development in DHH children are now better than ever before, it is to be expected that this may have also positive consequences for the building of social relationships by DHH children (with their parents, teachers, peers, and other persons in their environments). Research data are needed to support this assumption and to uncover what the challenges for deaf education are for the coming decades.

Theoretical and practical knowledge should be included in teacher training courses to prepare teachers for the challenges of teaching DHH students to relate effectively to other persons. This needs to be done under the supervision of skilled teachers who can share their expertise and their competencies in educating DHH students. In this regard the application of the social network map could be a fruitful instrument for practice; it enables teachers to obtain more qualitative information on the emotional situation of DHH children and how they experience social relations inside and outside of school.

Future research needs to study the long-term effects of early interventions in the social-emotional domain for later development. More research on the effects of family-centered early intervention as well as on the effects of social interaction experiences at preschool for later socioemotional development and academic success would be welcomed. More systematic interventions should be carried out and evaluated regarding their effects.

A further important point to consider is the increase in the number of DHH children who attend general schools in which they need to learn together with hearing peers. This group of DHH learners will need special attention in the coming years (cf. Antia et al., 2010). Since participation (in class as well as outside of school) has emerged as a key factor in DHH students' development, this should be a significant focus of future research. Research on the communicative participation of DHH with the CPQ, for example, has already shown that participation contributes to better academic and socioemotional outcomes (Antia et al., 2009; Hintermair & Lepold, 2010). It would broaden our knowledge if researchers were to collect data on participation not only from the perspective of the DHH children themselves, but also from teachers', peers', and parents' perspectives. Because DHH children often grow up with relatively impoverished language and education experiences, this may leave them unable to judge accurately whether and how much they comprehend of classroom content (Harrington, 2000) or from chatting with peers. Students may either be unaware of their comprehension failures (Strassman, 1997) or simply accept them as normal (Napier & Barker, 2004). Judgments from different perspectives may contribute to a more differentiated view on DHH students' participation at school. In this regard Elanjimattom and Hintermair (2009) conducted a study with 41 DHH students at general schools with a short form of the CPQ. The items were reformulated so that the classroom teacher answered the same items as the DHH child, but from his or her perspective. The results showed no significant differences between the teachers' and the students' evaluations, but there was a slight tendency by the DHH students to evaluate their communication with their teachers more positively than the teachers did. Therefore, DHH children may not know what information they are really missing from the teacher (cf. Knoors & Marschark, 2014).

Because most of the DHH students at general schools will be the single DHH child in a classroom, research should focus on this group of children, because their socioemotional situation and their peer relations may be at risk in particular. Research needs to focus on the potential benefits for these children of opportunities outside the school environment to meet other DHH children to strengthen their socio-emotional development. More information is needed on whether all DHH children would profit from such extracurricular meetings or, alternatively, to reveal what the characteristics of those children who do need this the most (e.g., grade of hearing loss) may be. The psychosocial and academic benefits of co-enrollment programs for DHH children need to be better substantiated by research (cf. Marschark, Tang, & Knoors, 2014).

Finally, some studies have revealed specific student characteristics or specific life situations that need to be investigated more closely, such as gender and school transitions (e.g., from kindergarten to primary school, or from junior high school to high school; cf. Wolters et al., 2011, 2012). Also of interest are studies that explain what factors influence the decision of DHH children to change from a general school to a school for the deaf (often when they are at a secondary school).

All this could broaden our knowledge about factors leading to the success of inclusive education. The social relations, and subsequently the social-emotional well-being, of DHH students at general schools (in oral as well as in bilingual settings) will become one of the biggest challenges for deaf education and research in the coming years.

REFERENCES

Antia, S. D., Jones, P. B., Reed, S., & Kreimeyer, K. H. (2009). Academic status and progress of deaf and hard-of-hearing students in general education classrooms. *Journal of Deaf Studies and Deaf Education, 14*, 293–311.

Antia, S. D., & Kreimeyer, K. H. (1996). Social interaction and acceptance of D/HH children and their peers. *Volta Review, 98*, 157–180.

Antia, S. D., Kreimeyer, K. H., Metz, K. K., & Spolsky, S. (2011). Peer interactions of deaf and hard-of-hearing children. In M. Marschark & P. E. Spencer (Eds.), *Oxford handbook of deaf studies, language, and education* (Vol. 1, 2nd ed., pp. 173–187). New York: Oxford University Press.

Antia, S. D., Kreimeyer, K. H., & Reed, S. (2010). Supporting students in general classrooms. In M. Marschark & P.E. Spencer (Eds.), *Oxford handbook of deaf studies, language, and education* (Vol. 2, pp. 72–92). New York: Oxford University Press.

Antia, S. D., Sabers, D. L., & Stinson, M. S. (2007). Validity and reliability of the Classroom Participation Questionnaire with deaf and hard of hearing students in public schools. *Journal of Deaf Studies and Deaf Education, 12*, 158–171.

Antonucci, T. C. (2001). Social relations. An examination of social networks, social support and sense of control. In J. E. Birren & K. W. Schaie (Eds.), *Handbook of the psychology of the aging* (5th ed., pp. 427–453). San Diego, CA: Academic Press.

Bat-Chava, Y., & Deigman, E. (2001). Peer relationships of children with cochlear implants. *Journal of Deaf Studies and Deaf Education, 6*, 186–199.

Blumer, H. (1969). *Symbolic interactionism: Perspective and method*. Englewood Cliffs, NJ: Prentice-Hall.

Braeges, J., Stinson, M., & Long, G. (1993). Teachers' and deaf students' perceptions of communication ease and engagement. *Rehabilitation Psychology, 38*, 235–246.

Calderon, R., & Greenberg, M. (2011). Social and emotional development of deaf children: Family, school, and program effects. In M. Marschark & P. E. Spencer (Eds.), *Oxford handbook of deaf studies, language, and education* (Vol. 1, 2nd ed., pp. 188–199). New York: Oxford University Press.

Cohen, S., Gottlieb, B. H., & Underwood, L. G. (2000). Social relationships and health. In S. Cohen, L. G. Underwood, & B. H. Gottlieb (Eds.), *Social support measurement and intervention* (pp. 3–25). Oxford: Oxford University Press.

Ducharme, D., & Holborn, S. (1997). Programming generalization of social skills in preschool children with hearing impairments. *Journal of Applied Behavior Analysis, 30*, 639–651.

Durlak, J. A., Weissberg, R. P., Dymnicki, A. B., Taylor, R. D., & Schellinger, K. B. (2011). The impact of enhancing students' social and emotional learning: A meta-analysis of school-based universal interventions. *Child Development, 82*, 405–432.

Economic & Social Research Council. (2013). Mental health and social relationships. Retrieved February 7, 2013, from http://www.esrc.ac.uk/_images/ESRC_Evidence_Briefing_Mental_health_social_rel_tcm8-26243.pdf

Elanjimattom, S., & Hintermair, M. (2009). Kommunikative und psychosoziale Partizipation hörgeschädigter Kinder in der Regelschule—Eine Pilotstudie mit einer deutschen Kurzversion des Classroom Participation Questionnaire

(CPQ) [Communicative and psychosocial participation of mainstreamed deaf and hard of hearing children. A pilot study with a German short version of the Classroom Participation Questionnaire (CPQ-D). *Sonderpädagogische Förderung, 54*, 53–71.

Freeman, L. C. (2006). *The development of social network analysis.* Vancouver: Empirical Press.

Gergen, K. J. (1990). Die Konstruktion des Selbst im Zeitalter der Postmoderne [Construction of self in postmodern age]. *Psychologische Rundschau, 41*, 191–199.

Gerich, J., & Fellinger, J. (2011). Effects of social networks on the quality of life in an elder and middle-aged deaf community sample. *Journal of Deaf Studies and Deaf Education, 17*, 102–115.

Greenberg, M. T., & Kusché, C. (1998). Preventive intervention for school-age deaf children: The PATHS curriculum. *Journal of Deaf Studies and Deaf Education, 3*, 49–63.

Guardino, C., & Antia, S. D. (2012). Modifying the classroom environment to increase engagement and decrease disruption with students who are deaf or hard of hearing. *Journal of Deaf Studies and Deaf Education, 17*, 518–533.

Gugel, J., Blochius, P., & Hintermair, M. (2012). Erfahrungen einzelintegriert beschulter hörgeschädigter Kinder aus Begegnungen mit anderen hörgeschädigten Kindern—Evaluation des Jugendtreffs Hörnix [Experiences of single included hard of hearing children when meeting other hard of hearing children—Evaluation of the youth club "Hörnix"]. *Zeitschrift für Heilpädagogik, 63*, 381–388.

Harrington, F. (2000). Sign language interpreters and access for deaf students to university curricula: The ideal and the reality. In R. P. Roberts, S. E. Carr, D. Abraham & A. Dufour (Eds.), *The critical link 2: Interpreters in the community* (pp. 219–273). Amsterdam: John Benjamins.

Hermans, D., de Klerk, A., Wauters, L., & Knoors, H. (2014). The Twinschool: A co-enrollment program in the Netherlands. In M. Marschark, G. Tang, & H. Knoors (Eds.), *Bilingualism and bilingual deaf education* (pp. 396–423). New York: Oxford University Press.

Hermans, D., Wauters, L., de Klerk, A., & Knoors, H. (2014). Quality of instructions in bilingual schools for deaf children: Through the children's eyes and the camera's lens. In M. Marschark, G. Tang, & H. Knoors (Eds.), *Bilingualism and bilingual deaf education* (pp. 272–291). New York: Oxford University Press.

Hintermair, M. (2009). The social network map as an instrument for identifying social relations in deaf research and practice. *American Annals of the Deaf, 154*, 300–310.

Hintermair, M. (2011). Health-related quality of life and classroom participation of deaf and hard-of-hearing students in general schools. *Journal of Deaf Studies and Deaf Education, 16*, 254–271.

Hintermair, M. (2014). Psychosocial development in deaf and hard of hearing children in the twenty-first century: Opportunities and challenges. In M. Marschark, G. Tang, & H. Knoors (Eds.), *Bilingualism and bilingual deaf education* (pp. 152–186). New York: Oxford University Press.

Hintermair, M., Krieger, L., & Mayr, T. (2011). Beziehungsqualitäten zwischen hörgeschädigten Kindern und ihren Erzieherinnen im Kindergarten. Eine Studie mit der Student Teacher Relationship Scale (STRS) [Relationship

qualities between deaf and hard-of-hearing children in kindergarten and their educators. A study with the Student Teacher Relationship Scale (STRS)]. *Heilpädagogische Forschung, 37*, 62–73.
Hintermair, M., & Lepold, L. (2010). Partizipationserleben hörgeschädigter Kinder in der allgemeinen Schule—Eine Studie mit der deutschen Version des Classroom Participation Questionnaire (CPQ-D) [Participation experiences of deaf and hard of hearing students at general schools—a study with a German version of the Classroom Participation Questionnaire (CPQ-D)]. *Empirische Sonderpädagogik, 2*, 40–63.
Jòkay. E. (2004). *Peer Counseling: Mentoren an deutschen Schulen für Hörgeschädigte* [Peer Counseling: Mentors at German schools for the deaf]. Hamburg: Signum.
Keupp, H. (2005). Welche Prioritäten wollen wir setzen?—Psychosoziales Arbeiten in einer Gesellschaft im Umbruch [Psychosocial work in a society undergoing radical change—What will our priorities be?]. *Psychoneuro, 31*, 35–41.
Knoors, H., & Hermans, D. (2010). Effective instruction for deaf and hard-of-hearing students: Teaching strategies, school settings and student characteristics. In M. Marschark & P. E. Spencer (Eds.), *Oxford handbook of deaf studies, language, and education* (Vol. 2, pp. 72–92). New York: Oxford University Press.
Knoors, H., & Marschark, M. (2014). *Teaching deaf learners: Psychological and developmental foundations*. New York: Oxford University Press.
Kushalnagar, P., Topolski, T. D., Schick, B., Edwards, T. C., Skalicky, A. M., & Patrick, D. L. (2011). Mode of communication, perceived level of understanding and perceived quality of life in youth who are deaf or hard of hearing. *Journal of Deaf Studies and Deaf Education, 18*, 47–61.
Lang, H. G., Stinson, M. S., Kavanagh, F., Liu, Y., & Basile, M. L. (1999). Learning styles of deaf college students and instructors' teaching emphases. *Journal of Deaf Studies and Deaf Education, 4*, 16–27.
Luckner, J. L., & Ayantoye, C. (2013). Itinerant teachers of students who are deaf or hard of hearing: Practices and preparation. *Journal of Deaf Studies and Education, 18*, 409–420.
Marschark, M. (2007). *Raising and educating a deaf child. Second edition.* New York: Oxford University Press.
Marschark, M., Bull, R., Sapere, P., & Lee, C. (2013). Supporting deaf students' mathematics learning in the college classroom. Unpublished manuscript.
Marschark, M., Sapere, P., Convertino, C., & Pelz, J. (2008). Learning via direct and mediating instruction by deaf students. *Journal of Deaf Studies and Deaf Education, 13*, 546–561.
Martin, D., Bat-Chava, Y., Lalwani, A., & Waltzman, S. B. (2011). Peer relationships of deaf children with cochlear implants: Predictors of peer entry and peer interaction success. *Journal of Deaf Studies and Deaf Education, 16*, 108–120.
Mattejat, F., & Remschmidt, H. (2006). *ILK. Inventar zur Erfassung der Lebensqualität bei Kindern und Jugendlichen* [ILC. Inventory of Life Quality of Children and Youth]. Bern: Huber.
Most, T., & Aviner, C. (2009). Auditory, visual, and auditory-visual perception of emotions by individuals with cochlear implants, hearing aids, and normal hearing. *Journal of Deaf Studies and Deaf Education, 14*, 449–464.
Mukherji, P., & Albon, D. (2009). *Research methods in early childhood. An introductory guide.* London: Sage Publishers.

Napier, J. & Barker, R. (2004). Access to university interpreting: Expectations and preferences of deaf students. *Journal of Deaf Studies and Deaf Education, 9*, 228–238.

Nestmann, F., & Wehner, K. (2008). Soziale Netzwerke von Kindern und Jugendlichen [Social networks of children and youth]. In F. Nestmann, J. Günther, S. Stiehler, K. Wehner, & J. Werner (Hrsg.), *Kindernetzwerke. Soziale Beziehungen und soziale Unterstützung in Familie, Pflegefamilie und Heim* (pp. 11–40). Tübingen: DGVT-Verlag.

Paul, P., & Jackson, D. (1993). *Toward a psychology of deafness: Theoretical and empirical perspectives*. Boston, MA: Allyn & Bacon.

Pianta, R. C., Nimetz, S. L., & Bennett, E. (1997). Mother-child relationships, teacher-child relationships and school outcomes in preschool and kindergarten. *Early Childhood Quarterly, 12*, 263–280.

Piso, F., Knoors, H., & Vervloed, M. (2009). Vriendschapsrelaties van dove en slechthorende adolescenten. [Friendship relations of deaf and hard of hearing adolescents]. *Van Horen Zeggen, 50*, 10–17.

Pressman, L. J., Pipp-Siegel, S., Yoshinaga-Itano, C., & Deas, A. (1999). Maternal sensitivity predicts language gain in preschool children who are deaf and hard-of-hearing. *Journal of Deaf Studies and Deaf Education, 4*, 294–304.

Pressman, L. J., Pipp-Siegel, S., Yoshinaga-Itano, C., Kubicek, L., & Emde R.N. (2000). A comparison of the links between emotional availability and language gain in young children with and without hearing loss [monograph]. *Volta Review, 100*(5), 251–277.

Punch, R., & Hyde, M. (2011). Social participation of children and adolescents with cochlear implants: A qualitative analysis of parent, teacher, and child interviews. *Journal of Deaf Studies and Deaf Education, 16*, 474–493.

Qi, S., & Mitchell, R. E. (2012). Large-scale academic achievement testing of deaf and hard-of-hearing students: Past, present, and future. *Journal of Deaf Studies and Deaf Education, 17*, 1–18.

Rogoff, B. (2003). *The cultural nature of human development*. New York: Oxford University Press.

Sass-Lehrer M. (2012). Early intervention for children birth to 3: Families, communities, and communication. In L. A. Schmeltz (Ed.), *A resource guide for early hearing detection and intervention* (pp. 10-1–10-16). Retrieved February 7, 2013, from http://www.infanthearing.org/ehdi-ebook/2012_ebook/Chapter10.pdf

Schmidt-Denter, U. (1996). *Die soziale Entwicklung: Ein Lehrbuch über soziale Beziehungen* [Social development: A textbook on social relations]. Weinheim: Psychologie Verlags Union.

Sen, A. (2006). *Identity and violence: The illusion of destiny*. New York: W.W. Norton & Company.

Stern, D. (2004). *The present moment in psychotherapy and everyday life*. New York: W.W. Norton & Company.

Stinson, M. S., & Antia, S. D. (1999). Considerations in educating deaf and hard-of-hearing students in inclusive settings. *Journal of Deaf Studies and Deaf Education, 4*, 163–175.

Strassman, B. (1997). Metacognition and reading in children who are deaf: A review of the research. *Journal of Deaf Studies and Deaf Education, 2*, 140–149.

Tang, G., Lam, S., & Yiu, C. (2014). Language development of deaf children in a sign bilingual and co-enrollment environment. In M. Marschark, G. Tang, & H. Knoors (Eds.), *Bilingualism and bilingual deaf education* (pp. 313–341). New York: Oxford University Press.

Umberson, D., & Montez, J.K. (2010). Social relationships and health: A flashpoint for health policy. *Journal of Health and Social Behavior, 51* (Suppl.), S54–S66.

van Gent, T., Goedhart, A. W., Knoors, H. E. T., Westenberg, P. M., Philip, D. A., & Treffers, P. D. A. (2012). Self-concept and ego development in deaf adolescents: A comparative study. *Journal of Deaf Studies and Deaf Education, 17*, 333–351.

Wauters, L. N., & Knoors, H. (2008). Social integration of deaf children in inclusive settings. *Journal of Deaf Studies and Deaf Education, 13*, 21–36.

Wolters, N., Knoors, H. E. T., Cillessen, A. H. N., & Verhoeven, L. (2011). Predicting acceptance and popularity in early adolescence as a function of hearing status, gender, and educational setting. *Research in Developmental Disabilities, 32*, 2553–2565.

Wolters, N., Knoors, H. E. T., Cillessen, A. H. N., & Verhoeven, L. (2012). Impact of peer and teacher relations on deaf early adolescents' well-being: Comparisons before and after a major school transition. *Journal of Deaf Studies and Deaf Education, 17*, 464–482.

Yetman, M., & Brice, P. J. (2002). *Peer relations and self-esteem among deaf children in a mainstream school environment.* Unpublished manuscript, Gallaudet University.

14

Reciprocity in School Peer Relationships of Deaf and Hard-of-Hearing Early Adolescents

Promoting Empowerment

Nina Wolters and Jet Isarin

Theoretical views on peer relationships share an important commonality. The one basic element in peer relationships, whether specified as cooperation, equity, intimacy, or attraction, is mutual exchange, or reciprocity (Hartup, 2009). Reciprocity concerns responsiveness with directional actions, where one peer performs an action and the other peer responds to this action. This responsiveness is often symmetrical, with equal contribution of peers to the interaction (Bukowski, Motzoi, & Meyer, 2009). For deaf and hard-of-hearing (DHH) youth, an imbalance in reciprocity in peer relationships is likely to occur. Considering potential communication and behavior problems (Antia & Dittillo, 1998; Antia, Kreimeyer, Metz, & Spolsky, 2011; Brown & Foster, 1991; Suárez, 2000; Wolters, Knoors, Cillessen, & Verhoeven, 2011b, 2014), creating and maintaining positive peer relationships encompasses extra challenges for DHH youth. In early adolescence, a period with increased contact with peers and intensification of peer relationships, these challenges prove particularly difficult for DHH adolescents, even for those with cochlear implants (CIs) and better spoken language skills (Bukowski, Hoza, & Boivin, 1993; Punch & Hyde, 2011; Steinberg, 2008). By exploring peer relationships and specifically those of DHH early adolescents, as well as reciprocity in peer relationships, the support we should provide DHH early adolescents in school can be more clearly identified.

PEER RELATIONSHIPS AND FRIENDSHIP

The importance of peer relationships has been underscored by several studies. Positive peer relationships foster social, emotional, and cognitive development and academic growth (e.g., Flook, Repetti, & Ullman, 2005; Rubin, Bukowski, & Parker, 2006), which in turn affect well-being in the short and long terms (e.g., Rubin et al., 2006). In contrast, poor peer relationships in childhood and adolescence predict maladjustment, academic disengagement, and poor well-being (Flook et al., 2005; Steinberg, 2008).

When discussing youth's success in peer relationships, at least two elements need to be understood (Parker, Rubin, Erath, Wojslawowicz, & Buskirk, 2006). First, it is important to recognize the difference between levels of acceptance and popularity. Both are types of high status in the peer group and represent ways of being socially successful or competent in relationships with peers, although at a different level (LaFontana & Cillessen, 1998; Parkhurst & Hopmeyer, 1998). Youth are extremely aware of their own positions in the social hierarchies in the classroom; high social status creates social support, friends, and self-confidence and buffers against stress (e.g., Bukowski et al., 1993).

Acceptance, or sociometric popularity, refers to likeability or social preference. It reflects success at the dyadic level in the classroom. Popularity, or perceived popularity, reflects visibility and being a central and influential member of a peer group and is a measure of social success at the group level in the classroom (e.g., Cillessen, 2009, 2011). Thus, the term *acceptance* refers to sociometric popularity, but *popularity* refers to perceived popularity (Cillessen & Marks, 2011), where different attributions and expectations are ascribed to peers being accepted compared to peers perceived as popular. Accepted youths are cooperative and prosocial, whereas popular youths have influence in a group and are prosocial but also aggressive and manipulative. Popular peers have more influence in a group than accepted peers. Accepted youths experience positive social opportunities such as friendships and academic achievement. Popular youths have the same short-term benefits but may be at risk for health-risk behaviors and academic disengagement in the long term (Bukowski, 2011; Mayeux, Houser, & Dyches, 2011).

Hearing classmates' perspectives are crucial when determining whether DHH students are socially accepted or popular; they implicitly use (hearing) group norms to judge peers. A standard procedure for assessing acceptance is by asking children whom they like most and least in their peer group. Based on these nominations, children are ascribed a sociometric status—accepted, average, rejected, controversial, neglected—or are ranked according to their social preference in the group (e.g., Cillessen, 2009). With regard to popularity, students nominate most and least popular classmates (e.g., Cillessen, 2011).

The second element in understanding peer relationships is friendship. As with the emergence of a group social hierarchy (i.e., role of peer status), friendships change significantly when children move into adolescence. Friendships become closer and more distinctive from other peer relationships, reflected in the behavior and interactions of the friends (Berndt & McCandless, 2009). Although acceptance and friendship are connected in significant ways, friendships serve different functions than acceptance, and acceptance does not guarantee successful friendships (Parker et al., 2006). Friendships are the closest of youth's relationships with peers (Rubin et al., 2006) and serve functions such as attachment, reliable alliance, enhancement of worth, companionship, guidance, and nurturance (Bukowski et al., 2009). Mutual friendships have also been found to predict social competence, self-esteem, achievement in school, and positive adjustment in times of transition (Rubin et al., 2006). They protect youth from victimization and externalizing and internalizing problems, provide self-confidence, and make youth perform better academically (Bukowski et al., 2009). Important to recognize, though, is that besides the positive protective effects, friendships can also cause tension, for example when friends fight or one disappoints the other (Parker et al., 2006).

A very basic definition of friendship is (assumed) reciprocal knowing and a high level of liking (Berndt & McCandless, 2009; Bukowski et al., 2009). It reflects a strong positive bond between two persons (Bukowski et al., 2009). The level of reciprocity can be viewed on a friendship continuum (Berndt & McCandless, 2009). This continuum reflects the position of a friendship as defined by the friends' knowledge and liking of each other. The positive pole on this continuum represents "the best of friends," whereas the negative part of the continuum represents a range of acquaintances, with strangers at the pole. Reciprocal friendships are near the end of the positive pole, represented by high levels of positive relationship properties and a stronger affective tie than unilateral friendships. In the latter, one peer nominates the other as a friend, but not vice versa. Both types of friendship should be recognized; where the reciprocal friendship has positive outcomes, nonreciprocated friendships have their effects as well, for example when one peer considers a popular though aggressive peer as a friend, looks up to this friend, and copies this peer's behavior (Berndt & McCandless, 2009).

When considering the quality of friendships, important positive and negative features, their quality, and types of interactions should be recognized. Positive characteristics are, for example, companionship, intimacy, closeness, and trust, whereas co-rumination, frequency of conflict, and rivalry are negative features (Berndt & McCandless, 2009; Bukowski et al., 2009). A pair of friends may judge these features differently, reflecting the asymmetry in friendships.

A basic measure of friendship is the level of liking between two individuals. Most measures are nomination and/or rating based, acknowledging youth's own judgment (Bukowski et al., 2009). In the nomination procedure a peer chooses whom he or she considers his or her best friends in the classroom. In the rating scale procedure, the peer rates all classmates according to how much he or she likes them. Variations on these procedures are used, where, for example, an unlimited nomination procedure expands the range on the friendship continuum of the friendships identified, compared to a limited procedure of often three nominations per classmate.

Early Adolescence

Going through adolescence means facing cognitive, psychological, biological, and social changes (Blakemore, 2008; Steinberg, 2008). Biologically, for example, there are hormonal and physical changes, even on the neurobiological level, reflecting the difference between a young adolescent and an adult. Brain regions involved in social cognition, particularly in understanding other people, undergo structural development during adolescence (Blakemore, 2008). Regarding social changes, there is a shift with increased contact with peers and decreased contact with adults and a change in family functions. Here, an adolescent desires family to become supportive, guiding, and directive as opposed to the earlier functions of nurturance, protection, and socialization, mainly in light of the increased value ascribed to peer relationships (Steinberg, 2008). The latter is signified by an intensification of peer interest and peer relationships becoming more important and dyadic in nature. Today's teenagers spend twice as much time in the company of peers than of adults, even if we exclude time in the classroom, with about half of an adolescent's waking hours being spent with peers as opposed to 15% with adults. There is a decrease in adult supervision, and early adolescents become less emotionally dependent on parents and start to rely on their peers instead (Bukowski et al., 1993; Steinberg, 2008).

The social context in which an adolescent develops changes as well (Steinberg, 2008). In early adolescence, the school classroom is a very important context. Youth spend a vast amount of time with peers at school. Peer relationships in the classroom context are embedded in a group with defined boundaries (Rubin et al., 2006). Relationships with peers are a person's first true experience with dyadic relationships and closeness (Rubin et al., 2006), distinct from the hierarchical relationship with parents (Bukowski et al., 2009). Also, the peer group changes in structure, with the emergence of cliques and crowds in school (Rubin et al., 2006; Steinberg, 2008).

One major social contextual change is school transition from a smaller elementary school into a larger secondary school, where the situation is more dynamic and complex. This challenges all early adolescents, since they face a new social context with unfamiliar peers and a larger social system than the one in elementary education. Elementary school represented a well-known context with familiar classmates, since children often share classrooms with the same peers for several years. In contrast, at the start of secondary school, the majority, if not all, of the classmates are unfamiliar peers. Thus, new peer relationships have to be formed and a place in the class hierarchy has to be conquered. Generally, the new peer group is used to assess what is "normal," and being different, even if it just means you cannot hear well, is simply not valued by peers (Coyner, 1994; see Tijsseling, Chapter 3 in this volume). School transition is also marked by shifts from one primary teacher to multiple teachers and larger classrooms.

Thus, in early adolescence (ages 10 to 14), while dealing with inevitable mental and physical changes, social life considerably changes as well, especially in the area of peer relationships. Facing adolescence therefore dares all children—but what is it like for someone who cannot hear well? The challenge that comes with early adolescence and school transition has an extra problematic dimension for DHH youth.

Deaf and Hard-of-Hearing Early Adolescents' Peer Relationships

Communication and interaction with peers become increasingly important in the life of adolescents; interaction is a prerequisite for healthy relationships to emerge. However, for DHH youth, their hearing losses affect their interaction and thus their relationships with peers. With respect to educational setting, DHH children now more frequently attend mainstream education where they share a classroom with hearing peers. Since deafness has a relatively low incidence (Antia, Kreimeyer, & Reed, 2010; Stinson & Antia, 1999), DHH youth are often the only student with a hearing loss in the classroom, a phenomenon tagged as the "solitary mainstream experience" by Oliva (2004). In special education settings, often separate from mainstream schools, they share classrooms with DHH peers or hearing peers with disabilities. In co-enrollment settings, a general and a special education teacher teach both DHH and hearing students (see Tang, Lam, & Yiu, Chapter 6 in this volume).

In all types of educational settings, DHH peers may experience problems in their peer relationships due to communication and interaction challenges. "The sheer effort of communication is often tiring on both sides so the easy option is to avoid it altogether or restrict it to basics and superficial niceties" (Davis, 2003, p. 184). In all settings, a communication barrier lies at the forefront. This barrier constitutes more than just different preferred communication modes such as spoken versus signed language or diversity in sign language skills. The degree of hearing loss, however, is not a key factor in determining success in peer relationships (e.g., Stinson & Antia, 1999). For example, even DHH mainstream children with a mild hearing loss are at risk (Isarin, 2006, 2008). Whereas young children might fare well with relatively simple language, early adolescents need to be equipped with much more complex language to function in social interactions with peers. Communication with hearing peers requires not only (speech) perception and production, but also the ability to participate actively and incidentally, whether in spoken or signed language. It thus entails several communicative skills and social aspects that become more and more important in early adolescence (Fabes, Martin, & Hanish, 2009).

A hearing loss directly affects communication with hearing peers. Many aspects of communication are simply not easily available to DHH adolescents, affecting incidental learning in general (Calderon & Greenberg, 2011) but also specifically the "incidental participation" in communicative acts in the social environment. Incidental learning is the process by which information is learned not through direct instruction, but by overhearing things, or by passive exposure to situations, affecting the understanding of rules for how people communicate and behave (Calderon & Greenberg, 2011). Incidental, or secondary, participation in communicative acts refers to passive participation in communicative acts. One can unconsciously overhear a conversation, process the information overheard, and decide to continue participation actively. Even those situations affect a student's position in the classroom hierarchy.

DHH youth's communicative skills are often less well developed than those of their hearing peers (Antia et al., 2011; Stinson & Antia, 1999; Suárez, 2000; Wolters, Blom, Knoors, & Verhoeven, 2011a; Wolters et al., 2011b). The somewhat restricted interaction with hearing peers limits the variety of peer interactions in which DHH youth can learn social skills and behavior (Antia & Dittillo, 1998). Their social behavior and their communicative skills have been found to be the main predictor of peer status (Asher & McDonald, 2009; Wolters et al., 2011b; Wolters, Knoors, Cillessen, & Verhoeven, 2012, 2014). DHH early adolescents are likely to experience more problems with making friends than younger DHH children (Antia et al., 2010). Punch and Hyde (2011), for example, specifically found adolescence to be a difficult time for DHH youth, even for those with a CI. The DHH adolescents in their study stressed communication in groups and social skills as causes of them feeling self-conscious and worrying about friendships. Relationships with peers are an important determiner of well-being (e.g., Blom, Marschark, Vervloed, & Knoors, 2014; Moeller, 2007; Wolters et al., 2012), and DHH youth have been found to experience victimization, depression, and psychiatric problems more often than hearing youth (e.g., Kouwenberg, Rieffe, Theunissen, & De Rooij, 2012; Moeller, 2007; Van Gent, Goedhart, Hindley, & Treffers, 2007; Weiner, Day, & Galvan, 2013).

The above illustrates that DHH youth, and especially DHH early adolescents, face challenges in establishing a positive position in the classroom social hierarchy and making friends (see Hintermair, Chapter 13 in this volume). Since poor peer relationships often go hand in hand with maladjustment and poor well-being (e.g., Steinberg, 2008), it is important to consider whether DHH early adolescents indeed experience lower peer status and problems with making friendships in the classroom. This is particularly important since acceptance by hearing peers has been identified as the best predictor of DHH peers' academic success (Coyner, 1994).

RECIPROCITY: A CYCLE OF INFLUENCE

Parker and colleagues (2006) described a model reflecting a cycle of influence, referring to the reciprocal process in peer relationships. It is by no means the aim of this chapter to fully describe this reciprocal model. The model, however, stresses important general aspects of peer relationships, providing insight into the earlier-described problems in peer relationships between hearing and DHH early adolescents.

The model recognizes that peers "form certain impressions and perceptions of one another that guide their behavioral responses toward each other and determine the nature of their relationships" (Parker et al., 2006, p. 462). In other words, the social outcomes—peer status and friendships—follow from peer perceptions, which are formed during interactions. Relationships are composed of a history of interactions and the interaction partners' thoughts and feelings about those previous interactions (Berndt & McCandless, 2009). From the first interaction between peers, peer perceptions are shaped and consist of expectations and representations regarding peers in the peer group. These expectations and representations, as well as the representation of the self, guide future interaction and affect the interpretation of behavioral cues of the interaction partner. The expectations and representations are established by a person's cognition, emotions, and behaviors (see Rieffe, Netten, Broekhof, and Veiga, Chapter 16 in this volume). Importantly, the social behavior of both the peer and the members of the peer group contribute to (un)successful peer relationships (Parker et al., 2006). Thus, both the DHH and the hearing peer contribute to the position of a DHH early adolescent in the social hierarchy in the classroom.

The components of the reciprocity model include the child's cognitions about himself or herself, the child's characteristic behavior toward peers, the influence of the child's behavior on the peer group's shared evaluation of the child, and the resulting influence of these attitudes on the peer group's collective behavior toward the child (Parker et al., 2006). In the following paragraphs, these components will be discussed with the DHH early adolescent as the "child" and the hearing classmates as the "peer group." The behavior of the peer group will be discussed in terms of acceptance and popularity of the DHH classmates as well as peer friendships in the classroom.

The Self: The Deaf and Hard-of-Hearing Early Adolescent

Parker and colleagues (2006) described the first component of reciprocity as incorporating the child's self, social cognition, and emotions. During interaction, one's knowledge about the self, one's knowledge about relationships in general, and one's prior experiences come into play. They create expectations one has about interactions with (specific) peers, fed by personal and emotional general efficacy, but also with regard to specific relationships. Through this, one's self-efficacy and self-regard affect how one initiates and maintains social exchanges with peers. Thus, social behavior is largely affected by one's prior social experiences, with these experiences affecting how one interprets and processes social information or cues.

One's self-image represents the perception of the self as a socially desirable being (Kluwin, Stinson, & Colarossi, 2002). In her study of DHH adolescents in special and mainstream education, Isarin (2006) distinguished four types of *self*: the solitary, the lost, the searching, and the solidary. She found that the first two types were dominant in early adolescence. The *solitary self* is lonely and withdrawn. Such children have a negative identity based on internalized prejudices about deafness and resulting in feelings of shame, incompetency, and distress. The *lost self* is disoriented and confused. This self identifies with a world that is only partially understood and strives for a sense of belonging. The *searching self* is in search of an identity of which deafness is part. The searching self does not know yet where it wants to belong and is actively trying to find out by "traveling" between different worlds. The *solidary self* is connected, internally and externally. This self is confident and has found its way in (social) life.

All participants in a survey on the "solitary mainstream experience" of DHH students (Oliva, 2004) started off feeling excluded and lonely in middle and high school due to a change in social dynamics. A combination of less activity, more verbalization, and the hearing peers' lack of willingness or patience to communicate effectively on an ongoing basis made them outsiders. The strategies they used to fit in when younger no longer worked, resulting in a pervasive feeling of being different and left out. Most participants reported desperately trying to fit in and be like their hearing peers, but failing. As a result they felt inadequate, "a burden to others," and unable to make a contribution in activities or conversations.

> As I grew up I had more and more a feeling that I was different. I had the feeling that people talked to me as their "good deed of the day." (Robinson, 2003, p. 97)

In the context of disability studies, low self-esteem in people with disabilities has been described in terms of internalized oppression (Reeve, 2002; Shakespeare, 1996). Daily experiences with negative attitudes, prejudices, exclusion, and low expectations cannot but influence self-image.

> We harbour inside ourselves the pain and the memories, the fears and the confusions, the negative self-images and the low expectations, turning them into weapons with which to re-injure ourselves, every day of our lives. ("Mason," in Reeve, 2002, p. 495)

DHH adolescents have been found to perceive themselves as less socially accepted and having fewer close friendships than hearing adolescents (Stinson, Whitmire, & Kluwin, 1996; Van Gent, Goedhart, Knoors, Westenberg, & Treffers, 2012). When DHH adolescents feel incompetent in the social domain, this low self-confidence also hinders them from feeling adequate in other domains (Van Gent et al., 2012). Although self-esteem seems not to be related to the extent of mainstreaming (Bat-Chava, 1993; Kluwin et al., 2002), mainstreamed adolescents have been found to experience lower levels of feeling socially accepted, pointing toward a socially difficult time and lack from support of hearing classmates (Van Gent et al., 2012; Wolters et al., 2012). Yetman (2000) found that the more time DHH children spent with hearing children, the lower their self-esteem is. This is because the way we perceive ourselves is derived from our interactions with our social environment; DHH youth's self-concept is affected by comparison with hearing peers (Van Gurp, 2001; Yiu & Tang, 2014).

DHH people generally have been found to have lower self-esteem than hearing people, although studies have shown variability (e.g., higher self-esteem for DHH youth with DHH parents). Stinson and colleagues (1996) found DHH adolescents to be less satisfied with their social skills at the end of high school, experiencing low social competence, but also giving lower ratings of emotional security with hearing peers than with DHH peers. Repeated frustration and socially discouraging situations in contact with hearing peers, perceiving the hearing peers' negative attitude, might have contributed to this situation (Kluwin et al., 2002; Stinson & Liu, 1999). For example, DHH youth think the potential communication obstacle with hearing peers can be more easily overcome than do hearing peers (Nunes et al., 2001).

For DHH early adolescents, a positive attitude toward their hearing losses supports positive relationships with peers (Yiu & Tang, 2014). Being self-conscious about a hearing loss creates withdrawal and difficulty in establishing healthy peer relationships (Martin & Bat-Chava, 2003); withdrawn youth also display negative self-evaluations in attributing peer relationship difficulties to themselves (Hymel, Bowker, & Woody, 1993). Identification and contact with DHH peers seems to foster positive self-esteem (Bat-Chava, 1993).

Deaf and Hard-of-Hearing Adolescents' Behavior Toward Peers

The second component of the reciprocal influence model is the characteristic behavior the DHH early adolescent displays toward his or her classmates. This behavior affects the perception of the hearing classmates toward the DHH peer. Even the earliest interactions with classmates predict later peer status and friendships. From earlier studies we can conclude that problems may arise for DHH youth as both social behavior and communicative skills impede their peer status and friendships (e.g., Antia & Dittillo, 1998; Antia et al., 2011b; Stinson & Antia, 1999; Suárez, 2000; Wauters & Knoors, 2007; Wolters et al., 2011b, 2014).

Social behavior is usually divided in prosocial, antisocial, and withdrawn behaviors. Prosocial behaviors refer to socially desirable voluntary behaviors such as helping and caring (Eisenberg et al., 1999). Antisocial behavior includes being overtly or relationally aggressive and disruptive or impulsive (Warden, Cheyne, Christie, Fitzpatrick, & Reid, 2003). Passive withdrawn behavior refers to isolating oneself from a group (Rubin, Burgess, & Coplan, 2002). Social behavior affects peer interactions (Fabes et al., 2009) and is an important determinant of peer status and friendships (e.g., Asher & McDonald, 2009; Kouwenberg, 2013). Norm-breaking behaviors (e.g., withdrawal and immaturity) are considered increasingly deviant by peers with increasing age, especially during early adolescence.

Generally, less age-appropriate or less mature behavior is found in DHH than hearing peers, often accompanied by more problematic behavioral profiles among students in separate special classes compared to mainstreamed classes (Kluwin et al., 2002; Stinson & Kluwin, 2011; Wolters et al., 2011b, 2014). Antia, Jones, Luckner, Kreimeyer, and Reed (2011a) found social skills and problem behavior for 191 DHH second- through eighth-grade students in mainstream classrooms to be within average range. For DHH early adolescents in mainstream settings specifically, passive withdrawn behavior appears to be an important determinant for peer acceptance and popularity (Wolters et al., 2014). Wolters and colleagues found that hearing students perceived DHH classmates to show more withdrawn behavior than hearing classmates. In their study, passive withdrawn behavior reflected the preference of a classmate to be alone during recess or complete school tasks alone, rather than in companionship with classmates. This passive withdrawn behavior proved to be the main predictor of acceptance and popularity both in the short term (in grade 7) as well as the long term (into grade 8). In the study by Wauters and Knoors (2007), withdrawn behavior was operationalized not as passive withdrawn behavior but as reflecting a combination of active isolation by the peer group (being bullied) and social ineffectiveness of the DHH peer (seeking help). This type of withdrawn behavior, however, was also found to be important for DHH peers' social status. In contrast with mainstream education and the importance of withdrawn behavior, in separate special settings, prosocial behavior appears to be a main predictor of peer status, but not withdrawn behavior (Wolters et al., 2014).

Less is known about specific behaviors and their relation with peer friendships (Parker et al., 2006). Prosocial behavior has a strong positive association with friendship quality in hearing youth (Berndt, 2002). Furthermore, high levels of positive features and low levels of negative features create high-quality friendships (Berndt, 2002). Kouwenberg (2013) found social behavior to affect the quality of peer friendships of DHH (and hearing) peers; an increase in empathic skills (e.g., prosocial behavior, understanding) and a decrease in antisocial behavior improved friendship quality for both DHH and hearing youth. One can expect DHH youth who are considered withdrawn in mainstream education, or less prosocial in separate special settings, to both engage in fewer prosocial acts with peers. This likely is one factor explaining the lower quality of their peer relationships compared to hearing peers.

In the domain of communicative skills, in particular, strategic and pragmatic communicative skills are important for positive and effective interaction, regardless of the mode of communication (e.g., spoken or signed). Pragmatic skills refer to the appropriateness of language use, or the appropriate interpretation of a message in a particular situation (Nærland, 2011). Strategic skills involve metacognitive strategies for managing effective interaction (Verhoeven & Vermeer, 1992). Pragmatic skills have been found to promote peer relationships (Nærland, 2011); strategic communicative skills have been studied rarely in this context.

Generally, communicative skills are learned by being exposed to proficient language users, which is often a problem for children with a hearing loss. In that regard, DHH children's pragmatic communication is less clear than that of hearing children, although comparable to that of younger children. Also, in direct dyadic communication DHH children experience difficulties (e.g., Jeanes, Nienhuys, & Rickards, 2000). In early adolescence, DHH mainstreamed youth's pragmatic skills have been found to be less well developed compared to those of their hearing classmates, as were their strategic communicative skills (e.g., monitoring a conversation, improvisation, initiating and maintaining a conversation; Wolters et al., 2011b).

DHH youth's communicative skills are positively related to peer relationships; both pragmatic and strategic communicative skills have been found to affect DHH youth's acceptance by hearing peers as well as their popularity (Batten, Oakes, & Alexander, 2013; Wolters et al., 2011b). Gender effects have to be recognized, though (Murphy & Faulkner, 2006): Communicative skills for DHH early adolescent girls are more important for peer acceptance than for boys at that age (Wolters et al., 2011b). Regarding friendships, Martin and Bat-Chava (2003) found that actively interacting with hearing peers helped DHH girls to make friends, but for DHH boys this made no difference. Both studies (Martin & Bat-Chava, 2003; Wolters et al., 2011b) found that for girls, communication equals social connectedness. For them, considerate and polite language use fosters peer relationships. In boys' peer friendships verbal communication is less emphasized due to the competitive nature of their interactions. Boys have a competitive interaction style, often revolving around activities such as sports. Here, commands, providing information, or telling jokes is more important (Rose & Smith, 2009). Telling jokes, being a part of improvisation, plays a significant role in the number of friendships, regardless of gender (Wolters et al., 2011b). Although this part of the reciprocity model focuses on the behavior of the child, and behavior plays an overriding role in peer relationships, peers' social status and friendships can also be affected due to nonbehavioral reasons (Parker et al., 2006). For example, for DHH early adolescents, merely having a hearing loss negatively predicted their peer status in the classroom in the study by Wolters and colleagues (2011b, 2014). As Coyner (1994) pointed out, being different, even if it is just by being DHH, is simply not valued in early adolescence. Also, DHH youth have been found to be less socially mature than hearing peers in public schools (Brown & Foster, 1991; Kluwin et al., 2002). Their more childish behavior compared to that of their hearing peers likely has a negative effect on the way they come across to early adolescent peers who strive to be mature and independent. Appearance is a strong determiner of peer status (Hymel et al., 1993; LaFontana & Cillessen, 2002).

Peers' Social Cognitions: Hearing Classmates' Perspective

Reputations, or representations and perceptions people have of each other, are quite stable over time (LaFontana & Cillessen, 1998, 2002). The foundation of these reputations lies in the contact between peers, from the first contact on, as well as one's own reputation (Parker et al., 2006). In this process, the behaviors that peers display play an important role. This entire cognitive process represents the third factor in the model by Parker and colleagues (2006).

For hearing classmates, this means that their (collective) opinion about DHH classmates is strongly affected by their experience with the classmates with a hearing loss. In mainstream general education classes, it is likely that hearing peers are inexperienced with communicating with a DHH classmate. In general, this means that there is a lack of understanding, or knowledge, about hearing loss on the part of hearing peers (Hung & Paul, 2006; Stinson & Kluwin, 2011). Unfamiliarity and a lack of meaningful contact foster a negative attitude on the part of hearing peers toward DHH peers (Brown & Foster, 1991; Hung & Paul, 2006; Stinson & Liu, 1999), affecting their acceptance of DHH classmates (Batten et al., 2013).

Although hearing classmates' attitudes seem to relate to contact experience with DHH classmates (Hung & Paul, 2006), a negative attitude may reflect a hearing classmate's frustration, misinterpretation, communication breakdowns, unfamiliarity, and fear (Stinson & Liu, 1999). Also, youth who are "different," in this case early adolescents with a hearing loss, seem to face obstacles in positive peer judgment by definition (Coyner, 1994; Stinson & Liu, 1999; Wolters et al., 2011b).

Hung and Paul (2006) found in American inclusive or general education classrooms a more positive attitude toward DHH classmates in their older hearing participants than younger participants. Cambra (2002), in contrast, found that in a comparable age sample of Spanish student (grades 6 through 12), the older hearing students were less positive. The older students thought that DHH classmates (1) would be better off in a special education setting, (2) showed more problem behaviors, and (3) were not as hard-working as their hearing peers. Importantly, when DHH peers are considered less socially competent, this might be attributable to hearing peers unconsciously using hearing norms (Brown & Foster, 1991). For example, waving to get someone's attention is normal for DHH peers, but for hearing peers who are unfamiliar with this, it might be interpreted as impolite.

Chinese hearing students in a co-enrollment program with DHH classmates (Yiu & Tang, 2014) expressed quite positive attitudes toward their DHH classmates. They provided care and support. The latter finding, although positive, questions the quality of the relationships between the DHH and hearing peers; for example, it does not reflect the traditional role of friendships. Nunes and colleagues (2001) mentioned that American hearing peers described their roles as friends in the context of being an interpreter, helping DHH classmates by acting as role models. They felt empathy for DHH classmates but still preferred hearing classmates as friends to share enjoyment and intimacy. The finding that girls, in particular, were among the hearing classmates with more positive attitudes toward DHH peers (Cambra, 2002; Hung & Paul, 2006) seems in line with previous findings: Girls foster cooperation and social connectedness in peer relationships (Rose & Smith, 2009). Regardless of positive attitudes, understanding and accepting communication difficulties are always challenges for hearing peers (Yiu & Tang, 2014). These communication obstacles were specifically mentioned by hearing classmates as forming barriers in initiating friendships with DHH classmates (Nunes et al., 2001). Interaction is a prerequisite for peer relationships to emerge; a hearing loss is hard to ignore when this directly affects interaction (Brown & Foster, 1991). Not surprisingly, both DHH and hearing youth have been found to prefer to interact with peers with the same hearing status (e.g., Antia et al., 2011b; see Antia, Chapter 23 in this volume).

Peer Behavior Toward Deaf and Hard-of-Hearing Early Adolescents: Peer Status and Friendships

The fourth and final component of the model by Parker and colleagues (2006) represents the peer behavior toward the child, or, with regard to the current chapter, the responses by the hearing classmates toward the DHH early adolescent. The reputations of DHH early adolescents, through the eyes of the classmates, guide the classmates' collective behavior toward them. The question is what the classmates' shared evaluation of their DHH peer comprises, reflected in the DHH classmate's peer status and friendships.

Peer Status: Acceptance and Popularity

When we sum up earlier findings on acceptance based on four reviews, DHH children have been found to be accepted by their hearing classmates in some but not all studies (Antia et al., 2010; Kluwin et al., 2002; Stinson & Antia, 1999; Stinson & Kluwin, 2011). When they are not as accepted as hearing classmates, they are often neglected (i.e., not nominated as either "liked" or "disliked") or rejected (often nominated as "disliked" but not as "liked") and feel lonely. The four reviews together considered seven studies reflecting DHH peers' acceptance or likeability (Antia & Kreimeyer, 1996; Bowen, 2008; Capelli, Daniels, Durieux-Smith, McGrath, & Neus, 1995; Coyner, 1994; Kluwin & Gonsher, 1994; Nunes et al., 2001; Wauters & Knoors, 2007). Most of these, and some other studies, have concerned elementary school children and/or consider a broad age range and relatively small groups; this complicates the generalization of findings. Factors explaining the mixed results, though, may be age, gender, and educational setting.

With regard to age, Antia and colleagues (2010) mentioned that peers might socially accept younger DHH children, but not older ones. DHH adolescents seem to have more difficulty feeling emotionally secure, with social isolation as a possible consequence. Punch and Hyde (2011) interviewed 24 parents, 15 teachers, and 11 DHH children and adolescents (aged 10 to 17 years) from Australia with a CI with regard to social participation. The adolescents in their study experienced particular difficulties regarding peer relationships in the classroom. In a Spanish adolescent sample of 10- to 20-year-old DHH students, Cambra (2002) found that DHH students were mainly accepted by female and younger hearing peers. Even within a group of elementary-aged children (grades 1 through 6), age effects can be found. Capelli and colleagues (1995) studied 23 Canadian DHH children and 23 hearing classmates, matched by gender. Overall, the DHH students were more often rejected than their hearing classmates. Interestingly, this was especially true for the younger children in grades 1 through 3, but not in grades 4 through 6. An intervention study among DHH preschool and first-grade children even showed the rigidity of lower peer acceptance;

an intervention did not affect the acceptance of 45 4- to 6-year-old DHH children by their 91 hearing classmates (Antia & Kreimeyer, 1996).

A few studies have pointed to the role of gender in DHH early adolescents' peer acceptance (Coyner, 1994; Wolters et al., 2011b, 2012). Coyner (1994) found a hearing-status-by-gender interaction for acceptance in a group of 10 American 13- to 17-year-old (early) adolescents in mainstream education, compared to 25 hearing classmates. As in the study by Wolters and colleagues (2011b) concerning 35 Dutch mainstreamed DHH children and 672 hearing classmates in grade 6 of elementary school (age 11 and 12), DHH girls were more accepted by their hearing classmates than DHH boys. Wolters and colleagues (2012), however, found that such acceptance of DHH mainstream girls decreased over the subsequent school transition to mainstream secondary school, diminishing the gender difference. DHH boys were even somewhat more accepted in grade 7 in their subsequent study regarding the first two years of secondary school (Wolters et al., 2014). No gender effect for hearing classmates in mainstream education was found in that study.

The role of educational setting seems important as well. DHH children in separate classrooms seem to have more positive social experiences, with fewer reports of loneliness than mainstreamed DHH peers (Stinson & Kluwin, 2011). Wolters and colleagues (2011b, 2012, 2014) specifically compared DHH peers in mainstream regular classes with DHH peers in separate schools for the DHH on acceptance. In addition to the 35 to 42 Dutch DHH early adolescents in mainstream education in their studies, 52 to 62 DHH participants attended special schools. In all three studies, despite fewer reports of loneliness (Stinson & Kluwin, 2011), DHH early adolescents in mainstream education were equally accepted as their DHH peers in separate schools for the DHH. Considering that the DHH peers in mainstream schools were less accepted than their hearing classmates, this suggests that peer acceptance in both school settings could be better.

In co-enrollment settings, DHH students have been found to be accepted (Bowen, 2008; Kluwin & Gonsher, 1994; Wauters & Knoors, 2007; Yiu & Tang, 2014) as well as neglected (Nunes et al., 2001). These results are based on relatively small samples from kindergarten to grades 1 through 6, however, of five, seven, four, 16, and nine DHH children respectively, who were in actual co-enrollment settings. In the study by Nunes and colleagues (2001), although the DHH children were more often neglected, they were equal in play preference compared to their hearing classmates. In a recent study by Yiu and Tang (2014), 16 DHH children in grades 4 through 6 in a Chinese co-enrollment setting were judged quite positively by their peers. Still, there was a higher preference for DHH peers by DHH peers (higher intragroup than intergroup ratings).

These results all concern peer acceptance. So far, only Wolters and colleagues (2011b, 2012, 2014) studied the popularity of DHH early adolescents. The DHH participants attended either mainstream or separate special education settings in grade 6 (Wolters et al., 2011b). Two follow-up studies followed these students during school transition to secondary school (grade 6 to 7; Wolters et al., 2012) and the first two years (grade 7 and 8) of secondary school (Wolters et al., 2014). In all three studies, DHH early adolescents in mainstream education were less popular not only compared to their hearing classmates, but also compared to DHH peers in separate special education settings. No gender effects were found.

Little is known about the stability of acceptance and popularity of DHH youth. In hearing children, popularity is more stable than acceptance overall, but acceptance is more stable for boys and popularity is more stable for girls (Mayeux et al., 2011). Also, acceptance has been found to be more stable for older than younger children, although generally there is lower stability over time (Jiang & Cillessen, 2005). Regarding DHH youth, in a Dutch study (Wauters & Knoors, 2007), the acceptance of 11 DHH first- to fifth-grade children was relatively stable over a year. Two other Dutch studies (Wolters et al., 2012, 2014) confirmed this. Although the school transition from primary to secondary education temporarily disrupts the stability of acceptance by hearing peers (Wolters et al., 2012), after the transition to secondary school both the lower acceptance and lower popularity of DHH adolescents were quite stable (Wolters et al., 2014). Specifically, popularity was more stable than acceptance for DHH adolescents in mainstream education, and vice versa in separate special education settings. Popularity represents a group reputation and is generally quite stable due to the hardiness of reputations. Acceptance is based on personal preference and is more easily affected by small behavioral changes, for example (Mayeaux et al., 2011). In smaller groups, like special education classrooms, a popularity hierarchy or having favorites in the classroom is less likely to occur. Also, different contexts (i.e., mainstream vs. special education setting) create different norms for behavior, which again affects peer status differently.

The conclusion can be drawn that overall, although one has to recognize youth's age and gender, peer status (i.e., acceptance and popularity) is less favorable for DHH youth in mainstream education than for hearing classmates and than DHH peers in separate special education settings. In regular, mainstream classes, DHH youth are more often less accepted by peers, and also less popular. This means that on the dyadic level, they less often are considered as "liked most" by hearing classmates and more often as "liked least." On a group level, they have little influence in the peer group and are less visible in the classroom than hearing classmates.

Quantity and Quality of Peer Friendships

Few studies have focused on the number of friends of DHH youth in early adolescence. The nine DHH early adolescents, aged 11 to 13 years, in the study by Nunes and colleagues (2001) were more likely to have no friends (i.e., reciprocal positive nominations) than their hearing classmates. In contrast, Wauters and Knoors (2007) concluded that DHH children (grades 1 to 5) in the Netherlands did not differ from hearing classmates on the number of reciprocal friendships. Although they seemed to be more often involved in a network without friendships, the differences were not significant. In another Dutch study (Wolters et al., 2011a), DHH early adolescents in mainstream classes also had equal numbers of reciprocal friendships as their hearing classmates. DHH peers in separate special education settings, when acknowledging differences in class size and thus potential number of friends, also did not differ from DHH peers in mainstream settings. To conclude, one Dutch study focused on DHH adolescents' general relationship network, thus including peers in school and outside of school, as well as adults (Piso, Knoors, & Vervloed, 2009). Participants were 12 hearing and 12 DHH 13- to 19-year-old adolescents, matched by age and gender. Although the number of persons in the social network was equal for the hearing and DHH participants, the DHH adolescents had fewer friends than their hearing peers.

As pointed out earlier, when discussing the quality of friendships, the presence and quality of positive and negative features can be considered, as well as the interaction between friends. Piso and colleagues (2009) used the Network of Relationships Inventory (NRI) to assess the quality of Dutch DHH adolescents' social networks, reflecting both positive and negative relationship features. Although the average network quality of DHH and hearing peers did not differ from each other, the friendship quality of peer relationships turned out to be less well evaluated; DHH youth scored lower than hearing youth on, for example, intimacy and companionship. The quality of DHH youth's best friendships also was found to be lower in another Dutch study of 127 DHH (aged eight to 14 years) and 121 hearing (aged eight to 16 years) youth, reflecting less positive and more negative features in best friendship dyads of DHH than hearing peers (Kouwenberg, 2013). This effect was larger for DHH peers in separate special schools than DHH peers in mainstream settings, however. In a qualitative study, 35 American DHH children aged five to 11 years, attending full or partial mainstream school settings, established reasonable relationships with hearing peers; a third of the children had good relationships, a half had fair relationships, and five children (14%) had poor relationships with their hearing peers (Martin & Bat-Chava, 2003). In 113 older (aged 18 to 26 years) DHH Dutch and American students, Blom and colleagues

(2014) found no difference in friendship quality between the DHH and hearing students.

The interaction patterns between friends differ from nonfriends on coordination, responsiveness, and similarity in their affect and behavior (Bukowski et al., 2009). Antia and colleagues (2011b) reviewed studies on the quality and quantity of peer interactions of DHH youth. They concluded that DHH children often interact less frequently with peers. The duration of these interactions is also less than for hearing peers. DHH as well as hearing peers prefer to interact with peers of similar hearing status. Both are interested in interacting with peers. Potentially, nonlinguistic initiations by DHH peers are not always noticed by hearing classmates.

Although the relatively limited number of studies makes it difficult to generalize the findings regarding DHH early adolescents' friendships, one can cautiously state that they are at risk for having fewer friends, although not all studies confirm this. This conclusion is based on studies focusing on reciprocal friendships, but not the friendship continuum. The quality of DHH youth's friendships seems less than their hearing peers' friendships.

RECIPROCITY IN PEER RELATIONSHIPS BETWEEN HEARING CHILDREN AND DEAF AND HARD-OF-HEARING ONES: PROMOTING EMPOWERMENT

Peer relationships foster social, emotional, and cognitive development but also academic growth, while poor peer relationships in childhood and adolescence predict maladjustment, poor well-being, and academic disengagement. Peer relations thus affect academic performance. Acceptance by hearing peers has even been identified as the best predictor of DHH peers' academic success. Also, low scores on self-esteem correlate negatively with academic competence.

The reciprocity model, interpreted in light of DHH–hearing peer relationships in school, underscores that the focus has to lie on the cognitive level of both the DHH as well as the hearing peer if one wants to positively affect their relationships. As Yiu and Tang (2014) explained, the attitude of DHH youth regarding their own hearing loss and how this affects their social life, and hearing peers' attitudes toward deafness, are related in significant ways. Merely focusing on the behavioral level seems equivalent to tackling symptoms (i.e., lower peer status and friendship quality of DHH peers, as well as their withdrawn behavior and communicative skills) but fails to tackle an important cause of the relationship problem (both DHH and hearing peers' perspectives and attitudes). Both parties need to come to a certain level of mutual understanding, where the perceptions and attitudes of both are important (Yiu & Tang, 2014). In reaching this, help of (at least) teachers and itinerant services is important; simple physical proximity will not change attitudes (Hung & Paul, 2006).

Regarding DHH early adolescents with a CI, one is inclined to expect them to have fewer problems engaging in positive peer relationships or positive peer status. However, having a CI does not equate to hearing "as hearing peers do." For those DHH peers with better-developed speech production and perception skills attributable to their CI, communication in groups, for example, remains a challenge (e.g., Punch & Hyde, 2011). Although CIs often improve the communication with their (hearing) classmates, it will, as the visible device that it is, make many young people feel different and awkward.

To increase familiarity, or mutual understanding, between DHH and hearing youth, the interpretation of behavior is of relevance. Often displaying withdrawn behavior, for example, can create social expectations and prejudice by classmates (LaFontana & Cillessen, 1998). Not only should youth be made aware of their own biases when interpreting others' behaviors, but they should also realize that their own behavior is subjected to others' interpretation (Wolters et al., 2014); one tends to confirm rather than disconfirm existing opinions (Parker et al., 2006). Do DHH peers indeed prefer to spend time alone, possibly pointing to internalizing problems, or is there another reason for their withdrawn behavior? It is reasonable to expect the communication barrier or lack of DHH peers' communicative skills to (co)create the situation where DHH youth in mainstream education are considered withdrawn by their hearing classmates, whose misunderstanding of communication difficulties also plays a role (Martin & Bat-Chava, 2003). Antia and colleagues (2011a) found classroom communication participation to be a major predictor of social outcomes. Thus, DHH early adolescents should be aware of how their behavior might be (mis)interpreted by hearing classmates, while hearing classmates should be aware of potential prejudice guiding their interpretation of DHH peers' behavior (Brown & Foster, 1991).

For DHH early adolescents, it seems important to focus on empowerment. Empowerment is a collective struggle for power on a personal (self-esteem and self-knowledge), interpersonal (support, advocacy and sharing), and political (attitudes, access) level (Van Houten & Bellemakers, 2002), or as Morris (1991) defined it: "pride against prejudice." For DHH early adolescents, a positive attitude toward their hearing loss supports their relationships with peers (Yiu & Tang, 2014). In contrast, self-consciousness and low self-esteem negatively affect their social behavior (i.e., withdrawal) and with that their peer relationships (Martin & Bat-Chava, 2003).

To promote positive attitudes, itinerant services and teachers should start helping students to understand each other's perspectives (Nunes et al., 2001) at the start of secondary school, considering the fact that the social climate in a classroom remains the same throughout the school year (Mainhard, Brekelmans, Den Brok, & Wubbels, 2011). When doing this, it is important to acknowledge gender differences and the ways in which young adolescents attribute positive characteristics to peers. For girls, interactions fostering collaboration (Martin & Bat-Chava, 2003; Murphy & Faulkner, 2006), or considerate language use (Wolters et al., 2011b), have been found to increase their acceptance. Actively participating in interactions with hearing peers facilitates establishing friendships for DHH girls (Martin & Bat-Chava, 2003). For DHH boys, such interaction characteristics made no difference in their peer relationships. The nature of their interactions is competitive and their socialization often revolves around activities such as sports. The attribution of positive characteristics is a mutual process of which both DHH and hearing students should be aware. To increase self-esteem it can help students to know what positive social qualities are ascribed to them and what they can actually do to become more accepted. Cooperative behavior, friendliness, getting along with teachers, and being academically competent have been found to be considered positive characteristics, also in withdrawn classmates (Hymel et al., 1993; Punch & Hyde, 2011).

To develop a positive attitude and higher self-esteem, DHH peers need social-emotional support (Yiu & Tang, 2014) from parents, teachers, and itinerant services and opportunities for identification and contact with DHH peers (Bat-Chava, 1993; Isarin, 2006, 2008). Openness and self-esteem start with self-knowledge and knowledge about the meaning and consequences of a hearing loss for the self and others. Personal empowerment cannot exist without interpersonal and political empowerment. In the Netherlands the educational program CIDS is used to stimulate a positive identity and enhance self-esteem (Van Gils, Voor in 't Holt, Van den Bogaerde, n.d.). DHH students and their hearing classmates learn about DHH culture, communities for the deaf and hard of hearing, sign language, DHH role models, and having multiple identities. By sharing experiences and knowledge about hearing loss, culture, and identity, the burden of communicative difficulties is shifted from DHH adolescents to the social environment of which they are part. Inclusive education thus requires not only the personal empowerment of DHH adolescents, but also the removal of prejudice and negative attitudes and the fostering of positive attitudes in both teachers and peers (Hung & Paul, 2006). "Only the individuals involved can fashion the 'ideal mainstream'" (Oliva, 2004, p. 160).

REFERENCES

Antia, S. D., & Dittillo, D. A. (1998). A comparison of the peer social behavior of children who are deaf/hard of hearing and hearing. *Journal of Children's Communication Development*, *19*, 1–10.

Antia, S. D., Jones, P., Luckner, J., Kreimeyer, K. H., & Reed, S. (2011a). Social outcomes of students who are deaf and hard of hearing in general education classrooms. *Exceptional Children*, *77*, 489–504.

Antia, S. D., & Kreimeyer, K. H. (1996). Social interaction and acceptance of deaf or hard-of- hearing children and their peers: A comparison of social-skills and familiarity based interventions. *Volta Review*, *98*, 157–180.

Antia, S. D., Kreimeyer, K. H., Metz, K. K., & Spolsky, S. (2011b). Peer interactions of deaf and hard-of-hearing children. In M. Marschark & P. E. Spencer (Eds.), *The Oxford handbook of deaf studies, language, and education* (2nd ed., Vol. 1, pp. 173–187). New York: Oxford University Press.

Antia, S. D., Kreimeyer, K. H., & Reed, S. (2010). Supporting students in general education classrooms. In M. Marschark & P. E. Spencer (Eds.), *The Oxford handbook of deaf studies, language, and education* (Vol. 2, pp. 72–92). New York: Oxford University Press.

Asher, S. R., & McDonald, K. L. (2009). The behavioral basis of acceptance, rejection, and perceived popularity. In K. H. Rubin, W. M. Bukowski & B. Laursen (Eds.), *Handbook of peer interactions, relationships, and groups*. New York: Guilford.

Bat-Chava, Y. (1993). Antecedents of self-esteem in deaf people: A meta-analytic review. *Rehabilitation Psychology*, *38*, 221–234.

Batten, G., Oakes, P. M., & Alexander, T. (2013). Factors associated with social interactions between deaf children and their hearing peers: A systematic literature review. *Journal of Deaf Studies and Deaf Education*. doi:10.1093/deafed/ent052.

Berndt, T. J. (2002). Friendship quality and social development. *Current Directions in Psychological Science*, *11*, 7–10. doi:10.1111/1467-8721.00157.

Berndt, T. J., & McCandless, M. A. (2009). Methods for investigating children's relationships with friends. In K. H. Rubin, W. M. Bukowski, & B. Laursen (Eds.), *Handbook of peer interactions, relationships, and groups* (pp. 63–81). New York: Guilford.

Blakemore, S. J. (2008). Development of the social brain during adolescence. *Quarterly Journal of Experimental Psychology*, *61*, 40–49.

Blom, H., Marschark, M., Vervloed, M. P. J., & Knoors, H. (2014). Finding friends online: online activities by deaf students and their influence on their well-being. *PLoS ONE*, *9*(2), e88351. doi: 10.1371/journal.pone.0088351.

Bowen, S. K. (2008). Coenrollment for students who are deaf or hard of hearing: Friendship patterns and social interactions. *American Annals of the Deaf*, *153*, 285–293.

Brown, P. M., & Foster, S. B. (1991). Integrating hearing and deaf students on a college campus. Successes and barriers as perceived by hearing students. *American Annals of the Deaf*, *136*, 21–27.

Bukowski, W. M. (2011). Popularity as a social concept. In A. H. N. Cillessen, D. Schwartz, & L. Mayeux (Eds.), *Popularity in the peer system* (pp. 3–24). New York: Guilford.

Bukowski, W. M., Hoza, B., & Boivin, M. (1993). Popularity, friendship, and emotional adjustment during early adolescence. *New Direction for Child Development*, *60*, 23–37. doi:10.1002/cd.23219936004.

Bukowski, W. M., Motzoi, C., & Meyer, F. (2009). Friendship as process, function, and outcome. In K. H. Rubin, W. M. Bukowski, & B. Laursen (Eds.), *Handbook of peer interactions, relationships, and groups* (pp. 217–231). New York: Guilford.

Calderon, R., & Greenberg, M. (2011). In M. Marschark & P. E. Spencer (Eds.), *The Oxford handbook of deaf studies, language, and education* (2nd ed., Vol. 1, pp. 188–199). New York: Oxford University Press.

Cambra, V. (2002). Acceptance of deaf students by hearing students in regular classrooms. *American Annals of the Deaf, 147*, 38–43.

Capelli, M., Daniels, D., Durieux-Smith, A., McGrath, P., & Neus, D. (1995). Social development of children with hearing impairments. *Volta Review, 97*, 197–208.

Cillessen, A. H. N. (2009). Sociometric methods. In K. H. Rubin, W. M. Bukowski, & B. Laursen (Eds.), *Handbook of peer interactions, relationships, and groups* (pp. 82–99). New York: Guilford.

Cillessen, A. H. N. (2011). Toward a theory of popularity. In A. H. N. Cillessen, D. Schwartz, & L. Mayeux (Eds.), *Popularity in the peer system* (pp. 273–299). New York: Guilford.

Cillessen, A. H. N., & Marks, P. E. L. (2011). Conceptualizing and measuring popularity. In A. H. N. Cillessen, D. Schwartz, & L. Mayeux (Eds.), *Popularity in the peer system* (pp. 25–56). New York: Guilford.

Coyner, L. S. (1994). *Comparison of the relationship of academic success to self concept, social acceptance, and perceived social acceptance for hearing, hard-of-hearing and deaf adolescents in a mainstream setting.* Doctoral dissertation, Tucson, University of Arizona. Retrieved from http://arizona.openrepository.com/arizona/bitstream/10150/186158/1/azu_td_9322659_sip1_m.pdf.

Davis, M. (2003). Integration from strength. In G. Taylor & A. Darby (Eds.), *Deaf identities* (pp. 184–186). Coleford: Douglas-McLean.

Eisenberg, N., Guthrie, S. J., Murphy, B. C., Shephard, S. A., Cumberland, A., & Carlo, G. (1999). Consistency and development of prosocial dispositions: A longitudinal study. *Child Development, 70*, 1360–1372. doi:1310.1111/1467-8624.00100.

Fabes, R. A., Martin, C. L., & Hanisch, L. D. (2009). In K. H. Rubin, W. M. Bukowski, & B. Laursen (Eds.), *Handbook of peer interactions, relationships, and groups* (pp. 45–62). New York: Guilford.

Flook, L., Repetti, R. L., & Ullman, J. B. (2005). Classroom social experiences as predictors of academic performance. *Developmental Psychology, 41*, 319–327. doi:310.1037/0012-1649.1041.1032.1319.

Hartup, W. W. (2009). Critical issues and theoretical viewpoints. In K. H. Rubin, W. M. Bukowski, & B. Laursen (Eds.), *Handbook of peer interactions, relationships, and groups* (pp. 3–19). New York: Guilford.

Hung, H., & Paul, P. V. (2006). Inclusion of students who are deaf or hard of hearing: Secondary school hearing students' perspectives. *Deafness Education International, 8*, 62–74.

Hymel, S., Bowker, A., & Woody, E. (1993). Aggressive versus withdrawn unpopular children: Variations in peer and self-perceptions in multiple domains. *Child Development, 64*, 879–896.

Isarin, J. (2006). *Hoor hen! Participatieonderzoek: virtueel en in real life.* Amsterdam: Van Tricht.

Isarin, J. (2008). *Zo hoort het. Dove kinderen in het CI-tijdperk: een participatieonderzoek.* Amsterdam: Van Tricht.

Jeanes, R. C., Nienhuys, T. G. W. M., & Rickards, F. W. (2000). The pragmatic skills of profoundly deaf children. *Journal of Deaf Studies and Deaf Education, 5*, 237–247.

Jiang, X. L., & Cillessen, A. H. N. (2005). Stability of continuous measures of sociometric status: A meta-analysis. *Developmental Review, 25*, 1–25.

Kluwin, T. N., & Gonsher, W. (1994). A single school study of social integration of children with and without hearing loss in a team taught kindergarten. *ACEHI/ACEDA Journal, 20*, 4–86.

Kluwin, T. N., Stinson, M. S., & Colarossi, G. M. (2002). Social processes and outcomes of in- school contact between deaf and hearing peers. *Journal of Deaf Studies and Deaf Education, 7*, 200–213.

Kouwenberg, M. (2013). *Social-emotional factors underlying internalizing problems and peer relations in deaf or hard-of-hearing youth.* Unpublished doctoral dissertation.

Kouwenberg, M., Rieffe, C., Theunissen, S. C. P. M., & De Rooij, M. (2012). Peer victimization experienced by children and adolescents who are deaf or hard of hearing. *PLoS One, 7*, e52174.

LaFontana, K. M., & Cillessen, A. H. N. (1998). The nature of children's stereotypes of popularity. *Social Development, 7*, 301–320.

LaFontana, K. M., & Cillessen, A. H. N. (2002). Children's perceptions of popular and unpopular peers: A multimethod assessment. *Developmental Psychology, 38*, 635–647.

Mainhard, M. T., Brekelmans, M., Den Brok, P., & Wubbels, T. (2011). The development of classroom social climate during the first months of the school year. *Contemporary Educational Psychology, 36*, 190–200.

Martin, D., & Bat-Chava, Y. (2003). Negotiating deaf and hearing friendships: coping strategies of deaf boys and girls in mainstream schools. *Child: Care, Health & Development, 29*, 511–521.

Mayeux, L., Houser, J. J., & Dyches, K. D. (2011). Social acceptance and popularity: Two distinct forms of peer status. In A. H. N. Cillessen, D. Schwartz, & L. Mayeux (Eds.), *Popularity in the peer system* (pp. 79–102). New York: Guilford.

Moeller, M. P. (2007). Current state of knowledge: Psychosocial development in children with hearing impairment. *Ear and Hearing, 28*, 729–739.

Morris, J. (1991). *Pride against prejudice: transforming attitudes to disability.* London: Women's Press.

Murphy, S. M., & Faulkner, D. (2006). Gender differences in verbal communication between popular and unpopular children during an interactive task. *Social Development, 15*, 82–108.

Nærland, T. (2011). Language competence and social focus among preschool children. *Early Child Development and Care, 181*, 599–612.

Nunes, T., Pretzlik, U., & Olsson, J. (2001). Deaf children's social relationships in mainstream schools. *Journal of Deaf Education International, 3*, 123–136.

Oliva, G. (2004). *Alone in the mainstream. A Deaf woman remembers public school.* Washington, DC: Gallaudet University Press.

Parker, J. G., Rubin, K. H., Erath, S. A., Wojslawowicz, J. C., & Buskirk, A. A. (2006). Peer relationships, child development, and adjustment: A developmental psychopathology perspective. In Cicchetti, D., & Cohen, D. J. (Eds.), *Developmental psychopathology, Vol. 1: Theory and method* (2nd ed., pp. 419–493). Hoboken, NJ: Wiley.

Parkhurst, J. T., & Hopmeyer, A. (1998). Sociometric popularity and peer-perceived popularity: Two distinct dimensions of peer status. *Journal of Early Adolescence, 18*, 125–144.

Piso, F., Knoors, H., & Vervloed, M. (2009). Vriendschapsrelaties van dove en slechthorende adolescenten. *Van Horen Zeggen, 50*(6), 10–17.
Punch, R., & Hyde, M. (2011). Social participation of children and adolescents with cochlear implants: A qualitative analysis of parent, teacher, and child interviews. *Journal of Deaf Studies and Deaf Education, 16*, 474–493.
Reeve, D. (2002). Negotiating psycho-emotional dimensions of disability and their influence on identity constructions. *Disability & Society, 17*, 493–508.
Robinson, J. (2003). Integration from strength. In G. Taylor & A. Darby (Eds.), *Deaf identities* (pp. 96–102). Coleford: Douglas-McLean.
Rose, A. J., & Smith, R. J. (2009). Sex differences in peer relationships. In K. H. Rubin, W. M. Bukowski, & B. Laursen (Eds.), *Handbook of peer interactions, relationships, and groups* (pp. 379–393). New York: Guilford.
Rubin, K. H., Bukowski, W. M., & Parker, J. G. (2006). Peer interactions, relationships, and groups. In N. Eisenberg, W. Damon, & R. M. Lerner (Eds.), *Handbook of child psychology* (6 ed., Vol. 3, pp. 571–645). Hoboken, NJ: Wiley.
Rubin, K. H., Burgess, K. B., & Coplan, R. J. (2002). Social withdrawal and shyness. In P. K. Smith & C. H. Hart (Eds.), *Blackwell handbook of childhood social development* (pp. 329–352). Oxford: Blackwell.
Shakespeare, T. (1996). Disability, identity, difference. In C. Barnes & G. Mercier (Eds.), *Exploring the divide: illness and disability* (pp. 94–113). Leeds: Disability Press.
Steinberg, L. (2008). *Adolescence*. New York: McGraw-Hill.
Stinson, M. S., & Antia, S. D. (1999). Considerations in educating deaf and hard-of-hearing students in inclusive settings. *Journal of Deaf Studies and Deaf Education, 4*, 163–175.
Stinson, M. S., & Kluwin, T. N. (2011). Educational consequences of alternative school placements. In M. Marschark & P. E. Spencer (Eds.), *Oxford handbook of deaf studies, language, and education* (pp. 47–62). New York: Oxford University Press.
Stinson, M., & Liu, M. (1999). Participation of deaf and hard-of-hearing students in classes with hearing students. *Journal of Deaf Studies and Deaf Education, 4*, 191–202.
Stinson, M. S., Whitmire, K., & Kluwin, T. N. (1996). Self-perceptions of social relationships in hearing-impaired adolescents. *Journal of Educational Psychology, 88*, 132–143.
Suárez, M. (2000). Promoting social competence in deaf students: The effect of an intervention program. *Journal of Deaf Studies and Deaf Education, 5*, 323–336.
Van Gent, T., Goedhart, A. W., Hindley, P. A., & Treffers, P. D. A. (2007). Prevalence and correlates of psychopathology in a sample of deaf adolescents. *Journal of Child Psychology and Psychiatry, 48*, 950–958.
Van Gent, T., Goedhart, A. W., Knoors, H., Westenberg, P. M., & Treffers, P. D. A. (2012). Self-concept and ego development in deaf adolescents: A comparative study. *Journal of Deaf Studies and Deaf Education, 17*, 333–351.
Van Gils, G., Voor in 't Holt, A., & Van den Bogaerde, B.(2014, January). Sprong Vooruit, CIDS. Retrieved from http://www.sprongvooruit.nl
Van Gurp, S. (2001). Self-concept of deaf secondary school students in different educational settings. *Journal of Deaf Studies and Deaf Education, 6*, 54–69.
Van Houten, D., & Bellemakers, C. (2002). Equal citizenship for all. Disability politics in the Netherlands: empowerment of marginals. *Disability & Society, 17*, 171–185.

Verhoeven, L., & Vermeer, A. (1992). Modeling communicative second language competence. In L. Verhoeven & J. H. A. L. De Jong (Eds.), *The construct of language proficiency* (pp. 163–173). Amsterdam/Philadelphia: John Benjamins Publishing Company.

Warden, D., Cheyne, B., Christie, D., Fitzpatrick, H., & Reid, K. (2003). Assessing children's perceptions of prosocial and antisocial peer behavior. *Educational Psychology, 23*, 547–567. doi: 510.1080/0144341032000123796.

Wauters, L., & Knoors, H. (2007). Social integration of deaf children in inclusive settings. *Journal of Deaf Studies and Deaf Education, 13*, 21–36.

Weiner, M. T., Day, S. J., & Galvan, D. (2013). Deaf and hard of hearing students' perspectives on bullying and school climate. *American Annals of the Deaf, 158*, 324–343.

Wolters, N., Blom, H. C., Knoors, H., & Verhoeven, L. (2011a). Vriendschap hoort: De rol van communicatieve vaardigheden in vriendschappen van dove en slechthorende kinderen in groep 8. *Van Horen Zeggen, 52*(3), 10–18.

Wolters, N., Knoors, H., Cillessen, A. H. N., & Verhoeven, L. (2011b). Predicting acceptance and popularity in early adolescence as a function of hearing status, educational setting, and gender. *Research in Developmental Disabilities, 32*, 2553–2565.

Wolters, N., Knoors, H., Cillessen, A.H.N., & Verhoeven, L. (2012). Impact of peer and teacher relations on deaf early adolescents' well-being: Comparisons before and after a major school transition. *Journal of Deaf Studies and Deaf Education, 17*, 463–482.

Wolters, N., Knoors, H., Cillessen, A. H. N., & Verhoeven, L. (2014). Social adjustment of deaf early adolescents at the start of secondary school: The divergent role of withdrawn behavior in peer status. *Exceptional Children, 80*, 438–453. doi: 10.1177/0014402914527242.

Yetman, M. (2000). *Peer relations and self-esteem among deaf children in a mainstream school environment*. Ph.D. dissertation. Washington, DC: Gallaudet University.

Yiu, C., & Tang, G. (2014). Social integration of deaf and hard-of-hearing students in a sign bilingual and co-enrollment environment. In Marschark, M., Tang, G., & Knoors, H. (Eds.), *Bilingualism and bilingual deaf education*. New York: Oxford University Press.

15

Stress Among Children Who are Deaf or Hard of Hearing and Their Families

Anat Zaidman-Zait

Children and adolescents with hearing loss face unique challenges and stressors that can adversely affect their developmental outcomes and well-being. Their parents and caregivers often also experience their own stresses related to raising children with such unique needs. The majority of parents of children with hearing loss (approximately 90% to 95%) are themselves hearing. Hence, these parents are overwhelmed with the identification and the new experience they are about to face of raising a child with a hearing loss (Kurtzer-White & Luterman, 2003). They have limited information about hearing loss, sensory devices, communication options, early intervention programs, and service provision (Fitzpatrick, Angus, Durieux-Smith, Graham, & Coyle, 2008). Research demonstrates that parental stress is not a direct outcome of child deafness but rather that individual differences in parental stress stem from differences in the context, the child experiences, and parental characteristics, including parental perceptions and coping resources (Lederberg & Golbach, 2002). Similarly, hearing loss among children and adolescents is also associated with risk for a number of adverse outcomes (Greenberg & Kusché, 1989; Marschark, 1997). Yet among children as well, hearing loss itself was not found to bear the greatest influence on adjustment outcomes; rather, factors such as the quality of the family environment, family and child coping patterns, school and community resources available to the family, and individual characteristics yield the greatest impact (Calderon & Greenberg, 2003). Models of child/adolescent psychopathology recognize the potential importance of stressors in the etiology and maintenance of both internalizing and externalizing symptoms (e.g., Cicchetti & Toth, 1997; Haggerty, Sherrod, Garmezy, & Rutter, 1994; Rutter, 1994). According to Mash and Barkley(2003), stressors represent the environmental contribution of risk, which interacts with individual characteristics, including genetic predisposition, to lead to psychological problems in children and adolescents.

The Developmental System model (Guralnick, 2005) highlights the important role of stressors associated with parenting children with disabilities. Parenting a child with a disability can threaten various patterns of interactions within families, harming the chances of achieving children's optimal social and cognitive competence. Stressors might include parental lack of information, interpersonal and family distress, lack of resources, and threats to parenting confidence. In addition, stressors can be generated by family characteristics, including parents' mental health, financial circumstances, marital relationship, and availability of social support.

According to the contextual model of stress, researchers must examine stressors embedded within a specific context, including factors related to the child, the family, and the specific tasks and demands that must be mastered for successful functioning (Quittner & DiGirolamo, 1998). While the experience of parenting a child with hearing loss can lead to positive parental outcomes, such as new insights into family priorities and a renewed sense of purpose, early childhood deafness also presents unique and long-term challenges for hearing parents (Lederberg & Golbach, 2002; Quittner et al., 2010; Zaidman-Zait, 2008). Parenting a DHH (i.e., Deaf and Hard of Hearing) child can make some of the common parenting demands more challenging, or might establish a completely new set of unique daily demands. Specific problems and concerns experienced by parents of deaf children should be considered (Lederberg & Golbach, 2002; Quittner, Glueckauf, & Jackson, 1990). The experience of such everyday frustrations may leave parents with a diminished sense of competence and satisfaction and may ultimately adversely affect the quality of parenting, parent–child relationships, and the child's functioning (Belsky, Woodworth, & Crnic, 1996). A more comprehensive understanding of parental stressors may have a positive impact on children who are deaf or hard of hearing by empowering parents to develop competence and involvement in their child's education and development (Dunst, Trivette, Boyd, & Brookfield, 1994; Minke & Scott, 1995). Furthermore, identification and understanding of these stressors is crucial for professionals who provide family-centered care to families of children with hearing loss. Indeed, under the family-centered care approach, supporting and empowering families is a key component of professional practices. Hence, the family-centered care approach advocates participatory practices that are individually tailored, flexible, and responsive to concerns and priorities of each family and provide families with opportunities (Bruder & Dunst, 2008; Sass-Lehrer, 2002). Although stressful, the experience of parenting a child with a disability can lead to positive outcomes. These outcomes are denoted as stress-related growth or eustress. Stress-related growth refers to positive changes people make in their lives as a result of their efforts to cope with adverse situations or negative events (Park, 2004). These positive outcomes could include improved relationships with family and friends, changes in priorities and values, new insights into family priorities, a renewed sense of purpose, and an increased sense of one's own strength (Joseph & Linley, 2006).

This chapter will review research examining the various stressors that DHH children and their parents might face. First, I will discuss the definitions of stress and parenting stress, including their conceptualization and measurement. Second, I will review stressors experienced by parents of DHH children. Next, I will discuss stressors faced by DHH children and adolescents across multiple domains of life. I will conclude the chapter with a summary and suggested implications.

WHAT IS STRESS?

Stress is a construct that has been difficult to define (Kahn, 1987). Numerous definitions have been suggested, most of which were criticized as too vague, too broad, or too difficult to operationalize for the purpose of scientific inquiry (Cohen, Kessler, & Gordon, 1995). Generally, the concept of stress is an overarching heading for concerns with "how individuals adjust to their environments; achieve high levels of performance and health; and become distressed in various physiological, medical, behavioral, or psychological ways" (Quick, Wright, Adkins, Nelson, & Quick, 2013, p. 12). The term *stress* can refer to a variety of personal states, including cognitive tension, physiological strain, and emotional dysfunction. Despite the diverse ways in which stress is defined and measured, it is commonly agreed that stress encompasses environmental circumstances or conditions that threaten, challenge, exceed, or harm the psychological or biological capacities of the individual (Cohen et al., 1995).

Some main concepts that are used under the rubric of the term *stress* include stressor (or demand) and distress (or strain). Stressors or demands are physical or psychological stimuli to which an individual responds. Stressors and demands can be universally agreed upon, or can be individually based on the roles of appraisal, coping, and individual response. Stressors might be general, or they can be specific to a particular role, event, or task. Distress and strain, on the other hand, refer to the unhealthy, negative, destructive outcomes of stressful events or the stress response. In other words, individual distress (strain) refers to the degree of physiological, psychological, and behavioral deviation from an individual's healthy functioning, in reaction to stressors. Individual distress and strain can be expressed physiologically (e.g., cardiovascular disease), psychologically (e.g., negative feelings or emotions, such as depression), or behaviorally (e.g., violent conduct) (Quick et al., 2013).

Grant and colleagues (2003) refer to two approaches that distinguish between the various stress definitions. One approach relies exclusively on objective measurable changes in, or characteristics of, individuals' environments. This approach conceives of stress as a stimulus (Holmes & Rahe, 1967) of stressors (McCubbin & Patterson, 1983) or as objective stress (Rudolph & Hammen, 1999). The latter authors define stressors as "environmental events or chronic conditions that objectively threaten the physical and/or psychological health or wellbeing of individuals of a particular age in a particular society" (p. 449). This perspective emphasizes the environmental events and conditions independent of the process of cognitive appraisals (Brown & Harris, 1989; Cohen et al., 1995).

The second approach emphasizes the psychological processes that occur in response to the environment, and views stress as a relationship between environmental events or conditions and the individual's cognitive appraisals of the degree and type of challenge, threat, harm, or loss (Lazarus & Folkman, 1984). This approached is known as the transactional perspective, mostly associated with the work of Lazarus and Folkman (1984). Lazarus and Folkman offer the following definition: "Psychological stress involves a particular relationship between the person and the environment that is appraised by the person as taxing or exceeding his or her resources and endangering his or her wellbeing" (1984, p. 19). According to the transaction approach, individuals experience the same demands and stressors differently, based on how they cognitively assess these influences; hence, a stress reaction depends on whether a person judges a situation to be "taxing or exceeding his or her resources" (Lazarus & Folkman, 1984, p. 10). This assessment includes both primary and secondary appraisal processes. Primary appraisals occur when an individual evaluates the potential harm or benefit of an event. Secondary appraisal involves the person's assessment of his or her coping options; for example, a person may consider what resources are available to deal with the event or circumstance. When a person believes he or she lacks the resources or skills to cope with the event, the person may perceive the situation as stressful.

Finally, Quittner and colleagues (1990) highlight a third approach, involving two important distinctions among stressor characteristics. The first distinction is the temporal nature of the stressor, specifically acute versus chronic stress. Acute, discrete, time-limited stress, usually referred to as stressful life events, typically occurs at a low frequency. In contrast, chronic stress refers to ongoing, long-term strains. The second distinction Quittner describes refers to life-stress versus specific stressors. Life-stress may be considered an overarching (i.e., global) rather than a specific type of stress, which in itself is not descriptive of the context in which these events occur or how they are likely to influence current roles and daily circumstances. An alternative to the life-stress approach is to study stressors embedded within a particular context, such as parenting a child, while taking into account everyday problems or daily hassles that occur during the parent–child interactions (Kanner, Coyne, Schaefer, & Lazarus, 1981).

In the current chapter, I highlight the stressors experienced by children who are deaf or hard of hearing and their families. These stressors are conceptualized within the specific context of childhood hearing loss, within a developmental framework and—following the transactional approaches to stress and coping—highlighting the importance of the subjective individual experience of stress.

DEFINITION, CONCEPTUALIZATIONS, AND EVALUATION MECHANISMS OF PARENTING STRESS

Parenting stress can be defined as an "aversive psychological reaction to the demands of being a parent" (Deater-Deckard, 1998, p. 315). This specific type of stress arises when parents' perceptions of the demands of parenting outstrip their resources (Abidin, 1992; Deater-Deckard & Petrill, 2004; Östberg & Hagekull, 2000). Parenting stress is a distinct type of stress related to the strain individuals face in their role as parents. Chang and Fine (2007) identified it as one of the most common daily concerns parents face. Parenting stress is triggered by a wide variety of stressors, including task-specific demands, role demands, interpersonal demands, and physical demands. These demands may or may not be inherently or necessarily harmful. In line with Lazarus's approach (Lazarus & Folkman, 1984), the degree of stress a person experiences depends in part on his or her cognitive appraisal of that demand. Parenting stress may place parents at risk of psychological distress if it is too intense, frequent, or chronic.

Parenting stress has been assessed in multiple ways. The Parenting Stress Index (PSI) (Abidin, 1995) and its short form, the PSI-SF, are among the self-report rating scales most commonly used to measure parenting stress in deaf studies. In addition to its wide use in research, the PSI is a popular clinical tool to identify parents in need of counseling services. The PSI was developed in accordance with Abidin's theory of parenting stress, according to which parental stress stems from complex interactions among child characteristics, parent characteristics, and problematic situations within the family. The PSI is divided into two main domains: child-related stress (stress reflecting child characteristics that make it difficult to fulfill the parenting role) and parent-related stress (stress as a consequence of parental functioning). The parent stress domain includes various scales that examine stress related specifically to parenting aspects (e.g., sense of parenting competence) but also taps into other psychological distress spheres (e.g., depression) and related issues such as social support, health, and spousal relations. The PSI-SF provides a brief assessment comprising three scales: parental distress, child difficulty, and parent–child dysfunctional interactions.

Both the original and short forms of the PSI raise conceptualization and methodological concerns. First, coinciding with a broad definition of parenting stress that includes perceived resources and demands associated with parenting (Deater-Deckard & Scarr, 1996), the PSI includes a wide range of issues such as social support and parental health. This broad conceptualization makes it hard to distinguish between stress in general and stress that specifically emerges from the act of parenting. In addition, some of the predicators the PSI examines (e.g., child behavior, social support) overlap with the PSI's outcome measure. It would be useful to include a more narrow definition of parenting stress that specifically captures parents' feelings about their parenting skills, tapping into the demands of parenting (Anthony et al., 2005; Deater-Deckard & Scarr, 1996; Zaidman-Zait et al., 2011). Second, the PSI contains items describing child behaviors, whose endorsement reflects parent agreement; however, the scale fails to account for parental appraisals of these items' impact in term of the parents' own degree of stress. This approach overlooks parents' subjective appraisals following the conceptualization of the transactional model of stress and coping. Last, the PSI does not examine parenting stress in the context of childhood hearing loss, ignoring stressors specific to the actual tasks and demands of parenting a child with hearing loss (Quittner et al., 2010).

Another frequently used measure is the Questionnaire on Resources and Stress (QRS; Friedrich, Greenberg, & Crnic, 1983). The QRS was designed to assess the stress experienced by parents of young children with disabilities. However, this scale is not always applicable to issues related to childhood hearing loss. The QRS is divided into four subscales, covering parent and family problems, pessimism, and physical problems. Like the PSI, its conceptualization does not fully correspond with a definition of parenting stress and it fails to account for parental subjective evaluation of some situations described by the scale items in term of the parents' own degree of stress.

The Parenting Daily Hassles scale (Crnic & Greenberg, 1990) provides a third measure of parenting stress. This measure was based on the minor event perspective, which addresses the impact of everyday frustrations and irritations that accompany childrearing and children's behavior. Research into parenting daily hassles has demonstrated this notion to be a meaningful stress evaluation framework for families (Belsky et al., 1996; Creasey & Reese, 1996; Crnic & Booth, 1991). The measure examines specific stressors of everyday tasks and events associated with parenting young children (e.g., children's nagging, whining, and complaining; homemaking tasks). However, once again, these stressors are not specifically associated with childhood hearing loss.

Three measures were developed specifically to measure parenting stress in the context of having a child with hearing loss. The first, the Family Stress Scale (Quittner et al., 1990) was developed to assess perceived parenting stress for parents of young deaf and hearing children. The questionnaire comprises 11 items addressing general family stressors and five items addressing challenges of early childhood deafness. These items are rated on a Likert scale asking about the parents' stress level regarding each stressor. Similarly, Zaidman-Zait (2008) used an open question to identify parents' stressors in the context of parenting a child with hearing loss and to rate each stressor by its perceived stress level. Last, Meinzen-Derr and colleagues (2008) used an "expert panel" consisting of professionals caring for deaf or hard of hearing children and individual interviews with caregivers of deaf or hard of hearing children to identify stressors experienced by families of such children. These stressors fall under the following domains: communication, education, emotional well-being, resources, financial abilities, health care, social networks, and support mechanisms. Parents are asked to indicate the level of stress they experience in response to the items representing each of these domains.

UNIQUE DEMANDS AND STRESSORS FACING PARENTS OF DEAF OR HARD-OF-HEARING CHILDREN

For virtually all parents, caring for a child is an experience full of successes and joys, as well as challenges and stress. The experiences of parents of DHH children are similar in many ways to the experiences of parents of hearing children, but there are some important distinctions that can cause parents of DHH children to be at greater risk for elevated levels of parenting stress (e.g., Lederberg & Golbach, 2002; Quittner et al., 2010; Zaidman-Zait, 2008). Parents of children who are deaf or hard of hearing face a variety of unique demands and long-term challenges in raising their children. Receiving the news of the hearing loss diagnosis can be a stressful and difficult experience for hearing parents (Gilbey, 2010). Indeed, hearing parents often perceive the period immediately after the diagnosis as the most stressful one (Burger et al., 2005). Most parents are initially stunned and unprepared for the accommodations they must make to provide a meaningful and mutually accessible communication environment for their child. Furthermore, parents experience emotional stress caused by the discrepancies between their expectations for their child and their child's actual developmental competence (Kurtzer-White & Luterman, 2003).

As DHH children grow, their parents continue to face numerous stressors and challenges (Calderon & Greenberg, 1999; Lederberg & Golbach, 2002; Quittner et al., 1990, 1991, 2010; Zaidman-Zait, 2008). Some of these stressors are related to child characteristics, including communication difficulties, learning difficulties, and behavior problems. Communication difficulties in particular have a negative impact on daily interactions between parents and their deaf or hard of hearing children and lead to frustrations for both the parents and the child (Freeman, Dieterich, & Rak, 2002; Hintermair, 2000). In turn, these everyday problematic transactions might lead to cumulative parental stress (Zaidman-Zait, 2008). Parents of deaf children have cited their children's language and communication difficulties (Kluwin & Stewart, 2000; Zaidman-Zait, 2008) as well as concerns with their children's behavior and social-emotional competence (Sach & Whynes, 2005; Wodehouse & McGill, 2009) as major stressors. Quittner and colleagues (2010) suggested that language and communication difficulties influence parenting stress through child behavior problems (Topol, Girard, Pierre, Tucker, & Vohr, 2011). Topol and colleagues (2011) supported the contribution of children's behavior problems to parenting stress through a study involving mothers of toddlers with congenital hearing loss.

Meinzen-Derr and colleagues (2008) found that over 20% of all caregivers of DHH children reported high levels of stress related to the child's own frustration, worrying about the child's safety, and worrying that others might take advantage of the child. In addition, mothers felt they had little time for themselves, which intensified their stress. Results from this study also indicated that over time, stressors increased or diminished according to the child's development and changing needs. For example, education-related stressors grew as children began to enter the school system, whereas stressors related to health issues decreased with time following diagnosis. At the same time, stress related to child communication skills remained high in the long run.

Other stressors are associated with the demands of the parenting role or with specific task demands that can be challenging to parents. Some examples include learning sign language (Takala, Kuusela, & Takala, 2000; Young, 1997), the provision of increased medical and audiological care, therapy and language training demands, medical and educational decisions, and learning about the various assistive technologies (such as cochlear implantation [CI]). Pediatric CI, for example, has become a commonly selected habilitation option for children who are deaf (Spencer & Marschark, 2003). The CI process among children involves potentially stressful decision making, detailed assessment, surgery, a demanding rehabilitation process, and the need for lifelong technical support. These decisions entail a great deal of personal investment by the parents and child (Archbold, Sach, Lutman, & Gregory, 2006; Christiansen & Leigh, 2002; Most & Zaidman-Zait, 2001; Thoutenhoofd et al., 2005; see also Bruin, Chapter 5 in this volume). Moreover, the parents' role throughout the implantation and habilitation processes strongly influences the child's progress in aural habilitation and the perceived benefit from the CI by parents (Allegretti, 2002; Geers, Brenner, & Davidson, 2003; Spencer, 2004). Zaidman-Zait (2008) reported that parents continued to have concerns with their child's language development and behavior even after the child received a CI, while also experiencing challenges managing CI equipment, therapies, and associated financial costs. In a recent study using the context-specific measure of parenting stress (i.e., the Family Stress Scale mentioned previously), parents of children with CI reported communication difficulties with their children, educational concerns, hearing device maintenance, and teaching their children language as high on their list of stressors (Quittner et al., 2010). Sarant and Garrard (2014) found a negative correlation between language outcomes of children with CI and parenting stress and a positive correlation between child behavior problems and parenting stress.

Stressors related to interpersonal relationship include relationships with the child, spouse, other children in the family, and professionals working with the child. For example, higher levels of parental stress correlated with less satisfactory parental relationships with professionals (Zaidman-Zait & Most, 2005). Finally, parents experience contextual and personal stressors, including seeking the provision of adequate services, as well as strains related to the cost and time spent in frequent visits to language clinics. Parents of DHH children, like other parents, also experience work-related stressors, physical and mental health challenges, and other ongoing life events. However, these parents also have to deal with the notion that their child is "different" and are often called upon to explain their child's hearing loss and associated needs (Sarant & Garrard, 2014; Zaidman-Zait, 2008). Parents of children who have disabilities in addition to hearing loss may experience even more stressors in childrearing. This group of children accounts for approximately 30% to 40% of children born with hearing loss (Picard, 2004) and may pose unique or perhaps intensified challenges to parents that require additional research attention. Few studies have highlighted the stressors experienced by parents of children with hearing loss and additional disabilities regarding service provision, treatment, and collaboration with professionals. Research findings indicate that parents of deaf children with additional disabilities often face greater demands than parents of deaf children without additional needs, as the former must deal with lack of adequate educational services, multiple therapies, and multiple professionals, often with little coordination between services (Curle & Zaidman-Zait, 2013; Huttunen et al., 2009; Myck-Wayne, Robinson, & Henson, 2011; Zaidman-Zait, Curle, Jamieson, Chia, & Kozak, 2012). In our study most parents of children with additional needs who were also CI users believed that their child was not receiving adequate services, especially regarding speech-language therapy and behavioral support. Furthermore, in interviews, parents also noted stressors related to accessing and locating services. Parents found it time-consuming to manage the associated paperwork, find information about services, coordinate multiple professional visits, and follow numerous (sometimes contradictory) recommendations from different professionals (Zaidman-Zait et al., 2012).

EVERYDAY STRESSORS AND CHALLENGES AMONG CHILDREN AND ADOLESCENTS WITH HEARING LOSS

School-age children and adolescents growing up with hearing loss may encounter a variety of stressors that could place them at increased risk for the development of adjustment problems. Several studies consistently indicate that in comparison to hearing peers, children who are deaf or hard of hearing experience lower levels of wellbeing (Wolters, Knoors, Cillessen, & Verhoeven, 2012) and poorer quality of life (Gilman, Easterbrooks, & Frey, 2004). They are more prone to have mental health difficulties and behavioral problems (Barker et al., 2009; Hindley, 2005; Theunissen et al., 2011). Thus, they may experience greater stress and challenges than typically developing children.

DHH children and adolescents experience not only the everyday stressors typical for their development stage, such as problems related to academic demands at school (Nurmi, Lerner, & Steinberg, 2004; Seiffge-Krenke, 1995; Skinner & Zimmer-Gembeck, 2007), but also unique, difficult situations and problems. Indeed, hearing loss represents an intrusive, nonnormative demand that can interfere with the many age-specific developmental tasks. For example, children with hearing loss often experience delays in cognitive development (Marschark & Wauters, 2003), communication skills (Spencer & Marschark, 2006), literacy (Trezek, Wang, & Paul, 2009), age-appropriate behavior (Barker et al., 2009), and socioemotional development (Calderon & Greenberg, 2011). They need to function in a hearing environment that does not always meet their special auditory and visual needs (Leigh, Maxwell-McCaw, Bat-Chava, & Christiansen, 2009), while dysfunctional communication skills hinder successful internal and interpersonal processes (Stinson & Whitmire, 2000). Overall, these challenges may lead to stressful situations within school, home, or community environments.

One of the first contextual milestones presenting a new set of challenges for children and their families is the transition to school. School is one of the most important developmental contexts for contemporary young people (Eccles, 2009). Academic achievement, along with peer competence, is a core developmental task for school-age children and adolescents in many economically advanced countries (Masten & Motti-Stefanidi, 2009). School presents a different ecological environment than early education programs or home environments, with explicit goals for children's academic skills and socialization. It presents a new set of expectations from teachers and peers regarding children's responsibilities, independent behavior, and academic and socialization skills (Rimm-Kaufman & Pianta, 2000). Although a child's transition to school may be an exciting, anticipated event in the family's life, the new social, cognitive, and behavioral expectations can be stressful for children (Quas, Murowchick, Bensadoun, & Boyce, 2002). Above and beyond the normative stressors associate with attending school, children with hearing loss and their families might experience additional stressors.

Research findings indicate that parents of children with and without special needs share similar concerns regarding their children's transitioning to school. In many cultures, children between the ages of four and seven years are expected to take on greater independence and responsibility (Sameroff & Haith, 1996). In kindergarten, children are expected to get along with peers, learn and follow routines, and remain alert and active for longer periods of time (Rimm-Kaufman & Pianta, 2000). McIntyre, Eckert, Fiese, DiGennaro, and Wildenger (2007) surveyed a group of 132 families of children entering kindergarten and found that the majority of parents had concerns over their child's ability to meet the school's academic and behavioral expectations.

Parents of special-needs children face additional stressors regarding their child's transition to school. One stressor involves the shift from the family-centered approach of early intervention programs to the largely child-centered education system, which replaces the family focus with a more singular focus on the child's education and development (Jamieson, Zaidman-Zait, & Poon, 2011). Children with special needs, including hearing loss, often receive early intervention services to support their development and to help families adjust to and manage the child's special needs. Researchers found that the shift from these services to schools was a jarring and confusing time for parents of special-needs children (Giallo, Treyvaud, Matthews, & Kienhuis, 2010). Parents of special-needs children in general have reported dissatisfaction with the services available for their children in integrated school settings, where the most frequent complaints involve the scarcity of specialized personnel or programs (Valeo, 2003) and the lack of school-level services (Janus, Kopechanski, Cameron, & Hughes, 2008).

Parents of children who are deaf or hard of hearing similarly have specific concerns about their children's transition to school. A survey of parents of children with hearing loss who were just entering school found that over 50% reported concerns regarding their child's abilities, including the ability to communicate and follow directions, pursue needs, and form relationships with peers, as well as concerns regarding the child's academic performance and social skills, including problem solving and managing emotions and behaviors (Zaidman-Zait, Poon, Curle, Norman, & Jamieson, 2013).

Families are also faced with new challenges as they learn how to best support their children's education, collaborate with their child's teachers, and adjust to new elementary school routines. Parents of children with hearing loss reported concerns regarding their own adjustment to the new school and the new professionals, their involvement in decision making at the school, the support they will receive from the classroom teacher, and their own ability to assist with their children's peer relationships (Zaidman-Zait et al., 2013).

Another important factor that can elicit daily stress is the ability to actively and fully participate in school and classroom activities and discussions (Antia, Sabers, & Stinson, 2007; Wheeler, Archbold, Gregory, & Skipp, 2007; see also Hintermair, Chapter 13 in this volume, and Antia, Chapter 23 in this volume). As Antia and colleagues (2007) noted: "the ability to communicate with teachers and peers can be a major component of academic success as teacher–student communication and student–student communication are the primary means of learning in classrooms" (p. 158). Research findings indicate that parental participation is an important factor in children's learning and academic success (Antia et al., 2007; Antia, Jones, Reed, & Kreimeyer, 2009; Kluwin, Stinson, & Colarossi, 2002). Deaf college students reported that they experience challenges related to classroom communication, such as lecturer's unclear speech, rapid turn-taking among students during discussions, lack of topic coherence, and frequent interruption (Stinson, Liu, Saur, & Long, 1996). In addition, students who use sign language interpreters might also experience problems regarding communication in the classroom, such as understanding the content of the lesson and delivering their own comments (Antia et al., 2007). The Classroom Participation Questionnaire (Antia et al., 2007) enables exploration of cognitively and emotionally subjective experiences that can elicit stress among students. It investigates the ability to understand teachers (e.g., "I understand when my teacher tells me what to study for a test") and students (e.g., "I understand the other students in class"). In addition, it reflects students' emotional experiences, including positive affect (e.g., "I feel relaxed when I talk to my teacher") and negative affect (e.g., "I feel frustrated because it is difficult for me to communicate with other students").

At present, the majority of children with hearing loss attend school alongside hearing children (Antia, Kreimeyer, & Reed, 2010; Antia, Chapter 23 in this volume). Inclusive educational programs strive to provide the least restrictive and stigmatized learning environment possible and aim to enhance children's communication skills to better prepare them for interactions with the hearing world (Eriks-Brophy et al., 2006; Most, 2007). Although mainstreaming has been associated with stronger academic outcomes and improved development of social skills (Stinson & Antia, 1999), attending an inclusive educational setting might be stressful for children with hearing loss. In a school system designed for hearing children, the peers and teachers are usually unfamiliar with hearing loss and the adaptations needed for accessible communication with a student who is deaf or hard of hearing (Jamieson et al., 2011). In this sense, an inclusive environment may create greater stress for a deaf child than a specialized program where teachers and support staff are familiar with the needs of a student with hearing loss (Angelides & Aravi, 2006).

Another potential stressor for children with hearing loss is peer relations. Interactions with peers create opportunities for developing social competencies, validating emerging self-identity, and promoting positive adjustment (Gifford-Smith & Brownell, 2003). However, stressful peer interactions (e.g., rejection, harassment, and victimization) are associated with poor behavioral adjustment and academic problems (Boivin, Hymel, & Hodges, 2001; Juvonen, Nishina, & Graham, 2000).

For children and youth with hearing loss, spoken language skills have been found to positively affect relationships because they ease communication with hearing peers (Antia et al., 2010). When communication difficulties arise, peer interactions can be stressful for children who are deaf or hard of hearing, who face a lack of understanding of hearing loss and negative attitudes among hearing peers (Antia & Stinson, 1999; Bat-Chava & Deignan, 2001; Eriks-Brophy et al., 2006; Leigh et al., 2009; Stinson & Kluwin, 2003) and fewer opportunities to create meaningful friendships (Most, Weisel, & Tur-Kaspa, 1999). A number of studies indicate that DHH children in mainstream schools are more rejected and neglected than their hearing peers (see reviews in Antia, Kreimeyer, Metz, & Spolsky, 2011; Stinson & Kluwin, 2003), have fewer friendships with hearing peers (Kouwenberg, 2013, in Blom, Marschark, Vervloed, & Knoors, 2014), and are more likely to have a complete lack of friends than their hearing peers (Nunes, Pretzlik, & Olson, 2001). At the same time, in a recent study Wauters and Knoors (2008) found no differences between the deaf children and their hearing peers in terms of peer acceptance, social status, the number of mutual friendships, or the number of mutual antipathies. Although no differences were found in peer acceptance, deaf and hearing children differed on some dimensions of social competence. The deaf children scored lower than their hearing peers on prosocial behavior and higher on socially withdrawn behavior. In addition, deaf children seemed to be more often involved in a network without any friendships. Being the only child with hearing loss in a class with hearing peers can be a negative experience. Overall, DHH children in mainstream schools reported fewer positive social experience than deaf children in special schools (Stinson & Kluwin, 2003). Feeling different from the peer group may lead to unique negative feelings about oneself and about hearing loss (Most, 2007). Stinson and Liu (1999) found negative attitudes among hearing peers toward deafness that focused on communication breakdowns, fear, lack of familiarity with deaf peers, and an unwillingness to befriend children who are "different." Indeed, some of the arguments against integrating children with hearing loss into regular schools include lack of opportunities for making friends and having social interaction with other children with hearing loss (Cerney, 2007; Foster, 1988; Leigh et al., 2009; Musselman, Mootilal, & MacKay, 1996; Oliva, 2004). This lack of opportunities is particularly problematic given that relationships with deaf peers are important for deaf children's well-being (Musselman et al., 1996). Leigh (1999) argued that interacting with other children with hearing loss is essential for the formation of an identity that includes a healthy perspective about oneself. In a recent study, differences were found in two dimensions of peer relations (peer acceptance and popularity) between grade six DHH children who were in mainstream programs and DHH children who attended special schools. Specifically, DHH boys in mainstream education were less accepted and popular compared with their hearing classmates and with their deaf peers in special education programs. DHH girls in mainstream education were also less popular than their hearing peers (Wolters, Knoors, Cillessen, & Verhoeven, 2011). Differences were also evident in changes in children's well-being during the transition from grade 6 to secondary education. The well-being of DHH children in mainstream schools increased for boys but decreased for girls. In contrast, school well-being increased for DHH girls in special education schools but decreased for DHH boys. Overall, it seems that gender and educational setting also need to be considered when accounting for stressors faced by DHH children and adolescents.

Challenges During Adolescence

School-aged children with hearing loss and their families face new challenges and demands due to different developmental issues that affect both the child and the family. In particular, adolescence is a unique and challenging period during a person's life, in which a young person must negotiate rapid changes across physical, cognitive, and social domains (Forman, 1993). Adolescence has been recognized as a frequently turbulent transition from childhood to adulthood, even among typically developing youth. The rapid physical changes and dramatic psychosocial changes that occur during this period lead to the emergence of diverse age-specific normative stressors that affect adolescents' well-being (Seiffge-Krenke, Weidemann, Fentner, Aegenheister, & Poeblau, 2001). An impressive body of evidence has demonstrated that adolescents perceive stress in their lives (Grant et al., 2003) and that elevated levels of stressors are associated with psychopathology (Grant et al., 2006). Notably, such adolescent stressors refer to stressful everyday situations (e.g., conflicts with parents or peers), which represent the majority of stressful events in the lives of young people (Seiffge-Krenke et al., 2001), as opposed to adverse circumstances or major stressful life events that affect only a relatively small number of adolescents (e.g., a major illness, parental divorce, or the death of a close friend or relative). As noted earlier, however, most adolescents confront mildly stressful situations in their everyday lives, which pertain to interpersonal relationships (Seiffge-Krenke, 2011), perception of self and identity formation (e.g., dissatisfaction with changes in one's body, appearance, traits, and characteristics), and tension regarding their future educational, occupational, and career goals (Nurmi, Poole, & Kalakoski, 1994; Seiffge-Krenke, Overbeek, & Vermulst, 2010; Sentse, Lindenberg, Omvlee, Ormel, & Veenstra, 2010).

While adolescence is widely considered a challenging period for young people in general, it may be especially challenging for those with disabilities (e.g., Todd & Jones, 2005). Clearly, DHH adolescents experience many of these everyday stressors that are typical for their developmental stage. However, similar to other adolescents facing difficult conditions (e.g., chronic illness) (Seiffge-Krenke, 2001), minority adolescents in mostly white areas (Farrell et al., 2007), or those with divorcing parents (Sheets, Sandler, & West, 1996), DHH adolescents' daily life may be complicated by additional stressors specific to hearing loss and its related consequences. A new quality-of-life instrument was developed recently specifically for DHH youth (Patrick et al., 2011), based on semistructured concept elicitation interviews with youth and adults who are deaf or hard of hearing and their parents. The scale reflects some of the unique challenges this group faces in participating in social activities, self-acceptance and advocacy, and perceived stigma.

INTERPERSONAL RELATIONSHIP STRESSORS

An important aspect of young people's development is forming close interpersonal relationships, including those with parents, peers, and teachers. During adolescence, the relationships with parents and peers change in their functions and meaning (Laursen & Collins, 2004; Steinberg, 2001). Not surprisingly, interpersonal stressors are among the most salient ones for adolescents (Seiffge-Krenke, Aunola, & Nurmi, 2009) and are the most common type of stressful situation investigated in child and adolescent coping research (see review by Compas, Connor-Smith, Saltzman, Thonmsen, & Wadsworth, 2001).

Regarding parental relationships, adolescents frequently seek to become more autonomous and often attempt to establish more mature relationships to gain more equal power relations with their parents. This quest, in turn, can challenge the stability of a warm and cohesive relationship and lead to frequent conflicts and stressful interactions between adolescents and their parents (Branje, van Doorn, van der Valk, & Meeus, 2009; Seiffge-Krenke et al., 2001; Steinberg & Silk, 2002). Among typical adolescents, a high level of perceived stress relates to interactions and relationships with parents. These situations include parent–adolescent arguments about adolescent autonomy, communication difficulties, and parental pressure to succeed in school (Seiffge-Krenke et al., 2009).

For adolescents with hearing loss, communication with parents may be even more complicated. Most individuals with hearing loss are born to hearing parents who have little or no prior knowledge or experience with providing an accessible communication environment to the child who is deaf or hard of hearing (Mitchell & Karchmer, 2004). Parents often find effective communication with their deaf or hard of hearing child to be difficult, frustrating, and demanding (Freeman et al., 2002; Zaidman-Zait, 2008). In a study examining parents of deaf children with a CI (ranging in age from 12 months to 13 years), nearly 40% of the parents indicated that communication problems between their children and themselves were a major source of daily stress. Parents related this challenge either to the child's immature speech perception and language level or to the fact that they themselves did not share an easily understood, mutually accessible language with their child (Zaidman-Zait, 2008). Gregory (1995) reported that some youth with hearing loss struggle in communicating with their parents and feel left out, not knowing about issues in their own families. Wheeler and colleagues (2007) reported that young people with a CI noted improvement in their interactions with family and friends following the implantation.

Typically, parent–adolescent communication practices during adolescence are perceived to be fraught with ambiguity (Sillars, Koerner, & Fitzpatrick, 2005). This situation likely escalates when there is limited shared language competence between parent and child. The ongoing difficulty of struggling to communicate effectively with parents can have an adverse impact on the adolescent's well-being (Hintermair, 2006) and often creates a daily source of stress. Leigh and colleagues (2009) found a positive correlation between perceived satisfaction with communication at home and deaf adolescents' social and academic self-esteem, as well as their overall life satisfaction. In a recent study, the quality of parent–child communication predicted global self-worth level, which was also associated with the prevalence of psychopathology (Van Gent, Goedhart, Knoors, Westenberg, & Treffers, 2012)

Similarly, a study by Kushalnagar and colleagues (2011) found that better communication between hearing-impaired adolescents and their parents was related to adolescents' lower level of depression, higher level of quality of life in terms of self-acceptance and advocacy, participation, and lower perceived stigma. These findings underscore the importance of effective mutual communication methods at home (by either sign or spoken language) among adolescents with hearing loss and their parents. However, the communication barrier that exists between many deaf or hard of hearing adolescents and their parents may make it difficult for the young people to comfortably express their concerns or fears to parents and can create adverse consequences for adolescents' social-emotional development and well-being, causing a perceived lower quality of life with higher stress.

Moreover, parent–adolescent communications involve conflicts, which also play a role in promoting the renegotiation of familial roles, creating opportunities to communicate about interpersonal issues (Collins, 1995; Smetana, 1988; Youniss, 1980), and teaching negotiation and conflict-resolution skills (Steinberg & Silk, 2002). Indeed, moderate experiences of conflict during adolescence have been associated with better adjustment than either no conflict or frequent intense conflicts (Adams & Laursen, 2001). However, these gains may be lost when the adolescent and parents cannot communicate at a level that allows for questioning, reasoning, and negotiation.

Adolescents' relationships with their peers change dramatically during this developmental stage. This change is marked by increased time spent with peers and the growing importance of peer relationships (Brown & Larson, 2009). It is characterized by the emergence of friendships with greater intimacy than those found in middle and early childhood (Bowker, Bukowski, Hymel, & Sippola, 2000). The increased complexity in the nature of peer relationships places greater demands on adolescents' social skills (Brown & Larson, 2009). Negotiating interactions may prove more difficult during adolescence than it is in childhood (Rubin et al., 2006). As adolescents place greater expectations on their relationships with peers, they become more concerned with peer acceptance ("fitting in") (Buhrmester, 1990), with fear of rejection becoming a greater stressor (Sentse et al., 2010). Given the significance of peer relationships during adolescence, the ability to manage problem situations among peers may be particularly important (Allison et al., 1999; Farrell et al., 2007). As discussed earlier, peer interactions and relationships might be especially challenging for DHH youth. Adolescents with hearing loss frequently have communication difficulties and communication barriers, which have a negative impact on their peer interactions (Antia, Jones, Luckner, Kreimeyer, & Reed, 2011; Stinson & Kluwin, 2003; Wolters et al., 2011). In a recent study, Wolters and colleagues (2011) found that compared with their hearing peers, DHH adolescents received lower ratings on peer acceptance, regardless of educational setting. DHH youth in mainstream settings scored lower on popularity in comparison to their hearing peers. Furthermore, adolescents with hearing loss have reported challenges in forming and maintaining meaningful friendships with their hearing peers (Israelite, Ower, & Goldstein, 2002; Stinson & Antia, 1999). It is important to note that peer relations (both acceptance and popularity) were found to predict well-being in school (Wolters et al., 2012). Gilman, Easterbrooks, and Frey (2004) examined multidimensional life satisfaction among youth who are deaf or hard of hearing (ages eight to 18, mean = 13.04 years) across five life domains: family, friends, school, living environment, and self. The results showed that deaf or hard of hearing youth scored lower on satisfaction with friends than did the hearing group. Another study used a quality-of-life instrument developed specifically for youth who are DHH (Patrick et al., 2011). Early adolescents (11 to 14 years) had higher positive scores on the participation domain (i.e., participation in social activities) than did their older peers (15 to 19 years). The authors suggested that this finding reflects greater challenges in communication and social interactions among older adolescents (Schick et al., 2013). These studies highlight the challenges and stressors that youth with hearing loss face as they navigate the complexity of interpersonal communication and relationship formation with peers through adolescence.

Currently, given recent advances in audiological devices such as CI, adolescents' spoken communication skills can lead to more satisfying socialization among hearing peers. However, socialization outcomes do vary across children with CI (Bat-Chava & Martin, 2002; Bat-Chava, Martin, & Kosciw, 2005), mostly due to delays in oral communication skills, limited access to communication within group situations, and the attitudes of hearing peers (Bat-Chava & Deignan, 2001; Bat-Chava et al., 2005; Chmiel, Sutton, & Jenkins, 2000; Kluwin & Stewart, 2000; Nicholas & Geers, 2003). In a study of 30 parents of children with CI, one third referred to their children's immature social competence and lack of peer relationships as problematic (Zaidman-Zait, 2008). Wheeler and colleagues (2007) discussed bullying and other incidents of unpleasant peer behavior experiences among young people using CI. Archbold and Wheeler (2010) suggested that bullying may arise from difficulty interacting with peers, given that young people with hearing loss are perceived as different. Overall, research indicates that among deaf youth who are CI users, acceptance by hearing peers is linked to good spoken communication skills (Bat-Chava & Deignan, 2001; Stinson & Kluwin, 2003). Apparently, challenges in forming relationships with hearing peers, as well as the difficulties associated with class participation and learning, create additional stressors among young people with hearing loss compared to hearing adolescents.

In our recent mixed-method study (Zaidman-Zait, Most, & Dotan, 2014), we examined the stress perception of 36 DHH youth and 73 hearing adolescents in mainstream schools. Adolescents' stress perception was measured by the Problem Questionnaire (PQ; Seiffge-Krenke, 1995), which assesses adolescence-specific stressors in seven domains: problems with school, perceptions of the future, parents, peers, leisure time, self-related issues, and romantic relationships. Findings showed that adolescents with hearing loss had the highest levels of stress in the domain of problems related to their future, followed by stress related to school and peer relationships.

The study illuminated the unique stress experienced among adolescents who are deaf or hard of hearing. Because the PQ was not developed to measure stressors in the specific context of being an adolescent with a hearing loss, we conducted semistructured interviews with 12 adolescents about the challenges and problems they had had during the two weeks prior to the interview. Thematic analysis of the interview transcripts revealed that similar domains of stress were represented in the interviews, with stressors specific to hearing loss apparent in each domain. Evidently, relationships with peers were a major source of stress. In the interviews, adolescents with hearing loss expressed difficulty in initiating conversations with peers, embarrassment at asking their peers to repeat and clarify their words when communication breakdowns occurred, and impatience and negative attitudes from their peers on such occasions. They felt insecure about peer acceptance and at times felt lonely. In the domain of school-related stress, some of the unique stressors deaf adolescents experienced involved the acoustic conditions of the classroom, which made learning very difficult; lack of awareness and understanding of hearing loss on the part of teachers and students; lack of consideration and accessibility; and difficulty participating in classroom discussion and following teachers and students during lessons. Similarly, the deaf adolescents found communicating with their parents to be stressful and had problems that related to their hearing condition during leisure activities (e.g., listening to music, communicating with friends, or even spending time at a swimming pool). This made them feel different, which led to further stress, frustration, and anger. Finally, adolescents faced some unique stressors involving not their peers, schools, and parents but rather themselves. Some of the interviewees held negative feelings about their hearing loss, expressed lack of confidence, and struggled with their identity.

Overall, it seems that while adolescents with hearing loss face many of the everyday stressors that most youth are bound to experience, they must also cope with unique stressors directly related to their hearing loss and the challenges they face while functioning in a hearing world. The study reveals the dual difficulties these youngsters deal with on a daily level and calls for further research on the ways in which they can be assisted in handling the difficulties associated with hearing loss and deafness in adolescence.

SUMMARY AND IMPLICATIONS

Research demonstrates that stress among either parents or children is not a direct outcome of child deafness. Rather, individual differences in stress stem from differences across a number of contextual factors, including the child's experiences, parental and family characteristics, coping patterns, as well as the school and community resources available to the family. DHH children and their parents face unique challenges and stressors that can hinder their functioning, adjustment, and well-being. We must identify specific stressors in order to provide support that best matches the recipient's needs based on his or her expectations or desires (Logsdon, Birkimer, Ratterman, Cahill, & Cahill, 2002). To prevent these stressors from adversely affecting family patterns of interaction, any intervention must include assessment and identification of stressors as a crucial first stage. In particular, we must examine the many challenges that DHH children and their parents experience, which may differ from those reported by parents and children unaffected by hearing loss. Service providers need to be sensitive to contextual issues and major events along the life course such as the identification of the child's hearing loss or the transition to school. Moreover, we must consider stressors within the context of the child's developmental stage. For example, adolescence is a particularly critical time when multiple changes occur, such as an increased desire for autonomy, greater focus on peer groups, salience of identity issues, development of abstract cognitive abilities, and rapid physical changes. Last, we must take into account children's individual characteristics and competencies. Overall, we must identify stressors so that we can better explicate the child's and the family's processes of adaptation to hearing loss and develop interventions to enhance their coping and adjustment.

When implementing stress management programs, health professionals and educators should consider the interdependency between the parents and their children. In other words, parents' stressors can put children at risk for distress, and vice versa. Parents are important socialization agents, teaching their children how to regulate and cope with negative feelings by providing valuable information to their children about appropriate emotional displays and successful coping strategies (Eisenberg, Cumberland, & Spinrad, 1998). At the same time, parenting stress levels are associated with parent management of their children's negative emotions. Specifically, the more parents experience stress, the more nonsupportive their techniques are for teaching their children coping strategies (Nelson, O'Brien, Blankson, Calkins, & Keane, 2009). Furthermore, parents who experience high levels of stress may be less able to implement interventions to help their children (Kazdin, 1995). Indeed, elevated levels of parenting stress appear to be related to poorer improvement following early intervention among young children with disabilities (Osborne, McHugh, Saunders, & Reed, 2008; Robbins, Dunlap, & Pleinis, 1991). Similarly, children who experience elevated levels of stress will be less capable of succeeding academically. Research findings demonstrate that students who manage their stress effectively learn more and get better grades (Elliot & Dweck, 2005). Overall, promoting children's social and emotional learning increases academic performance and leads to healthy development and well-being (Durlak, Weissberg, Dymnicki, Taylor, & Schellinger, 2011). Hence, intervention programs and schools have an important role in promoting parent and child well-being. This is a significant component for professionals who are providing family-centered care to families of children with hearing loss. The family-centered care approach to supporting and empowering families is a key component of professional practice (Bruder & Dunst, 2008). School-based prevention efforts have been indicated as an effective way to promote children's positive mental health (Greenberg, 2006). Specifically, programs that promote coping with normative stress have been considered to represent a promising direction for preventing social-emotional difficulties (Frydenberg & Brandon, 2002).

It would be valuable to adopt prevention principles, namely to identify and modify preventable sources of parent and child stress. As Quick and colleagues stated, "It is more difficult to avert distress when its consequences are already being experienced at the individual level" (Quick et al., 2013, p. 105). Therefore, we should anticipate the specific challenges faced by DHH children and their parents, as well as protect them from harmful effects. When implementing prevention and intervention strategies, we should consider how individuals differ in their perceptions and responses to demands and challenges, in their recognition of distress, and in their response to stress management interventions (Quick et al., 2013). Last, we should pay attention to the changes occurring in deaf education and in the nature of DHH learners. This includes early identification, technological changes, mainstream education for the majority of students, and programming and social advances (Marschark & Spencer, 2006).

Interventions that both reduce stressors and enhance children's and parents' adaptive capacities should be given priority. Once the stressors are identified, professionals should work together with families and children to provide adequate services and support, enhancing their protective mechanisms and resources and targeting their specific needs. Such support strengthens families so they can optimize their patterns of interaction and helps to enhance child development (Guralnick, 2004). As suggested by Quick and colleagues (2013), all levels of preventions should include the following: (a) preventive interventions focused on reducing and managing stressors; (b) secondary prevention focusing on the responses to the stressors, moderating the stress responses, and promoting stress growth; and (c) when necessary, providing psychological intervention to minimize distress and enhance the well-being of families. Interventions such as these will strengthen children and their families to meet the challenges in their daily lives in the context of childhood hearing loss.

REFERENCES

Abidin, R. R. (1992). The determinants of parenting behavior. *Journal of Clinical Child Psychology, 21*(4), 407–412.

Abidin, R. (1995). *Parenting stress index* (3rd ed.). Odessa, FL: Psychological Assessment Resources.

Adams, R., & Laursen, B. (2001). The organization and dynamics of adolescent conflict with parents and friends. *Journal of Marriage and Family, 63*(1), 97–110.

Allegretti, C. M. (2002). The effects of a cochlear implant on the family of a hearing-impaired child. *Pediatric Nursing, 28*(6), 614–620.

Allison, K. W., Crawford, I., Leone, P. E., Trickett, E., Perez-Febles, A., Burton, L. M., & Le Blanc, R. (1999). Adolescent substance use: Preliminary examinations of school and neighborhood context. *American Journal of Community Psychology, 27*(2), 111–141.

Angelides, P., & Aravi, C. (2006). A comparative perspective on the experiences of deaf and hard of hearing individuals as students at mainstream and special schools. *American Annals of the Deaf, 151*(5), 476–487.

Anthony, L. G., Anthony, B. J., Glanville, D. N., Naiman, D. Q., Waanders, C., & Shaffer, S. (2005). The relationships between parenting stress, parenting behaviour and preschoolers' social competence and behaviour problems in the classroom. *Infant and Child Development, 14*(2), 133–154.

Antia, S. D., Kreimeyer, K. H., Metz, K. K., & Spolsky, S. (2011). Peer interactions of deaf and hard-of-hearing children. In M. Marschark & P. E. Spencer (Eds.), *The Oxford handbook of deaf studies, language, and education* (Vol. 1, 2nd ed., pp. 173–187). New York: Oxford University Press.

Antia, S. D., Jones, P. B., Reed, S., & Kreimeyer, K. H. (2009). Academic status and progress of deaf and hard-of-hearing students in general education classrooms. *Journal of Deaf Studies and Deaf Education, 14*(3), 293–311.

Antia, S. D., Jones, P., Luckner, J., Kreimeyer, K. H., & Reed, S. (2011). Social outcomes of students who are deaf and hard of hearing in general education classrooms. *Exceptional Children, 77*(4), 489–504.

Antia, S. D., Kreimeyer, K. H., & Reed, S. (2010). Supporting students in general education classrooms. In M. Marschark & P. E. Spencer (Eds.), *The Oxford handbook of deaf studies, language, and education* (vol. 2, pp. 72–92). New York: Oxford University Press.

Antia, S. D., Sabers, D. L., & Stinson, M. S. (2007). Validity and reliability of the classroom participation questionnaire with deaf and hard of hearing students in public schools. *Journal of Deaf Studies and Deaf Education, 12*(2), 158–171.

Archbold, S., Sach, T., Lutman, M., & Gregory, S. (2006). Deciding to have a cochlear implant and subsequent after-care: Parental perspectives. *Deafness & Education International, 8*(4), 190–206.

Archbold, S., & Wheeler, A. (2010). Cochlear implants: Family and young people's perspectives. In M. Marschark & P. E. Spencer (Eds.), *Oxford handbook of deaf studies, language, and education* (2nd ed., pp. 226–240). Oxford: Oxford University Press.

Barker, D. H., Quittner, A. L., Fink, N. E., Eisenberg, L. S., Tobey, E. A., & Niparko, J. K. (2009). Predicting behavior problems in deaf and hearing children: The influences of language, attention, and parent-child communication. *Development and Psychopathology, 21*(2), 373–392.

Bat-Chava, Y., & Deignan, E. (2001). Peer relationships of children with cochlear implants. *Journal of Deaf Studies and Deaf Education*, *6*(3), 186–199.

Bat-Chava, Y., & Martin, D. (2002). Sibling relationships for deaf children: The impact of child and family characteristics. *Rehabilitation Psychology*, *47*(1), 73–91.

Bat-Chava, Y., Martin, D., & Kosciw, J. G. (2005). Longitudinal improvements in communication and socialization of deaf children with cochlear implants and hearing aids: Evidence from parental reports. *Journal of Child Psychology and Psychiatry*, *46*(12), 1287–1296.

Belsky, J., Woodworth, S., & Crnic, K. (1996). Trouble in the second year: Three questions about family interaction. *Child Development*, *67*(2), 556–578.

Blom, H., Marschark, M., Vervloed, M. P., & Knoors, H. (2014). Finding friends online: Online activities by deaf students and their well-being. *PLoS One*, *9*(2), e88351.

Boivin, M., Hymel, S., & Hodges, E. V. (2001). Toward a process view of peer rejection and harassment. In J. Juvonen & S. Graham (Eds.), *Peer harassment in school: The plight of the vulnerable and victimized* (pp. 265–289). New York: The Guilford Press.

Bowker, A., M. Bukowski, W., Hymel, S., & K. Sippola, L. (2000). Coping with daily hassles in the peer group during early adolescence: Variations as a function of peer experience. *Journal of Research on Adolescence*, *10*(2), 211–243.

Branje, S. J., van Doorn, M., van der Valk, I., & Meeus, W. (2009). Parent–adolescent conflicts, conflict resolution types, and adolescent adjustment. *Journal of Applied Developmental Psychology*, *30*(2), 195–204.

Brown, B. B., & Larson, J. (2009). Peer relationships in adolescence. In R. M. Lerner & L. Steinberg (Eds.), *Handbook of adolescent psychology: Contextual influences on adolescent development* (3rd ed., pp. 74–103). New York: Wiley.

Brown, G. W., & Harris, T. O. (1989). *Life events and illness*. New York: Guilford Press.

Bruder, M. B., & Dunst, C. J. (2008). Factors related to the scope of early intervention service coordinator practices. *Infants & Young Children*, *21*(3), 176–185.

Buhrmester, D. (1990). Intimacy of friendship, interpersonal competence, and adjustment during preadolescence and adolescence. *Child Development*, *61*(4), 1101–1111.

Burger, T., Spahn, C., Richter, B., Eissele, S., Löhle, E., & Bengel, J. (2005). Parental distress: The initial phase of hearing aid and cochlear implant fitting. *American Annals of the Deaf*, *150*(1), 5–10.

Calderon, R., & Greenberg, M. (2003). Social and emotional development of deaf children. In M. Marschark & P. E. Spencer (Eds.), *The Oxford handbook of deaf studies, language, and education* (pp. 177–189). Oxford: Oxford University Press.

Calderon, R., & Greenberg, M. T. (1999). Stress and coping in hearing mothers of children with hearing loss: Factors affecting mother and child adjustment. *American Annals of the Deaf*, *144*(1), 7–18.

Calderon, R., & Greenberg, M. T. (2011). Social and emotional development of deaf children: Family, school, and program effects. In M. Marschark & P. E. Spencer (Eds.), *The Oxford handbook of deaf studies, language, and education* (Vol. 1, 2nd ed., pp. 188–199). New York: Oxford University Press.

Cerney, J. (2007). *Deaf education in America*. Washington, DC: Gallaudet University Press.

Chang, Y., & Fine, M. A. (2007). Modeling parenting stress trajectories among low-income young mothers across the child's second and third years: Factors accounting for stability and change. *Journal of Family Psychology*, *21*(4), 584–594.

Chmiel, R., Sutton, L., & Jenkins, H. (2000). Quality of life in children with cochlear implants. *Annals of Otology, Rhinology & Laryngology (Supplement), 185*, 103–105.

Christiansen, J. B., & Leigh, I. (2002). *Cochlear implants in children: Ethics and choices*. Washington, DC: Gallaudet University Press.

Cicchetti, D. E., & Toth, S. L. (1997). *Developmental perspectives on trauma: Theory, research, and intervention*. Rochester, NY: University of Rochester Press.

Cohen, S., Kessler, R. C., & Gordon, L. U. (1995). Strategies for measuring stress in studies of psychiatric and physical disorders. In S. Cohen, R. C. Kessler, & L. U. Gordon (Eds.), *Measuring stress: A guide for health and social scientists* (pp. 3–26). New York: Oxford University Press.

Collins, W. A. (1995). Relationships and development: Family adaptation to individual change. In Shulman, S. (Ed.), *Close Relationships and Socioemotional Development* (pp. 128–154). Norwood, NH: Ablex.

Collins, W. A., & Laursen, B. (2004). Changing relationships, changing youth interpersonal contexts of adolescent development. *Journal of Early Adolescence, 24*(1), 55–62.

Compas, B. E., Connor-Smith, J. K., Saltzman, H., Thomsen, A. H., & Wadsworth, M. E. (2001). Coping with stress during childhood and adolescence: Problems, progress, and potential in theory and research. *Psychological Bulletin, 127*(1), 87–127.

Creasey, G., & Reese, M. (1996). Mothers' and fathers' perceptions of parenting hassles: Associations with psychological symptoms, nonparenting hassles, and child behavior problems. *Journal of Applied Developmental Psychology, 17*(3), 393–406.

Crnic, K. A., & Booth, C. L. (1991). Mothers' and fathers' perceptions of daily hassles of parenting across early childhood. *Journal of Marriage and the Family, 53*(4), 1042–1050.

Crnic, K. A., & Greenberg, M. T. (1990). Minor parenting stresses with young children. *Child Development, 61*(5), 1628–1637.

Curle, D., & Zaidman-Zait, A. (November, 2013). *Use of signed communication among parents of cochlear-implanted children with additional disabilities*. Presented at ASHA Annual Convention, Chicago, Illinois.

Deater-Deckard, K. (1998). Parenting stress and child adjustment: Some old hypotheses and new questions. *Clinical Psychology: Science and Practice, 5*(3), 314–332.

Deater-Deckard, K., & Petrill, S. A. (2004). Parent–child dyadic mutuality and child behavior problems: An investigation of gene–environment processes. *Journal of Child Psychology and Psychiatry, 45*(6), 1171–1179.

Deater-Deckard, K., & Scarr, S. (1996). Parenting stress among dual-earner mothers and fathers: Are there gender differences? *Journal of Family Psychology, 10*(1), 45–59.

Dunst, C. J., Trivette, C. M., Boyd, K., & Brookfield, J. (1994). Help-giving practices and the self-efficacy appraisals of parents. In C. J. Dunst, C. M. Trivette, & A. G. Deal (Eds.), *Supporting & strengthening families, vol. 1: Methods, strategies and practices* (pp. 212–220). Cambridge, MA: Brookline Books.

Durlak, J. A., Weissberg, R. P., Dymnicki, A. B., Taylor, R. D., & Schellinger, K. B. (2011). The impact of enhancing students' social and emotional learning: A meta-analysis of school-based universal interventions. *Child Development, 82*(1), 405–432.

Eccles, J. (2009). Who am I and what am I going to do with my life? Personal and collective identities as motivators of action. *Educational Psychologist*, *44*(2), 78–89.

Eisenberg, N., Cumberland, A., & Spinrad, T. L. (1998). Parental socialization of emotion. *Psychological Inquiry*, *9*(4), 241–273.

Elliot, A. J., & Dweck, C. S. (2005). Competence and motivation: Competence as the core of achievement motivation. In A. J. Elliot & C. S. Dweck (Eds.), *Handbook of competence and motivation* (pp. 3–12). New York: Guilford Press.

Eriks-Brophy, A., Durieux-Smith, A., Olds, J., Fitzpatrick, E., Duquette, C., & Whittingham, J. (2006). Facilitators and barriers to the inclusion of orally educated children and youth with hearing loss in schools: Promoting partnerships to support inclusion. *Volta Review*, *106*(1), 53–88.

Farrell, A. D., Erwin, E. H., Allison, K. W., Meyer, A., Sullivan, T., Camou, S., . . . Esposito, L. (2007). Problematic situations in the lives of urban African American middle school students: A qualitative study. *Journal of Research on Adolescence*, *17*(2), 413–454.

Fitzpatrick, E., Angus, D., Durieux-Smith, A., Graham, I. D., & Coyle, D. (2008). Parents' needs following identification of childhood hearing loss. *American Journal of Audiology*, *17*(1), 38–49.

Forman, S. G. (1993). *Coping skills interventions for children and adolescents*. San Francisco, CA: Jossey-Bass.

Foster, S. (1988). Life in the mainstream: Deaf college freshmen and their experiences in the mainstreamed high school. *Journal of the American Deafness and Rehabilitation Association*, *22*(2), 27–35.

Freeman, B., Dieterich, C. A., & Rak, C. (2002). The struggle for language: Perspectives and practices of urban parents with children who are deaf or hard of hearing. *American Annals of the Deaf*, *147*(5), 37–44.

Friedrich, W. N., Greenberg, M. T., & Crnic, K. (1983). A short-form of the questionnaire on resources and stress. *American Journal of Mental Deficiency*, *88*(1), 41–48.

Frydenberg, E., & Brandon, C. M. (2002). *The best of coping*. Melbourne: Oz Child.

Geers, A., Brenner, C., & Davidson, L. (2003). Factors associated with development of speech perception skills in children implanted by age five. *Ear and Hearing*, *24*(1), 24S–35S.

Giallo, R., Treyvaud, K., Matthews, J., & Kienhuis, M. (2010). Making the transition to primary school: An evaluation of a transition program for parents. *Australian Journal of Educational & Developmental Psychology*, *10*(1), 1–17.

Gifford-Smith, M. E., & Brownell, C. A. (2003). Childhood peer relationships: Social acceptance, friendships, and peer networks. *Journal of School Psychology*, *41*(4), 235–284.

Gilbey, P. (2010). Qualitative analysis of parents' experience with receiving the news of the detection of their child's hearing loss. *International Journal of Pediatric Otorhinolaryngology*, *74*(3), 265–270.

Gilman, R., Easterbrooks, S. R., & Frey, M. (2004). A preliminary study of multidimensional life satisfaction among deaf/hard of hearing youth across environmental settings. *Social Indicators Research*, *66*(1-2), 143–164.

Grant, K. E., Compas, B. E., Thurm, A. E., McMahon, S. D., Gipson, P. Y., Campbell, A. J., . . . & Westerholm, R. I. (2006). Stressors and child and adolescent psychopathology: Evidence of moderating and mediating effects. *Clinical Psychology Review*, *26*(3), 257–283.

Grant, K. E., Compas, B. E., Stuhlmacher, A. F., Thurm, A. E., McMahon, S. D., & Halpert, J. A. (2003). Stressors and child and adolescent psychopathology: Moving from markers to mechanisms of risk. *Psychological Bulletin, 129*(3), 447–466.

Greenberg, M. T. (2006). Promoting resilience in children and youth: Preventive interventions and their interface with neuroscience. *Annals of the New York Academy of Science, 1094*, 139–150.

Greenberg, M. T., & Kusché, C. A. (1989). Cognitive, personal, and social development of deaf children and adolescents. In M. C. Wang, M. C. Reynolds, & H. J. Walberg (Eds.), *Handbook of special education: Research and practice, vol. 3: Low incidence conditions. advances in education* (pp. 95–129). Elmsford, NY: Pergamon Press.

Gregory, S. (1995). *Deaf young people and their families: Developing understanding*. New York: Cambridge University Press.

Guralnick, M. J. (2004). Family investments in response to the developmental challenges of young children with disabilities. In A. Kalil & T. DeLeire (Eds.), *Family investments in children's potential: Resources and parenting behaviors that promote success. monographs in parenting* (pp. 119–137). Mahwah, NJ: Lawrence Erlbaum Associates Publishers.

Guralnick, M. J. (2005). Early intervention for children with intellectual disabilities: Current knowledge and future prospects. *Journal of Applied Research in Intellectual Disabilities, 18*(4), 313–324.

Haggerty, R. J., Sherrod, L. R., Garmezy, N., & Rutter, M. (1994). *Stress, risk, and resilience in children and adolescents: Processes, mechanisms, and interventions*. New York: Cambridge University Press.

Hindley, P. A. (2005). Mental health problems in deaf children. *Current Paediatrics, 15*(2), 114–119.

Hintermair, M. (2000). Hearing impairment, social networks, and coping: The need for families with hearing-impaired children to relate to other parents and to hearing-impaired adults. *American Annals of the Deaf, 145*(1), 41–53.

Hintermair, M. (2006). Parental resources, parental stress, and socioemotional development of deaf and hard of hearing children. *Journal of Deaf Studies and Deaf Education, 11*(4), 493–513.

Holmes, T. H., & Rahe, R. H. (1967). The social readjustment rating scale. *Journal of Psychosomatic Research, 11*(2), 213–218.

Huttunen, K., Rimmanen, S., Vikman, S., Virokannas, N., Sorri, M., Archbold, S., & Lutman, M. (2009). Parents' views on the quality of life of their children 2–3 years after cochlear implantation. *International Journal of Pediatric Otorhinolaryngology,73*(12), 1786–1794.

Israelite, N., Ower, J., & Goldstein, G. (2002). Hard-of-hearing adolescents and identity construction: Influences of school experiences, peers, and teachers. *Journal of Deaf Studies and Deaf Education, 7*(2), 134–148. doi:10.1093/deafed/7.2.134

Jamieson, J. R., Zaidman-Zait, A., & Poon, B. (2011). Family support needs as perceived by parents of preadolescents and adolescents who are deaf or hard of hearing. *Deafness & Education International, 13*(3), 110–130.

Janus, M., Kopechanski, L., Cameron, R., & Hughes, D. (2008). In transition: Experiences of parents of children with special needs at school entry. *Early Childhood Education Journal, 35*(5), 479–485.

Joseph, S., & Linley, P. A. (2006). Growth following adversity: Theoretical perspectives and implications for clinical practice. *Clinical Psychology Review, 26*(8), 1041–1053.

Juvonen, J., Nishina, A., & Graham, S. (2000). Peer harassment, psychological adjustment, and school functioning in early adolescence. *Journal of Educational Psychology*, *92*(2), 349–359.

Kahn, R. (1987). Work stress in the 1980s: Research and practice. In J. C. Quick, R. S. Bhagat, J. E. Dalton, & J. D. Quick (Eds.), *Work stress: Health care systems in the workplace* (pp. 311–320). New York: Praeger Publishers.

Kanner, A. D., Coyne, J. C., Schaefer, C., & Lazarus, R. S. (1981). Comparison of two modes of stress measurement: Daily hassles and uplifts versus major life events. *Journal of Behavioral Medicine*, *4*(1), 1–39.

Kazdin, A. E. (1995). Child, parent and family dysfunction as predictors of outcome in cognitive-behavioral treatment of antisocial children. *Behaviour Research and Therapy*, *33*(3), 271–281.

Kluwin, T. N., & Stewart, D. A. (2000). Cochlear implants for younger children: A preliminary description of the parental decision process and outcomes. *American Annals of the Deaf*, *145*(1), 26–32.

Kluwin, T. N., Stinson, M. S., & Colarossi, G. M. (2002). Social processes and outcomes of in-school contact between deaf and hearing peers. *Journal of Deaf Studies and Deaf Education*, *7*(3), 200–213.

Kurtzer-White, E., & Luterman, D. (2003). Families and children with hearing loss: Grief and coping. *Mental Retardation and Developmental Disabilities Research Reviews*, *9*(4), 232–235.

Kushalnagar, P., Topolski, T., Schick, B., Edwards, T., Skalicky, A., & Patrick, D. (2011). Mode of communication, perceived level of understanding, and perceived quality of life in youth who are deaf or hard of hearing. *Journal of Deaf Studies and Deaf Education*, *16*(4), 512–523.

Lazarus, R. S., & Folkman, S. (1984). *Stress, appraisal, and coping*. New York: Springer Publishing Company.

Lederberg, A. R., & Golbach, T. (2002). Parenting stress and social support in hearing mothers of deaf and hearing children: A longitudinal study. *Journal of Deaf Studies and Deaf Education*, *7*(4), 330–345.

Leigh, I. (1999). Inclusive education and personal development. *Journal of Deaf Studies and Deaf Education*, *4*(3), 236–245.

Leigh, I. W., Maxwell-McCaw, D., Bat-Chava, Y., & Christiansen, J. B. (2009). Correlates of psychosocial adjustment in deaf adolescents with and without cochlear implants: A preliminary investigation. *Journal of Deaf Studies and Deaf Education*, *14*(2), 244–259.

Logsdon, C. M., Birkimer, J. C., Ratterman, A., Cahill, K., & Cahill, N. (2002). Social support in pregnant and parenting adolescents: Research, critique, and recommendations. *Journal of Child and Adolescent Psychiatric Nursing*, *15*(2), 75–83.

Marschark, M. (1997). *Raising and education a deaf child: A comprehensive guide to the choices, controversies, and decisions faced by parents and educators*. New York: Oxford University Press.

Marschark, M., & Spencer, P. E. (2006). Spoken language development of deaf and hard-of-hearing children: Historical and theoretical perspectives. In P. E. Spencer & M. Marschark (Eds.), *Advances in the spoken-language development of deaf and hard-of-hearing children* (pp. 3–21). New York: Oxford University Press.

Marschark, M., & Wauters, L. (2003). Cognitive functioning in deaf adults and children. In M. Marschark & P. E. Spencer (Eds.), *Oxford handbook of deaf studies, language, and education* (pp. 464–477). New York: Oxford University Press.

Mash, E. J., & Barkely, R. A. (Eds.). (2003). *Child psychopathology* (2nd ed.). New York: Guilford.

Masten, A. S., & Motti-Stefanidi, F. (2009). Understanding and promoting resilience in children: Promotive and protective processes in schools. In C. R. Reynolds & T. B. Gutkin (Eds.), *The handbook of school psychology* (4th ed., pp. 721–738). Hoboken, NJ: John Wiley & Sons, Inc.

McCubbin, H. I., & Patterson, J. M. (1983). The family stress process: The double ABCX model of adjustment and adaptation. *Marriage & Family Review*, *6*(1-2), 7–37.

McIntyre, L. L., Eckert, T. L., Fiese, B. H., DiGennaro, F. D., & Wildenger, L. K. (2007). Transition to kindergarten: Family experiences and involvement. *Early Childhood Education Journal*, *35*(1), 83–88.

Meinzen-Derr, J., Lim, L. H., Choo, D. I., Buyniski, S., & Wiley, S. (2008). Pediatric hearing impairment caregiver experience: Impact of duration of hearing loss on parental stress. *International Journal of Pediatric Otorhinolaryngology*, *72*(11), 1693–1703.

Minke, K. M., & Scott, M. (1995). Parent-professional relationships in early intervention A qualitative investigation. *Topics in Early Childhood Special Education*, *15*(3), 335–352.

Mitchell, R. E., & Karchmer, M. A. (2004). Chasing the mythical ten percent: Parental hearing status of deaf and hard of hearing students in the united states. *Sign Language Studies*, *4*(2), 138–163.

Most, T. (2007). Speech intelligibility, loneliness, and sense of coherence among deaf and hard-of-hearing children in individual inclusion and group inclusion. *Journal of Deaf Studies and Deaf Education*, *12*(4), 495–503.

Most, T., Weisel, A., & Tur-Kaspa, H. (1999). Contact with students with hearing impairments and the evaluation of speech intelligibility and personal qualities. *Journal of Special Education*, *33*(2), 103–111.

Most, T., & Zaidman-Zait, A. (2001). The needs of parents of children with cochlear implants. *Volta Review*, *103*(2), 99–114.

Musselman, C., Mootilal, A., & MacKay, S. (1996). The social adjustment of deaf adolescents in segregated, partially integrated, and mainstreamed settings. *Journal of Deaf Studies and Deaf Education*, *1*(1), 52–63.

Myck-Wayne, J., Robinson, S., & Henson, E. (2011). Serving and supporting young children with a dual diagnosis of hearing loss and autism: The stories of four families. *American Annals of the Deaf*, *156*(4), 379–390.

Nelson, J. A., O'Brien, M., Blankson, A. N., Calkins, S. D., & Keane, S. P. (2009). Family stress and parental responses to children's negative emotions: Tests of the spillover, crossover, and compensatory hypotheses. *Journal of Family Psychology*,*23*(5), 671–679.

Nicholas, J. G., & Geers, A. E. (2003). Personal, social, and family adjustment in school-aged children with a cochlear implant. *Ear and Hearing*, *24*(1), 69S–81S.

Nunes, T., Pretzlik, U., & Olsson, J. (2001). Deaf children's social relationships in mainstream schools. *Deafness & Education International*, *3*(3), 123–136.

Nurmi, J., Lerner, R., & Steinberg, L. (2004). Socialization and self-development. In R. M. Lerner & L. Steinberg (Eds.), *Handbook of adolescent psychology* (2nd ed., pp. 85–124). Hoboken, NJ: John Wiley & Sons.

Nurmi, J., Poole, M. E., & Kalakoski, V. (1994). Age differences in adolescent future-oriented goals, concerns, and related temporal extension in different sociocultural contexts. *Journal of Youth and Adolescence*, *23*(4), 471–487.

Oliva, G. (2004). *Alone in the mainstream: A deaf woman remembers public school.* Washington, DC: Gallaudet University Press.

Osborne, L. A., McHugh, L., Saunders, J., & Reed, P. (2008). Parenting stress reduces the effectiveness of early teaching interventions for autistic spectrum disorders. *Journal of Autism and Developmental Disorders, 38*(6), 1092–1103.

Östberg, M., & Hagekull, B. (2000). A structural modeling approach to the understanding of parenting stress. *Journal of Clinical Child Psychology, 29*(4), 615–625.

Park, C. L. (2004). The notion of growth following stressful life experiences: Problems and prospects. *Psychological Inquiry, 15*, 69–76.

Patrick, D. L., Edwards, T. C., Skalicky, A. M., Schick, B., Topolski, T. D., Kushalnagar, P., . . . & Sie, K. (2011). Validation of a quality-of-life measure for deaf or hard of hearing youth. *Otolaryngology-Head and Neck Surgery, 145*(1), 137–145.

Picard, M. (2004). Children with permanent hearing loss and associated disabilities: Revisiting current epidemiological data and causes of deafness. *Volta Review, 104*(4), 221–236.

Quas, J. A., Murowchick, E., Bensadoun, J., & Boyce, W. T. (2002). Predictors of children's cortisol activation during the transition to kindergarten. *Journal of Developmental & Behavioral Pediatrics, 23*(5), 304–313.

Quick, J. C., Wright, T. A., Adkins, J. A., Nelson, D. L., & Quick, J. D. (2013). *Stress in organizations* (pp. 11–26). Washington, DC: American Psychological Association. doi:10.1037/13942-001

Quittner, A. L., Barker, D. H., Cruz, I., Snell, C., Grimley, M. E., Botteri, M., & Team, C. I. (2010). Parenting stress among parents of deaf and hearing children: Associations with language delays and behavior problems. *Parenting: Science and Practice,10*(2), 136–155.

Quittner, A. L., & DiGirolamo, A. M. (1998). Family adaptation to childhood disability and illness. In R. T. Ammerman & J. V. Campo (Eds.), *Handbook of pediatric psychology and psychiatry, vol. 2: Disease, injury, and illness* (pp. 70–102). Needham Heights, MA: Allyn & Bacon.

Quittner, A. L., Glueckauf, R. L., & Jackson, D. N. (1990). Chronic parenting stress: Moderating versus mediating effects of social support. *Journal of Personality and Social Psychology, 59*(6), 1266–1278.

Quittner, A. L., Steck, J. T., & Rouiller, R. L. (1991). Cochlear implants in children: A study of parental stress and adjustment. *Otology & Neurotology, 12*(3), 95–104.

Rimm-Kaufman, S. E., & Pianta, R. C. (2000). An ecological perspective on the transition to kindergarten: A theoretical framework to guide empirical research. *Journal of Applied Developmental Psychology, 21*(5), 491–511.

Robbins, F., Dunlap, G., & Pleinis, A. (1991). Family characteristics, family training, and the progress of young children with autism. *Journal of Early Intervention, 15*(2), 173–184.

Robbins, F. R., Dunlap, G., & Plienis, A. J. (1991). Family characteristics, family training, and the progress of young children with autism. *Journal of Early Intervention, 15*(2), 173–184.

Rubin, K. H., Bukowski, W., & Parker, J. G. (2006). Peer interactions, relationships, and groups. In W. Damon, R. M. Lerner, & N. Eisenberg (Eds.), *Handbook of child psychology: Social, emotional, and personality development* (6th ed., pp. 571–645). Hoboken, NJ: John Wiley & Sons.

Rudolph, K. D., & Hammen, C. (1999). Age and gender as determinants of stress exposure, generation, and reactions in youngsters: A transactional perspective. *Child Development*, *70*(3), 660–677.

Rutter, M. (1994). Comorbidity: Meanings and mechanisms. *Clinical Psychology: Science and Practice*, *1*(1), 100–103.

Sach, T. H., & Whynes, D. K. (2005). Paediatric cochlear implantation: The views of parents: Implantación coclear pediátrica: Los punto de vista de los progenitores. *International Journal of Audiology*, *44*(7), 400–407.

Sameroff, A. J., & Haith, M. M. (Eds.). (1996). *The five to seven year shift: The age of reason and responsibility*. Chicago, IL: University of Chicago Press.

Sarant, J., & Garrard, P. (2014). Parenting stress in parents of children with cochlear implants: Relationships among parent stress, child language, and unilateral versus bilateral implants. *Journal of Deaf Studies and Deaf Education*, *19*(1), 85–106.

Sass-Lehrer, M. (2002). *Early beginnings for families with deaf and hard of hearing children: Myths and facts of early intervention and guidelines for effective services*. Washington, DC: Laurent Clerc National Deaf Education Center, Gallaudet University.

Schick, B., Skalicky, A., Edwards, T., Kushalnagar, P., Topolski, T., & Patrick, D. (2013). School placement and perceived quality of life in youth who are deaf or hard of hearing. *Journal of Deaf Studies and Deaf Education*, *18*(1), 47–61.

Seiffge-Krenke, I. (1995). *Stress, coping, and relationships in adolescence*. Mahwah, NJ: Erlbaum.

Seiffge-Krenke, I. (2001). *Diabetic adolescents and their families: Stress, coping, and adaptation*. New York: Cambridge University Press.

Seiffge-Krenke, I. (2011). Coping with relationship stressors: A decade review. *Journal of Research on Adolescence*, *21*(1), 196–210.

Seiffge-Krenke, I., Aunola, K., & Nurmi, J. (2009). Changes in stress perception and coping during adolescence: The role of situational and personal factors. *Child Development*, *80*(1), 259–279.

Seiffge-Krenke, I., Overbeek, G., & Vermulst, A. (2010). Parent–child relationship trajectories during adolescence: Longitudinal associations with romantic outcomes in emerging adulthood. *Journal of Adolescence*, *33*(1), 159–171.

Seiffge-Krenke, I., Weidemann, S., Fentner, S., Aegenheister, N., & Poeblau, M. (2001). Coping with school-related stress and family stress in healthy and clinically referred adolescents. *European Psychologist*, *6*(2), 123–132.

Sentse, M., Lindenberg, S., Omvlee, A., Ormel, J., & Veenstra, R. (2010). Rejection and acceptance across contexts: Parents and peers as risks and buffers for early adolescent psychopathology: the TRAILS study. *Journal of Abnormal Child Psychology*, *38*(1), 119–130.

Sheets, V., Sandler, I., & West, S. G. (1996). Appraisals of negative events by preadolescent children of divorce. *Child Development*, *67*(5), 2166–2182.

Sillars, A., Koerner, A., & Fitzpatrick, M. A. (2005). Communication and understanding in parent–adolescent relationships. *Human Communication Research*, *31*(1), 102–128.

Skinner, E. A., & Zimmer-Gembeck, M. J. (2007). The development of coping. *Annual Review of Psychology.*, *58*, 119–144.

Smetana, J. G. (1988). Concepts of self and social convention: Adolescents' and parents' reasoning about hypothetical and actual family conflicts. In

M. R. Gunnar & W. A. Collins (Eds.), *Development during the transition to adolescence* (pp. 79–122). Hillsdale, NJ: Lawrence Erlbaum Associates.
Spencer, P. E. (2004). Individual differences in language performance after cochlear implantation at one to three years of age: Child, family, and linguistic factors. *Journal of Deaf Studies and Deaf Education, 9*(4), 395–412.
Spencer, P. E., & Marschark, M. (2006). *Advances in the spoken language development of deaf and hard-of-hearing children.* New York: Oxford University Press.
Spencer, P., & Marschark, M. (2003). Cochlear implants; issues and implications. In M. Marschark & P. E. Spencer (Eds.), *Oxford handbook of deaf studies, language, and education* (pp. 434–448). New York: Oxford University Press.
Steinberg, L. (2001). We know some things: Parent–adolescent relationships in retrospect and prospect. *Journal of Research on Adolescence, 11*(1), 1–19.
Steinberg, L., & Silk, J. S. (2002). Parenting adolescents. In M. H. Bornstein (Ed.), *Handbook of parenting: Volume I: Children and parenting* (pp. 103–133). Mahwah, NJ: Lawrence Erlbaum Publishers.
Stinson, M., & Kluwin, T. (2003). Educational consequences of alternative school placements. In M. Marschark & P. E. Spencer (Eds.), *Oxford handbook of deaf studies, language, and education* (pp. 52–62). New York: Oxford University Press.
Stinson, M. S., & Whitmire, K. A. (2000). Adolescents who are deaf or hard of hearing: A communication perspective on educational placement. *Topics in Language Disorders, 20*(2), 58–72.
Stinson, M., & Antia, S. (1999). Considerations in educating deaf and hard-of-hearing students in inclusive settings. *Journal of Deaf Studies and Deaf Education, 4*(3), 163–175.
Stinson, M., & Liu, Y. (1999). Participation of deaf and hard-of-hearing students in classes with hearing students. *Journal of Deaf Studies and Deaf Education, 4*(3), 191–202.
Stinson, M., Liu, Y., Saur, R., & Long, G. (1996). Deaf college students' perceptions of communication in mainstream classes. *Journal of Deaf Studies and Deaf Education, 1*(1), 40–51.
Takala, M., Kuusela, J., & Takala, E. (2000). "A good future for deaf children": A five-year sign language intervention project. *American Annals of the Deaf, 145*(4), 366–374.
Theunissen, S. C., Rieffe, C., Kouwenberg, M., Soede, W., Briaire, J. J., & Frijns, J. H. (2011). Depression in hearing-impaired children. *International Journal of Pediatric Otorhinolaryngology, 75*(10), 1313–1317.
Thoutenhoofd, E. D., Archbold, S. M., Gregory, S., Lutman, M., Nikolopoulos, T., & Sach, T. (2005). *Paediatric cochlear implantation: Evaluating outcomes.* London: Whurr.
Todd, S., & Jones, S. (2005). Looking at the future and seeing the past: The challenge of the middle years of parenting a child with intellectual disabilities. *Journal of Intellectual Disability Research, 49*(6), 389–404.
Topol, D., Girard, N., Pierre, L. S., Tucker, R., & Vohr, B. (2011). The effects of maternal stress and child language ability on behavioral outcomes of children with congenital hearing loss at 18–24 months. *Early Human Development, 87*(12), 807–811.
Trezek, B. J., Paul, P. V., & Wang, Y. (2009). *Reading and deafness: Theory, research, and practice: Theory, research, and practice.* Clifton Park, NY: Cengage Learning.
Valeo, A. (2003). Special education tribunals in Ontario. *International Journal of Special Education, 18*(2), 18–30.

Van Gent, T., Goedhart, A. W., Knoors, H. E., Westenberg, P. M., & Treffers, P. D. (2012). Self-concept and ego development in deaf adolescents: A comparative study. *Journal of Deaf Studies and Deaf Education*, *17*(3), 333–351.

Wauters, L. N., & Knoors, H. (2008). Social integration of deaf children in inclusive settings. *Journal of Deaf Studies and Deaf Education*, *13*(1), 21–36.

Wheeler, A., Archbold, S., Gregory, S., & Skipp, A. (2007). Cochlear implants: The young people's perspective. *Journal of Deaf Studies and Deaf Education*, *12*(3), 303–316.

Wodehouse, G., & McGill, P. (2009). Support for family carers of children and young people with developmental disabilities and challenging behaviour: What stops it being helpful? *Journal of Intellectual Disability Research*, *53*(7), 644–653.

Wolters, N., Knoors, H. E. T., Cillessen, A. H., & Verhoeven, L. (2011). Predicting acceptance and popularity in early adolescence as a function of hearing status, gender, and educational setting. *Research in Developmental Disabilities*, *32*(6), 2553–2565.

Wolters, N., Knoors, H., Cillessen, A. H., & Verhoeven, L. (2012). Impact of peer and teacher relations on deaf early adolescents' well-being: Comparisons before and after a major school transition. *Journal of Deaf Studies and Deaf Education*, *17*(4), 463–482.

Young, A. (1997). Conceptualizing parents' sign language use in bilingual early intervention. *Journal of Deaf Studies and Deaf Education*, *2*(4), 264–276.

Youniss, J. (1980). *Parents and peers in social development: A Sullivan-Piaget perspective*. Chicago: University of Chicago Press.

Zaidman-Zait, A. (2008). Everyday problems and stress faced by parents of children with cochlear implants. *Rehabilitation Psychology*, *53*(2), 139–152.

Zaidman-Zait, A., Curle, D., Jamieson, J., Chia, R., & Kozak, F. (2012, November). *Cochlear implants for children with disabilities: Parent perspectives & satisfaction*. Presented at the ASHA Annual Convention, Atlanta, GA.

Zaidman-Zait, A., Mirenda, P., Zumbo, B. D., Georgiades, S., Szatmari, P., Bryson, S., . . . & Vaillancourt, T. (2011). Factor analysis of the parenting stress Index-Short form with parents of young children with autism spectrum disorders. *Autism Research*, *4*(5), 336–346.

Zaidman-Zait, A., & Most, T. (2005). Cochlear implants in children with hearing loss: Maternal expectations and impact on the family. *Volta Review*, *105*(2), 129–150.

Zaidman-Zait, A., Most, T., & Dotan, A. (2014). Perceived Stress of everyday problems among adolescents with and without hearing loss and its association to subjective well-being. Manuscript in preparation.

Zaidman-Zait, A., Poon, B., Curle, D., Norman, N., & Jamieson, J. (2013, April). *Kindergarten transition among children with hearing loss: Parents' experiences*. Presented to the Society for Research in Child Development, Seattle, WA.

16

The Role of the Environment in Children's Emotion Socialization

The Case of Deaf and Hard-of-Hearing Children

Carolien Rieffe, Anouk P. Netten, Evelien Broekhof, and Guida Veiga

THE IMPORTANCE OF PLAY

Humans are social beings. We like to be in the company of others, share our thoughts and feelings, plan activities together, play together, belong somewhere, and feel wanted by others. Most people also desire stable, long-lasting relationships, including friendships. Friendships in childhood have an additional function: They form a good platform to playfully practice all kinds of social skills, such as how to cooperate with others, resolve conflicts, take turns, obtain and keep a position in the peer group, and not be bullied or worse: forgotten or neglected (Hodges, Boivin, Vitaro, & Bukowski, 1999).

Yet, emotions can run high in children's play. Sometimes this is planned. For example, in pretend play (i.e., play situations in which different roles are taken on by the players involved, such as a policeman and a crook), situations are usually created to evoke different kinds of emotional situations that can then be acted out (Evans, Galyer, & Smith, 2001). The ability to take one's losses during a game of backgammon is not planned, but equally essential to master when the child is interested in maintaining good friendships. In fact, we use online computer games in our studies in which the opponent cheats in order to test children's ability for emotion regulation.

For deaf and hard-of-hearing (DHH) children, play experiences might be quite different than for hearing children. Yet there is little research on this topic, so we can only speculate. Playing with hearing children will be difficult, without a doubt. As Sue Archbold has said: "How do you know what you did not hear? Missing out the word 'not' in a sentence will make a complete difference." Parents are not always patient and thoughtful in their interactions with their DHH child (Vaccari & Marschark, 1997), let alone their hearing peers. For this reason, pretend play, in which different roles are taken but also switched again, will be more challenging for DHH children, even when playing with other DHH peers, because language and mutual understanding are crucial for the course of the storyline that is acted out. Games that require good motor skills or balance, such as climbing and skating, can be more demanding for DHH children, not to mention hide-and-seek games. From another perspective, board games such as Ludo, which in Dutch is rightfully called "Mens-Erger-Je-Niet," meaning "Control Yourself," will be more difficult for DHH children as interactions go quickly and changes of rules are sometimes negotiated during the play situation.

Hypothetically, falling behind in play situations with others can work out in two different directions. Being the one who misses out on much of the (verbally communicated) information is like being the youngest one in the family: being tolerated by other more advanced players. To stay in the game, this could mean that DHH children will have to try even harder to control themselves, hiding any frustration or anger. Alternatively, DHH children might end up playing alone and prefer solitary play, or even being actively isolated by their peers, who perceive them as less desirable play partners. The DHH child thus misses out on this important opportunity to learn and practice the skills that help to make him or her emotionally competent.

WHY EMOTIONS?

So why do we have these emotions? Can we not do without them? Why do children need so much time to practice their emotional skills? There are many everyday misconceptions about emotions among professionals, and we will discuss a few of the most common. And based on these misconceptions, indeed, it might be better to have no emotions at all. First, books, television commercials, and newspapers often imply that emotions are the opposite of rational thinking; they disturb our ability to reason logically and coherently. These different forms of media make us believe we have to choose between our "heart" and our "head." Second, many people think that it is better not to have certain emotions, especially negative ones such as anger or jealousy. In a conversation about a peer conflict in the classroom, a teacher was asked: "Imagine you come home feeling furious after work because you had a conflict with your manager. Now how would you react if your partner tells you in a patronizing voice that you do not need to be angry about something like that?" Yet, this is what children hear from adults regularly: "Don't be scared," "Don't get angry about this," "Come on, get over it." Third, as repeatedly noted by Nico Frijda (1986), one of the founding fathers of our current emotion theory, the idea that "time heals" is a fallacy.

For example, try to retell an anger-causing situation to a close friend or partner, and even years later, the anger will rise again.

An alternative approach to emotions is based on recognition of why they help us, guide us, and assist us in our daily social interactions. Emotions help to "smooth out" and maintain these social relationships. First, an emotion is an indicator, like pain, that something meaningful has happened, is going on, or might happen in the future. So first of all, an emotion has a signaling function by focusing our attention. Emotions tell us that other things can wait; this situation has priority. Then the tricky part comes in: What do I feel, and why? Let's first make clear that we are not talking here about mood states, such as waking up in the morning and feeling all happy to start a new, sunny day. Nor are we talking about sensations such as those evoked when eating chocolate or having a warm bath. Second, an emotion involves a readiness for action, a willingness to do something, to change something or protect something, which is not necessarily acted out: wanting to hit someone (anger), wanting to run away (fear), or wanting to hide oneself (shame). Consequently, every emotion also includes a bodily change that corresponds with this action tendency and usually can be felt physically. So, by definition, emotions are linked to the situations that evoke them. Now if I want to know what I feel, and why, I need to find this link between my feeling and the situation. I need to identify the element(s) in the situation that make me want to act. In other words, I need to find what is so important to me and understand what it is I want to protect or obtain.

Emotion Awareness

The capacity for *emotion identification*, or *emotion awareness*, is a basic element in emotional competence, but not always easily achieved. Children need their social environment to help them understand what they feel and why. Young children might complain about a stomachache, and a parent or teacher might be inclined to look for a medical solution (Rieffe, Terwogt, & Bosch, 2004). A schoolteacher once described a four-year-old girl in her class who had a stomachache every time something exciting was planned. Once the teacher understood this pattern, she guided the child in identifying her excitement with the situation and explaining that she could also notice excitement as a feeling in her body, like tension in her belly. Once we learn this, the bodily sensations that accompany the action tendency most times are not consciously felt anymore. Similarly, we know that the tension in our muscles is a part of anger, and that this tension will vanish once the emotion-evoking situation is adequately resolved. In fact, we consistently see in our studies that the children who pay more attention to these bodily sensations and who are more aware of them during an emotional episode are less able to deal with emotion-evoking situations adequately and develop internalizing symptoms, such as symptoms of depression (Rieffe & De Rooij, 2012).

Emotion identification can be a problem for DHH children, because achieving this capacity depends partly on emotion socialization and thus on input from the social environment (see Fellinger & Holzinger, Chapter 17 in this volume; Hintermair, Chapter 13 in this volume). As in the schoolteacher example, parents can help their children understand that physical symptoms can be a part of the emotion process. Yet, hearing parents with a DHH child talk less often about abstract concepts, such as feelings, with their DHH child (Koester & Lahti-Harper, 2010; Vaccari & Marschark, 1997). Incidental learning (i.e., learning by observing or overhearing others, reading or while watching movies with no educational intentions) is less obvious or accessible for DHH children. Nonetheless, two studies that examined emotion identification or emotional awareness in DHH children found no differences between DHH children (mean age 12 years old) and their hearing peers (Kouwenberg, Rieffe, & Theunissen, 2011; Rieffe, 2012).

In the study by Kouwenberg and colleagues (2011), children and young adolescents were asked to fill out a self-report questionnaire, the Emotion Awareness Questionnaire (Rieffe, Oosterveld, Miers, Meerum Terwogt, & Ly, 2008), consisting of items regarding their ability to differentiate between emotions ("It is difficult to know whether I feel sad or angry or something else"); their ability to link their emotions to the situations that caused them ("I always want to know why I feel bad about something"); their tendency to pay attention to the bodily symptoms of the emotion episode ("When I am scared or nervous, I feel something in my tummy"); and their ability to communicate these emotions to others ("I find it difficult to explain to a friend how I feel"). DHH children rated themselves equally capable compared to a hearing control group.

In another study (Rieffe, 2012), DHH children (mean age 11 years old) were asked to describe situations in which they had experienced certain emotions (e.g., anger, sadness, fear, and happiness) and to rate the intensity of these emotions. Again, there were no differences between DHH and hearing children. DHH children are sometimes compared to children with an autism spectrum disorder (ASD) owing to their comparable communication difficulties. In a similar study, children with ASD did show more difficulties than typically developing children in identifying in what kinds of situations they had felt these emotions (Rieffe, Meerum Terwogt, & Kotronopoulou, 2007). The children with ASD never mentioned a social event—for example, happiness ("Happy? When reading my maths book")—whereas DHH and hearing children most often reported concrete and social situations ("Happy? Yesterday, when I had my birthday party"). Taken together, the outcomes of these studies suggest no impairments in many DHH children's capacities to identify their own emotions and locate the antecedents.

Nevertheless, a much younger group of deaf children of approximately four years of age using cochlear implants (CIs; mean CI use was 25 months) did fall behind a hearing comparison group when asked how other children would feel in prototypical emotion-evoking situations (i.e., participants were shown a drawing of a child in front of a scary dog or of another child pulling the protagonist's T-shirt) (Wiefferink, Rieffe, Ketelaar, De Raeve, & Frijns, 2013). This disappointing outcome was unrelated to children's language ability or the duration of CI use. These results could indicate that DHH children need more time than hearing children to develop their emotion knowledge, or, alternatively, that DHH children understand their own emotions equally well but find it more difficult to predict or reason about other children's emotions.

Yet another important aspect of emotion awareness is understanding *which* emotion is felt, and this might be different for DHH and hearing children, even when the emotion-evoking situation is the same. A very simple example to explain this phenomenon is the fight-or-flight reaction in a situation that is perceived as life-threatening. Various intrapersonal factors can affect this decision to opt for one or the other action tendency, such as one's judgment of the possibility to run into safety, one's own capacities (e.g., a black belt in any form of martial arts will help to defeat an attacker), or one's former experiences.

In one study (Rieffe, Meerum Terwogt, & Smit, 2003), we presented children with profound hearing loss (>90-dB loss in the better ear) and hearing children (mean age 11 years old) with vignettes in which one child broke the toy of another child (the protagonist), and we asked our participants how the protagonist, the owner of the toy, would feel and why. Children were given a forced choice between anger and sadness. These two emotions denote different action tendencies. Sadness reflects a focus on the loss, when there is no hope to reinstate the desired goal, and one needs some time to come to terms with the loss. Sadness about the broken toy in this case would reflect feelings of helplessness. Anger, on the other hand, indicates a focus on the process or, in this case, on the aggressor who broke the toy. Anger is aimed at reinstating the desired goal, or at least getting some kind of compensation (Saarni & Harris, 1991). The deaf children in our study more often reported sadness than their hearing peers, who more often reported anger. Children's explanations for their choices indeed reflected these different action tendencies. In case of sadness, a typical answer for a deaf child was "She wants to play with her toy, but it is broken," whereas typical explanations by hearing children for an angry response were focused on the aggressor: "The other child has to say sorry," or "The other child should ask her mother to buy her friend a new one."

These results were in line with our expectations that deaf children would feel less able to negotiate and feel more helpless than their hearing peers, and consequently that deaf children more often would report sadness than their hearing counterparts. When generalizing these findings to the larger and more heterogeneous group of DHH children, this suggests that DHH children seem to be aware of their position in their social environment and adapt their (emotional) behavior accordingly. In other words, the results of this study emphasize that an emotion is the outcome of an appraisal process, based on an evaluation in which one strategically opts for one action tendency over another, with the aim of achieving the best outcome.

In addition to these results, Rieffe and colleagues (2003) found that hearing children more often reported both emotions, anger and sadness, occurring simultaneously than their deaf peers. Emotion-evoking situations can indeed elicit more than one emotion. One can have different desired goals in mind, and different emotions reflect the different action tendencies aimed at these different goals. The ability to identify various emotions within one emotion-evoking situation therefore implies a more thorough and detailed understanding of the goals and action tendencies involved. A limited capacity to identify multiple emotions in one situation was confirmed with another group of deaf children in a follow-up study (Rieffe, 2012). When the multiple emotions were both negative, deaf children again more often identified only one negative emotion compared to hearing children, who more often reported two or more negative emotions.

In sum, the outcomes of studies that examine children's capacity for emotion awareness suggest that DHH children can identify their own emotions; they know what they feel and when to the same extent as their hearing peers. Nevertheless, their ability for emotion awareness seems less thorough. Possibly, DHH children stop their appraisal process once they have identified one possible aspect causing them to feel what they feel. Alternatively, DHH children might make a more global appraisal of the emotion-evoking situation, such as "bad," instead of the more specific emotions like "angry" or "jealous." Either way, this might negatively reflect on their capacity for emotion regulation, which is the second important capacity within the domain of emotional competence.

Emotion Regulation

So, emotions have a function: They make us aware that something important is going on, focus our attention, and motivate us to act to improve our (social) world. That would imply that we should just "live up to" our emotions and that we should just act them out as we feel them. Some emotional responses are so quick and automatized that they are indeed beyond control, which is good, because they help us to survive (Levenson, 1999). It is not wise to first observe the situation, come to the decision that this really is a huge truck coming toward you, look again, and then decide to get out of its way as quickly as possible. There are many instances where it is much better to first react and think afterward (perhaps it was only a shadow), but better to be safe than sorry. Yet, there are also situations where it will be much better to control either the expression of emotions or the intensity with which they are felt. Especially when we talk about emotions in a social context, as is the focus of this chapter, it is much more difficult to find examples of situations where it would be good or justified to act upon the first impulse, the so-called *primary appraisal*. You might think that the person approaching you is holding a knife, but maybe it is just a shadow. The court cases that follow these acts of "self-defense" are closely watched in the media and often cause heated public debates.

Most studies on emotion regulation are focused on emotions with a negative valence (anger, sadness, jealousy, guilt), all implying something you do not want. These are more often the ones that need to be regulated compared with ones with a positive valence, such as happiness, pride, or joy. If the other person involved would do exactly what we wanted or had expected, we would not have these negative emotions. So, obviously, we have here a conflict of interest or a conflict of perspective, but either way, there is a tension between two parties. Automatically, more than one objective comes into play, and this usually involves an idiosyncratic objective ("I want my promotion at work" or "I want to be first to pick a car to play with") in conflict with a socially oriented objective ("I want to stay on good terms with my manager" or "I want to stay friends with the other boys"). Fully expressing one's emotions based on an idiosyncratic objective might harm the relationship, and thus one needs to find a balance between these various objectives with their different emotions and accompanying action tendencies. Consequently, the initial feelings based on the idiosyncratic objective should not be acted out with the intensity felt at that moment if one wants to keep the relationship intact. Young infants have not yet mastered the skills necessary to control these initial levels of arousal, but children's emotion socialization starts very early in life and can already be observed in toddlers. Parental input is an important factor here, teaching the child to calm down or, even better, to avoid the stressful stimulus when the level of arousal is running too high (Gottman, Katz, & Hooven, 1996).

Emotion regulation skills are commonly studied in infants and toddlers with the so-called closed box paradigm, designed to frustrate or upset the child (Calkins, Smith, Gill, & Johnson, 1998). In this task, the child, in the presence of the mother, can play for only a very short period of time with an attractive toy. The experimenter then takes back the toy and locks it away in a box in front of the child. Observers rate the extent to which the child expresses a negative emotion and to which the child can distract or divert his or her attention to something else. We applied this paradigm in a slightly altered form to young deaf children with CIs (Wiefferink, Rieffe, Ketelaar, & Frijns, 2012). In that study, we examined children's capacity to control negative feelings that were evoked when they could not open a bottle with a safety lock containing a small gift. The outcomes showed that children with CIs were less able than the hearing control group to calm themselves by diverting their attention away from the negative stimulus.

Other indices for emotion regulation also pointed to a more difficult development in this respect for the CI group than the hearing children. The toddlers with CIs in this study were also rated higher on negative emotionality by their parents, indicating more negative affect in these children on a day-to-day basis. In another task, children were shown pictures of stressful events, such as a boy in a dark forest, a boy in front of a scary dog, or a child pulling the main character's clothes. Children were asked what kinds of emotion regulation strategies they could think of—how the boy in the story could become happy again. Relevant answers, such as "when the dog leaves" were all focused on solving the situation. Yet, this task relies heavily on children's verbal abilities, and it might not come as a surprise that the children with CIs fell behind their hearing peers again. Only 12% of the children with CIs, compared to 45% of the hearing control group, were able to formulate an adequate response (Wiefferink et al., 2013).

An impaired capacity for emotion regulation in the DHH population also has been observed in late childhood on a similar task. In a study with young deaf teenagers (mean age 12 years old), the participants were read (or signed) various peer conflict situations and asked how angry or sad they would feel, what they could do to feel less angry/sad, and how angry/sad they would feel then. The teenagers could rate the intensity of their feelings on a 5-point scale, from "not at all" to "very much" (Rieffe, 2012). Although the initial levels of arousal did not differ between the deaf and hearing group, deaf participants came up with fewer strategies for emotion regulation; consequently, their levels of arousal decreased less over time than for their hearing peers.

The capacity for emotion regulation is obviously something that society asks for. It is a clear case of social learning, because others will tell you, for example, to reduce your anger or to control yourself. A toddler throwing a temper tantrum is not a pleasant experience for parents or other caregivers but is acceptable because "it fits the age." Yet, a teenager doing the same is socially unacceptable and will be condemned by others. Emotions thus can be expressed, but in culturally or socially acceptable ways, especially the negative emotions. So why is it that DHH children do not seem to have accomplished this capacity for emotion regulation as well as hearing children? This is especially striking because uncontrolled emotion expression will harm rather than help their relationships. For example, children who express their negative emotions more bluntly are less popular with their peers or have less stable friendships (Dougherty, 2006; Spinrad et al., 2004).

A first possible explanation for the discrepancy between DHH and hearing children in expressing emotions is an inability for emotion regulation, for example due to oversensitivity or lower cognitive abilities. Children with ASD are often noted for their oversensitivity and overarousal. As a preventive strategy, children with ASD seem to avoid or withdraw from social situations that might evoke negative emotions (Pouw, Rieffe, Stockmann, & Gadow, 2013). Yet, as far as we know, the DHH children in the studies mentioned above had cognitive levels equal to their hearing peers, and there were no signs pointing to oversensitivity or other neurological causes. A second possibility is that DHH children have less understanding of how emotions are used in our daily conversations and how they are shape our daily social interaction. In other words, perhaps DHH children have fewer insights into the function of emotion communication: Why learn something that does not seem that important?

Emotion Communication

There are many arguments about why DHH people are expected to have an impaired understanding of the function and form of emotion communication. Emotion communication can take various forms. Emotions can be communicated through facial expression, intonation, one's posture, the content of speech, the tone in which it is said, or a combination of these. It will be obvious that DHH children miss the vocal information from others. This can apply to misunderstanding the tone or the so-called affective speech prosody (Hopyan-Misakyan, Gordon, Dennis, & Papsin, 2009; Nakata, Trehub, & Kanda, 2012; Volkova, Trehub, Schellenberg, Papsin, & Gordon, 2013) but also in combination with the content. Sarcasm and irony, for example, will be very difficult to get—not only to understand in others, but also to express and use to influence the course of a conversation. How often do you hear DHH people explain to a hearing conversation partner: "I was not serious, I made a joke," because they did not see the hearing person laugh at the right moment? So instead of the tone in which something is said, DHH children will have to rely more on visual cues and the content of the message.

The ability to recognize facial expression has recently been examined by Wiefferink and colleagues (2013). A nonverbal task was used in which children were asked to sort cards into one or the other category. This card sorting was first trained with cards showing either a car and a flower. Young toddlers with CIs in this study performed equally well as their hearing peers. It was hypothesized that the CI and hearing children would perform equally well on the facial emotion sorting task to follow the flower and car task, or possibly the CI children were expected to outperform the hearing group in recognizing faces and facial expressions because they might be more focused than hearing children on visual cues. Yet, the opposite was true: The hearing children were better in sorting faces than their CI peers in this study, despite the fact that language was not involved in this task. This finding is consistent with various recent studies indicating that DHH children have difficulties identifying facial emotion expressions (e.g., Ambert-Dahan, Giraud, Sterkers, & Samson, 2011; Ludlow, Heaton, Rosset, Hills, & Deruelle, 2010; Wang, Su, Fang, & Zhou, 2011).

However, this outcome should not come as a surprise. Some time ago, the (hearing) first author of this chapter was reading a book on cats with her (hearing) son. The book showed four facial expressions cats can present to signal others what they want. Narrowing the eyes, ears flat on the head, bared teeth was one of them. We understood what this behavior meant, but only because we had read the text explaining the faces. In other words, facial expressions have to be interpreted; understanding them does not come automatically. We need a social context, providing exposure and feedback, in which they are taught and trained. This relies on incidental learning. For example, in the Netherlands, the name "Bokito" became a phenomenon because a Dutch woman who regularly visited the zoo where Bokito, an alpha-male gorilla, lives misinterpreted his bared teeth for a smile. In fact, bared teeth are a dominance display for gorillas. The woman went a few times a week to visit Bokito and smiled at him, thinking that she was bonding with him, because Bokito smiled back. But one day, Bokito displayed his dominance in another way than just showing his teeth, jumping over the canal separating the gorillas from visitors, attacking the woman, and hurting several other people as well. Similarly, DHH children often are at a disadvantage in understanding emotions solely from facial expressions, because the input they receive from their environment teaching them how to interpret them will be less frequent and also less sophisticated than for hearing children.

So, assuming that DHH children have less understanding and are less skilled at reading emotions correctly in others, what could this mean for their own emotion expression? In hearing toddlers, we can observe how they already use their emotion expression in their contact with the mother. For example, Buss and Kiel (2004) used the locked box paradigm and other frustrating or fear-evoking situations while toddlers were sitting on their mothers' laps. The researchers videotaped and coded the looks of the toddlers in response to the stressful event before, during, and after they looked at their mothers. Many of these two-year-old participants showed a basic understanding of emotion communication, because they intensified their sadness when they looked at their mother, which suggests that they were expecting more support from their mothers when looking sadder.

In comparison to sadness, anger is a more complicated emotion to express. Anger expression intends to set one's limits and show one's disapproval with the other person, in order to change the other person's behavior in the desired direction (Rieffe & Meerum Terwogt, 2006). Anger can evoke anger and is thus easily responded to with anger. It is important that one can deal with the anger of the other person and still try to affect the other person's behavior as originally desired. The fact that toddlers in the study by Buss and Kiel (2004) intensified their sadness when looking at their mother suggests that even children this young already know from experience that it is better to show sadness, rather than anger, to evoke the mother's sympathy and support.

We have not yet adapted this paradigm to young children with CIs, but we did carry out a study on young deaf teenagers (mean age twelve years) and examined how and why they would communicate anger in a peer conflict situation (Rieffe & Meerum Terwogt, 2006). Children were given (either in Dutch or in Sign Supported Dutch) peer conflict situations designed to evoke so-called justified anger. In other words, the vignettes were designed in a way that adults would understand why the child would become angry. For example, "Imagine you are dressed up for a party, and on the way there your friend shakes a can of Coke and opens it in a way that it all sprays over you. Even your hair is soaked with Coke." Children were asked if they would feel angry, how strongly (on a 5-point scale starting with "not at all"), what they would say or do, what the friend would say or do in return, and if they met the next day on the schoolyard, whether they would play with him or her.

The outcomes showed that children in both groups reported equal levels of anger intensity, suggesting they both were equally angered by these vignettes. Both expressed their anger toward their friend, but hearing teenagers more often also explained why they were angry, focusing the friend on the negative consequences of their actions for them. Consequently, the hearing teenagers also expected more empathic reactions from their friend than the deaf group. These reactions contained apologies, or attempts to restore the relationship ("I will help you to clean up"). In both groups, boys more often reacted angrily, without explaining ("You are stupid, look what you did"). When asked what they thought the friend would say in return, these kinds of responses also more often led to similar responses ("You are stupid yourself"). But most strikingly, the deaf group was less realistic in their expectations concerning the continuation of this friendship. For example, a hearing boy who simply reacted angrily and also expected a negative response also thought that he would not play with this child again. But when asked what would happen the next day, deaf children more often expected the friendship to continue, despite the course of the discussion after the cola incident.

Expressing emotions can be seen as like playing tennis, albeit not with the intention to win: You hit the ball, and you expect the ball to be played back into your court. The game is to anticipate this: where to hit, and what to expect back—in other words, how to play. It seems as if DHH children perceive emotion communication more as a way of sending out information, but without considering the fact that this information does something with the other person, changes his or her ideas, feelings, and thoughts, and thus that the other person will also react, not just act, but indeed "re-act." This observation is supported by their impaired understanding of display rules (Hosie et al., 2000), knowing when to show an appropriate emotion and knowing when to hide anger, fear, or happiness. This impaired understanding of the interactive aspect of emotion communication has its roots in the frequently noted delays in Theory of Mind (ToM) in the DHH population, in which delay is already present in two-year-olds with CIs (Ketelaar, Rieffe, Wiefferink, & Frijns, 2012). Having less attention for and understanding of others' thoughts and feelings also undermines children's basic capacity for empathy (see Wiefferink et al., Chapter 20 in this volume).

CONSEQUENCES FOR DEAF AND HARD-OF-HEARING CHILDREN'S SOCIAL FUNCTIONING

Although it might be alarming to note the impairments in DHH children's emotional competence that have been described in this chapter so far, the key question is how these impairments affect children's mental health and their social lives. Does poor emotion regulation have the same impact on DHH children's friendships or level of depression as in hearing children (Wright, Banerjee, Hoek, Rieffe, & Novin, 2010)? Or are these relationships different?

Problems in DHH children's social lives are frequently reported and are well known to professionals and parents. Especially their contact with peers, either hearing or deaf, goes less smoothly. DHH children are less popular within the group (Wolters, Knoors, Cillessen, & Verhoeven, 2011); they report more loneliness (Schorr, 2006); and although they do not report that they are more often bullied than their hearing peers (Kouwenberg, Rieffe, Theunissen, & De Rooij, 2012a), there are also signs that they feel more frequently neglected or ignored by their peers (Nunes, Pretzlik, & Olsson, 2001). Having friends, even just one good friend, is a strong protective factor in children's development. Unfortunately, the quality of DHH children's friendships seems also to be affected by their limited opportunity for emotion socialization. DHH friends report more rivalry, jealousy, and anger in their friendship compared to hearing friends, who report more support and sharing good times together (Kouwenberg, 2013). This is very unfortunate indeed because good friends offer a safe place to express oneself freely, share one's inner thoughts and worries, and find support that can strengthen the child's self-esteem while also increasing his or her repertoire for different emotion regulation strategies.

It is unclear to what extent impairments in emotion identification, regulation, and communication can explain these social problems in the DHH group. Researchers have just begun to unravel these patterns for this particular group. Obviously, many underlying factors (e.g., the capacity for adaptive emotion regulation) will work equally for all children, deaf or hearing. For example, higher levels of negative emotions are related to more victimization. Especially anger is a good emotion for bullies, because they need their victim to be easily agitated or unbalanced (Camodeca, Goossens, Terwogt, & Schuengel, 2002). Victims of bullying also show more sadness. This sadness can be the result, but it can also be the trigger for the bully and his or her helpers to pick exactly this child (Spence, De Young, Toon, & Bond, 2009). Yet, these patterns between negative emotions and peer relationships are not unique to either group: They can be observed in hearing and DHH children alike (Kouwenberg, 2013).

Poor emotion competence is related to more social problems in hearing children, and again this also has been confirmed for DHH children. Wiefferink and colleagues (2012) showed that toddlers, hearing or with CIs, who showed more negative emotions on a day-to-day basis also had more behavioral problems. Another study asked DHH and hearing teenagers whether they had been aggressive toward peers lately. Children in both groups who reported more aggression also reported more negative friendships later on (Kouwenberg, 2013). Nevertheless, the reason for this relationship could be different for hearing or DHH children. For example, reactive aggression or negative emotion expressions in DHH children could be related to a less-than-complete understanding of social rules for emotion communication. Future studies could look more closely into the exact basis for this relationship between negative emotionality and behavioral problems. The expression of negative emotions in the DHH children could also be related to a less profound understanding of the strategies or social rules for emotion communication. Future studies could look more closely into the exact basis for this relationship between negative emotionality and behavioral problems.

Happy children are rated more positively by their peers; they are more often invited to play dates and birthday parties, and other children like to play with them (Denham et al., 2003). It does not need much elaboration to understand that most people, including children, are more attracted to a happy person to hang out with than to one with many problems and worries, of which negative emotionality can be an indication. Also, someone who is easily angered or upset, for example while playing a game, is less fun to play with. There is no reason to assume this would be different for the DHH population. To date, only one study has looked at the effect of positive emotions on DHH children's social competence (Wiefferink et al., 2012). And indeed, hearing toddlers who showed more happiness were also perceived as more socially competent. Yet, the outcomes failed to show this for the CI group. The capacity to solve a problem and change a negative emotion into a positive one, or decrease the impact of the negative emotion, was also related to better social competence, but again only in the hearing group of toddlers. Although future studies should examine the absence of an effect of positive emotion expression on CI children's social competence, we speculate that the use of positive emotions in daily communication might require more than just the expression. Perhaps the child should also know when and how to express this to improve the quality of the relationship, and this might be more challenging for children with CI.

Note that these studies are the first in this area, and these outcomes are only indicative of the way in which emotional competence affects the development of DHH children's social functioning. Based on these outcomes, the picture emerges that risk factors such as impairments in emotion regulation and emotion communication work the same way in DHH and hearing children. Negative emotions are related to more social problems in all children. However, the role of protective factors, such as positive emotions and adaptive emotion regulation skills, seems more helpful for hearing children, improving the quality of their social development. In other words, emotions can be a hindrance in their social lives for all children, but when used adaptively, emotions seem to be more beneficial for hearing than DHH children. Future studies should examine this into more detail.

CONSEQUENCES FOR DEAF AND HARD-OF-HEARING CHILDREN'S MENTAL HEALTH

The mental health problems in DHH children are well documented (see overview in Hintermair, Chapter 13 in this volume; Theunissen et al., 2014b). Impaired emotion identification and regulation are both strong contributors to the development of all kinds of internalizing symptoms (depression, anxiety, and somatization) in the general population (Rieffe & De Rooij, 2012). Problems with emotion identification prevent a thorough analysis of the emotion-evoking situation and the elements in the situation that should be dealt with. Consequently, the negative emotion lingers or does not sufficiently decrease in intensity. Impaired emotion regulation skills also prevent a sufficient decrease of the arousal level. It is assumed that emotions that are not adequately dealt with but linger become detached from the original emotion-evoking situation. Moreover, this heightened level of arousal can cause long-lasting hormonal and other physiological changes that can put the individual at risk for these internalizing symptoms (Stewart, Mazurka, Bond, Wynne-Edwards, & Harkness, 2013). Again, there is no reason to assume that this would be different for the DHH population. The few studies that looked into this confirm that lower emotion identification and negative emotionality contribute equally to more symptoms of depression and somatic complaints in both groups (Kouwenberg et al., 2011; Theunissen et al., 2011). In the study by Kouwenberg and colleagues (2011), the protective role of happiness was stronger in the hearing group. The role of poor emotion communication in the development of internalizing symptoms has not yet been studied, and this could be a focus for future studies.

INDIVIDUAL DIFFERENCES IN THE DEAF AND HARD-OF-HEARING POPULATION

In this chapter, we have not disentangled the extent to which language impairments and a limited opportunity for incidental learning (which involves more than language development, but for example also understanding nonverbal cues and the implicit rules for adaptive emotion communication) are influential factors underlying this impaired emotional competence. Nor have we distinguished between children with CIs or hearing aids, or in different types of school; nor have we taken into account degree of hearing loss, socioeconomic status, or cognitive abilities. Further, since the start of early intervention programs, hearing losses are being detected earlier, and therefore the effect of rehabilitation programs and family support becomes increasingly important. All these factors might cause important individual differences within the DHH group. Instead, we described the DHH population as a more or less homogeneous population, which by no means reflects the complexity and variability within this group.

One important factor that needs attention is the dichotomy of hearing aid versus CI. Studies comparing these two groups either find no difference (Kouwenberg, Rieffe, Theunissen, & Oosterveld, 2012b; Kouwenberg et al., 2011; Theunissen et al., 2011) or find an advantage of children with CI over children with a hearing aid (Theunissen et al., 2012; Theunissen et al., 2014a). Children with CIs are doing increasingly well, but even in young implanted children, we still find impairments compared to their hearing peers as soon as the tasks measure abilities for which language skills are (indirectly) needed (Ketelaar et al., 2012; Wiefferink et al., 2013). This might denote a delay, and these children will catch up, but future studies need to examine more in depth the role of language in the development of emotion socialization.

HOW CAN CAREGIVERS AND PROFESSIONALS FOSTER EMOTION SOCIALIZATION IN DEAF AND HARD-OF-HEARING CHILDREN?

We want to conclude this chapter with suggestions for caregivers and professionals on how to facilitate opportunities for emotion socialization in DHH children. Back to the starting point of this chapter: Emotions shape our social relationships, and in childhood, interactions established with equals (siblings or peers) provide a crucial context for emotion socialization. As children grow up, the ability to play and get on well with others becomes increasingly important. There is a perceived sense of freedom and safety during play that encourages children to achieve and express their competences without fear for failure. Within this safe atmosphere, children can engage in social play activities that push them to explore and expand their emotional capacities. For example, in pretend play children can act out previously experienced real-life situations and use the play situation to learn how to emotionally regulate and deal with these kinds of (stressful) situations (Moore & Russ, 2008). These play situations can involve different perspectives on complex emotional situations and different reaction patterns (Galyer & Evans, 2001). Therefore, pretend play creates an important context for children to gain a better awareness of emotion communication, it deepens children's emotion knowledge, and it provides the opportunity to practice their emotion skills. In other words, social play offers a good opportunity for emotion socialization.

It is important that caregivers and professionals facilitate situations in which DHH children can participate in social play. Playing with peers is more demanding for DHH children. For example, they lack the same level of language and communication skills as their hearing peers (e.g., using abstract meanings), which are essential to sustain pretend play situations (Brown, Prescott, Rickards, & Paterson, 1997). Research with young DHH children showed similar frequencies of initiated interactions as for hearing children, but hearing and DHH children used different initiation strategies. DHH children interrupted more often but rarely succeeded in their mission to start an interaction (Brown, Remine, Prescott, & Rickards, 2000; DeLuzio & Girolametto, 2011; Duncan, 1999). Given the benefits of social play for children's social development and the difficulties DHH children have successfully initiating interactions, it might be important to teach DHH children specific social entry strategies (DeLuzio & Girolametto, 2011) and support the practice of these strategies in small peer groups before moving to larger groups (Timler, Olswang, & Coggins, 2005).

Emotion socialization takes place in large part through incidental learning. Since the opportunities for incidental learning in DHH children are limited compared to their hearing peers, caregivers and professionals could put more emphasis on the various aspects of emotional coaching (acknowledging, labeling, and emphasizing with the child's emotion; discussing different strategies for emotion regulation and dealing with the emotion-evoking situation), which is based on the notion that there are no "right" or "wrong" emotions, but that every emotion first of all reveals what is important to that person (Gottman, 1999). It is particularly important for DHH children to learn how to analyze what they feel and talk about their emotions in a safe and open environment, in which they can freely explore different ways for communicating their emotions. Next, DHH children need to experience how others react to their emotion expressions, and they need to learn how this can change their interactions and eventually their relationships. New developments, such as participatory video in which children are trained into making their own storyboard about a topic that they choose, filming and editing it, and eventually showing it to the intended audience to evoke discussion about the theme in the film, can help to develop awareness of the effect of emotion communication (Rieffe et al., 2014). Combined, we think that these techniques can lay the foundation for a more advanced emotional and social competence in DHH children and adolescents.

REFERENCES

Ambert-Dahan, E., Giraud, A. L., Sterkers, O., & Samson, S. (2011). Impaired dynamic facial emotion recognition in deaf participants. *Perception, 40,* 138–139.

Brown, P. M., Prescott, S. J., Rickards, F. W., & Paterson, M. M. (1997). Communicating about pretend play: a comparison of the utterances of 4-year-old normally hearing and deaf or hard-of-hearing children in an integrated kindergarten. *Volta Review, 99,* 5–17.

Brown, P. M., Remine, M. D., Prescott, S. J., & Rickards, F. W. (2000). Social interactions of preschoolers with and without impaired hearing in integrated kindergarten. *Journal of Early Intervention, 23,* 200–211.

Buss, K. A., & Kiel, E. J. (2004). Comparison of sadness, anger, and fear facial expressions when toddlers look at their mothers. *Child Development, 75,* 1761–1773.

Calkins, S. D., Smith, C. L., Gill, K. L., & Johnson, M. C. (1998). Maternal interactive style across contexts: Relations to emotional, behavioral and physiological regulation during toddlerhood. *Social Development, 7,* 350–369.

Camodeca, M., Goossens, F. A., Terwogt, M. M., & Schuengel, C. (2002). Bullying and victimization among school-age children: Stability and links to proactive and reactive aggression. *Social Development, 11,* 332–345.

DeLuzio, J., & Girolametto, L. (2011). Peer interactions of preschool children with and without hearing loss. *Journal of Speech, Language, and Hearing Research, 54,* 1197–1210.

Denham, S. A., Blair, K. A., DeMulder, E., Levitas, J., Sawyer, K., Auerbach-Major, S., & Queenan, P. (2003). Preschool emotional competence: Pathway to social competence? *Child Development, 74,* 238–256.

Dougherty, L. R. (2006). Children's emotionality and social status: a meta-analytic review. *Social Development, 15,* 394–417.
Duncan, J. (1999). Conversational skills of children with hearing loss and children with normal hearing in an integrated setting. *Volta Review, 101,* 193–212.
Evans, I. M., Galyer, K. T., & Smith, K. J. H. (2001). Children's perceptions of unfair reward and punishment. *Journal of Genetic Psychology, 162,* 212–227.
Frijda, N. H. (1986). *The emotions.* Cambridge: Cambridge University Press.
Galyer, K. T., & Evans, I. M. (2001). Pretend play and the development of emotion regulation in preschool children. *Early Child Development and Care, 166,* 93–108.
Gottman, J. M. (1999). *Hart voor je kind.* Utrecht: Kosmos.
Gottman, J. M., Katz, L. F., & Hooven, C. (1996). Parental meta-emotion philosophy and the emotional life of families: Theoretical models and preliminary data. *Journal of Family Psychology, 10,* 243–268.
Hodges, E. V., Boivin, M., Vitaro, F., & Bukowski, W. M. (1999). The power of friendship: protection against an escalating cycle of peer victimization. *Developmental Psychology, 35,* 94.
Hopyan-Misakyan, T. M., Gordon, K. A., Dennis, M., & Papsin, B. C. (2009). Recognition of affective speech prosody and facial affect in deaf children with unilateral right cochlear implants. *Child Neuropsychology, 15,* 136–146.
Hosie, J. A., Russell, P. A., Gray, C. D., Scott, C., Hunter, N., Banks, J. S., & Macaulay, M. C. (2000). Knowledge of display rules in prelingually deaf and hearing children. *Journal of Child Psychology and Psychiatry and Allied Disciplines, 41,* 389–398.
Ketelaar, L., Rieffe, C., Wiefferink, C. H., & Frijns, J. H. M. (2012). Does hearing lead to understanding? Theory of Mind in toddlers and preschoolers with cochlear implants. *Journal of Pediatric Psychology, 37,* 1041–1050.
Koester, L. S., & Lahti-Harper, E. (2010). Mother-infant hearing status and intuitive parenting behaviors during the first 18 months. *American Annals of the Deaf, 155,* 5–18.
Kouwenberg, M. (2013). *Social-emotional factors underlying internalizing problems and peer relations in deaf or hard of hearing youth* (unpublished doctoral dissertation). Leiden University, Leiden.
Kouwenberg, M., Rieffe, C., & Theunissen, S. C. P. M. (2011). Intrapersonal and interpersonal factors related to self-reported symptoms of depression in DHH youth. *International Journal of Mental Health and Deafness, 1,* 46–57.
Kouwenberg, M., Rieffe, C., Theunissen, S. C., & De Rooij, M. (2012a). Peer victimization experienced by children and adolescents who are deaf or hard of hearing. *PLoS One, 7,* e52174.
Kouwenberg, M., Rieffe, C., Theunissen, S. C., & Oosterveld, P. (2012b). Pathways underlying somatic complaints in children and adolescents who are deaf or hard of hearing. *Journal of Deaf Studies and Deaf Education, 17,* 319–332.
Levenson, R. W. (1999). The intrapersonal functions of emotion. *Cognition & Emotion, 13,* 481–504.
Ludlow, A., Heaton, P., Rosset, D., Hills, P., & Deruelle, C. (2010). Emotion recognition in children with profound and severe deafness: Do they have a deficit in perceptual processing? *Journal of Clinical and Experimental Neuropsychology, 32,* 923–928.

Moore, M., & Russ, S. W. (2008). Follow-up of a pretend play intervention: Effects on play, creativity, and emotional processes in children. *Creativity Research Journal, 20*, 427–436.

Nakata, T., Trehub, S. E., & Kanda, Y. (2012). Effect of cochlear implants on children's perception and production of speech prosody. *Journal of the Acoustic Society of America, 131*, 1307–1314.

Nunes, T., Pretzlik, U., & Olsson, J. (2001). Deaf children's social relationships in mainstream schools. *Deafness and Education International, 3*, 123–136.

Pouw, L. B. C., Rieffe, C., Stockmann, L., & Gadow, K. D. (2013). The link between emotion regulation, social functioning, and depression in boys with ASD. *Research in Autism Spectrum Disorders, 7*, 549–556.

Rieffe, C. (2012). Awareness and regulation of emotions in deaf children. *British Journal of Developmental Psychology, 30*, 477–492.

Rieffe, C., & De Rooij, M. (2012). The longitudinal relationship between emotion awareness and internalising symptoms during late childhood. *European Child & Adolescent Psychiatry, 21*, 349–356.

Rieffe, C., & Meerum Terwogt, M. (2006). Anger communication in deaf children. *Cognition & Emotion, 20*, 1261–1273.

Rieffe, C., Meerum Terwogt, M., & Kotronopoulou, K. (2007). Awareness of single and multiple emotions in high-functioning children with autism. *Journal of Autism and Developmental Disorders, 37*, 455–465.

Rieffe, C., Meerum Terwogt, M., & Smit, C. (2003). Deaf children on the causes of emotions. *Educational psychology, 23*, 159–168.

Rieffe, C., Oosterveld, P., Miers, A. C., Meerum Terwogt, M., & Ly, V. (2008). Emotion awareness and internalising symptoms in children and adolescents: The Emotion Awareness Questionnaire revised. *Personality and Individual Differences, 45*, 756–761.

Rieffe, C., Pieper, I., van den Bedem, N., Wolthuis, K., de Vries, M., & Uilenburg, N. (2014). Kijk mij nou. *Van Horen Zeggen, 55*, 10–18.

Rieffe, C., Terwogt, M. M., & Bosch, J. D. (2004). Emotion understanding in children with frequent somatic complaints. *European Journal of Developmental Psychology, 1*, 31–47.

Saarni, C., & Harris, P. L. (1991). *Children's understanding of emotion*. Cambridge: Cambridge University Press.

Schorr, E. A. (2006). Early cochlear implant experience and emotional functioning during childhood: Loneliness in middle and late childhood. *Volta Review, 106*, 365–379.

Spence, S. H., De Young, A., Toon, C., & Bond, S. (2009). Longitudinal examination of the associations between emotional dysregulation, coping responses to peer provocation, and victimisation in children. *Australian Journal of Psychology, 61*, 145–155.

Spinrad, T. L., Eisenberg, N., Harris, E., Hanish, L., Fabes, R. A., Kupanoff, K., . . . & Holmes, J. (2004). The relation of children's everyday nonsocial peer play behavior to their emotionality, regulation, and social functioning. *Developmental Psychology, 40*, 67–80.

Stewart, J. G., Mazurka, R., Bond, L., Wynne-Edwards, K. E., & Harkness, K. L. (2013). Rumination and impaired cortisol recovery following a social stressor in adolescent depression. *Journal of Abnormal Child Psychology, 41*, 1015–1026.

Theunissen, S. C. P. M., Rieffe, C., Kouwenberg, M., De Raeve, L., Soede, W., Briaire, J. J., & Frijns, J. H. (2012). Anxiety in children with hearing aids or cochlear implants compared to normally hearing controls. *Laryngoscope, 122*, 654–659.

Theunissen, S. C. P. M., Rieffe, C., Kouwenberg, M., De Raeve, L., Soede, W., Briaire, J. J., & Frijns, J. H. M.(2014a). Behavioral problems in school-aged hearing-impaired children: the influence of sociodemographic, linguistic, and medical factors. *European Child & Adolescent Psychiatry, 4*, 187–196.

Theunissen, S. C. P. M., Rieffe, C., Kouwenberg, M., Soede, W., Briaire, J. J., & Frijns, J. H. (2011). Depression in hearing-impaired children. *International Journal of Pediatric Otorhinolaryngology, 75*, 1313–1317.

Theunissen, S. C. P. M., Rieffe, C., Netten, A. P., Briaire, J. J., Soede, W., Schoones, J. W., & Frijns, J. H. (2014b). Psychopathology and its risk and protective factors in hearing-impaired children and adolescents: A systematic review. *JAMA Pediatrics, 168*, 170–177.

Timler, G. R., Olswang, L. B., & Coggins, T. E. (2005). *Social communication interventions for preschoolers: Targeting peer interactions during peer group entry and cooperative play.* Paper presented at the Seminars in Speech and Language.

Vaccari, C., & Marschark, M. (1997). Communication between parents and deaf children: Implications for social-emotional development. *Journal of Child Psychology and Psychiatry, 38*, 793–801.

Volkova, A., Trehub, S. E., Schellenberg, E. G., Papsin, B. C., & Gordon, K. A. (2013). Children with bilateral cochlear implants identify emotion in speech and music. *Cochlear Implants Int, 14*, 80–91.

Wang, Y. F., Su, Y. J., Fang, P., & Zhou, Q. X. (2011). Facial expression recognition: Can preschoolers with cochlear implants and hearing aids catch it? *Research in Developmental Disabilities, 32*, 2583–2588.

Wiefferink, C. H., Rieffe, C., Ketelaar, L., De Raeve, L., & Frijns, J. H. M. (2013). Emotion understanding in deaf children with a cochlear implant. *Journal of Deaf Studies and Deaf Education*, 175–186.

Wiefferink, C. H., Rieffe, C., Ketelaar, L., & Frijns, J. H. M. (2012). Predicting social functioning in children with a cochlear implant and in normal-hearing children: The role of emotion regulation. *International Journal of Pediatric Otorhinolaryngology, 76*, 883–889.

Wolters, N., Knoors, H. E. T., Cillessen, A. H. N., & Verhoeven, L. (2011). Predicting acceptance and popularity in early adolescence as a function of hearing status, gender, and educational setting. *Research in Developmental Disabilities, 32*, 2553–2565.

Wright, M., Banerjee, R., Hoek, W., Rieffe, C., & Novin, S. (2010). Depression and social anxiety in children: Differential links with coping strategies. *Journal of Abnormal Child Psychology, 38*, 405–419.

17

Social Relations, Mental Health, and Deaf Learners

Approaches to Intervention

Johannes Fellinger and Daniel Holzinger

INTRODUCTION

Mental health in the sense of mental well-being is often understood as the absence of mental illness. Recent definitions, however, are based on a two-continua model of mental health and mental illness as related but distinct phenomena (Westerhof & Keyes, 2010). According to this concept a person with a psychiatric disorder can still be in the state of positive mental health in the sense of well-being and meaning in life.

Mental health is defined by the World Health Organization (WHO) as "a state of well-being in which the individual realizes his or her abilities, can cope with the normal stresses of life, can work productively and fruitfully, and is able to make a contribution to his or her community" (WHO, 2005, p. 2). This definition of mental health was historically included in Aristotle's concept of *eudaimonia*, in which not happiness but the realization of one's own potentials was considered to be the essential element of a good life (Waterman, 1993). Similarly, recent research on well-being distinguishes between hedonic well-being (happiness, life satisfaction, and interest in life) and eudaimonic well-being (Keyes, Shmotkin, & Ryff, 2002; Ryan & Deci, 2001; Waterman, 1993; Westerhof & Keyes, 2010).

In her conceptual and empirical work, Ryff (1989; Ryff & Keyes, 1995) includes six elements in her definition of psychological well-being (Westerhof & Keyes, 2010) that guide our efforts to promote mental health in people who are deaf and hard of hearing (DHH):

1. Self-acceptance: a positive and acceptant attitude toward aspects of self in past and present;
2. Purpose in life: goals and beliefs that affirm a sense of direction and meaning in life;
3. Autonomy: self-direction as guided by one's own socially accepted internal standards;

4. Positive relations with others: having satisfying personal relationships in which empathy and intimacy are expressed;
5. Environmental mastery: the capability to manage the complex environment according to one's own needs; and
6. Personal growth: the insight into one's own potential for self-development.

While this definition of mental well-being emphasizes a person and his or her strengths, typical definitions of mental illness refer to conditions that negatively affect cognition, emotion, and behavior. Symptoms of various mental illnesses are categorized according to several patterns of pathology as groups of diagnoses with degrees of severity from subsyndromal states or nonspecific psychological distress to serious and disabling mental illnesses.

Emphasizing individual strengths and maintaining a positive, strengths-based approach to address mental health problems and disorders is the mission of our interventions, which will be described later (Keyes, 1998). As suggested by the WHO (2002), we follow the three overlapping approaches to prevention of mental health disorders:

- Primary prevention aims at improving the mental health of the population at large and promotes positive mental health.
- Secondary prevention refers to interventions of early recognition and effective management of mental health problems and disorders.
- Tertiary prevention includes interventions that reduce disability and all forms of rehabilitation.

MENTAL HEALTH PROBLEMS IN DEAF CHILDREN

Numerous studies of different populations of DHH children show an 1.5 to 2 times elevated rate of internalizing and externalizing mental health problems compared to hearing peers (Dammeyer, 2009; Fellinger, Holzinger, Beitel, & Goldberg, 2009b; Fellinger, Holzinger, Sattel, Laucht, & Goldberg, 2009a; Hindley, 2000; Van Gent, Goedhart, Hindley, & Treffers, 2007; Stevenson et al., 2011). Psychiatric interviews reveal particularly high rates of depression among deaf children (Van Gent et al., 2007). Among a representative sample of children with a hearing loss greater than 40 dB and a mean age of 11 years, 26% had experienced at least one depressive episode in their lifetime (Fellinger et al., 2009a). A recent Dutch study examined self-reports of students with a mean age of 11 years and found higher rates of depressive symptoms in deaf children compared to hearing peers (Theunissen et al., 2011).

Most recent studies use the Strengths and Difficulties Questionnaire (SDQ) as a research instrument to identify the degree of overall mental health problems as well as subcategories of emotional symptoms, behavior problems, hyperactivity, peer problems, conduct problems, and prosocial behavior (Goodman, Meltzer, & Bailey, 1998).

High levels of peer relationship problems are perhaps the most common findings worldwide (Dammeyer, 2009; Fellinger, Holzinger, Sattel, & Laucht, 2008; Hintermair, 2007; Stevenson et al., 2011).

Various factors were found to be associated with higher levels of mental health problems. Several studies report lower levels of internalizing and externalizing symptoms in children with better language abilities independent of language modality (Barker et al., 2009; Dammeyer, 2009; Percy-Smith et al., 2008; Polat, 2003; Sinkkonen, 1994; Stevenson, McCann, Watkin, Worsfold, & Kennedy, 2010; Theunissen et al., 2012, 2014; van Eldik, Treffers, Veerman, & Verhulst, 2004).

The quality of the language and communicative environment of the family is a crucial variable affecting the mental health of DHH children; a study from Austria helps to illustrate this point. DHH children who cannot make themselves understood in the family are four times more likely to be affected by mental health disorders than those from families who communicate successfully. These children are also more likely to be victims of maltreatment at school (Fellinger et al., 2009a). Peer problems found in teenagers in Upper Austria were associated with the level of language used in conversation, such that lower levels of language ability were correlated with higher rates of peer problems (Fellinger et al., 2009b). However, in most studies the degree of hearing loss did not correlate with the degree of mental health problems (Dammeyer, 2009; Fellinger et al., 2008; Hintermair, 2007; Theunissen et al., 2012).

Additional neurodevelopmental problems that occur in about a quarter of DHH children (Gallaudet Research Institute, 2008; van Naarden, Decouflé, & Caldwell, 1999) increase the risk for psychopathology (Bond, 2000; Dammeyer, 2009; Hartshorne, Grialou, & Parker, 2005; Polat, 2003). Results from a Danish study revealed that deaf children with additional neurodevelopmental complications had a three times greater prevalence of psychosocial difficulties than other DHH children (Dammeyer, 2009). In terms of assistive hearing technologies, studies have not found clear correlations between type of hearing device and level of psychopathology; however, favorable mental health outcomes for children with cochlear implantation are reported (Sahli, Arslan, & Belgin, 2009; Theunissen et al., 2012).

Educational placement seems to be associated with the occurrence of mental health problems. DHH students in special education settings have more psychosocial difficulties (Keilmann, Limerger, & Mann, 2007; Kouwenberg, Rieffe, Theunissen, & Oosterveld, 2012; Van Gent et al., 2007). However, the choice of school setting might be affected by the child's characteristics (Fellinger et al., 2009b).

In addition to these factors, various sociodemographic factors contribute to the quality of life, mental health, and academic achievement of DHH children, each in a unique and individual way as described by Knoors and Marshark (2014, Chapter 7) in their chapter on learning and social and emotional development.

Before describing four approaches to fostering positive mental health and the treatment of mental health problems in DHH children, we will offer a background discussion of deaf education in Upper Austria and Salzburg as well as the clinical department involved.

EDUCATION OF DEAF OR HARD-OF-HEARING CHILDREN IN UPPER AUSTRIA AND SALZBURG

Upper Austria, one of nine Austrian provinces, has a current population of about 1.4 million inhabitants (Fig. 17.1). All schoolchildren with a hearing loss are registered for public school at the Center for Special Education for Children with Sensory Impairments. This center is based in Linz, the capital of Upper Austria, and employs four itinerant teachers who serve all 246 children who have assistive hearing devices. These DHH children are mainstreamed either as a single student with special needs or together with other children with different kinds of disabilities. The itinerant teachers give information to the local teachers about the use of assistive technology, how to make adaptions to the classroom, and how to prepare teaching materials.

Ninety-three DHH children are enrolled in the special school setting at the center. This school offers two primary approaches to education. One approach is to teach mainly profoundly deaf children using sign language as the primary mode of instruction. In this case, class sizes are small (five to nine students). In addition, there are two specialized classes for children with additional disabilities. Children with spoken German as their preferred language are mainstreamed in classes with

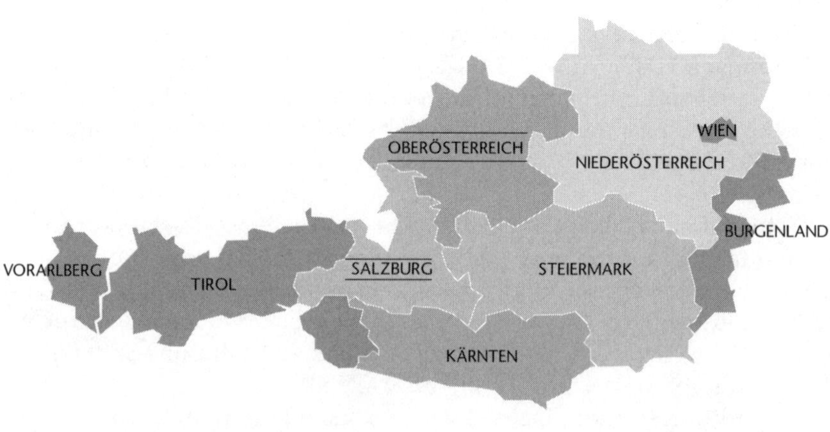

Figure 17.1 The provinces of Austria.

three to five DHH children together with children with normal hearing and without any disabilities from neighboring parts of the city at the special school center in Linz. In this case, two teachers work together simultaneously to educate both the deaf and hearing children. At the same location, another organization provides care for those who stay overnight in two residential living groups. In addition, this organization also runs the kindergarten and provides vocational training and occupational placement for adolescents.

Since 2003, therapists from various disciplines, including psychology, speech language therapy, and occupational therapy, as well as a deaf assistant for mental health promotion work at that same location (Fig. 17.2). They are employed by and members of the team of Institut fuer Sinnes- und Sprachneurologie, which is a clinical department of the Hospital of St. John of God in Linz. With respect to the importance of developing a healthy deaf identity, the role of having deaf people in responsible leadership positions cannot be overestimated. With the presence of a deaf professional in the school for the deaf, the Deaf community is represented and teachers, therapists, and parents can gain a deeper understanding of deafness and of being deaf. Furthermore, sign language skills of students and of team members are enhanced.

In the province of Salzburg with 532,000 inhabitants, the Center for Deaf Education comprises a home-based early intervention program, a preschool for DHH children in a mainstreamed setting, a school for grades one to nine, and apprenticeship trainings.

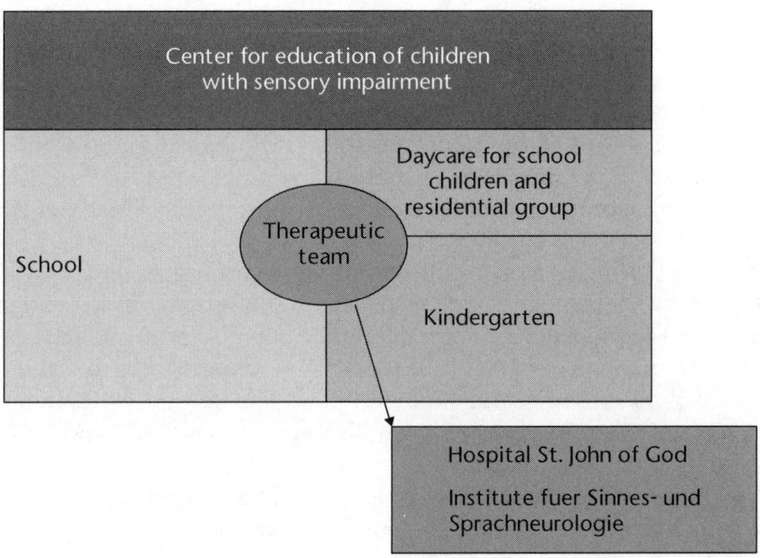

Figure 17.2 Organizational structure of stakeholders involved in the education of deaf children in Linz.

Currently, about 60 DHH students, a group of 60 with normal hearing similar to Linz's reversed mainstreaming. and a group of about 20 with auditory processing or severe speech-language disorders are enrolled at the special school. In almost all classes there is an equal distribution of children with hearing loss and with normal hearing. DHH children with severe learning disabilities are taught in segregated settings. In addition, there are two special classes for profoundly deaf children with sign language used as language of instruction. Usually there are two teachers present in all the classes for most of the time.

Salzburg's therapeutic team of the Institut fuer Sinnes- und Sprachneurologie comprises a psychologist, a speech-language therapist, an occupational therapist, and a deaf professional who serves as a role model and sign language teacher. The team collaborates closely on a regular basis with a psychotherapist, who specializes in working with students with hearing loss. These therapeutic services have been available for about the past seven years.

The therapeutic teams in Linz and Salzburg work independently from the educational system as far as team affiliation is concerned. Their contributions to mental health will be described further in the following section after a short introduction to the clinical Institut fuer Sinnes- und Sprachneurologie they belong to.

THE INSTITUT FUER SINNES- UND SPRACHNEUROLOGIE

The Institut fuer Sinnes- und Sprachneurologie serves DHH people and people with disorders of communication and language, including autism (Fellinger & Holzinger, 2014) (Fig. 17.3). Multidisciplinary teams provide comprehensive assessments that cover developmental domains such as cognitive, psychosocial, physical health, and language and communication. In addition, audiological assessments are included. The assessments focus not only on the individual's developmental profile, but also on the resources found within his or her social network.

At the institute, two major intervention programs focusing on young children and their families are used. The first is a home-based program called the Family-Centered Linz Intervention Program, which serves the whole province of Upper Austria with respect to early intervention for DHH children and their families. The second program, Linz Intervention Autism, focuses on children with autism and follows the Early Start Denver Model Curriculum. This is the first time a German-speaking country has implemented the curriculum.

The institute is also responsible for the Health Center for Deaf People, which offers direct access to health care, mental health care, and social services by staff members who are able to communicate directly with the patients in sign language and can also adapt their mode and speed

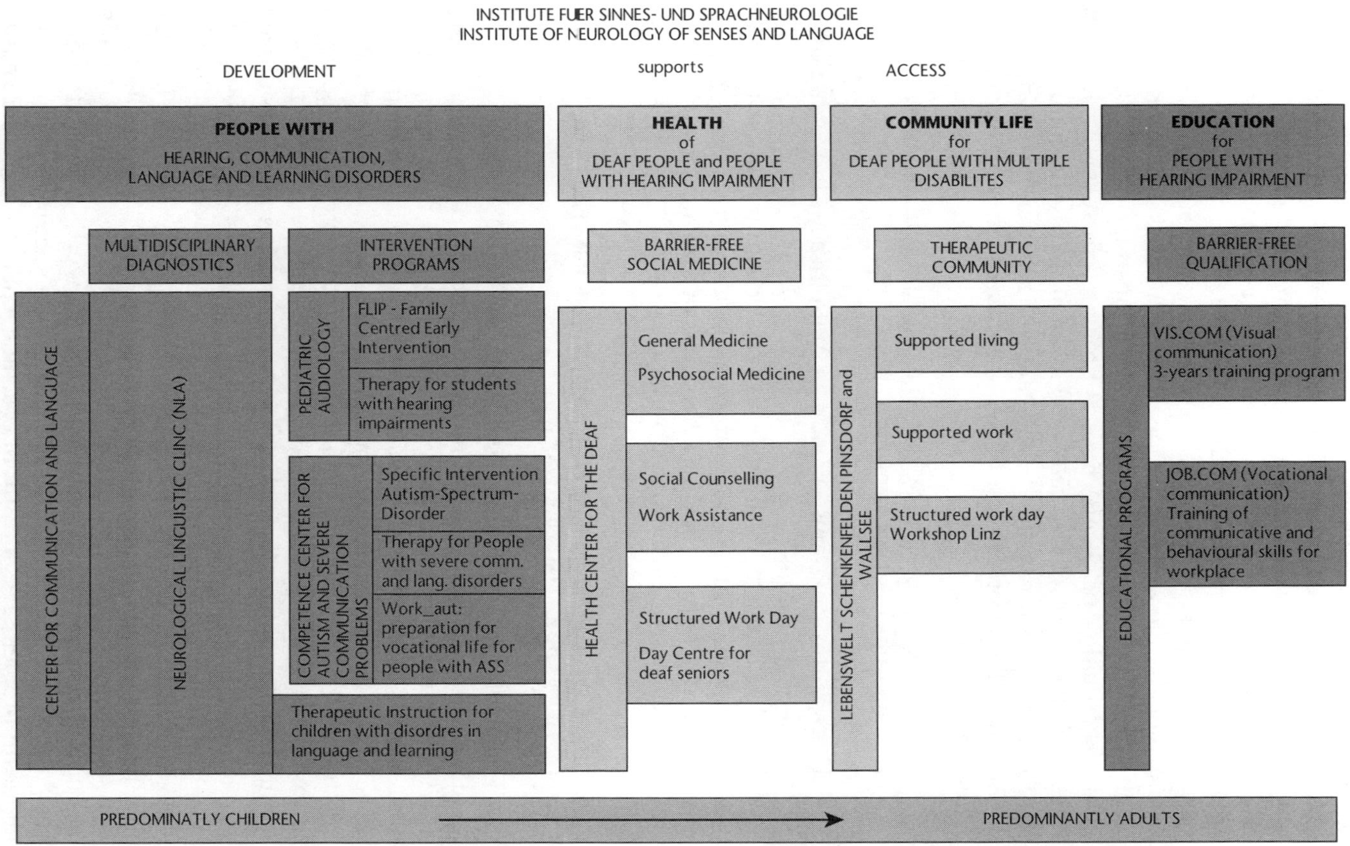

Figure 17.3 Working fields of the Institut fuer Sinnes- und Sprachneurologie.

of communication to the level the patient needs (Fellinger, Holzinger, Schobesberger, & Lenz, 2005).

Residential facilities, where DHH people with multiple disabilities live together in therapeutic communities, are also provided by the institute, as well as a three-year training program for DHH persons to become professionals in the psychosocial field.

All staff members, regardless of their specific professional background, collaborate to meet the mental health needs and improve the quality of life of the individuals and the groups they serve within the teams. The quality of clients' lives is promoted in several important ways. Like the DNA of any cell in the human body, our guiding values and principles for mental health care embedded in the practices at the institute. These principles, which are embedded in all our efforts, include the following:

- Mental health care is provided in a transdisciplinary way.
- Therapeutic interventions are based on multidisciplinary assessments.
- Therapeutic programs encourage self-efficacy and enhance social relationships.
- The development of abilities in social communication is an overarching approach toward mental health.
- Professionals must be specialized in both mental health care and deafness in order to treat clinical cases.

PRINCIPLES OF MENTAL HEALTH CARE OF THE INSTITUT FUER SINNES- UND SPRACHNEUROLOGIE

Mental Health Care Is Provided in a Transdisciplinary Way

Mental health and quality of life are central outcome dimensions of any intervention and therefore are approached not only by mental health professionals but by all staff members in an transdisciplinary way (King et al., 2009). Especially in the field of communication disorders as covered by the Institute fuer Sinnes- und Sprachneurologie, high rates of comorbidity with mental health problems can be observed. These mental health problems become obvious in assessment sessions as well as during therapeutic programs offered, for instance, by specialists in language and communication. Instead of sending the patient to a psychologist who should "fix" the mental health problem, the language therapist is coached by mental health professionals within the team. This coaching process with respect to mental health issues is actually an ongoing teaching process in mental health work for all staff members and widens their awareness of and competence to deal with mental health problems. As a result of coaching, children with more easily treated, common mental health problems don't have to be sent to a mental health professional. In this way, the likelihood that the child is stigmatized by others can be reduced, given that issues of mental health are still negatively stereotyped in our cultural context.

However, when the mental health problem is more serious, having a positive, trusting relationship with the professional who is not a specialist in mental health can support the client's willingness to seek special mental health care according to the predecisional phase in the Rubicon model. This model of action phases refers to Roman history, where Caesar committed himself, after a long period of doubt, to cross the river Rubicon and to take the full risk (Achtzinger & Gorlowitzer, 2007; Grawe, 2000; Heckhausen & Heckhausen, 2006). Therefore, the trusting and constant relationship can be used as a bridge for becoming willing to accept professional psychological support in the field of mental health.

Mental Health Interventions Are Guided by the Individual's Needs and Are Based on Multidimensional Assessments

In our work, we frequently observe how inadequately the language comprehension level, intellectual abilities, or social networks of DHH people are understood; as a result of this, we see that others' expectations about the abilities of DHH people need adjustment. Therefore, regular assessments with a strong inclusion of parents, teachers, and the deaf student himself or herself are planned at developmental milestones such as kindergarten entrance, school entrance, transition from primary school to secondary school, and transition into work and further education. This service is available for all DHH children regardless of whether they are enrolled in mainstream or special school settings.

Mental Health Interventions Stimulate Self-Efficacy

Self-efficacy means the belief of individuals about their abilities to control their own lives. More specifically, it "refers to beliefs in one's capabilities to organize and execute the courses of action required to manage prospective situations" (Bandura, 1995, p. 2). This definition includes not only aspects of identity, self-worth, and self-determination, but also the growth of skills in how to manage personal stress situations. Efficacy beliefs are enhanced by four primary sources (Bandura, 1996; O'Leary, 1985): mastery experience, vicarious experience or modeling, verbal persuasion, and physiological states. Most importantly, successfully dealing with challenges and difficult situations helps a person to believe that he or she can deal with similar situations in the future and to believe that he or she has control over his or her environment. Observing and working together with other children who are going through similar developmental tasks and observing a deaf teaching assistant as a role model who has already mastered those tasks strengthen students' self-efficacy. Findings from Berkman and Glass (2000) on the mediating role of self-efficacy between social integration and quality of life in general population samples were shown to be valid as well in a sample of elderly DHH people (Gerich & Fellinger, 2011).

Mental Health Interventions Focus on Social Relationships

A wealth of previous research has shown that social proximity and interaction promote health and longevity (Beals, Peplau, & Gable, 2009; Cohen & Janicki-Deverts, 2009; Gallagher & Vella-Brodick, 2008; Holt-Lunstad, Smith, & Layton, 2010; Simpson, Rholes, Campbell, Tran, & Wilson, 2003). The Social Baseline Theory suggests that the human brain is designed to assume that it is embedded within a relatively predictable social network characterized by familiarity, joint attention, shared goals, and interdependence (Beckes & Coan, 2011; Coan, Schaefer, & Davidson, 2006). Neuroscientific investigations of social support show that the presence of other people helps individuals to conserve important somatic and neural resources through the social regulation of emotion.

Various studies show that DHH children are at higher risk of lacking satisfying peer relationships (Batten, Oakes, & Alexander, 2013; Knoors & Marschark, 2014; Wauters & Knoors, 2007; Wolters, Knoors, Cillessen, & Verhoeven, 2011). Therefore, improving social relations in DHH children is a central element of all interventions provided by the Institut fuer Sinnes- und Sprachneurologie over the lifespan, starting in infancy with a family-centered approach in early intervention programs and ending with programs for Deaf people in our geriatric center.

Developing Abilities in Social Communication Supports Mental Health

Efforts to strengthen communicative abilities are the main approach in our attempt to improve mental health. Interdisciplinary practice and research over the past two decades has increased our understanding of the relationship among language, cognitive, and social development of DHH children. Language delays are often associated with difficulties in pragmatics, the use of language in social contexts. For children with hearing loss, pragmatics was found to be an area of particular challenge. Research demonstrated that for DHH children, difficulties using language in natural conversations were usually much greater than any delays in linguistic knowledge, such as vocabulary or morphosyntactic skills (Goberis et al., 2012). The relationship between difficulties in social communication and psychosocial problems such as social isolation, anxiety, and low self-esteem persisting into adulthood was found to be highly significant. Whitehouse and colleagues (2009) compared adult psychosocial outcomes of individuals with a history of specific language impairment, pragmatic language impairment, or autism spectrum disorder. The results showed deficits in establishing social relations in all of the three groups, but most prominent in the autistic spectrum disorder group and in the pragmatic language impairment group (more prominent than in the specific language impairment group). Van Agt (2011) conducted a study on the impact of different types of language disorders on psychosocial development and health-related quality of life, in which 4,745 parents and 4,771 teachers of eight-year-old children completed a questionnaire. Eight and a half percent of the parents stated that their child had some form of language impairment. Interestingly, the children with pragmatic language impairment (and those with autism spectrum disorder) turned out to have the lowest levels of health-related quality of life at the age of eight years. Fellinger and colleagues (2009a) studied a group of DHH children, examining the relationship between linguistic competence and psychosocial functioning. The results showed that peer problems at school were associated mainly with low levels in conversation skills, not with low linguistic competence per se. Taken together, this research proves that there are significant associations between pragmatic (conversational) language skills and mental health.

There is some empirical evidence that training of social communication skills results in an improved quality of life. Dahlberg and colleagues (2007) investigated 52 individuals with traumatic brain injury participating in a treatment efficacy study. The participants received 12 weeks of training in social communication. Quality of life was measured before the intervention started, immediately after the intervention, and three, six, and nine months after the intervention with the Satisfaction With Life Scale (Diener, Emmons, Larsen, & Griffin, 1985). A significant improvement of quality of life was maintained until nine months after the intervention had ended.

As a consequence of the previous research, the Institut fuer Sinnes- und Sprachneurologie has started to emphasize the importance of social communication in its assessment procedures, intervention planning, therapeutic activities, and counseling of parents as well as school and kindergarten teachers. Communication assessments refer not only to the language levels achieved in the different domains (expressive and receptive semantic and grammatical competence) but also to the scope of communicative functions expressed by a student, such as requiring information, expressing personal opinions, explaining, arguing for something, or narrative skills. In addition, conversational skills (e.g., turn-taking, initiating conversations, joining conversations of peers, use of repair strategies in case of communication breakdowns), individual styles of interaction (e.g., passive, interested and reactive, dominating) and communication contexts (communication partners, situations, topics, and special interests), all of which can be used to enhance social communication skills, are taken into account.

Social communication intervention is regarded as a primary responsibility of all members of the multidisciplinary team. Speech-language therapists might focus more on direct work on language skills and the development of pragmatics (e.g., active listening skills, clarifications, turn-taking, topic management, and matching communication styles to the context) in one-to-one and small group situations by illustrating good and bad examples in role plays. Psychologists may be more involved in the development of social understanding (e.g., understanding emotions, stated and nonstated social information, social flexibility, and problem-solving or friendship skills) in individual and (more usual) group settings. Occupational therapists try to use the vehicles of practical problem-solving activities for cognitive interactions. Siraj-Blatchford and colleagues (2002) have described this approach as "sustained shared thinking" (p. 10). In the "Effective Pedagogy in the Early Years Project," the authors focused on verbal parent–child interactions and their impact on the children's learning. It was concluded that sustained shared thinking—that is, the process of cognitive and verbal co-construction (creative thinking aloud between adults and children)—extends the learning mechanisms of children. In our own approach, interventionists are engaged to support children's learning by offering verbal explanations about what they or the children are doing while working on a specific task. The same approach can be used when discussing feelings, thus supporting the children's recognition, processing, and discussion of their own emotions.

All of the therapists are trained in language facilitation strategies (e.g., responsiveness, expansions, corrective feedback, open questions) that enhance the students' active participation in conversation and their linguistic and pragmatic language skills. Decontextualization skills help the student to go beyond the direct experience and include his or her personal perspective by reflecting past experiences, thinking about the future, abstract thinking, or nonreal contents (fantasy).

In summary, as a consequence of the strong relationship between pragmatic language and mental health outcomes, social communication intervention is a key factor in mental health interventions for children with hearing loss. Individual therapy sessions in various disciplines and in multidisciplinary group settings, school-based programs, and parent counseling from a very early age can all work toward this objective (Fig. 17.4).

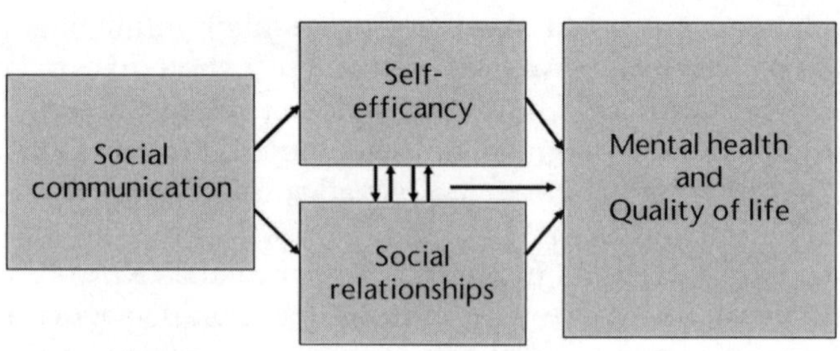

Figure 17.4 Models of contributors to mental health.

SPECIFIC PROGRAMS OF MENTAL HEALTH PROMOTION

This section resembles more a visit to a craftsman's workshop rather than to an exhibition hall, where perfect products are displayed. Interventions focus on the development of inner strengths and well-being (primary prevention) as well as on prevention of mental health problems (secondary prevention) and the treatment of mental health disorders (tertiary prevention). So in this craftsman's workshop quite a number of pieces are unfinished, perhaps even just starting to be developed, whereas others are in use but still awaiting evaluation. However, with this section an ongoing discussion can be stimulated, and practitioners are encouraged to proceed in developing practical support, including systematic evaluation.

Primary Prevention

Interdisciplinary Development Plan

For children enrolled in primary school, interdisciplinary meetings of parents, teachers, and therapists are organized twice a year. During these sessions parents, educators, and teachers are asked substantial questions focusing on the child's communicative skills in different settings (family, kindergarten/school/daycare, and out-of-school context). This semistructured questionnaire was developed by the Institut fuer Sinnes- und Sprachneurologie for clinical use and comprises questions like "Can your child initiate a dialogue?", "How does the child react if he/she doesn't understand?", and "How does the child communicate with peers?" Parents are asked about their current concerns and goals for their child pertaining to academic learning as well as social-emotional development, behavior, communication, self-care, or any other dimension of development. Starting with the child's strengths, major objectives for the school year are formulated and roles and responsibilities are allocated to teachers, therapists, and parents. Using this approach, the focus on mental health has increased significantly. Preventive aspects of socioemotional health are now considered regularly. Family communication, self-esteem, self-efficacy, and identity are some of the topics frequently discussed in these meetings. This approach is greatly appreciated by the families, as evidenced when a parent who had limited contact with the school shows an increase in involvement, participation, and responsibility for the support of the child's development.

The PATHS Curriculum

The PATHS curriculum is well known as an evidence-based program that promotes social competence and emotional development in DHH students (Greenberg, 2000; Greenberg & Kusche, 1993). The program is grounded in a theory of development of social cognitive understanding that influences behavior. It is planned as a multiyear curriculum mainly for DHH students between six and 12 years of age. Children are taught by their teachers how to develop and maintain self-control, how to identify their own and other people's feelings, and how to solve problems and conflicts. The program was introduced to the teachers in Linz and Salzburg in 2011 by our therapeutic teams and a training course was held. Unfortunately we were not able to get both special schools for DHH children completely involved, mainly due to restrictions in the educational system. In Linz only a few teachers committed themselves to use of the curriculum. In Salzburg teachers of six classes decided to use PATHS on a regular and ongoing basis. Institut fuer Sinnes- und Sprachneurologie therapists who had undergone PATHS training modified some procedures and materials to set up the program for the teachers who are willing to use it. In addition to the classroom-based implementation for students with hearing loss and with normal hearing in the social learning interventions, the psychologist and deaf assistant offer extra group interventions for students who struggle to master PATHS principles as well as for those with more pronounced social or emotional difficulties. This combination turned out to be effective for the students, according to reports from teachers and parents and observations by the therapists. As we are quite successful in implementing PATHS elements in all groups of the special kindergarten for DHH children, we still hope that PATHS will become implemented in all classes of the special schools as well and will eventually become an integral element of teaching deaf learners, and even one day will be acknowledged by the educational authorities.

Summer Camps

At our institute, there is a long tradition of organizing summer camps for children and adolescents with hearing loss. The camps are organized by a deaf staff member who is supported by clinical therapists, the local organization of the deaf, and the parents' organization. Children with hearing loss and children of Deaf adults who attend schools for the deaf or regular schools spend a week in different attractive surroundings during their summer vacation. An adventure program with enough space for informal exchange and play activities is offered. Local Deaf representatives are invited one day of the week to provide children with the opportunity to meet successful deaf adults and to learn about Deaf culture. These interactions foster discussions on identity and self-worth of the participants. For many DHH children the summer camp has become an annual event they look forward to and greatly enjoy. Most of the former participants who have become young adults report that their summer camp experiences were essential for their lifelong development of friendships, self-esteem, and identity.

Secondary Prevention

Screening

School-based screenings help to identify children who are considered to be at high risk. So far, children whose parents had asked for one or more therapeutic interventions from the clinical staff (80% speech-language, 10% psychology, 50% occupational therapy) were screened for mental health problems using the SDQ. The respective therapists (speech-language, occupational, psychology) used the results to adjust their treatment plan. The parents were informed in a sensitive way about the results and invited for further assessments.

In autumn 2014 a paradigmatic shift will take place in Linz. The educational authorities have agreed that all schoolteachers will fill out the screening questionnaires themselves and will then invite all the parents at the regular parent conference day to respond to the questions of the SDQ. The questionnaires will be evaluated by the psychologists, who also will give feedback to parents of children whose scores are in the abnormal range.

Kindergarten children (aged three to six) are screened using the VBV (Verhaltensbeurteilungsbogen fuer Vorschulkinder), a behavior questionnaire for preschool children (Doepfner, Berner, Fleischmann, & Schmidt, 1993), filled in by parents and educators. This instrument provides information about social-emotional competences, oppositional and aggressive behavior, attention problems, hyperactivity, and duration of play.

Psychoeducational Support for Teachers and Educators

By request, the members of the therapeutic staff provide teaching sessions on various important topics such as prevention of bullying or sexual harassment. Teachers and educators also feel free to approach the clinical psychologist to discuss psychosocial problems they observe in their classes. If necessary and wanted, they are coached by the psychologist in dealing with these problems.

Tertiary Prevention

Management of Mental Health Disorders

As previously mentioned, easy accessibility to professional mental health care is one of the primary objectives of the clinical staff based at the school for the deaf. This requires high levels of sign language skills and other visual techniques such as drawing comics that may support adequate communication (Caby & Caby, 2011; Mills & Crowley, 1996).

Another primary role of clinical psychologists is clinical case management. They are supported by the medical staff of the institute. The first author, a trained neurologist and psychiatrist, visits the special school for the deaf once a month or when necessary for case consultation.

The treatment of children with mental health needs is complex; there are various ways in which clinical experts become involved in treatment. At the beginning of the school year parents can request language, occupational, or psychological therapy for the children, which is provided by the clinical team at the school. Most parents apply for language therapy; fewer request psychological therapy. However, during the school year behavior and emotional problems become more evident, warranting behavioral observation by the psychologists, who stay in the classroom or day center and observe the students. Behavioral observations can be done only if the parents give written consent that information can be shared among teachers, educators, and clinical staff. Almost all parents appreciate this service. Language and occupational therapists introduce those children with pronounced mental health problems to the psychologists, as mentioned before. If the consultations between the different disciplines lead to the conclusion that specific therapeutic psychological or medical interventions are necessary, the parents are invited to give their consent and to agree to be involved if necessary. Sometimes children themselves approach the psychologists and ask for specific help. Regular therapeutic sessions are planned, and the treatment goals are clearly defined and evaluated together with parents and involved partners.

Individual Therapy Settings

Treatment has been provided for a wide range of mental health disorders that occur in childhood and adolescence. We have found that the school environment is an appropriate ecosystem to provide psychological therapy, especially when considering treatment effectiveness (Zirkelback & Reese, 2010). Teacher involvement has proven to be effective, although involving teachers is not always easy to put into practice (Calear & Christensen, 2010). We have not yet systematically evaluated the impact of the inclusion of a clinical team at the school, but we can report on how this service functions and on the feedback we have received from parents, teachers, and patients.

We most frequently observe emotional and disruptive behavior problems, including inattention and hyperactivity. As far as the psychological interventions are concerned, a mixed-method approach is used by the psychologists, who are able to adapt to the special needs of the DHH patient. In particular, elements of dialectical behavior therapy are frequently used with respect to the development of emotional regulation skills and stress management (mindfulness) (Glickman, 2009). The psychologists are fluent in sign language and can use different ways of visualizations and role-play techniques. When working with children with limited sign language skills and rather idiosyncratic signing, the deaf staff members are called on to facilitate communication. Individual therapeutic sessions are supported by additional group therapies. In some cases group therapeutic approaches are the first choice.

Case Vignette
A 14-year-old girl approached the psychologist and disclosed that she was being sexually harassed by her classmates. Intervention started with a discussion of possible courses of action (including informing her teacher and parents) with the girl and helping her prepare for these conversations by role playing. Therapy sessions then focused on the topic of "my body and I" and setting boundaries (see Dietzel, 2004, for further material on the prevention of sexual abuse in the field of DHH). A course of action for dealing with the situation in class was discussed with the teacher, including awareness training and confrontation of abusive classmates and their parents. Fortunately, the intervention brought an end to the abusive situation.

Multidisciplinary Group Therapies

Group therapy, in addition to individual counseling, gives students the chance to express themselves in a manageable and safe social setting, where the group process itself is the most important aspect of therapy (Oaklander, 2013; Rahm, 2004). The key element in group therapy is social learning through the observation of others, as proposed by Bandura (Bandura, 1977; Bandura, Grusec, & Menlove, 1966). Observing others is essential for the group therapeutic approach and is based on the theoretical concepts of behavioral modification and problem solving (Furman, 2005; Petermann & Petermann, 2005, 2008). Problems do arise when a therapist's attention must be divided among multiple children during a group session, which can incite rivalry or jealousy among the students. When addressed effectively, this envy can also create solidarity and group cohesion because students learn to experience their strengths and abilities, approaching problems in the actual setting they occur (e.g., social interaction). Using conflict resolution interventions helps them to develop new coping strategies and to better understand their actions and feelings. The feeling of being able to help others also promotes self-efficacy (Yalom, 2001).

Various group therapies with slightly different objectives are used to enhance students' social interaction, social communication skills (and social relationships), and self-efficacy. Parents are given information about the concept and objectives of the group therapy to avoid misunderstandings (as some parents may think the group is for gardening or cooking) and to make them aware of the potential for ongoing inclusion of the family and a generalization to family contexts.

In these so-called AT groups ("acting together"), there is a focus on practical everyday group activities (e.g., gardening, shopping, cooking, use of public transport, climbing) that require planning, social communication, and social skills (Borg-Laufs & Hungerige, 2010; Hobday & Ollier, 2001; Karpfhammer & Nachtrab, 2000; Maur-Lambert, Landgraf, & Oehler, 2004). In small groups two therapists from different professional backgrounds (frequently involving the deaf staff member), assign a challenging task or situation in a series of ten sessions of 1.5 hours each to three to five students with hearing loss. They are required to create and discuss ideas and make decisions. The students develop a chronological action plan, distribute roles, and find problem-solving strategies along the way and reflect on their experiences afterward. In the reflection and documentation part, a special emphasis is given to the social aspects of the children's experiences (social peer interaction, interaction with and among therapists, distribution of roles) as well as a discussion on "social rules." Although we observe that this group concept improves social skills (social communication, social strategies, cooperation, awareness of social rules, impulse control, introspection), emotional development (awareness of feelings of oneself and peers, dealing with individual frustrations and weaknesses), and everyday problem solving and independence, we have not been able to fully evaluate the program's effectiveness. However, our DHH students are eager to participate, and parental acceptance for this group intervention has increased.

SUMMARY

The promotion of mental health and quality of life in deaf children within educational settings is crucial for successful life outcomes. However, the educational systems are often not prepared to focus on these dimensions. The model of a group of therapists who are linked to a clinical institute but serve at the locations of special schools for DHH children in Linz and Salzburg shows how DHH children can be fully and holistically supported, and that a systemic focus on mental health can support life outcomes. Programs that are easily accessible strengthen self-efficacy and enhance social relationships by improving social communication skills. In children with clinical dimensions of mental health disorders, the psychologists play a key role in providing treatment within the natural school setting by paying attention not only to the individual but also to the social environment and by using the resources available in a multiprofessional team. Programs to foster satisfying peer relationships for children who are taught in mainstream settings need to be further developed. There is an urgent need not only to promote programs focusing on mental health but also to provide scientific evidence for their efficacy and effectiveness. The vision of a healthy, socially competent DHH child can direct our steps in education, health care, and research.

ACKNOWLEDGMENTS

We want to thank our colleagues who contributed to this book chapter, especially Maria Primetzhofer, Anna Hofstaetter, Peter Holzinger, Stephanie Handstanger, Birgit Stelzer, Paul Fellinger, Sarah Schoffstall, and the Hospital of St. John of God in Linz.

REFERENCES

Achtzinger, A., & Gorlowitzer, P. (2007). Rubicon model of action. In R. Baumeister & K. Vohs (Eds.), *Encyclopedia of social psychology*(vol. 2, pp. 769–770). Thousand Oaks, CA: Sage.

Bandura, A. (1977). *Social learning theory*. Englewood Cliffs, NJ: Prentice-Hall.

Bandura, A. (1995). *Self-efficacy in changing societies*. Cambridge: Cambridge University Press.

Bandura, A. (1996). *Social foundations of thought and action: A social cognitive theory*. Englewood Cliffs, NJ: Prentice Hall.

Bandura, A., Grusec, J., & Menlove, F. (1966). Observational learning as a function of symbolization and incentive set. *Child Development*, *37*(3), 499–506.

Barker, D., Quittner, A., Fink, N., Eisenberg, L., Tobey, E., Niparko, J., & The CDaCI Investigative Team. (2009). Predicting behavior problems in deaf and hearing children: The influences of language, attention, and parent–child communication. *Development and Psychopathology*, *21*(2), 373–392.

Batten, G., Oakes, P., & Alexander, T. (2013). Factors associated with social interactions between deaf children and their hearing peers: A systematic literature review. *Journal of Deaf Studies and Deaf Education*, *19*(3), 285–302.

Beals, K., Peplau, L., & Gable, S. (2009). Stigma management and wellbeing: The role of perceived social support, emotional processing, and suppression. *Personality and Social Psychology Bulletin*, *35*, 867–879.

Beckes, L., & Coan, J. A. (2011). Social Baseline Theory: The role of social proximity in emotion and economy of action. *Social and Personality Psychology Compass*, *5*(12), 976–988.

Berkman, L., & Glass, T. (2000). Social integration, social networks, social support, and health. In L. Berkman, & I. Kawachi (Eds.), *Social epidemiology* (pp. 137–173). New York: Oxford University Press.

Bond, D. E. (2000). Mental health in children who are deaf and have multiple disabilities. In P. Hindley, & N. Kitson (Eds.), *Mental health and deafness* (pp. 127–148). London: Whurr Publishers.

Borg-Laufs, M., & Hungerige, H. (2010). *Selbstmanagementtherapie mit Kindern. Ein Praxishandbuch* (2nd ed.). Stuttgart: Klett-Cotta.

Caby, A., & Caby, F. (2011). *Die kleine psychotherapeutische Schatzkiste: Tipps und Tricks für kleine und große Probleme vom Kindes- bis zum Erwachsenenalter*. Borgmann Media.

Calear, A., & Christensen, H. (2010). Systematic review of school-based prevention and early intervention programs for depression. *Journal of Adolescence*, *33*(3), S. 429–438.

Coan, J., Schaefer, H., & Davidson, R. (2006). Lending a hand: Social regulation of the neural response to threat. *Psychological Science*, *17*(12), 1032–1039.

Cohen, S., & Janicki-Deverts, D. (2009). Can we improve our physical health by altering our social networks? *Perspectives on Psychological Science*, *4*, 375–378.

Dahlberg, C., Cusick, C., Hawley, L., Newman, J., Morey, C., Harrison-Felix, C., & Whiteneck, G. (2007). Treatment efficacy of social communication skills training after traumatic brain injury: a randomized treatment and deferred treatment controlled trial. *Archives of Physical Medicine and Rehabilitation*, *88*(12), 1561–1573.

Dammeyer, J. (2009). Psychosocial development in a Danish population of children with cochlear implants and deaf and hard-of-hearing children. *Journal of Deaf Studies and Deaf Education*, *15*(1), 50–58.

Diener, E., Emmons, R., Larsen, R., & Griffin, S. (1985). The Satisfaction With Life Scale. *Journal of Personality Assessment*, *49*(1), 71–75.

Dietzel, A. (2004). *Gehoerlos—sprachlos—missbraucht?! Eine Untersuchungsreihe für die praeventive Arbeit mit hoergeschaedigten Maedchen und Jungen*. Hamburg: Verlag Dr. Kovac.

Doepfner, M., Berner, W., Fleischmann, T., & Schmidt, M. (1993). *Verhaltensbeurteilungsbogen für Vorschulkinder*. Goettingen: Beltz Test Gesellschaft.

Fellinger, J., & Holzinger, D. (2014). Creating innovative clinical and service models for communication: Institut fuer Sinnes- und Sprachneurologie. *Journal of Developmental and Behavioral Pediatrics*, *35*(2), 148–153.

Fellinger, J., Holzinger, D., Beitel, C., & Goldberg, D. (2009b). The impact of language skills on mental health in teenagers with hearing impairments. *Acta Psychiatrica Scandinavica*, *120*(2), 153–159.

Fellinger, J., Holzinger, D., Sattel, H., & Laucht, M. (2008). Mental health and quality of life in deaf pupils. *European Child & Adolescent Psychiatry*, *17*(7), 414–423.

Fellinger, J., Holzinger, D., Sattel, H., Laucht, M., & Goldberg, D. (2009a). Correlates of mental health disorders among children with hearing impairments. *Developmental Medicine & Child Neurology*, *51*(8), 635–641.

Fellinger, J., Holzinger, D., Schobesberger, R., & Lenz, G. (2005). Psychosocial characteristics of deaf people: evaluation and data from a special oupatient clinic for the deaf. *Nervenarzt*, *76*, 43–51.

Furman, B. (2005). *Ich schaffs! Spielerisch und praktisch Loesungen mit Kindern finden—Das 15-Schritte-Programm für Eltern, Erzieher und Therapeuten*. Heidelberg: Carl-Auer-Systeme Verlag.

Gallagher, E., & Vella-Brodick, D. (2008). Social support and emotional intelligence as predictors of subjective well-being. *Personality and Individual Differences*, *44*, 1551–1561.

Gallaudet Research Institute. (2008). *Regional and national summary report of data from the 2007-08 annual survey of deaf and hard of hearing children and youth*. Washington, DC: GRI, Gaullaudet University.

Gerich, J., & Fellinger, J. (2011). Effects of social networks on the quality of life in an elder and middle-aged deaf community sample. *Journal of Deaf Studies and Deaf Education*, *17*(1), 102–115.

Glickman, N. (2009). *Cognitive-behavioral therapy for deaf and hearing persons with language and learning challenges*. New York: Routledge.

Goberis, D., Beams, D., Dalpes, M., Abrisch, A., Baca, R., & Yoshinaga-Iatno, C. (2012). The missing link in language development. *Seminars in Speech and Language*, *33*(4), 297–309.

Goodman, R., Meltzer, H., & Bailey, V. (1998). The Strengths and Difficulties Questionnaire: a pilot study on the validity of the self-report version. *European Child & Adolescent Psychiatry*, *7*(3), 125–130.

Grawe, K. (2000). *Psychologische Therapie*. Göttingen: Hogrefe Verlag.

Greenberg, M. (2000). Educational interventions: Prevention and promotion of competence. In P. Hindley & N. Kitson (Eds.), *Mental health and deafness* (pp. 311–336). London: Whurr Publishers.

Greenberg, M., & Kusche, C. (1993). *Promoting social and emotional development in deaf children: The PATHS project*. Seattle, WA: University of Washington Press.

Hartshorne, T., Grialou, T., & Parker, K. (2005). Autistic-like behavior in CHARGE syndrome. *American Journal of Medical Genetics. Part A*, *133A*(3), 257–261.

Heckhausen, J., & Heckhausen, H. (2006). Motivation und Handeln: Einführung und Überblick. In J. Heckhausen & H. Heckhausen (Eds.), *Motivation und Handeln* (pp. 1–9). Berlin, Heidelberg: Springer.

Hindley, P. (2000). Child and adolescent psychiatry. In P. Hindley & N. Kitson (Eds.), *Mental health and deafness* (pp. 42–74). London: Whurr Publishers.

Hintermair, M. (2007). Prevalence of socioemotional problems in deaf and hard of hearing children in Germany. *American Annals of the Deaf*, *152*(3), 320–330.

Hobday, A., & Ollier, K. (2001). *Helfende Spiele. Kreative Lebens- und Konfliktberatung von Kindern und Jugendlichen*. Winheim, Basel: Beltz.

Holt-Lunstad, J., Smith, T., & Layton, J. (2010). Social relationships and mortality risk: A meta-analytic review. *PLOS Medicine*, *7*, 1–20.

Karpfhammer, C., & Nachtrab, M. (2000). *Entspannungsspiele für hoergeschaedigte und sprachbehinderte Kinder* (A. Leonhardt, Ed.). Neuwied, Kriftel, Berlin: Luchterhand Verlag.

Keilmann, A., Limerger, A., & Mann, W. (2007). Psychological and physical well-being in hearing-impaired children. *International Journal of Pediatric Otorhinolaryngology*, *71*(11), 1747–1752.

Keyes, C. (1998). Social well-being. *Social Psychology Quarterly*, *61*, 121–140.

Keyes, C., Shmotkin, D., & Ryff, C. (2002). Optimizing well-being: The empirical encounter of two traditions. *Journal of Personality and Social Psychology*, *82*, 1007–1022.

King, G., Strachan, D., Tucker, M., Duwyn, B., Desserud, S., & Shillington, M. (2009). The application of a transdisciplinary model for early intervention services. *Infants & Young Children*, *22*(3), 211–223.

Knoors, H., & Marschark, M. (2014). Learning and social and emotional development. In H. Knoors & M. Marschark (Eds.), *Teaching deaf learners. Psychological and developmental foundations* (pp. 132–158). New York: Oxford University Press.

Kouwenberg, M., Rieffe, C., Theunissen, S., & Oosterveld, P. (2012). Pathways underlying somatic complaints in children and adolescents who are deaf or hard of hearing. *Journal of Deaf Studies and Deaf Education*, *17*(3), 319–332.

Maur-Lambert, S., Landgraf, A., & Oehler, K.-U. (2004). *Gruppentraining für aengstliche und sozial unsichere Kinder und ihre Eltern*. Dortmund: Borgmann.

Mills, J., & Crowley, R. (1996). *Therapeutic metaphors for children and the child within*. New York: Brunner/Mazel.

Oaklander, V. (2013). *Gestalttherapie mit Kindern und Jugendlichen*. Klett-Cotta.

O'Leary, A. (1985). Self-efficacy and health. *Behaviour Research and Therapy*, *23*(4), 437–451.

Percy-Smith, L., Jensen, J., Cayé-Thomasen, P., Thomsen, J., Gudman, M., & Lopez, A. (2008). Factors that affect the social well-being of children with cochlear implants. *Cochlear Implants International*, *9*(4), 199–214.

Petermann, F., & Petermann, U. (2005). *Training mit aggressiven Kindern*. Winheim, Basel: Beltz.

Petermann, F., & Petermann, U. (2008). *Training mit sozial unsicheren Kindern. Einzeltraining, Kindergruppen, Elternberatung*. Weinheim, Basel: Beltz.

Polat, F. (2003). Factors affecting psychosocial adjustment of deaf students. *Journal of Deaf Studies and Deaf Education*, *8*(3), 325–339.

Rahm, D. (2004). *Integrative Gruppentherapie mit Kindern*. Paderborn: Jufermannsche Verlagsbuchhandlung.

Ryan, R., & Deci, E. (2001). On happiness and human potentials: A review of research on hedonistic and eudaimonic well-being. *Annual Review of Psychology*, 52, 141–166.

Ryff, C. (1989). Happiness is everything, or is it? Explorations on the meaning of psychological well-being. *Journal of Personality and Social Psychology*, *57*, 1069–1081.

Ryff, C., & Keyes, C. (1995). The structure of psychological well-being revisited. *Journal of Personality and Social Psychology*, *69*, 719–727.

Sahli, S., Arslan, U., & Belgin, E. (2009). Depressive emotioning in adolescents with cochlear implant and normal hearing. *International Journal of Pediatric Otorhinolarynology*, *73*(12), 1774–1779.

Simpson, J., Rholes, W., Campbell, L., Tran, S., & Wilson, C. (2003). Adult attachment, the transition to parenthood, and depressive symptoms. *Journal of Personality and Social Psychology*, *84*, 1172–1187.

Sinkkonen, J. (1994). Evaluation of mental health problems among Finnish hearing-impaired children. *Psychiatria Fennica*, *25*, 52–65.

Siraj-Blatchford, I., Sylva, K., Muttock, S., Gilden, R., & Bell, D. (2002). *Researching effective pedagogy in the early years. Research report 356*. London: Department for Education and Skills.

Stevenson, J., McCann, D., Law, C., Mullee, M., Petrou, S., Worsfold, S., . . . & Kennedy, C. (2011). The effect of early confirmation of hearing loss on the behaviour in middle childhood of children with bilateral hearing impairment. *Developmental Medicine and Child Neurology*, *53*(3), 269–274.

Stevenson, J., McCann, D., Watkin, P., Worsfold, S., & Kennedy, C. (2010). The relationship between language development and behaviour problems in children with hearing loss. *Journal of Child Psychology and Psychiatry, and Allied Disciplines*, *51*(1), 77–83.

Theunissen, S., Rieffe, C., Kouwenberg, M., De Raeve, L., Soede, W., Briaire, J., & Frijns, J. (2012). Anxiety in children with hearing aids or cochlear implants compared to normally hearing controls. *Laryngoscope*, *122*(3), 654–659.

Theunissen, S., Rieffe, C., Kouwenberg, M., De Raeve, L., Soede, W., Briaire, J., & Frijns, J. (2014). Behavioral problems in school-aged hearing-impaired children: the influence of sociodemographic, linguistic, and medical factors. *European Child & Adolescent Psychiatry*, *23*(4), 187–196.

Theunissen, S., Rieffe, C., Kouwenberg, M., Soede, W., Briaire, J., & Frijns, J. (2011). Depression in hearing-impaired children. *International Journal of Pediatric Otorhinolaryngology*, *75*(10), 1313–1317.

van Agt, H. (2011). *Language disorders in children. Impact and the effects of screening*. Proefschrift (Doctoral Dissertation). Erasmus Universiteit Rotterdam.

van Eldik, T., Treffers, P., Veerman, J., & Verhulst, F. (2004). Mental health problems of deaf Dutch children as indicated by parents' responses to the Child Behavior Checklist. *American Annals of the Deaf, 148*(5), 390–395.

Van Gent, T., Goedhart, A., Hindley, P., & Treffers, P. (2007). Prevalence and correlates of psychopathology in a sample of deaf adolescents. *Journal of Child Psychology and Psychiatry, 48*(9), 950–958.

van Naarden, K. P., Decouflé, P., & Caldwell, K. (1999). Prevalence and characteristics of children with serious hearing impairment in metropolitan Atlanta, 1991–1993. *Pediatrics, 103*(3), 570–575.

Waterman, A. (1993). Two conceptions of happiness: Contrasts of personal expressiveness (eudaimonia) and hedonic enjoyment. *Journal of Personality and Social Psychology, 64*, 678–691.

Wauters, L., & Knoors, H. (2007). Social integration of deaf children in inclusive settings. *Journal of Deaf Studies and Deaf Education, 13*, 21–36.

Westerhof, G., & Keyes, C. (2010). Mental illness and mental health: The two continua model across the lifespan. *Journal of Adult Development, 17*(2), 110–119.

Whitehouse, A., Watt, H., Line, E., & Bishop, D. (2009). Adult psychosocial outcomes of children with specific language impairment, pragmatic language impairment and autism. *International Journal of Language and Communication Disorders, 44*(4), 511–528.

Wolters, N., Knoors, H. E. T., Cillessen, A. H., & Verhoeven, L. (2011). Predicting acceptance and popularity in early adolescence as a function of hearing status, gender, and educational setting. *Research in Developmental Disabilities, 32*(6), 2553–2565.

World Health Organization. (2002). *Prevention and promotion in mental health*. Geneva: WHO.

World Health Organization. (2005). *Promoting mental health: Concepts, emerging evidence, practice*. Geneva: WHO.

Yalom, I. (2001). *Theorie und Praxis der Gruppenpsychotherapie. Ein Lehrbuch*. Stuttgart: Klett-Cotta.

Zirkelback, E., & Reese, R. (2010). A review of psychotherapy outcome research: Considerations for school-based mental health providers. *Psychology in the Schools, 47*(10), S. 1084–1100.

Part 4

Technology for Learning and Development

18

Enhancing Emergent Literacy in Preschool Deaf and Hard-of-Hearing Children Through Interactive Reading

Evelien Dirks and Loes Wauters

Reading has consistently been found to be challenging for many deaf and hard-of-hearing (DHH) students. It is still unclear why these reading difficulties occur and how we can improve the reading levels of our students. In recent decades, with the introduction of universal newborn hearing screening and better and earlier fitting of hearing aids and cochlear implants, more attention has been given to the importance of early intervention in order to improve the development of DHH children (Yoshinago-Itano, 2003). In 1998, the International Reading Association (IRA) and the National Association for the Education of Young Children (NAEYC) of the United States formulated a position statement on early literacy development to provide guidance to parents and teachers of young children from birth to age eight. This statement emphasizes the importance of experiences in the early years to develop children's basic understandings of concepts about print and its functions, the stage of emergent literacy. These experiences can be provided through storybook reading. The focus of this chapter is on interactive reading as an important factor in enhancing emergent literacy skills.

EMERGENT LITERACY

Emergent literacy refers to the concepts, skills, and knowledge that young children have about reading and writing before they start formal reading instruction (Vukelich & Christie, 2009; Whitehurst & Lonigan, 1998). These emergent literacy skills provide the foundation for later literacy and academic development. Storch and Whitehurst (2002) distinguished two components of emergent literacy: oral language skills and code-related skills. Oral language skills include semantic skills (word knowledge, expressive and receptive vocabulary), syntactic skills (knowledge of word order and grammatical rules), conceptual knowledge, and narrative skills. Code-related skills are about the conventions of print (reading from left to right, front to back of a book), beginning forms of writing, letter knowledge, grapheme–phoneme correspondence (understanding the link between sounds and letters), and phonological awareness. The code-related skills conventions of print, forms of print (letter knowledge, word knowledge), and functions of print are often referred to as print knowledge. Both code-related skills and oral language skills are essential to reading and work simultaneously in skilled readers (Storch & Whitehurst, 2002; Whitehurst & Lonigan, 1998).

The stage of emergent literacy starts as early as birth when children start to develop their language and communication skills. Babies immediately begin to "read" the world around them (Barton & Brophy-Herb, 2006). They learn from several kinds of sensory input, such as seeing, hearing, touching, tasting, and feeling. This helps them in understanding the world around them, a necessary precursor of language development. In developing their language, they learn about the complex system of symbols and rules of the language, learn to distinguish different sounds, and relate those to meaning differences. They also increase their vocabularies and develop their communicative skills (Barton & Brophy-Herb, 2006; Roskos, Tabors, & Lenhart, 2009). As children grow older, they develop their print knowledge. They learn about the functions, structure, and rules of written language and about the concepts of print (Vukelich & Christie, 2009). Part of learning about the functions of print is that children learn that print conveys meaning.

Emergent Literacy and Later Reading Skills

In their position statement, the IRA and NAEYC stated that reading and writing acquisition is a developmental continuum rather than an "all-or-nothing phenomenon" (IRA & NAEYC, 1998, p. 3). The notion of emergent literacy thus is based on that idea of a continuum between prereading and reading, where literacy activities in the preschool period are important aspects of literacy development (Storch & Whitehurst, 2002). Experiences in the early years are important precursors for later reading and writing skills and are essential for children's motivation toward learning to read and write. Storch and Whitehurst (2002) described a model to explain how emergent literacy skills in preschool and kindergarten are related to later reading acquisition. This model showed a strong relationship between and within code-related and oral language skills in the preschool years. Oral language skills in earlier grades accounted for a large part (88% to 90%) of the variance in oral language skills in later grades. Code-related skills were measured in preschool and kindergarten: 38% of the variance in kindergarten was explained by the skills in preschool. This shows that early differences between children in emergent literacy skills are relatively stable over time. The model further confirmed results from an earlier model by Whitehurst and Lonigan (1998) as code-related skills in kindergarten were directly related to reading ability in first and second grade. And oral language skills were significantly related to reading comprehension skills in grades 3 and 4. These models show that code-related skills are most important when children start reading and learn to "crack the code," whereas oral language skills seem more important for reading comprehension.

Emergent Literacy in Children with Hearing Loss

In hearing children, language development starts as early as the sixth month in the womb (Barton & Brophy-Herb, 2006). That is when fetuses start to detect noises in the environment, and once they are born they will recognize familiar sounds or voices that they heard often in the womb (DeCasper & Fifer, 1980). Young hearing infants have amazing capacities to hear and learn language. This early development of language is an important precursor of later language and literacy development (Zupan & Dempsey, 2013). This natural way of detecting noise and language is not so obvious for children who are born with hearing loss. They will need more explicit language access to develop their language skills and as a result to acquire emergent literacy skills. Research into precursors of reading skills of children with hearing loss has shown that both code-related and oral language skills are important for their reading acquisition and thus need attention in the emergent literacy period (Easterbrooks, Lederberg, & Connor, 2010; Zupan & Dempsey, 2013). DesJardin and Ambrose (2010) mention that many young DHH children do not have the spoken language skills they need to be ready for kindergarten. When it comes to phonological awareness, huge variability exists among children before they enter school. No data seem to be available for other code-related skills in DHH children.

In her review on emergent literacy in DHH children, Williams (2004) found only a few studies on DHH children's emergent reading and writing skills. Although scarce, these studies pointed out that DHH children can participate in and profit from literacy activities and learn emergent literacy concepts as hearing children do, given that they get sufficient opportunities to do so. However, Webster (2000) mentioned that the lack of a shared language between DHH children and their hearing parents may impede these opportunities. Studies on emergent writing showed that children learned about written language through authentic activities and that social interaction was supportive of the emergent writing development. The emergent writing skills of the young DHH children described in these studies were similar to those of hearing children, which suggests that emergent literacy instruction that supports hearing children's emergent writing may also be appropriate for DHH children.

Gathoo and Kulkarni (2013) studied the emergent literacy skills prior to school in five- and six-year-old children in India with and without hearing loss. They found that children with hearing loss showed a delay in both script-related and non–script-related emergent reading skills. Children with hearing loss performed worse than hearing children on non–script-related activities measuring conceptual skills and phonemic awareness but did not differ on non–script-related reading activities measuring perceptual skills and paired association. They also performed worse on script-related reading activities measuring visual matching, picture–word association, spelling, and comprehension (picture–sentence matching). Unfortunately, a clear description of the measured constructs was not provided, but these results show that even though DHH children should be able to develop their emergent reading skills if they get sufficient opportunities (Williams, 2004) they seem to start formal reading instruction with a delay in both script- and non–script-related skills.

Emergent Literacy and Parent Involvement

Easterbrooks, Lederberg, and Connor (2010) mentioned that one of the critical factors in the development of emergent literacy skills is parent involvement. Children develop language skills and learn about reading and writing mostly from their interactions with adults and other children. A great deal of these interactions happen informally in daily activities, such as storytelling, reading, playing games, drawing, writing (or scribbling), and singing. In these interactions, children develop their code-related and oral language skills, and they learn that there are many ways of expressing their ideas, for example by writing a note to someone or by telling them a story that they have read. Because these interactions are so important, children need the opportunities to engage in these kinds of activities in the home and preschool environment. Factors that are important in creating these opportunities are access to print and books, adult demonstrations of literacy behavior, adults who are supportive of early attempts at literacy (without directly teaching), and storybook reading (Vukelich & Christie, 2009). Parents of children who started to read early reported that their children had an early interest in print and writing (print motivation) and that they often read stories to their children and took time to answer their children's questions about written language. These home experiences seem to be important in promoting early reading (Vukelich & Christie, 2009; Whitehurst & Lonigan, 1998).

Several studies have shown the importance of home literacy activities for children's early reading skills (e.g., Aram, Korat, & Hassunah-Arafat, 2013; Xu, Chin, Reed, & Hutchinson, 2013) and of parent training in promoting children's emergent literacy skills (e.g. Jordan, Snow, & Porche, 2000; Xu et al., 2013). In their review of 16 intervention studies in which parents were trained to improve their children's early reading skills, Sénéchal and Young (2008) found that parent involvement had a positive effect on children's reading acquisition. Whitehurst and Lonigan (1998) suggested that interventions should target both the code-related and the oral language skills (which they called inside-out and outside-in skills) because both are found to be important for later reading success. Interventions that focus on increasing children's experience with picture books (and other literacy materials) and the frequency of their verbal interactions with adults around these materials, such as interactive reading, have their primary effect on the oral language skills of emergent literacy. Interventions focusing on improving phonological processing skills in children have effects on the code-related skills of emergent literacy.

Storch and Whitehurst (2002) claimed that children with minimal interactive reading activities and exposure to print materials in the home environment are likely to have poor oral language skills. According to them, "the strong relationship between preschool oral language and code-related skills and the strong continuity between code-related skills and later reading achievement places children with early deficits at risk for later reading difficulties" (p. 944). Therefore, we must not wait until formal reading instruction to help those who are at risk for reading difficulties.

DesJardin and Ambrose (2010) suggested that DHH children may need additional support in their home environment to obtain the same literacy skills as their hearing counterparts. Therefore, professionals must empower parents to promote their DHH child's emergent literacy skills. Stobbart and Alant (2008) also emphasize the early acquisition of literacy skills in deaf children and the specific role that parents have to play in engaging in meaningful text-based interaction with their children, in a literacy-rich environment with high expectations for literacy development. They claimed that parents need to highly prioritize acquisition of reading and writing skills. Zupan and Dempsey (2013) suggested that to do so, parents and professionals need to be aware of the necessary code-related and oral language skills and need to collaborate to ensure that these skills are maximally targeted.

INTERACTIVE READING

One of the most important activities in the home environment to promote emergent literacy is storybook reading. In this section we describe the effect of storybook reading on literacy skills in both hearing and DHH children. The importance of the quality of storybook reading is also discussed together with reading programs that enhance storybook reading skills in parents.

Storybook reading in young children has been linked to children's later reading performance (Bus, van Ijzendoorn, & Pellegrini, 1995). During storybook reading, a child learns how to handle books and is exposed to new vocabulary and concepts. Adults use more formal language during storybook reading than in other settings (DeTemple & Snow, 2003)—for example, talking about topics beyond the here and now or using vocabulary outside the child's usual daily experiences. Further, storybook reading promotes children's letter identification skills and knowledge of conventions of print. Both the quantity and quality of book reading have been shown to be important for child language outcomes (Aram & Levin, 2002; Bus et al., 1995). The more frequently a child is read to, the better the outcomes.

The quality of storybook reading is just as important. It seems that storybook reading is most effective when a child is actively involved (Mol, Bus, de Jong, & Smeets, 2008). Asking questions about the story, having conversations with the child during storybook reading, and responding actively to a child's initiatives are examples of actively involving the child in storybook reading. Discussing events and characters in the book, asking open-ended questions before and after reading, and linking prior experiences to the story have a beneficial effect on the development of emerging literacy skills in preschool-aged children (Huebner & Meltzoff, 2005). This so-called *interactive reading* requires the adult to read *with* the child instead of reading *to* the child. The book is thus used as a basis for a conversation about the story.

DeBruin-Parecki (2007) defined interactive reading as reading aloud that includes conversation, turn taking, and involving the child in the process. She stated that interactive reading serves multiple purposes—for example, clarifying a child's understandings of a book, familiarizing a child with concepts of print, providing opportunities for letter and sound identification, prompting a child to use new vocabulary words from a book in conversations, and encouraging a child to enjoy reading. Interactive reading proved to be more effective in improving language skills than traditional storybook reading, in which the adult simply reads the story to the child with minimal interaction (Chow, McBride-Chang, Cheung, & Chow, 2008; Huebner, 2000; Mol et al., 2008; Whitehurst & Lonigan, 1998). In the literature different terms are used for describing adult–child storybook reading—for example, shared reading, joint book reading, storybook reading, dialogic reading, and interactive reading. In this chapter the term *interactive reading* will be used when the emphasis is on the interactive aspect during the reading activity; otherwise the term *storybook reading* will be used. In citing other studies, the term from those studies will be used.

Children whose adult reading partners engage them more during reading made greater gains in expressive vocabulary (Sénéchal, 1997;Whitehurst & Lonigan, 1998) and narrative skills (Zevenbergen,

Whitehurst, & Zevenbergen, 2003) and expanded their knowledge about written language (DeBruin-Parecki, 1999).

Given the view that an active role of the child during storybook reading is important, most researchers in this field have adopted a Vygotskian framework in interpreting their results (Aram, Most, & Mayafit, 2006). Vygotsky (1978) stated that human development results from a dynamic interaction between individuals and society. Through this interaction, children learn gradually from parents and teachers. Parents and teachers can foster this learning by supporting a child to achieve just beyond his or her current level of mastery. In the case of interactive reading, this means that children acquire knowledge through the interaction with an adult that would not be acquired if the child read alone (Robertson, Dow, & Hainzinger, 2006).

Interactive reading with young children occurs in different settings (in the home, daycare, and preschool) and with different partners (parents, grandparents, and preschool teachers). Given that parents interact daily with their children and are aware of their interests, it is important to consider how parents can stimulate their child's emergent literacy development. Storybook reading is considered to be a joyful parent–child interaction, and in the preschool years children spend most of their time with their parents. After all, parents are a child's first teacher, and they are uniquely motivated to promote their child's development.

Interactive Reading with Children with Hearing Loss

Only a few studies have investigated the relationship between interactive book reading activities and literacy outcomes in DHH children (Aram et al., 2006; DesJardin, Ambrose, & Eisenberg, 2009; DesJardin & Eisenberg, 2007; DesJardin et al., 2014; Fung et al., 2005). Fung and colleagues (2005) investigated whether dialogic reading was effective in improving the receptive vocabulary in Chinese children (kindergarten to second-graders) with hearing loss. Three groups of children (a control group, a typical storybook reading group, and a dialogic reading group) were compared on a pretest and posttest (after eight weeks) of receptive vocabulary. Parents in the dialogic reading group followed an eight-week training to learn and practice the techniques of dialogic reading. The dialogic reading group showed greater improvement in vocabulary scores compared to the other two groups.

Aram and colleagues (2006) studied mother–child storybook telling as a predictor of early literacy skills in Israeli kindergartners. They found that interactive reading predicted DHH children's phonological awareness, general knowledge, and receptive vocabulary at the end of kindergarten. Similar results were found by DesJardin and colleagues (2009) in their three-year longitudinal study of literacy skills in two- to seven-year-old children with cochlear implants. They found that mothers' early use of facilitative language techniques (open-ended questions) during storybook reading was positively related to children's reading skills. In their 2014 study, DesJardin and colleagues found that parental use of higher-level facilitative language techniques was also related to higher oral language abilities in children with moderate to severe hearing loss. In short, although the evidence is scarce, interactive reading in DHH children seems to have the same beneficial effects on literacy skills as in hearing children. Since parents of hearing children do not use the techniques of interactive reading automatically, we can probably expect the same for parents of DHH children. These parents have even more challenges in communication with their child that influence the storybook reading interaction.

Interactive reading with DHH children challenges parents because of aspects such as positioning, attracting and maintaining the child's attention, and communication. Often parents experience storybook reading as a pleasant interaction with their child, sitting physically close to each other and having joint attention. For parents of DHH children, the positioning of how they will sit together could itself be a challenge. While some parents (and children) have a preference for a child sitting on the parent's knee, this might not be ideal for the purposes of eye contact of the child with the parent and the book. Techniques related to attracting and maintaining visual attention may not be familiar to them. Parents thus sometimes feel inadequate in this regard and may even experience storybook reading as frustrating because of the communication mismatch with their child (Swanwick & Watson, 2005).

Research has found that hearing parents do not read often to their DHH child (Marschark & Harris, 1996). When they do, differences are found compared to parents of hearing children. Stobbart and Alant (2008) investigated the home literacy experiences of preschool DHH children with their hearing parents. Parents were found to focus more on the text rather than engaging their child in a conversation about the story. They often pointed to the pictures and labeled them or asked their child to point and label. These parents also used closed-ended questions rather than open-ended questions during joint book reading (DesJardin et al., 2014). The use of open-ended questions elicited more words from children and was positively related to language growth. Further, parents were more in control concerning turn taking and choosing topics of conversations, and they asked more directive questions. The children took the initiative less frequently than the parents did. Research by Aram and colleagues (2006) also found that hearing parents were more dominant and DHH children were less responsive and active during storybook reading. This finding is in line with other research on parent–DHH child interaction showing shorter interactions and parents being more directive in the interactions (Pressman et al., 1999). Swanwick and Watson (2005) explained this more directive style during storybook reading by the tendency of parents to repeat words several times to be sure the child heard it. Storybook reading thus could result in a language lesson instead of a joyful parent–child activity.

Considering the fact that even parents of hearing children find it difficult to apply interactive reading strategies, it is not surprising that this is more challenging for parents of DHH children. Interactive reading programs can train them in applying these strategies.

Interactive Reading Programs

Several studies have investigated the effects of interactive reading programs (Huebner, 2000; Huebner & Meltzoff, 2005; Fung, Chow, & Chang, 2005; Reese, Sparks, & Leyva, 2010; Sénéchal & Young, 2008; Whitehurst et al., 1988). In these programs parents are trained in using evocative techniques (use of open-ended questions, repetition, expansion, pause for response), book management (child turning the pages), and print-referencing behaviors (comments, questions, pointing to print; Ezell, Justice, & Parsons, 2000). Huebner and colleagues (2000, 2005) showed that parent reading style before interactive reading instruction included few interactive reading behaviors. Most commonly, parents just "read the text directly without engaging the child in the story" (Huebner et al., 2005, p. 297). Parent reading style changed enormously after instruction, with an increase in interactive reading behaviors. A meta-analysis (Mol et al., 2008) of nine interactive reading intervention studies with parents of preschool or kindergarten children concluded that these types of reading intervention programs explained about 8% of the expressive language skills of the children. Further, the authors found parent–child interactive reading to be more effective for children's expressive than receptive vocabulary and more beneficial for younger than older children.

DeBruin-Parecki (2009) developed an interactive reading intervention program for parents and their young children (three- to five-year-olds). This program is based on three categories of parent and child behavior: (1) enhancing attention to the text, (2) promoting interactive reading and supporting comprehension, and (3) using literacy strategies. Examples of behaviors in these categories are given in Table 18.1. DeBruin-Parecki studied the effects of this program on parent and child behavior in 24 families. She found that both parents and children improved on the behaviors described in Table 18.1.

To sum up, interactive reading has a positive effect on a child's literacy development, however, because parents do not use interactive reading techniques automatically, instruction or training is needed (Huebner & Meltzoff, 2005; Mol et al., 2008; Sénéchal, 1997). Interactive reading programs have shown to be effective, with parents using more interactive reading strategies after following the program and the child showing better language performance. These findings are, however, based on research with hearing children; can the same conclusions be drawn for DHH children?

Table 18.1 Parent Behavior in Interactive Reading

Category	Parent Behavior
Enhancing attention to the text	Promote and maintain physical proximity Sustain interest and attention Give opportunity to hold book and turn pages Share book with the child
Promoting interactive reading and supporting comprehension	Pose and solicit questions about book content Point to pictures and words to assist in identification Relate book content to personal experiences Pause to answer questions of the child
Using literacy strategies	Identify visual cues Solicit predictions Ask child to recall information from story Elaborate on child's ideas

From DeBruin-Parecki, 2007.

Interactive Reading Programs for Children with Hearing Loss

The positive outcomes of interactive reading on literacy development in DHH children were described earlier. These outcomes call for including an interactive reading program in early family intervention programs.

Interactive reading programs for hearing children cannot simply be copied for DHH children but need to be adapted to the needs of DHH children and their parents. The program of DeBruin-Parecki (2009) as described earlier in this chapter may serve as a basis for a program for DHH children. We know from previous research that interactive reading with DHH children calls for specific strategies (e.g., DesJardin et al., 2014).

Based on the interactive reading program of DeBruin-Parecki (2009) and the specific insights of DesJardin and colleagues (2014) for reading with DHH children, we propose 13 strategies for interactive reading with DHH children (Table 18.2). The principles as identified by the Laurent Clerc Center at Gallaudet University (see Mueller & Hurtig, 2010) were also taken into account. However, not all of their principles focus specifically on the interactive aspect of reading but rather on reading in sign language. Our focus is on *interactive* reading with DHH children in any language, and the strategies we propose can be applied by both deaf and hearing adults. Strategies to focus the child's attention and to give the child the opportunity to be in charge of the reading activity are the main ingredients here. A description of the strategies will be given below, and then an interactive reading program based on these strategies will be described.

Table 18.2 Thirteen Strategies for Interactive Reading with Children with Hearing Loss

1	Give the child the opportunity to hold the book and turn the pages.
2	Follow the child's lead.
3	Introduce the book by discussing the cover.
4	Use materials and/or toys.
5	Allow enough time to observe, process, and respond.
6	Elaborate on the child's ideas.
7	Praise and reinforce.
8	Ask questions about the story.
9	Relate book content to personal prior experiences of the child.
10	Point to pictures and/or words.
11	Use mimicry, body posture, voice, and signs.
12	Reflect on the story.
13	Reread stories.

Allowing a child to hold the book and turn the pages empowers the child in leading the interaction. This is specifically important in DHH children because they tend to be less active in interactions with their hearing parents. Holding a book can also be helpful in enhancing the attention to the book.

Another way to give DHH children the opportunity to be in charge in the activity is to follow their lead. In following the child's lead, the child is allowed to make choices, and the adult responds to the child's initiatives (pointing or looking at pictures, and vocalizations). It is okay if a child skips pages in the book, because focusing on those pages that have a child's interest can be a valuable reading experience. The focus is on the interaction, not on finishing the book.

Introducing the story by discussing the cover is a good way to attract a child's attention and to trigger the child's prior knowledge about the topic. For example, the parent may point to the cover and say, "Look at this picture, I see the beach, what do you think the story is about?" Talking about the cover triggers the child's curiosity to read the book together.

The use of toys and materials before, during, and after reading the story can be very helpful in focusing a child's attention on a book. For example, materials and toys can be used during the introduction of the story to evoke a child's curiosity. Playing with thematically related toys before reading leads to increased interaction, increased participation and satisfaction, and more positive emotions during reading for DHH children (Pataki, Metz, & Pakulski, 2014).

Giving the child the time to look at pages/pictures, to process the information, and to respond before continuing helps in the child's understanding and gives the child the opportunity to initiate the interaction. It is important to wait for the child to initiate the interaction to let the child be in charge. This calls for patience in the adults, who will have to pause and wait. DHH children may need extra time to look at the pictures and then at the adult to start the interaction.

Elaborating on a child's ideas is another important strategy. It gives the child the feeling of being important, to be a part of the reading process, and it promotes the child's language development and narrative skills. This also means that the printed text is not always literally read, but that it is used as a guideline in building the story together. By following a child's lead and elaborating on his or her ideas, the story can be constructed in interaction with the child.

Within the interactions between parent and child, the amount of joy they have together is vital. A child who experiences reading with his or her parent as a pleasant and fun activity will ask to read with him or her again and again. The child is the best motivator for a parent. Giving a child positive feedback and reinforcement during reading improves the child's joy of reading. Children's initiatives must be praised to encourage them to show even more initiatives and be in charge of the interaction.

A key aspect of interactive reading is asking questions that are related to the child's interest and that evoke answers of more than one word. Open-ended questions in particular encourage participation and conversation during storybook reading and are positively related to language skills in children with hearing loss (DesJardin & Eisenberg, 2007; DesJardin et al., 2014). Wh-questions (what, where, when, who, and why) are types of questions that elicit rich conversations and evoke abstract language (Aram et al., 2006). Asking a child to predict what will happen next in the story stimulates his or her imagination and engages the child in the interaction.

Linking the book content to the child's prior life experiences enhances comprehension and understanding. For example, when reading a book about the beach, the story could be related to a child's visit to the beach in the past. For a child, it is fun when a story is made relevant to his or her life. Further, talking about previous experiences allows the child to practice with conversations beyond the here and now.

Another important strategy to focus the child's attention is pointing to pictures or words. For DHH children, visual input may be even more important than for hearing children. In young children, pointing to pictures is important to achieve joint attention and to enhance their comprehension. For example, pointing to a dog in the book and saying, "Look, that is Max, he has a lot of spots on his fur, and this is Joe, he has black fur," helps a child keep characters in the book apart. When children get older, pointing can be used to relate the printed words to the content of the story.

Interactive reading with DHH children requires even more techniques from parents compared to interactive reading with hearing children. Signs, mimicry, body posture, and voice are helpful tools that parents can use during interactive reading. Apart from the use of signs in the communication between parent and child, they can be used to get a child's attention, for example by making signs on the child's body. The creative use of mimicry, body posture, and voice brings the characters to life and helps maintain the child's attention.

Reflecting on the story after finishing reading helps the child to process the story. Talking about what happened in the story and the child's feelings about it are helpful strategies for processing the story. Different kinds of activities can be done to reflect on the story—for example, drawing, acting out the story, or singing a song (in sign or voice, as appropriate) related to the topic.

Children enjoy reading the same book again and again, and this practice may build a feeling of familiarity and comfort. Repeated reading also has advantages in the context of interactive reading because it enhances comprehension. Every time the book is read again, something new is added to the child's understanding of it. As mentioned before, the child is the best motivator for a parent.

Effects of an Interactive Reading Program for Children with Hearing Loss

We developed an interactive reading program in the Netherlands for parents of DHH children that was built on these strategies. The effect of the program on parent behavior has been examined and the first results are promising.

The interactive reading program consisted of three group sessions in which parents were taught the strategies of interactive reading with DHH children. At the start of the program parents received two print books and materials/toys related to the stories to practice at home with their child. Parents were also given fact sheets for each book with suggestions for reading the story—for example, introducing the story, asking questions about the story, and activities to do after reading the story. During the sessions parents practiced the interactive reading strategies and gave each other feedback. For example, they practiced in attracting and maintaining a child's attention, formulating open-ended questions, introducing the cover, and using materials. They were trained in using the text in the book as a guide in building the story without always literally reading that text. Because the reading activity should be a pleasant experience, parents were taught that they must praise their child's reading-related initiatives and give positive feedback.

At home, the parents practiced applying the strategies with their children. One of the strategies they learned was to wait for their child's reaction, for example after a page was turned. They were taught to wait for 10 seconds before starting the interaction. Within these 10 seconds most children showed an initiation (pointing, eye gaze, or vocalization).

Parents brought a video of a reading activity with their child to the third group session and discussed it with the other parents. Sharing experiences and challenges of interactive reading with a DHH child with other parents was considered valuable by most parents.

As part of our study, parents followed the interactive reading program at home. After completing the sessions, parents received five books (print books or electronic books [e-books]) to read with their DHH children in the following five weeks. Parent behavior and experience was measured in a pretest–posttest design through video observations. This part of our study focused on the application of the interactive reading strategies by parents of DHH toddlers. We examined whether parents applied more interactive reading strategies after participating in the interactive reading program. Twenty-five parent–child dyads participated in the total study. The children were two- to five-year-old toddlers with hearing loss. All children were identified as having hearing losses by universal newborn hearing screening and participated in a family-centered early intervention program. Here the data from the first 12 parent–child dyads who participated are described.

The videos were coded using the Responsive Adult–Child Engagement During Joint Book Reading Scale (RACED-JBR; DesJardin et al., 2014). The RACED-JBR scale consists of four adult and three child behavior categories; here we focus on the parent behavior only. The parent categories are (a) engagement (e.g., sustaining attention, providing positive feedback, engaging the child in interaction), (b) literacy strategies (e.g., pointing to pictures/objects in the book, soliciting questions), (c) teacher: techniques (e.g., relating a story to the child's personal experience, elaborating on the child's ideas), (d) interactive reading (e.g., following the child's lead, giving the child the opportunity to hold the book, allowing time for observing, processing, and responding). These categories cover almost all interactive reading strategies we introduced before. We added the use of toys/materials and discussion of the cover to the coding system. Strategies 12 and 13 were not coded because the parent and child were videotaped during book reading only, not during what happened after they finished reading the book.

Analyses comparing use of the interactive reading techniques before and after the sessions for the first 12 parents showed that the program was effective for some aspects of interactive reading. Significant differences were found on strategies 2, 5, 7, and 8. After participating in the program, parents responded more to a child's initiatives; gave their child more time to process, observe, or respond to the story; praised their child more; and asked more open-ended questions about the book content.

No differences were found on strategies 1, 3, 6, 9, 10, and 11. Parents showed some improvement on relating the book content to personal prior experiences and on the use of mimicry, body posture, voice, and signs, but this was not statistically significant. Parents did not improve in giving their child the opportunity to hold the book and turn the pages: they did somewhat apply this strategy at pretest and posttest, but for parents who did not do it, old habits seem to die hard. The strategies of introducing the book by discussing the cover and elaborating on their child's ideas seem to be difficult for parents to apply. The strategy of pointing to pictures already was being used at the time of pretest, so no improvement could occur there. Although parents mentioned during the sessions that they used materials/toys during reading activities with their child (strategy 4), it was only seen on the videos of one parent.

On program evaluation forms, parents reported that they found the program very useful and that they had experienced that reading together can be very pleasant. In sum, parents made more efforts in engaging their child in the reading activity and managed to improve their use of the interactive reading strategies after following the interactive reading program. Some of these parents read e-books in the five weeks of reading at home. We will now describe the potential of e-books for interactive reading with DHH children. Results of a comparison between print books and e-books will be discussed later in this chapter.

DIGITAL MEDIA AND STORYBOOK READING

Most interactive reading programs are based on the use of traditional print books. New digital technologies have made it possible to read books in different media. Apart from traditional print books, e-books on computers and tablets have become available.

With the introduction of digital media and electronic e-books, storybook reading with young children is not what it used to be (Hoffman & Paciga, 2013). In 2011, Eagle stated that it was time to rethink the design of digital technologies in a way that they support the participation of children and allow them to express and share their ideas. With all the possibilities of digital media, there is a new variety of materials to read with children. E-books are now very popular, and so are the devices used to read these books. The ownership of mobile media devices in particular has increased significantly. A survey among 1,463 parents of zero- to eight-year-olds in the United States (Rideout, 2013) showed that 40% of the households owned a tablet, with 7% of the children having their own tablet. In addition, smartphones were present in 63% of the homes. Similar findings were reported in a Dutch survey with 1,100 parents of newborns to seven-year-olds (Stichting Mijn Kind Online,

2013), where tablets were present in 67% of the homes. Although access to mobile devices has also increased in lower-income families, the gap between rich and poor still exists, with 20% of lower-income families owning a tablet compared to 63% of higher-income families (Rideout, 2013).

Children now start using mobile media at a young age. In the United States, 38% of the children under age two have at some point used a mobile device (tablet, smartphone, or iPod) according to the Common Sense Media (Rideout, 2013) study. Among the two- to four-year-olds, 80% had used one and 83% of the five- to eight-year-olds had done so. In the Netherlands, Stichting Mijn Kind Online reported that about half of the children (both zero- to three-year-olds and four- to seven-year-olds) frequently used a tablet, and about 40% frequently used a smartphone. Both surveys found that although the use of mobile devices has increased, television is still the number-one media activity among young children and the most widely used platform for educational content. Luckily, both surveys also showed that, in addition to using screen media, children were still reading or being read to. Eighty-two percent of the Dutch zero- to three-year-olds and 95% of the four- to seven-year-olds were frequently read to by their parents. Of the American zero- to eight-year-olds, 60% were reading or being read to every day.

Because interactive reading with children is so important for their emergent literacy skills, the presence of these e-books and mobile devices makes it important to explore their possibilities for interactive reading with DHH children. Little is known about the efficacy of e-books for the development of emergent literacy and as tools for interactive reading. We will first give an overview of the available research with hearing children and then relate these findings to interactive reading with DHH children.

Efficacy of E-books

E-books are available in many sorts and vary in their degree of interactivity. Usually an e-book includes the reading of the story out loud, with or without showing the printed text. Multimedia additions to these books can be sound/music, animations, or highlighting of the text. The visual interface varies from static pictures to a video of the story. Often, one can choose between reading the story or listening to the story being read out loud (with or without highlighting of the text). Several studies have looked at the effects of e-books as a useful means for supporting children's literacy and language development (e.g., Korat & Shamir, 2008).

Most studies focused on children's independent reading of e-books, not on adult–child interactive reading activities. Results of these studies show that the available interactive features in e-books affect the emergent literacy skills (Salmon, 2013). Verhallen, Bus, and de Jong (2006) found that five-year-old second-language learners profited more from animated e-books (video with sound and music) than from static e-books (static pictures). The children showed a greater increase in their story understanding and vocabulary and syntax knowledge when reading animated books than when looking at books with static pictures (see also Verhallen & Bus, 2010).

Although animations are found to be effective, Labbo and Kuhn (2000) warned that children can shift to passive cognitive modes when interactive features are not congruent with the text (see Segers & Verhoeven, Chapter 21 in this volume). De Jong and Bus (2004) also found that children could profit as much from independent reading of e-books as from being read to by adults *if* e-books were developed in such a way that the animations adhere to the content of the story instead of distracting children from the content. Animations that have been found to be effective are highlighting of the text and interactive dictionaries (hotspots that activate additional information) (Salmon, 2013). Highlighting of the text during narration had an effect on concepts of print and letter knowledge. Hotspots with word definitions were found to improve vocabulary and word reading. Korat and Shamir (2008, 2012) found that children who read a story with dictionary hotspots showed greater improvement in vocabulary knowledge than children who only read the story or read the story with other kinds of hotspots. Smeets and Bus (2012) found that hotspots increased children's receptive and expressive vocabulary knowledge compared to reading alone, but they also found that asking questions about word meaning was even more effective.

Results from these (and other) studies call for critical evaluation of e-books to make sure that children can develop their emergent literacy skills from engaging with e-books. Eagle (2011) mentioned that digital technologies should facilitate, support, and stimulate interaction in order to let children engage in meaning-making activities, and we now turn to that issue.

E-books and Storybook Reading

Hoffman and Paciga (2013) stated that most studies on e-books focus on the effects of the technology such as hotspots or other animations, not on the quality of the adult–child interaction that is so important in developing language and literacy skills. De Jong and Bus (2004) also mentioned that e-books for independent reading are effective if they are used as a supplement to adult–child storybook reading. There have been only a few studies on adult–child interactions during storybook reading of e-books (e.g., Salmon, 2013). These studies provide evidence that adult support is beneficial in addition to the interactive features in e-books. Korat and Or (2010) found that mother–child e-book reading showed more child initiations and maternal mediations (e.g., relating book to personal experience, pointing to and labeling illustrations, relating illustrations to the story, explaining word meanings) than print book reading, where more maternal initiations and child responses occurred. However, print book reading showed more expanding talk about the content of the story. The authors concluded that different reading contexts evoke different kinds of adult–child interactions. They also suggested that the lower incidence of expanding talk in the e-books may be influenced by the fact that the embedded animations already expand on the content of the story.

Salmon's review of the literature on the efficacy of e-books in supporting literacy development (2013) showed that apart from the quality of the interactive features of e-books and repetitive readings, adult support was an important aspect of the beneficial effect of e-books.

Storybook Reading on a Tablet

Most studies on the efficacy of e-books are about books read independently on a computer. With the increase of tablets, more and more e-book applications for tablets are being developed. These could provide even more promising ways to improve children's emergent literacy skills, because tablets are easier to handle than computers and have a more intuitive interface (Neumann & Neumann, 2013). But what do we know about tablet e-books?

A parent–child co-reading survey by the Joan Ganz Cooney Center (Vaala & Takeuchi, 2012) showed that 72.5% of the parents owning a tablet did read e-books with their child, but these parents mostly still preferred reading print books. Reasons given for not reading e-books on the tablet are preference for traditional print books, finding reading on a tablet too difficult, worries that the child will want to use the tablet all the time, and so forth.

Parents who did read e-books with their child felt that certain features in e-books could help their children learn to read. Positive features included clicking on a word to sound it out, audio narration (allowing the child to read the e-book on his or her own), and highlighting of words during narration. Features that were thought to distract were animations in illustrations, games in e-books, and videos in e-books (Vaala & Takeuchi, 2012).

In a related study from the Joan Ganz Cooney Center (Chiong, Ree, Takeuchi, & Erickson, 2012), the differences among print books, basic e-books, and enhanced e-books were studied. Basic e-books were just digitized versions of the print books, whereas enhanced e-books had extra features such as animations or hotspots embedded in the illustrations and games. Although child engagement was higher for e-books than for print books, there were no differences between the books in the frequency of children's explaining critical elements from the story.

They recalled fewer details from the enhanced e-books than from the print books, though. The experiences of parents and children were also found to be different for the enhanced e-books than for basic e-books and print books. Basic e-books and print books elicited more content-related interactions (labeling, pointing, elaborating) between parent and child, whereas interactions while reading enhanced e-books were more likely to be related to something other than the content (focusing more on handling the tablet). Hoffman and Paciga (2013) also stated that shared reading of e-books with animations and interactive features led the conversation away from the meaning-making goal of shared reading.

Data from these studies showed that parents and their children spend a lot of time on storybook reading and even though they use both, parents still prefer to read print books over e-books. However, parents who do not read e-books with their children also indicate that they find it difficult to read on a tablet. Maybe we do not know enough about interactive reading on a tablet for parents to be convinced about the possibilities of using this medium in addition to reading print books. Neumann and Neumann (2013), indeed, stated that many tablet e-books are available but that we know little about the effects of these tablet e-books. From what we know, optimal use of tablets for developing emergent literacy skills seems dependent upon the support given by parents or teachers. For example, at home parents could model the use of tablet apps by writing e-mails or reading the newspaper. Also, parents or teachers can scaffold the child's development of print knowledge by pointing to and explaining the meaning of digital print and by providing positive feedback to the child's app use.

Interactive Reading of E-books with Children with Hearing Loss

We can learn lessons from the research that has been done on the efficacy of e-books with hearing children to promote interactive reading of e-books with DHH children. Conclusions from studies with hearing children tell us that digital technologies should facilitate, support, and stimulate interaction in order to let children engage in meaning-making activities; that adult support is an important aspect of the beneficial effect of e-books; that animations that are not related to the content of the story are distracting and elicit more non–content-related interactions between the adult and the child; and that parents may have difficulty providing qualitative interactive reading experiences for their children. The intuitive and attractive interface of tablets may be beneficial for interactive reading experiences between DHH children and their parents. Because a tablet is so attractive to young children, it may be a perfect medium to attract the attention of a DHH child and to involve the child in the interaction. However, because initiation of the interaction with DHH children is so important, the choice of the right e-book is essential. The e-book should elicit interaction between the parent and child, and animations in the e-book should be related to the content of the story so that children do not watch a movie or play a game instead of interacting with their parent about the book.

To our knowledge, only a few e-books have been developed specifically for DHH children. The Science of Learning Center on Visual Language and Visual Learning (VL2) at Gallaudet University has developed two bilingual storybook apps for deaf children. These apps include a sign narrator of the story and an American Sign Language glossary. The same options hold for the Iowa signing e-book, the only e-book for DHH children whose effects have been studied (Mueller & Hurtig, 2010). The Iowa signing e-book is actually a multimedia tool that creates electronic books from text, with or without a video of a narrator. The narrator tells the story (in any modality), makes comments on the story, asks questions, and gives feedback. The e-book should ideally be read by the parent and child together to provide the necessary interaction, but it can also be read independently by the child. The e-book may also serve as an instruction tool for hearing parents to improve their signing skills when interacting with their child during the shared reading process. Mueller and Hurtig studied the effect of the signing narrator in the e-book on the frequency of shared reading sessions between four two- to five-year-old DHH children and their hearing parents. They found that only slightly more time was spent on reading e-books with a sign narrator than e-books without a sign narrator. The mothers in this study reported that they found the sign narration helpful in learning how to sign the story themselves. The authors mentioned that not only the quantity of shared reading should be studied but also the quality. As research on this quality issue is scarce, nothing is known about the quality of storybook reading experiences with e-books between DHH children and their parents. Therefore, in our interactive reading study described earlier, we also focus on the use of tablets in interactive reading with DHH toddlers. We discuss some preliminary data from that study here.

Mueller and Hurtig (2010) studied the effect of e-books on a computer on the *quantity* of shared reading with DHH children. The effect of tablet e-books on the *quality* of interactive reading with DHH children has not been previously studied. We do know from the above-mentioned studies that e-books must be developed with the child's abilities in mind and should not include animations that are not related to the text (Segers & Verhoeven, Chapter 21 in this volume). For example, from a study with children with specific language impairments (Smeets, van Dijken, & Bus, 2012), we know that music/sound is not beneficial for word learning. Kindergartners with specific language impairments learned as many words from static e-books as from video stories, but they learned fewer words when music/sound was included in the e-books.

In our study on interactive reading with DHH toddlers, insights from previous studies on the effects on e-books and the attribution or distraction of animations were taken into account. This resulted in the development of e-book apps with the following features:

- The printed text was visible in the e-book.
- No narration was included, even if the child had sufficient hearing (because we wanted the parent and child to read together).
- There was no automatic page turning; the child or parent had to swipe to new pages.
- There was the possibility of going both forward and backward in the story.
- A sign dictionary for key words was included.
- There were built-in zoom effects to focus attention or to build suspense (automatic, not instigated by the reader).
- Information and tips about interactive reading were provided for the specific book.

The focus of this part of the study was on the potential of a tablet for interactive reading with DHH toddlers. We examined whether parents were able to apply the interactive reading strategies in reading e-books on a tablet as well as in reading print books. Further, the frequency of reading and the reading experience were examined for both print books and e-books. The same 25 parent–child dyads participated in this part of the study, and we will again discuss the results of the first 12 dyads.

As mentioned before, parents received five print books or five e-books on a tablet after they completed the sessions of the interactive reading program. After five weeks of reading these materials at home, a reading activity between parent and child was videotaped at home and the parents filled out a questionnaire about the frequency and experiences of reading. They then received new books to read in the following five weeks. Parents who received the print books in the first five weeks now received the e-books, and vice versa. After these five weeks, they were videotaped again and the parents filled out another questionnaire. Again, the RACED-JBR (DesJardin et al., 2014) was used to score the interactive reading behavior. This time, we also added the use of the sign dictionary to the coding system.

When we looked at differences between the tablet and print books in applying the interactive reading strategies, it seemed that both conditions were useful. No differences were found in parents' interactive reading behavior between the print books condition and the tablet condition, with one exception: Parents less frequently pointed to pictures in e-books on the tablet than they did when reading print books. This could be related to the other options of the e-books on the tablet, such as the sign button or the built-in zoom function, that draw the attention of both parent and child. The fact that they already have to swipe to turn pages may also impede pointing behavior. In conclusion, a tablet definitely has potential for interactive reading with DHH toddlers. However, are parents also willing to read on the tablet with their child? The questionnaires revealed a slight preference for the print books compared to the tablet when we asked how much they enjoyed reading with their child. No differences were found in reported frequency of reading, though.

SUMMARY AND CONCLUSIONS

Emergent literacy refers to skills and knowledge children have about reading and writing before they start formal reading instruction. Components of emergent literacy include semantic skills, syntactic skills, conceptual knowledge, narrative skills, print knowledge, phonological awareness, letter knowledge, and beginning reading and writing. These emergent literacy skills form a firm foundation for later reading skills and motivation. Because DHH children are at risk for developing reading difficulties, it is important to focus on enhancing the emergent literacy skills in the preschool period.

To develop emergent literacy skills, children need sufficient opportunities to engage with print in interaction with adults. If DHH children get these opportunities, they should be able to develop these skills as hearing children do (Williams, 2004). However, to provide DHH children with these opportunities, parents may need to invest more than parents of hearing children (DesJardin & Ambrose, 2010). One way they can achieve this is through interactive reading. In this chapter, we introduced 13 strategies for interactive reading with young DHH children: Give the child the opportunity to hold the book and turn the pages; follow the child's lead; introduce the book by discussing the cover; use materials and/or toys; allow enough time to observe, process, and respond; elaborate on the child's ideas; praise and reinforce; ask questions about the story; relate book content to personal experiences; point to pictures and words; use mimicry, body posture, voice, and signs; reflect on the story; and reread stories.

Applying these strategies is not easy for most parents, a situation that makes an interactive reading program for them imperative. Interactive reading programs for parents of DHH children should focus on these strategies. Therefore, we developed a program based on them. The first results of our study show that parents are able to apply the strategies after participating in an interactive reading program. They are better able to engage their child in the interaction by following their child's lead; asking open-ended questions; responding to their child's utterances; allowing time for their child to observe, process, and respond; and praising and reinforcing the child's initiatives.

The introduction of new digital technologies such as tablets in the homes of children called for research on the potential of these technologies for interactive reading with DHH children. The literature on the effectiveness of e-books points to some important implications for their use with DHH children. E-books should evoke meaningful interaction between the parent and the child, parent–child reading should be the focus instead of independent reading by the child, and animations should be used only if they are related to the story and add meaning to the interaction. Based on these indications, we developed five e-books for our study in which the strategies of interactive reading with DHH children are taken into account and the focus is on parent–child interaction.

The initial results of our study showed that parents are able to apply the interactive reading strategies on a tablet as well as in print books. The only exception was in the strategy of pointing to pictures: Parents pointed more to pictures when reading print books than when reading e-books. As mentioned before, this could be related to the fact that the attention of the parent and child is already pulled to the signs provided in the e-books or to the pictures that the e-book automatically zooms in on. Another explanation could be that parents are so busy with swiping to turn the pages that they do not find the time to point to pictures. Because this strategy is important in focusing the attention of the child, parents should be explicitly trained in applying it when reading e-books on a tablet with their child.

Storybook reading has been found to be one of the most important activities in enhancing emergent literacy skills. The effect on these skills is even larger when the child is actively involved (Mol et al., 2008). Components of this so-called interactive reading are asking open-ended questions, allowing the child enough time to respond, following the child's lead, and positively reinforcing the child. Parents can learn to apply interactive reading strategies with their DHH child. Besides reading print books, parents can also use a tablet. To create opportunities to enhance a child's emergent literacy skills, e-books on a tablet should elicit parent–child interaction about the story. This interaction between parent and child is what makes storybook reading so successful in enhancing emergent literacy skills. Participating in an interactive reading program helps parents in applying effective strategies in the reading activity with their child.

REFERENCES

Aram, D., Korat, O., & Hassunah-Arafat, S. (2013). The contribution of early home literacy activities to first grade reading and writing achievements in Arabic. *Reading and Writing*, *26*, 1517–1536.

Aram, D., Most, T., & Mayafit, H. (2006). Contributions of mother-child storybook telling and joint writing to literacy development in kindergartners with hearing loss. *Language, Speech, and Hearing Services in Schools*, *37*(3), 209.

Barton, L. R., & Brophy-Herb, H. E. (2006). Developmental foundations for language and literacy from birth to 3 years. In S. E. Rosenkoetter & J. Knapp-Philo (Eds.), *Learning to read the world: Language and literacy in the first three years* (pp. 15–58). Washington, DC: ZERO TO THREE Press.

Bus, A. G., Van Ijzendoorn, M. H., & Pellegrini, A. D. (1995). Joint book reading makes for success in learning to read: A meta-analysis on intergenerational transmission of literacy. *Review of Educational Research, 65*(1), 1–21.

Chiong, C., Ree, J., Takeuchi, L., & Erickson, I. (2012). *Print books vs. e-books: Comparing parent-child co-reading on print, basic, and enhanced e-book platforms*. New York: The Joan Ganz Cooney Center.

Chow, B. W., McBride-Chang, C., Cheung, H., & Chow, C. S. (2008). Dialogic reading and morphology training in Chinese children: Effects on language and literacy. *Developmental Psychology, 44*(1), 233–244.

DeBruin-Parecki, A. (2007). *Let's read together: Improving literacy outcomes with the adult/child interactive reading inventory*. Baltimore, MD: Brookes.

DeBruin-Parecki, A. (2009). Establishing a family literacy program with a focus on interactive reading: The role of research and accountability. *Early Childhood Education Journal, 36*(5), 385–392.

DeCasper, A., & Fifer, W. P. (1980). Of human bonding: Newborns prefer their mothers' voices. *Science, 208*, 1174–1176.

De Jong, M. T., & Bus, A. G. (2004). The efficacy of electronic books in fostering kindergarten children's emergent story understanding. *Reading Research Quarterly, 39*(4), 378–393.

DesJardin, J. L., & Ambrose, S. E. (2010). The importance of the home literacy environment for developing literacy skills in young children who are deaf or hard of hearing. *Young Exceptional Children, 13*, 28–44.

DesJardin, J. L., Ambrose, S. E., & Eisenberg, L. S. (2009). Literacy skills in children with cochlear implants: The importance of early oral language and joint storybook reading. *Journal of Deaf Studies and Deaf Education, 14*(1), 22–43.

DesJardin, J. L., Doll, E. R., Stika, C. J., Eisenberg, L. S., Johnson, K. J., Ganguly, D. H., . . . & Henning, S. C. (2014). Parental support for language development during joint book reading for young children with hearing loss. *Communication Disorders Quarterly, 35*(3), 167–181.

DesJardin, J. L., & Eisenberg, L. S. (2007). Maternal contributions: Supporting language development in young children with cochlear implants. *Ear and Hearing, 28*(4), 456–469.

DeTemple, J., & Snow, C. E. (2003). Learning words from books. In A. van Kleeck, S. A. Stahl, & E. B. Bauer (Eds.), *On reading books to children: Parents and teachers* (pp. 16–36). Mahwah, NJ: Erlbaum.

Eagle, S. (2011). Learning in the early years: Social interactions around picture books, puzzles and digital technologies. *Computers & Education, 59*, 38–49.

Easterbrooks, S. R., Lederberg, A. R., & Connor, C. M. (2010). Contributions of the emergent literacy environment to literacy outcomes for young children who are deaf. *American Annals of the Deaf, 155*(4), 467–480.

Ezell, H. K., Justice, L. M., & Parsons, D. (2000). Enhancing the emergent literacy skills of preschoolers with communication disorders: A pilot investigation. *Child Language Teaching and Therapy, 16*, 121–140.

Fung, P., Chow, B. W., & McBride-Chang, C. (2005). The impact of a dialogic reading program on deaf and hard-of-hearing kindergarten and early primary school-aged students in Hong Kong. *Journal of Deaf Studies and Deaf Education, 10*, 82–95.

Gathoo, V., & Kulkarni, K. (2013). Emergent literacy skills of children with and without hearing loss in India. *Infants and Young Children, 26*(1), 42–56.

Hoffman, J. L., & Paciga, K. A. (2013). Click, swipe, and read: sharing e-books with toddlers and preschoolers. *Early Childhood Education Journal*, DOI10.1007/s10643-013-0622-5.

Huebner, C. E. (2000). Promoting toddlers' language development through community-based intervention. *Journal of Applied Developmental Psychology, 21*, 513–535.

Huebner, C. E., & Meltzoff, A. N. (2005). Intervention to change parent–child reading style: A comparison of instructional methods. *Journal of Applied Developmental Psychology, 26*(3), 296–313.

International Reading Association & National Association for the Education of Young Children. (1998). Learning to read and write: Developmentally appropriate practices for young children. *The Reading Teacher, 52*, 193–216.

Jordan, G. E., Snow, C. E., & Porche, M. V. (2000). Project EASE: The effect of a family literacy project on kindergarten students' early literacy skills. *Reading Research Quarterly, 35*(4), 524–546.

Korat, O., & Or, T. (2010). How new technology influences parent-child interaction: The case of e-book reading. *First Language, 30*(2), 139–154.

Korat, O., & Shamir, A. (2008). The educational electronic book as a tool for supporting children's emergent literacy in low versus middle SES groups. *Computers & Education, 50*, 110–124.

Korat, O., & Shamir, A. (2012). Direct and indirect teaching: using e-books for supporting vocabulary, word reading, and story comprehension for young children. *Journal of Educational Research, 46*(2), 135–152.

Labbo, L. D., & Kuhn, M. R. (2000). Weaving chains of affect and cognition: A young child's understanding of CD-ROM talking books. *Journal of Literacy Research, 32*(2), 187–210.

Marschark, M., & Harris, M. (1996). Success and failure in learning to read: The special (?) case of deaf children. In C. Cornoldi & J. Oakhill (Eds.), *Reading comprehension difficulties: Processes and intervention* (pp. 279–300). Hillsdale, NJ: Lawrence Erlbaum.

Mol, S. E., Bus, A. G., de Jong, M. T., & Smeets, D. J. (2008). Added value of dialogic parent–child book readings: A meta-analysis. *Early Education and Development, 19*(1), 7–26.

Mueller, V., & Hurtig, R. (2010). Technology-enhanced shared reading with deaf and hard of hearing children: The role of a fluent signing narrator. *Journal of Deaf Studies and Deaf Education, 15*, 72–101.

Neumann, M. M., & Neumann, D. L. (2013). Touch screen tablets and emergent literacy. *Early Childhood Education Journal*, DOI 10.1007/s10643-013-0608-3.

Pataki, K. W., Metz, A. E., & Pakulski, L. (2014). The effect of thematically related play on engagement in storybook reading in children with hearing loss. *Journal of Early Childhood Literacy, 14*(2), 240–264.

Pressman, L. J., Pipp-Siegel, S., Yoshinaga-Itano, C., & Deas, A. (1999). Maternal sensitivity predicts language gain in preschool children who are deaf and hard of hearing. *Journal of Deaf Studies and Deaf Education, 4*, 294–304.

Reese, E., Sparks, A., & Leyva, D. (2010). A review of parent interventions for preschool children's language and emergent literacy. *Journal of Early Childhood Literacy*, 10(1), 97–117.

Rideout, V. (2013). *Zero to eight: Children's media use in America 2013*. San Francisco, CA: Common Sense Media.

Robertson, L., Dow, G. A., & Hainzinger, S. L. (2006). Story retelling patterns among children with and without hearing loss: Effects of repeated practice and parent- child attunement. *Volta Review*, *106*(2), 147–170.

Roskos, K. A., Tabors, P. O., & Lenhart, L. A. (2009). *Oral language and early literacy in preschool: Talking, reading, and writing*. Newark, DE: International Reading Association.

Salmon, L. G. (2013). Factors that affect emergent literacy development when engaging with electronic books. *Early Childhood Education Journal*, *42*(2), 85–92.

Sénéchal, M. (1997). The differential effect of storybook reading on preschoolers' acquisition of expressive and receptive vocabulary. *Journal of Child language*, *24*, 123–138.

Sénéchal, M., & Young, L. (2008). The effect of family literacy interventions on children's acquisition of reading from kindergarten to grade 3: A meta-analytic review. *Review of Education Research*, *78*(4), 880–907.

Smeets, D. J., & Bus, A. G. (2012). Interactive electronic storybooks for kindergartners to promote vocabulary growth. *Journal of Experimental Child Psychology*, *112*(1), 36–55.

Smeets, D. J., van Dijken, M. J., & Bus, A. G. (2012). Using electronic storybooks to support word learning in children with severe language impairments. *Journal of Learning Disabilities*, *47*(5), 435–449.

Stichting Mijn Kind Online. (2013). *Ienemiene media: een onderzoek naar mediagebruik door kleine kinderen, van 0 t/m 7 jaar* [Eenymeeny media: a study into media use by young children, aged 0 to 7 years]. Mediawijzer.net.

Stobbart, C., & Alant, E. (2008). Home-based literacy experiences of severely to profound deaf preschoolers and their hearing parents. *Journal of Developmental and Physical Disabilities*, *20*, 139–153.

Storch, S. A., & Whitehurst, G. J. (2002). Oral language and code-related precursors to reading: Evidence from a longitudinal structural model. *Developmental Psychology*, *38*(6), 934–947.

Swanwick, R., & Watson, L. (2005). Parents sharing books with young deaf children in spoken English and BSL: The common and diverse features of different language settings. *Journal of Deaf Studies and Deaf Education*, *12*(3), 385–405.

Vaala, S., & Takeuchi, L. (2012). *Parent co-reading survey: Co-reading with children on iPads: Parents' perceptions and practices*. New York: The Joan Ganz Cooney Center.

Verhallen, M. J., & Bus, A. G. (2010). Low-income immigrant pupils learning vocabulary through digital picture storybooks. *Journal of Educational Psychology*, *102*(1), 54.

Verhallen, M. J., Bus, A. G., & de Jong, M. T. (2006). The promise of multimedia stories for kindergarten children at risk. *Journal of Educational Psychology*, *98*(2), 410.

Vukelich, C., & Christie, J. (2009). *Building a foundation for preschool literacy: Effective instruction for children's reading and writing development*. Newark, DE: International Reading Association.
Vygotsky, L. S. (1978). *Mind in society: The development of higher psychological processes*. Cambridge, MA: Harvard University Press.
Webster, A. (2000). An international research review of literacy intervention strategies for children with severe to profound deafness. *Deafness and Education International*, 2(3), 128–141.
Whitehurst, G. J., Falco, F., Lonigan, C. J., Fischel, J. E., DeBaryshe, B. D., Valdez-Menchaca, M. C., & Caulfield, M. (1988). Accelerating language development through picture-book reading. *Developmental Psychology, 24*, 552–558.
Whitehurst, G. J., & Lonigan, C. J. (1998). Child development and emergent literacy. *Child Development*, *69*, 848–872.
Williams, C. (2004). Emergent literacy and deaf children. *Journal of Deaf Studies and Deaf Education*, *9*(4), 352–365.
Xu, Y., Chin, C., Reed, E., & Hutchinson, C. (2013). The effects of a comprehensive early literacy project on preschoolers' language and literacy skills. *Early Childhood Education Journal*, DOI 10.1007/s10643-013-0613-6
Zevenbergen, A. A., Whitehurst, G. J., & Zevenbergen, J. A. (2003). Effects of a shared-reading intervention on the inclusion of evaluative devices in narratives of children from low-income families. *Journal of Applied Developmental Psychology*, *24*(1), 1–15.
Zupan, B., & Dempsey, L. (2013). Facilitating emergent literacy skills in children with hearing loss. *Deafness and Education International*, *15*(3), 130–148.

19

Language Skills and Literacy of Deaf Children in the Era of Cochlear Implantation

Suggestions for Teaching through E-learning Visual Environments

Maria Cristina Caselli, Pasquale Rinaldi, Daniela Onofrio, and Elena Tomasuolo

LINGUISTIC SKILLS OF DEAF CHILDREN WITH COCHLEAR IMPLANTS

Thanks to hearing screening programs for newborns, a growing number of infants with severe to profound hearing loss are being identified very early in their lives. This timely identification provides children with the opportunity to receive hearing aids very early and to be implanted with a cochlear implant by the first two years of age and thus to benefit from the most important periods of neural development, allowing for a relatively normal maturation of the auditory pathways (May-Mederake, 2012). Moreover, in many Western countries, the standard procedure is bilateral implantation between eight and 12 months (e.g., Norway; see Bruin, Chapter 5 in this volume). Especially when cochlear implantation (CI) takes place at an early age, age-appropriate spoken language levels are feasible (Nicholas & Geers, 2007). However, CI does not ensure "typical" language development nor a homogeneous developmental profile in the different linguistic domains. Data collected after CI have shown contrasting results and large individual variability, which can be attributed to diverse factors, including age at diagnosis of deafness (e.g., Blamey et al., 2001; Rinaldi, Baruffaldi, Burdo, & Caselli, 2013), age at CI activation (e.g., Geers, Moog, Biedenstein, Brenner, & Hayes, 2009), family environment (e.g., Spencer, 2004; Szagun & Stumper, 2012), and specific language(s) the child is acquiring (for a recent review on this topic, see Crowe & McLeod, 2014).

Duchesne, Sutton, and Bergeron (2009) reported data on the linguistic skills of 27 French deaf children with CI between three and eight years of age. It was not the authors' primary interest for the paper, but they reported the outcomes in terms of the percentage of children who were within normal limits in each of the linguistic domains evaluated. To determine whether language skills are within normal limits, a threshold of –1 standard deviation is frequently used. Their data showed that the percentage of children who performed within normal limits in expressive vocabulary (about 86%) was higher than for children who performed within normal limits in receptive vocabulary (about 56%) or in comprehension of syntactic structures (about 36%).

Similar findings have been reported on deaf preschool children with CI in the United States (Geers et al., 2009). In this research also, the authors reported the outcomes in terms of the percentage of children who were within normal limits in each of the linguistic domains evaluated, even if this was not their primary interest for the paper. The percentage of children who were within normal limits when expressive vocabulary was assessed (58%) was higher than the percentage of children who were within normal limits when receptive vocabulary (50%), word structure (33%), or sentence structure (40%) was evaluated.

Similar results emerged in a recent study on Italian deaf children between 18 and 36 months (Rinaldi et al., 2013). The percentage of children who were within normal limits when lexical production was assessed (45%) was higher than the percentage of children who were within normal limits when morphosyntactic aspects were evaluated, in particular when the complexity and accuracy of the sentences produced (14%) were considered. Furthermore, about 36% of the children fell below normal range in all the skills assessed. With respect to pragmatic skills, 25% of the children were within normal limits and 17% were within normal limits in both pragmatic and lexical skills.

Similar difficulties remain in older Italian deaf children, until school age. Children with CI aged 44 to 65 months performed similarly to their hearing peers and better than younger hearing children matched for time elapsed since CI activation in lexical production. These are younger hearing children with the same hearing experience. For example, a deaf child evaluated at four years whose cochlear implant was activated when he was one year old was compared with a hearing child aged three years; both children were exposed to spoken language for three years. In lexical comprehension and in morphosyntactic comprehension and production, children with CIs performed significantly worse than their hearing peers and similar to younger hearing children (Caselli, Rinaldi, Varuzza, Giuliani, & Burdo, 2012). Italian children with CIs aged 50 to 82 months still performed worse than their hearing peers in lexical comprehension and morphosyntactic comprehension and production and had a specific difficulty in production of clitic pronouns (Guasti et al., 2014).

These studies highlighted that language development of deaf children with CIs follows a delayed and atypical pattern, with lexical comprehension more impaired than lexical production and morphosyntactic aspects more impaired than lexicon (Caselli et al., 2012; Duchesne et al., 2009; Geers et al., 2009; Guasti et al., 2014; Rinaldi et al., 2013).

With respect to specific parameters affecting language development, Geers and colleagues (2009) assessed 153 deaf children in the United States aged five years to six years and 11 months. After controlling for the effects of nonverbal intelligence and parent education level, the strongest predictor for language development was age at CI activation. Children who received their CIs at younger ages had higher scores on language tests than children who were older at implantation. The range of age at implantation in this study was quite extended and varied from 11 months to five years of age.

Contrasting results were found in another study on 96 children, also in the United States (Holt & Svirsky, 2008). The authors found that children implanted in the first year of life had linguistic skills similar to those of children implanted in the second year of life. Furthermore, children from both these groups taken together, implanted before two years of age, had higher performances than children implanted in the third or fourth years of life. An overall reading of the results of these research studies suggests that age at CI activation as a strong predictor of outcome emerges when children studied and compared have large differences in age at implant activation. It did not emerge between children implanted within 12 months of age and those implanted in the second year of age.

Another study evaluated Italian preschool children with CIs (Rinaldi et al., 2013). All children enrolled in this research received their CIs by 26 months of age, so that the range in age of CI activation was relatively restricted. As found in other research that evaluated children in short ranges of age at CI activation, the authors found that the only predictor of lexical skills was age at diagnosis of hearing loss: the earlier the diagnosis, the higher the linguistic performance. Neither the duration of the CI experience, nor the age at CI activation, or preimplant residual hearing with hearing aids entered the model in the regression analysis.

Other studies have focused on family environment as a parameter influencing language development. Szagun and Stumper (2012) longitudinally followed 25 deaf German children who were between six and 42 months old at the time of CI. The children's language was assessed at four data points: 12, 18, 24, and 30 months after implantation. Language was assessed by measures based on spontaneous speech and on parental questionnaires. The authors found that age at implantation did not have an overall effect, but maternal education and some properties of maternal input were associated with the children's linguistic development. In particular, mothers who produced longer sentences and who more frequently expanded the child's utterance, by repeating it and by adding elements and the correct grammatical markings, had children with faster linguistic progression.

The focus on the role of CI on spoken language outcomes presents only a partial picture in the case of deaf children who also know and use a sign language. Children can be exposed to signs in various ways: from the use of signs to support spoken language, as in Total Communication programs, to the sign language as a complex linguistic system. A deaf child who is exposed to both sign language and spoken language could be considered to be a "bimodal bilingual." As for hearing bilingual children exposed to two spoken languages, skills in each of the two languages and the relationship between them are affected by characteristics such as the time of onset of bilingualism, the amount and quality of linguistic input, and the contexts in which the languages are acquired and used (e.g., speech therapy, school, home) (Rinaldi, Caselli, Onofrio, & Volterra, 2014). Exposure to signs has been identified as a factor that could influence spoken language outcomes. In recent studies, researchers found that early exposure to sign language did not prevent subsequent spoken language development using a CI and that using sign language after CI might even lead to greater success in spoken language acquisition (Davidson, Lillo-Martin, & Chen Pichler, 2014; Hassanzadeh, 2012; Jiménez, Pino, & Herruzo, 2009; Rinaldi & Caselli, 2014). In particular, Davidson and colleagues (2014) studied spoken language development of four native signing children with CIs (bimodal bilinguals, deaf children of deaf parents). They found that all of these children were within normal limits in both comprehension and production, following a typical development in spoken language acquisition. Their performances were better than those of monolingual deaf children with CIs exposed only to spoken language and similar to those of hearing bimodal bilingual children (hearing children of deaf parents) in both comprehension and production.

In another study, researchers evaluated spoken language and sign language development of a deaf child with CI, of hearing parents, who was exposed at an early age to Italian Sign Language (Lingua dei Segni Italiana [LIS]) (Rinaldi & Caselli, 2014). His skills in spoken Italian were within normal limits (with respect to hearing peers) and the vocabulary growth rate in spoken Italian was equivalent to that of his hearing peers. Before CI, the child relied almost exclusively on sign language; after CI, he gradually shifted to spoken Italian, yet he still used sign language when unable to retrieve words in spoken Italian. The authors concluded that bimodal bilingualism might scaffold the development of spoken language, at least in these aspects, in these early developmental stages (Rinaldi & Caselli, 2014). These results suggest that also in deaf children with hearing parents, the onset of language(s) exposure during development could enhance the ability to learn spoken language, regardless of the sensorimotor form of the early language experience (Mayberry & Lock, 2003; Mayberry, Lock, & Kazmi, 2002).

Notwithstanding findings documenting the positive effects of early bimodal bilingualism (sign language and spoken language) even in children with CI, either with deaf parents (Davidson et al., 2014) or hearing parents (Rinaldi & Caselli, 2014), the jury is still out on the positive outcomes of this coexistence because the long-term implications of early sign language for academic abilities remain unclear. Research studies that have been mainly based on children exposed to signs in Total Communication programs (instead of to a full language, like sign language is) have shown that the use of signs impedes spoken language mastery in deaf children.

Otherwise, bimodal bilingualism could contribute to CI efficacy, both by providing language to multimodal language circuits and by giving the child a gateway to understanding auditory signals (see also Knoors & Marschark, 2012; Lyness, Woll, Campbell, & Cardin, 2013; Rinaldi & Caselli, 2014, for a more detailed discussion on this topic).

Academic Achievement of Deaf Pupils

Linguistic skills in deaf as well as in hearing children have a strong relationship with academic skills, in particular with reading skills. The delay that deaf children show in language development in preschool years could have cascading effects on later academic outcomes.

Only a few studies have examined classroom performance and academic achievements of students with CIs, and findings were heterogeneous. Damen, van den Oever-Goltstein, Langereis, Chute, and Mylanus (2006) used the SIFTER (Screening Instrument for Targeting Educational Risk) questionnaire to assess the school performance of students with CIs and showed that they scored significantly lower than their hearing peers in most domains (academics, attention, communication, classroom participation, and school behavior). Both the earlier age at implantation and the duration of CI use contributed to better outcomes, yet large individual variability was reported. Weisi and colleagues (2013) investigated the reading skills in 24 second-and third-grade deaf students with CIs and in 24 of their hearing peers. Students with CIs showed weak performance in reading skills in comparison to hearing peers due to their lower accessibility to phonological information. For children who received a CI before age three years, the age at implantation was not strongly correlated with reading skills that the child exhibited at age eight or nine years. One possible explanation was that there might be an advantage for early implantation that is no longer apparent by the age of eight years (Weisi et al., 2013). Individually, some deaf children performed at similar levels to their hearing peers in school-related domains, but in a large-scale study on academic achievement of thousands of deaf children in the United States, they were more likely to have age-appropriate levels when they were young; median academic achievement fell significantly behind that of their hearing peers by the time they reached high school (Qi & Mitchell, 2012). Similar results were found in a previous study (Geers, Tobey, Moog, & Brenner, 2008). Deaf participants had age-appropriate reading levels at eight and nine years of age, but they faced an average delay of two years in reading levels at fifteen and sixteen years of age. The results suggested that reading abilities at an early stage after implantation might not be maintained over time, confirming previous research that found that the lag between deaf and hearing children tends to increase with age (Harris & Moreno, 2004; Johnson & Goswami, 2010; Pisoni & Geers, 2000). One possible explanation, again, is that there might be an advantage for early implantation that is no longer apparent at older ages on academic achievement.

With respect to sign language, some studies found limited improvement in academic outcomes of deaf students attending classrooms in which sign language was used. In these situations it is relevant to know whether the pupils were exposed to sign language early in life and whether they were exposed to a full sign language or to a form of sign supported speech. Some researchers found that the reading abilities of deaf children of deaf parents were associated with their early sign language skills; as in hearing children, early spoken language skills were associated with reading abilities (Knoors & Marschark, 2014). Thus, early language experience, either spoken or signed, appears to have positive cascading effects on learning supporting academic achievement.

In conclusion, considerable individual differences in both language and academic skills remain in children and adolescents with CIs, with specific difficulties in reading and writing. Researchers have reported difficulties in several linguistic aspects involved in reading comprehension, for example in vocabulary knowledge and in grammar (Hermans, Knoors, Ormel, & Verhoeven, 2008; Trezek, Wang, & Paul, 2011), as was found in deaf children with hearing aids (Marschark & Spencer, 2006; Rinaldi & Caselli, 2009). These difficulties could hinder school performance in general. For these reasons, as pointed out by some authors, deaf students need explicit instruction in academically relevant skills (e.g., reading strategies) (Borgna, Convertino, Marschark, Morrison, & Rizzolo, 2011), and new technologies may effectively support literacy learning (Lachs, 2000; Cedric Wachholz, 2006).

In the past few decades, the use of multimedia tools with deaf students to enhance learning, and in particular to enhance the accessibility of written texts to deaf students, has widely increased. It is a common assumption that the use of multiple visual information, such as pictures, animations, and/or movies, enhances learning in deaf students using their unimpaired sensory channel. However, studies on hearing students have demonstrated that processing information from multiple sources of information requires considerable cognitive effort (Baddeley, 2007). As reported by Knoors and Marschark (2014), little empirical research into the educational efficacy of the use of multimedia tools with deaf students is available, and there are no definitive conclusions on the role that some sources of information could have in terms of facilitating or interfering with learning. Lang and Steely (2003) conducted a series of studies to verify the effectiveness of Web-based science instruction for deaf students. The multimedia environment contained short texts, related animations, and American Sign Language translation of the texts. The authors found a significantly higher level of knowledge in students who used these interactive multimedia and Web-based materials than in students provided with traditional classroom experiences. Gentry, Chinn, and Moulton (2004-2005) supported the findings that multimedia tools based on various combinations of print, pictures, sign language-enhanced video, graphics, and animation might be enjoyable and interesting supplements to standard reading practices. On the other hand, Reitsma (2008) demonstrated that neither the use of pictures nor the use of sign videos in a multimedia program facilitated single word reading in deaf children.

In the following section, we will describe some multimedia tools developed to improve the learning abilities of Italian deaf students, preceded by a brief review of different school contexts in Italy in which deaf students could be enrolled.

MULTIMEDIA LEARNING ENVIRONMENTS DEVELOPED FOR ITALIAN DEAF STUDENTS

In Italy, deaf children are provided with different types of schooling. The great majority of them attend mainstream public schools along with hearing children. In these schools, the family has the right by law to request a support teacher. In most of these schools, Italian (spoken and written) is the only language used both in providing instructions and for communication purposes (see Caselli, Maragna, & Volterra, 2006; Trovato, 2014). There are no sign language interpreters, the support teacher of the classroom does not use sign language, and teachers and students in the classroom communicate in spoken Italian. Since 1992, children's families may request the additional presence in the classroom of a teaching assistant for a maximum of 20 hours a week. Depending on the family's request, the teaching assistant can use LIS or Signed Italian (SI) or rarely Sign Supported Italian (SSI).[1] In most cases, there is only one deaf child in a class of hearing children.

Very few public schools offer a bilingual curriculum that implies constant use of Italian and LIS within the classroom. In these schools, teachers use LIS or SI or there is an LIS interpreter who simultaneously translates the teachers' and pupils' messages from Italian to LIS and vice versa. In these schools, LIS is also taught as a subject to deaf and hearing pupils, for a minimum of one hour per week to a maximum of six hours per week. Usually two or more deaf children are present in the same classroom (Russo Cardona & Volterra, 2007; Teruggi, 2003).

In recent years in Italy, as in other countries, a growing number of deaf children received CI in their early years and attend mainstreamed classes, often only with the help of a support teacher. Only a few of these families requested that their implanted children have a signing teaching assistant and/or a bilingual curriculum. As previously reported, there are large individual differences in the spoken Italian competencies of deaf children with CI; some have poor skills on some linguistic measures, in particular morphosyntactic abilities, and this could have negative cascading effects on their academic achievement.

No studies have been conducted on the reading and writing skills of Italian deaf students with CI. Researchers studying Italian deaf students using hearing aids reported serious difficulties in reading comprehension (Rinaldi et al., 2014). Furthermore, in writing production, with respect to their hearing peers, deaf students produced shorter sentences, avoided more complex syntactical structures (e.g., relative, subordinate, and pronominal clauses), and made errors of omission and substitution in several morphosyntactic aspects (e.g., articles, clitic pronouns, prepositions). The typology and severity of difficulties were very similar in signing and nonsigning students (Ajello, Marotta, Mazzoni, & Nicolai, 2001; Arfé & Boscolo, 2006; Fabbretti & Caselli, 2001; Fabbretti, Volterra, & Pontecorvo, 1998).

Also in Italy, some multimedia tools have been developed to improve the reading and writing abilities of deaf students so they can obtain better academic achievement. The Lode project provided a Web application to support deaf children in working on their reading comprehension skills and in particular on the comprehension of temporal relations (Arfé, Gennari, & Mich, 2009). The application is based on animated stories and exercises developed as games. The language used in Lode's stories is simplified to assist the children's focus on the inference aspects. In a preliminary evaluation study with 18 deaf children and 12 hearing peers (attending primary and middle schools), researchers assessed the usability and effectiveness of the Lode application. The results showed that hearing children performed better than deaf participants in comprehension exercises. Simplified stories, illustrated with drawings and extended with definitions, resulted in greater effectiveness for the reading comprehension of deaf children than did the original version of the text or the simplified stories without images (Mich, Pianta, & Mana, 2013). More recently, the Terence project involved the creation of an adaptive learning system to help students with poor comprehension skills (deaf and hearing) to reason about stories and to improve their comprehension of the written materials (Cofini, Di Giacomo, Di Mascio, Gennari, & Vittorini, 2013b). The Terence learning materials are books of stories (in Italian and in English) and games. The "smart games" serve to stimulate story comprehension and to assist with reasoning about the events of a story and their relationships with each other. Each story is written at four difficulty levels. The levels are designed to make a story less difficult at the following levels: first of global coherence, then of global cohesion, and finally of lexicon and grammar. Terence has been used with hearing and deaf students from primary schools who have poor text comprehension skills, and who are older than seven years and without cognitive and/or neurosensorial difficulties. Research on the effectiveness of this project for deaf students' reading comprehension is ongoing, but preliminary results show improvements in reading comprehension in hearing students as well as in children's interest and motivation in reading and writing activities (Cofini et al., 2013a).

Since the 1990s some multimedia tools have been developed by our research group at the Institute of Cognitive Sciences and Technologies of the Italian National Research Council (ISTC-CNR), to offer deaf students more enjoyable learning environments and to support their reading abilities. We will describe two of these tools: Savannah and Dele. Unlike other multimedia applications created for deaf pupils in Italy, both are designed according to the bimodal bilingual educational model. In particular, video in LIS is employed, along with other visual sources of information, to facilitate deaf children's access to written materials.

Savannah

Savannah was developed in the early 1990s as a multimedia approach in providing information on a topic known to be interesting for children of various ages (between seven and fourteen years) (Volterra et al., 1994). The selected topic was animals living in the savannah portion of the African continent. The application involves setting up a multimedia learning environment in which the learner might follow different paths independently. Exploration of the environment stimulates the pupil to access and to integrate four sources of visual information, two nonlinguistic (videos and graphic explanations) and two linguistic (texts in written Italian, and LIS descriptions). The information provided in the various forms was only partially equivalent and retained some differences in content, depending on its source. For example, the two linguistic sources provided more detailed information than did those provided by the videos and graphic explanations, which, on the other hand, might offer a more direct access to a character or to an event. Children could freely choose any path without feeling excessively constrained.

The pathway was organized as follows: the savannah environment was presented, 10 animals were introduced as a group, and then the pathway presented three main topics: physical characteristics, feeding habits, and special living habits. For each topic, children could choose the animal or the animals they wished to see. Children entered the application guided by a lion mascot who introduced the first film, which presented the savannah environment. As soon as the film sequence ended, children were presented with a menu that gave them access to the following environments: Italian written text, comments in LIS, and graphics-based explanations. This menu reappeared at various stages of the journey along the pathway, and children could make their choices.

Most of the vocabulary used was carefully chosen, and some scientific terms relevant to the topics were included. Particular attention was paid to syntactic organization, characterized by using short sentences, coordinated clauses (rather than embedded clauses), subject repetition, and the present tense. Words or sentences that might need further explanation appeared in boldface type; clicking on them caused nonwritten explanations to appear near the text in the form of fixed images (graphics or photographs) or of short film sequences. If the LIS option was selected, the child saw a short film sequence of a deaf adult explaining and commenting in LIS the images the child had just seen in the introductory film. In addition, children could access a free space in which they could write information about the animals, their thoughts and feelings, or their preferences. Children were also engaged in games that proposed different kinds of activities related to the content of the multimedia application. The activities included making a poster about the savannah by cutting and pasting predrawn animals, taking and pasting photographs from the virtual environment, and answering various types of questions (e.g., specific questions, fill-in-the-blank by choosing the correct word from a word list, and judging the semantic acceptability of sentences).

The prototype of this application has been used with 25 deaf pupils (from second elementary school grade to third middle school grade) with different linguistic and educational backgrounds, for about nine months, in weekly sessions. The children used the application on an individual basis with the presence of an adult observer (tutor) who could give explanations or help when the child requested such. The experiment was structured into three phases. In the first phase, the pupils were asked to explore the application and to get acquainted with it (five to eight sessions of 30 minutes to one hour maximum each). In the second, students were asked to answer some questions about information contained in the application and related to one of the animals previously described, such as "What does it eat?" and so on (at least three sessions). In the last phase, students were engaged in the different activities provided in the application related to the contents of the savannah. Data reported on the evaluation study on 12 deaf pupils showed that a variety of visual information sources, including LIS, offered deaf children wider access to information and improved their retention of contents, in relation to their linguistic and educational backgrounds/skills. The application was also able to maintain the children's interest and motivation in reading and writing activities that are usually difficult and tiring for deaf children of school age (Volterra, Pace, Pennacchi, & Corazza, 1995).

For its time (the final version was released in 1994), Savannah was a pioneer in the learning environment, using the more advanced technologies available in those years (interactive videodisk and CD-ROM). In the following years, other learning environments based on new developing technologies and using Web facilities were developed by our research group at ISTC-CNR; the most recent is Deaf-centered E-Learning Environment (DELE).

Dele

Dele is an e-learning environment for promoting reading skills in high school-aged deaf students (regardless of their linguistic abilities and their preference for using spoken and/or sign language) that takes into account the potential these learners possess and the abilities they can take advantage of, relying on their unimpaired visual modality. Dele was developed as part of the project "E-learning, Deafness, Written Language: A Bridge of Letters and Signs towards Knowledge Society" (www.visel.cnr.it) (conceived by Dr. Elena Pizzuto). In Dele, didactic tools are available in different forms: written Italian and LIS, in accordance with the bimodal bilingual educational approach. Written texts are presented and explained to the students using the interactive "easification" methodology (Bhatia, 1983). "Easification" does not modify the text; the text remains in its original form for both content and lexical, morphosyntactic, and textual characteristics. Different sources of information, aimed to support and promote text comprehension, are added. Unlike "simplification," in which the complexity of the written text is reduced in several aspects (e.g., lexicon, grammar, content) with replacements or paraphrases/cut words and/or phrases, the easification methodology guides the reader through the text, making it more accessible with signifying images, videos, comics, definitions, synonyms, short stories, and whatever else can be of any help to comprehension (for further details about the application of this methodology in Dele, see Roccaforte & Giunchi, 2013).

To introduce students to the Dele environment, the metaphor of a university campus is used, and the students are requested to achieve graduate levels (to be implemented by teachers) and to have positive results on virtual examinations with story-specific goals. Inside the story, several other substories (e.g., home, university, building, coffee shop) were provided, building up a story-based path for all learning activities.

These have been adapted to increase deaf people's comprehension and interaction in the system through cooperative activities. Access to each course is given by the virtual university building, which contains the learning units as well as recreational and discussion areas such as the forum (Main Square) and the chat room. The learners can at any time cooperate with their peers through these collaboration tools. Moreover, the students can require the support of a tutor, asking for clarification or assistance. Proceeding independently or in cooperation with peers or with the tutor, the learner performs a series of educational activities related to the text and designed to promote understanding.

Once the student has read the text, he or she is introduced to different activities (exercises) aimed to support and improve the comprehension of the text as well as to evaluate reading comprehension. All the activities are presented in a realistic and dynamic context, aimed at encouraging deaf learners to interact with and manipulate texts. Through this interaction, students can gain skills that allow them to achieve educational goals, as well as to navigate daily linguistic situations.

Students are faced with the original text, without any easification. By clicking a button, students can visualize the original text, in which are highlighted all the elements for which easification cues are provided. He or she can have access to some of them, choosing the preferred type of support. When carrying out these activities, the learner can ask the tutor for specific support on the underlined text, leaving notes and/or posting a video, or asking for additional help for sections of the text for which specific support is not provided. The learner can receive the requested assistance through the range of tools provided, including:

- Teaching material that already exists in Dele's library, which the tutor can select;
- Teaching material created ad hoc;
- Sign language videos;
- Written answers; and
- Multimedia content such as illustrations, tables, cartoons, animations.

The platform was implemented with the constant involvement of deaf colleagues with teaching experience who were part of the ISTC research team. The platform was modified based on the feedback received from a group of deaf teachers of sign language and deaf research assistants who experienced the platform before its release.

The e-learning environment was tested with a group of 19 deaf users who attended high school or university and had very different sign language skills. Detailed information about the participants (degree and onset of deafness, family, linguistic and educational background, everyday linguistic choices, and reading habits) was collected. At the end of the testing period (about one month), the accessibility of the platform and its appreciation by the deaf students were evaluated through semistructured interviews. The results of the testing enabled the resolution of some critical problems in browsing highlighted by the participants. The results of the interviews showed that deaf students highly appreciated the e-learning environment and asked to continue to use the platform autonomously. Results on the effectiveness of the platform for comprehension of the written texts are still in progress. However, preliminary observations suggested that the visual cues and facilities offered provided students with a high motivation to explore all the available materials and to answer the questions. Dele was designed as a container, allowing it to be implemented or customized by professionals such as teachers, teaching assistants, and speech therapists who are involved in educating deaf learners.

CONCLUSION

Linguistic and academic outcomes of deaf children in the CI era continue to be characterized by wide variability. Some deaf children and adolescents, a few years after CI, catch up with their hearing peers, while others still show difficulties in linguistic abilities, with lexical comprehension being more impaired than lexical production and morphosyntactic aspects being more impaired than lexicon. The delay deaf children show in language development may have effects on their later academic outcomes, with specific difficulties in reading and writing. Weakness in literacy could also seriously limit these youth's educational and career possibilities since without literacy, one's professional opportunities are highly circumscribed.

New technologies, in particular Web-based multimedia environments, that take into account the peculiarities of deaf learners and the variability that characterizes their linguistic and educational backgrounds and skills might effectively support learning. However, these tools must be designed according to educational models with solid theoretical backgrounds. Deaf students have the right to full access to the same didactic materials as their hearing peers, without any simplification and reduction in either form or content. In light of these considerations, we suggest that educators offer deaf students the original written materials, providing special tools that could ease their access to all the information included. Multimedia e-learning tools must be developed in flexible and dynamic environments in which each deaf student, based on his or her strengths and weaknesses, can access easification strategies when he or she is struggling with the original source of information. Tools designed for deaf students should take into account the opportunities that the use of sign language can offer as added value for their academic achievement, at least for bimodal bilingual students. The Savannah and Dele tools offer deaf students the opportunity to understand the content of the original written texts, also taking advantage of their sign language knowledge. In such environments, deaf students can choose the preferred type of support to use, setting reasonable learning goals for themselves and adopting productive learning strategies. All these activities could improve metacognitive skills in both deaf and hearing students.

Finally, we suggest that educators use new technologies to develop environments in which collaborative learning among students, along with their tutors, is encouraged. Cooperative learning provides deeper comprehension of the content, increases academic achievements, improves self-esteem, and raises the student's motivation to remain on task. Cooperative learning helps students to become actively and constructively involved in content, to take ownership of their own learning, and to improve their teamwork skills and inclusion (Tolmie et al., 2010).

In conclusion, various e-learning tools for deaf students, as well as Web based tools for teachers and clinicians to assess deaf students' spoken and signed linguistic skills are now available, and their potential for educational purposes is widely recognized. However, the effectiveness and usability of most of these tools have not yet been demonstrated through evidence-based research.

ACKNOWLEDGMENTS

This work was partially funded by Fondazione Telecom Italia, Project "VOLIS," to Pasquale Rinaldi, Education, Audiovisual and Culture Executive Agency—EACEA no. 543264-LLP-1-2013-1-ITKA2-KA2MP "SignMET" to Pasquale Rinaldi and by Italian Ministry of University and Research, programme FIRB 2012, "MODELACT," project code RBFR12C6O8 to Elena Tomasuolo. We wish to thank Virginia Volterra for her insightful comments.

NOTE

[1] SI and SSI both rely on spoken Italian words simultaneously accompanied by the corresponding LIS signs. In addition, SSI uses fingerspelling for Italian function words.

REFERENCES

Ajello, R., Marotta, G., Mazzoni, L., & Nicolai F. (2001). Morphosyntactic fragility in the spoken and written Italian of the deaf. In E. Fava (Ed.), *Clinical linguistics. Theory and applications in speech pathology and therapy* (pp. 49–74). Amsterdam, Philadelphia: John Benjamin Publishing Company.

Arfé, B., & Boscolo, P. (2006). Causal coherence in deaf and hearing students' written narratives. *Discourse Processes*, *42*, 271–300.

Arfé, B., Gennari, R., & Mitch, O. (2009). Evaluations of the LODE temporal reasoning tool with hearing and deaf children. *Cognitive and Metacognitive Educational Systems*: Papers from the AAAI Fall Symposium (FS-09-02).

Baddeley, A. D. (2007). *Working memory, thought and action*. New York: Oxford University Press.

Bhatia, V. K. (1983). Simplification vs. easification. The case of legal texts. *Applied Linguistics*, *4*, 42–54.

Blamey, P., Barry, J., Bow, C., Sarant, J., Paatsch, L., & Wales, R. (2001). The development of speech production following cochlear implantation. *Clinical Linguistics and Phonetics*, *15*, 363–382.

Borgna, G., Convertino, C., Marschark, M., Morrison, C., & Rizzolo, K. (2011). Enhancing deaf students' learning from sign language and text: Metacognition, modality, and the effectiveness of content scaffolding. *Journal of Deaf Studies and Deaf Education*, *16*, 79–100.

Caselli, M. C., Maragna, S., & Volterra, V. (2006). *Linguaggio e sordità. Gesti, segni e parole nello sviluppo e nell'educazione* [Language and deafness. Gestures, signs and words in development and education]. Bologna, Italy: Il Mulino.

Caselli, M. C., Rinaldi, P., Varuzza, C., Giuliani, A., & Burdo, S. (2012). Cochlear implant in the second year of life: lexical and grammatical outcomes. *Journal of Speech Language and Hearing Research*, *55*, 382–394.

Cedric Wachholz, E. E. M. (Ed.), (2006). *Using ICT to develop literacy*. Bangkok: UNESCO.

Cofini, V., De la Prieta, F., Di Mascio, T., Gennari, R., Marenzi, I., & Vittorini, P. (2013a). The design of learning material for poor comprehenders: lessons learnt from experts. *Jurnal Teknologi*, *63*, 45–51.

Cofini, V., Di Giacomo, D., Di Mascio, T., Gennari, R., & Vittorini, P. (2013b). *The pedagogical evaluation of TERENCE: Preliminary results for hearing learners in Italy*. In Proceedings of the Third International Workshop on Evidence-Based and User-Centred Technology. Fondazione Bruno Kessler, Trento, Italy, September 16, 2013.

Crowe, K., & McLeod, S. (2014). A systematic review of cross-linguistic and multilingual speech and language outcomes for children with hearing loss. *International Journal of Bilingual Education and Bilingualism*, *17*, 287–309.

Damen, G. W. J. A., van den Oever-Goltstein, M. H. L., Langereis, M. C., Chute, P. M., & Mylanus, E. A. M. (2006). Classroom performance of children with cochlear implants in mainstream education. *Annals of Otology, Rhinology and Laryngology*, *115*, 542–552.

Davidson, K., Lillo-Martin, D., & Chen Pichler, D. (2014). Spoken English language development in native signing children with cochlear implants. *Journal of Deaf Studies and Deaf Education*, *19*, 238–250.

Duchesne, L., Sutton, A., & Bergeron, F. (2009). Language achievement in children who received cochlear implants between 1 and 2 years of age: Group trends and individual patterns. *Journal of Deaf Studies and Deaf Education*, *14*, 465–485.

Fabbretti, D., & Caselli, M. C. (2001). Scrivere senza sentire. Analisi delle scritture di bambini sordi di scuola elementare [Writing without hearing. Analysis of the written productions of elementary school deaf children]. *Età Evolutiva [Developmental Age]*, *68*, 72–80.

Fabbretti, D., Volterra, V., & Pontecorvo, C. (1998) Written language abilities in deaf Italians. *Journal of Deaf Studies and Deaf Education, 3*, 231–244.

Geers, A. E., Moog, J. S., Biedenstein, J., Brenner, C., & Hayes, H. (2009). Spoken language scores of children using cochlear implants compared to hearing age-mates at school entry. *Journal of Deaf Studies and Deaf Education, 14*, 371–385.

Geers, A., Tobey, E., Moog, J., & Brenner, C. (2008). Long-term outcomes of cochlear implantation in the preschool years: from elementary grades to high school. *International Journal of Audiology, 47*, 21–30.

Gentry, M. M., Chinn, K. M., & Moulton, R. D. (2004-2005). Effectiveness of multimedia reading materials when used with children who are deaf. *American Annals of the Deaf, 149*, 394–403.

Guasti, M. T., Papagno, C., Vernice, M., Cecchetto, C., Giuliani, A., & Burdo, S. (2014). The effect of language structure on linguistic strengths and weaknesses in children with cochlear implants: Evidence from Italian. *Applied Psycholinguistics, 35*, 739–764.

Harris, M., & Moreno, C. (2004). Deaf children's use of phonological coding: evidence from reading, spelling, and working memory. *Journal of Deaf Studies and Deaf Education, 9*, 253–268.

Hassanzadeh, S. (2012). Outcomes of cochlear implantation in deaf children of deaf parents: Comparative study. *Journal of Laryngology & Otology, 126*, 989–994.

Hermans, D., Knoors, H., Ormel, E., & Verhoeven, L. (2008). The relationship between the reading and signing skills of deaf children in bilingual education programs. *Journal of Deaf Studies and Deaf Education, 13*, 518–530.

Holt, R. F., & Svirsky, M. A. (2008). An exploratory look at pediatric cochlear implantation: Is earliest always best? *Ear and Hearing, 29*, 492–511.

Jiménez, M. S., Pino, M. J., & Herruzo, J. (2009). A comparative study of speech development between deaf children with cochlear implants who have been educated with spoken or spoken + sign language. *International Journal of Pediatric Otorhinolaryngology, 73*, 109–114.

Johnson, C., & Goswami, U. (2010). Phonological awareness, vocabulary and reading in deaf children with cochlear implants. *Journal of Speech, Language, and Hearing Research, 53*, 237–261.

Knoors, H., & Marschark, M. (2012). Language planning for the 21st century: Revisiting bilingual language policy for deaf children. *Journal of Deaf Studies and Deaf Education, 17*, 291–305.

Knoors, H., & Marschark, M., (2014). *Teaching deaf learners. Psychological and developmental foundations*. New York: Oxford University Press.

Lachs, V. (2000). *Making multimedia in the classroom: A teacher's guide*. London: Routledge.

Lang, H., & Steely, D. (2003). Web-based science instruction for deaf students: What research says to the teacher. *Instructional Science, 31*, 277–298.

Lyness, C. R., Woll, B., Campbell, R., & Cardin, V. (2013). How does visual language affect crossmodal plasticity and cochlear implant success? *Neuroscience and Biobehavioral Reviews, 37*, 2621–2630.

Marschark, M., & Spencer, P. E. (2006). Spoken language development a deaf and hard of hearing children: historical and theoretical perspectives. In P. E. Spencer & M. Marschark (Eds.), *Advances in the spoken language development of deaf and hard of hearing children* (pp. 3–21). New York: Oxford University Press.

May-Mederake, B. (2012). Early intervention and assessment of speech and language development in young children with cochlear implants. *International Journal of Pediatric Otorhinolaryngology, 76*, 939–946.

Mayberry, R. I., & Lock, E. (2003). Age constraints on first versus second language acquisition: evidence for linguistic plasticity and epigenesis. *Brain and Language, 87*, 369–384.

Mayberry, R. I., Lock, E., & Kazmi, H. (2002). Linguistic ability and early language exposure. *Nature, 417*, 38.

Mich, O., Pianta, E., & Mana, N. (2013). Interactive stories and exercises with dynamic feedback for improving reading comprehension skills in deaf children. *Computers & Education, 65*, 34–44.

Nicholas, J. G., & Geers, A. E. (2007). Will they catch up? The role of age at cochlear implantation in the spoken language development of children with severe to profound hearing loss. *Journal of Speech, Language, and Hearing Research, 50*, 1–15.

Pisoni, D. D., & Geers, A. E. (2000). Working memory in deaf children with cochlear implants: correlations between digit span and measures of spoken language processing, *Annals of Otology, Rhinology, and Laryngology, 109*, 92–93.

Qi, S., & Mitchell, R. E. (2012). Large-scale academic achievement testing of deaf and hard-of-hearing students: Past, present, and future. *Journal of Deaf Studies and Deaf Education, 17*, 1–18.

Reitsma, P. (2008). Computer-based exercises for learning to read and spell by deaf children. *Journal of Deaf Studies and Deaf Education, 14*, 178–189.

Rinaldi, P., Baruffaldi, F., Burdo, S., & Caselli, M. C. (2013). Linguistic and pragmatic skills in toddlers with cochlear implant. *International Journal of Language & Communication Disorders, 48*, 715–725.

Rinaldi, P., & Caselli, M. C. (2009). Lexical and grammatical abilities in deaf Italian preschoolers: The role of duration of formal language experience. *Journal of Deaf Studies and Deaf Education, 14*, 63–75.

Rinaldi, P., & Caselli, M. C. (2014). Language development in a bimodal bilingual child with cochlear implant: A longitudinal study. *Bilingualism: Language and Cognition, 17*, 798–809.

Rinaldi, P., Caselli, M. C., Onofrio, D., &Volterra, V. (2014). Language acquisition by bilingual deaf preschoolers: Theoretical, methodological issues and empirical data. In M. Marschark, G. Tang, & H. Knoors (Eds.), *Bilingualism and bilingual deaf education* (pp. 85–116). New York: Oxford University Press.

Rinaldi, P., Onofrio, D., Pennacchi, B., Petitta, G., Del Gesso, V., Lauria, E., . . . & Caselli, M. C. (2014), *Comprensione del linguaggio e abilità cognitive in bambini bilingui bimodali [Linguistic comprehension and cognitive abilities in bimodal bilingual children]*. Giornate di Neuropsicologia dell'età evolutiva [Conference on Developmental Neuropsychology], Brixen, Italy, January 15–19, 2014.

Roccaforte, M., & Giunchi, P. M. (2013). Strategie nello sviluppo di un ambiente e-learning per giovani e adulti sordi. [Strategies to design e-learning environments for deaf learners]. In C. Bosisio & S. Cavagnoli (Eds.), *Atti del XII Congresso della Associazione Italiana di Linguistica Applicata (AITLA) [Proceedings of the XII Congress of the Italian Association of Applied Linguistics (AITLA)]* (pp. 229–241). Guerra Edizioni, Perugia (Italy).

Russo Cardona, T., & Volterra, V. (2007). *Le lingue dei segni: Storia e Semiotica [Sign languages: History and semiotics]*. Rome, Italy: Carocci.

Spencer, P. E. (2004). Individual differences in language performance after cochlear implantation at one to three years of age: Child, family, and linguistic factors. *Journal of Deaf Studies and Deaf Education, 9*, 395–412.

Szagun, G., & Stumper, B. (2012). Age or experience? The influence of age at implantation and social and linguistic environment on language development in children with cochlear implants. *Journal of Speech, Language, and Hearing Research, 55*, 1640–1654.

Teruggi, L. A. (Ed.) (2003). *Una Scuola, due lingue: l'esperienza di bilinguismo della scuola dell'Infanzia ed Elementare di Cossato [One school, two languages: Bilingual experience in Cossato's kindergarten and primary school]*. Milan, Italy: Franco Angeli.

Tolmie, A. K., Topping, K. J., Christie, D., Donaldson, C., Howe, C., Jessiman, E., & Thruston, A. (2010). Social effects of collaborative learning in primary schools. *Learning and Instruction, 20*, 177–191.

Trezek, B. J., Wang, Y., & Paul, P. V. (2011). Processes and components of reading. In M. Marschark & P. Spencer (Eds.). *Handbook of deaf studies, language and education* (2nd ed., pp. 99–114). New York: Oxford University Press.

Trovato, S. (2014). *Insegno in segni. Linguaggio, cognizione, successo scolastico per gli studenti sordi [Teaching through signs. Language, cognition and academic achievement of deaf students]*. Milan, Italy: Raffaello Cortina Ed.

Volterra, V., Caselli, M. C., Corazza, S., Pace, C., Pennacchi, B., & Rampelli, S. (1994). *Gli animali della Savana. Un'esplorazione multimediale interattiva (CD-Rom) [The animals of the Savannah. An interactive multimedia tool (CD-Rom)]*. Milan, Italy: Opera Multimedia, & Rome, Italy: CNR.

Volterra, V., Pace, C., Pennacchi, B., & Corazza, S. (1995). Advanced learning technology for a bilingual education of deaf children. *American Annals of the Deaf, 140*, 402–409.

Weisi, F., Rezaei, M., Rashedi, V., Heidari, A., Valadbeigi, A., & Ebrahimi-Pour, M. (2013). Comparison of reading skills between children with cochlear implants and children with typical hearing in Iran. *International Journal of Pediatric Otorhinolaryngology 77*, 1317–1321.

20

EmotionWeb

From Fundamental Research to a Functional Tool for Professionals

Karin Wiefferink, Meinou de Vries, and Lizet Ketelaar

Everyone experiences emotions on a day-to-day basis. Emotions serve an important function: They alert us that something is at stake and prepare us to deal with the situation at hand (Frijda, 1986). They also inform others in our surroundings about our goals, intentions, needs, and so on (Keltner & Haidt, 1999). Emotions can be confusing for young children, but as they grow older their emotional competence increases. Children learn how to recognize and understand their own emotions and those of others. They also learn how to strategically communicate their emotions in line with the social rules and moral codes of their social environment. In other words, children's increasing emotional competence promotes their social functioning. Emotionally competent children are more likely to respond appropriately to other people, which improves their social relationships and other aspects of development (e.g., school performance). Forming and maintaining positive relationships not only with adults but in particular with peers is one of the most important developmental tasks for young children (Denham et al., 2003).

Usually, children acquire social-emotional skills in interaction with their environment, partly by observing and overhearing others and partly through direct feedback, instructions, and explanations. This process is called emotion socialization (Saarni, 1999). Emotion socialization can take place only when children have access to their social environment. Deaf and hard-of-hearing (DHH) children with hearing parents often have limited access to their social environment. They experience difficulties overhearing conversations between other people, which severely limits their potential for incidental learning (Vaccari & Marschark, 1997). This implies that social-emotional learning in DHH children occurs only when they are addressed directly. Yet, interacting with their DHH child is challenging for hearing parents because they frequently do not communicate in the same language or do not do so with sufficient fidelity or consistency for the child's understanding (Hosie, Gray, Russell, Scott, & Hunter, 1998; Rieffe & Meerum Terwogt, 2006). In comparison to hearing parents of hearing children, hearing parents of DHH children interact less frequently with their child, and these interactions are less extensive (Barker et al., 2009; Gale & Schick, 2009; Prezbindowski, Adamson, & Lederberg, 1998).

Disruptions of the emotion socialization process could result in impaired emotional competence and in more behavioral and social problems. DHH children are indeed found to more often experience behavioral problems (Barker et al., 2009; Van Eldik, Treffers, Veerman, & Verhulst, 2004), internalizing problems (Kouwenberg, 2013; Van Eldik et al., 2004; Van Gent, 2012), and peer interaction problems (Kouwenberg, 2013; Wolters, Knoors, Cillessen, & Verhoeven, 2011) than their hearing peers. Teachers, family counselors, social workers, and other professionals working with DHH children must know which aspects of social-emotional development are impaired or are developing differently. This knowledge enables them to offer these children better support. We have developed a screening tool called EmotionWeb to identify delays in key aspects of individual children's social-emotional development. EmotionWeb enables professionals to compare the presence of behavioral problems and the level of emotional functioning in an individual child with normative scores of hearing children and normative scores of DHH children.

We will first describe the various aspects of emotional functioning that can be screened with EmotionWeb. Next, we describe how EmotionWeb was developed, followed by how it can be used in daily practice. Finally, we provide examples of how information from EmotionWeb can be interpreted and how it can be used to improve the social-emotional development of DHH children.

ASPECTS OF EMOTIONAL FUNCTIONING

Emotion Identification

For a healthy social-emotional development it is important that children can recognize and understand their own emotions. They have to learn to recognize that certain physical sensations and nonverbal signals are part of emotional experiences. This helps children to understand the nature of their emotions and in what situations a certain emotion may occur. In other words, they learn the causes and consequences of their emotions. Hearing preschool children already understand causes and consequences of emotions. A child who understands that a present arouses happiness already anticipates this pleasant feeling when he expects to get a present at his birthday. He thus can connect an emotion to a specific situation and therefore understands why and when someone experiences the emotion "happy."

Learning to identify one's own emotions usually starts during the preschool period. As children get older, the following aspects of identifying emotions can be seen (Denham, 1998):

- Verbal and nonverbal expressions of emotions;
- Recognizing situations that can provoke emotions;
- Understanding the causes and consequences of emotions in specific situations;
- Using emotion words to clarify one's own emotions;
- Awareness that it is possible to experience more than one emotion at the same time, even though these might be contradictory; and
- Recognizing complex emotions, such as shame or guilt.

Many DHH children have more difficulties in learning nonverbal cues of their emotions, because they do not know how to interpret these cues because they cannot understand the spoken language accompanying these cues (Wiefferink, 2012). For example, they may experience physical sensations, such as abdominal pain or goose bumps, without knowing how to interpret these sensations. If no one explains to them that these physical sensations belong to an emotional experience, these children might focus on the physical sensations instead of the emotion-arousing situation (Rieffe & De Rooij, 2012). Consequently, these children may not know how to deal with the emotion-arousing situation, which in turn may negatively influence the emotion regulation and may cause stress, leading to, for example, somatic complaints (Jellesma, Rieffe, & Meerum Terwogt, 2007). Therefore, DHH children often need to explicitly be taught how they can identify their emotions and which emotions they feel in specific situations.

Emotion Communication

Children not only have to be aware of their own emotions but also have to learn the words for them. Developing an emotion vocabulary usually starts when the child is about two years old and continues until the end of primary school (Izard, 2009). At the age of two or three years, most hearing children can communicate their (emotional) needs, such as a need for comfort, support, or attention. For example, when a child comes home telling his mother that he had cried at school, he might be seeking attention and comfort from his mother. Toddlers can also make clear what they want or do not want by expressing their emotions. About 75% of three-year-old hearing children can verbally express emotions such as happy, sad, fear, and anger (Denham, 1998). When they reach the age of six they also know the meaning of words such as excited, surprised, disappointed, relieved, bored, lonely, shy, and concerned.

Children learn new emotion words by conversing with others and by receiving feedback about emotions and the causes of emotions. Learning to converse about emotions is a challenge for DHH children. Hearing children mostly learn how to talk about emotions from overhearing conversations between others, whereas DHH children have fewer opportunities to learn from these conversations. They experience the same emotions as other children but do not communicate them as well as hearing children and are not always aware of how their emotional behavior affects others (Rieffe & Meerum Terwogt, 2006). In their study, Rieffe and Meerum Terwogt (2006) found that DHH children, more than hearing children, tended to communicate their anger rather bluntly to other children, without explaining why they were angry. At the same time, DHH children were as optimistic as hearing children with respect to continuation of the friendship, even when they did not try to resolve the conflict. This may harm their relations with other children and adults.

Understanding Emotions of Others

Human beings have an innate capacity to attend to other people's emotions, also called empathy. Empathy refers to the ability to understand and share another's emotional state. It allows us to understand how other people are feeling and to react appropriately to these feelings. It is therefore important for social interactions. The level of empathy influences the quality of social relationships. For example, lower levels of empathy in 15-year-old hearing children were found to be related to higher levels of bullying (Jolliffe & Farrington, 2006), whereas hearing children with a higher level of empathy tend to be better liked by their peers and teachers and are judged to be more socially competent (Eisenberg, Spinrad, & Sadovsky, 2006).

Empathy can be divided into two components: *affective* empathy and *cognitive* empathy (Baron-Cohen & Wheelwright, 2004). *Affective* empathy can already be seen in infants. They are prone to display the emotions of others as though they automatically feel what others feel, which is called "emotion contagion." Infants are usually overwhelmed by this emotional experience. They do not know that it is not their own feeling they are responding to, but someone else's feeling. Gradually, over the course of their first year, children learn to differentiate between self and other, which enables them to focus their attention to the other person's experience.

In their second year of life, *cognitive* empathy starts to play a role. Around this age, most hearing children learn to identify the emotions of other people, and more importantly they start to understand the causes of these emotions. This allows them to select the appropriate response to relieve other people's distress. In other words, children start showing prosocial behavior, implying that they are concerned about the well-being of other people (Rieffe, Ketelaar, & Wiefferink, 2010).

To develop cognitive empathy, children need a Theory of Mind (ToM) (Baron-Cohen & Wheelwright, 2004). ToM refers to the ability to understand, predict, and explain the (emotional) behavior of others by taking the perspective of the other. When children grow older, they learn the different mental concepts of ToM, starting with *intentions*, followed by *desires* and finally *beliefs*. Children need to understand these mental concepts to know that someone else can have different intentions, desires, and beliefs than they have, and that people's behavior is governed by these mental states (see Morgan, Chapter 12 in this volume).

Awareness of *intentions* can be seen in young children. One-year-old hearing children already realize that the behavior of others is intentional. These toddlers look in the same direction as someone else because they understand that the other is not just looking at an object but has certain intentions, for example picking it up or showing it (Colonessi, Rieffe, Koops, & Perucchini, 2008).

Wellman (1990) demonstrated that two-year-old hearing children understand that the emotions and behavior of others may originate from desires, such as hopes, wishes, and needs. However, whether children at this age also understand the subjective nature of desires was not measured. A study by Rieffe, Meerum Terwogt, Koops, Stegge, and Oomen (2001) showed that three- and four-year-old hearing children still think that their own desires predict the emotions and behavior of others. For example, they may think that their brother would choose candy instead of an apple, because they themselves prefer candy. They do not take into account that their brother does not like candy but instead is very fond of apples.

Three-year-old hearing children already can predict that the emotions and behavior of others are caused by *beliefs*, such as notions, ideas, and views of people (Wellman, 1990). For example, if Mom wants a cookie and thinks that there are still cookies in the cupboard, the child will predict that she will go to the cupboard. The child also understands that she will be disappointed when she does not find cookies. However, not all three-years-olds realize that these beliefs are subjective or, in other words, that someone can hold a false belief. When they know that the cookies are finished, because Dad ate them, they do not understand that Mom does not have this knowledge and will therefore still go to the cupboard for cookies. Four- to five-year-old hearing children usually do understand this (Ketelaar, Rieffe, Wiefferink, & Frijns, 2012).

Because language is considered a prerequisite for the development of ToM skills (Astington & Jenkins, 1999), DHH children may experience difficulties in acquiring a ToM. A child needs to reason why someone else feels certain emotions or shows a specific behavior, and language is needed for this reasoning. Indeed, many studies show that the ToM development of DHH children is seriously hampered (for an overview, see Peterson & Siegal, 1995, 2000). When the development of ToM is disturbed, children may experience problems interacting with peers or may have behavioral problems such as aggression or withdrawal (Ketelaar et al., 2012). Older children also may develop internalizing problems such as depression (Kouwenberg, 2013).

Emotion Regulation

Controlling or diminishing the intensity of an emotion is an important skill in social situations. By learning how to regulate their emotions, children can avoid inappropriate behavior and can find a balance between their personal needs and their social needs (Gottman & Declaire, 1997). Most children learn how to regulate their emotions during interactions with peers: They learn to share, to handle a conflict, and to take into account the feelings and needs of others.

Even infants regulate their emotions to some extent. Their primary means of avoiding overarousal is to turn their head away from an emotion-arousing situation. Toddlers can divert themselves in a stressful or frustrating situation, for example by starting to do something completely different. While avoidance is an adequate strategy in young children, it is not for older children, who have to learn to confront a negative situation and find a way to solve it. Instead of avoiding a friend after a conflict, they should learn how to solve the conflict. Adequate problem-solving strategies improve children's mental health. Research shows that children who often use problem-solving strategies are less prone to develop depression or other internalizing problems (Wright, Banerjee, Hoek, Rieffe, & Novin, 2010).

Although problem-solving strategies are important for coping with negative situations, in some situations avoidance strategies are in fact more appropriate. Problem-solving strategies are effective only if it is possible to solve the problem. If this is not the case, for example when a beloved pet dies, it is better to draw attention away from the negative situation and try not to think about it too much. DHH children are less capable of discriminating between social situations that can be solved and ones that cannot (Rieffe, 2012). Consequently, they more often use inappropriate strategies, reflecting cognitive as well as social challenges.

Once children have developed sufficient metacognitive skills, around the age of 10 years, they start applying mental strategies when regulating their emotions (Rieffe, Meerum Terwogt, & Jellesma, 2008). Children from this age up can change their beliefs about situations. They know how to see things in perspective (e.g., "He didn't mean to hurt me") or can reappraise the situation ("It wasn't that important to me"). The ability to reappraise the situation is a particularly important factor in preventing depression and anxiety in children (Wright et al., 2010).

DEVELOPMENT OF EMOTIONWEB

The data in EmotionWeb were collected between 2009 and 2011. In total, 824 children participated in the study (224 DHH children and 600 hearing peers). The study was conducted by researchers from the Developmental Psychology department of the University of Leiden, the ENT department of the Leiden University Medical Center, Center for Autism, and the Dutch Foundation for the Deaf and Hard of Hearing Child.

Children participating in the project fell into three age groups: one to two-and-a-half years, two-and-a-half to five years, and nine to 14 years; see Table 20.1 for demographic characteristics. DHH children in all age groups were born to hearing parents and had no other disabling conditions. DHH children in the two youngest age groups all had cochlear implants (CIs). In line with their preferred mode of communication, approximately half of the children in the younger age groups were tested by means of some form of spoken Dutch, combined with signs; about a third of the children were tested in spoken Dutch; and the remaining children were tested in sign language. The DHH children in the oldest age group had a hearing loss of at least 40 dB, which was detected pre- or perilingually. These children either had hearing aids (57%) or CIs (43%). As in the youngest age groups, most DHH children in this group preferred to communicate in spoken language (70%) or a combination of sign (supported) and spoken language (30%). Just two children preferred to communicate fully in sign language. Children in the oldest group were also addressed using their preferred mode of communication. Moreover, children in the oldest group could choose between two ways of questionnaire presentation. They could either read the questions (which were presented one by one on a laptop computer), or they could choose for the written questions to be accompanied by video clips showing the questions in sign language.

Questionnaires as well as observation tasks were used to assess the different aspects of social-emotional development. Some aspects were assessed with an observation task, others with a questionnaire, and some with both a questionnaire and an observation task. Examples of these three types are described below. More detailed information on questionnaires, observation tasks, and the test procedure is available in the literature (Ketelaar et al., 2012, 2013; Kouwenberg, 2013; Rieffe et al., 2010; Theunissen, 2013; Wiefferink, 2012) or can be obtained online (www.emotieweb.nl). All questionnaires and observation tasks consist of one or more "scales." Each scale consists of several items, together measuring a specific aspect of social-emotional functioning.

Observations were used to assess whether children aged one to five years could identify the emotions of others in specific situations. The task consisted of eight vignettes depicting prototypical emotion-eliciting situations; for each basic emotion (happiness, anger, sadness, and fear), two vignettes were designed. After the children had been asked to look at the drawing and had been offered, either in spoken or in signed

Table 20.1 Demographic Characteristics of the Children

	Mean (SD)	Range	Missing values
Hearing children 1–2.5 years old (*n* = 128)			
Age (in months)	20.56 (5.46)	12–29	0
% Boys	46.1%	n.a.	0
Socioeconomic status:			
Education mother*	3.67 (0.67)	1–4	26
Annual income**	3.65 (0.97)	1–5	45
Deaf and hard-of hearing children 1–2.5 years old (*n* = 31)			
Age (in months)	19.16 (4.31)	14–27	0
% Boys	64.5%	n.a.	0
Socioeconomic status:			
Education mother*	3.78 (0.43)	3–4	13
Annual income**	3.92 (0.99)	2–5	19
Hearing children 2.6–5 years old (*n* = 343)			
Age (in months)	46.86 (11.45)	30–76	0
% Boys	56.9 %	n.a.	0
Socioeconomic status:			0
Education mother*	3.61 (0.64)	1–4	105
Annual income**	3.74 (1.05)	1–5	172
Deaf and hard-of-hearing children 2.6–5 years old (*n* = 61)			
Age (in months)	46.69 (9.92)	30–77	0
% Boys	60.7%	n.a.	0
Socioeconomic status:			
Education mother*	3.38 (0.88)	1–4	19
Annual income**	3.48 (1.23)	1–5	28
Hearing children 9–14 years old (*n* = 129)			
Age (in months)	139.40 (16.37)	99–176	0
% Boys	45%	n.a.	0
Socioeconomic status:			
Education mother*	3.16 (0.83)	1–4	48
Annual income**	3.55 (1.24)	1–5	65
Deaf and hard-of-hearing children 9–16 years old (*n* = 132)			
Age (in months)	143.23 (21.69)	100–197	0
% Boys	50%	n.a.	0
Socioeconomic status:			
Education mother*	3.17 (0.83)	1–4	69
Annual income**	3.33 (1.19)	1–5	86

*1 = no education; 2 = low; 3 = medium; 4 = high.

**1 = < €15,000; 2 = €15,000–30,000; 3 = €30,000–45,000; 4 = €45,000–60,000; 5 = > €60,000.

language, very simple illustrative words (e.g., "Boy sees dog"), they were first asked to say or sign how the protagonist would feel, and then to point to the drawing with the correct facial expression.

Empathy in children aged one to five years was assessed with the Empathy Questionnaire for infants and toddlers (19 items), which measures empathic behavior displayed in daily situations. Parents rated the degree to which each item represented their child's behavior over the past two months (0 = never, 1 = sometimes, 2 = often). The Empathy Observation task examines children's empathic responses to three emotions that are acted out nonverbally by the experimenter: happiness when clicking with a pen, anger with a pen that fails to write, and pain/sadness upon hurting one's finger. Children's responses were scored on a 20-item checklist (0 = not at all, 1 = a little, 2 = a lot).

A shortened version of the Fear Survey Schedule for Children–Revised (Ollendick, 1983) was used to measure general levels of fearfulness (i.e., aspect of internalizing problems) and was suitable for children aged seven to 17 years. This self-report consists of 25 items that measure the intensity of children's fears of failure and criticism (e.g., making mistakes), the unknown (e.g., going to bed in the dark), small animals (e.g., spiders), danger and death (e.g., being hit by a car or truck), and medical affairs (e.g., getting an injection from the physician). Each item consisted of a self-evaluation sentence with a score in the direction of severity from 1 (no fear) to 3 (a lot of fear).

EmotionWeb Findings

The data collected for EmotionWeb confirmed previous studies by demonstrating that the social-emotional development of DHH children differs from that of their hearing peers. Table 20.2 shows outcomes in the various domains of social-emotional development for DHH children in the three different age groups as compared to hearing children. The youngest DHH children showed more internalizing and externalizing behavior than their hearing peers; we did not find this difference in children above two-and-a-half years old. In contrast, DHH children over the age of two-and-a-half years were found to be less socially competent than their hearing peers, which was not the case for children between one and two-and-a-half years old. Furthermore, DHH children were less emotionally mature (tested only in children between nine and 14 years) than their hearing peers. Although we did not find differences in the youngest group concerning Emotion Identification, Emotion Communication, and Emotion of Others, DHH children between two-and-a-half and five years also performed less well than their hearing peers on Emotion Communication and Emotion of Others.

As DHH children can differ from each other considerably, for example regarding their preferred mode of communication or the type of hearing device they use, we also compared DHH children on these factors. In none

Table 20.2 Social-Emotional Development of Different Age Groups, Comparing Deaf and Hard-of-Hearing (DHH) Children with Hearing Peers

Component	1–2.5 years	2.5–5 years	9–16 years
Internalizing Behavior	*	-	-
Externalizing Behavior	*	-	-
Social Functioning	-	*	*
Emotion Regulation	*	-	*
Emotional Intelligence	n.a.	n.a.	*
Emotion Identification	-	-	n.a.
Emotion Communication	-	*	n.a.
Emotions of Others	-	*	n.a.

* DHH children differ at least half a standard deviation from their hearing peers.

- No difference between DHH and hearing children.

n.a. No data are available for the age group on that domain.

of the age groups did we find any differences regarding social-emotional skills among DHH children who used sign language, those who used spoken language, and those who used a combination of signed and spoken language. This supports Hintermair's (2006, p. 493) point of view that "the child's communicative competence makes for a more sound prediction [of the child's social-emotional development] than its linguistic medium (spoken language or sign)" (see Hintermair, Chapter 13 in this volume). In our sample, it seems that DHH children in each of these subgroups were just as likely to acquire social-emotional skills.

In the older group of DHH children, just under half of the children were fitted with CIs and the remainder were using conventional hearing aids. Candidacy criteria for either of these hearing devices depends largely on the level of hearing loss. Children with hearing loss in the severe to profound region do not benefit sufficiently from conventional hearing aids and could therefore become candidates for CIs. Children with lower levels of hearing loss typically do benefit from conventional hearing aids. We did find some differences between these two subgroups regarding their social-emotional skills. Remarkably, the subgroup that initially had higher levels of hearing loss, those with CIs, attained better psychosocial outcomes than the subgroup that initially had lower levels of hearing loss and were wearing conventional hearing aids (Theunissen, 2013).

Note, however, that "higher" and "lower" levels of hearing loss refer to children's unaided hearing thresholds (thus without CI or conventional hearing aid). It is very conceivable that the children who were fitted with CIs ended up with lower levels of aided hearing loss than children who were wearing conventional hearing aids. Furthermore, these positive outcomes for children with CIs versus children with conventional hearing aids could also be the result of factors related to the intensive rehabilitation track these children are involved in for several years after surgery. Moreover, on other aspects of social-emotional development, these positive outcomes for children with CIs versus children with conventional hearing aids were not found. For example, the groups' scores were equal on internalizing problems and peer relations (Kouwenberg, 2013).

USING EMOTIONWEB IN DAILY PRACTICE

EmotionWeb is a tool that can help professionals gain more insight into the social-emotional development of the DHH children in their care. Professionals can test the children using the questionnaires and observation tasks incorporated in EmotionWeb and can compare the individual child with normative scores of other DHH children as well as with normative scores of their hearing peers. It is possible to use all tests together, but professionals can also choose to test certain aspects of social-emotional functioning they think the child is falling behind on.

Part of the website is accessible to everyone, providing general information on the social-emotional development of (DHH) children. But there is also a secured part, accessible only to licensed professionals, where test results can be entered and compared with normative scores. Figure 20.1 shows the structure of the website.

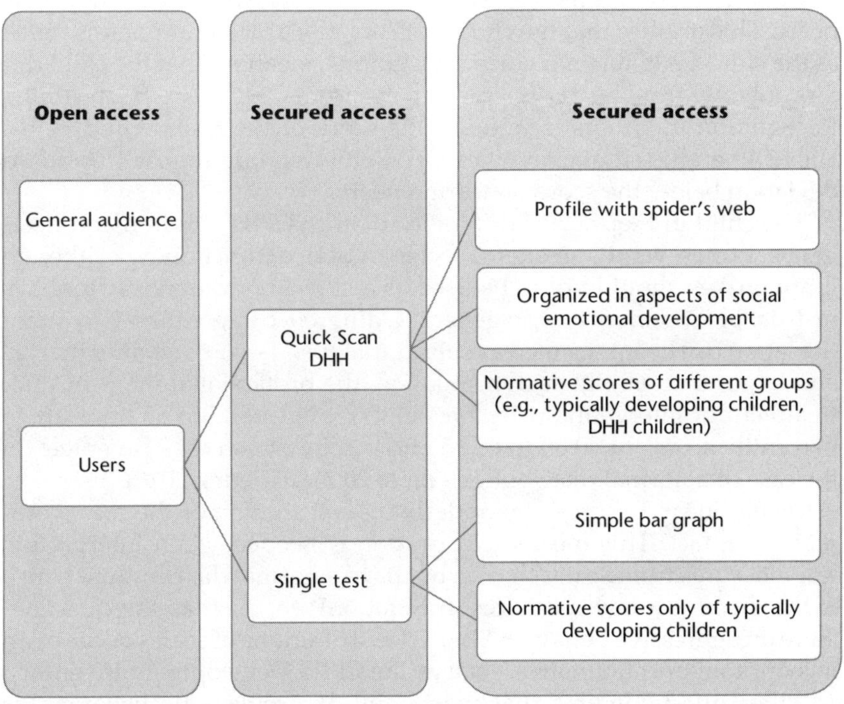

Figure 20.1 Structure of EmotionWeb website.

Interpreting the Outcomes

For all tests, EmotionWeb uses standard scores (linear T-scores) with a mean of 50 and a standard deviation of 10, and denoting the deviation from the norm group. T-scores are useful for test interpretation as they allow for comparisons between an individual child and a normative group, as well as comparisons between different tests. The latter is relevant when generating development profiles, one of EmotionWeb's aims. An example of how the results are presented in EmotionWeb is the spider's web (Fig. 20.2). The spider's web shows at first glimpse the child's strengths and difficulties on several dimensions of social-emotional functioning. Is the child falling behind on all dimensions or on only one or two of them? The dark-gray line represents the scores of hearing peers on all domains of social-emotional functioning. Because we used standard scores, this is always 50. The light-gray line represents the normative scores of DHH children, and the dashed line represents the scores of the individual child.

If we compare the child in Figure 20.2 with both normative groups, we can easily see that on the Prosocial behavior scale of Social Functioning, the child shows the same prosocial behavior as other DHH children and hearing peers: all three lines are close to the mean score of 50. It is also clear from the spider's web, however, that the score of this child on Emotion Communication: Talking about emotions is about 0.5 standard deviation below the mean score of both the hearing peers and DHH peers. This implies that the child does not talk about emotions as much as the children in the two normative groups, meaning that the child differs not only from hearing peers but also from DHH peers. Concerning Recognition of Others' Emotions, the score of the tested child is just above 40 and is similar to other DHH children but almost 1 standard deviation below the score of hearing peers.

The child in Figure 20.2 differs from other DHH children and hearing peers on several domains of social-emotional functioning. Although EmotionWeb should not to be used as a clinical or diagnostic tool, we instruct practitioners that, in general, a difference larger than 1 standard deviation can be interpreted as substantial (i.e., T-scores smaller than 40 and larger than 60). In such a situation, the professional may consider treatment or intervention. T-scores in the range of 45 to 55 translate to percentile scores of 30.85 to 69.15 and can be denoted as "average" in the case of a normal distribution (Table 20.3; De Beurs, 2010).

Using linear T-scores, the underlying distribution of the raw scores remains intact. This means that caution is needed when interpreting test measures from scales that do not have a normal distribution, which is the case for a few measures in EmotionWeb, such as the questionnaire on aggressive behavior. Skewed distributions of scales occur often in symptom questionnaires, such as the Child Development Inventory, or other questionnaires that may point at problematic behavior, as

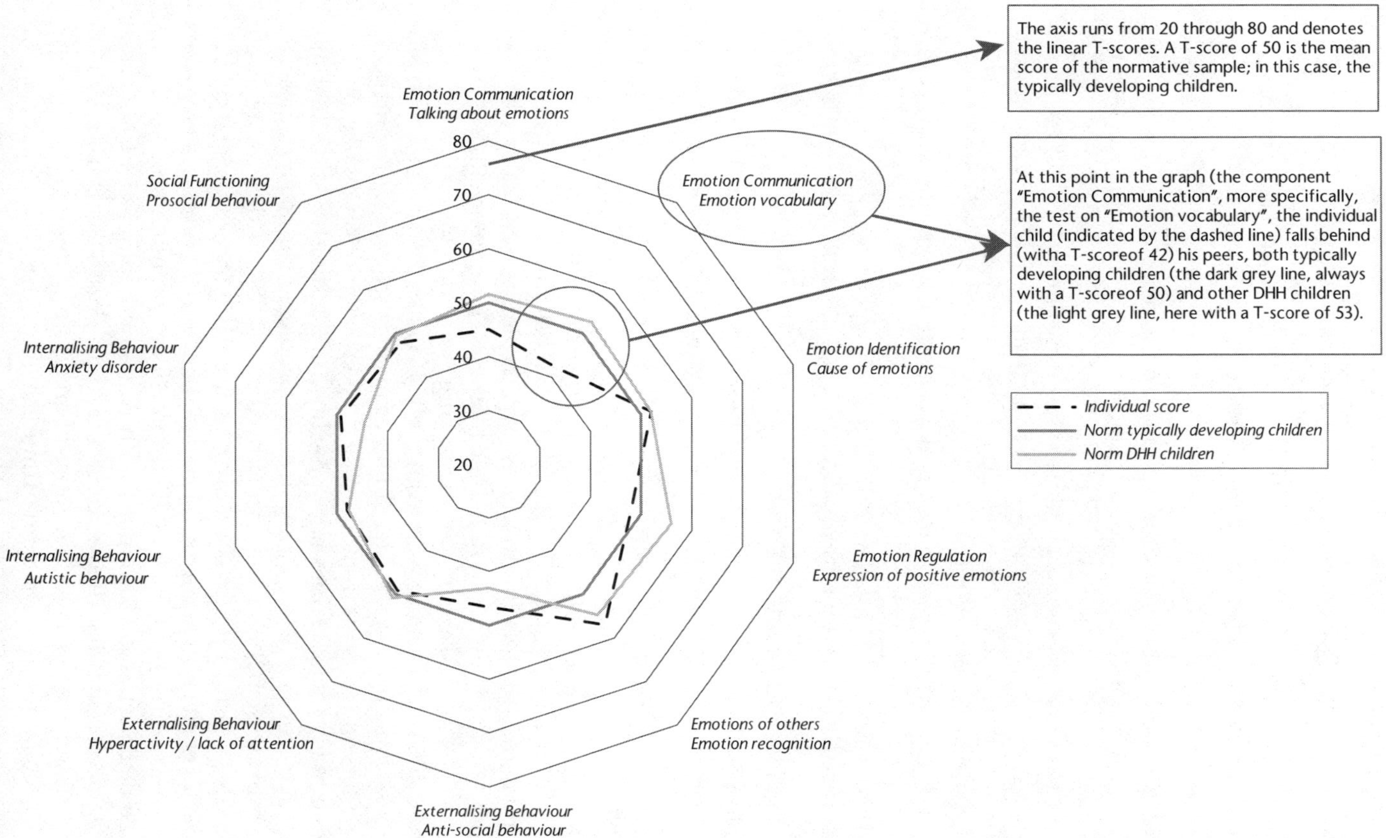

Figure 20.2 Example of a spider's web (fictitious case Bob).

Table 20.3 When Is a Difference Relevant?

Score	Interpretation
45–55	Difference is not relevant.
40–45 and 55–60	Difference is not substantial, but be alert.
Lower than 40 and higher than 60	Difference is substantial.

only a small proportion of the population experiences a specific trait. However, linear T-scores are still preferable above normalized T-scores, as they are more precise (Frick et al., 2010).

When the professional chooses to test only one or two dimensions of social-emotional development, the results are presented in a histogram in which the score of the individual child is compared with normative scores of hearing children.

It is important to realize that a relevant difference is not always negative. A child who displays more empathic behavior than his or her peers probably does not have any difficulties. However, when a child shows less empathic behavior, he or she might develop behavioral problems.

Examples: Two Fictitious Cases

In this section we consider two fictitious cases of DHH children. We discuss the outcomes of the spider's web, followed by suggestions for treatment.

Case 1

Anna is a 14-year-old hard-of-hearing girl. From the spider's web (Fig. 20.3) it is immediately clear that she has internalizing problems. She has high levels of anxiety as well as depression, as can be seen from her scores, which are higher than 60. These internalizing symptoms may be caused by not expressing her emotions or by not handling stressful situations appropriately. Because the spider's web also shows that she expresses her emotions just as well as her hearing peers, no intervention is warranted in the domain of emotion regulation. It is more likely that she does not know how to handle stressful situations, in other words that she lacks adequate problem-solving strategies.

A professional can help Anna by discussing with her strategies to handle stressful situations adequately. Anna can try out these strategies whenever she is in a stressful situation. Because it is important for Anna to have positive experiences, the professional should discuss and evaluate recent stressful situations with Anna and compliment her when she successfully handled such a situation. Positive experiences may contribute to a decrease in feelings of anxiety and depression for Anna.

A technique to help Anna diminish her anxiety is "exposure," a cognitive-behavioral therapy technique. Exposure means that Anna is

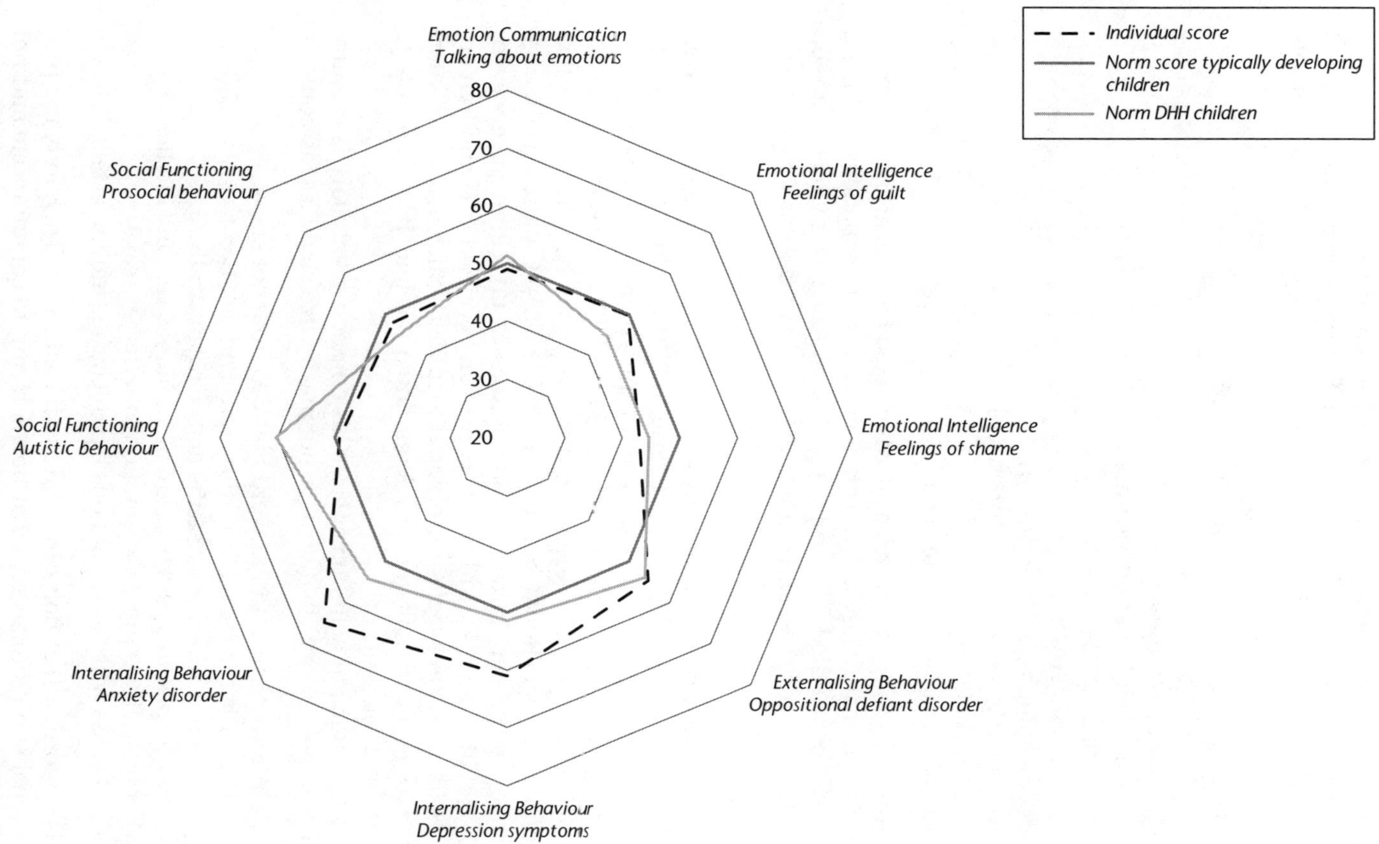

Figure 20.3 Example of a spider's web (fictitious case Anna).

confronted with situations that frighten her in a stepwise fashion. The professional explains to Anna how it helps to get used to frightening situations. Next, Anna, together with the professional, makes a list of 10 situations that frighten her and that she usually avoids. For example (see Bögels, 2008):

1. Asking questions in the classroom;
2. Traveling by bus alone;
3. Going to the swimming pool;
4. Calling a friend on the phone;
5. Swimming in the sea;
6. Traveling by train alone;
7. Sleeping with the lights off;
8. Staying the night at a friend's place;
9. Touching a spider; and
10. Being alone at home at night.

Anna has to try all of these situation, step by step, at her own pace. The goal is that she experiences that even difficult situations and great fears can be handled. The professional helps Anna by giving her tips on how to approach these situations, and by evaluating Anna's experiences.

Case 2

Bob is a four-year-old deaf boy with a CI. Looking at the spider's web of Bob's scores (see Fig. 20.2), we see that he has low scores on emotion communication and emotion vocabulary, not only compared to his hearing peers but also compared to his DHH peers. His scores are 45 and 42, which means that the difference may be relevant and that the professional should be alert (see Table 20.3). Children at this age develop at different paces, so Bob might catch up with his peers eventually without any outside help. However, because DHH children are more likely to have communication difficulties, which may cause internalizing and externalizing problems down the line, it is advisable to work on these skills.

A technique to help Bob enlarge his emotion vocabulary is to introduce emotion words that he does not master in a stepwise fashion:

1. Introduce an emotion word that Bob does not know.
2. Describe the meaning of the word and ask Bob to say or sign the word and to express the emotion physically.
3. Show pictures and photos of human faces and bodies that physically express the emotion in different ways.
4. Discuss with Bob situations in which the emotion is felt.

It is important that Bob can express himself freely. Therefore, the professional should focus on what Bob is trying to communicate and not whether he is expressing himself grammatically or articulates clearly.

Another way of helping Bob enlarge his emotion vocabulary and to learn how to communicate about emotions is to ask his parents to talk with Bob about emotions. For example, the parents could read books with Bob and ask questions about how the character in the book would feel and why he feels like that. But they can also talk with Bob about Bob's emotions. Another technique is that parents explicitly mention their own emotions during everyday activities and the reasons for their emotions.

CONCLUSION

The data that we collected for EmotionWeb has given us an overview of DHH children's current social-emotional development in various areas, whereas previous studies often focused on just one aspect of social-emotional development. The data suggest that DHH children (except for the youngest ones) do not show mental health issues (i.e., internalizing and externalizing problems). They do, however, have more social problems than hearing children. As social interactions are such an important part of our lives, we should be on the lookout for other problems that may be arising later on, including mental health problems. If DHH individuals continue to encounter social problems, this may impair their future romantic relationships and work relationships, and failures in these areas could lead to feelings of worthlessness and correspondingly lower levels of mental health.

Throughout this chapter, many aspects of emotional development have been discussed as well as how these could affect children's social development. Areas of emotional development that turn out to be problematic for DHH children include their ability to regulate their emotions, the ability to communicate their emotions adaptively, their level of emotional intelligence, and their understanding of other people's emotions and behavior. These, then, seem to be the areas of development on which professionals should focus their attention. Improvements that can be realized in these areas will, it is hoped, result in corresponding improvements in DHH children's social functioning. At the same time, we should avoid lumping all DHH children together. Some DHH children might indeed fit the normative profile perfectly, but most will deviate from it in one way or another. So while the normative data provide us with valuable knowledge about the DHH group as a whole, the added value of EmotionWeb lies in the fact that professionals can identify the strengths and weaknesses in the social-emotional development of each individual DHH child.

As is well known, the DHH population is a very heterogeneous one, and one that is changing over time. For example, candidacy criteria for CIs are expanding, meaning more and more DHH children are eligible to receive a CI. Moreover, over the past years, the age at which children receive their implant has gone down considerably, and at the same time the technology has become more and more sophisticated. Currently, a debate revolves around whether bilateral (vs. unilateral) implantation would benefit children's social-emotional development. These changes, especially in the field of CI, pose the question of whether the younger and the older age groups in our dataset are fully comparable. The answer is a definite "no." Only about half of the children in the older age group had CIs; the others were wearing conventional hearing aids. Moreover, children in the older age group had received their CIs up to several years later than children in the younger age group. And finally, the CIs of the older children were probably less sophisticated than those of the younger children. However, both groups are representative of the DHH population in each of these particular age groups. Our aim was not to draw comparisons between younger and older DHH children, and thus between those who are implanted earlier versus later for example, but to provide normative scores against which individual children's social-emotional competence could be judged. We should, however, keep in mind that these normative scores might have an "expiration date." In another couple of years, our youngest group will reach the current age of the oldest group, and it is by no means certain that this youngest group will show the same pattern of social-emotional strengths and difficulties by then. Therefore, we consider EmotionWeb to be a work in progress. We feel compelled to continue to monitor DHH children's development over time.

REFERENCES

Astington, J. W., & Jenkins, J. M. (1999). A longitudinal study of the relation between language and theory-of-mind development. *Developmental Psychology*, *35*, 1311–1320.

Barker, D. H., Quittner, A. L., Fink, N. E., Eisenberg, L. S., Tobey, E. A., Niparko, J. K., & CDaCI Investigative Team. (2009). Prediction behaviour problems in deaf and hearing children: The influence of language, attention, and parent-child communication. , *21*, 373–392.

Baron-Cohen, S., & Wheelwright, S. (2004). The empathy quotient: An investigation of adults with Asperger syndrome or high functioning autism, and normal sex differences. *Journal of Autism and Developmental Disorders*, *34*, 163–175.

Colonnesi, C., Rieffe, C., Koops, W., & Perucchini, P. (2008). Precursors of a theory of mind: A longitudinal study. *British Journal of Developmental Psychology*, *26*, 561–577.

De Beurs, E. (2010). De genormaliseerde T-score: een "euro" voor testuitslagen. *Magazine voor GGZ en verslavingszorg*, *65*(9), 684–695.

Denham, S. A. (1998). *Emotional development in young children*. New York: Guilford Press.

Denham, S. A., Blair, K. A., DeMulder, E., Levitas, J., Sawyer, K., Auerbach–Major, S., & Queenan, P. (2003). Preschool emotional competence: Pathway to social competence? *Child Development*, *74*(1), 238–256.

Eisenberg, N., Spinrad, T. L., & Sadovsky, A. (2006). Empathy-related responding in children. In M. Killen & J. Smetana (Eds.), *Handbook of moral development* (pp. 517–549). Mahwah, NJ: Lawrence Erlbaum Associates.

Frijda, N. H. (1986). *The emotions*. Cambridge: Cambridge University Press.

Gale, E., & Schick, B. (2009). Symbol-infused joint attention and language use in mothers with deaf and hearing toddlers. *American Annals of the Deaf, 153*, 484–503.

Gottman, J. M., & Declaire, J.(1997). *Hart voor je kind: de vijf stappen naar de emotionele intelligentie van je kind*. Utrecht: Kosmos-Z&K.

Hintermair, M. (2006). Parental resources, parental stress, and socioemotional development of deaf and hard of hearing children. *Journal of Deaf Studies and Deaf Education, 11*(4), 493–513.

Hosie, J. A., Gray, C. D., Russell, P. A., Scott, C., & Hunter N. (1998). The matching of facial expressions by deaf and hearing children and their production and comprehension of emotion labels. *Motivation and Emotion, 22*, 293–313.

Izard, C. E. (2009). Emotion theory and research: Highlights, unanswered questions, and emerging issues. *Annual Review of Psychology, 60*, 1–25.

Jellesma, F. C., Rieffe, C., & Meerum Terwogt, M. (2007). The Somatic Complaint List: Validation of a self-report questionnaire assessing somatic complaints in children. *Journal of Psychosomatic Research, 63*, 399–401.

Jolliffe, D., & Farrington, D.P. (2006). Examining the relationship between low empathy and bullying. *Aggressive Behavior, 32*, 540–550.

Keltner, D., & Haidt, J. (1999). Social functions of emotions at four levels of analysis. *Cognition & Emotion, 13*, 505–521.

Ketelaar, L., Rieffe, C., Wiefferink, C. H., & Frijns, J. H. M. (2012). Does hearing lead to understanding? Theory of mind in toddlers and preschoolers with cochlear implants. *Journal of Pediatric Psychology, 37*, 1041–1050.

Ketelaar, L., Rieffe, C., Wiefferink, C. H., & Frijns, J. H. M. (2013). Social competence and empathy in young children with cochlear implants and with normal hearing. *Laryngoscope, 123*, 518–523.

Kouwenberg, M. (2013). *Social-emotional factors underlying internalizing problems & peer relations in deaf or hard of hearing youth.* Dissertation, University of Leiden.

Ollendick, T. H. (1983). Reliability and validity of the revised Fear Survey Schedule for Children (FSSC-R). *Behaviour Research and Therapy, 21*, 685–692.

Peterson, C. C., & Siegal, M. (1995). Deafness, conversation, and theory of mind. *Journal of Child Psychology & Psychiatry, 36*, 459–474.

Peterson, C. C., & Siegal, M. (2000). Insights into theory of mind from deafness and autism. *Mind & Language, 15*, 123–145.

Prezbindowsky, A. K., Adamson, L. B., & Lederberg, A. R. (1998). Joint attention in deaf and hearing 22 month-old children and their hearing mothers. *Journal of Applied Developmental Psychology, 19*, 377–387.

Rieffe, C. (2012). Awareness and regulation of emotions in deaf children. *British Journal of Developmental Psychology, 30*, 477–492.

Rieffe, C., & De Rooy, M. (2012). The longitudinal relationship between emotion awareness and internalizing symptoms during late childhood. *European Child & Adolescent Psychiatry, 21*(6), 349–356.

Rieffe, C., Ketelaar, L., & Wiefferink, C. H. (2010). Assessing empathy in young children: Construction and validation of an Empathy Questionnaire (EmQue). *Personality and Individual Differences, 49*, 362–367.

Rieffe, C., & Meerum Terwogt, M. (2006). Anger communication in deaf children. *Cognition and Emotion*, *20*, 1261–1273.

Rieffe, C., Meerum Terwogt, M., & Jellesma, F. C. (2008). Emotional competence and health in children. In J. Denollet, I. Nyklicek, & A. Vingerhoets (Eds.), *Emotion regulation: Conceptual and clinical issues*. New York: Springer.

Rieffe, C., Meerum Terwogt, M., Koops, W., Stegge, H., & Oomen, A. (2001). Pre-schoolers' appreciation of uncommon desires and subsequent emotions. *British Journal of Developmental Psychology*, *19*, 259–274.

Saarni, C. (1999). *The development of emotional competence*. New York: Guilford Press.

Theunissen, S. C. P. M. (2013). *Psychopathology in hearing impaired children*. Dissertation, University of Leiden.

Vaccari, C., & Marschark, M. (1997) Communication between parents and deaf children: Implications for social-emotional development. *Journal of Child Psychology and Psychiatry and Allied Disciplines*, *38*, 793–801.

Van Eldik, T., Treffers, P. D. A., Veerman, J. W., & Verhulst, F. C. (2004). Mental health problems of deaf Dutch children as indicated by parents' responses to the child behavior checklist. *American Annals of the Deaf*, *148*, 390–395.

Van Gent, T. (2012). Mental health problems in deaf children and adolescents. *Mental health problems in deaf and severely hard of hearing children and adolescents*. Dissertation, University of Leiden.

Wellman, H. M. (1990). *The child's theory of mind*. Cambridge, MA: MIT Press.

Wiefferink, C. H. (2012). *Cochlear implants in children: Development in interaction with the social context*. Dissertation, University of Leiden.

Wolters, N., Knoors, H. E. T., Cillessen, A. H. N., & Verhoeven, L. (2011). Predicting acceptance and popularity in early adolescence as a function of hearing status, gender, and educational setting. *Research in Developmental Disabilities*, *32*, 2553–2565.

Wright, M., Banerjee, R., Hoek, W., Rieffe, C., & Novin, S. (2010). Depression and social anxiety in children: Differential links with coping strategies. *Journal of Abnormal Child Psychology*, *38*(3), 405–419

21

Benefits of Technology-Enhanced Learning for Deaf and Hard-of-Hearing Students

Eliane Segers and Ludo Verhoeven

Today's world of technology offers many opportunities and challenges for both learners and their learning environments. Learning has rapidly shifted from absorbing information from books to constructing knowledge on the Internet (Kuiper, Volman, & Terwel, 2005) to learning in an environment in which technology is omnipresent via tablets, smartphones, and so on. In such an environment, literacy and numeracy skills are more important than ever (Pagliaro, Chapter 8 in this volume); knowledge is mediated through these skills and created via social interaction (Scardamelia, Bransford, Kozma, & Quellmalz, 2012). The division between formal and informal learning is becoming less strict, and home and school are becoming more and more interconnected. Both schools and homes in Western society are largely connected to the Internet, with many people owning a smartphone and/or tablet and, as such, being always online. People keep in touch via social media, and e-mail is almost getting old-fashioned. For academic success, students need so-called 21st-century skills, which include critical thinking, communication, collaboration, and creativity, as well as information, media, and technology skills (Trilling & Fadel, 2009).

For deaf and hard-of-hearing (DHH) students, this new world opens new perspectives but also raises new barriers. A key question is how technology can help DHH students in their development of literacy and numeracy skills as tools for social interaction and knowledge acquisition. We will address this question by focusing on the role of information and communications technology support in emergent literacy and numeracy, learning basic and advanced literacy and numeracy skills, learning from multimedia texts, and learning from the Internet. We close with a perspective on future research and development in technology-enhanced learning for DHH students.

INFORMATION AND COMMUNICATIONS TECHNOLOGY-ENHANCED EMERGENT LITERACY AND NUMERACY

Language, literacy, and numeracy can be seen as foundational subjects for schooling, and it is important to note that their underlying competencies are to some extent related. There is evidence that the recursive capacity in grammar has evolved not only for the domain of human communication but also for other cognitive domains such as numeracy, spatial navigation, and logical reasoning. Just as symbolic relations are associated with relations between objects in language use, relations between numbers are associated with relations between empirical objects in mathematical thinking. Convergent evidence from neuroimaging studies has revealed that brain-based systems supporting approximate and exact arithmetic processing can be distinguished, and that the representation of exact number may recruit language-related networks (Dehaene, Molko, Cohen, & Wilson, 2004; Dehaene, Piazza, Pinel, & Cohen, 2003).

At the preschool level, children have already built up early literacy and numeracy skills thanks to informal learning experiences at home in domains such as storybook reading and field trips with parents (see Dirks & Wauters, Chapter 18 in this volume; Pagliaro, Chapter 8 in this volume). During the early school years the home environment also can be seen as an important predictor of school success. This goes for both the home literacy and the home numeracy environments (Segers, Kleemans, & Verhoeven, 2015). The home learning environment has rapidly changed with the entrance of computers, smartphones, and tablets. Even very young children use tablet computers, playing games, watching animations, or "reading" books. Young children prosper in rich learning environments, with lots of opportunities to interact with adults and peers.

Storybook reading can be seen as an effective means to enhance young children's language and literacy development. By fostering children's understanding of narratives, developmental shifts take place from intrasentential to intersentential abilities, from basic structures to additional functions, and from contextual to decontextualized abilities (cf. Karmiloff-Smith, 1997). For young children, there is an abundance of interactive e-book titles available. These multimedia books can be "read" independently by the child, for example on a tablet computer, and offer good learning opportunities (Korat & Shamir, 2007). Interactivity can be added, for example, by a "who" that asks vocabulary questions. This adds to the learning gain of young children (Smeets & Bus, 2012).

Research on emergent literacy has convincingly shown that interactive storybook reading has an impact on hearing children's oral and written language development (Mol, Bus, & De Jong, 2009). Both the quality of the book reading and its frequency turn out to be important for the development of spoken language and written language skills in young children. With respect to spoken language, children learn from interactive storybook reading new vocabulary and gain insight into the structure of narrative text. With regard to written language, interactive storybook reading fosters children's phonological awareness and letter knowledge (Mol & Bus, 2011). The development of all of these skills can be seen as an important predictor of children's later reading comprehension. Comparable results were found for parents' numeracy expectations as well as parent–child numeracy activities in predicting numeracy skills (e.g., Kleemans, Peeters, Segers, & Verhoeven, 2012; see Pagliaro, Chapter 8 in this volume).

Multimedia support has also been shown to have a positive impact on early literacy (Segers & Verhoeven, 2002) and numeracy learning (Praet & DeSoete, 2014). Interactive e-books, for example, can enhance the school learning environment. However, Nir-Gal and Klein (2004) showed that learning gains of five- and six-year-olds were positively correlated with the amount of assistance by the teacher; the computer cannot replace the teacher (Segers, Takke, & Verhoeven, 2004). Interactive e-books allow the child to repeatedly listen to the story, and as such enhance literacy learning. Especially when the story is accompanied by animations instead of static pictures, story comprehension can be enhanced (Verhallen, Bus, & De Jong, 2006). Besides, there is evidence that interactive storybooks may help hearing children become phonologically aware and learn to grasp the alphabetic principle, even in children from low socioeconomic status (Lefebvre, Trudeau, & Sutton, 2011) or at-risk children (Justice & Ezell, 2002). Interactive storybooks as well as computer games have potential in grounding logical operations and number concepts in young hearing children (LeFevre et al., 2009).

Research has shown that DHH children lag behind hearing children in literacy and mathematics from an early age. Some of the basic concepts that hearing children learn informally before starting school are still challenging for DHH children in the early school years. Computer games may help children to understand letter representations and basic literacy skills, on the one hand, and number concepts and basic arithmetic skills, on the other hand. Interactive storybook reading has shown to be similarly important for the language and literacy development of deaf and hearing children (Fung, Chow, & McBride-Chang, 2005; see Dirks & Wauters, Chapter 18 in this volume). Desjardin and Ambrose (2010) noted that even when children receive assistive listening devices such as cochlear implants at a young age, they are still at risk for emergent literacy delays. Mueller and Hurtig (2010) reported that hearing parents with DHH children face several problems when reading a storybook to their child, related to the various modalities necessary for interaction (e.g., using sign language). This leads to a poorer learning environment for deaf children. A signing e-book may be a very helpful tool in this respect (Mueller & Hurtig, 2010). Such a book provides a video of a narrator telling the story in sign language. The narrator also can ask questions to the child, and as such create an interactive reading experience. More and more of such books are now becoming available, and similar materials also are available on tablets (Parton & Hancock, 2011). Educational games using abundant visual cues may also help deaf children to understand the basic principles of early numeracy (Nunes, Barros, Evans, & Burman, 2012).

COMPUTER-SUPPORTED TRAINING OF LITERACY AND NUMERACY SKILLS

Basic Literacy and Numeracy Skills

Starting in grade 1, basic literacy and numeracy skills are taught with the goal of giving children highly specified orthographic and numeric representations. With respect to basic literacy skills, children must learn that words can be represented as strings of letters that can be mapped onto phonemes. And in the case of complex words, children must learn that morphologic constituents may underlie complex words (Verhoeven & Perfetti, 2011). With reference to basic numeracy skills, children must learn that numbers may refer to nominal, cardinal, and ordinal relations between objects and that number operations allow the addition or subtraction of numbers (Geary, Hamson, & Hoard, 2000). Basic arithmetic involves the addition and subtraction of numbers less than 10 (Cowan, Donlan, Newton, & Lloyd, 2005), and a distinction can be made between canonical problem types (i.e., arithmetic problems with a sum below ten), on the one hand, and advanced problems (i.e., arithmetic problems with sums and minuends above 10 and less than 20, that contain carryover operations), on the other hand (cf. Stanescu-Cosson et al., 2000). Both have a strong link to language representations (Kleemans, Segers, & Verhoeven, 2013). In literacy and numeracy education, classroom instruction is more and more often accompanied by computer games. Computer games not only provide a motivational context for skill improvement but also enhance the executive control in planning, monitoring, and evaluation of child behavior, which may result in greater cognitive flexibility and strategic competence on the part of the child. Moreover, games may also enhance active learning, especially when interaction between multiple players is involved.

DHH students are challenged in acquiring basic literacy and numeracy skills. For several decades, ample studies have documented reading problems in DHH students (see Knoors & Marschark, 2014, Chapter 6). On average, the reading achievement of deaf students leaving high school is significantly lower than that of hearing students, comparable to nine- to 10-year-old hearing students (Wauters, Van Bon, & Tellings, 2006). Most deaf students come to the classroom with an atypical linguistic background. It may help to see how the brains of signing deaf children respond to written words. Figure 21.1 shows how the neural network for word decoding and spelling in signing DHH children may look; it represents how different specialized parts of the brain may be interacting. To begin with, for children who sign there are the connections between sign language and semantics to constitute children's basic vocabulary. Via the emergence of literacy, connections are also made between semantics and second-language (L2) orthography and phonology. DHH children acquiring sign language as the first language (L1) and/or the spoken language as L2 may benefit greatly from sign supported word decoding feedback in computer games. For hard-of-hearing children and deaf children who do not use sign language, it will be helpful to support the grapheme–phoneme mapping and its automatization in word decoding by means of series of computer games that follow the principles of visual phonics.

Early reading difficulties for DHH students manifest themselves mainly in the following areas: poor phonologic awareness (i.e., awareness of the sound structure of words, especially phonemic awareness as manifested in the ability to analyze and manipulate sounds within a syllable); difficulty in learning to establish stable correspondence rules between graphemes and phonemes; poor orthographic word reading strategies; and problems in arriving at fluent word identification. The

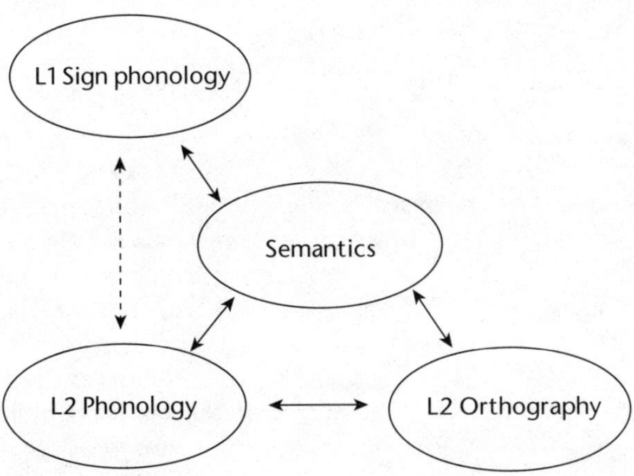

Figure 21.1 Neural network representing the relations between L1 sign phonology, semantics, L2 phonology, and L2 orthography.

result is that children are late in letter identification and word decoding accuracy and remain behind in word decoding speed (Perfetti & Sandak, 2000). It is highly important that beginning reading problems are identified at the earliest stages. There is research evidence that interventions started in the early years of hearing children's formal education show the best remediation effects (Hurry & Sylva, 2007).

Early math difficulties in deaf children become manifest as they often show delays in acquiring the number symbols and in gaining insight into the mental number line (see Pagliaro, Chapter 8 in this volume). Moreover, they show difficulties in acquiring the basic number operations (Nunes, Barros, Evans, & Burman, 2012). Figure 21.2 shows what the neural numeracy network in signing DHH children may look like. Numbers can be represented in terms of L1 sign phonology and L2 phonology and form the input for number operations. DHH children who do not use sign language may have weaker phonologic representations and need to rely more on the written form.

Now that we have seen how DHH children may respond to words and numbers, the question remains how optimal interventions can be thought of. Given that it is hard for teachers to conduct reading interventions for DHH students in mainstream classrooms, computer programs can be highly valuable. Computer programs offer many advantages for the learning process of these children and can be an additional remedial and time-freeing tool for (remedial) teachers. In the case of children with reading problems, who need extra time and much rehearsal to master certain skills and acquire automaticity in reading, the computer offers the limitless patience and extra exercise needed. Through the adaptability of the program, the learning skills can be presented step by

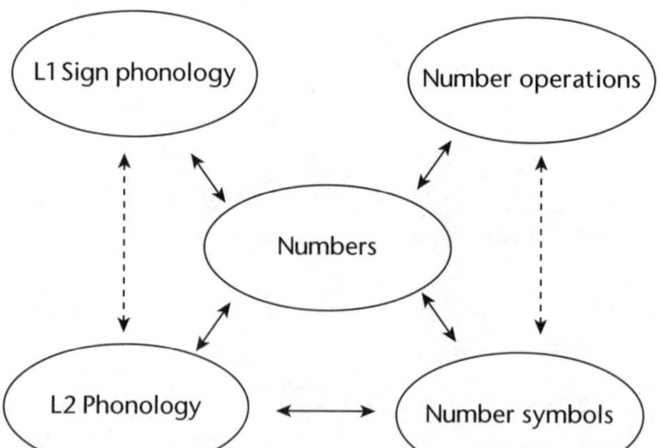

Figure 21.2 Neural network representing the relations between L1 sign phonology, numbers, L2 phonology, number symbols, and number operations.

step, preventing frustration and providing the necessary success experiences. By presenting auditory/signing and visual information simultaneously, more insight can be gained in correspondences between orthographic and phonologic information. Several studies involving hearing children have shown that technology-enhanced instruction is effective in improving word decoding and spelling skills (see for a review MacArthur, Ferretti, Okolo, & Cavalier, 2001).

More and more, interactive and adaptive computer programs have become available to respond to children's individual needs. Programs can be called *interactive* if they can guide the learning process by reacting continuously to the actions and responses of the user. Programs can be called *adaptive* if they can accommodate instructions and exercises according to the performance level of the student. Figure 21.3 represents the basic configuration of an interactive and adaptive computer program to foster the basic reading development of students with reading problems (cf. Irausquin & Verhoeven, 2008).

The program consists of a linguistic database, a navigation module, a student section, a teacher monitor, and a student database. The linguistic database provides the contents for the exercises, including signs, phonologic units, and orthographic units. The student database provides the student with a series of exercises in a game format, the outcomes of which are stored in the student database. The navigation

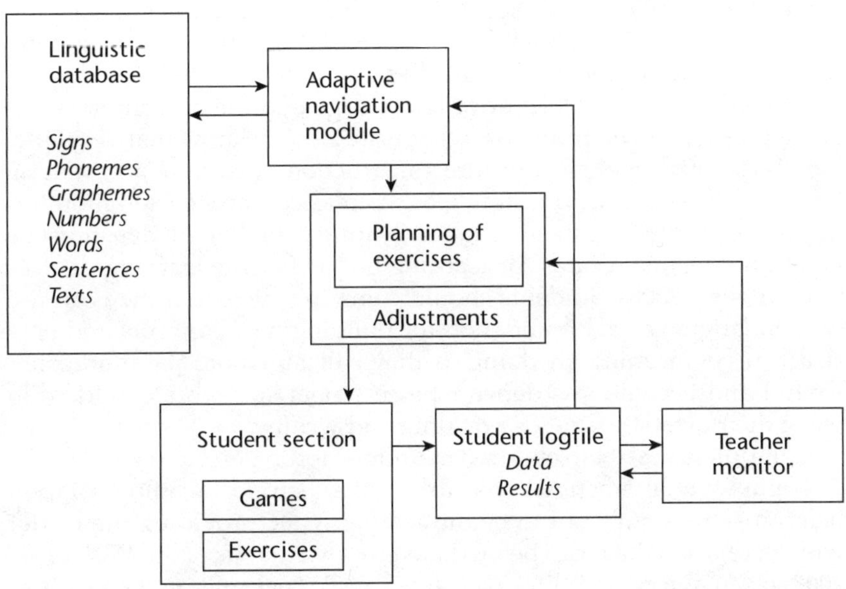

Figure 21.3 Multiple agents in computer programs to plan exercises adapted to the needs of individual children.

module adapts the order and levels of exercises based on the student's performance results. The teacher monitor allows the teacher to follow the student's performance and to make necessary adjustments. A pilot version of this program has successfully been implemented for dyslexic children (Irausquin, Drent, & Verhoeven, 2005). It can be expected that it may also help to support signing DHH children learning to read because an important strength is that sign representations can be part of the exercises. In a similar vein, Reitsma (2009) developed a computer program that used sign language to enhance children's spelling abilities. He found significantly positive effects on deaf children's spelling.

Higher-Order Literacy and Numeracy Skills

Advanced reading and writing demand the development of vocabulary; insight into the structure of sentences and larger textual structures, such as episodes and paragraphs; and knowledge of rules for punctuation. Comparisons of expert and novice learners have also called attention to the importance of control processes, such as planning and monitoring reading and writing processes. Literacy in advanced classes is fostered by teachers who plan lessons that have a clear conceptual focus. This enables students to (i) actively observe objects in reality, (ii) compare objects, events, and actions, (iii) find the connections between concepts in the form of semantic diagrams, and (iv) distinguish between semantic features. Rich learning situations are required that can stimulate the visual, auditory, psychomotor, and metacognitive functions (cf. Guthrie et al., 2009). Students should be given time to reflect, to practice relevant strategies, and to achieve depth of meaning and understanding. Instruction should focus on principles and ideas that help children to make connections between prior knowledge and the new information in the text. However, from observation studies we know that very little time is devoted to explicit or direct instruction of reading and writing strategies (Pressley, 2001). Strategies, such as comprehension monitoring, using graphic organizers, and activating prior knowledge, must be taught not just as recipes for learning but as flexible learning devices (see Pressley, 2000). Students should come to realize that they can use written language as a foundation for building new concepts and new structures of meaning. By doing so, they will gain more and more inner control and become less dependent on others and more confident in using their own strategies for reading and writing.

Computers may help children in understanding text in several ways. To begin with, interactive books for children support reading comprehension as they turn out to be motivating while providing the reader with feedback, which can be mediated by a virtual tutor (cf. Wise et al., 2008) or an automated tutor (Mostow, 2008). Focusing on the needs of deaf children, Mich, Pianta, and Mana (2013) designed computer storybooks that contain reading comprehension questions, a dictionary, intelligent feedback, and animations to improve reading comprehension. They found the program to be useful and effective for deaf children. Sign language was not part of their feedback system. With an eye on future programs, it can be assumed that the effects of such programs can be strengthened by incorporating sign language as additional feedback for deaf children who use sign language.

Computers may also facilitate children's mathematics learning. Hasselbring (2012) identified six purposes of technology use for supporting student mathematical learning, including converting symbols, notations, and text and building computational fluency. Creating conceptual understanding by using video technology to create scenarios of real-world math problems can easily be added to this (Cognition and Technology Group at Vanderbilt, 1996). Although the development of specific software for DHH students in this domain is still needed, existing mainstream software may help deaf students to overcome problems in advanced mathematics learning. A study by Liu, Chou, Liu, and Yang (2006) examined a wireless technology-enhanced classroom environment for mathematics teaching that included online, individualized scaffolds by the teacher during the lecture, a shared whiteboard, and tablet-PCs for all children. In a small sample of seven hard-of-hearing students, they found enhanced participation by the students and augmented interaction between the teacher and the students. The authors argued that this helped students to stay focused and decreased their cognitive load.

LEARNING FROM MULTIMEDIA TEXTS

Hypertext Comprehension

A new challenge in technology-enhanced learning is the processing of hypertexts. Hypertext reading comprehension is more complicated than reading comprehension of linear text. The reader has to construct his or her own reading path, deciding at each hyperlink whether to click on it or not (Amadieu, Tricot, & Mariné, 2010; DeStefano & LeFevre, 2007; Salmerón, Cañas, Kintsch, & Fajardo, 2005). Hypertexts are often preceded by graphic overviews in which the text structure is shown in a graph, including text sections, titles, and their connections. It is assumed that graphic overviews help to overcome disorientation and navigation problems while reading hypertexts. Most studies involving typically developing children examining the effectiveness of graphic overviews in hypertexts have yielded positive results, especially in cases of low prior knowledge (Destefano & Lefevre, 2007; Salméron, Cañas, Kintsch, & Fajardo, 2005). Due to its greater interactivity and hierarchical structure, hypertext comprehension increases cognitive load, so it is cognitively more challenging than linear text comprehension (Salmerón & García, 2012). As in the comprehension of linear texts, prior knowledge is highly important, as it helps readers to navigate through the text. Reading comprehension of linear text is largely predicted by the quality of lexical representations as indicated by high levels of word decoding skills and vocabulary knowledge (Perfetti, 2007). This also pertains to the comprehension of hypertexts with or without overviews (Klois, Segers, & Verhoeven, 2015).

Numerous studies have been conducted on reading comprehension of hypertexts and how to facilitate this comprehension (e.g., by the use of graphic overviews; Bezdan, Kester, & Kirschner, 2013; Salmerón, Baccino, Cañas, Madrid, & Fajardo, 2009; Vörös, Rouet, & Pléh, 2011). Little research in this area has focused on children. Klois, Segers, and Verhoeven (2013) showed that in a small hypertext, reading comprehension of children was comparable across four conditions (digital linear texts with or without overview, hypertexts with or without overview), with higher comprehension of linear texts only with overview relative to hypertexts without overview. However, in hypertexts with or without overview, the reading order was less linear, and the mind maps (i.e., a representation of the text using words and small drawings that are linked in an organized manner) of the children who had read a hypertext indicated a richer situation model compared to the reading of linear texts. Researchers have also been examining the use of strategy training to overcome cognitive load and disorientation in digital text comprehension. Coiro and Dobler (2007), for example, found that digital text prompts helped hearing sixth-graders to search for information in digital text.

Studies on hypertext comprehension in DHH students are generally lacking. It can be predicted that hypertext reading puts a greater demand on deaf learners, given that they often lag behind in working memory capacities (Hintermair, 2013), course-related content, and general world knowledge (Marschark & Wauters, 2008). Therefore, structured overviews preceding the text may be highly beneficial for their hypertext comprehension. However, research is needed to disentangle how the structural layout of hypertext can be optimally attuned to the cognitive and linguistic abilities of deaf students.

Learning from Multimedia

In learning from multimedia, children have to combine different input modalities: visual texts, pictures, and animations, as well as auditory texts for those who can hear, or narrations. An influential paradigm in multimedia learning research is the Cognitive Theory of Multimedia Learning (CTML) by Mayer (2009) and colleagues. The theory is based on the dual coding approach of Paivio (1986) and claims that the limited capacity of the working memory places boundaries on learning from multimedia. The working memory has both a visual and auditory system, both of which can contain only a certain amount of information. When too much information has to be processed, cognitive overload is created (cf. Sweller, 2005), which impedes learning. A lot of research in relation to the CTML has been devoted to the so-called modality effect, referring to optimal learning occurring when a narrative text is accompanied by a picture (Mayer, 2009). In that situation, both the auditory and visual channels of the short-term memory are being used. On the contrary, when a learner is being presented with a written text and a picture, the visual channel can become overloaded. The modality effect has mostly been evidenced in a system-paced paradigm (and not learner-paced), both in direct learning and in transfer effects (i.e., being able to use what has been learned in a new situation).

The modality effect is quite a robust effect, but there are boundary conditions (see Schüler, Scheiter, & Schmidt-Weigand, 2011). One boundary condition is that not all pictures facilitate learning in a similar vein; indeed, decorative pictures may even have a negative effect (Carney & Levin, 2002). Picture types that facilitate learning the most are mnemonics and interpretive pictures (i.e., pictures that explain how things work, such as the weather cycle). The latter type is most often used in research on modality effects. However, a picture has an additional value only when the learner recognizes its relevance and needs it for understanding. A student with high prior knowledge may not need the picture to understand the text (see Schnotz, 2011). A picture in this case becomes redundant (and thus decorative) and hence may have a negative effect on learning.

Another boundary condition of the modality effect is that when learning in a multimedia environment is paced by the learner instead of by the system, the effect tends to disappear or even reverse. This was shown in university students by Tabbers (2002) and in primary school hearing children by Segers, Verhoeven, and Hulstijn-Hendrikse (2008) and Segers and Witteman (2010). Immediately after learning, a modality effect was found by Segers and colleagues, but after a week and even after just a single night (Witteman & Segers, 2010), the modality effect reversed: Children had higher scores in the written-text-with-picture condition than in the narrative-text-with-picture condition. We believe this effect is caused by the fact that in the written condition, children have a deeper processing of the text. They can look back at a piece of text they did not completely understand, can pause reading to look at the picture, and so on. When the material is narrated, the learner can listen to the text of a page again but cannot go back so easily to a particular phrase. Van den Broek, Segers, and Verhoeven (2014) showed that, for adult learners, these effects are not caused by longer learning times in the written-text-with-picture condition. Learners, however, tend to return to a page more often in the written condition and may learn in a more efficient manner.

With respect to DHH children's opportunities in multimedia learning, Marschark and Hauser (2008) noted that deaf learners cannot optimally benefit from the combination of auditory and visual information. Furthermore, it was noted earlier that deaf learners may have lower working memory than their hearing peers (Hintermair, 2013), which has a direct impact on their language skills. Even children with cochlear implants still have lower digit span and vocabulary scores (Fagan, Pisoni, Horn, & Dillon, 2007). For DHH students, cognitive overload thus may be an extra risk when multimedia lessons are implemented that also may include sign language. They then have to process both a visual picture and the (visual) sign language, and often also the written text. According to the CTML, this would lead to cognitive overload via the visual short-term memory. The recent evidence of work by Segers and colleagues, however, suggests otherwise—that in the long run optimal learning occurs when combining only visual media. This would mean that the (signing) DHH children may not be disadvantaged by the combination of written text, pictures, and sign language. Of course, research is needed to support this hypothesis. Nikolaraizi and Vekiri (2012) implemented the principles from, among others, the CTML in a multimedia learning environment for deaf students and their teachers ("See and See"), including concept maps, sign language, and pictures, in an effort to enhance (signing) DHH students' reading comprehension in hypertexts as well as multimedia formats. They reported a pilot study with 15 teachers who had used the software with two students each. In interviews that were done afterward, the teachers reported that the children were all very motivated to use the computer and seemed to like reading more than usual. They did not yet make full use of all graphic options, but the teachers felt the program could be a very useful tool in their reading comprehension lessons. In a follow-up study with eight deaf students aged seven to 12 years, Nikolaraizi, Vekiri, and Easterbrooks (2013) analyzed the viewing behavior of the children and again found that the children did not make strategic use of the visual aids to aid their reading comprehension. The authors argued for mediated instruction to help improve the "visual literacy skills" of DHH children to improve their reading comprehension. It was unclear whether the tool actually improved text comprehension.

LEARNING FROM THE INTERNET

Multimedia documents are only one facet of the diamond of learning in the 21st century. When going online, however, children face several challenges. First, they must be able to find relevant information. Second, they have to deal with combining information from various resources. And third, they have to be able to comprehend hypertexts. This makes learning from the Internet a complex challenge for children, and even more so for children with learning difficulties, including some DHH children.

Many children have difficulties in finding information relevant to their goal on the Internet (Kuiper, Volman, & Terwel, 2005). But teenagers and adults also have difficulties in this area, finding it hard to come up with the optimal search terms and judging whether the information they find is relevant and trustworthy (Walraven, Brand-Gruwel, & Boshuizen, 2008). Interventions using Web-based inquiry-based learning environments, so-called WebQuests, have been proposed to help children overcome this problem (Segers & Verhoeven, 2009). WebQuests give children a meaningful assignment and prompt via assignments the reading of various predefined Internet pages. The WebQuest thus helps to organize the learning process (Chalmers, 2003). Segers and Verhoeven compared a traditional WebQuest with a WebQuest in which children had to search for relevant Internet sources themselves. The former, the closed-search condition, led to highest learning gains for boys, but for girls, the two conditions did not differ in terms of learning gains. Segers, Droop, and Verhoeven (2010) argued for a more integrated approach in using WebQuests, in which learning to search for meaningful information and processing this information are part of the more general educational curriculum. By focusing more on activating prior knowledge via the use of anchored instruction (cf. Bransford, Sherwood, Hasselbring, Kinzer, & Williams, 1990), the reading of Internet documents is facilitated. MacGregor and Lou (2004) added extra support to a WebQuest in the form of a concept map that needed to be filled in with information that children found on the Internet. This extra form of structure caused higher learning gains in an experimental group compared to a group that received a traditional WebQuest. Particularly for children with learning problems, this may be an optimal approach. However, it is interesting to note that Kleemans, Segers, Droop, and Wentink (2011) showed that a WebQuest with an ill-defined assignment produced higher learning gains for children in special education (with mild learning disabilities) than WebQuests with well-defined assignments. The ill-defined assignment gave children the opportunity to create their own path to learning, but within the safety of the sheltered environment.

Given their limited background knowledge and working memory skills, learning through the Internet may be especially challenging for DHH students. A learning environment that has the goal of providing children with ample opportunities to learn about the many different aspects of literacy will have to meet several conditions. To begin with, the use of WebQuests that contain Internet sources attuned to the students' level of reading comprehension may be quite helpful to start off learning from the Internet. It can be assumed that in an Internet environment that gives more structure, DHH students will be offered opportunities to learn with an optimal cognitive load.

A technology-enhanced learning environment for DHH students should meet some basic requirements. Figure 21.4 outlines such an environment (see Verhoeven, Segers, Bronkhorst, & Boves, 2006). To foster their motivation, "authentic" learning situations should be provided, in which children gather knowledge via anchored instruction. Anchored instruction starts from assignments with rich and cohesive informational contexts that help students to identify problem-based learning objectives and to generate strategies for solving identified problems (Bransford, Brown, & Cocking, 2000). In the environment, students should have access to information sources—that is, a language base (including online dictionaries) and a knowledge base that can provide them with possibilities for automated feedback. An important question is the extent to which sign language can support (signing) DHH children's learning in an Internet environment. Fajardo, Vigo, and Salmeron (2009) explored the possibilities of bilingual (written text + sign language) versus sign-language-only websites, resulting in a taxonomy of techniques for generating sign language on the Internet. Moreover, Fajardo, Parra, and Canas (2010) demonstrated that searching online was facilitated for signing deaf students when video-based sign language navigation aids were implemented. Online dictionaries (including sign language) to foster online reading comprehension may also be relevant sources of help for children learning in the Internet environment.

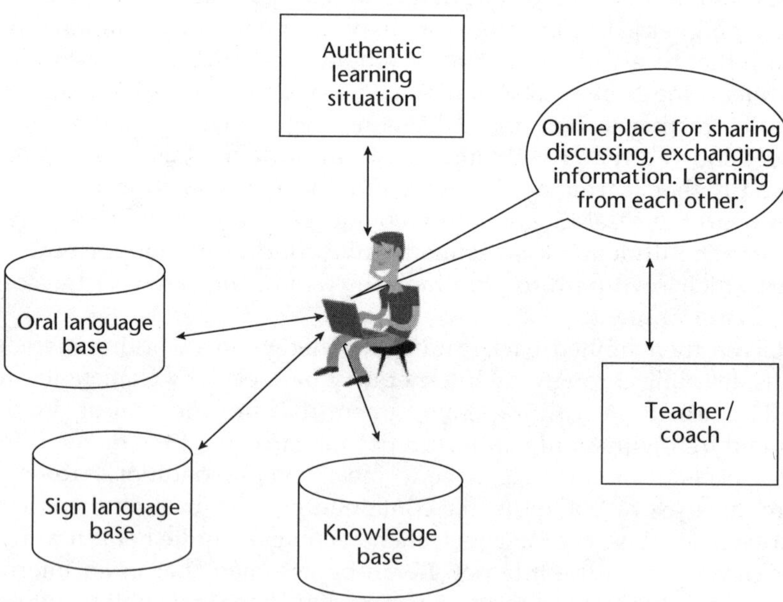

Figure 21.4 Technology-enhanced learning environment.

In such a learning environment, the teacher may fulfil the role of a coach who shares control with the students to promote higher-level thinking, communication skills, and deeper understandings of texts. That means that the teacher encourages discussion and provides detailed explanations about the identity, scope, and relevance of different strategies. Children can be offered opportunities to build on their own strategies for acquiring and using knowledge independently. Strategies, such as comprehension monitoring, using graphic organizers, and activating prior knowledge, need to be taught not just as recipes for learning but as flexible learning devices. Students should come to realize that they can use language as a foundation for building new concepts and new structures of meaning. They thus may gain more internal control, become less dependent on others, and gain confidence in their own strategies for reading, writing, and math. Learning is supposed to occur interactively. The Internet facilitates small group experimentation and small- and large-group discussions that support collaborative learning. The teacher also can support learning in this vein. In such groupings, disagreement about textual inferences may provoke genuine questions that may generate new ideas. Introducing students to new concepts in problem-solving situations provides them with the opportunity to experience changes in their own thinking and to elaborate on the new information.

Web 2.0 is different from the Web of the 1990s (Greenhow, Lobelia, & Hughes, 2009), as it requires even more learner participation and creativity. Being able to collaborate on learning activities is becoming more important than ever. Collaboration can involve two people at the same time at the same place (together behind the computer) or at different places (each behind his or her own computer, Skype, chat), as well as when people work together on a document at different times and places, working with tracked changes, and so on. Importantly, new technologies facilitate collaborative learning between hearing and DHH children, as the challenge of face-to-face talk is removed. Chen (2014), for example, implemented an online interactive self-regulated learning environment intended to stimulate attention, relevance, confidence, and satisfaction (ARCS). The students had multiple opportunities to interact online with peers and teachers in a forum, in which their hearing losses were not an issue (because forum discussions are asynchronous). The learning environment motivated the deaf students and had them engage in a positive learning behavior.

FUTURE PERSPECTIVE

The goal of the present chapter was to give an overview on the role of information and communications technology support in emergent literacy and numeracy, learning basic and advanced literacy and numeracy skills, learning from multimedia texts, and learning from the Internet, with a focus on DHH learners. Research is needed on the possibilities and challenges that have opened up for DHH learners, because of the ubiquity of multimedia in day-to-day life.

The population of DHH students is quite heterogeneous. They differ not only in the amount of hearing loss and mastery of sign language and spoken language, but also, for those who use cochlear implants, the age of implantation and the amount of time they have been able to use those devices. Besides these obvious characteristics, working memory capacity seems to be an important factor in predicting academic success in DHH children (Hintermair, 2013), and this factor may play a crucial role in learning from multimedia (Mayer, 2009).

A first main issue that emerges, then, is what individual differences within the DHH population predict the ability to benefit from multimedia that are also used by hearing children. Which children learn best from electronic storybooks? What are differences in understanding hypertexts? How can the CTML be applied to this special population? Although research has found generally poorer working memory skills among DHH children (Hintermair, 2013), it seems not entirely clear whether there is, indeed, a limited capacity or rather a higher cognitive load when performing certain tasks, which leads to poorer performance. So, for example, in studying differences in the understanding of hypertext, working memory capacity also needs to be taken into consideration. Further, when all or most of the information has to be processed via the visual-spatial channel, it is clear that design principles put forward by the CTML have to be adjusted for the DHH population. With the use of eye-trackers, more in-depth knowledge about the processing of multimedia can be gathered. This line of research has been thus far mostly done at the behavioral level, but advances in brain research may very well add to our understanding of how DHH students learn in a digital world and whether the proposed cognitive processes in literacy and numeracy learning indeed function as hypothesized in this chapter.

The second main issue is what technology can be added to facilitate learning in DHH children. Artificial intelligence research can benefit the development of online speech-to-sign synthesis and vice versa. Important questions to be addressed are: Can learning be enhanced when technology is added in the form of sign language, or does the extra stream of information cause overload of the visual-spatial sketchpad? When, where, and how should sign language be implemented to facilitate learning? Intervention studies are needed to arrive at evidence-based technology that enhances learning in DHH students.

Finally, the dissemination of online learning environments calls for carefully designed implementation studies in the school. Which interventions are successful implementation conditions? How can such a learning environment be implemented? What factors facilitate or hamper learning? How can the computer optimally adapt to the needs of deaf students? How can collaborative learning within the deaf community, and between the deaf and hearing communities, be optimized?

With the backup of behavioral and neurocognitive research, it can be expected that the 21st century will open up many possibilities for facilitating learning by DHH students and enabling better interactions between deaf and hearing students. This empowerment of DHH learners can strengthen their position in today's society.

REFERENCES

Amadieu, F., Tricot, A., & Mariné, C. (2010). Interaction between prior knowledge and concept-map structure on hypertext comprehension, coherence of reading orders and disorientation. *Interacting with Computers*, *22*, 88–97.

Bezdan, E., Kester, L., & Kirschner, P. A. (2013). The influence of node sequence and extraneous load induced by graphical overviews on hypertext learning. *Computers in Human Behavior*, *29*, 870–880.

Bransford, J. D., Brown, A. L., & Cocking, R. R. (2000). *How people learn. Brain, mind experience and school.* Washington, DC: Academic Press.

Bransford, J., Sherwood, R., Hasselbring, T. Kinzer, C., & Williams, S. (1990). Anchored instruction: why we need it and how technology can help. In: D. Nix & R. Spiro (Eds.), *Cognition, education and multimedia: Exploring ideas in high technology*. Hillsdale, NJ: Lawrence Erlbaum Associates.

Carney, R. N., & Levin, J. R. (2002). Pictorial illustrations still improve students' learning from text. *Educational Psychology Review*, *14*, 5–26.

Chalmers, P. A. (2003). The role of cognitive theory in human-computer interface. *Computers in Human Behavior*, *19*, 593–607.

Chen, Y-T. (2014). A study to explore the effects of self-regulated learning environment for hearing-impaired students. *Journal of Computer Assisted Learning*, *30*, 97–109.

Cognition and Technology Group at Vanderbilt. (1996). Looking at technology in context: A framework for understanding technology and education research. In D. C. Berliner & R. C. Calfee (Eds.), *Handbook of educational psychology* (pp. 807–840). New York: Macmillan.

Coiro, J., & Dobler, E. (2007). Exploring the online comprehension strategies used by sixth-grade skilled readers to search for and locate information on the Internet. *Reading Research Quarterly*, *42*, 214–257.

Cowan, R., Donlan, C., Newton, E. J., & Lloyd, D. (2005). Number skills and knowledge in children with specific language impairment. *Journal of Educational Psychology*, *97*, 732–744.

Dehaene, S., Molko, N., Cohen, L., & Wilson, A. J. (2004). Arithmetic and the brain. *Current Opinion in Neurobiology*, *14*, 218–224.

Dehaene, S., Piazza, M., Pinel, P., & Cohen, L. (2003). Three parietal circuits for number processing. *Cognitive Neuropsychology*, *20*, 487–506.

Desjardin, J. L., & Ambrose, S. E. (2010). The importance of the home literacy environment for developing literacy skills in children who are deaf or hard of hearing. *Young Exceptional Children*, *13*, 28–44.

DeStefano, D., & LeFevre, J.-A. (2007). Cognitive load in hypertext reading: A review. *Computers in Human Behavior*, *23*(3), 1616–1641.
Fagan, M. K., Pisoni, D. B., Horn, D. L., & Dillon, C. M. (2007). Neuropsychological correlates of vocabulary, reading, and working memory in deaf children with cochlear implants. *Journal of Deaf Studies and Deaf Education*, *12*, 461–471.
Fajardo, I., Parra, E., & Canas, J. J. (2010). Do sign language videos improve web navigation for deaf signer users? *Journal of Deaf Studies and Deaf Education*, *15*, 242–262.
Fajardo, I., Vigo, M., & Salmeron, L. (2009). Technology for supporting web information search and learning in sign language. *Interacting with Computers*, *21*, 243–256.
Fung, P-C., Chow, B. W-Y., & Mc-Bride Chang, C. (2005). The impact of a dialogic reading program on deaf and hard-of-hearing kindergarten and early primary school–aged students in Hong Kong. *Journal of Deaf Studies and Deaf Education*, *10*, 82–95.
Geary, D. C., Hamson, C. O., & Hoard, M. K. (2000). Numerical and arithmetical cognition: A longitudinal study of process and concept deficits in children with learning disability. *Journal of Experimental Child Psychology*, *77*, 236–263.
Greenhow, C., Robelia, E., & Hughes, J. (2009). Web 2.0 and classroom research: What path should we take *now? Educational Researcher*, *38*(4), 246–259.
Guthrie, J. T., McRae, A., Coddington, C. S., Klauda, S. L., Wigfield, A., & Barbosa, P. (2009). Impacts of comprehensive reading instruction on diverse outcomes of low-achieving and high-achieving readers. *Journal of Learning Disabilities*, *42*, 195–214.
Hasselbring, T. S. (2012). *Research foundation paper: FASTT Math Next Generation*. Retrieved March 25, 2014, from http://teacher.scholastic.com/math-fact-fluency/fastt-math-next-generation/files/FASTTMathNG_FoundationPaper.pdf.
Hintermair, M. (2013). Executive functions and behavioral problems in deaf and hard-of-hearing students at general and special schools. *Journal of Deaf Studies and Deaf Education*, *18*, 344–359.
Hurry, J., & Sylva, K. (2007). Long-term outcomes of early reading intervention. *Journal of Research in Reading*, *30*, 227–248.
Irausquin, R. S., Drent, J., & Verhoeven, L. (2005). Benefits of computer-presented speed training for poor readers. *Annals of Dyslexia*, *55*, 246–265.
Irausquin, R. S., & Verhoeven, L. (2008). Multiagent-based computer support for children with reading disabilities. In L. Verhoeven & C. Kinzer (Eds.), *Interactive literacy education. Facilitating literacy environments through technology.* (pp. 149–165). Mahwah, NJ: Lawrence Erlbaum Associates.
Justice, L. M., & Ezell, H. K. (2002). Use of storybook reading to increase print awareness in at-risk children. *American Journal of Speech-Language Pathology*, *11*, 17–29.
Karmiloff-Smith, A. (1997). *Beyond modularity*. Cambridge, MA: MIT Press.
Kleemans, M., Peeters, M., Segers, E., & Verhoeven, L. (2012). Child and home predictors of early numeracy skills in kindergarten. *Early Childhood Research Quarterly*, *27*, 471–477.
Kleemans, M., Segers, E., & Verhoeven, L. (2013). Relations between home numeracy experiences and basic calculation skills in children with and

without specific language impairment. *Early Childhood Research Quarterly*, *28*, 415–423.

Kleemans, T., Segers, E., Droop, M., & Wentink, H. (2011). WebQuests in special primary education: Learning in a web-based environment. *British Journal of Educational Technology*, *42*(5), 801–810.

Klois, S. S., Segers, E., & Verhoeven, L. (2013). How hypertext fosters children's knowledge acquisition: The roles of text structure and graphical overview. *Computers in Human Behavior*, *29*, 2047–2057.

Klois, S. S., Segers, E., & Verhoeven, L. (2015). Individual variation in children's reading comprehension across digital text types. Manuscript resubmitted for publication.

Knoors, H., & Marschark, M. (2014). *Teaching deaf learners.* New York: Oxford University Press.

Korat, O., & Shamir, A. (2007). Electronic books versus adult readers: effects on children's emergent literacy as a function of social class. *Journal of Computer Assisted Learning*, *23*, 248–259.

Kuiper, E., Volman, M., & Terwel, J. (2005). The web as an information resource in K-12 education: strategies for supporting students in searching an processing information. *Review of Educational Research*, *75*, 285–328.

Lefebvre, P., Trudeau, N., & Sutton, A. (2011). Enhancing vocabulary, print awareness and phonological awareness through shared storybook reading with low-income preschoolers. *Journal of Early Childhood Literacy*, *11*, 453–479.

LeFevre, J., Skwarchuk, S., Smith-Chant, B. L., Fast, L., Kamawar, D., & Bisanz, J. (2009). Home numeracy experiences and children's math performance in the early school years. *Canadian Journal of Behavioural Science*, 41, 55–66.

Liu, C-C., Chou, C-C., Liu, B-J., & Yang, J-W. (2006). Improving mathematics teaching and learning experiences for hard of hearing students with wireless technology-enhanced classrooms. *American Annals of the Deaf*, *151*, 345–355.

MacArthur, C. A., Ferretti, R. P., Okolo, C. M., & Cavalier, A. R. (2001). Technology applications for students with literacy problems: A critical review. *Elementary School Journal*, *101*, 273–301.

MacGregor, S. K., & Lou, Y. (2004). WebQuesting: Influence of task structure and web site design on learning. *Journal of Research on Technology in Education*, *37*, 161–175.

Marschark, M., & Hauser, P. C. (2008). Cognitive underpinnings of learning by deaf and hard-of-hearing students. Differences, diversity, and directions. In M. Marschark & P. C. Hauser (Eds.), *Deaf cognition: Foundations and outcomes* (pp. 3–23). New York: Oxford University Press.

Marschark, M., & Wauters, L. (2008). Language comprehension and learning by deaf students. In M. Marschark & P. C. Hauser (Eds.), *Deaf cognition: Foundations and outcomes* (pp 309–350). New York: Oxford University Press.

Mayer, R. E. (2009). *Multimedia learning* (2nd ed.). Cambridge: University Press.

Mich, O., Pianta, E., & Mana, N. (2013). Interactive stories and exercises with dynamic feedback for improving reading comprehension skills in deaf children. *Computers & Education*, *65*, 34–44.

Mol, S. E., & Bus, A. G. (2011). To read or not to read: A meta-analysis of print exposure from infancy to early adulthood. *Psychological Bulletin*, *137*(2), 267–296.

Mol, S. E., Bus, A. G., & De Jong, M. T. (2009). Interactive book reading in early education: A tool to stimulate print knowledge as well as oral language. *Review of Educational Research, 79*, 979–1007.

Mostow, J. (2008). Evaluation purposes, excuses, and methods: Experience from a reading tutor that listens. In Kinzer, C., & Verhoeven, L. (Eds.), *Interactive literacy education. Facilitating literacy environments through technology* (pp. 117–148). Mahwah, NJ: Lawrence Erlbaum Associates.

Mueller, V., & Hurtig, R. (2010). Technology-enhanced shared reading with deaf and hard-of-hearing children: The role of a fluent signing narrator. *Journal of Deaf Studies and Deaf Education, 15*, 72–101.

Nikolaraizi, M., & Vekiri, I. (2012). The design of a software to enhance the reading comprehension skills of deaf students: An integration of multiple theoretical perspectives. *Education and Information Technologies, 17*, 167–185.

Nikolaraizi, M., Vekiri, I., & Easterbrooks, S. R. (2013). Investigating deaf students' use of visual multimedia resources in reading comprehension. *American Annals of the Deaf, 157*, 458–473.

Nir-Gal, O., & Klein-Pnina, S. (2004). Computers for cognitive development in early childhood: The teacher's role in the computer learning environment. *Information Technology in Childhood Education Annual, 16*, 97–119.

Nunes, T., Barros, R., Evans, D., & Burman, D. (2012). A game-based working memory intervention for deaf children. In S. D. Wannemacker, S. Vandercruyse, & G. Clarebout (Eds.), *Serious games: The challenge* (pp. 31–39). Berlin: Springer-Verlag.

Paivio, A. (1986). *Mental representations: A dual coding approach*. New York: Oxford University Press.

Parton, B. S., & Hancock, R. (2011). EyeBooks on the iPad for deaf students. In M. Koehler & P. Mishra (Eds.), *Proceedings of Society for Information Technology & Teacher Education International Conference 2011* (pp. 3711–3712). Chesapeake, VA: AACE.

Perfetti, C. (2007). Reading ability: Lexical quality to comprehension. *Scientific Studies of Reading, 11*, 357–383.

Perfetti, C., & Sandak, R. (2000). Reading optimally builds on spoken language. *Journal of Deaf Studies and Deaf Education, 5*, 32–50.

Praet, M., & DeSoete, A. (2014). Enhancing young children's arithmetic skills through non-intensive, computerised kindergarten interventions: A randomised controlled study. *Teaching and Teacher Education, 39*, 56–65.

Pressley, M. (2000). What should comprehension instruction be the instruction of? In M. L. Kamil, P. B. Mosenthal, P. D. Pearson, & R. Barr (Eds.), *Handbook of reading research: Volume III* (pp. 545–561). Mahwah, NJ: Erlbaum.

Pressley, M. (2001). *Effective beginning reading instruction*. Executive Summary and Paper Commissioned by the National Reading Conference, Chicago, IL.

Reitsma, P. (2009). Computer-based exercises for learning to read and spell by deaf children. *Journal of Deaf Studies and Deaf Education, 14*, 178–189.

Salmerón, L., Baccino, T., Cañas, J. J., Madrid, R. I., & Fajardo, I. (2009). Do graphical overviews facilitate or hinder comprehension in hypertext? *Computers & Education, 53*, 1308–1319.

Salmerón, L., Cañas, J. J., Kintsch, W., & Fajardo, I. (2005). Reading strategies and hypertext comprehension. *Discourse Processes, 40*, 171–191.

Salmerón, L., & García, V. (2012). Children's reading of printed text and hypertext with navigation overviews: The role of comprehension, sustained attention, and visuo-spatial abilities. *Journal of Educational Computing Research, 47*, 33–50.

Scardamelia, M., Bransford, J., Kozma, B., & Quellmalz, E. (2012). New assessments and environments for knowledge building. In P. Griffin, B. McGaw, & E. Care (Eds.), *Assessment and teaching of 21st century skills* (pp. 231–300). Springer Netherlands.

Schnotz, W. (2011). Colorful bouquets in multimedia research: A closer look at the modality effect. *Zeitschrift für Pädagogische Psychologie, 25*, 269–276.

Schüler, A. Scheiter, K., & Schmidt-Weigand, F. (2011). Boundary conditions and constraints of the modality effect. *Zeitschrift für Pädagogische Psychologie, 25*, 211–220.

Segers, E., Droop, M., & Verhoeven, L. (2010). The integration of a WebQuest in a primary school using anchored instruction. *Computer Resources for Language Learning, 3*, 65–74.

Segers, E., Kleemans, M., & Verhoeven, L. (in press, 2015). Role of parent literacy and numeracy expectations and activities in predicting early numeracy skills. *Mathematical Thinking and Learning*.

Segers, E., Takke, L., & Verhoeven, L. (2004). Teacher-mediated versus computer-mediated storybook reading to children in native and multicultural classrooms. *School Effectiveness and School Improvement, 15*, 215–226.

Segers, E., & Verhoeven, L. (2002). Multimedia support of early literacy learning. *Computers & Education, 39*, 207–221.

Segers, E., & Verhoeven, L. (2009). Learning in a sheltered Internet environment: The use of WebQuests. *Learning & Instruction, 19*, 423–432.

Segers, E., Verhoeven, L., & Hulstijn-Hendrikse, N. (2008). Cognitive processes in children's multimedia text learning. *Applied Cognitive Psychology, 22*, 375–387.

Smeets, D. J. H., & Bus, A. G. (2012). Interactive electronic storybooks for kindergartners to promote vocabulary growth. *Journal of Experimental Child Psychology, 112*, 36–55.

Stanescu-Cosson, R., Pinel, P., Van de Moortele, P-F., Le Bihan, D., Cohen, L., & Dehaene, S. (2000). Understanding dissociations in dyscalculia: A brain imaging study of the impact of number size on the cerebral networks for exact and approximate calculation. *Brain, 123*, 2240–2255.

Sweller, J. (2005). Implications of cognitive load theory for multimedia learning. In R. E. Mayer (Ed.), *The Cambridge handbook of multimedia learning* (pp. 19–30) New York: Cambridge University Press.

Tabbers, H. K. (2002). *The modality of text in multimedia instructions—refining the design guidelines*. Unpublished dissertation, Open University of the Netherlands, Heerlen.

Trilling, B., & Fadel, C. (2009). *21st century skills: Learning for life in our times*. San Francisco: Jossey-Bass.

Van den Broek, G., Segers, E., & Verhoeven, L. (2014). Effects of text modality in multimedia presentations on written and oral performance. *Journal of Computer Assisted Learning, 30*, 438–449.

Verhallen, M. J. A. J., Bus, A. G., & De Jong, M. T. (2006). The promise of multimedia stories for kindergarten children at risk. *Journal of Educational Psychology, 98*, 410–419.

Verhoeven, L., & Perfetti, C. A. (2011). Introduction to this special issue: Vocabulary growth and reading skill. *Scientific Studies of Reading, 15*, 1–7.
Verhoeven, L., Segers, E., & Bronkhorst, J., & Boves, L. (2006). Toward interactive literacy education in the Netherlands. In M. McKenna, L. D. Labbo, R. D. Kieffer, & D. Reinking (Eds.), *International handbook of literacy and technology* (Vol. II, pp. 41–53). Mahwah, NJ: Lawrence Erlbaum Associates.
Vörös, Z., Rouet, J.-F., & Pléh, C. (2011). Effect of high-level content organizers on hypertext learning. *Computers in Human Behavior, 27*(5), 2047–2055.
Walraven, A., Brand-Gruwel, S., & Boshuizen, H. P. A. (2008). Information-problem solving: A review of problems students encounter and instructional solutions. *Computers in Human Behavior, 24*, 623–648.
Wauters, L. N., Van Bon, W. H. J., & Tellings, A. E. J. M. (2006). Reading comprehension of deaf children. *Reading and Writing, 19*, 49–76.
Wise, B., Cole, R., Van Vuuren, S., Schwartz, S., Snyder, L., Ngampatipatpong, N., Tuantranont, J., & Pellom, B. (2008). Learning to read with a virtual tutor: Foundations literacy. In C. Kinzer & L. Verhoeven (Eds.), *Interactive literacy education: Facilitating literacy environments through technology* (pp. 31–75). Mahwah, NJ: Lawrence Erlbaum Associates.
Witteman, M. J., & Segers, E. (2010). The modality effect tested in children in a user-paced multimedia environment. *Journal of Computer Assisted Learning, 26*, 132–142.

22

Click and Start Learning!

Innovative Development Programs for Professionals

Chantal Gervedink Nijhuis and Arie Terpstra

Like other people, deaf and hard-of-hearing (DHH) learners should have every opportunity to make best use of their capabilities and to build happy and prosperous lives. Parents, friends, teachers, and, in the case of DHH learners, health care providers, audiologists, and other professionals in their network, all have their own specific roles in stimulating and facilitating the learning process of learners. Contrary to the assumption that many deaf children do not have successful futures, Marschark (2007) showed that there are many ways in which the environment at home and school can increase a deaf child's chances of success in both academic and social life. Nevertheless, the tasks and duties of professionals with responsibilities for DHH children are complex and demanding. For example, although parent–child communication plays a central role in the social growth of a deaf child, many hearing parents of deaf children do not have a fully effective means of communicating with them (Vaccari & Marschark, 1997; Dirks & Wauters, Chapter 18 in this volume; Zaidman-Zait, Chapter 15 in this volume). Supporting DHH children in their personal growth and learning processes requires very specific expertise and lifelong learning on the part of the professional, in which the relationship between the professional and the deaf person is based on equality, respect, and mutual involvement. Professional development programs can help parents, teachers, health care providers, and other professionals to be better prepared and skilled for their responsibilities and tasks and to keep the acquired knowledge and skills up to date and appropriate over time.

In this chapter, the background, aims, and setup of development programs for professionals supporting DHH learners will be explained and discussed. Professional development programs developed by Royal Dutch Kentalis will be used as the primary examples. Royal Dutch Kentalis is a national organization in the Netherlands that provides care and education for DHH persons, persons who are deaf and blind, persons who have serious speech and language difficulties, and persons who have autism, sometimes combined with intellectual disabilities. The Kentalis development programs can be characterized as innovative and advanced, particularly because of the combination of e-learning and multimedia applications coupled with classroom contact and practical assignments. By way of illustration, the development and implementation of an innovative module for learning sign language according to the Common European Framework of Reference for Languages (CEFR) will be presented. At the end of the chapter, the results of the program to date from professionals who have completed this module will be shared. In addition, lessons learned for the development of such modules as part of professional development programs will be discussed.

PROFESSIONAL DEVELOPMENT AS A CONTINUOUS PROCESS

The Need for Lifelong Learning

Professionals working with DHH learners need a great deal of knowledge and skills about aspects such as communication, cultural issues, language acquisition, and interventions in order to become key players in the education process. Parents are usually the first to take responsibility and care for their DHH child. Having a child with hearing problems may initiate feelings of shock, denial, anger, guilt, and sadness (Hindley, 1997), and most parents do not have prior knowledge or experience in raising a DHH child. In the case of hearing parents, in particular, there is an immediate need for substantial amounts of information about hearing loss and for support from a variety of professionals (Marschark, 2007). As Moores and Meadow-Orlans (1990) described, parents often have no idea of the linguistic, psychological, social, and educational implications of early childhood hearing loss. For example, if the parents do not learn sign language, the child's opportunities to learn any language may be reduced, and this can have a lifelong impact on the child's communication, social, and cognitive development (e.g., Calderon, 2000; Courtin, 2000; Meadow, 2005). Results of studies reviewed by Vaccari and Marschark (1997) showed that providing greater social support to mothers and families led to more positivity when interacting with their deaf child, more frequent interaction with the child, and better social interactions of the deaf child with both family members and preschool-age peers. If the parents and child can communicate well, information and ideas can be shared, creating opportunities for inclusion, participation, and independence of the DHH child.

In the context of care, Harmer (1999) emphasized how important it is for care providers to understand appropriate communication strategies, the impact of hearing loss on an individual and his or her family, and Deaf culture (Fellinger & Holzinger, Chapter 17 in this volume). Many DHH children start visiting pediatricians, audiologists, speech and language specialists, surgeons, and other care providers when they are very young. Frequently, necessary information is not adequately offered alongside sufficient support for the family. The lack of deaf and hearing professionals who can use sign language, or interpreters to work with them, is also an obstacle to the deaf person receiving such services. Philips (1996) looked at aspects of Deaf culture, such as the tendency to relay information as a story, and greater use of facial expressions and affective display, that may result in misinterpretations and lack of appreciation in the busy, task- and hearing-oriented health care system. There is clearly a need for more (and more up-to-date) information on and exposure to hearing loss in preservice development programs, followed by continuing professional development, in which cultural and communication issues are addressed in addition to health issues per se. Such training leads to more mutual awareness and understanding, a stronger relationship between the DHH person and the care provider, and the delivery of higher-quality care services. Only if care providers have the necessary backgrounds and experiences with regard to hearing loss, they can incorporate those concerns into their interventions and services, and meet the needs of the DHH persons. As for the DHH person, he or she can become an active participant in the care system (Harmer, 1999).

In the context of education, congruent with the context of care, Luckner and Carter (2001) noted that one of the main challenges in providing education for learners who are deaf (sometimes with additional disabilities) is a shortage of well-prepared teachers (Swanwick, Chapter 26 in this volume). Kwakman and Van den Berg (2004) clearly stated that a career as a professional teacher requires further professional development in the work situation apart from preservice development programs. In general, teaching is a complex and situation-specific activity that requires continuous learning, changing, and improvement by the professional (Kwakman, 1999). But teachers of DHH children need to take even more account of factors such as characteristics of the learners, the context, and the curriculum. These teachers should be consummate professionals in constantly seeking the best solutions that make the maximum contribution to the learning of the DHH learners. Sheetz and Martin (2008) identified six characteristics of outstanding teachers of the deaf:

- Employing cognitive strategies;
- Being up to date;
- Having a passion for teaching;
- Working collaboratively;
- Demonstrating strong communication skills; and
- Creating independent learners.

Although some of these characteristics are included in regular preservice teacher training programs, the specific knowledge and skills needed to raise and educate DHH children are often not covered. Moreover, the role of teachers of the deaf is rapidly changing, as are the classroom settings, the demographics of the learners, and the possibilities offered by technologies such as cochlear implants. These changes not only demand adaptations in preservice teacher training programs (Mitchell & Karchmer, 2006) but also underline the importance of additional professional development programs for teachers so that they become lifelong learners and quality professionals.

Professional Development Programs

According to Guskey (2002, p. 381), referring to the context of education, "Professional development programs are systematic efforts to bring about change in the classroom practices of teachers, in their attitudes and beliefs, and in the learning outcomes of students." More generally, professional development programs are aimed at improving professional practice toward particular ends. These programs and activities can be provided by many organizations, communities, and networks and are characterized by their wide diversity of content, format, and duration. Examples include workshops for parents to learn what it means to be deaf so that they can better understand the feelings and emotions of their child, programs for unit managers in care organizations for DHH individuals to improve the efficiency of organizational processes, or coaching sessions in which teachers advance their interaction skills so they can communicate better with their students.

Despite all of the efforts made by organizations and the importance attached to professional development, many of these programs have turned out to be ineffective (Cohen & Hill, 2000; Wang, Frechtling, & Sanders, 1999). Possible factors adversely affecting the outcomes of professional development activities include the pressure of work, differences between training settings and work situations, shortages of facilitators, low-quality learning materials, and lack of management support (e.g., Baldwin & Ford, 1988; Gielen, 1995). Professionals also need to be motivated to apply their new knowledge and skills (Gegenfurtner, Veermans, Festner & Gruber, 2009). In this respect, two subfactors are not always addressed in professional development programs: the motivation of professionals to take part in professional development programs, and the motivation of professionals to change their practices. In relation to the first, according to Fullan (1991, 1993), teachers primarily see professional development programs as a promising means of professional growth. They believe that professional development expands their knowledge and skills and enhances their effectiveness with students (e.g., Fullan & Hargreaves, 1996). Through professional development, teachers look to gain specific, tangible, and practical ideas to improve their day-to-day practice (Fullan & Miles, 1992). According to Guskey (2002), development programs that fail to address these needs are unlikely to succeed.

In relation to the second subfactor, professional development activities frequently aim to change teachers' attitudes, beliefs and perceptions, based on the presumption that changes in professional practice will occur thereafter. However, significant changes in teachers' attitudes and beliefs primarily occur only after they have seen evidence of improvements in students' learning (Guskey, 2002). To achieve these improvements, teachers have to make changes in their classroom practices, for example by implementing a different instructional approach or using new learning materials. It is thus not primarily the professional development that leads to changes in teachers' attitudes and beliefs, but the experience of successful implementation. In other words, teachers believe that a new instructional approach or materials will work because they have seen that it works, and those experiences shape their attitudes and beliefs. According to Sparks (2002), high-quality professional development programs for teachers and administrators:

- Focus on deepening teachers' content knowledge and pedagogical skills;
- Include opportunities for practice, research, and reflection;
- Are embedded in educators' work and take place during the school day;
- Are sustained over time; and
- Are founded on a sense of collegiality and collaboration among teachers and between teachers and principals in solving important problems related to teaching and learning.

Timperley (2008) emphasized the importance of creating conditions that are responsive to the ways in which teachers (and other professionals) learn. To encourage learning, learners' prior conceptions about how the world works should be engaged, deep factual and conceptual knowledge should be developed and organized into frameworks that facilitate retrieval and application, and metacognitive and self-regulatory processes should be promoted that help learners define goals and then monitor their progress toward them. Related to metacognitive and self-regulatory processes, Holec (cited in Little, 2007) addressed learners' autonomy as "the ability to take charge of one's own learning" (pp. 27–28). Autonomy refers to the attitude of being able and willing to take responsibility for one's own learning process both in organized learning activities and in day-to-day situations. These two aspects are independent, so a learner may have the capacity but not be willing to take responsibility for the learning process or, conversely, the learner may be willing to do so but not have the ability. According to Little (2007), autonomous learners are characterized by their active involvement in the planning, monitoring, and evaluation of their learning. They reflect in a critical way on their learning process and can adjust the process if they think it is necessary. Nevertheless, autonomy is also an issue for teachers. They need to change their way of thinking about learning since classroom instruction by the teacher is no longer the only, or in some contexts even the most prominent, method of learning. Classroom-based activities are becoming more learner-driven, incorporating elements such as mentoring, coaching, and group assessments (Segers & Verhoeven, Chapter 21 in this volume). Teachers have the task of maintaining a balance between offering content and supporting the autonomy of the learner. Of course, they play an important role in providing the proper resources and opportunities for learners to learn and become proficient, but they also need to be aware of the different ways and possibilities for achieving the training objectives and discover how they can help their students to become independent learners in the classroom, at work, and in daily life.

Influence of Multimedia on Professional Development Programs

As mentioned earlier, professional development is a broad term that includes a wide array of possible learning activities. Although lessons provided by a teacher in a kind of authentic classroom setting can be a very effective way of learning, more and different ways of learning are available today. The introduction of multimedia, in particular, into the learning environment has created extensive possibilities in professional development programs. For example, multimedia applications have changed learning in terms of learning activities. The traditional method of a teacher lecturing in front of a group of learners has become just one possibility, and it is also possible to combine learning activities in what is called blended learning. Multimedia applications have also created more flexibility regarding where and when teaching and learning take place: at home, at the office, on the train, at the workplace, or at any other location, and at any time. Furthermore, the use of multimedia applications has generated new opportunities for other aspects of the programs, such as the role of the teacher, the rationale, content, aims and objectives, the grouping of learners, learning resources, and assessment (Van den Akker, 2003).

In the framework developed by Mishra and Koehler (2006), three bodies of knowledge are emphasized that are required to develop good teaching and professional development programs: knowledge about content, pedagogy, and technology. Content knowledge is knowledge about the actual subject matter that is to be learned or taught. Depending on the subject field, knowledge of key facts, concepts, theories, procedures, and frameworks should be acquired. Pedagogical knowledge is knowledge about methods of teaching and learning and, among other things, embraces knowledge of the overall educational goals, values, and aims. Pedagogical knowledge includes knowledge and skills about the nature of the target audience, lesson plan development and implementation, strategies for evaluating learners' understanding, and classroom management. Technology knowledge is knowledge about standard technologies, such as books, chalkboard and blackboard, as well as more advanced technologies, such as the Internet and digital video. This involves the skills required to operate particular technologies. Although the three bodies of knowledge can be analyzed separately, they can also be viewed in pairs or all three together, as Technological Pedagogical Content Knowledge. According to Mishra and Koehler (2006), there is a strong interplay among the three bodies of knowledge since they interact with, reinforce, and also can obstruct each other. A change in any one of the factors has to be "compensated" by changes in the other two and disrupts the dynamic equilibrium between them. In the context of professional development, this means that incorporating multimedia applications into teaching and learning in professional development programs also raises fundamental questions and concerns about content and pedagogy.

In recent decades, the introduction of multimedia applications in the different forms of e-learning and the use of Learning Management Systems, in particular, have increased the scope for program designers and instructors to develop effective professional development programs that address the learning needs of professionals. At the same time, new perspectives and ideas are emerging about the content and pedagogies of the programs. For instance, e-learning enables interaction among learners, and between instructors and learners, who are in different geographic locations (Fulford & Zhang, 1993; Wilson & Stacey, 2004); it also facilitates constructivist, collaborative, and community learning (Bonk & Cunningham, 1998; Holmes & Gardner, 2006; Jochems, Van Merriënboer, & Koper, 2004; Martens, Gulikers, & Bastiaens, 2004), blended learning (Littlejohn & Pegler, 2007), and "just-in-time" learning (Welsh, Wanberg, Brown, & Simmering, 2003).

PROFESSIONAL DEVELOPMENT AT ROYAL DUTCH KENTALIS

This section presents an example of in-service development programs for professionals supporting DHH learners, in which multimedia applications are integrated.

Professionals in Education and Care for Deaf and Hard-of-Hearing People

The national organization Royal Dutch Kentalis was founded in the Netherlands in 2010 as a merger of three regional organizations: Viataal, Royal Effatha Guyot Group, and Sint Marie. The various parts of the organization have specialized for the last 220 years in providing diagnostic, care, and educational services to people with a variety of hearing and/or communication challenges, including DHH persons. Two pillars of the organization are provision of high-quality services and continuous development and sharing of knowledge and expertise, including in hearing loss, both within and outside the organization (see www.kentalis.nl).

In dialogue with partners, parents, other family members, partner organizations, and external specialists, the 4,600 staff members aim to provide access to the best facilities in the fields of language and communication. They are part of multidisciplinary teams, consisting of teachers, care providers, psychologists, speech and language therapists, sign language specialists, and/or other professionals. Every professional is expected to be well educated, trained, and up to date in order to fulfill the needs of DHH learners and to meet the aims of the organization. Since preservice training programs usually do not cover the specific expertise needed by professionals, and since staff are required to engage in lifelong learning, Kentalis offers various opportunities for professional development. Facilitated by the Kentalis Academy, staff are encouraged to follow development programs (in-service training courses, workshops, coaching, and so on), to contribute to conferences and network meetings, to carry out research, and to exchange information and expertise with their colleagues. Parents, partner organizations, and other professionals who are interested can also subscribe to the professional development programs.

Toward More Innovative and Advanced Development Programs

The merger that created Kentalis offered the opportunity for a variety of in-service development programs that incorporated the knowledge and expertise present within the three former organizations. The following underlying educational principles for both the existing and proposed professional development programs were discussed and agreed on:

- Each professional is responsible for his or her own professional development. The organization facilitates learning in terms of time and facilities.
- Each professional starting a new job in the organization should become competent within three years.
- Each professional should continually deepen and update his or her expertise throughout his or her career within Kentalis.
- The in-service professional development programs must be relevant and useful for the day-to-day work of the professionals.
- Various learning methods and activities should be combined within the professional development programs (blended learning) to ensure that different learning styles are covered.
- Professional development programs should be offered on a "just-in-time" basis so that the professional can learn the right things at the right moment.

Three years ago, Kentalis started exploring the integration of a Learning Management System and e-learning in professional development. In particular, new opportunities available through the application of the Internet and multimedia in teaching and learning met the upcoming needs within the organization for internal and external information sharing, for learning at the professional's chosen time and place, and for constructing flexible learning programs. Although the underlying educational principles described above remained the same, the adoption of multimedia applications for professional development changed ideas about which content should be incorporated in the development programs, and about the underlying pedagogical principles. The next section describes the development and implementation of an innovative module developed by Kentalis for use by, among others, professionals working with DHH learners. This module about learning sign language at a basic level is illustrative of the change in the perspective on teaching and learning using multimedia applications and is part of a professional development program to learn sign language.

Principles and Design of a Development Program for Learning Sign Language

One of the most obvious, and very relevant, needs of parents and professionals working with DHH children is to learn sign language. As a center of expertise for the education of DHH learners, Kentalis has offered development programs on sign language since the start of its long history.

Until recently, Kentalis programs for learning signs or sign language consisted of a number of classroom sessions in which an instructor taught the signs by using pictures, short sentences, and stories. Information about grammatical issues was provided and exercises were performed to learn the signs. Occasionally, short conversations with grammatical structures were practiced. Long lists of signs were often used to improve the skills of the learners, who were expected to use those skills in their work without further support. Videos were mainly used for practicing signs at home. In this way, professionals learned sign language to some extent and were reasonably well able to communicate with DHH pupils and clients. Achieving a sufficient level of proficiency, however, also depended on personal interest and the willingness of the organization to facilitate learning.

With the introduction and availability of multimedia applications, in combination with new insights into learning a second language, the question arose at Kentalis: Can we find new, innovative ways of teaching and learning sign language that are effective and that will genuinely support those working with deaf children and adults?

Second-Language Learning

For a long time, sign language had been perceived as a method of communication with DHH individuals, and not as a language. As a result, signed systems were developed in the early days without any cultural or linguistic implications calling for the proper use of a National Sign Language. During the 1970s and 1980s, sign language increasingly came to be recognized in the Netherlands as a full and comprehensive language, based on the principle of equality with other languages (Commissie Nederlandse Gebarentaal, 1997). In addition, new perceptions of learning a second language in general, and sign languages in particular, were developing. Proficiency guidelines were established in different parts of the world for learning, teaching, and assessing foreign languages based on learners' successive levels of communicative achievement (for the United States ACRFL-PG; Canada CLB; Europe CEFR[1]). The development of these guidelines signified a major change in perspective on languages, and more specifically the learning of sign languages. In Europe, the growing cooperation between member states of the European Union and employee exchanges between European countries led to a need for an objective measurement instrument for foreign languages.

These guidelines all provide a means of measuring the achievements of learners of foreign languages. They describe various skill areas for spoken languages: expression, reception, reading, writing, and interaction. Each of these areas is described in terms of levels of proficiency and substages. For the skill areas, the levels of proficiency are specified in what are called "can-do" statements. A can-do statement is a user-oriented description of a language skill the learner should be able to perform. The can-do statements are worked up into detailed descriptors for different domains of life such as personal, public, and education.

Apart from the can-do statements, the guidelines describe strategies for language learning and cultural aspects. One of the four key advantages of these kinds of language guidelines is that they provide descriptions of proficiency levels that are transparent, absolute, functional, and international. The guidelines also provide clear information about what language levels mean to designers of development programs and teachers, as well as to learners themselves. The levels are moreover independent of the type of education, the country, and the level of interdependency of learners. The guidelines also describe what learners can do (not what they know about the language) and how they can learn to perform well.

The CEFR has formed the basis for the development of a new series of professional development programs of Sign Language of the Netherlands. The different CEFR levels are shown in Table 22.1. Table 22.2 shows two examples of can-do statements for different levels, A1 and C1.

Table 22.1 Levels of Language Proficiency According to the CEFR

A	Basic user	A1 Breakthrough
		A2 Waystage
B	Independent user	B1 Threshold
		B2 Vantage
C	Proficient user	C1 Effective operational
		C2 Mastery

Table 22.2 Examples of "Can-do" Statements

Two examples of can-do statements for the skill area: Expression—sustained monologue	
Level A1	The student can describe him/herself, what he/she does and where he/she lives.
Level C1	The student can give elaborate descriptions and narratives, integrating sub-themes, developing particular points and rounding off with an appropriate conclusion.

Three Main Design Principles

In 2010, a group of educational designers, sign language interpreters, instructors, and deaf professionals from Kentalis began designing and developing a new professional development program for learning sign language. They used the frameworks developed by Mishra and Koehler (2006) and the CEFR to formulate three main design principles: the content should be in line with the principles of second-language learning (CEFR); learners' autonomy should be the guiding principle in the elaboration of the program's pedagogies; and the possibilities offered by multimedia and new media[2] should be integrated as effective means of strengthening the content and pedagogies. These three principles are explained in more detail below.

First, the designers of the professional development program for learning sign language decided to design the program content in line with the second-language learning principles as formulated and described in detail in the CEFR. Since the CEFR was developed for spoken languages, the designers reformulated the descriptors in the CEFR to make them applicable for Signed Languages.[3] The first Kentalis sign language module designed as part of the development program is called Breakthrough and is based on the first level in the CEFR.

In addition, three subprinciples were regarded as very important in designing the second-language learning path of the learners. One subprinciple focused on receptive versus expressive skills. The CEFR describes the amount of time needed to learn a second language. A distinction is made between the time required for the acquisition of receptive language skills and the time needed for the acquisition of expressive language skills, taking into account the fact that receptive skills are needed to learn expressive skills. For the lower levels of sign language, more time is therefore needed to work on the acquisition of receptive skills, while for the higher the levels of language skills more time is needed for learning expressive skills. Since the potential learners in the Kentalis development program have daily contact with DHH persons as sign language users, the program actually needed to include the learning of both receptive and expressive skills. However, the program designers took the ratio between receptive and expressive skills for a "Basic" user as a starting point for the content of the Breakthrough module. Multimedia applications were expected to be very useful in facilitating the learning of receptive skills, for example by using video clips and guiding the learner though the learning materials in a reflective way.

A second subprinciple associated with second-language learning concerned the time needed to learn the language (Table 22.3). An important prerequisite for learning a language is that the learner has enough contact hours with the language. A contact hour is the amount of time for which the learner consciously has "contact" with the language in a reflective way. This contact can take various forms, for instance trying to understand what is being said on a video clip, following a classroom instruction in which the learner is actively involved, or having a conversation with another language user. The amount of time needed to progress from level 0 to A1, to A2, to B1, and so on increases exponentially. When designing the development program, the designers realized that most of the potential program learners have daily contact with DHH sign language users. This was seen as a good opportunity to learn sign language in a relatively short time and underlined the importance of a strong link between the program's content and learners' workplaces (although of course DHH persons should not continually be exploited for personal learning purposes).

The third second-language learning subprinciple recognized that there are a variety of learning strategies. People tend to use different learning strategies depending on their personal preferences, the time available or the moment at which learning takes place, and their personal or working environment. For instance, those in professional development who are working with young deaf children have different learning needs, opportunities, and strategies than those who work with young adults. Given this variety, the program designers decided that the learning path through the program should be flexible in terms of content and mode of instruction. The use of multimedia applications, in particular, was expected to facilitate this flexibility, possibly in combination with classroom-based learning (blended learning).

The second program design principle emphasized learners' autonomy. The CEFR emphasizes this autonomy because languages can be learned

Table 22.3 Average Amount of Time Spent on Receptive and Expressive Skills

Level	Receptive skills	Expressive skills
A. Basic user (A1 + A2)	70%	30%
B. Independent user (B1 + B2)	50%	50%
C. Proficient user (C1 + C2)	30%	70%

most effectively if the learner practices the language independently and spontaneously and displays personal responsibility and involvement during the learning process. For this reason, the program designers decided that the program should encourage learners to learn sign language in interaction with other people, facilitated by classroom sessions, new media applications such as the use of webcams, or day-to-day contact with DHH persons. In each learning activity, sign language is used in a variety of ways, such as taking initiative, reacting, or posing questions. In addition, the learners are encouraged to take responsibility for their own learning process in the program through flexibility and reflection facilitated by multimedia. From the beginning, learners can choose which content they would like to learn and in what order. Thereafter, learners are continuously challenged to think about what they have achieved, what they have learned through reflection, and how they will continue going forward. In this way, the learners assess and reflect on their own achievements as well as on the achievements of their fellow learners.

The third program design principle involved the possibilities offered by multimedia and new media and the idea that they should be integrated as effective means of strengthening content and pedagogy. Inspired by the framework developed by Mishra and Koehler (2006), the professional development program from Kentalis combines content, pedagogy, and technology. Given the implications of the other two design principles for the use of multimedia in the program, the module Breakthrough was also interlaced with multimedia.

Design of the Breakthrough Module

The Breakthrough module covers five blocks, each with its own theme (persons and professions; weather and transport; rhythm of the day; clothes and colors; celebrations throughout the year) and consists of online learning, a classroom session, and short exercises to be carried out at the workplace. The online learning has to be completed before the learners are allowed to take part in the classroom session, to ensure that they have gained enough receptive and expressive skills to participate actively. Each block and each learning activity affords scope for learners' autonomy.

Online learning is an important part of the module. It is divided into four elements, reflecting a variety of learning strategies and the two language skills (receptive and expressive). The four elements are called Watch, Know, Drill, and Sign (Fig. 22.1).

The Watch element encourages self-discovering learning (Fig. 22.2). Facilitated by videos, questions, and short exercises, learners learn what and how things are expressed in sign language. Apart from learning signs, they learn observation strategies to help them understand signs.

The Know element concerns background and factual information about aspects such as language, language use, grammatical issues, and

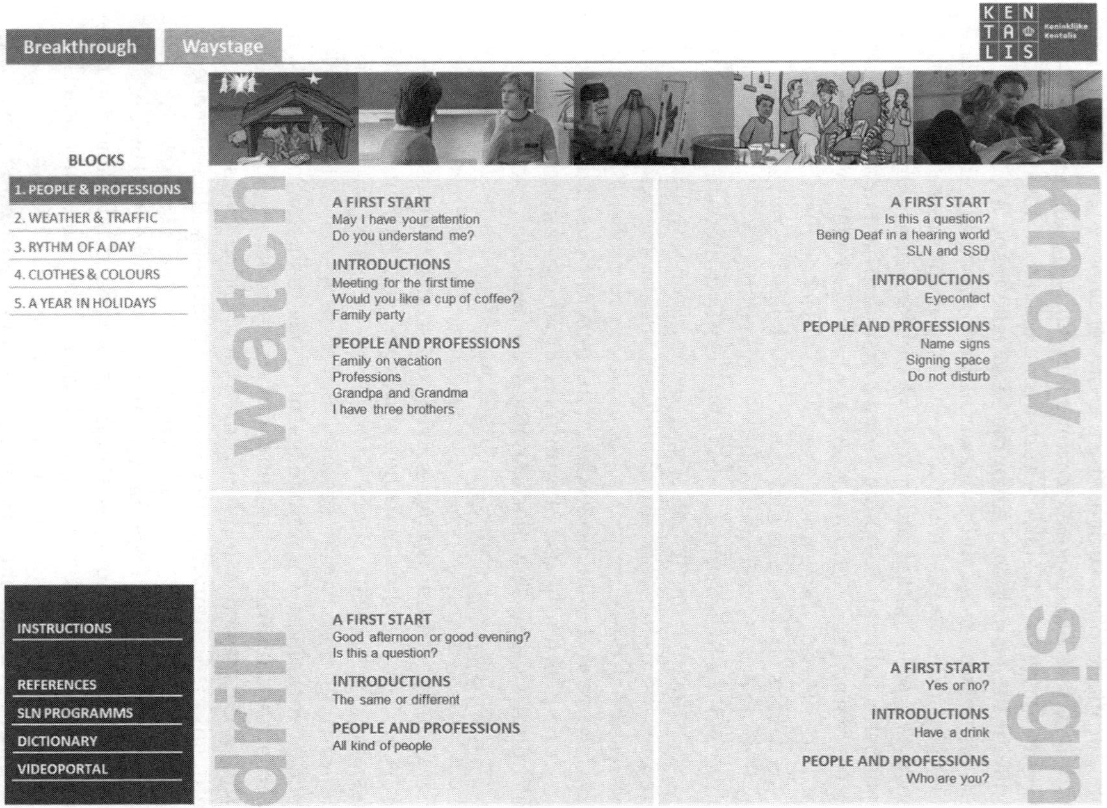

Figure 22.1 Interface of the Breakthrough module.
For this chapter the texts in the images are translated into English. All the texts in the original program are in Dutch.

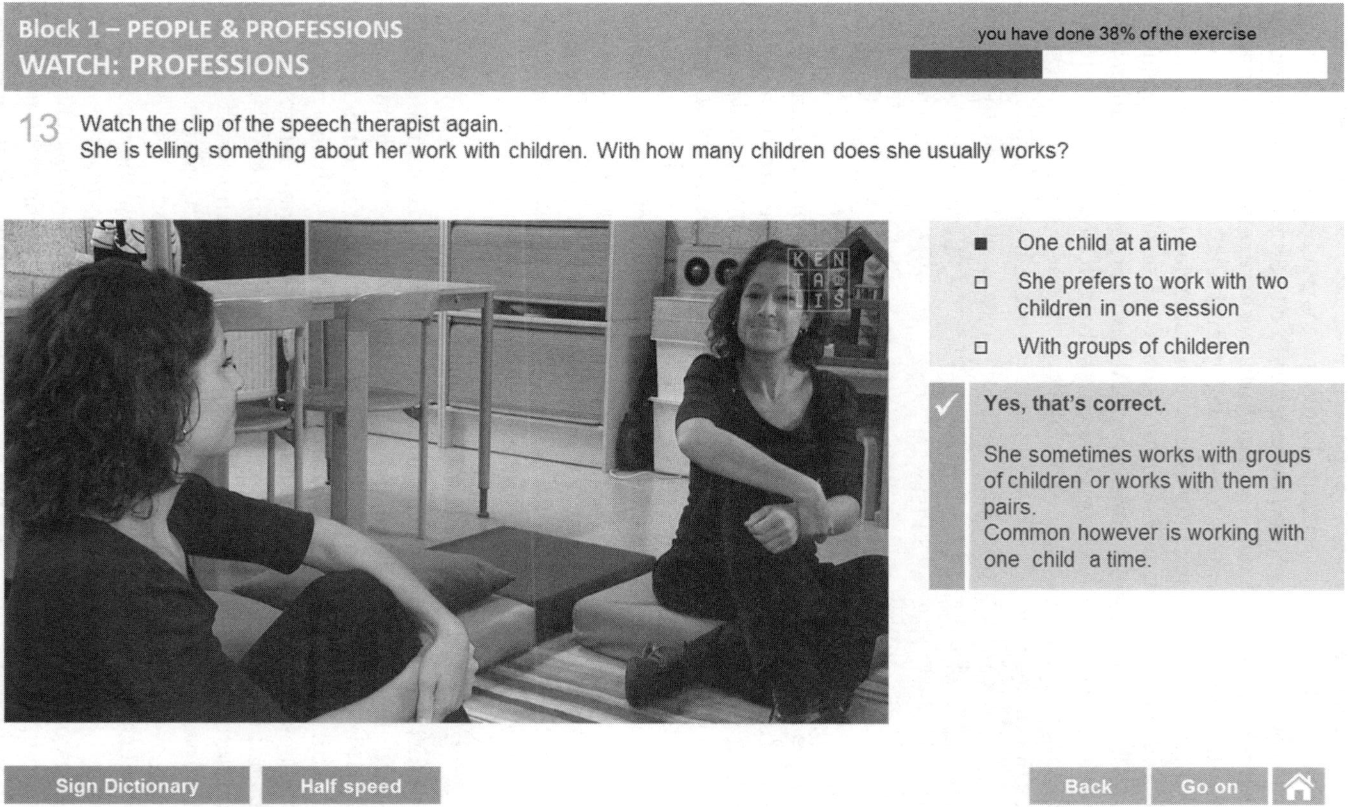

Figure 22.2 The Watch element in the Breakthrough module.

cultural aspects. The Drill element includes short, quick drills to train sign and routine recognition, and remembrance. The Sign element provides opportunities for learners to record themselves using webcams, and to compare the recorded material with correct examples. In future versions of the module, it will be possible to share self-recorded materials with peers and teachers for evaluation and feedback.

Expression and interaction skills are practiced through conversation and reflection exercises during classroom sessions. A large number of practical conversation exercises are performed together with other learners in these sessions. Learners have to interact, solve problems together, and play games against one another. After each exercise, reflection takes place. The instructor takes the role of a facilitator who encourages learners to interact and take responsibility for their own learning process, and who offers the means and opportunities to learn.

A wide variety of workplace exercises is included in this part of the module. For example, one exercise involves trying to discover the name signs of three colleagues and discussing why they have these name signs. In another exercise, participants learn to ask for coffee or learn the signs for other drinks and food they like. Some of the exercises are also discussed in the classroom sessions. Overall, the time investment for the module is approximately 35 to 45 hours. Online learning takes four to six hours for each block; each classroom session lasts two-and-a-half hours; and no time is specified for the exercises at the workplace. Compared to earlier development modules for learning sign language offered at Kentalis, consisting of 12 classroom sessions of two hours each and one hour's homework, the total amount of learning time remains the same. However, learners save time and travel expenses because of the reduced number of classroom sessions.

Evaluation of the Breakthrough Module

The Breakthrough module as part of the professional development program for learning sign language has been delivered several times since it was introduced just in 2013. After completing the module, learners and instructors are asked about their experiences with the program by means of a questionnaire and evaluation meetings. Although the data gathered through these evaluation activities are not yet extensive enough to perform reliable data analyses, the qualitative reactions and reflections have provided a lot of information about the effectiveness of the program, as well as ideas for further improvement.

In general, the motivation of professionals to follow the module significantly increased because of the e-learning component, the reduction of classroom time, and the linkages with the CEFR. The new way of learning sign language using multimedia applications greatly encouraged the learners to subscribe to the module, although some professionals were somewhat concerned about their computer skills and the "modern" character of the program. The instructors were already enthusiastic about the new setup and potential of the module during the design phase, especially the different ways of interacting with the learners and the extended variety of learning activities. The fact that some instructors were closely involved in designing and developing the module undoubtedly contributed to their enthusiasm in embracing the new module.

After completing the module, both learners and instructors were very positive about the way in which learning had taken place and about their learning outcomes. In particular, the ability to learn at their own pace and the diversity of learning activities were greatly appreciated. One learner said: "I am very pleased with the possibility offered by the module to plan my own time for online learning, and the different ways of learning [watching, knowing, drilling, signing] were also very inspiring." The flexibility in learning time and the limited number of classroom sessions also reduced learners' sense of having a high study load. As two learners commented: "The time investment needed to do the exercises online is substantial, but on the other hand I only had to go to the classroom meetings once a month," and "The online learning part was quite substantial, but it actually went well because I was able to plan my time to suit me." The close link between online learning and classroom practice was also appreciated. The learners recognized the signs they had learned online in the classroom sessions and felt comfortable in further improving their sign skills during the sessions. Some learners commented that they ran through the online learning session just before each of the classroom sessions started. They reflected on their own learning responsibility, as they intended to avoid this method of learning next time. The learners and instructors were also very satisfied with the learning outcomes, especially the skills they acquired in initiating and following a conversation in sign language, and in approaching DHH persons in a self-confident manner.

Depending on the professionals' workplace, many learners were already using the sign skills they had acquired in their day-to-day work practice and intended to subscribe to the follow-up module to learn the next level of sign language ("Waystage"). One very enthusiastic learner commented: "The communication with pupils and colleagues at my workplace has improved a lot since I took the module. The personal growth, progressing from only making a few signs in the beginning to having a full sign conversation was fantastic. As a result, my pupils and colleagues understand me better and I can easily communicate with them." The instructors realized that there was a discrepancy between the learning outcomes achieved with the previous module and the newly developed Breakthrough module. Although this suggested that the learners learned less than in the previous module, the instructors realized the learners' outcomes were different. Instead of mastering an extensive vocabulary of signs, learners were better equipped with the skills needed to understand and participate in sign conversations. This was precisely what the developers were aiming for when designing a development program for professionals working with DHH persons in day-to-day practice.

The learners and instructors also gave the program designers suggestions and ideas for improving the module. Some technical problems were experienced with the videos and online learning environment, which called for better availability of the multimedia elements in the module. In addition, some videos in the online learning section, some classroom sessions, and the time between classroom sessions were experienced as too long, leading to a lack of concentration on the part of the learners. Long-winded videos could be replaced and the classroom sessions and the time between them could possibly be shortened. The learners' own responsibility for the learning process and reflection could also be addressed more directly.

Based on the outcomes of this evaluation, the program designers decided to make some adjustments to the module. Since both learners and instructors had suggested reducing the length of the classroom sessions and the time between them, the duration of the classroom sessions was set at two-and-a-half instead of three hours. The time between classroom sessions was reduced to two weeks instead of the suggested three to four weeks, although this could be adjusted to suit the preference of the instructor or the logistical possibilities. However, less than two weeks was not recommended, because the learners would not have enough time to tackle the video exercises seriously. The designers also adapted the way in which the sign vocabulary was made available, and improvements were made in the learning material for some of the themes to meet the learning needs of specific groups of professionals more closely. For instance, although the module is not intended for professionals who already have a certain proficiency in sign language, many of them indicated that they would like to have access to the online learning materials to refresh their knowledge and skills. The module accessibility has been extended for that purpose. The technological problems experienced might be explained by a lack of experience on the part of the learners and instructors. Therefore, program designers made additional investments in good instruction, collegial support, and helpdesk instructions to overcome these problems. Another explanation might be a lack of technical resources such as a properly functioning Internet connection or webcam. To make sure that learners and instructors are not impeded in their learning process, the program designers made explicit the required organizational and other conditions for the module.

With regard to sign language quality, Kentalis still needs to make a major change in assessing professionals according to the CEFR. For example, which sign language level is required for a professional teacher of the deaf, or for a speech therapist? How do we assess them? The first steps in answering these questions are being taken in cooperation with other organizations. An important tool is an elaborate video portal in which professionals can share signed exercises with peers and instructors to obtain feedback. The portal can also be used in the evaluation and assessment of learners.

Much still has to be explored, however, including the use of sign language in social media: How can signing people benefit from social media developments as a learning tool? The possibilities are endless, but we need to remain critical to ensure that the media contributes to the effectiveness of the module. The focus should remain on quality; just as e-learning is a means, not an end, the same applies to future techniques. The important thing is to get the best out of what is offered.

CONCLUSIONS AND FUTURE PERSPECTIVES

The development of the Breakthrough module illustrates the innovative way in which organizations can support the development of their professionals. In particular, the combination of e-learning and multimedia applications with classroom sessions and practical assignments in the modules was described and stressed, leading to blended learning programs, high autonomy for the learners, and a flexible learning process. For example, learners were able to learn at their own place and time.

These types of development programs consisting of various modules not only expand the knowledge and skills of professionals but also seem to increase their motivation to learn and to change their practices. Being a professional (teacher, health care provider, or other professional) implies lifelong learning, for instance by participating in professional development programs. This enables professionals to stay up to date, prepared, and able to take on the specific responsibilities and tasks needed to raise and educate DHH learners. Continuing professional development is crucial in addition to regular preservice programs simply because the role of teachers of DHH students, the classroom settings, the demographics of the learners, and the possibilities offered by technology are changing so quickly.

Of course, developers of professional development programs are also professionals themselves who need to engage in lifelong learning and constantly seek to improve their own practices. Based on their experiences, new theoretical insights, improved technology, and program evaluations, professional development programs can be made more adaptive to and more effective for professionals and their organizations. For example, more specific design principles can be developed for particular target groups and organizations, and the integration of other new media can be explored. More research on the effectiveness of blended professional development programs (including the Breakthrough module) is also needed to validate the underlying design principles and to make clear the effect of professionals' learning on their daily practice. This also requires the development and availability of reliable learners' assessments and evaluation tools that go beyond the evaluation of learners' reactions and learning outcomes immediately after completing a program. Without doubt, the expanding possibilities of new media will also be explored and used to improve assessment and evaluation. Nonetheless, new media should always be supportive of the effectiveness of professional development programs, and the programs should always be supportive of the aims and goals of education and care. In other words, they are a means to an end, not ends in themselves. The mission of all professionals working with DHH children is and will always be to increase the deaf child's chances of success in both academic and social life.

NOTES

1 United States of America: American Council of the Teaching of Foreign Language-Proficiency Guidelines; Canada: Canadian Language Benchmarks; Europe: Common European Framework of Languages.

2 *New media* refers to on-demand access to content anytime, anywhere, and on any digital device, as well as interactive user feedback and creative participation. Another aspect of new media is the real-time generation of new and unregulated content (Schivinski & Dąbrowski, 2014).

3 Since 2009, Kentalis has worked on a version of the descriptors for Sign Language of the Netherlands as a basis for the development of a new series of sign language development programs. Since 2011, Kentalis has collaborated with the University of Ap plied Sciences Utrecht, the Association of Teachers of Modern Languages–Department of Sign Language Teachers, and the University of Amsterdam Sign Language Department to develop the Dutch CEFR for Signed Languages. This collaboration was supported by the Institute for Curriculum Development. Results were presented at a national symposium in November 2013.

REFERENCES

Academieteam ERK NGT. (2013). *Europees Referentiekader voor Talen: Gebarentalen.* Utrecht: Kenniscentrum Educatie Hogeschool Utrecht

Baldwin, T. T., & Ford, J. K. (1988). Transfer of training: A review and directions for future research. *Personnel Psychology, 41*(1), 63–105.

Bonk, C., & Cunningham, D. (1998) Searching for learner-centred, constructivist, and sociocultural components of collaborative educational learning tools. In C. J. Bonk & K. S. King (Eds.), *Electronic collaborators: Learner-centered technologies for literacy, apprenticeship, and discourse* (pp. 25–50). Mahwah, NJ: Erlbaum.

Calderon, R. (2000). Parental involvement in deaf children's education programs as a predictor of child's language, early reading, and social-emotional development. *Journal of Deaf Studies and Deaf Education*, *5*(2), 140–155.

Cohen, D. K., & Hill, H. C. (2000). Instructional policy and classroom performance: The mathematics reform in California. *Teacher College Record*, *102*(2), 294–343.

Commissie Nederlandse Gebarentaal. (1997). *Meer dan een gebaar*. Den Haag: SduUitgevers

Council of Europe. (2011). *Common European Framework of Reference for Languages: Learning, teaching, assessment*. Cambridge: Cambridge University Press.

Courtin, C. (2000). The impact of sign language on the cognitive development of deaf children: The case of theories of mind. *Journal of Deaf Studies and Deaf Education*, *5*(3), 266–276.

Fulford, C. P., & Zhang, S. (1993). Perceptions of interaction: The critical predictor in distance education. *American Journal of Distance Education*, *7*(3), 8–21.

Fullan, M. G. (1991). *The new meaning of educational change*. New York: Teachers College.

Fullan, M. G. (1993). *Change forces: Probing the depths of educational reform*. Bristol: Falmer.

Fullan, M. G., & Hargreaves, A. (1996). *What's worth fighting for in your school*. New York: Teachers College.

Fullan, M. G., & Miles, M. B. (1992). Getting reform right: What works and what doesn't. *Phi Delta Kappan*, *73*(10), 745–752.

Gegenfurtner, A., Veermans, K., Festner, D., & Gruber, H. (2009). Integrative literature review: Motivation to transfer training: An integrative literature review. *Human Resource Development Review*, *8*(3), 403–423.

Gielen, E. W. M. (1995). *Transfer of training in a corporate setting*. Doctoral dissertation. Enschede: University of Twente.

Guskey, T. R. (2002). Professional development and teacher change. *Teachers and Teaching: Theory and Practice*, *8*(3/4), 381–391.

Harmer, L. M. (1999). Health care delivery and deaf people: Practice, problems, and recommendations for change. *Journal of Deaf Studies and Deaf Education*, *4*(2), 73–110.

Hindley, P. (1997). Psychiatric aspects of hearing impairment. *Journal of Child Psychology & Psychiatry & Allied Health Disciplines*, *38*(1), 101–117.

Holmes, B., & Gardner, J. (2006). *E-learning: Concepts and practice*. London: Sage.

Jochems, W., Van Merriënboer, J., & Koper, R. (2004). *Integrated e-learning: Implications for pedagogy, technology, and organization*. London: RoutledgeFalmer.

Kwakman, K. (1999). *Leren van docenten tijdens de beroepsloopbaan. Studies naar professionaliteit op de werkplek in het voortgezet onderwijs*. Doctoral dissertation. Nijmegen: Katholieke Universiteit Nijmegen.

Kwakman, K., & Van den Berg, E. (2004). Professionele ontwikkeling als kennisontwikkeling door leraren: naar een betere interactie tussen praktijk en theorie. *Velon, Tijdschrift voor Lerarenopleiders*, *25*(3), 6–12.

Little, D. (2007, December). *Learner autonomy, inner speech and the European Language Portfolio*. Paper presented at the 14th International Conference of Applied Linguistics, Thessaloniki, Greece.

Littlejohn, A., & Pegler, C. (2007). *Preparing for blended e-learning*. New York: Routledge.

Luckner, J., & Carter, K. (2001). Essential competencies for teaching students with hearing loss and additional disabilities. *American Annals of the Deaf, 146*(1), 7–15.

Marschark, M. (2007). *Raising and educating a deaf child* (2nd ed.). New York: Oxford University.

Martens, R. L., Gulikers, J., & Bastiaens, T. (2004). The impact of intrinsic motivation on e-learning in authentic computer tasks. *Journal of Computer Assisted learning, 20*(5), 368–376.

Meadow, K. P. (2005). Early manual communication in relation to the deaf child's intellectual, social, and communicative functioning. *Journal of Deaf Studies and Deaf Education, 10*(4), 321–329.

Mishra, P., & Koehler, M. J. (2006). Technological pedagogical content knowledge: A framework for teacher knowledge. *Teachers College Record, 108*(6), 1017–1054.

Mitchell, R. E., & Karchmer, M. A. (2006). Demographics of deaf education: More students in more places. *American Annals of the Deaf, 151*(2), 95–104.

Moores, D. F., & Meadow-Orlans, K. P. (1990). *Educational and developmental aspects of deafness*. Washington, DC: Gallaudet University.

Philips, B. (1996). Bringing culture to the forefront: Formulating diagnostic impressions of deaf and hard of hearing people at times of medical crisis. *Professional Psychology Research and Practice, 27*(2), 137–144.

Schivinski, B., & Dąbrowski, D. (2014). The effect of social-media communication on consumer perceptions of brands. *Journal of Marketing Communications*. Advance online publication. doi: 10.1080/13527266.2013.871323.

Sheetz, N., & Martin, D. (2008). National study of master teachers in deaf education: Implications for teacher education. *American Annals of the Deaf, 153*(3), 328–343.

Sparks, D. (2002). *Designing powerful professional development for teachers and principals*. Oxford: National Staff Development Council.

Timperley, H. (2008). *Teacher professional learning and development*. Belley: Imprimerie Nouvelle Gonnet.

Van den Akker, J. (2003). Curriculum perspectives: An introduction. In J. van den Akker, W. Kuiper, & U. Hameyer (Eds.), *Curriculum landscapes and trends* (pp. 1–10). Dordrecht: Kluwer Academic Publishers.

Viccari, C., & Marschark, M. (1997). Communication between parents and deaf children: Implications for social-emotional development. *Journal of Child Psychology and Psychiatry, 38*(7), 793–801.

Wang, Y. L., Frechtling, J. A., & Sanders, W. L. (1999, April). *Exploring linkages between professional development and student learning: A pilot study.* Paper presented at the Annual Meeting of the American Educational Research Association, Montreal.

Welsh, E. T., Wanberg, C. R., Brown, K. G., & Simmering, M. J. (2003). E-learning: emerging uses, empirical results and future directions. *International Journal of Training and Development, 7*(4), 245–258.

Wilson, G., & Stacey, E. (2004). Online interaction impacts on learning: Teaching the teachers to teach online. *Australian Journal of Educational Technology, 20*(1), 33–48.

Part 5

Learning and Educational Context

23

Enhancing Academic and Social Outcomes

Balancing Individual, Family, and School Assets and Risks for Deaf and Hard-of-Hearing Students in General Education

Shirin D. Antia

Historically, deaf and hard-of-hearing (DHH) students have been educated in self-contained programs. These programs generally include only other DHH students; all students are taught by teachers of the deaf. Since the 1970s, however, such segregation of students with hearing loss has become less common. In many countries most DHH students are educated in general education programs with their hearing peers. In the United States, for instance, approximately 70% of students are educated in general education classrooms. Other countries, such as Australia and Israel, report even higher percentages.

A question that has plagued educators is whether DHH students can survive and thrive in educational environments that consist mostly of hearing students. Can DHH students achieve academically when educated with hearing peers? Can they make friends and feel socially accepted in schools attended by only a few DHH students?

The answer, as is usual for most complex questions, is "It depends." Having a hearing loss, even a mild hearing loss, puts a student at risk for poor academic and social outcomes. Many DHH students achieve at levels similar to their classmates, have friends, and are well liked by peers; others experience both academic and social difficulties. Instead of assuming that hearing loss alone accounts for all difficulties, it is valuable to explore the factors that contribute to these outcomes. Factors that contribute to positive outcomes are assets; those that negatively influence outcomes are risks. Once assets and risks are identified, it may be possible for families and educational professionals to enhance assets and mitigate risks. Clearly, not all risks can be mitigated. Cognitive ability and the family's socioeconomic status are not factors that can be changed easily. However, teachers can provide support commensurate with the child's cognitive ability; families can learn to communicate effectively with their children and take an interest in their schooling; professionals can find means of communicating with and encouraging the involvement of all family members.

This chapter draws from findings of a longitudinal study of academic and social outcomes of DHH students in general education classrooms who were followed for five years (Antia, Jones, Luckner, Kreimeyer, & Reed, 2011; Antia, Jones, Reed, & Kreimeyer, 2009; Antia et al., 2008). The students were drawn from school districts in two southwestern states in the United States. A total of 197 students were included in the study. Students with any degree of hearing loss were included if they received services from an itinerant teacher of the deaf. Of the 197 students, 17% had a unilateral loss, 36% had a mild or moderate bilateral hearing loss, and 36% had a severe or profound bilateral loss; information on the level of hearing loss was missing for 10%. The students were in grades 2 through 8 at the beginning of the study; therefore, most students were between eight and 13 years of age when they entered the study. The itinerant teachers serving these students consulted with the classroom teachers and also provided direct academic instruction and support to the DHH students as needed. The research team obtained annual academic and social assessment information on these students. The team also conducted extensive interviews with a randomly selected subsample of 25 students and their teachers, principals, and parents. Interviewers asked about the students' academic and social lives, the support they received from family and school personnel, and any reasons that might explain how they were doing. By examining all the information collected, quantitative and qualitative, the research team learned about the students' academic and social outcomes and how different individual, family, and school factors contributed to these outcomes.

ACADEMIC OUTCOMES

There are three ways in which one might examine the academic outcomes of DHH students. The first is to examine the standardized test scores, or academic achievement scores. Standardized test scores allow educators to compare the achievement of DHH students to other students of the same age or grade. These scores also allow educators to examine DHH students' progress in achievement from year to year and compare it to that expected of other students.

A second way to examine academic outcomes is to request teachers to provide information on students' achievement and progress compared to their classmates. Teachers' judgments are valid and reliable if they have frequent contact with the DHH student. For students in general education classrooms, the classroom teachers are good judges because they can compare the DHH student's academic performance with that of classmates who are the same age and who are (presumably) learning the same content.

A third way of looking at academic outcomes is to examine the ability of the DHH student to participate in the academic life of the classroom. This can be done by observing the student or by asking the student to complete a questionnaire that assesses how well he or she can understand and communicate with teachers and peers and join in classroom discussions.

Previous researchers have found that DHH students' academic test scores are far below the expectations for their age (Traxler, 2000) and that their progress is approximately one-third that of their peers of the same age and grade (Wolk & Allen, 1984). In contrast, the results of the longitudinal study of DHH students in general education showed that, as a group, these DHH students had reading, language/writing, and math scores within the low-average range. The DHH students scored highest in math and somewhat lower in reading and writing. In math, over two thirds of the DHH students scored in the average to above-average range, while in reading and writing approximately 50% to 60% scored in the average range each year. The researchers also examined the progress made by these students over the five-year time period. They found that, on average, the DHH students made a year of progress annually in reading and math. In writing they made more than one year's progress annually (Antia et al., 2009).

When teachers were asked about DHH students' achievement compared to classmates, they rated 70% to 80% of students as being in the average or above-average range in academic competence. When the researchers examined the ratings given by teachers over the five years, they found that almost 90% of students made a year's progress in a year's time (Antia et al., 2009). However, some of these students were achieving less than their peers to begin with, and so would need to make more rapid progress to catch up. Finally, an examination of classroom participation showed that, on average, the students rated themselves as "almost always" understanding their teachers and classmates (Antia, Sabers, & Stinson, 2007).

SOCIAL OUTCOMES

As with academic outcomes there are three main methods of examining social outcomes. The first is to examine peer relationships by observing how frequently DHH children interact with their peers, and whether these interactions are positive or negative. A second method is to assess the friendship patterns of DHH students by asking all students within a classroom or a program to identify or rate peers with whom they would like to play or work. A third method is for parents, teachers, and students to complete a questionnaire or a rating scale that includes positive and negative items about specific social skills and behaviors.

The research on social outcomes of DHH students in general education classrooms has yielded mixed results. An early study (Antia, 1982) found that DHH students who spent only some of the time in the general education classroom interacted infrequently with all peers whether they were DHH *or* hearing. Some researchers have reported that DHH students are less socially accepted than their hearing classmates (Cappelli, Daniels, Durieux-Smith, McGrath, & Neuss, 1995), while others have found no difference between the acceptance of DHH students and their hearing peers (Wauters & Knoors, 2008). Similarly, when it comes to ratings of social skills, some researchers have found no differences between DHH and hearing students (Mejstad, Heiling, & Svedin, 2008/2009), while others have found considerable differences (Dammeyer, 2010). The specific reasons for the varied results are not clear. There may be differences in the manner in which data were collected, differences among the students in the studies, and also differences in the social support provided by the educational programs.

For the longitudinal study, the researchers asked DHH students and their teachers to complete a social skills and problem behavior questionnaire each year for five years (Antia et al., 2011). Over the five-year period teachers rated 80% of students as average or above-average in social skills when compared to their peers in the same class and of the same age. Students rated themselves in a similar manner: 80% rated themselves as being average or above-average socially. Teachers rated fewer than 15% of DHH students as having above-average problem behaviors. This is similar to the percentage found in the general population. The teacher and student ratings did not change much over time, showing that the students continued to have age-appropriate social skills as they got older.

The information obtained from interviews showed that 16 of the 25 students (64%) who were interviewed had close friends in their school or their neighborhood. Six students did not have close friends, but only one student was described as being lonely and isolated. Some students were extremely popular and well known in their school because they excelled in academic work, sports, or other activities. As some of the younger students entered adolescence, their social life posed more challenges. Difficulties were encountered during the transition from elementary to middle school, or middle to high school. These findings are similar to those of Wolters, Knoors, Cillessen, and Verhoeven (2012). During transitions the DHH students had to find new friends, adapt to several new teachers, and become more self-reliant. This was also the time when many students felt singled out because of their hearing loss and decided not to use amplification. For most students, social issues (which parents attributed mostly to the onset of adolescence) resolved within a year or two.

RISK AND RESILIENCE FACTORS

The academic and social outcomes reported by Antia and colleagues are encouraging, especially when compared to other reports of the outcomes for DHH students. However, because average results seldom capture the outcomes for specific students, there are students for whom the outcomes are less than rosy. Academically about 35% to 38% of DHH students remained below average in reading and writing as measured by their test scores, and about 20% made less than a year's progress annually. Socially, about 16% were rated as below average. Some students continued to do well over the five-year period, while others fell behind their classmates early and stayed there. Some students interviewed were extremely popular and had close friends, but at least one was described as lonely and isolated. How are discrepancies in performance explained? What puts some students at risk while others, with similar or even greater hearing loss, are resilient and do well?

Usually one thinks of resilience as adaptation when faced with overwhelming adversity. However, a more encompassing definition is provided by Goldstein and Brooks (2005), who suggest that resilience is the manner in which individuals thrive emotionally, behaviorally, academically, and interpersonally. The fit between an individual and the environment affects the person's ability to thrive. Thus, resilience can be thought of as the ability to respond positively to emotional, environmental, and developmental challenges; it is a process that can be nurtured in all individuals.

For children born with a hearing loss, the hearing world is a poor fit. However, as shown by the results outlined earlier in this chapter, many do well in school despite the hurdles that likely exist in their environment. Teachers and parents know that children with an identical degree of hearing loss do not have the same outcomes. Are there specific assets that promote resilience because they cushion these children from adverse outcomes? Alternatively, what are the risks (apart from hearing loss itself) that result in some children's poor outcomes? Do some assets provide more protection and result in resilient and successful individuals? Similarly, which risks are most problematic? How does the balance between assets and risks influence outcomes?

Assets and risks include those internal to the child such as temperament and learned skills, as well as those external to the child, such as the characteristics and support of the family and the larger society, including schools and communities (Kaplan, 2005). These personal, familial, and environmental factors can be considered assets at one end of the spectrum, and risks at the other. Thus, for example, homework help provided by parents is an asset contributing to positive academic outcomes, while the lack of such support likely poses a risk resulting in limited success in school. Assets and risks might change over time. Expanding on the previous example, parental homework help might contribute to academic success for elementary school children, but a similar degree of homework help might promote learned helplessness during adolescence.

Researchers have shown that there is a relationship between the number of assets and risks encountered and the behavioral and academic outcomes of children. The next section examines the individual, family, and school and community assets and risks. Because it is not possible to look at all possible assets and risks, the focus will be mostly on those that can be changed (e.g., communication) rather than historical factors (e.g., age of identification) or those that teachers and parents are not in a position to change (e.g., family socioeconomic status).

Individual Assets and Risks

Individual assets found to promote resilience in all students (not just DHH students) include the skills to develop good interpersonal relationships and to solve problems. Other individual assets are good self-esteem, the ability to be autonomous, and a sense of self-determination (Mandleco & Peery, 2000; Masten, 2001). Interviews with DHH individuals, their parents, and the professionals who work with them reveal that being social, persistent, committed to succeed, and advocating for oneself are mentioned frequently as reasons for success (Luckner & Muir, 2001; Rogers, Muir, & Everson, 2003).

Motivation

Antia and colleagues found that students who were reported as doing well in school were often described by teachers and parents as motivated, independent, persistent, and having a good work ethic. One teacher mentioned, for example, "She is a kid who is determined to try anything and when she does she is usually successful." Some students were motivated to succeed because they saw that their classmates were doing well; others were motivated to obtain good grades. Students who attended school regularly and were consistent about turning in homework were academically successful (Reed, Antia, & Kreimeyer, 2008).

Communication

An asset that contributed to both academic and social success was good functional communication on the part of the student. Functional communication is the ability to appropriately communicate with peers and teachers and is not necessarily related to mode of communication. Students who used signed or spoken language were rated by teachers as having good functional communication (i.e., the ability to communicate fluently and easily). Students who had good expressive and receptive functional communication received high academic achievement scores and high social skills ratings and had a low occurrence of problem behaviors (Antia & Jones, 2010; Antia et al., 2011). Students with even mild problems in *either* expressive or receptive communication were at risk for below-average academic outcomes, whereas students who had mild problems in *both* expressive and receptive communication were at high risk for poor academic outcomes. Good functional communication was also related to better classroom participation, which was a factor in both academic and social success (Antia et al., 2007).

Functional Hearing and Amplification Use

Although it was expected that a greater degree of hearing loss would pose a risk, the degree of hearing loss as measured by pure tone average was not related to either academic or social outcomes. However, students' *functional hearing* was related to academic outcomes. Functional hearing is the ability of the child to obtain auditory information within the classroom environment and is a combination of the degree of hearing loss, the student's consistent use of amplification, and the classroom acoustic conditions. Poor functional hearing exists even for students with mild or moderate hearing loss. These students may not have visible difficulty in one-to-one communication, and thus teachers may not pay attention to the poor effects of acoustic conditions on their ability to understand classroom communication in noise. DHH students who were rated as having good functional hearing scored in the average range in math, reading, and language. Students who had even mild difficulties with functional hearing had low-average scores in math and below-average scores in reading and language (Antia & Jones, 2010).

As would be expected from the results on functional hearing, an individual asset that was seen as important to academic achievement was consistent use of amplification (Reed et al., 2008), while inconsistent use was a risk. Lack of consistent amplification use considerably reduced academic scores (Antia & Jones, 2010). Interestingly, the use of amplification by the students was influenced by their own feelings about their hearing loss. Almost all students interviewed reported, at some time during the five years, feeling embarrassed by their hearing loss or the manner in which it made them different. To avoid being seen as different, these students often refused to wear amplification.

Family Assets and Risks

Close relationships with family members and parenting practices that promote autonomy and initiative promote resilience in all children (Goldstein & Brooks, 2005). For DHH individuals, supportive families are crucial. Supportive families promote close relationships, communicate with the DHH child, and ensure that the child is involved in all aspects of family life (Luft, 2011).

Relationships

Antia and her colleagues found that most of the DHH students interviewed had close relationships with at least one family member, be it parent, grandparent, stepparent, or sibling. Parents who had close relationships with their DHH child conveyed important messages to them about their own values, and also messages that promoted self-confidence and autonomy. For example, many parents told their DHH children that they (the children) were capable and that hearing loss should not limit their ambitions or their expectations for success. One mother said that she never felt sorry for her daughter; instead she tried to convey to her that she would need to work hard to succeed. A father told his son that he should never be ashamed of having a hearing loss and should advocate for himself.

Support of Schooling

The family's commitment to the child's schooling was an asset. Such commitment was most obviously seen when families participated in school activities. Students whose family members participated in a large number of school activities had higher academic achievement, better social skills, and fewer problem behaviors than students whose families did not participate in school activities (Antia et al., 2009, 2011).

Parents supported schooling by their overt emphasis on the importance of school. Some families moved long distances to provide their DHH child with an education. They made getting good grades in school a condition for participating in preferred extracurricular activities. Parents chose school programs that challenged their child academically even when transportation to and from these schools took extra parental effort.

An indicator of the value parents put on doing well in school was their commitment to homework. Parents who expected their child to complete homework and who provided homework help were seen by teachers as having commitment to their child's schooling. A lack of parental commitment was evidenced by lack of supervision for homework. Frequent student absences from school for frivolous reasons were also a sign of low parental emphasis on schooling.

Parents who were committed to their child's schooling advocated for their child's education. Such advocacy included involvement in selecting their child's general education teacher and informing the teachers and administrators about their child's needs. Parents often advocated for specific services for their child. Occasionally, teachers or administrators perceived parental advocacy negatively, either because they felt that parents were overly involved or because parents wanted services that the schools did not routinely provide. Parents mentioned that they had to advocate more strongly when school districts, teachers, or administrators were reluctant to make accommodations for the child's hearing loss.

Relationship with the School

A good relationship between the parent and teacher was an asset, while a poor relationship was a risk. Communication between the parents and the teacher of DHH students kept parents apprised of how their child was doing in school and also let them tell the teacher about any specific issues that might affect their child. Teachers sometimes interpreted lack of parental communication as a lack of parental interest in the child's schooling. Interviews revealed that infrequent communication was due to language barriers between parents and teachers, lack of parental resources (telephones, transportation), or parents' work schedules rather than a lack of interest.

Typically parents communicated frequently with the teacher of DHH students, but less frequently with the general education teacher. Parents communicated more frequently with teachers when their child was in elementary school; they reduced direct involvement with teachers as their children grew older. The reduced involvement was often deliberate as it gave DHH students the opportunity to advocate for themselves.

Parental Resources

The presence of family resources, specifically time and money, is an asset to any child. For the DHH students, parents who had time, flexible work schedules, and transportation could meet with teachers or volunteer for school activities. Parents who did not have these resources were not able to communicate with teachers, to meet with administrators to advocate for their child's needs, or to get to know their child's capabilities by observing them at school. Parents with transportation and time were able to transport their children to chosen schools and to enroll their DHH children in extracurricular activities in the school and community. Student participation in extracurricular activities was strongly associated with good social skills.

Some families had extremely few resources. One mother who lived in a rural area had no transportation so she could not travel to her child's school for teacher–parent meetings. She also lacked a phone and could not talk to the teachers. However, even when families lacked transportation or material goods, they still had good relationships with their children and conveyed their support for schooling.

School and Community Assets and Risks

Schools can create environments where students can succeed, feel competent, and be welcome. They are also a place for students to develop relationships with supportive adults and peers outside their family circle (Olsson, Bond, Burns, Vella-Brodrick, & Sawyer, 2003). Schools provide opportunities for students to learn the skills that promote individual resilience, such as planning, self-determination, and problem solving (Masten, Herbers, Cutuli, & Lefavor, 2008). Successful DHH adults interviewed by Rogers, Muir and Everson (2003) mentioned that caring role models at school, encouraging and supportive teachers, and positive partnerships with hearing peers contributed to their success.

Public schools that provide systematic support for DHH students are perceived to be positive environments (Lytle, Oliva, Ostrove, & Cassady, 2011). Systematic support requires collaboration and communication among professionals and integration of services. On the other hand, when schools leave the decisions about support services solely to the teacher of DHH students, services are often fragmented and dependent on the teacher's time, ability, and beliefs.

The larger community also can be an asset or pose a risk to children. Churches and other organized groups provide opportunities for developing peer and adult relationships. Neighborhoods low in crime and those that provide opportunities for children to play and engage in sports can provide opportunities for social networking and contribute to positive social outcomes (Jaffee, Caspi, Moffitt, Polo-Tomas, & Taylor, 2007). Specifically, for DHH students, the ability to interact with the larger DHH community is an asset, as they and their parents can encounter positive role models and set their expectations for success.

Curriculum Access

For the DHH students in the longitudinal study, academic outcomes were related to the number of hours they spent in the general education classroom. Students who received most of their academic instruction in the general education classroom obtained higher academic achievement scores than students who spent little time in the general education classroom. Students who received most of their *academic instruction* (math, science, reading) from the teacher of DHH students were likely to be below average academically (Antia & Jones, 2010). However, students who received some *nonacademic instruction* such as auditory and speech skills, study skills, and self-advocacy from the teacher of DHH students received higher academic scores than those who received no instruction from a teacher of DHH students.

How can these findings about time in the general education classroom be interpreted? It was not possible to determine whether the kind of academic instruction received (in the general education classroom, or from a teacher of DHH students) was the cause or the effect of the academic outcomes of students. It is possible that DHH students were in the general education classroom because they were high achievers while others were pulled out for special instruction because they were not able to follow the general curriculum. However, it is also possible that DHH students who were not in the general education classroom did not have access to the curriculum and were therefore not able to make academic progress. In addition to receiving curricular instruction in the general education classroom, however, it was important that students received some support from a teacher of DHH students. The nonacademic instruction from the teacher of students was in areas that were important for the DHH students but were not addressed in the general education classroom.

Classroom Participation

Although having access to the general education curriculum can facilitate good academic outcomes, mere physical presence in a regular classroom does not provide such access. It is important for DHH students to participate in classroom communication (i.e., to understand and be understood by teachers and peers).

Classroom participation was related to both social and academic outcomes (Antia et al., 2009, 2011). DHH students who rated themselves as understanding teachers, understanding peers, and feeling positively toward communicating in the classroom received high academic achievement scores and high social ratings and had low problem behaviors. Students who perceived themselves as "always" participating in the classroom were at low risk for poor academic outcomes in reading and writing (Antia, 2010). Students who "almost always" participated were likely to have low-average achievement, while those who "sometimes" participated had below-average achievement. In a related study Hintermair (2011) reported that classroom participation was related to DHH students' ability to cope with the demands of school work, to their ability to get along with their peers, and to their overall quality of life.

School Support Services

Systematic support of DHH students within the school is an asset. Support services received by the DHH students in the longitudinal study included services from a teacher of DHH students, sign language interpreters, note-takers, and audiological services. In only one instance did a school administrator show reluctance to provide support services because the DHH student was receiving good grades.

An important school asset was the availability of sign language interpreters both during and after school hours. Sign language interpreters allowed DHH students to have access to classroom instruction and facilitated participation. Students who had sign language interpreters after school had access to extracurricular activities and after-school tutoring.

As mentioned earlier, the nonacademic services from a teacher of DHH students were important to academic outcomes. Schools also provided the same support to the DHH students that they offered to other students. One DHH student received support from a teacher of English as a second language. Others received support from special education teachers. In some schools all students had access to after-school tutoring.

Support from General Education Teachers and Administrators

The atmosphere of a school is often set by administrators who can either welcome and support inclusion of DHH students, or be indifferent or even hostile. The presence of supportive administrators was an invaluable asset. These administrators understood the importance of communication access. They allowed after-school interpreting and the use of FM systems outside of the classroom. In one elementary school the principal paid general education teachers to take sign language classes.

Classroom teachers who adapt their instruction in ways that allow DHH students to have access to content and discussions and who are interested in and take ownership of the DHH student are important assets. Some classroom teachers made attempts to learn to sign. Many had expectations for the DHH students similar to those they held for hearing students and were willing to help the DHH students academically as necessary. They consistently used FM systems. In one middle school general educators were described by the teacher of DHH students as "phenomenal" and aware of each student's strengths.

Some classroom teachers, however, were not willing or able to provide accommodations for the DHH students (Reed et al., 2008). Some were unwilling to make accommodations for a single student; others were unwilling to use visual aids while teaching. In some cases teachers had low expectations of the DHH students.

Collaboration Among Professionals

Good communication between the classroom teachers and all the professionals who supported the DHH student was an asset. In many schools the communication among the classroom teachers, teachers of DHH students, and sign language interpreters was explicitly mentioned as a factor that contributed to positive student outcomes. In contrast, difficulties in communication among school personnel was a risk. Evidence of poor collaboration and communication included the general education teacher not attending the DHH student's Individual Education Plan meetings, criticisms about general education teachers' instructional modifications, or the general education teachers' lack of knowledge of the role of the teacher of DHH students.

Stability of school personnel fostered staff relationships and facilitated collaboration. Often the same sign language interpreter and teacher of DHH students provided support for a student several years in a row. One teacher of DHH students mentioned that because she had been in the school district a long time, the teachers at the various schools knew who she was and what she did and thus felt comfortable asking her questions or expressing concerns about the DHH students in their classrooms.

Peers

The presence of supportive peers within the classroom was a school asset. Peers who communicate with the student and accept his or her hearing loss allow the DHH student to be comfortable in the classroom and the school. Conversely, peers who ignore, bully, or tease can create academic and social problems for the DHH student.

In several school peers learned sign language to communicate with the DHH students. The opportunity and motivation for hearing peers to learn to sign was enhanced by the presence of sign language clubs and classes run by parents, teachers, and sometimes students themselves. The presence of more than one DHH student was an asset, not only because of the support provided by DHH peers, but also because the presence of a number of DHH students "normalized" the use of sign language interpreters, amplification, or other accommodations.

A risk to DHH students was the presence of peers who bullied them or caused them to feel unwelcome. Several students in the longitudinal study reported present or past bullying. Parents mentioned the social difficulties created for their children by peer bullying. In some cases the bullying resolved itself over time, but other times parental intervention was needed.

Communities

The involvement of DHH students within their communities, including both the neighborhood and the Deaf community, was an asset. While the research team did not request specific information about the community, several community assets were mentioned by parents and teachers.

Involvement within the Deaf community, especially as it gave access to deaf peers, was an asset for the students who were deaf and who signed. Families went to some trouble to involve their child with other deaf individuals. One mother drove her daughter a long distance to keep in contact with deaf peers at the school for the deaf. Another family kept in constant touch with Deaf community members. One mother became an interpreter for the deaf individuals in her local area. For one student, the ability to attend a camp for deaf children was an important positive social experience mentioned frequently by his parents and teachers.

The resources and opportunities for involvement in the neighborhood community represented another asset. One DHH student took a job at a restaurant in his small community. While working he had to interact with supervisors, employees, and the general public. He reported that, as a result, he was no longer as shy or retiring as he had been. A similar change was seen in a student who had an opportunity to travel with a community group but needed to raise the money for travel from community organizations. The experience of meeting members of the community and having to speak to strangers caused her to become more confident and outgoing.

PUTTING IT ALL TOGETHER

Every DHH student has some assets and some risks. Research with hearing students shows that the presence of multiple risk factors increases the likelihood of poor academic outcomes (Gutman, Sameroff, & Cole, 2003). The issue is typically one of balance: Does the presence of individual, family, and school assets cancel or mitigate the influence of the risks?

Balance of Assets and Risks

In an attempt to examine the balance of assets and risks, Reed and colleagues (2008) contrasted DHH students who were above average academically with those who were below average. There was no single asset or risk that distinguished the two groups of students. However, the above-average students had assets in all three categories (individual, family, school) and few significant risks in any category. The below-average students also had assets in each category, but unlike the above-average students, they also had significant risks in each category. To illustrate, the authors provided two case studies that contrasted the balance of assets and risks of an academically above-average and below-average student.

Individual assets for the above-average student included motivation, hard work, and good communication; few individual risks were present. Family assets included high parental expectations, strong family commitment to and involvement in schooling, and good communication between the parents and the school. No family risks were found for this student. School assets included high expectations of the student by all teachers; good support services for the student, including a full-time sign language interpreter and services from a teacher of DHH students; good communication among professionals; excellent classroom participation; and a welcoming school atmosphere. A single school risk was the inconsistency of teachers' classroom adaptations.

Individual assets for the below-average student included consistent attendance and a motivation to learn in areas of interest. Individual risks included lack of persistence and a lack of consistent amplification use. Family assets included parental commitment to schooling, as shown by the family's move to an area where the child could receive an education. Family risks included the parents' inability to communicate with their child, lack of communication with the school, and low academic expectations of their child. School assets included services from a teacher of DHH students and a sign language interpreter, as well as a welcoming atmosphere in the classroom. School risks included poor communication among staff members, an interpreter who was not able to adequately interpret classroom communication, and poor classroom participation. The difference between the above- and below-average students appeared to be in the intensity and number of risks and the balance of assets and risks.

What Can Be Done?

The discussion of assets and risks should remind professionals and parents that no students are without assets and few are without risks. How can adults help DHH students build resilience and increase the chances of good academic and social outcomes? It is important not to let the presence of risks overshadow expectations for positive outcomes. Thus, it is important to systematically document individual, familial, school, and community assets and risks. After such a profile is completed both family members and professionals can take actions to enhance assets. The following (necessarily abbreviated) suggestions are adapted from the literature and from strategies that parents and teachers revealed during the interviews.

Enhancing Individual Assets

Motivation and persistence were individual assets commonly mentioned by parents and teachers as having a positive effect on academic outcomes. Although motivation is often seen as an intrinsic, biological trait, it is enhanced and maintained by supportive home and school environments (Ryan & Deci, 2000). These are environments in which adults promote competence and autonomy and provide positive feedback.

A powerful model that parents and educators can follow to develop autonomy and persistence is the self-directed model of learning developed by Wehmeyer and his colleagues (Lee, Palmer, Turnbull, & Wehmeyer, 2006; Wehmeyer, Palmer, Agran, Mithaug, & Martin, 2000). The self-directed model emphasizes making choices, setting goals, empowerment, and solving problems. Educators and parents can encourage DHH students to make choices and express preferences. DHH students can be systematically taught to select their personal academic and social goals, keep track of their progress toward these goals, recognize barriers to meeting their goals, and revise goals as necessary.

Adults can convey messages of competence, celebrate student successes, and also help the DHH student cope with inevitable failures. They can teach students to attribute success or failure to hard work instead of luck or purely external factors and so develop in the student an internal locus of control. One mother conveyed messages of competence and empowerment by telling her DHH daughter that her hearing loss, although it put at her certain disadvantages in some situations, was not an excuse for not working hard and trying to succeed academically. In contrast, the mother who told her DHH son that he should not be expected to complete his homework because of his hearing loss conveyed a message of disempowerment.

It was not surprising to find that good communication skills on the part of the DHH student were an important individual asset. Educators often think of communication as the ability to speak intelligibly, to use appropriate grammatical structures, or to have a large vocabulary. However, functional communication or communication competence appeared to be the crucial skill. Communicative competence is independent of mode of communication; it is the ability to communicate to others in a manner that is appropriate to the social context, and includes skills such as using a sign language interpreter, communication assertiveness, and the ability to engage in and repair conversations. DHH students learn communicative competence by participating in family conversations and having opportunities to interact with a wide variety of individuals inside and outside of school. The student who had to communicate with the public when working in a restaurant and the student who had to present to community groups to raise money were placed by their parents and educators in situations that helped increase their communicative competence. Parents can enhance student communicative competence by committing to communicate with their DHH child. Educators can help parents by respecting family choices and recognizing the effort it takes to communicate when families have a DHH child.

Enhancing Family Assets

Even though expending resources on families creates dividends, educators focus mainly on students. While families of DHH infants and toddlers receive support, the support often ceases once their children enter school. Educators should understand that providing support to families is one of their primary roles. This might include making home visits, teaching sign language (as necessary), and communicating regularly with families.

Parents can be assertive about developing a relationship and communicating with educators. They should share problems and solutions pertaining to their children. They can be models for advocacy and, over time, teach their children to advocate for themselves. Parents demonstrate the importance of schooling to their children by ensuring that they attend school consistently and that homework is given priority. Families can also encourage and make it possible for their children to be involved in extracurricular activities in the school and community.

Enhancing School and Community Assets

Schools must provide the supports the DHH student needs to succeed both academically and socially. It is important for professionals to develop systems to communicate with one another instead of communicating "on the fly," as frequently is the case. Some teachers of DHH students kept the general education teacher apprised of the support they provided the student while the work of others was a mystery to the general education teachers.

One way to both communicate with teachers and to learn about the DHH student's classroom participation is for the teacher of DHH students to observe the DHH student in the general education classroom. During these observations the teacher of DHH students can learn about classroom composition, teaching styles, classroom activities, and curriculum content being covered. The teacher of DHH students will be in a position to provide suggestions that are suited to the classroom culture. Classroom teachers are more likely to adopt modifications that assist all students, rather than just the DHH student.

Providing the DHH student access to curricular content similar to that of peers is important. Often the DHH student is pulled out of the classroom to receive instruction from the teacher of DHH students. Frequent pullouts can result in diminished access to the education curriculum (Knoors & Hermans, 2010). Thus, pullout instruction must be carefully designed. The teacher of DHH students needs to stay in close communication with the classroom teacher to determine the skills and content that will enhance the students' academic experience. However, this teacher needs to be more than a tutor in subject matter. During pullout instruction, the teacher of DHH students may need to focus on teaching those skills that are not usually taught in the curriculum but that the student needs to succeed in the classroom, such as communicative competence, self-determination, self-advocacy, study skills, and amplification use. *All* educators can help DHH students see themselves as capable individuals by holding high expectations, but also by encouraging and teaching the skills needed to meet these expectations.

Frequent pullouts can also cause the DHH student to feel like a visitor in the classroom. In contrast, "push-in" services or co-teaching can enhance teacher communication and develop the perception that the DHH student and the teacher of DHH students are valued members of the classroom. One teacher vividly commented on the pullout issue, "It is important for [the DHH student] socially to feel a part of the mainstream rather than staring at my face all day in the resource room." Finally, schools can enhance the social life of DHH students by ensuring access to extracurricular activities, providing sign language instruction to students and school personnel during or after school, and welcoming deaf adults in schools and classrooms.

CONCLUSIONS

The academic outcomes of DHH students in general education classrooms indicate that they achieved within the average range and made one year's progress annually. Although this is better than reported academic outcomes for students in self-contained environments, about 30% to 40% of DHH students had below-average reading scores. Socially, most DHH students are rated as average or above average by their general education teachers and by the students themselves. The DHH students were actively involved in their schools and communities and participated in many out-of-school activities.

To understand why some children had good outcomes while others did not, we analyzed the social and academic outcome data and interviews conducted with teachers, parents, administrators, and students to identify individual, family, and school assets and risks. Individual assets included high motivation, good communication, and good functional hearing and amplification use. Family assets included close relationships between family members and the DHH student; good family support of schooling; positive relationships and communication with school personnel; and resources that allowed parents to enroll their child in a program of choice and also in extracurricular activities. School assets included access to the general education curriculum; classrooms in which the DHH student could fully participate; support services from appropriate professionals, including a teacher of DHH students and sign language interpreters; support for inclusion from administrators and teachers; and collaboration and communication among school personnel. Community assets included involvement in neighborhood activities and with the Deaf community.

To maximize outcomes, it is important to look at all the assets surrounding a student rather than focusing only on risks. The difference between students who had good academic outcomes and those who did not was in the balance of assets and risks. Few students were without either assets or risks. Educators should focus on those assets that can be enhanced or maintained, while eliminating risk where and when possible.

REFERENCES

Antia, S. D. (1982). Social interaction of partially mainstreamed hearing-impaired children. *American Annals of the Deaf*, *127*, 18–25.

Antia, S. D. (2010). *Risk and resilience factors influencing academic and social outcomes*. Paper presented at the National Technical Institute for the Deaf, Rochester, NY.

Antia, S. D., & Jones, P. (2010). *Development of a risk scale to determine services to deaf and hard of hearing students in public schools*. Paper presented at the American Educational Research Association, Denver, CO.

Antia, S. D., Jones, P., Luckner, J., Kreimeyer, K. H., & Reed, S. (2011). Social outcomes of students who are deaf and hard of hearing in general education classrooms. *Exceptional Children, 77*, 487–502.

Antia, S. D., Jones, P. B., Reed, S., & Kreimeyer, K. H. (2009). Academic status and progress of deaf and hard-of-hearing students in general education classrooms. *Journal of Deaf Studies and Deaf Education, 14*, 293–311.

Antia, S. D., Jones, P., Reed, S., Kreimeyer, K. H., Luckner, J., & Johnson, C. (2008). *Longitudinal study of deaf and hard of hearing students attending general education classrooms in public schools.* Final report submitted to Office of Special Education Programs for grant H324C010142. University of Arizona, Tucson.

Antia, S. D., Sabers, D., & Stinson, M. S. (2007). Validity and reliability of the Classroom Participation Questionnaire with deaf and hard of hearing students in public schools. *Journal of Deaf Studies and Deaf Education, 12*, 158–171.

Cappelli, M., Daniels, T., Durieux-Smith, A., McGrath, P. J., & Neuss, D. (1995). Social development of children with hearing impairments who are integrated into general education classrooms. *Volta Review, 97*, 197–208.

Dammeyer, J. (2010). Psychosocial development in a Danish population of children with cochlear implants and deaf and hard-of-hearing children. *Journal of Deaf Studies and Deaf Education, 15*, 50–58.

Goldstein, S., & Brooks, R. B. (2005). Why study resilience? In S. Goldstein & R. B. Brooks (Eds.), *Handbook of resilience in children* (pp. 3–15). New York: Kluwer Academic/Plenum Publishers.

Gutman, L. M., Sameroff, A. J., & Cole, R. (2003). Academic growth curve trajectories from 1st grade to 12th grade: Effects of multiple social risk factors and preschool child factors. *Developmental Psychology, 39*, 777–790.

Hintermair, M. (2011). Health-related quality of life and classroom participation of deaf and hard-of-hearing students in general schools. *Journal of Deaf Studies and Deaf Education, 16*, 254–271.

Jaffee, S. R., Caspi, A., Moffitt, T. E., Polo-Tomas, M., & Taylor, A. (2007). Individual, family, and neighbourhood factors distinguish resilient from non-resilient maltreated children: A cumulative stressors model. *Child Abuse and Neglect, 31*, 231–253.

Kaplan, H. B. (2005). Understanding the concept of resilience. In S. Goldstein & R. B. Brooks (Eds.), *Handbook of resilience in children* (pp. 39–47). New York: Kluwer Academic/Plenum Publishers.

Knoors, H., & Hermans, D. (2010). Effective instruction for deaf and hard-of-hearing students: Teaching strategies, school settings, and students characteristics. In M. Marschark & P. Spencer (Eds.), *The Oxford handbook of deaf studies, language, and education* (Vol. 2, pp. 57–71). New York: Oxford University Press.

Lee, S., Palmer, S. B., Turnbull, A. P., & Wehmeyer, M. L. (2006). A model for parent-teacher collaboration to promote self-determination in young children with disabilities. *Teaching Exceptional Children, 38*, 36–41.

Luckner, J., & Muir, S. (2001). Successful students who are deaf in general education settings. *American Annals of the Deaf, 146*, 435–445.

Luft, P. (2011). Promoting resilience in deaf adolescents. In D. H. Zand & J. E. Pierce (Eds.), *Resilience in deaf children: Adaptation through emerging adulthood* (pp. 299–340). New York: Springer.

Lytle, L. R., Oliva, G. A., Ostrove, J. M., & Cassady, C. (2011). Building resilience in adolescence: The influences of individual, family, school, and community perspectives and practices. In D. H. Zand & J. E. Pierce (Eds.), *Resilience in deaf children: Adaptation through emerging adulthood* (pp. 251–277). New York: Springer.

Mandleco, B., & Peery, C. (2000). An organizational framework for conceptualizing resilience in children. *Journal of Child and Adolescent Psychiatric Nursing, 13,* 99–111.

Masten, A. S. (2001). Ordinary magic: Resilience processes in development. *American Psychologist, 56,* 227–238.

Masten, A. S., Herbers, J. E., Cutuli, J. J., & Lefavor, T. L. (2008). Promoting competence and resilience in the school context. *Professional School Counseling, 12,* 76–84.

Mejstad, L., Heiling, K., & Svedin, C. G. (2008/2009). Mental health and self-image among deaf and hard of hearing children. *American Annals of the Deaf, 153,* 504–515.

Olsson, C. A., Bond, L., Burns, J. M., Vella-Brodrick, D. A., & Sawyer, S. M. (2003). Adolescent resilience: a concept analysis. *Journal of Adolescence, 26,* 1–11.

Reed, S., Antia, S. D., & Kreimeyer, K. H. (2008). Academic status of deaf and hard-of-hearing students in public schools: Student, home, and service facilitators and detractors. *Journal of Deaf Studies and Deaf Education, 13,* 485–502.

Rogers, S., Muir, K., & Everson, C. R. (2003). Signs of resilience: Assets that support deaf adults' success in bridging the deaf and hearing worlds. *American Annals of the Deaf, 148,* 222–232.

Ryan, R. M., & Deci, E. L. (2000). Self-determination theory and the facilitation of intrinsic motivation, social development, and well-being. *American Psychologist, 55,* 68–78.

Traxler, C. B. (2000). The Stanford Achievement Test, 9th Edition: National norming and performance standards for deaf and hard-of-hearing students. *Journal of Deaf Studies and Deaf Education, 5,* 337–339.

Wauters, L., & Knoors, H. (2008). Social integration of deaf children in inclusive settings. *Journal of Deaf Studies and Deaf Education, 13,* 21–36.

Wehmeyer, M. L., Palmer, S. B., Agran, M., Mithaug, D. E., & Martin, J. E. (2000). Promoting causal agency: The self-determined learning model of instruction. *Exceptional Children, 66,* 439–453.

Wolk, S., & Allen, T. E. (1984). A 5-year follow-up of reading-comprehension achievement of hearing-impaired students in special education programs. *Journal of Special Education, 18*(2), 161–176.

Wolters, N., Knoors, H., Antonius, H. N., Cillessen, H. N., & Verhoeven, L. (2012). Impact of peer and teacher relations on deaf early adolescents' well-being: comparisons before and after a major school transition. *Journal of Deaf Studies and Deaf Education, 17,* 463–482.

24

Classroom Adaptations for Effective Learning by Deaf Students

Leo De Raeve

RECENT CHANGES IN DEAF EDUCATION

Changing Population

With the introduction of universal neonatal hearing screening in many countries, hearing loss in children is being identified earlier in life than ever before (Van Kerschaver, Boudewyns, Stappaerts, Wuyts, & Van de Heyning, 2007). Many studies to date provide strong evidence of the benefits of early identification and intervention for the development of expressive and receptive language, listening, and reading skills and for social and emotional development (Boons et al., 2012; Dettman, Wall, Constantinescu, & Dowel, 2013; Kennedy et al., 2006; Moeller, 2000; Niparko et al., 2010; Philips et al., 2009; Verhaert, Willems, Van Kerschaver, & Desloovere, 2008; Vermeulen, van Bon, Schreuder, Knoors, & Snik, 2007; Yoshinaga-Itano, 2006; Yoshinaga-Itano & Sedey, 2000).

Greater numbers of deaf children are receiving cochlear implants (CIs) to improve their hearing skills substantially: In Flanders, the Dutch-speaking part of Belgium, 93% of all newborn deaf children receive them (De Raeve & Lichtert, 2012). Not only has the rate been increasing, but the age of implantation has also been falling steadily, and the use of bilateral implants or binaural hearing (CI + conventional hearing aid) is becoming common (De Raeve, Vermeulen, & Snik, 2015). Studies on the effects of CIs in children show a positive influence on their auditory perception (De Raeve, 2010; Kirk, Miyamoto, Ying, Perdew, & Zuganelis, 2000), speech recognition, speech intelligibility, and other aspects of spoken language development (Boons et al., 2013; De Raeve, 2010; Schauwers, Gillis, Daemers, De Beukelaer, & Govaerts, 2004; Svirsky, Su-Wooi, & Neuburger, 2004). Evidence shows that children who receive a CI at a younger age do better on a range of auditory, speech, and language measures than children who are implanted at an older age (Kirk et al., 2000; Svirsky et al., 2004). Yoshinago-Itano (2006) concluded that early identification of profound hearing loss combined with early implantation and a high-quality auditory stimulation program results in outcomes that are similar to those of children with an early identified mild to severe hearing loss and using conventional hearing aids.

The heterogeneity of the population of deaf children is another major factor emphasized in the research literature. In addition to factors associated with the cause of the hearing loss (e.g., maternal illness, childhood infections, toxins, syndromes) itself influencing the outcomes, there is also huge variability in early auditory, linguistic, family, and educational environment.

In the recent literature, 30% to 40% of deaf children are reported to have additional disabilities (Fortnum, Marshall, & Summerfield, 2002; Nikolopoulos, Archbold, & Gregory, 2005; Verhaert et al., 2008). The main reason for the increase of this group is the fact that more extremely preterm babies survive. In the United States, 80% of babies born at 26 weeks (extremely preterm) and 96% of those born between 28 and 31 weeks (very preterm) survive. The risk of hearing loss or other additional disabilities is three to four times higher in this group than in the general newborn population (National Center for Health Statistics, 2008). The EPICure study, which has followed all children born prematurely in England in 1995, found that, at age six years, over 50% of children born very or extremely premature survive with disabilities (Johnson et al., 2009). Even premature children who do not show apparent difficulties early in life have persistent and mildly poorer grammatical skills and verbal working memory (Lee et al., 2011).

In the early years of CI use, children with additional disabilities were not candidates. The number of children with additional disabilities receiving CIs has now increased substantially (Meinzen-Derr, Wiley, Grether, & Choo, 2011), although outcomes are often poorer than for children with no additional disability (Boons et al., 2012; Duchesne, Bergeron, & Sutton, 2008; Geers, Nicholas, & Sedey, 2003).

Many deaf children are raised by parents whose first language is not that of the country in which they are living, or who may speak multiple languages proficiently. Some of these children are born in the country where they are educated; others (parents changing work conditions, refugees) enter the local educational system during their school years. In these situations, hearing children will learn their parents' first language, as well as the national language. Studies of young implanted deaf children (Boons et al., 2012; De Raeve, Vermeulen, & Snik, 2015; Robbins, Green, & Waltzman, 2004) showed that multilingualism in the family, often in combination with low socioeconomic status of the parents, was related to lower language and verbal cognition scores even when taking into account their knowledge in both languages.

This all implies that the range of educationally relevant individual differences is large, much larger than it would be in a population of hearing children (Swanwick & Marschark, 2010).

Adapting Our Communication Approaches to the Changing Population

For this heterogeneous population, no one approach will meet the needs of all deaf children and their families. A combination of communication approaches may be used and modified over time depending on the needs of the child and family. The language and communication approaches and strategies for a young implanted deaf child may be different from those for a child obtaining a CI when he or she is older and at a later stage of language development (Archbold, 2010). The challenge is to develop effective strategies for identifying which option is best at a specific moment for a specific child (Leigh, 2008).

The improved auditory experiences provided by CIs over hearing aids has facilitated the acquisition of spoken language in children with profound deafness, not only for those in oral educational settings but also for those in total communication and sign bilingual approaches, although also these results are very heterogeneous (Geers, 2006).

There are many reports of children attending oral communication programs achieving higher speech perception and language scores than children in total communication settings (El-Hakim et al., 2001; Geers, Nicholas, & Sedey, 2003; Moog & Geers, 2003). Chin and Kaiser (2002) found that children educated through oral communication had better articulation than did those educated through a total communication approach. This is confirmed by Tobey and colleagues (2003), who found teaching methods that emphasized speaking and listening to be the most influential factors in determining speech production development in implanted deaf children. Percy-Smith and colleagues (2012) found significant regional differences in speech and language outcomes after implantation in Denmark, based on the rehabilitation approach used. Although the age of implantation and the level of audition were comparable between the group from western and from eastern Denmark, there were significant differences on all speech and language tests in favor of children with implants from eastern Denmark. Further analysis of the data showed that these differences in speech and language outcomes could be explained by the fact that the parents from western Denmark were less involved in the auditory rehabilitation of their children, and they were using more signs and less spoken language. It is also remarkable that in the western part of Denmark, the children had even more individual speech therapy and more learning support assistance, yet the children from the eastern part of the country scored more highly on speech and language measures.

Comparable results were found in a study by Wiefferink and colleagues (2008), who compared children using CIs in a spoken monolingual environment in Belgium with a group of children from the Netherlands in a signed bilingual environment. In this study the auditory perception, speech intelligibility, and spoken language development were also better in the monolingual spoken language environment. These authors also concluded that despite possible alternative explanations, such as better residual aided hearing before implantation or more professional support, it is plausible that the differences are partly caused by the linguistic environment.

In contrast, other (but fewer) research findings indicate that children with CIs educated with some form of sign language have significantly higher vocabulary levels than those educated orally (Connor, Hieber, Arts, & Zwolan, 2000; Robbins, Bollard, & Green, 1999). Some studies suggest that when signs support spoken words, they do not hinder the auditory speech perception in children with CIs. However, both in the perception of perceptually confusable words (Giezen, 2011; Giezen, Baker, & Escudero, 2014) and in reading comprehension (Spencer, Gantz, & Knutson, 2004), children using CIs appear to benefit from the availability of bimodal input. This is confirmed by Davidson, Lillo-Martin, and Pichler (2014), who investigated the spoken English language skills of five deaf children with CIs (they had deaf signing parents). These children received exposure to a full natural sign language (American Sign Language) from birth, in addition to spoken English after implantation. The researchers compared their spoken language skills with those of hearing American Sign Language/English bilingual children of deaf parents and concluded that natural sign language input does no harm and may even mitigate negative effects of early auditory deprivation for spoken language development. Tait (2003) found that children who are good communicators before implantation, whether gestural or vocally, are likely to have good speech perception abilities in later years after implantation.

Mayer and Leigh (2010, p. 177), in discussing sign bilingual programs, stated that "the key point is that there is no data to suggest that, as a group, students in bilingual programs are achieving at the age-appropriate language and literacy levels that were predicted when bilingual models were first implemented and that for the first time in history, spoken language has become accessible as the first language for many, arguably the vast majority of profoundly deaf children."

Wheeler and Archbold (2009) described the communication journey of parents, based on parent interviews. Prior to implantation parents wanted the most effective form of communication, which (for 95% of the hearing parents) was spoken language with or without some signed support. Following implantation parents reported a reduction of signed support as spoken language developed through increased access to speech through audition. Later parents and young deaf people themselves showed interest in the use of some sign support or sign language itself, once spoken language had been established. So parents recognize that different approaches may be appropriate at different times or in different settings. These young people using the latest technology report being both "deaf" and "hearing" (Wheeler & Archbold, 2009). These deaf children and young people are functioning not like those with a significant hearing loss did in the past, but also not quite like hearing children.

Changing Educational Placement

This heterogeneous population of deaf children is being educated in a variety of settings using a variety of communication approaches. Although there is variation in outcomes, more children with CIs go to mainstream schools and use spoken language as their primary means of communication (Archbold & Mayer, 2012). Regular education is now considered to be a realistic option for the majority of children using CIs with normal learning potential, by both parents and professionals. Many parents hope their child will be able to attend a regular school in their home environment so they can be part of their community, with siblings, neighbors, and classmates. However, we do not know whether these expectations on the part of parents and professionals are always realistic, knowing the amount of deaf children (and families) with special needs (Nikolopoulos, Archbold, & Gregory, 2005).

For many of these children their speech perception in quiet is often excellent (Kirk et al., 2000), but speech perception in noise is known to remain difficult for children with (unilateral) CIs (Dunn, Tyler, Oakley, Gantz, & Noble, 2008). The excellent levels of speech intelligibility typically achieved by those implanted early in life may mask their language delay or difficulties with the more complex grammatical and pragmatic communication skills required in the classroom (Archbold & Mayer, 2012). Although they may have access to greater levels of spoken language through hearing than ever before, they continue to require support as learners in the classroom.

NATURAL LEARNING

There are two crucial milestones in language and development of verbal cognition in both hearing and deaf children.

First is the development of joint attention around the age eight to 12 months, in which children start to look actively at another person's intention. Caregivers play a crucial role in learning to interpret linguistic symbols as referring to the focus of joint attention. They talk about things the child is looking at. Hearing children are able to look at the object the adult is talking about while listening to the adult. This combined input results in comprehension of the language of the adult. In the past, profoundly deaf children with conventional hearing aids had difficulty achieving joint attention through audition, because they had no or unclear auditory input. If one wanted to accomplish joint attention in these situations, it was important to bring the object one was talking about into the visual field between the adult and the child and to support the spoken language with signs or use sign language (Loots, Devise, & Jacques, 2005).

Today most children receiving CIs early in life have the auditory skills to achieve joint attention the way that typical hearing children do. With access to audition given by the CI, the child can receive the spoken language input at the same time that he or she is looking at or playing with the object, rather than having to divide his or her attention between the object and the (subsequent) communication (Tait, De Raeve, & Nikolopoulos, 2007; Tasker, Nowakowsk, & Schmidt, 2010). So now hearing parents of deaf toddlers can do what comes most naturally to someone caring for the very young: to supply the language for whatever is occupying the child's attention at any one time without having to attract his or her visual attention all time (Tait et al., 2010). If this auditory joint attention is not possible for one reason or the other, we still have to use additional visual communication strategies (Loots & Devisé, 2003).

Second, 80% to 90% of the vocabulary of normal hearing children is learned incidentally (Gillis & Schaerlaekens, 2000). This incidental or random learning refers to unintentional learning occurring at any time and in any place, usually by overhearing conversation. Children need good auditory conditions to stimulate and develop the cognitive skills needed for incidental learning. Children who use CIs and who have good binaural hearing skills are often able to hear speech from distance and in challenging listening situations, which are precursors to incidental learning (De Raeve, Vermeulen, & Snik, 2015). These auditory incidental learning precursors can be assessed using Tait's Non-Looking Vocal Turns (Tait, De Raeve, & Nikolopoulos, 2007). Incidental learning and better access to spoken language also stimulate the development of executive functions, Theory of Mind (Wiefferink, Rieffe, Ketelaar, De Raeve, & Frijns, 2013), pragmatic skills (Boons et al., 2013), and cognitive development (Pisoni & Cleary, 2003). To enable incidental learning, the ideal acoustic environment for children with a hearing loss would have minimal background noise and low-level reverberation with a signal-to-noise ratio of +15 dB (i.e., the speech is 15 dB louder than the surrounding noise level) (Boothroyd, 2004). Assessing speech perception in noise and at a soft speech intensity of 45 dB hearing level [HL]) is advised (De Raeve, 2014).

It is important that deaf children access incidental learning for language, verbal cognition, and social-emotional development. This can be on an auditory basis by picking up spoken language from the environment, or visually by picking up sign language from the environment. To enable this to happen, all children should have fully accessible language and communication during the sensitive period for linguistic development at home and in school (Leigh, 2008). Before the time of implantation, deaf children from deaf families may have had an advantage in access to incidental learning (Brackenbury, Ryan, & Messenheimer, 2006). Now it is also possible for deaf children from hearing families (95% of the deaf population), especially for those wearing bilateral CIs or having bimodal hearing early in life, giving them good access to auditory information (De Raeve, Vermeulen, & Snik, 2015).

Binaural Hearing

In recent years increasing numbers of deaf children are receiving bilateral CIs (De Raeve, 2014; Litovsky, Jones, & Agrawai, 2010; Sparreboom et al., 2010), with benefits shown for localization of sound (Beijen, Snik, & Mylanus, 2007; Greco-Alub, Litovsky, & Werner, 2008; Van Deun et al., 2009), the perception of soft speech (De Raeve, Vermeulen, & Snik, 2015), and speech discrimination in noise (De Raeve, Vermeulen; & Snik, 2015; Dunn et al., 2008; Kuhn-Inacker, Shehata-Dieler, Muller, & Helms, 2004; Litovsky, Johnstone, & Godar, 2006).

When interviewed, young deaf learners using mostly unilateral CIs reported that listening in groups and listening in noise in school can be extremely challenging and resulted in missing important parts of lessons or instructions (Wheeler & Archbold, 2009). As CI users wearing bilateral devices achieve better speech perception in noise, one might expect that these students may have a little less difficulty than previously in an educational setting. Being able to use both ears enables easier location of the speaker and increase the likelihood that the student will understand speech in a mainstream educational setting.

Historically, the consequences of hearing with one ear only, called unilateral hearing loss, have been underestimated. Children with unilateral hearing loss show language delays in preschool (Borg, Edquist, Reinholdson, Risberg, & McAllister, 2007), have more academic failure (a 22% to 35% rate of repeating at least one grade), and have additional need for educational assistance (12% to 41%) in comparing to bilateral hearing children (Lieu, 2004). Parents and teachers reported persistent behavioral problems and academic weaknesses or areas of concern in about 25% of children with unilateral hearing loss (Lieu, Tye-Murray, & Qiang Fu, 2012). The same challenges may occur in children with unilateral hearing through one CI (Boons et al., 2012; Spencer, Gantz, & Knutson, 2004).

The positive effect of binaural hearing is demonstrated by Tait and colleagues (2010), who showed significantly more use of vocalization to communicate and more use of audition when interacting vocally with an adult in bilaterally implanted infants compared to the unilateral ones, and by a recent study by De Raeve, Vermeulen, and Snik (2015), who showed that these binaural "hearing" deaf children can acquire complex spoken language and verbal cognition skills that are age equivalent to their hearing peers at five years after implantation.

Suggestions Regarding Checking the Hearing Devices

The most important issue for children using digital hearing aids or CIs is the correct functioning of these devices. Devices must function all the time and should be repaired as soon as possible in case of a problem. Deaf learners should be empowered to take care of the devices themselves. For younger deaf children, parents and educators need knowledge regarding troubleshooting in case these devices break down. The following suggestions for parents and teachers are meant to optimize the functional use of amplification devices:

- Check amplification daily to ensure that it is working properly.
- One frequently used procedure to check that the child can hear all the sounds of speech is the Ling 6 Sound Test. The teacher says each of the six sounds (oooh, aaah, m, sh, ee, s) at 4 feet (1.2 m) distance in random order, varying intervals, and presenting the sound as it would appear in speech, at normal speaking volume (60 dB sound pressure level [SPL]) and length of sound. The sound is presented through audition alone, without speech reading cues. The child imitates the sound that is heard or points to a picture that represents the sound.
- Consult resource personnel (e.g., hearing aid manufacturers, CI companies, CI teams) to determine proper procedures for daily device checks.
- Be alert for the flashing (alarm) lights of the hearing device, which give feedback on its functioning.
- Contact the audiologist or CI fitting team to learn about troubleshooting and care of the hearing device, which can differ from device to device.
- Consult the manufacturer's website for maintenance and troubleshooting guides.
- Have some spare parts (e.g., cables, batteries) on hand at home and school, and have the clinic phone number/email address available.
- Avoid exposure to moisture or dust, and ensure that any long cables are worn beneath clothing.
- Try to repair device problems as soon as possible so the child does not miss important language and learning opportunities.

CLASSROOM LEARNING

Changes in Classroom Learning

This new population of deaf children (early screened and early fitted [binaurally] with hearing aids and/or CIs) are not functioning like deaf children did in the past, nor do they function like hearing children.

Success at capturing information in the classroom and assimilating it into learning relies on an intertwined set of language, cognitive, and social skills. These include joint attention, working memory, executive function, Theory of Mind, and pragmatics. These skills are typically present at a high level in hearing children's psychology when they arrive for the first time in the classroom, but are often absent or delayed in children with a hearing loss. Recent research shows that some early screened and young bilaterally implanted children can acquire these skills on a level that is age equivalent to their hearing peers, but there is still a huge variability in outcomes, which confirms again the heterogeneity of the population (Beer, Kronenberger, & Pisoni, 2011; Boons et al., 2012; Ketelaar, Rieffe, Wiefferink, & Frijns, 2012; Leigh, 2008).

Learning also varies from grade to grade (Bednar, 2005). Preschool and kindergarten classrooms are busy and noisy places. Children learn to share toys and materials, work in small groups, and often relate to more than one adult. There is a lot of language input from the environment, which means that a lot of incidental learning can take place. In the lower elementary grades, making friends, planning games, and solving conflicts through negotiation require sophisticated social language skills. Children learn to listen to the teacher for a longer period of time (training their attention span) and learn to work in small groups, where discovery takes place in joint discussions. They are expected to master reading and writing skills. In the upper elementary grades, children sometimes change classes and teachers, and they are expected to read information and to write for self-expression. A foreign language may be introduced, and current events are discussed. At secondary level, children change classes and teachers nearly every hour, and some of these class groups can be very noisy. Depending on the curriculum, more foreign languages or vocational training may be introduced, and discussion groups and group work take place. Teachers talk a lot and write less on the board. All this is very hard for most deaf learners, even for those using CIs (Archbold, 2010; De Raeve, 2014).

In addition to the differences in learning from grade to grade, there are also differences between special schools and regular schools. Special schools should be more adapted to the needs of deaf children: they have fewer children in one class, offer more individual teacher support, have better classroom acoustics, use assistive listening devices, offer more visual support and individual therapy, and provide better communication and interaction with the students. In reality, this is not always the case. On the other hand, more and more deaf children are now being educated in mainstream settings than in special schools or special classes for deaf children.

The following are suggestions for good communication techniques:

- Face the student and be in close proximity (3 to 5 feet [1 to 1.5 m]).
- Encourage students with a hearing loss to seat themselves toward the front of the room and slightly to the side, where they will have an unobstructed line of vision of the teacher but can also see some of the students. This is particularly important if the student is using an interpreter, lip-reading, relying on visual clues, or using a hearing aid that has a limited range.
- Speak clearly and at a slow/moderate level. Pause after asking a question to allow the student processing time.
- Give clear indications of the topic of conversation, and alert the student to a change in topic.
- Gain the student's attention prior to giving directions.
- Stand in one place if possible and don't walk around all the time.
- Avoid speaking while writing on the board.
- Beards and moustaches can make speech-reading more difficult; keep beards and moustaches trimmed and keep hair, pencils, and hands away from the mouth when speaking.
- Use facial expressions, body language, gestures, and so forth when appropriate.
- Rephrase (rather than repeat) the message if the student has difficulty understanding.
- In tutorials, assist students who lip-read by having them sit directly opposite you. Ensure that they can see all other participants. Control the discussion so that only one person is speaking at a time and echo back comments from students.
- If the student is wearing one hearing device, sit on the same side as the child's hearing device.
- Use a FM (frequency modulation) or induction loop hearing system if available in the classroom.
- Use a sign language interpreter or note-taker.

Speech Perception in the Classroom

Classrooms are intended for learning, and most of that learning is mediated by speech, especially in regular schools, where most of our current population of deaf children are educated. Boothroyd (2012) states that if these assumptions are correct, students in a classroom need to hear speech clearly, both the speech of the teacher and the speech of the other students. The amount of information in a talker's speech that actually reaches the ear of the listener depends not only on the intensity and the intelligibility of the talker's speech but also on the acoustic properties of the room. Poor acoustics can undermine the very purpose for which the classroom was intended. The effect of poor acoustic environments is seen in decreased speech perception in typical hearing children with auditory processing disorders, hyperactive behavior, or auditory neuropathy; second-language learners; and children with hearing loss (Whitelaw, 2004).

Perfectly clear hearing is difficult to achieve, but fortunately there is a high level of redundancy in spoken language. It is generally assumed, for example, that hearing adults can function adequately when only around 60% of the useful information in speech is available (Smaldino & Flexer, 2012). However, this requires that the listener takes full advantage of mature language knowledge and processing skills. Performance will break down if the language becomes more complex and unfamiliar.

This is not the case for children, who are acquiring language and who do not have mature language proficiency. They cannot take full advantage of context and do not have the mature speech processing skills that might enable them to keep pace with the talker while absorbing the meaning of what is being said. Also, much of the language used in a classroom is unfamiliar. For that reason, Boothroyd (2012) concluded that children in a learning environment have to receive 90% to 100% of the useful information carried by the sounds of speech. He also listed three main enemies of good speech perception: distance, noise, and reverberation.

The first of these is the distance from the talker. As speech sounds travel away from the talker, 6 dB of amplitude is lost for every doubling of distance. A listener standing 10 feet (3 m) away might perceive speech at an average level of 56 dB SPL, but a listener 20 feet (6 m) away would hear the same speech at only 50 dB SPL. In open air at 40 feet (12 m) it is perceived as only 44 dB SPL. Inside a classroom, this 6-dB rule applies up to a certain critical distance and then the level of sound is determined by reflected sound and remains fairly constant despite increasing distance. Thus, the same speech can still be perceived at 50 dB SPL at 40 feet (12 m) inside a classroom. Although the intensity of the speech can be the same, the quality of the speech signal is poorer because the sound is being reflected via wall and ceiling (Smaldino, 2011).

Second, classrooms tend to be very noisy places. To avoid speech being obscured by noise, the average level of speech needs to be at least 15 dB above that of the noise (Boothroyd, 2012). Consider a classroom with background noise of 55 dB SPL (which is not unusual) and the teacher's speech of 60 dB SPL (+ 5 dB SPL above the background noise). In this setting it is likely that only 50% of the speech will be perceived, which is far below the criterion of 90% to 100% audibility required by children for understanding speech in a learning environment. In addition to preventing audibility of information in the speech signal, noise can be distracting. This is especially the case if the noise carries interesting (speech) information. Individuals differ in terms of their ability to ignore distractions and focus attention on a specific talker. Distractible students with a hearing loss and students with attention-deficit/hyperactivity disorder may require a speech-to-noise ratio that is higher than 15 dB (Taub, Kanis, & Kramer, 2003).

A third enemy of good speech perception is reverberation in the classroom—that is, the persistence of sound in a room because of multiple, repeated reflections from the room surfaces. At each reflection some of the sound energy is absorbed and the strength of the reflected sound is reduced. As a result, by the time it reaches the listener, the reflected sound is weaker than that traveling directly from the talker. We measure the persistence of sound in a room in terms of reverberation time, the time it takes for the sound level to decrease by 60 dB after the sound stops. A reverberation time of 0.25 seconds means that it takes the speech sound 0.25 seconds to fall by 60 dB. A reverberation time of up to 0.5 second is still reasonable, but when it comes closer to 1 second the sound quality may be poorer due to the late reflection of sound (Boothroyd, 2012).

Hard surfaces such as ceramic tile, plasterboard, glass, and varnished wood are efficient sound reflectors. Other surfaces, such as carpeting, acoustic tiles, curtains, and clothing, absorb most of the sound hitting them. Room size also affects reverberation time. In a large room the sound has to travel farther between reflections; as a result, it takes longer for sound to be absorbed at the reflecting surfaces. In a small to medium-sized classroom, these guidelines call for a maximum noise level of 35 dB SPL and a maximum reverberation time of 0.6 second. These specifications are for an unoccupied room. Ones the room is occupied, the reverberation time will be somewhat lower because of sound absorption by the children and their clothing. The goal of standard norms for deaf learners is to attain at least a 15-dB speech-to-noise ratio and a reverberation time of less than 0.6 seconds (American National Standards Institute [ANSI], 2002).

Despite these standard regulations for noise and reverberation levels for educational settings, the reality is that mainstream kindergarten or educational settings are often very noisy and the reverberation is high. An example reported by Buch and Fielding (2001) showed that noise in a kindergarten during 11 of 14 daily educational situations that were measured reached peak intensities over 80 dB SPL. This occurred not only in the situations that were expected to be noisy (e.g., collecting children, free play time, and eating) but also during painting and drawing and in circle time sessions when children were having a conversation together on a certain topic.

Many children achieve excellent speech perception in quiet, and teachers may underestimate the difficulties they have listening in noise. Children do not have the sophisticated auditory or language skills to "fill in the blanks" where auditory information is missed.

In a study by Taub and colleagues (2003), the influence of classroom acoustics on language learning was studied using the Screening Instrument for Targeting Educational Risk (SIFTER), developed by Anderson (1989). The SIFTER was used to study the effect on children of improvement in the acoustic environment in a kindergarten located in a low socioeconomic area. The researchers concluded that the risk for language/learning problems decreased significantly when sound-field systems, in which a teacher speaks into a microphone and the speech is amplified and distributed through several loudspeakers, are used to improve classroom acoustics.

Environments with poor acoustics are known to have a detrimental impact on learning capacity, concentration, and listening skills in typical hearing children, and even more so in children with a hearing loss, whose speech perception decreases more in environments with poorer acoustics than typical hearing children. Researchers have documented the negative effects of excessive classroom noise and reverberation levels on speech recognition ability and educational/social development (e.g., Crandell & Smaldino, 2000; Davis, Elfenbein, Schum, & Bentler, 1986; Finitzo-Hieber, 1988; Johnson, 2000).

Suggestions Regarding Classroom Acoustics

Many things can be done to improve listening conditions in a classroom (National Deaf Children Society, 2001):

- Encourage children to maintain a quiet working atmosphere and try to make hearing children aware of various noises that a hearing aid can amplify, such as chairs scraping, doors banging, general chatter, shouting, and dropping objects.
- Avoid placing a deaf child in a noisy part of the classroom. For example, make sure deaf children are away from radiators, noisy equipment, or windows that overlook busy areas.
- Reduce background noise. Close doors and windows to reduce noise from outside.
- Use wall displays to cover and soften large flat surfaces, and carpet floors where possible, as this will help to reduce reverberation.
- Where possibly, have a "quiet" area in the mainstream classroom that can be used for individual, paired, or small group work.
- Have acoustic tiles on the ceiling.
- Modify chairs (i.e., attach soft materials to chair legs) or desks (i.e., felt cloth/rubber cushions) to reduce noise level.
- Remember the ANSI guidelines of a signal-to-noise ratio of +15 dB SPL and a reverberation time less than 0.6 seconds.
- Use Classroom Audio Distribution Systems (CADS).

Classroom Audio Distribution Systems

All children require a louder signal and a quieter environment than adults to distinguish words. Flexer (2004) recommended using sound distribution systems in every classroom. There is evidence that the poor acoustics of many classrooms can be ameliorated using classroom amplification systems. Deaf children can be fitted with a personal system. Both sound distribution and personal systems can be used in a complementary way.

Most personal amplification systems used by deaf students are FM systems using a wireless FM transmission; infrared systems using infrared light for wireless transmission of the acoustic signal; or electromagnetic induction loops, in which an amplifier transmits the electrical signal from a microphone to a wire encircling the room. The electrical current flowing through the wire creates an electromagnetic field that can be picked up by a telecoil, which is included in most hearing aids or CIs.

The technology used in CADS is evolving and promises to further improve in the near future. As described by Smaldino and Flexer (2012), several manufacturers have started using new ways to transmit sound: digital transmission technology using the 2.4-GHz frequency band, Bluetooth technology, and automatic noise compensation technology that can automatically adapt the intensity of the speech to the level of the background noise.

The choice of the most appropriate CADS for deaf students is complex and is influenced by many variables: the number of students per classroom, the acoustic characteristics of the classroom, the number and position of loudspeakers (in case of a sound-field system), the number of microphones needed, the teacher's teaching style, the availability of different CADS (FM system, infrared system, electromagnetic induction loop system), the need for in-service and follow-up maintenance, and possible connections to other amplification devices (e.g., hearing aids, CIs) by deaf students. Armed with adequate information on all these variables, an audiologist should be able to guide you in choosing the best CADS. Always try the system for several weeks before buying it; have different teachers use it in different lessons. More detailed information on the advantages and disadvantages of various CADS can be found in the *Handbook of Acoustic Accessibility* by Smaldino and Flexer (2012, pp. 72–88).

In addition to speech perception improvement, CADS have been shown to improve literacy skills (Darai, 2000; Flexer, Biley, Hinkley, Harkema, & Holcomb, 2002), social behaviors (Massie, Theodoros, McPherson, & Smaldino, 2004), and educational outcomes (Langlan, Socalingam, Caissie, & Kreisman, 2009; Massie & Dillon, 2006). Teachers have reported several benefits of CADS use as well, including reduction in vocal strain, less need for sick leave, and better attentiveness and behavior among students (Edwards & Fuen, 2005; Sapienza, Crandell, & Curtis, 1999).

Other (but fewer) studies have noted a lack of benefit from using CADS. Schafer and Kleinek (2009) found that sound-field amplification systems provided no significant speech recognition benefit over CI use alone, but benefit was seen for direct-audio-input FM systems coupled with CI. Wilson, Marinac, Pitty, and Burrows (2011) reported that sound-field amplification may not be beneficial in acoustically unsuitable rooms such as an open classroom. Finally, Smaldino and Flexer (2008) argue that classroom amplification systems should never be regarded as a substitute for appropriate noise control in the classroom.

Visual Support

In addition to poor classroom acoustics, there are often few visual cues given in regular schools. Teachers should provide deaf children with the visual cues they need to help maintain attention and guide them toward information in order to provide them with full access to instruction. Teachers need to be aware of the needs of deaf students in ongoing classroom activities (Knoors & Marschark, 2012). Cawthon (2001) found that teachers in mainstream classrooms directed less communication to deaf children compared to hearing children and were more likely to ask deaf children yes-or-no questions rather than open-ended questions. Such limitations are a frequent consequence of mainstream teachers' lack of familiarity with deaf children, sign language interpreters, and assistive listening devices (Knoors & Marschark, 2012).

Suggestions Regarding Visual Support

When teaching deaf children, it is important to think visually. Using visual clues and resources will help a deaf child access a lesson and develop his or her understanding. Using visual materials can give context to a subject or situation.

- If practical, have the students sit in a circle. This will allow the deaf student to observe and interact with classmates.
- Make sure that the lighting in the classroom is good. If you plan to turn off the lights, for example, to show a video, then consider the best place for a deaf child to sit. Also remember to give any instructions or explanations before you turn down the lights.
- Provide a written summary for videos and films, as they provide considerable difficulties for deaf students.
- Avoid sitting or standing in front of a light source, as this puts your face in shadow and interferes with speech-reading.
- Wherever possible, support what you are teaching by using visual clues as well as written texts. Visual clues might include

demonstrating a technique; using drama such as acting out a scene from history; using pictures, diagrams, illustrations, objects, and artifacts; and showing videos with subtitles.
- Write key words, topic headings, or questions on the board or overhead projector. Also smart boards can be very useful.
- Point to the objects or pictures you are using.
- Identify a few key places to stand in the classroom where a deaf child will be able to see you clearly. Don't walk around all the time.
- Make sure that when you are writing on the white board, you face the children when you are speaking. This will help them to lip-read and to see your facial expression.
- Allow time for a deaf child to look at the visual clue before you start talking again to give him or her time to focus attention back on you or the teaching assistant, especially when you use slide shows, a data projector, a computer, or a video.
- Provide support staff with copies of lesson plans, and set aside some time to discuss these with them so that they can carry out tutoring sessions effectively.
- Have homework tasks written on a sheet that pupils can take home. This is particularly useful for deaf children, because they cannot write down the homework assignment and watch you or the support worker at the same time.
- Recognize that some students require the services of an interpreter (sign or oral) or note-taker.

The following tips will make communication easier when using an interpreter (National Institutes of Health, 2013):

- Always speak directly to the student, not the interpreter. It is normally best if the interpreter is standing next to the main speaker and opposite the deaf person.
- Provide the student and interpreter with a glossary of new terms before the class to allow them to negotiate appropriate signs.
- If written material is presented, allow time for the deaf person to read it before continuing. Deaf people cannot watch the interpreter and read at the same time.
- Remember that the interpreter always lags a little behind the speaker. You may have to pause or speak more slowly to ensure the interpreter is keeping up.

Teacher Training

The challenge for the field is to embrace the diversity of the current population of deaf learners and to address the specific needs of each child and family in a specific country. This is particularly relevant to children whose home language is not the national language or those who have additional needs. Just as the population of deaf children has changed very rapidly in locations with access to advanced technology, and as more children attend mainstream schools, the demand for professional development opportunities and for specialized staff training increases. As Leigh (2008, p. 10) suggested, "there is currently more knowledge and skill required of a teacher of the deaf than at any time in the history in the field." Cochlear implantation has served to expand the range of this diversity within the student population, and of the competencies teachers need to meet learners' needs, which has implications for teachers and for teacher training.

Teachers of the deaf need to know how to manage today's hearing devices and should be able to teach others how to do so. This can be challenging given the variety of hearing devices and CADS from different manufacturers and the rapid changes in technology. Ongoing professional development for teachers of the deaf who are already in the field is also vital (Archbold & Mayer, 2012).

Many support staff start to work as itinerant support teachers as soon as they complete their teacher training, with little or no specific experience in educating or supporting deaf children. With more students in mainstream classes, more specialist staff are needed to support them in their mainstream school, while fewer staff are required to educate the smaller population in the special schools for the deaf. Mainstream teachers in regular schools also need some basic knowledge about children with hearing loss. Training courses for teachers of the deaf vary widely. Some countries have a very specialized training, while others lack a specific training (Lichtert & van Wieringen, 2010). With higher levels of academic achievement and involvement in mainstream education, rather than teaching a separate curriculum or one designed for deaf learners, teachers of the deaf need to know how to appropriately differentiate the mainstream program for deaf learners.

SUMMARY AND CONCLUSION

Universal neonatal hearing screening and cochlear implantation have changed not only the choices for parents but also the early intervention approach, the language and communication approach, and school placement for deaf children. Deaf children are a particularly heterogeneous population, and cochlear implantation has added even more to the diversity, which results in considerable variations in outcomes. All health professionals and educators of deaf children must be aware of this change so that they can provide appropriate support and advice for the diverse group of children, many of whom have additional needs and whose families have complex expectations regarding the educational placement and expected outcomes for their children (Powell & Wilson, 2011).

This variability in outcomes necessitates regular documentation of the child's progress to monitor device functioning, to inform the tuning process, to monitor progress in language development and learning, and to identify additional problems or areas of difficulty, as well as specific abilities and skills. It is critical to keep monitoring the child's classroom performance closely, because difficulties may be subtle in mainstreamed deaf children. The SIFTER has proven to be a useful instrument for this purpose (Vermeulen, De Raeve, Langereis, & Snik, 2012).

As a result of early identification and intervention of hearing loss, early cochlear implantation, and increased belief in inclusion of students with disabilities, there has been a notable increase in the number of deaf students in mainstream schools (De Raeve & Lichtert, 2012). However, the reality, contrary to many parents' expectations, is that mainstream teachers have little or no specific knowledge about deaf learners. In addition, speech perception in regular schools can be poor, hindered by a noisy classroom environment. Schools should follow ANSI guidelines that recommend a maximum noise level of 35 dB SPL, a maximum reverberation time of 0.6 seconds, and at least a 15-dB speech-to-noise ratio (ANSI, 2002).

Teachers of the deaf need to know how to manage today's hearing devices and should be able to teach others (e.g., classroom teachers, educational assistants) to manage the technology as well. This can be a challenge given the range of technologies and devices they will encounter and the rapid pace at which the technology changes. Therefore, heightened emphasis on technology and on classroom acoustics in teacher training is warranted. To guarantee a high standard of education for all students with a hearing loss, the outcomes of research need to feed back into the development of training courses in order to inform good practice. Ongoing professional development for teachers of the deaf who are already in the field is vital.

In addition to the poor listening conditions, there are often few visual cues provided in regular schools. Children may have relatively good speech intelligibility and appear to have good basic conversational language skills but lack the depth of language demanded in an academic situation. Visual cues cannot only increase language comprehension but may also create a longer attention span.

Newborn hearing screening and cochlear implantation have provided new opportunities for profoundly deaf children, have changed their educational choices and options, and as a consequence have created new challenges for teachers of the deaf. Teachers need to increase their expectations regarding what deaf children can achieve. They have to adapt their way of working and ensure that they have the skills to meet the challenges. Teachers need to be flexible and continually updated with the technology and changing expectations. They need to be able to provide (auditory and visual) classroom adaptations to create a fully accessible learning environment. They also need to meet the psychosocial needs of this group of children as they grow through adolescence. And finally, teachers need to be able to work with other professionals.

The challenge for the field is to embrace the diversity of this population of deaf students and to address the specific needs of each child and family in each specific country. As the population of deaf children has changed very rapidly in locations with access to advanced technology, and as more children attend mainstream schools, the demand for effective teaching in the classroom, for professional development opportunities, and for specialized staff training is higher than ever before.

REFERENCES

American National Standards Institute (ANSI). (2002). *Acoustical performance criteria, design requirements, and guidelines for schools.* (S12.6-2002). New York: American National Standards Institute.

Anderson, K. (1989). *SIFTER: Screening Identification for Targeting Educational Risk in children with identified hearing loss.* Tampa, FL: Educational Audiology Association.

Archbold, S., & Mayer, C. (2012). Deaf education: the impact of cochlear implantation? *Deafness & Education International, 14*(1), 2–15.

Bednar, A. (2005). Practical tips for the classroom teacher. *Volta Voices* (July/August), 41–44.

Beer, J., Kronenberger, W., & Pisoni, D. (2011). Executive function in everyday life: implications for young cochlear implant users. *Cochlear Implants International, 12*(Suppl. 1), S89–S91.

Beijen, J., Snik, A. & Mylanus, E. (2007). Sound localization ability of young children with bilateral cochlear implants. *Otology & Neurotology, 28*(4), 479–485.

Boons, T., Brokx, J., Frijns, J., De Raeve, L., Peeraer, L., Philips, B., ... & van Wieringen, A. (2012). Effect of pediatric bilateral cochlear implantation on language development. *Archives of Pediatrics and Adolescent Medicine, 166*, 28–34.

Boons, T., De Raeve, L., Langereis, M., Peeraer, L., Wouters, J., & van Wieringen, A. (2013). Expressive vocabulary, morphology, syntax and narrative skills in profoundly deaf children after early cochlear implantation, *Research in Developmental Disabilities, 34*(6), 2008–2022.

Boothroyd, A. (2004). Measuring auditory speech perception capacity in very young children. In R. Miyamoto (Ed.), *International Congress Series: Cochlear Implants: Proceedings of the 8th International Cochlear Implant Conference* (Vol. 1273, pp. 292–295). Amsterdam: Elsevier.

Boothroyd, A. (2012). Speech perception in the classroom. In J. Smaldino & C. Flexer (Eds.), *Handbook of acoustic accessibility: Best practices for listening, learning and literacy in the classroom* (pp. 18–33). New York: Thieme-Stratton.

Borg, E., Edquist, G., Reinholdson, A., Risberg, A., & McAllister, B. (2007). Speech and language development in a population of Swedish hearing-impaired preschool children, a cross-sectional study. *International Journal of Pediatric Otorhinolaryngology, 71*, 1061–1077.

Brackenbury, T., Ryan, T., & Messenheimer, T. (2006). Incidental word learning in a hearing child of deaf adults. *Journal of Deaf Studies and Deaf Education, 11*(1), 76–93.

Cawthon, S. (2001). Teaching strategies in inclusive classrooms with Deaf students. *Journal of Deaf Studies and Deaf Education, 6*(3), 212–225.

Chin, S., & Kaiser, C. (2002). Measurements of articulation in pediatric users of cochlear implants. *Volta Review, 102*(4), 145–156.

Connor, C., Hieber, S., Arts, A., & Zwolan, T. (2000). Speech, vocabulary, and the education of children using cochlear implants: oral or total communication? *Journal of Speech, Language, and Hearing Research, 43*, 1185–1204.

Crandell, C., & Smaldino, J. (2000). Classroom acoustics for children with normal hearing and with hearing impairment. *Language, Speech, and Hearing Services in Schools, 31*, 362–370.

Darai, B. (2000). Using sound field FM-systems to improve literacy scores. *ADVANCE for Speech-Language Pathologists & Audiologists, 10*(27), 5–13.

Davidson, K., Lillo-Martin, D., & Pichler, D. C. (2014). Spoken English language development in native signing children with cochlear implants. *Journal of Deaf Studies and Deaf Education, 19*(2), 238–250.

Davis, J., Elfenbein, J., Schum, R., & Bentler, R. (1986). Effects of mild and moderate hearing impairments on language, educational, and psychosocial behavior of children. *Journal of Speech and Hearing Disorders, 51*, 53–62.

De Raeve, L. (2010). A longitudinal study on auditory perception and speech intelligibility in deaf children implanted under the age of 18 months, in comparison to those implanted at later ages. *Otology & Neurotology, 31*(8), 1261–1267.

De Raeve, L. (2014). *Paediatric cochlear implantation: outcomes and current trends in education and rehabilitation*, PhD thesis, Radboud University Nijmegen.

De Raeve, L., & Lichtert, G. (2012). Changing trends within the population of children who are deaf or hard of hearing in Flanders (Belgium): effects of 12 years of universal newborn hearing screening, early intervention, and early cochlear implantation. *Volta Review, 112*(2), 131–148.

De Raeve, L., Vermeulen, A., & Snik, A. (2015). Verbal cognition in deaf children using cochlear implants: effect of unilateral and bilateral stimulation. *Audiology & Neurotology*, under review.

Dettman, S., Wall, E., Constantinescu, G., & Dowel, R. (2013). Communication outcomes for groups of children using cochlear implants enrolled in auditory-verbal, aural-oral and bilingual-bicultural early intervention programs. *Otology & Neurotology, 34*, 451–459.

Duchesne, I., Bergeron, F., & Sutton, A. (2008). Language development in young children who received cochlear implants: a systematic review. *Communicative Disorders Review, 2*(2), 33–78.

Dunn, C., Tyler, R., Oakley, S., Gantz, B., & Noble, W. (2008). Comparison of speech recognition and localization performance in bilateral and unilateral cochlear implant users match on duration of deafness and age at implantation. *Ear & Hearing, 29*(3), 352–359.

El-Hakim, H., Levasseur, J., Papsin, B., Paneasar, J., Mount, R., Stevens, D., & Harrison, R. (2001). Assessment of vocabulary development in children after cochlear implantation. *Archives of Otolaryngology Head & Neck Surgery, 27*(9), 1053–1059.

Finitzo-Hieber, T. (1988). Classroom acoustics. In R. Roeser (Ed.), *Auditory disorders in school children* (2nd ed., pp. 221–233). New York: Thieme-Stratton.

Flexer, C. (2004). Integrating sound distribution systems and personal FM technology. In D. Fabry. & C. DeConde Johnson (Eds.), *ACCESS, Achieving Clear Communication Employing Sound Solutions 2003, Proceedings of the first international Phonak conference* (pp. 101–119). Phonak AG: Cambrian Printers Ltd.

Flexer, C., Biley, K., Hinkley, AZ., Harkema, C. & Holcomb, J. (2002). Using sound-field systems to teach phonemic awareness to pre-schoolers. *Hearing Journal, 55*(3), 38–44.

Fortnum, H., Marshall, D., & Summerfield, Q. (2002). Epidemiology of the UK population of hearing-impaired children, including characteristics of those with and without cochlear implants-audiology, aetiology, comordibidity and affluence. *International Journal of Audiology, 41*, 170–179.

Geers, A. (2006). Spoken language in children with cochlear implants. In P. Spencer & M. Marschark (Eds.), *Advances in the spoken language development of deaf and hard-of-hearing children* (pp. 244–70). New York: Oxford University Press.

Geers, A., Nicholas, J., & Sedey, A. (2003). Language skills of children with early cochlear implantation. *Ear & Hearing, 24*(Suppl. 1), 46S–58S.

Giezen, M. (2011). *Speech and sign perception in deaf children with cochlear implants*. Utrecht, Netherlands: Lot Publisher Utrecht.

Giezen, M., Baker, A., & Escudero, P. (2014). Relationship between spoken word and sign processing in children with cochlear implants. *Journal of Deaf Studies and Deaf Education, 19*(1), 107–125.

Gillis, S., & Schaerlaekens, A. (2000). *Kindertaalverwerving: Een handboek voor het Nederlands*. Groningen, Netherlands: Martinus Nijhoff.

Greco-Alub, T., Litovsky, R., & Werner, L. (2008). Using the observer-based psychophysical procedure to assess localization acuity in toddlers who use bilateral cochlear implants. *Otology & Neurotology, 29*, 235–239.

Johnson, C. E. (2000). Children's phoneme identification in reverberation and noise. *Journal of Speech, Language, and Hearing Research, 43*, 144–157.

Johnson, S., Hennessy, E. M., Smith, R. M., Trikic, R., Wolke, D., & Marlow, N. (2009). Academic attainment and special educational needs in extremely preterm children at 11 years of age: the EPICure Study. *Archives of Diseases in Childhood, Fetal Neonatal Edition, 94*, F283–F289.

Kennedy, C., McCann, M., Campbell, C., Law, C., Mullee, M., Petrou, S., . . . & Stevenson, J. (2006). Language ability after early detection of permanent childhood hearing impairment. *New England Journal of Medicine, 354*, 2131–2141.

Ketelaar, L., Rieffe, C., Wiefferink, K., & Frijns, J. (2012). Does hearing lead to understanding? Theory of Mind in toddlers and preschoolers with cochlear implants. *Journal of Pediatric Psychology, 37*(9), 1041–1050.

Kirk, K., Miyamoto, R., Ying, E., Perdew, A., & Zuganelis, H. (2000). Cochlear implantation in young children: Effect of age of implantation and communication mode. *Volta Review, 102*(4), 127–144.

Knoors, H., & Marschark, M. (2012). Language planning for the 21st century: revisiting bilingual language policy for deaf children. *Journal of Deaf Studies and Deaf Education, 17*(3), 291–305.

Kuhn-Inacker, H., Shehata-Dieler, W., Muller, J., & Helms, J. (2004). Bilateral cochlear implants: a way to optimize auditory perception abilities in deaf children? *International Journal of Pediatric Otorhinolaryngology, 68*, 1257–1266.

Langlan, L., Socalingam, R., Caissie, R., & Kreisman, B. (2009). The benefit of sound-field amplification on the signal-to-noise ratio in First Nations elementary school children in Nova Scotia, Canada. *Australian and New Zealand Journal of Audiology, 31*, 55–71.

Lee, E. S., Yeatman, J., Luna, B., & Feldman, H. (2011). Specific language and reading skills in school-aged children and adolescents are associated with prematurity after controlling for IQ. *Neuropsychologia, 49*(5), 906–913.

Leigh, G. (2008). Changing parameters in deafness and deaf education. In M. Marschark & P. Hauser (Eds.), *Deaf cognition: foundations and outcomes* (pp. 24–51). New York: Oxford University Press.

Lichtert, G., & Van Wieringen, A. (2010). *Development of PAN-European competencies of teachers of the deaf through partnerships*, Leuven, Belgium: K.U. Leuven.

Lieu, J. (2004). Speech-language and educational consequences of unilateral hearing loss in children. *Archives of Otolaryngology Head & Neck Surgery, 130*, 524–530.

Lieu, J., Tye-Murray, N., & Qiang Fu, D. (2012). Longitudinal study of children with unilateral hearing loss. *Laryngoscope, 122*, 2088–2095.

Litovsky, R., Johnstone, P., & Godar, S. (2006). Benefits of bilateral cochlear implants and/or hearing aids in children. *International Journal of Audiology, 45* (Suppl. 1), 78–91.

Litovsky, R., Jones, G., & Agrawai, S. (2010). Effect of age at onset of deafness on binaural sensitivity in electric hearing in humans, *Journal of Acoustic Society America, 127*(1), 400–414.

Loots, G., & Devisé, I. (2003). The use of visual-tactile communication strategies by deaf and hearing fathers and mothers of deaf infants. *Journal of Deaf Studies and Deaf Education, 8*(1), 31–42.

Loots, G., Devise, I., & Jacques, W. (2005). The impact of visual communication on the intersubjective development of early parent-child interaction with 18- to 24-month-old deaf toddlers. *Journal of Deaf Studies and Deaf Education, 10*(4), 357–375.

Massie, R., & Dillon, H. (2006). The impact of sound-filed amplification in mainstream cross-cultural classrooms, Part 1: educational outcomes. *Australian Journal of Education, 50*(1), 62–77.

Massie, R., Theodoros, D., McPherson, B., & Smaldino, J. (2004). Sound-field amplification: enhancing the classroom listening environment for Aboriginal and Torres Strait Islander children. *Austrian Journal of Indigenous Education, 33*, 47–53.

Mayer, C., & Leigh, G. (2010). The changing context for sigh bilingual education programs: issues in language and the development of literacy. *International Journal of Bilingual Education and Bilingualism, 13*(2), 175–186.

Meinzen-Derr, J., Wiley, S., Grether, S., & Choo, D. (2011). Children with cochlear implants and developmental disabilities: a language skills study with developmentally matched hearing peers. *Research in Developmental Disabilities, 32*, 757–767.

Moeller, M.-P. (2000). Early intervention and language development in children who are deaf and hard of hearing. *Pediatrics, 106*(3), 1–9.

Moog, J., & Geers, A. (2003). Epilogue: major findings, conclusions and implications for deaf education. *Ear & Hearing*, *24*(1), 121S–125S.

National Center for Health Statistics. (2008). *2004 period linked birth/infant death data*. Prepared by March of Dimes Perinatal Data Center. Retrieved February 8, 2014, from http://www.marchofdimes.com/baby/premature_indepth.html.

National Deaf Children Society. (2001). *Deaf-friendly schools: a guide for teachers & governors in England and Wales*. London, UK: Author.

National Institutes of Health, Division of Amenities and Transportation Services. (2013). *Interpreters services: user manual*. Retrieved February 8, 2014, from http://www.ors.od.nih.gov/pes/dats/interpret/Documents/2013_NIH_Interpreting_Services_User_Manual.pdf.

Nikolopoulos, T., Archbold, S., & Gregory, S. (2005). Young deaf children with hearing aids or cochlear implants: Early assessment package for monitoring progress. *International Journal of Pediatric Otorhino-laryngology*, *69*, 175–186.

Niparko, J., Tobey, K, Thal, D., Eisenberg, L., Wang, N., Quittner, A. & CDaCI Investigative Team. (2010). Spoken language development in children following cochlear implantation. *Journal of the American Medical Association*, *300*, 1498–1506.

Percy-Smith, L., Busch, G., Sandahl, M., Nissen, L., Josvassen, J., Bille, M., . . . & Cayé-Thomasen, P. (2012). Significant regional differences in Denmark in outcome after cochlear implants in children. *Danish Medical Journal*, 59 (5), 1–5.

Philips, B., Corthals, P., De Raeve, L., D'haenens, W., Maes, L., Bockstael, A., . . . & Dhooge, I. (2009). Impact of newborn hearing screening comparing outcomes in pediatric cochlear implant users. *Laryngoscope*, *119*, 974–979.

Pisoni, D., & Cleary, M. (2003). Measures of working memory span and verbal rehearsal speed in deaf children after cochlear implantation. *Ear & Hearing*, *24*, 106–120.

Powel, J., & Wilson, J. (2011). The impact of childhood cochlear implantation on deaf education. *Clinical Otolaryngology*, *36*, 417–418.

Robbins, A., Bollard, P., & Green, J. (1999). Language development in children implanted with the Clarion cochlear implant. *Annals of Otology, Rhinology, and Laryngology*, *108*, 113–118.

Robbins, A., Green, J., & Waltzman, S. (2004). Bilingual oral language proficiency in children with cochlear implants. *Archives of Otology- Head & Neck Surgery*, *130*, 644–647.

Sapienza, C., Crandell, C., & Curtis, B. (1999). Effects of sound fields frequency modulation amplification on reducing teachers' sound pressure level in the classroom. *Journal of Voice*, *13*(3), 375–381.

Schafer, E., & Kleinek, M. (2009). Improvements in speech-recognition performance using cochlear implants and three types of FM-systems: a meta-analytic approach. *Journal of Educational Audiology*, *15*, 4–14.

Schauwers, K., Gillis, S., Daemers, K., De Beukelaer, C., & Govaerts, P. (2004). Cochlear implantation between 5 and 20 months of age: the onset of babbling and the audiological outcome. *Otology & Neurology*, *25*(3), 263–270.

Smaldino, J. (2011). New developments in classroom acoustics and amplification. *Audiology Today* (Jan–Feb), 30–36.

Smaldino, J., & Flexer, C. (2012). *Handbook of acoustic accessibility: best practices for listening, learning and literacy in the classroom*. New York: Thieme-Stratton.

Sparreboom, M., van Schoonhoven, J., van Zanten, B., Scholten, R., Mylanus, E., Grolman, W., & Maat, B. (2010). The effectiveness of bilateral cochlear implants for severe-to-profound deafness in children: A systematic review. *Otology and Neurotology, 31*, 1062–1071.

Spencer, L., Gantz, B., & Knutson, J. (2004). Outcomes and achievement of students who grew up with access to cochlear implants. *Laryngoscope, 114*(9), 1576–1581.

Svirsky, M., Su-Wooi, T, & Neuburger, H. (2004). Development of language and speech perception in congenitally, profoundly deaf children as a function of age at cochlear implantation. *Audiology & Neuro-Otology, 9*, 224–233.

Swanwick, R., & Marschark, M. (2010). Enhancing education of deaf children: Research into practice and back again. *Deafness & Education International, 12*, 217–235.

Tait, M. (2003). Using video analysis to monitor progress in young cochlear implant users. In B. Mc Cormick & S. Archbold (Eds.), *Cochlear implants for young children* (2nd ed., pp. 214–236). London: Whurr Publishers.

Tait, M., De Raeve, L., & Nikolopoulos, T. (2007). Deaf children with cochlear implants before the age of one year: comparison of preverbal communication with normal hearing children; *International Journal of Pediatric Otolaryngology, 71*, 1605–1611.

Tait, M., Nikolopoulos, T., De Raeve, L., Johnson, S., Datta, G., Karltorp, E., . . . & Frijns, J. H. (2010). Bilateral versus unilateral cochlear implantation in young children. *Journal of Pediatric Otorhino-laryngology, 74*(4), 206–211.

Tasker, S., Nowakowski, M., & Schmidt, L.A. (2010). Joint attention and social competence in profoundly deaf children with cochlear implants. *Journal of Developmental and Physical Disabilities, 22*, 509–532.

Taub, C., Kanis, R., & Kramer, L. (2003). Reducing acoustic barriers in classrooms: a report comparing two kindergarten classrooms in an inner-city school. *Journal of Educational Audiology, 11*, 69–74.

Tobey, E., Geers, A., Brenner, C. Altuna, D. & Gabbert, G. (2003). Factors associated with development of speech production skills in children implanted by age five. *Ear & Hearing, 24*(1), 36S–45S.

Van Deun, L., van Wieringen, A., Van den Bogaert, T., Scherf, F., Offeciers, E., Van de Heyning, P., . . . & Wouters, J. (2009). Sound localization, sound lateralization, and binaural masking level differences in young children with normal hearing. *Ear & Hearing, 30*(2), 178–90.

Van Kerschaver, E., Boudewyns, A., Stappaerts, L., Wuyts, F., & Van de Heyning, P. (2007) Organisation of a universal newborn hearing screening programme in Flanders. *B-ENT, 3*, 185–190.

Verhaert, N., Willems, M., Van Kerschaver E., & Desloovere C. (2008). Impact of early hearing screening on language development and education level: Evaluation of 6 years of universal hearing screening in Flanders-Belgium. *International Journal of Pediatric Otorhinolaryngology, 72*, 599–608.

Vermeulen, A., De Raeve, L., Langereis, M., & Snik, A. (2012). Changing realities in the classroom for hearing-impaired children with cochlear implant. *Deafness & Education International, 14*(1), 36–47.

Vermeulen, A., van Bon, W., Schreuder, R., Knoors, H., & Snik, A. (2007). Reading skills of deaf children with cochlear implants. *Journal of Deaf Studies and Deaf Education, 12*(3), 283–302.

Wheeler, A., & Archbold, A. (2009). Children with cochlear implants. The communication journey. *Cochlear Implant International, 10*(1), 41–62.

Whitelaw, G. (2004). FM candidacy issues and the 'alphabet soup'. In D. Fabry & C. DeConde Johnson (Eds.), *ACCESS, Achieving Clear Communication Employing Sound Solutions 2003, Proceedings of the first international Phonak conference* (pp. 101–119). Phonak AG: Cambrian Printers Ltd.

Wiefferink, K., De Raeve, L., Spaai, G., Vermeij, B., & Uilenburg, N. (2008). Influence of linguistic environment on children's language development: Flemish versus Dutch children. *Deafness and Education International, 10*(4), 226–243.

Wiefferink, C., Rieffe, C., Ketelaar, L., De Raeve, L., & Frijns, J. (2013). Emotion understanding in deaf children with a cochlear implant. *Journal of Deaf Studies and Deaf Education, 18*(2), 175–186.

Wilson, W., Marinac, J., Pitty, K., & Burrows, C. (2011). The use of sound-field amplification devices in different types of classrooms. *Language, Speech, and Hearing Services in Schools, 42*(4), 395–407.

Yoshinaga-Itano, C. (2006). Early identification, communication modality, and the development of speech and spoken language: patterns and considerations. In P. Spencer & M. Marschark (Eds.), *Advances in the spoken language development of deaf and hard-of-hearing children* (pp. 298–327). New York: Oxford University Press.

Yoshinaga-Itano, C., & Sedey, A. (2000). Language, speech and social–emotional development of children who are deaf or hard of hearing: The early years. *Volta Review, 100*(3), 286–95.

25

Curriculum Design in Dutch Deaf Education

Annet de Klerk, Connie Fortgens, and Annelies van der Eijk

CURRICULUM

Good-quality deaf education requires highly trained specialist teachers as well as curricula and learning materials that can meet the needs of deaf and hard-of-hearing (DHH) students (Knoors & Marschark, 2014). For the purpose of this chapter, we define "curriculum" as intended classroom actions: educational aims and objectives, activities to achieve these objectives, the organization of activities, and the evaluation necessary to determine whether the educational goals are being achieved. Power and Leigh (2011, p. 33) called this a narrow definition of curriculum, in contrast to a broader definition that incorporates "all of the arrangements that are made for students' learning, both planned and ad hoc."

Too often, teachers of the deaf lack suitable curricula and learning materials. This makes it difficult to deliver a feasible and sound program for DHH students. According to Marzano (2003), such a program is one of the most important factors for school success. A feasible and sound program guarantees that specific topics will be taught regardless of which teacher delivers them. It also means there will be sufficient time to teach the content adequately.

In trying to meet the needs of DHH students, it was quite common in the Netherlands during the last century for teachers to develop lessons themselves or to adapt mainstream curricula and/or learning materials. The educational needs of DHH students have been extensively described in the literature (see, e.g., Knoors & Marschark, 2014). They include specific and extra attention for the development of the lexicon, (morpho) syntactic structures, and pragmatic skills in spoken and written language curricula. There is often also a need for suitable textual material for reading comprehension lessons: less complex texts and age-appropriate material. Smaller steps, more practice with curriculum content, more visual information, and more hands-on activities are important in most curricula that are offered to DHH students in special education.

In the Netherlands, we have often seen a variety of adaptations designed to meet these needs in materials originally developed for hearing students. For subjects such as spoken language and literacy, math, history, or geography, the amount of material was reduced, texts were simplified or rewritten, or some parts of the material were deleted. When it came to subjects like Sign Language of the Netherlands (SLN) or Deaf Culture (now called Cultural Identity for DHH Students [CIDS]), learning materials were totally lacking in the Netherlands. Teachers therefore developed their own materials.

In light of the discussion about the quality of deaf education, this raises many questions. Who decides which adaptations facilitate the development of deaf students? On what basis are these decisions made? Leigh (2001) pointed out that the perspective that is adopted toward deafness—medical or a more sociocultural attitude—influences the objectives that are chosen in the curriculum. There are more questions: How is continuing development guaranteed? Which general didactic theories support the adaptations? How do we deal with the increasing variety of needs of DHH students in our classrooms? In the Netherlands, a nationwide approach to curriculum development made it possible to answer these questions in a more structured and substantiated way.

A NATIONWIDE APPROACH TO CURRICULUM DESIGN IN DEAF EDUCATION

In the late 1990s, the Dutch government provided financial support for the implementation of bilingual education for deaf students. A condition for this financial support was that all schools for the deaf in the Netherlands would cooperate in the development of good-quality curricula and learning materials. To realize appropriate bilingual deaf education, schools needed curricula for SLN, for spoken and written Dutch as a second language, and for Deaf Culture. A national curriculum development team was therefore established in 1999. This expert team was called *Sprong Vooruit* ("Leap Forward"). The momentum this generated made it possible to improve and/or develop curricula and learning materials that are still used in special schools for the deaf. When Sprong Vooruit started, there were five schools for the deaf in the Netherlands. Later, more DHH units were established, and today nine schools participate in the Sprong Vooruit initiative.

SPRONG VOORUIT

Adapting or developing curricula is something that requires experts. There are several advantages to developing or adapting curricula using a team of experts. The most important advantage is the pooling and sharing of expertise so that new materials are supported by current educational theories, or at least by good practices. The expertise that is needed for curriculum development taps into knowledge in the field of deaf education but also in the field of curriculum development, the latter type of knowledge not being automatically available in deaf education. The members of Sprong Vooruit are experts in deaf education. They include linguists, school psychologists, speech and language therapists, teachers of sign language, and supervisors from schools of the deaf. Some of them are also involved in research activities. Together, their knowledge and experience bridge the gap between research and practice.

To bring in expertise in the field of curriculum development, Sprong Vooruit initiated cooperation with a center specializing in developing curricula and educational materials, the Rotterdam-based CED group. Sprong Vooruit also established effective cooperation with the Dutch Sign Language Centre and with the teacher training program for Sign Language and Deaf Culture at Utrecht University of Applied Sciences (Hogeschool Utrecht).

Sprong Vooruit still exists 15 years after its formation, thanks to the success of the products it has delivered over the years. The team is still financed by the government.
The aims of Sprong Vooruit are as follows:

- To develop national frameworks and curricula for language education (SLN, spoken and written Dutch) and CIDS;
- To improve the quality of the content of these subjects and to share knowledge and expertise about these subjects in the field of deaf education, thereby bridging the gap between research and practice;
- To safeguard a national approach to the education of DHH students in language, reading, and cultural identity;
- To develop, evaluate, and publish educational products (aims and objectives, curricula and learning materials) for language, reading, cultural identity, and related subject areas (e.g., English language, language concepts in math);
- To implement new products; and
- To manage and maintain the products that have been developed.

The starting point for curriculum development by Sprong Vooruit is a bilingual and bicultural view of deafness and deaf education. For Sprong Vooruit, this means that sign language and Deaf studies are incorporated in the program and that ample attention is also given to developing expressive spoken language skills, written language, and reading skills. Flexibility and variety are the core concepts in the curricula developed by Sprong Vooruit. They are aimed at a group of DHH students with varying skills, but with IQs above 70, and with differing orientations toward the hearing and the Deaf worlds.

Procedures

Sprong Vooruit is an expert team that brings together knowledge in an efficient way. Decisions about things such as the starting points for curriculum development or development of educational materials are based on consensus. The team searches for and focuses on commonality in approaches and can deal with differences in opinion. Sprong Vooruit works with the "plan-do-check-act" cycle. Products are developed on the basis of theoretical knowledge and good practices. They are then piloted in practice, evaluated, and optimized.

All projects are financed by grants from the government. Sprong Vooruit supervises all projects and activities that are in progress. Other experts may be brought in for the development of specific products—for example, teachers, curriculum developers, writers or editors, website builders, and others. They all work under the supervision of Sprong Vooruit. After some years, and having gained a fair amount of experience, Sprong Vooruit established a fairly intensive structural cooperation arrangement with Duo Decimo, an educational consultancy and editorial bureau, which acts as a project coordinator and edits materials that are developed by teachers and others. Working with teachers as developers who have to write lessons on the basis of predetermined goals turned out to be a complex task, both for the teachers and for Sprong Vooruit in supporting them. Many of these teachers did not find it easy to write down their ideas on paper in the form of lessons and to stick to the goals. They often operated in a more activity-driven than a goal-driven way. They therefore required intensive support in the writing process and in editing the material. Learning from this, Sprong Vooruit and Duo Decimo now organize meetings in which problems and possible solutions are discussed and frameworks for lessons are established before developers start creating new methods and materials. At the end of the process, Sprong Vooruit feeds back all the material that has been developed, and Duo Decimo writes the final version.

When materials are developed on the basis of existing materials for hearing students, for example the material for spoken and written Dutch and for SLN, Sprong Vooruit officially asks publishers for permission to use their material. So far, the publishers have always been willing to give their permission, and Sprong Vooruit is grateful to them for this.

Products

The products that have been developed in Sprong Vooruit since 1999 are as follows:

- An educational framework together with aims and objectives for SLN, spoken and written Dutch, reading, and Deaf Culture (Wallien, Drubbel, & Soeters, 2001);
- A teachers' manual and educational materials for SLN for preschool and grade 1 to grade 6 (ages four to 12 years);

- A teachers' manual and adapted educational materials for spoken and written Dutch for preschool and grade 1 to grade 6;
- A teachers' manual and a small set of educational materials for Deaf Culture. This curriculum has recently been updated and expanded (it is now CIDS). The material has been developed for grade 1 to the end of secondary school.
- Reading Miles: digital reading materials for grade 2 to grade 6.

Currently Sprong Vooruit is working on the implementation and evaluation of Reading Miles and a digital instruction pack for preschool teachers for the teaching of language concepts in arithmetic. Sprong Vooruit also cooperates with the National Institute for Educational Testing and Assessment to improve assessments for DHH students.

In the following sections we will discuss the development of the products that have been created for SLN, spoken and written Dutch, reading, and cultural identity.

THE LANGUAGE CURRICULUM: SIGN LANGUAGE OF THE NETHERLANDS AND DUTCH

Acquiring or learning a spoken language is not easy for most deaf children because it is not easily accessible to them. A sign language, on the other hand, is accessible, but most of the time it is not readily available. Most parents of deaf children are hearing and do not have a mastery of a sign language when their deaf child is born. Even when parents do attend sign language courses, the majority of them does not become proficient signers. One reason for this is that it takes years to become fluent in a language. Another reason is the limited availability of sign language courses for parents in the Netherlands; there are only five courses of about ten lessons each. Consequently, neither spoken language nor sign language can be easily acquired at home by most deaf children (Knoors & Marschark, 2012).

Until the mid-1980s, schools for the deaf in the Netherlands were monolingual (Dutch-only) schools. They remained so after the introduction of Sign Supported Dutch (SSD) in the mid-1980s: Dutch, both spoken (with or without supporting signs) and written, was the language of instruction and the only language used in the curriculum. SSD proved to be very useful in conveying information and also improved the communication between teachers and students and among students. However, their Dutch language skills still lagged behind, and their signing skills also did not meet the level of native sign language users (Knoors, 1992). So, despite the introduction of signs in the form of SSD, students did not become proficient language users in any language, spoken or signed. The schools decided this had to change.

Bilingual Education

To help deaf students become proficient language users in a sign language—in the mid-1990s, their most accessible language—and to become proficient users in a spoken language, the monolingual schools for the deaf in the Netherlands transformed themselves into bilingual schools—that is, schools where SLN and Dutch are both used as languages of instruction and where both languages are part of the curriculum. This development may be seen as a follow-up of earlier pilot projects, experimenting with ways in which both sign and spoken language could be used effectively in deaf education, mainly in preschool (Knoors & Fortgens, 1995). As mentioned earlier, at that time there were no methods of language instruction for deaf students available. For Dutch language instruction, teachers used either (parts of) regular methods or made their own materials, as before in the monolingual era. For SLN, a new subject at the schools, teachers created their own lessons and materials, sometimes inspired by what they found in Dutch language methods or in SLN courses developed for parents and teachers. There were no age-appropriate goals for SLN and Dutch for deaf students, so the content of the lessons was based purely on what the individual teachers considered relevant. Moreover, the content of the language lessons was more often than not driven by activities rather than goals—not an ideal situation.

Bilingual Curriculum

As a first step to improve bilingual education, Sprong Vooruit developed a bilingual language curriculum for primary special education: a practical, clear document for teachers to help them organize and create their lessons in Dutch and SLN. This curriculum contains a description of how bilingual language education should take place, goals for both SLN and Dutch, and the criteria that language methods in Dutch and SLN should meet. The document was instrumental in the later writing of the language methods for SLN and Dutch (see the section on "Language Methods") and the method for Deaf Culture (see the section on "Cultural Education and Identity for Deaf and Hard-of-Hearing Students").

In the first place, it was felt to be important that SLN, a minority language, should be given full status in the schools. As the first language of most deaf children at that time, a time when few deaf children received cochlear implants (CIs), SLN is crucial for rapid development, not only of children's language skills but also for their social-emotional and cognitive development (see Wiefferink, de Vries, & Ketelaar, Chapter 20 in this volume). Because the SLN skills of DHH children vary greatly when they start going to school at the age of three, it was considered important to focus on this language with young students to begin with. Further, because of the age of these youngsters, this focus at school tries to imitate normal language development situation as far as possible—that is, preferably without explicit teaching of grammar and other domains of language education. In fact, this guideline was accepted for all ages: deaf students do have to learn a lot, and more effort on their part often is needed relative to hearing students in almost all subjects. It was therefore thought best for SLN to focus on means that would facilitate incidental learning rather than focusing on intentional learning with grammatical explanations.

Sprong Vooruit emphasizes that Dutch, most DHH students' second language, is also very important because it is the language of the majority and the language that is used in reading and writing. The starting point for relevant methods and material is that the acquisition of Dutch as a second language could benefit from vocabulary skills already acquired or learned in SLN. Teachers can use explicit didactic strategies to link signs to spoken words—although we know now (but not at the time when the material was developed) that this only occurs from the age of eight years onward (Hermans, Ormel, & Knoors, 2010).

Bilingual Language Goals

At the outset of Sprong Vooruit, no curricular language goals were available either for SLN or for Dutch as far as deaf students were concerned. So Sprong Vooruit compiled a set of goals for both languages. The question was for whom precisely the goals should apply. As in every other sphere, the population of the special schools was and is highly heterogeneous, encompassing students with severe and milder hearing losses, with and without CIs, with and without additional special needs, with and without (potential) spoken language skills, with and without SLN skills, with hearing parents and with deaf parents, with and without Dutch-speaking parents, and so on. Sprong Vooruit approached these issues in a pragmatic way to develop the required goals within an acceptable period of time.

Because not all the subgroups mentioned above could be included in one curriculum with one set of goals, it was decided to concentrate on the group of students in the age group four to 12 years without additional needs and with (potential) spoken language skills (for the Dutch part) and with a more or less rich SLN environment at school (for SLN).

For the language goals, Sprong Vooruit started with the attainment goals for Dutch for hearing 12-year-old students and the goals referred to in mainstream Dutch language teaching methods. The regular attainment goals for Dutch for 12-year-old hearing students cover the following domains:

- Spoken language skills such as conversation skills, listening, and giving information;
- Print literacy skills such as reading, writing, and spelling; and
- (Meta-)linguistic aspects related to vocabulary and grammar.

Mainstream language methods all use these domains to organize their goals and content. Sprong Vooruit used the same domains instead of creating new ones (in which vocabulary would, for example, not have been be part of the metalinguistics domain in order to align with commonly used approaches. Another pragmatic decision initially was to leave out the second domain (print literacy) because for technical reading and reading comprehension and for spelling, the schools for the deaf were fairly satisfied with the methods they were already using. However, when years later the schools did feel the need for a curriculum for reading, Sprong Vooruit was involved in creating one (see the section on "Reading").

For SLN there were no goals at all at the outset of Sprong Vooruit. Thus, the domains for Dutch were adapted and transformed into the following:

- Manual skills such as conversation skills, looking, and giving information;
- Discourse skills, such as understanding and composing SLN texts; and
- (Meta-)linguistic aspects related to signed vocabulary, grammar, and language use.

Again, the goals used in the Dutch language methods were transformed into SLN goals where possible.

What was considered age-appropriate was decided with the help of what little was known about the Dutch and SLN language development of deaf children, both from research (for a summary for Dutch, see Knoors, 2001; for SLN, see Baker, Van den Bogaerde, Pfau, & Schermer, 2008) and teachers' first-hand experience.

Starting Points for Development of Methods

There was and is no overall consensus in the Netherlands about how to organize bilingual deaf education. Sprong Vooruit therefore does not prescribe any single approach and does not give advice on what the language(s) of instruction should be. As a consequence of the different bilingual approaches in schools for the deaf, Sprong Vooruit did not opt for one method or one teachers' manual with alternating SLN and Dutch lessons. Such a book might be useful for schools with bilingual teachers who teach both languages and thus organize their own language lessons, but not for schools with, say, a one-person-one-language approach. Two manuals are therefore available, one for SLN and one for Dutch, with just occasional instructions like "this lesson should be given after/before this or that lesson in Dutch or SLN." There is a thematic cohesion between the SLN and Dutch lessons to facilitate positive transfer of the concepts. Another important principle is that special attention and intentional learning are needed for Dutch vocabulary and Dutch grammar, since at the time this material was developed, the Dutch language was (and for some pupils still is) not very easily accessible and thus difficult to acquire spontaneously. Learning the language instead of just acquiring it is conditional.

The most important didactic principle is the Model of Direct Instruction. This model has proven to be very useful, especially for students who need extra instruction (Veenman, Denessen, Van Den Oord, & Naafs, 2003; see also Hermans, Wauters, De Klerk, & Knoors, 2014). To follow the Model of Direct Instruction, all lessons use the following script:

- Start with a retrospective to retain the existing knowledge.
- Explain the goals of the lesson so that the students can focus.
- Use supervised practice to give extra support.
- Give students the opportunity for independent processing so they can apply what has been learned independently.
- Evaluate the lesson: What did we learn (or fail to learn, but will come back in a subsequent lesson), and how did we learn it?

Of course, various didactic methods are included, as well as opportunities to learn together, especially for SLN, but preferably also for the more difficult language (Dutch) since collaborative learning can be a fruitful learning strategy (Kirschner, Paas, & Kirschner, 2009). And as mentioned earlier, small steps, opportunity for rehearsal, and hands-on activities are included as well.

Language Methods

The bilingual language curriculum with the language goals and the starting points for the development of materials was finished and introduced in the schools in 2001. This curriculum was a leap forward, for it provided for the first time a set of nationwide goals and principles for bilingual language education for deaf students in the Netherlands aged between four and 12 years. What was missing, however, were real language methods like those used by teachers in mainstream education. The next step was therefore to develop language methods for SLN and Dutch. Again, pragmatism was the guideline. Instead of trying to write completely new methods, Sprong Vooruit looked for existing ones that it could adapt or rewrite for use in deaf education. Existing methods were investigated to see whether they met the principles mentioned in the bilingual language curriculum.

It was relatively easy to decide on the method for preschool children (four to six years old). There were not many mainstream methods to start with, and the two most popular methods incorporated all aspects of learning in the preschool phase. In other words, they also included aspects such as social and emotional development and preparatory math education. In addition, language education using these methods did not focus on intentional learning but on incidental learning. What was chosen instead was a language method specially designed for schools with many students with weak Dutch language development (mainly because they were immigrant children). This method is called *Ik & Ko* ("Me & Ko"). Ko is a puppet who plays an important role in the lessons and elicits use of language by the students. After some trials in adapting and rewriting selected methods for older students, a method was chosen that was fairly straightforward, with clear goals and without an incorporated spelling section: *Taal op Maat* (Made-to-Measure Language).

The publishers of both methods lent their full cooperation to the adaptation and rewriting of their methods. The methods were adapted and rewritten by experienced teachers who planned the lessons, and a professional author who wrote the ideas down. Adapting and rewriting *Ik & Ko* for the young deaf children was relatively easy because the method involves teachers' instructions only. It was much harder to make adequate revisions for the older students, especially as written texts and instructions for the students were more frequent in the mainstream method. This meant that the higher the level, the more rewriting—rather than "simply adapting"—was necessary. For SLN it meant that written texts had to be replaced by visual ones—in other words, filmed SLN texts.

As mentioned earlier, to facilitate purposeful learning, Dutch vocabulary and grammar needed to be given a more prominent place than would be the case in mainstream methods. Vocabulary lists were compiled both for Dutch words and for SLN signs. The vocabulary lists for Dutch and for SLN were not identical. For deaf children, Dutch words are harder to learn than signs (at least this was the case in the period when the methods were written), so the lists of signs contained more, and more complex, items than the lists of words. A program is available for the teaching of Dutch grammar (Matrix) that had proven useful in improving the correct grammatical use of Dutch, not only while using the program but also in spontaneous language use (Veenker, 1996a, 1996b). Matrix supplies three matrices in which all grammatical structures of Dutch sentences can be visualized. Matrix can be used on paper or the computer, and the author, Herman Veenker, made it available to Sprong Vooruit. Thus, Matrix has been incorporated in the Dutch language method for deaf students from seven or eight years of age.

For SLN, explicit grammar lessons were limited. Because this is the accessible language for deaf children, explicit teaching was deemed to be unnecessary, or needed only to a limited extent, because the language could be acquired instead of learned (see the section "A Bilingual Curriculum"). Today, with more and more students with CIs, these starting points for both vocabulary and grammar education might need some reinterpretation.

Ik & Ko was introduced in 2005 for preschool children, and *Taal op Maat* was introduced in 2008 for older students. Although there has been no formal evaluation of these programs, a few general remarks can be made. The experienced teachers who had been making their own material were very happy with the methods, the first that had been created specifically for teaching deaf students. Any shortcomings were easily remedied. New teachers were more critical, however, and were sometimes disappointed that the methods did not contain more material such as worksheets, training materials, and, for SLN, signed instructions for the students. Despite these reservations, the methods are still being used at all schools for the deaf in the Netherlands.

It would be helpful if a formal evaluation could be carried out as a starting point for new, improved methods. However, the resources to set up such a costly new project are not available. Moreover, the group of students who need and use the adapted methods is shrinking because of universal newborn hearing screening and the increase in the number of students with CIs and digital hearing aids. As things stand now, there is already a group of students at Dutch schools for the deaf who, with support, can use the original methods created for hearing students. Whether this group will grow in size is as yet uncertain.

READING

Educators of deaf students know that learning to read is very difficult for most of their students. Conrad's study (1979) was one of the first to demonstrate on a large scale that few deaf adolescents are proficient readers, a finding confirmed by many other studies and the experiences of parents, educators, and deaf adults (for a summary see Easterbrooks & Beal-Alvarez, 2013). One of the main reasons for this poor performance is the fact that our alphabetical writing is based on the spoken language; in other words, reading is a sound-based activity. It is therefore no wonder that many deaf students struggle to learn word decoding. Furthermore, reading comprehension requires knowledge of the language that is written, and many deaf children lack proficiency in various aspects of Dutch.

Since the introduction of CIs, much has changed with regard to the hearing possibilities of many deaf children and their acquisition of spoken language. As a result, their reading skills are on average considerably better than those of deaf children in the past (Vermeulen, van Bon, Schreuder, Knoors, & Snik, 2007), although they still do not yet match those of hearing children (Marschark, Sarchet, Rhoten, & Zupan, 2010). The disappointing reading results also apply for the Netherlands, as demonstrated in the nationwide research by Wauters, van Bon, and Tellings (2006). Since being able to read is essential for school success and has a major influence on social well-being, Sprong Vooruit felt it necessary to consider what might help to mitigate this problem. The first step was to gather evidence about effective interventions. To gain a full insight, evidence from studies involving deaf students as well from studies involving hearing students was used. We will mention just a few of the most influential factors here (other than child-dependent factors such as intelligence, hearing loss, speech intelligibility, and speech reading abilities).

Effective Reading Interventions

Something that must be considered for all children is the home setting. The more reading and writing materials there are at home, the more likely it is that a child will become a fluent reader (Easterbrooks & Beal-Alvarez, 2013). Other important factors relate to the schools. For example, the more time spent on a certain subject, the better the results will be (i.e., time on task; Marzano, 2003). Reading methodology and methods are also important (Wauters & De Klerk, 2014; Wauters, De Klerk, Van der Eijck, & Knoors, 2008). It is not entirely clear what the best approach is to obtain high reading comprehension levels for deaf students. Reading a lot improves reading abilities, but many deaf children lack sufficient reading experience because of a shortage of suitable reading material (i.e., material they can understand and enjoy). When they have to read books that are not appealing to them (too difficult or too childish), their motivation drops—and motivation is essential for the development of reading skills, especially in children with low reading ability (Logan, Medford, & Hughes, 2011).

Reading Material

The schools for the deaf in the Netherlands all have their own (mainstream or adapted) reading methods and methodologies. None of these methods has been proven to be more effective than the others, so it was not an option to recommend one new or existing approach or method. Instead, Sprong Vooruit focused on the lack of reading material. The aim was to create age-appropriate reading materials that match the reading abilities of the students, materials that make reading fun and can be used to read individually, without the help of a teacher, and at home. When such reading material is readily available, there is a reasonable chance that deaf students will learn to read more fluently and that their reading comprehension scores will improve.

Sprong Vooruit is well aware of research that pinpoints the dangers of written texts prepared especially for poor readers (Marschark, Lang, & Albertini, 2002). The principal criticism is that in texts that have been adapted for poor readers, important function words are more often than not eliminated to create short, simple sentences. These sentences and texts thus lose important information and lack cohesion. Understanding these "simplified" texts then becomes more difficult instead of easier. The new reading material for deaf readers would have to deal with this pitfall, for example by not avoiding conjunctions.

The group of students who need extra reading material is diverse: deaf, hard of hearing, with and without additional needs such as dyslexia, learning problems, attention deficits, and so forth. It was impossible to create sufficient reading material for all the students in grades 1 through 6 (age six to 12 years), so a pragmatic choice was made. The reasonably good readers were excluded from the target population as they can use existing materials, books created for hearing readers with some kind of reading difficulty. The very poor readers, students who hardly learn to read at all, also were excluded, because they can benefit to a greater or lesser degree from some of the material aimed at the middle group. Moreover, it was thought best that reading materials for very poor readers should be combined with hands-on activities. The middle group, which is also the largest group, therefore was selected as the main focus, because it was felt that they would derive most benefit from adequate reading material.

Reading Miles

Although little is yet known about the effects of digital reading, Sprong Vooruit decided to make the reading material Web based, because this enables the use of visual support material such as photos, drawings, films, speech, and sign language to back up the reading process. Another advantage is that Web-based material can easily be used at home, and it enables teachers to keep track of the students' progress. The material is intended to give deaf students the opportunity to read more. Using a travel analogy to enhance practice, the name "Reading Miles" (*Leeskilometers*) was coined for this program.

Other decisions concerning the content of Reading Miles had to do with the question of how to facilitate the reading of the texts. First, the fact that deaf readers struggle with a limited set of vocabulary words was addressed. Comprehending the words in texts is extremely important, since it is known that for a good understanding of a text, a large percentage of words should be familiar to the reader. Using familiar words in the texts is thus crucial. The problem, of course, is knowing which words are known to the deaf students and which are not. Fortunately, all the schools for the deaf use the same Dutch language teaching method developed by Sprong Vooruit, a method that includes vocabulary lists. The texts in the Reading Miles program thus contain words already learned using this language method.

The sentence structures and the grammar used in the texts also follow the lessons in the language method to facilitate the reading of the texts. The challenge was to compose appealing stories with a limited set of words and with familiar grammatical structures that deaf students can read independently. To achieve that goal, the stories are either informative or contain a so-called O. Henry effect (or both). Stories with an O. Henry effect have an unexpected, funny ending that compensates for the effort invested in reading the story. Most poor readers prefer informative stories over narratives. Informative texts also appeal to a wider age range than most fiction.

However, even texts with many known words and with familiar syntax pose problems for many deaf readers. The meaning of the word might be slightly different from what they have learned earlier, or the form of the word might differ (e.g., plurals or verb conjugations). It also proved to be impossible to create texts without adding new, unfamiliar words and grammatical structures. The students thus need extra support. To enhance the knowledge of the students, to explain possible difficulties, and to stimulate their curiosity, all texts are accompanied by short clips in SLN. For example, accompanying a text about the symbols and colors of flags, information is given in SLN about the flag of Suriname. In other cases, the SLN text gives a summary of the text. Watching the SLN text is an option and is not obligatory.

In a pilot of Reading Miles, many students appeared to struggle with the meaning of verbs, including the special inflections Dutch verbs can have (e.g., *lezen, lees, leest, lazen, las, gelezen*; all forms of the verb *lezen*, to read). The students can therefore opt for an SLN explanation of the verbs used in the text. Another option for grade 1 and 2 students is the possibility to have the text read out loud: The students see the text, can read the text, and can hear a voice that reads the text to them. The passages that are being read out loud are marked in the text. The voice is female because in the experience of the Nijmegen CI team, deaf children fitted with a CI understand a female voice better than a male voice (personal communication, Nijmegen CI team). There are also games revolving around word meanings and comprehension of texts. The students have to play the games, but they can choose the order in which they do so. It is recommended that they play the word meaning games before reading the text and do the comprehension quiz after reading. Since positive feedback often motivates more than negative feedback, the feedback is kept positive and encouraging. Finally, there is a quiz in which the students can test how well they read the text. They themselves give the definition of what "well" means in this context: They can decide whether 60%, 80%, or 100% correct answers is sufficient. The score for the quiz is marked on an "odometer," and the session is ended. The teachers can keep track of the results in the school office.

Reading Miles was ready in early 2013 and was available for schools for the deaf, for parents, and for deaf students in mainstream schools through their peripatetic teacher. Teachers can visit the Sprong Vooruit website (www.sprongvooruit.nl), apply for an access code, enter their students, and open the texts for them to read. Of course, not everyone can use such a program without instruction; thus, one of the program developers travels to the schools to instruct teachers. This is proving to be a fruitful approach: After instruction at a school, the number of subscriptions rose significantly (Gerritsen & Van Grafhorst, 2013).

Sprong Vooruit would like to know whether Reading Miles really works. Is it used at home and at school? What are the results? Above all, do the students become better readers? A qualitative research project recently received government funding and started in early 2014; results are expected to be published in 2015. The project aims to answer the following questions:

- Is Reading Miles used by teachers the way it is intended? If not, what type of deviations from the instruction occur, and for what reason?
- Is Reading Miles sufficiently accessible and user friendly that teachers and students can use it without additional instruction?
- Are the exercises in Reading Miles appropriate for pupils' age and reading level?
- Are the exercises in Reading Miles motivating enough, and do they contribute to growth of reading comprehension in deaf students?

CULTURAL EDUCATION AND IDENTITY FOR DEAF AND HARD-OF-HEARING STUDENTS

Approximately 95% of DHH students grow up in hearing families. Their experience of living in a predominantly hearing world as a DHH person is something they cannot share with most family members, and this brings the risk that they may experience feelings of failure, loneliness, or "being different" (Beck & De Jong, 1990; de Klerk, 1998). Sprong Vooruit therefore considers it important to challenge DHH students to explore aspects of their hearing loss, to internalize those aspects in their personal identity, and to share experiences about being DHH. The purpose of these activities is to stimulate the formation of a positive and realistic self-image and to promote the well-being of DHH students.

CIDS is a recent expansion of the curriculum and educational materials that Sprong Vooruit had developed in 2001 (Soeters & Wallien, 2001). At that time, this subject area was called Deaf Culture. Deaf Culture was aimed at the group of deaf students who were predominantly using sign language in the early years of bilingual education. During the past decade deaf education has changed considerably (Knoors & Marschark, 2014). Due to universal newborn hearing screening and early use of CIs, schools for the deaf in the Netherlands today have to deal with an even greater variety of students in terms of the degree of hearing loss, students' language preference (SLN, spoken Dutch, or SSD), and the degree of acculturation in the hearing society and/or the Deaf community. In addition, DHH students increasingly attend regular schools, and often at an earlier age, or will do so in the future. The original materials for Deaf Culture were developed for a relatively limited age group of students (nine to 16 years). However, teachers of Deaf Culture found that students began asking questions about their hearing loss and identity at a much younger age. In addition, the goals of the Deaf Culture program no longer met the general national educational standards. It therefore was decided that it was time to adapt and expand the material and to create CIDS.

CIDS has been developed for students from grade 1 (six-year-olds) to the end of secondary school (18-year-olds). The lessons can be used by teachers in special education but also by peripatetic teachers in regular schools. The lessons are built on a dynamic concept of culture and its meanings. DHH students are not a homogeneous group, so not all of them will participate in the Deaf community. Some will never choose that community and will take part in other communities. Others will participate in communities where they feel at home in a certain phase of their lives and will switch between communities at different times. Many of them have fluid identities. What unites them all is the lack of experience of being able to hear in a dominantly hearing world. CIDS offers them a means for reflection and a way of sharing their experiences. Being aware of the possible ways of dealing with this experience is the essence of CIDS.

Program Content: A Journey into a Diverse Landscape

CIDS aims to stimulate the development of a positive and realistic self-image. It offers students knowledge of, insight into, and an awareness of their identity as a DHH person in a society that consists predominantly of hearing persons. It offers possibilities for contact, bonding, and sharing experiences with other DHH students and adults.

The CIDS curriculum consists of six domains: citizenship (in line with the new development of this subject area in mainstream education); communication; deaf history; own identity; assistive listening devices and techniques; and arts, sports, culture, and leisure time. These domains are a combination of existing domains for all students (e.g., citizenship and the arts) and domains specific to deaf students (e.g., assistive listening devices and techniques). All domains are approached from a DHH perspective.

Didactics

Like the other Sprong Vooruit curricula, the web-based CIDS lessons follow the direct instruction model. Where possible, the lessons are delivered to groups of students so they can reflect on each other's thoughts and experiences. Parents must receive information about the program or be involved in it so they can support their child in the development of a positive and realistic self-image.

The teacher or peripatetic teacher has the specific task of providing DHH students with the tools to determine their own identity and make their own choices. They teach students that not being able to hear is not something to be ashamed of. Students learn to be their own advocates for a rightful place in society. This approach calls for teachers who are open to diversity and who know the different cultural and other aspects of deafness. There is a strong preference for teachers who are DHH themselves, since they can serve as positive role models for the students.

IMPLEMENTATION AND EVALUATION OF THE MATERIALS DEVELOPED BY SPRONG VOORUIT

The implementation of all the curricular materials is initiated by the members of Sprong Vooruit. They all work at schools for the deaf. They organize national symposia where teachers are informed about the Sprong Vooruit website, new materials, and the underlying educational concepts. The members also inform their colleagues at the schools for the deaf where they work.

In the 1990s and the early years of the 21st century, the products developed by Sprong Vooruit for SLN and for spoken and written Dutch (*Ik & Ko* and *Taal op Maat*) were originally published in print, whereas the materials for CIDS and Reading Miles were published in digital format on the Sprong Vooruit website. Currently all curriculum materials are downloadable from the website. Only the recently developed Reading Miles is an interactive program; the other materials are online versions of printed materials.

In 2012 there were 1,667 DHH students at primary or secondary school level in the Netherlands. Six hundred four of these students were profoundly deaf without multiple disabilities. Seventy percent attended special schools and 30% went to mainstream schools (Hermans et al., 2014). The only formal evaluation of the effectiveness of Sprong Vooruit's efforts so far has been the recent tracking of website statistics (Gerritsen & van Grafhorst, 2013). In the period from September 1, 2012, to June 24, 2013, there were 5,701 visitors to the website, 2,351 of whom were unique visitors. Altogether, they visited over 35,000 pages. It is hard to determine who those visitors are. They may be peripatetic or school-based teachers of the deaf, sign language teachers, parents or grandparents, or others with an interest in the materials. They could also be people who visited the site by accident, so these statistics need to be interpreted with care.

DHH students can access the site using the student login to use the Reading Miles program. A recent evaluation showed that schools that provided an introduction to and explanation of Reading Miles had a much higher percentage of users than schools that had not done so. Instructing teachers about the materials therefore seems to be essential.

OTHER ACTIVITIES OF SPRONG VOORUIT

Beyond developing curricula and educational materials, Sprong Vooruit is involved in several other activities, such as developing a protocol for the assessment of deaf students and giving advice about adaptations of assessments for deaf students. Both are being developed together with the National Institute for Educational Testing and Assessment. Sprong Vooruit is also involved in developing a protocol for examinations in secondary education and vocational training. The curriculum aims and objectives developed by Sprong Vooruit for SLN, spoken and written Dutch, and CIDS will be incorporated in the near future in a routine outcome monitoring system.

FUTURE DEVELOPMENTS

Educational policy is changing in the Netherlands. A new law came into force on August 1, 2014, the Appropriate Education Act (*Wet Passend Onderwijs*). Its aim is to ensure that as many students as possible are taught in mainstream schools; special schools will increasingly be reserved for students with complex needs. For DHH students, there will be three placement options: in special schools, in mainstream schools on an individual basis with extra support, or in mainstream schools together with several other deaf students with more intensive support. The possibilities for providing support are more extensive in the latter case because there are more resources available. These are referred to as "co-enrollment programs" (Hermans, De Klerk, Wauters, & Knoors, 2014). There will still be special schools for students who need highly specialized education in smaller groups. This latter setting will suit students who are predominantly orientated toward SLN and students with additional needs and/or those with developmental lags in both SLN and spoken Dutch. The new Appropriate Education Act does bring the risk of fragmenting expertise. With this in mind, the national organization of schools for students with hearing and language impairments, Simea, has organized an infrastructure for intensive collaboration between all schools and support services. This collaboration is aimed at maintaining and further developing specific expertise in the field of deaf education (and in education for students with specific language impairment). Sprong Vooruit will be incorporated in this infrastructure. Currently it seems that Sprong Vooruit will continue to be funded by the Ministry of Education. The team has just received funding for the implementation of Reading Miles and for the evaluation of this program and has prepared a new application for a project focusing on language concepts in math education at the preschool level.

Interestingly, not only secondary schools for DHH students are currently contemplating joining Sprong Vooruit: Simea is also investigating the possibility of organizing a Sprong Vooruit expert team for the schools for students with specific language impairment.

SUMMARY AND CONCLUSIONS

What can we conclude about Sprong Vooruit's experiences? Educating DHH students calls for highly specialized knowledge for what in relative terms is a very small group of students. The same is true for the development of curricula and learning materials for this group. Regular publishers of educational materials typically are not interested in developing products for this small group, for financial reasons, so there is a need for intensive cooperation in the field itself to fulfill this task, preferably in a national context. The limited financial resources can only be used once, and it is also more efficient to bring the available knowledge and expertise together. Increasingly, deaf students receive their education in different settings, in special or general education. This brings the risk of fragmentation or even erosion of the specific knowledge that is needed for this group. To secure and further develop the existing knowledge in this changing educational landscape, collaboration is needed at the national level.

As part of this collaboration, evidence-based practices and practice-based evidence need to be shared and used to improve the quality of education. Where such evidence is not available, we must discuss and choose the most appropriate and flexible options, always keeping in mind the need to maintain a relationship with what is known from general educational practice.

Sprong Vooruit also recommends building a network of relevant experts inside and outside the field of deaf education. These partners have already been mentioned in this chapter; they include a professional editor, an information and communication technology expert, an illustrator, or a writer. These partners have the additional expertise that is needed for curriculum development and have contributed to raising the professional standard of the products that have been developed. Efficient use of the materials developed is conditional on solid implementation, and teachers need sound instruction to help them achieve this.

Evaluation of the impact of the materials is necessary to establish whether they lead to better educational outcomes for DHH students. Sprong Vooruit has just received a grant to evaluate the Reading Miles program. We hope that the results of this evaluation will contribute to even better practices in curricular development for DHH students who have inadequate access to mainstream learning materials.

REFERENCES

Baker, A., Van den Bogaerde, B., Pfau, R., & Schermer, T. (2008). *Gebarentaalwetenschap. Een inleiding* [Sign language studies. An introduction]. Deventer: Van Tricht.

Beck, G., & de Jong, J. (1990). *Opgroeien in een horende wereld* [Growing up in a hearing world]. Twello: Van Tricht.

Conrad, R. (1979). *The deaf schoolchild*. London: Harper and Row.

De Klerk, A. (1998) Deaf identity in adolescence. In A. Weisel (Ed.), *Issues unresolved: New perspectives on language and deaf education* (pp. 206–214). Washington, DC: Gallaudet University Press.

Easterbrooks, S. R., & Beal-Alvarez, J. (2013). *Literacy instruction for students who are deaf and hard of hearing*. New York: Oxford University Press.

Gerritsen, C., & Van Grafhorst, M. (2013). *Rapportage Leeskilometers* 2012–2013. Duo Decimo Advies- en redactiebureau.

Hermans, D., Ormel, E., & Knoors, H. (2010). On the relation between the signing and reading skills of deaf bilinguals. *International Journal of Bilingual Education and Bilingualism*, *13*(2), 187–199.

Hermans, D., de Klerk, A., Wauters, L., & Knoors, H. (2014). The twin-school: A co-enrollment program in the Netherlands. In M. Marschark, G. Tang, & H. Knoors (Eds.), *Bilingualism and bilingual deaf education* (pp. 396–423). New York: Oxford University Press.

Hermans, D., Wauters, L., De Klerk, A., & Knoors, H. (2014). Quality of instruction in bilingual schools for deaf children: Through the children's eyes and the camera's lens. In M. Marschark, G. Tang, & H. Knoors (Eds.), *Bilingualism and bilingual deaf education* (pp. 272–291). New York: Oxford University Press.

Kirschner, F., Paas, F., & Kirschner, P. A. (2009). A cognitive load approach to collaborative learning: unites brains for complex tasks. *Educational Psychology Review*, *21*, 31–42.

Knoors, H. (1992). *Exploratie van de gebarenruimte* [Exploration of the signing space]. PhD dissertation, University of Amsterdam.

Knoors, H. (2001). Taalontwikkelingsstoornissen ten gevolge van doofheid [Impairments in language development as a consequence of deafness]. *Handboek Stem-, Spraak- en Taalstoornissen* (af. 16, B8.1.4.2, pp. 1–34). Houten: Bohn Stafleu & Van Loghum.

Knoors, H., & Fortgens, C. (1995). Het Rotterdamse tweetaligheidsproject: twee talen voor dove kleuters [The Rotterdam Bilingual Project: two languages for deaf toddlers]. *Van Horen Zeggen*, *35*(1), 4–11.

Knoors, H., & Marschark, M. (2012). Language planning for the 21st century: Revisiting bilingual language policy for deaf children. *Journal of Deaf Studies and Deaf Education*, *17*(3), 291–305.

Knoors, H., & Marschark, M. (2014). *Teaching deaf learners: Psychological and developmental foundations*. New York: Oxford University Press.

Leigh, G. R. (2001). Curriculum considerations. In R. G. Beattie (Ed.), *Ethics in deaf education: The first six years* (pp. 143–166). San Diego, CA: Academic Press.

Logan, S., Medford, E., & Hughes, N. (2011). The importance of intrinsic motivation for high and low ability readers' reading comprehension performance. *Learning and Individual Differences*, *21*(1), 124–128.

Marschark, M., Lang, H. G., & Albertini, J. A. (2002). *Educating deaf students: From research to practice*. New York: Oxford University Press.

Marschark, M., Sarchet, T., Rhoten, C., & Zupan, M. (2010). Will cochlear implants close the gap in reading achievement for deaf students? In M. Marschark & P. Spencer (Eds.), *The Oxford handbook of deaf studies, language, and education* (vol. 2, pp. 127–143). New York: Oxford University Press.

Marzano, R. J. (2003). *What works in schools. Translating research into action*. Alexandria, VA: ASCD.

Power, D., & Leigh, G. (2011) Curriculum: Cultural and communicative contexts. In M. Marschark & P. E. Spencer (Eds.), *The Oxford handbook of deaf studies, language, and education* (2nd ed., Vol. 1, pp. 32–46). New York: Oxford University Press.

Soeters, M., & Wallien, M. (2001). *Leerplan Dovencultuur* [Curriculum Deaf culture]. Rotterdam: CED/Het Projectbureau.

Veenker, H. (1996a). *De zinnen verzetten: Taaldidactiek voor secundaire taalverwervers in modulair perspectief* [Moving sentences: A language method for second language learners in modular perspective]. PhD Dissertation, Rijksuniversiteit Groningen.

Veenker, H. (1996b). Leren segmenteren met Ortho en Matrix [Learning to segment with Ortho and Matrix]. In G. J. van der Lem & C. Fortgens (Eds.), *Totale communicatie en lezen* (pp. 218–229). Twello: Van Tricht.

Veenman, S., Denessen, E., Van Den Oord, I., & Naafs, F. (2003). Direct and activating instruction: Evaluation of a pre-service course. *Journal of Experimental Education, 71*(3), 197–225.

Vermeulen, A. M., van Bon, W., Schreuder, R., Knoors, H., & Snik, A. (2007). Reading comprehension of deaf children with cochlear implants. *Journal of Deaf Studies and Deaf Education, 12*(3), 283–302.

Wallien, M., Drubbel, A., & Soeters, M. (2001). *Leerplan tweetalig onderwijs. Nederlandse Gebarentaal en Nederlandse taal in primair dovenonderwijs* [Curriculum bilingual education: Sign Language of the Netherlands and Dutch in primary education]. Rotterdam: CED/Het projectbureau.

Wauters, L., & De Klerk, A., (2014). Improving reading instruction to deaf and hard-of-hearing students. In M. Marschark, G. Tang, & H. Knoors (Eds.), *Bilingualism and bilingual deaf education* (pp. 242–271). New York: Oxford University Press.

Wauters, L., De Klerk, A., van der Eijk, A., & Knoors, H. (2008). *Lezen bij dove en slechthorende leerlingen: Naar goede praktijken voor het leesonderwijs* [Reading of deaf and hard of hearing students: Towards good practices in reading instruction]. Nijmegen: Pontem.

Wauters, L. N., Van Bon, W. H., & Tellings, A. E. (2006). Reading comprehension of Dutch deaf children. *Reading and Writing, 19*(1), 49–76.

26

Re-Envisioning Learning and Teaching in Deaf Education

Toward New Transactions Between Research and Practice

Ruth Swanwick

The aim of this chapter is to provide a different perspective on teaching deaf learners in order to expand existing conceptions and approaches, but not to replace them. The chapter takes a multilingual perspective, recognizing the increasingly plural and dynamic use of sign and spoken languages in deaf children's daily lives in the United Kingdom (UK) and the need for pedagogies that respond to these interesting and complex language and learning issues. Deaf children's multilingual (and bimodal) language use has hitherto only really been considered within the construct of bilingual education. Our thinking has advanced in this area, but we also need to look again at languages in deaf education within the context of the increasingly linguistically diverse UK. On average, 15% of schoolchildren use a language other than spoken English at home (this figure is 45% in London), and the proportion and relative commonness of languages continue to change in response to increasing diversity and migration patterns.

The strides we have made in language research in bilingualism and deafness are exciting and have broadened our understanding of how deaf children develop sign and spoken languages in different contexts and circumstances and what factors influence early and later language acquisition. Neurological studies probing bilingual and bimodal language use have given insights into how languages are activated, organized, and processed in the brain, and this work has extended into cognition and bilingualism (e.g., Casey & Emmorey, 2009; Emmorey, Borinstein, Thompson, & Gollan, 2008; Shook & Marian, 2012). Linguistics studies have expanded our knowledge of the structure of sign languages, the ways in which they and the social and cultural contexts of their use can be described (Baker, Van den Bogaerde, & Woll, 2005; Brennan, 2005; Hohenberger, 2008; Wilbur, 2009), and the sociolinguistic issues and cultural contexts of their use (Behares, Brovetto, & Peluso Crespi, 2012;

Branson & Miller, 2004; De Quadros, 2012; Geraci, 2012; McKee & McKee, 2011; Parisot & Rinfret, 2012; Quer, 2012; Schermer, 2012).

Taking this work forward into learning and teaching issues requires consideration of the bilingual and bimodal language practices of deaf children and bilingual and bimodal pedagogies. The most fulsome exploration of this relationship between language and learning has been in the bilingualism and literacy research. Although much of the discussion of bilingualism and literacy has sought to address theoretical questions, some studies have begun to probe the relationship between sign language and literacy development in more applied ways by exploring the interaction between sign and spoken language in deaf children's learning approaches, strategies, behaviors, and performance (Chamberlain & Mayberry, 2008; Emmorey & Petrich, 2012; Hermans, Knoors, Ormel, & Verhoeven, 2008; Ormel, Hermans, Knoors, & Verhoeven, 2012; Piñar, Dussias, & Morford, 2011). Bilingualism and literacy research has also yielded some directions for pedagogy on ways to build bridges between sign language and text for deaf learners through the use of specific language interventions and enhanced learning experiences and opportunities (Haptonstall-Nykaza & Schick, 2007; Humphries & MacDougall, 2000; Niederberger & Prinz, 2005). This body of work helps us to apply some of the fundamental research into being deaf and bilingual and learning, but more extended enquiry into bilingual teaching and learning in deaf education is scarce.

Some studies describe bilingual "instruction" in the classroom, but these are often policy oriented and do not generally connect language issues with learning or teaching. Some work focuses on developing tools and approaches to bridge sign language and English, but learning outcomes are sometimes difficult to extrapolate from these studies (Andrews & Rusher, 2010; DeLana, Gentry, & Andrews, 2007; Mayer & Akamatsu, 2000; Moores, 2008; Wilbur, 2000). Sometimes, in the research literature, learning seems to become synonymous with notions of access (e.g., Marschark et al., 2006; Marschark, Sapere, Convertino, Seewagen, & Maltzen, 2004; Tevenal & Villanueva, 2009). This body of work can help us understand how information can best be delivered and comprehended in the classroom and how technologies and sign language input can support this. This is only the tip of the iceberg in terms of learning, which is a more complex interaction among learner competencies, engagement, and opportunities in the learning environment (e.g., Knoors & Renting, 2000; Molander, Halldén, & Lindahl, 2010; Smith & Ramsey, 2004).

A THEORETICAL PERSPECTIVE

Missing from the research thus far is a "way of looking" or a theoretical perspective on deafness and learning that provides a framework for considering the development of practice and professional skills. The deaf education literature tends to deal in separate entities such as the audiological aspects of being deaf, language development issues, cognition and deafness, inclusive provision, and language policies. Knoors and Marschark's (2014) book *Teaching Deaf Learners* signifies a change in this regard, as they place an ecological model of learning at the start, providing a framework for integrating these issues that places the individual at the center. This chapter will extend the use of this model to explore the range of influences on deafness and learning and the role of professionals in mediating and supporting learning.

Understanding learning is about understanding a whole person and a whole life (Jarvis, 2006). As such, it is a complex and multidisciplinary area of study concerned with the physical, cognitive, social, and affective domains of (life-long) human experience. Learning is often described as a process that leads to a change that is relatively permanent and not accounted for by maturation and aging (Illeris, 2007, 2012). The term "relatively" provides an important nuance to this distinction because it stresses the dynamic and continuing nature of change over time as we learn new things, build on what we know, and modify and expand our learning. Jarvis (2009, p. 25) describes human learning as

> The combination of processes throughout a lifetime whereby the whole person—body (genetic, physical and biological) and mind (knowledge, skills, attitudes, values, emotions, meaning, beliefs and senses)—experiences social situations, the content of which is then transformed cognitively, emotively or practically (or through any combination) and integrated into the individual person's biography resulting in a continually changing (or more experienced) person.

This holistic view of learning provokes more rounded thinking about deafness and learning. Particularly pertinent to the study of deafness and learning is the emphasis here on the importance of the body as well as the mind, recognizing that cognitive theories only deal with one side of human learning (it's not all in the mind!). As individuals, we bring our whole person to the learning situation, and this includes the senses as the vehicle through which we engage with and interpret our surroundings. This contrasts with the more traditional placement of cognitive aspects of learning as separate from the more affective aspects of the mind and the thesis that knowledge gained through our senses is essentially unreliable.

Attention to the noncognitive aspects of learning emphasizes that the psychological processes of learning are embedded in a social context. In this sociocultural model, language and interaction are seen as the key mediators between the natural/biological and cultural influences on the individual (Vygotsky, 1978). This emphasis on interaction recognizes the crucial role played by adults and peers in shaping learning. This attention to the way in which learning is mediated through language-based interactions between adults and children has driven influential research with hearing children and has influenced educational policy. However, apart from seminal work done in the 1980s by David Wood and colleagues (1986), this is an underdeveloped avenue of research in deaf education.

Looking at learning in this situated way takes us beyond attention to the immediate interaction in learning situations to a perspective that acknowledges the wider societal context. All learners are part of a society or group or community with particular ways of seeing and understanding. The concept that that learning is "shaped by our language, culture and personal experience" (Mezirow, 1991, p. 1) widens our attention to the resources, life experiences, and identities that deaf learners bring to the classroom.

This acknowledgment of the complex set of influences on children's (and adults') learning can be usefully conceptualized using an ecological model that provides a framework for envisaging the learning issues associated with deafness and for planning learning interventions. This model derives from Bronfenbrenner's (1979) ecological systems framework. Bronfenbrenner's thesis was that to understand learning and development, we have to be able to understand the interaction between the individual and his or her environment and the characteristics of the environment. This framework helps us to think about deaf learners and the contexts of their learning in a way that encompasses the contextual influences (the home, the classroom, and the wider environment and culture). This model also brings into play the established constructs in the research and discourses that have thus far guided teaching and assessment approaches in deaf education. As such, this perspective helps us to analyze deafness and learning but also to consider the development of practice and research in deaf education in an integrated way.

In his ecological systems theory Bronfenbrenner identifies five socially organized environmental systems that influence human development and learning (Fig. 26.1).

The *microsystem* concerns the developing person in close and face-to-face "proximal" interactions with those closest to him or her in the environment (usually home and school), such as close family and peers. The person's own biology may be considered part of the microsystem (Bronfenbrenner, 2005). The *mesosystem r*efers to the interaction across a person's different environments or settings and the bidirectional influences between these environments (e.g., the effect the home environment can have on school experience). The *exosystem* casts the circle wider still and brings in contextual factors that, although external to the individual and the microsystem, will have an influence, such as the wider social network at home, the parents' workplace, or the religious community. The *macrosystem* develops the characteristics of

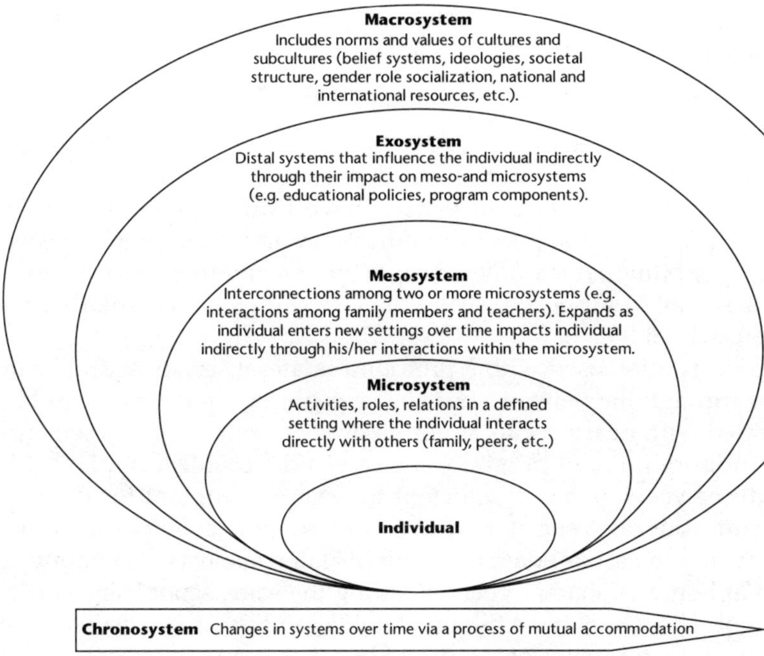

Figure 26.1 Bronfenbrenner's ecological systems theory.

the environment further to include factors that are more remote from the individual but that provide the infrastructure for the microsystem, such as cultural constructs of education, culture, or community. The microsystem is embedded in the macrosystem, so as the macrosystem evolves over time, this will have an impact on the microsystem. The next dimension, the *chronosystem*, recognizes that individuals grow and change and that time passes historically and the world changes.

CASE STUDIES

To explore the use of this model, we present three case studies of deaf learners that illustrate how these layers of influence are interwoven. The adults' roles described in these studies reflect the UK educational context, where support teams for deaf pupils usually comprise qualified teachers of the deaf, non-qualified teaching assistants, and educational interpreters, usually referred to as communication support workers. British Sign Language (BSL) is used in these settings alongside a range of manually coded English systems, usually Sign Supported English (SSE). Some cases refer to schools for the deaf, where individuals can join mainstream classes for some of their learning; this is commonly described as a co-location model. The other inclusive model described here is where deaf pupils are educated in a specially designated and resourced center within a mainstream school.

Case 1

Aisha lives at home with her mother. She is an only child. The family is hearing and there is no known family history of deafness. The home language is English, and both parents have learned BSL. The family members proactively support her education and have high expectations for her bilingual learning of language. The mother works closely with the school to support this, and the family members regularly contribute to school life.

Aisha was diagnosed with a profound bilateral sensorineural hearing loss through the newborn hearing screening protocol. She was initially fitted with hearing aids at age six weeks. Following assessments at the auditory implant program, she received a cochlear implant (CI) at age three years. She was reluctant to wear the implant for the first six months, but once she started attending school, she wore it consistently during the school day; four months later, she was also happy to wear it at home. Aisha has been attending the same school since nursery school. The school has a bilingual policy, and she is in a class of five children led by a teacher of the deaf. She attends a mainstream school two or three days every week, where she accesses the mainstream teacher's spoken language through the use of a radio aid (FM system) and is supported by the itinerant teacher of the deaf.

At home Aisha is exposed to both spoken English and BSL. Her parents have learned BSL to a good level, and some of her wider family members have learned to sign. Her mother will follow Aisha's lead in her choice of communication. For example, at the weekends, Aisha may choose not to wear her implant in the morning and will choose sign as the mode of communication, but when going out, she will put her device on and switch to spoken English or SSE.

The school's communication policy is bilingual. BSL and English are treated as separate and equal languages. The curriculum is taught in BSL, and English vocabulary is reinforced in one-to-one sessions with a hearing teacher and in speech and language therapy sessions. Aisha is confident about negotiating and conversing in social interactions with her peers in BSL or spoken English, depending on the communication partner, and can appropriately code switch between communication partners.

Case 2

Shazia lives at home with her mother, her father, and two brothers. Her parents are hearing, one of her brothers is profoundly deaf, and she also has a deaf cousin. The family members use a combination of English, Urdu, BSL, and SSE at home. Shazia is bilingual and uses a combination of the above, depending on the situation. Shazia's mother is very engaged in her education and language development; she has BSL intermediate skills and is very deaf aware.

Shazia was diagnosed with profound, bilateral, sensorineural loss at birth. She was fitted with two hearing aids, which she wore consistently. The residual hearing in the right ear began to deteriorate further, so Shazia was fitted with a CI at age three years. This was a difficult decision for Shazia and the family. She still wears her hearing aid on the left ear and gains a great deal of benefit from it.

Shazia attends a school for deaf children that is co-located in a mainstream school, where Shazia receives specialist teaching from a teacher of the deaf in small groups in acoustically treated classrooms. The school has a bilingual approach that recognizes and uses English and/or BSL as a first language, based on individual needs and preference. Shazia joins her mainstream class for about 50% of her learning, where she uses an FM system and is supported by a communication support worker.

At home Shazia is exposed to BSL, English, and Urdu. She can switch between BSL, spoken English, and SSE depending on the environment and her communication partner. At school the curriculum is delivered in spoken English with simultaneous BSL interpretation. Shazia switches her attention between the speaker and the signer in class. She benefits from the use of an FM system and receives weekly speech and language therapy sessions focusing on developing her English vocabulary and use of colloquial language.

Case 3

Zak lives with his hearing mother, younger sister, aunt, uncle, and cousin. His father and older sister live in Gambia. The spoken language used at home is Wolof; English is the family's second language. His mother and the extended family have good spoken and written English skills, and Zak's mother is studying intermediate-level BSL. There is excellent communication between Zak and his mother, and information between home and school is successfully relayed by Zak. His younger sister uses some beginner sign language, but the members of the extended family do not use any BSL. Zak's mother supports him fully with reading and math skills and accessing the world around him (e.g., news events, family news). The family is Muslim, and Zak attends mosque school every Saturday. Their faith is extremely important to the family members, and Zak has a very strong network of friends and families in this community, including other families with deaf children. Zak states that he is learning to read Arabic at mosque school but that it is hard. In his local social circle outside of school (he loves to play football), he communicates using SSE, gesture, and some speech.

Zak has a bilateral severe to profound sensorineural hearing loss. He was diagnosed at age three years and three months and was first aided at age three years and four months. Zak wears bilateral hearing aids, which are FM enabled. He is an independent hearing aid user: He checks and maintains his aids independently.

Zak has attended a designated resourced provision in a large mainstream school since nursery school. He is part of a small group taught by teachers of the deaf and specialist teachers, and he joins his year 6 mainstream class for over 60% of the day. In the mainstream class he has a teacher of the deaf and a teaching assistant for interpretation. The school has a bilingual approach, and both BSL and English are used throughout the school day. Staff explicitly teach BSL and English and identify which languages are being used and for what purpose. Zak learns about the differences in structure between English and BSL and is taught how to code switch and translate.

Each of these case studies illustrates the complexity of the microsystem in terms of the relationships and the language and communication practices at home and brings to light particular challenges and opportunities for these individuals. These can be analyzed at different levels of the ecological model. In each microsystem we can see the responsive and dynamic use of sign and spoken languages by the close family members, peers, and professionals in their daily interactions with Aisha, Zak, and Shazia. Within this microsystem we also have the organic nature of individual deafness to consider, which has a direct impact on these interactions in different ways.

Each case study also illustrates diverse examples of the mesosystem, where we see the interplay between experiences at home and school. An example of this interconnection is seen in Aisha's gradual use of her CI at school and the influence this has on her use of it at home. For Shazia, her bilingual interactions at home and school influence her ability to code switch among English, BSL, and SSE. Zak's interaction with his mother facilitates his learning engagement at school.

The external influences of the exosystem are clearly illustrated in Zak's case, where the family's Muslim faith exerts a significant influence on his life at home and his interactions with close and extended networks of family and friends. In all the cases the children are being educated in bilingual settings, and this factor, also external to the individuals, strongly influences their language and learning experiences at home and at school. The importance of context is prominent for all of the pupils, especially in terms of how it affects language exposure and use and individual technology choices. For example, Aisha removes or makes more use of her CI for quiet at home or socializing, respectively. She can also adjust her spoken interaction style with her hearing teacher (uses SSE) if there is background noise or the conversation concerns less familiar content. Shazia uses her FM system in the mainstream context but not in the small group, and Zak switches between the use of BSL from the educational interpreter for accessing the communication in the mainstream classroom and spoken English voice to make his own contributions.

Aspects of the macrosystem that, although they are more remote from these children, present further influences on learning and development include their home communities' cultures, values, and beliefs and the characteristics of the educational contexts, which share a bilingual and inclusive ethos. The influencing discourses and ideologies can be seen in the value that the different families attach to their children's education, their home cultures, and their faith. Taking this through into the educational context, it is apparent that high importance is attached in these settings to inclusivity and linguistic and cultural plurality.

In terms of the chronosystem, the pupils will of course be growing, changing, and maturing and becoming more experienced individuals day by day. As this happens, their learning competencies and needs will change. In this sense they are their own most powerful influence. We can see individual change, for example, in Aisha's initial response to and later engagement with and benefits from her CI and in the increasing development of the pupils' access to the mainstream curriculum.

Historical change also plays a part in the chronosystem. For example, we see the influence of globalization on the increasing cultural and linguistic diversity of the deaf school population. Medical advances and intervention protocols now secure early access to sophisticated and flexible technological support for deaf learners. And the growth of deaf awareness and sign language research has made BSL a language of learning in school and accessible to hearing families and the wider society.

THE ROLE OF THE TEACHER OF THE DEAF

Using the ecological model in this way not only serves as a way of thinking about deaf children's learning but also helps us to consider the role of teachers of the deaf as mediators within and across these different layers of influence and their role in mediating the individual challenges and opportunities illustrated above. The use of the term "mediator" communicates the particular complexities of the role of these teachers in these ecologies of learning; they must work to span, bridge, link, and connect these layers of influence and even sometimes must serve as the bridge themselves. Teachers cannot control all of these influences, but they can be aware of them and therefore play a major part in navigating them for the benefit of deaf learners.

At the microsystem level, teachers of the deaf engage daily in face-to-face communication with and teaching of deaf learners. In this role they must constantly make decisions about language use and teaching approaches to ensure a match with the student's learning needs, taking into account the impact of deafness and individual language competencies. The teacher thus mediates between the learner and the learning environment at the micro level of communication. Working with multilingual (and bimodal) pupils adds further layers of decisions regarding language choices for particular interactions and learning activities and the role of mixed and blended use of sign and spoken languages. Deaf learners may switch between using sign and spoken language for different purposes and audiences and also combine sign and spoken language to achieve a communicative goal. Being able to combine the spoken and sign modalities simultaneously (e.g., though the use of SSE) brings flexibility but also adds complexity to the communication and requires the teacher to mediate languages and modalities.

At this level the teacher is also managing relationships between the learner, the parents, and other professionals. In the case studies we can see that each of the teachers involved in supporting Aisha, Shazia, and Zak would need to be cognizant of the language experience and styles of interaction in the home settings as well as individual language practices so they could make their own decisions about spoken and sign language use and advise other colleagues.

In the mesosystem layer, we see teachers of the deaf as a central and instrumental link between all the proximal and more distal networks of the individual. They mediate between the individual and his or her learning environment and provide links across different learning environments to ensure appropriate and successful learning experiences. This might involve working between an inclusive and special school, connecting various professionals involved in the child's education (e.g., the speech and language therapist and teaching assistant or interpreter), and ensuring partnership with parents at all these levels, not forgetting the child's voice in the decisions. The way in which the teacher makes these links at the mesosystem level has a significant impact on learning. In the case studies we see that as the pupils move between home and school and between the small group and mainstream learning context, someone needs to ensure that there is communication between these environments and that the learning experiences and opportunities are congruent with the individual's needs and expectations.

At the exosystem level, the teacher mediates between the child's home culture and life out of school and all aspects of the learning environment. In the educational context this will include the wider school community as well as the policies and practices of the setting, such as the approach to inclusion, the language and communication used, specific curriculum areas of focus, or intervention initiatives. The teacher mediates between these aspects of the exosystem but also within them and between the exosystem and the mesosystem, always with the individual at the center, with the goal of maintaining the stability and effectiveness of the microsystem. As we can see from the case studies, this entails engaging with the whole school or service policy as well as understanding the cultural and community expectations and experiences of the individual.

At the level of the macrosystem, the teacher of the deaf seems to navigate more than mediate. This is perhaps the layer of the system where teachers have less control and less agency. At this level their own ideas and actions will be influenced by aspects of the macrosystem at the same time as they navigate this with the learner at the center. At this level we are concerned with the cultural and social constructs within which we operate and the political, educational, and cultural discourses of our daily lives. At the most fundamental level this taps into our understanding of what education and learning is. The case studies illustrate the extent to which cultural constructs of deafness and education will be at play here, as well as the discourses in deaf education involving language, technology, attainment, and research priorities.

Finally, for teachers of the deaf, the influence of the chronosystem for their mediating role cannot be overemphasized. The rate of change in educational policy as well as advances in hearing technology and digital learning is rapid, meaning that educational priorities and research directions are constantly in flux. Each child will also be changing, growing, and learning and moving on to different stages of development with different learning needs and priorities. Successful mediation of these influences is essential for the closer and wider systems around the child to facilitate his or her development and learning. The case studies provide examples of these changes at an individual level as well as in terms of policy and practice in deaf education.

This analysis reveals the complexities of the learning context and the extent of the mediating role of the teacher of the deaf. Operating at all these levels involves particular challenges for teachers and requires certain competencies. Teachers need to be able to critically navigate the different layers of influence that affect the individual, maintaining awareness of their own agency as mediators as well as participants at all levels. Operating across these levels needs a full understanding of the language and learning issues for deaf pupils; knowledge of how these issues interact with the learning environment; and an engagement with the educational, political, cultural, and social discourses involved. This includes an interaction with the priorities and dialogue in deaf education research and active involvement in linking these with practice. Teachers can be supported to develop the confidence and competencies to work effectively across these levels through training and professional development programs and, beyond training, by establishing research practice partnerships that foster a critical engagement with the learning and teaching process.

PROFESSIONAL DEVELOPMENT AND TRAINING

One way to support teachers of the deaf to develop these skills is by extending our understanding of teacher (adult) learning for training and professional development routes. Theories of adult learning popularized in the 1980s place the accumulated experience of adults as central to the learning process. However, just acquiring experience is not enough; in Kolb's (1984) influential model of adult learning, reflecting on that experience enables us to move to generalization, abstraction, and experimentation (i.e., for an actual change or transformation to take place). Jarvis (2012) extends this by suggesting a difference between primary and secondary experience. Primary experience is what we actually live through—our acts and the way we touch the world and derive meaning from it. As children we learn by imbibing experience with meaning because we don't always know the meaning of the experiences we have. However, as adults we more often learn through secondary experience, which is mediated through interaction and sharing with others. We create discourses from primary experiences and the interpreted primary experiences of others and thus learn within our own social world. This transformation occurs at the nexus of the individual and the wider society, as we saw in the ecological model.

Working with adult learners requires teachers to provide opportunities for them to reflect critically on the discourses they have created around their secondary experiences. Outside of formal learning contexts, these moments of transformation for adults (the "ah-hah" moments) typically occur when our lived experience of the world is challenged and the reality we trust or take for granted is disrupted. Mezirow describes this dissonance as a "disorientating dilemma" (1991, p. 197). From this disjuncture we begin a new learning experience. This is an ongoing process, and we continually reshape and redefine perceptions of the world and what they mean.

As part of teacher training, we can create conditions that foster this transformative learning. An effective way to do this is to use individual experience as a starting point to raise teachers' awareness of their own experience and to think about why they experience as they do and how it informs their actions. Exposing teachers to different points of view is a useful way to challenge the learning that has come from this experience and to create disjuncture. It is important to do this in a learning environment where there is meaningful and open dialogue in supporting relationships and to be cognizant of individual ecologies of learning—that is, their working context, life, and societal influences (Cranton & Taylor, 2012).

Practical ways of achieving this transformative learning were explored in a collaborative project between four UK institutions providing postgraduate programs in deaf education. This project examined the concepts of critical thinking and reflective practice as essential skills for teachers of the deaf and also for postgraduate-level study (Swanwick et al., 2013). Through a critical review and synthesis of current theories of critical thinking and reflective practice in higher education, the project team identified seven areas of skills or domains of development. Table 26.1 presents these as a framework of principles using key words to encapsulate the essence of each skill or domain. Learning activities to target these skills were tested across the different institutions, and teachers were asked to reflect on how successfully the activities promoted the skills.

The findings revealed that the students valued being exposed to different perspectives and that this broadened their knowledge. Students emphasized the importance of a supportive learning environment that included group and interactive work through which to explore these new ideas. In relation to notions of dissonance and disjuncture, uncertainty was a recurrent concern in their feedback. A paradox emerged here: Students reported difficulty in tolerating uncertainty and engaging with unknowns but associated this with risk taking and spontaneity, which they generally described as positive and creative aspects of their work. In terms of transformative learning, the students noted that new thinking and ideas came to the surface. A sense of critical awakening was evident in the comments; they described questioning their own values and beliefs and recognizing personal development and enlightenment.

Table 26.1 Principles of Critical Thinking and Reflective Practice

Keywords	Principles
Willingness	Being open to inquiry and adapting practice; being committed to experimentation as a learning process
Lenses	Recognizing and engaging with different viewpoints; ability to "look through another's eyes" and creatively synthesize multiple perspectives
Unknown	Tolerating uncertainty and unpredictability; being prepared to "get it wrong"; ability to engage with and negotiate unknowns (knowing what you don't know)
Self	Developing personal lines of inquiry; having the self-awareness to interrogate or critically assess instinct, intuition, and feelings
Metacognition	Identifying and reconceptualizing abstract ideas that synthesize theory and practice
Communication	Articulating and presenting ideas that synthesize theory and practice
Teacher-Researcher	Seeing oneself as a contributor to the wider research community

We learned from this project that by encouraging teachers of the deaf to work together on common issues; to experience different points of view; to be exposed to contradiction, tensions, or unknowns; and to innovate, reimagine, and re-envision their work, they begin to describe what we might call expansive learning (Engeström, 2001). This can be defined as a collective activity that leads to new sense making and change (Gutiérrez, Baquedano-López, Alvarez, & Chiu, 1999). It is transformative and boundary-crossing learning through which people and organizations work with new ideas to learn new forms of activity. An overarching goal of training should therefore be to create expansive learning communities that can adapt to unknowns, contradictions, and new contextual influences or demands to create new ways of looking at deafness and learning and to imagine new ways of working.

OTHER PROFESSIONALS

This goal is admittedly more problematic in contexts where no specific training is required for teaching or supporting deaf children in school. Qualified teachers of the deaf are not the only professionals mediating the different layers of influence in a deaf children's life on a daily basis. In the UK, special training is still mandated for teachers of the deaf, but such teachers account for less than half of the workforce supporting deaf children's learning. The remainder are deaf and hearing professionals with diverse skills and experience, for whom there is a lack of recognized professional training, status, and associated qualifications. This includes teaching assistants and communication support workers (CRIDE, 2013). Training needs to be developed that could be shared internationally through a research-to-practice "Teaching Deaf Learners" network. This would provide a forum to identify professional development priorities and develop training approaches that build on local expertise but that are also internationally relevant. Such a network would provide avenues for importing knowledge from research into classroom practice to improve deaf children's learning and achievement.

TRANSACTIONS BETWEEN RESEARCH AND PRACTICE

A second way to support teachers of the deaf is to develop more effective transactions between research and practice. The potential of action research is proposed here as a collaborative means of working that combines the different skills and expertise of researchers and practitioners. For example, in the UK the University of Leeds set up national workshops with practitioners to explore the use of an action research model to investigate their questions about reading comprehension (Carter & Swanwick, 2012). This began as a small group of schools and services. Gradually, national interest in this way of working grew, and more schools, services, and individuals began to design and implement their own action research projects. As a result, an action research culture has developed in a number of schools and services as a means of testing and evaluating whole-school and individual interventions. This work is led by practitioners; the role of the researchers is to sustain the momentum of the activities, to hold the shape of the projects, and to disseminate the findings nationally and internationally. Productive research–practice partnerships have developed, opening up dialogue both nationally and internationally about new ways of envisioning transactions between research and practice in deaf education (Swanwick, Kitchen, & Clarke, 2013).

A next step is to establish collaborative methodologies between researchers and practitioners. As part of the Deafness and Reading for Meaning (DReaM) project at the University of Leeds, a collaborative methodology was developed to test a process for developing a whole-school approach to reading comprehension intervention (Swanwick, Kitchen, & Clarke, 2012). This entailed establishing a research partnership by bringing in two practitioner-researchers from two deaf education settings to work with the two university investigators. The project took advantage of the different skills, expertise, and perspectives that the researchers and practitioners brought to the problem. Researchers and practitioners alike have reported that this was a very successful way to share research questions and methodological design and to make a difference to practice (Swanwick & Carter, 2013).

CONCLUSIONS

A conceptual shift that would make an immediate difference to developing these transactions between research and practice would entail rethinking the way we categorize researchers and practitioners. Instead of seeing ourselves as one or the other, we can see ourselves as belonging to one community, or a number of communities, of practice, all engaged in a shared endeavor to improve education for deaf children. The concept of a community of practice extends the notion of a network to a more coherent sense of a group whose members may not work together directly but are all working toward the same end and share the same concerns, interests, professional experiences, and tools (Wenger, 1998). This might be an interesting and fruitful way of looking at how we co-produce and exchange knowledge where the "hybridity" of the research/practice community is a resource for creating new learning.

This type of expansive learning community would create opportunities for new knowledge and new practices that actually change the learning context or the learning ecology for deaf children (Engeström, 2001). Expansive learning assumes that in this process everyone is learning (the pupils, the researchers, and the practitioners) and that including multiple voices arising from diverse perspectives and histories leads to a sideways learning, new conceptualizations, and transformative thinking. With this landmark volume, and following the inaugural conference on teaching deaf learners, we are poised to do this as we look again, and globally, at the learners and the teachers in deaf education. We shouldn't just ask ourselves what we can do—but imagine what we could do.

ACKNOWLEDGMENTS

The author gratefully acknowledges the work of the teachers of the deaf in the Language Planning project and particularly thanks Blanche Nevile, Frank Barnes, and James Wolfe Schools for the case studies.

REFERENCES

Andrews, J. F. A., & Rusher, M. (2010). Codeswitching techniques: Evidence-based instructional practices for the ASL/English bilingual classroom. *American Annals of the Deaf, 155*(4), 407–424.

Baker, A., Van Den Bogaerde, B., & Woll, B. (2005). Methods and procedures in sign language acquisition studies. *Sign Language and Linguistics (Online), 8*(1-2), 7–58.

Behares, L. E., Brovetto, C., & Peluso Crespi, L. (2012). Language policies in Uruguay and Uruguayan Sign Language (LSU). *Sign Language Studies, 12*(4), 519–542.

Branson, J., & Miller, D. (2004). The cultural construction of linguistic incompetence through schooling: Deaf education and the transformation of the linguistic environment in Bali, Indonesia. *Sign Language Studies, 5*(1), 6–38.

Brennan, M. (2005). Conjoining word and image in British Sign Language (BSL): An exploration of metaphorical signs in BSL. *Sign Language Studies, 5*(3), 360–382.

Bronfenbrenner, U. (1979). *The ecology of human development: Experiments by nature and design*. Cambridge, MA: Harvard University Press.

Bronfenbrenner, U. (2005). *Making human beings human: Bioecological perspectives on human development*. Thousand Oaks, CA: Sage Publications.

Carter, A., & Swanwick (2012). Action research makes a difference. *British Association of Teachers of the Deaf Magazine* (March), 40–41.

Casey, S., & Emmorey, K. (2009). Co-speech gesture in bimodal bilinguals. *Language and Cognitive Processes, 24*(2), 290–312.

Chamberlain, C., & Mayberry, R. I. (2008). American Sign Language syntactic and narrative comprehension in skilled and less skilled readers: Bilingual and bimodal evidence for the linguistic basis of reading. *Applied Psycholinguistics, 29*(3), 367–388.

Cranton, P., & Taylor, E. (2012). Transformative learning. In P. Jarvis (Ed.), *The Routledge international handbook of learning* (pp. 194–204). New York: Routledge.

CRIDE (Consortium for Research into Deaf Education). (2013). Report on 2013 survey on educational provision for deaf children. Retrieved from the

National Deaf Children's Society Website, January 2014. http://www.ndcs.org.uk/document.rm?id=8604

DeLana, M., Gentry, M. A., & Andrews, J. (2007). The efficacy of ASL/English bilingual education: Considering public schools. *American Annals of the Deaf, 152*(1), 73–87.

De Quadros, R. M. (2012). Linguistic policies, linguistic planning, and Brazilian sign language in Brazil. *Sign Language Studies, 12*(4), 543–564.

Emmorey, K., Borinstein, H. B., Thompson, R., & Gollan, T. H. (2008). Bimodal bilingualism. *Bilingualism, 11*(1), 43–61.

Emmorey, K., & Petrich, J. A. F. (2012). Processing orthographic structure: Associations between print and fingerspelling. *Journal of Deaf Studies and Deaf Education, 17*(2), 194–204.

Engeström, Y. (2001). Expansive learning at work: Toward an activity theoretical reconceptualization. *Journal of Education and Work, 14*(1), 133–161.

Geraci, C. (2012). Language policy and planning: The case of Italian sign language. *Sign Language Studies, 12*(4), 494–518.

Gutiérrez, K. D., Baquedano-López, P., Alvarez, H. H., & Chiu, M. M. (1999). Building a culture of collaboration through hybrid language practices. *Theory Into Practice, 38*(2), 87–93.

Haptonstall-Nykaza, T. S., & Schick, B. (2007). The transition from fingerspelling to English print: Facilitating English decoding. *Journal of Deaf Studies and Deaf Education, 12*(2), 172–183.

Hermans, D., Knoors, H., Ormel, E., & Verhoeven, L. (2008). The relationship between the reading and signing skills of deaf children in bilingual education programs. *Journal of Deaf Studies and Deaf Education, 13*(4), 518–530.

Hohenberger, A. (2008). The word in sign language: Empirical evidence and theoretical controversies. *Linguistics, 46*(2), 249–308.

Humphries, T., & MacDougall, F. (2000). "Chaining" and other links: Making connections between American Sign Language and English in two types of school settings. *Visual Anthropology Review, 15*(2), 84–94.

Illeris, K. (2007). *How we learn: Learning and non-learning in school and beyond*. London: Routledge.

Illeris, K. (2012). Learning and cognition. In P. Jarvis (Ed.), *The Routledge international handbook of learning* (pp. 18–27). New York: Routledge.

Jarvis, P. (2006). *Towards a comprehensive theory of human learning*. London: Routledge.

Jarvis, P. (2009). *Learning to be a person in society*. London: Routledge.

Knoors, H., & Marschark, H. (2014). *Teaching deaf learners: Psychological and developmental foundations*. New York: Oxford University Press.

Knoors, H., & Renting, B. (2000). Measuring the quality of education: The involvement of bilingually educated deaf children. *American Annals of the Deaf, 145*(3), 268–274.

Kolb, D. A. (1984). *Experiential learning: Experience as a source of learning and development*. Englewood Cliffs, NJ: Prentice-Hall.

Marschark, M., Leigh, G., Sapere, P., Burnham, D., Convertino, C., Stinson, M., & Noble, W. (2006). Benefits of sign language interpreting and text alternatives for deaf students' classroom learning. *Journal of Deaf Studies and Deaf Education, 11*(4), 421–437.

Marschark, M., Sapere, P., Convertino, C., Seewagen, R., & Maltzen, H. (2004). Comprehension of sign language interpreting: Deciphering a complex task situation. *Sign Language Studies*, *4*(4), 345–366, 405–406.
Mayer, C., & Akamatsu, C. T. (2000). Deaf children creating written texts: Contributions of American sign language and signed forms of English. *American Annals of the Deaf*, *145*(5), 394–401.
McKee, R., & McKee, D. (2011). Old signs, new signs, whose signs? Sociolinguistic variation in the NZSL lexicon. *Sign Language Studies*, *11*(4), 485–527.
Mezirow, J. (1991). *Transformative dimensions of adult learning*. Oxford: Jossey-Bass.
Molander, B. O., Halldén, O., & Lindahl, C. (2010). Ambiguity—A tool or obstacle for joint productive dialogue activity in deaf and hearing students' reasoning about ecology. *International Journal of Educational Research*, *49*(1), 33–47.
Moores, D. (2008). Research on Bi-Bi instruction. *American Annals of the Deaf*, *153*(1), 3–4.
Niederberger, N., & Prinz, P. (2005). Does the knowledge of a natural sign language facilitate deaf children's learning to read and write? [La connaissance d'une langue des signes peut-elle faciliter l'apprentissage de l'écrit chez l'enfant sourd?]. *Enfance*, *57*(4), 285–297.
Ormel, E., Hermans, D., Knoors, H., & Verhoeven, L. (2012). Cross-language effects in written word recognition: The case of bilingual deaf children. *Bilingualism*, *15*(2), 288–303.
Parisot, A. M., & Rinfret, J. (2012). Recognition of langue des signes Québécoise in Eastern Canada. *Sign Language Studies*, *12*(4), 583–601.
Piñar, P., Dussias, P. E., & Morford, J. P. (2011). Deaf readers as bilinguals: An examination of deaf readers' print comprehension in light of current advances in bilingualism and second language processing. *Linguistics and Language Compass*, *5*(10), 691–704.
Quer, J. (2012). Legal pathways to the recognition of sign languages: A comparison of the Catalan and Spanish sign language acts. *Sign Language Studies*, *12*(4), 565–582.
Schermer, T. (2012). Sign language planning in the Netherlands between 1980 and 2010. *Sign Language Studies*, *12*(4), 467–493.
Shook, A., & Marian, V. (2012). Bimodal bilinguals co-activate both languages during spoken comprehension. *Cognition*, *124*(3), 314–324. doi: 10.1111/j.1551-6709.2012.01243.x;
Smith, D. H., & Ramsey, C. L. (2004). Classroom discourse practices of a deaf teacher using American Sign Language. *Sign Language Studies*, *5*(1), 39–62.
Swanwick, R., & Carter, A. (2013). Practitioners making a difference. *British Association of Teachers of the Deaf Magazine* (December), 6–7.
Swanwick, R. A., Kitchen, R., & Clarke, P. J. (2012). Practitioner talk on deaf children's reading comprehension: Analysing multiple voices. *Deafness and Education International*, *14*(2), 100–120.
Swanwick, R., Kitchen, R., & Clarke, P. (2013). A design-based approach for research into deaf children's reading comprehension *Hillary Place Papers*, 1(1); available at http://hpp.education.leeds.ac.uk/
Swanwick, R., Kitchen, R., Jarvis, J., McCracken, W., O'Neil, R., & Powers, S. (2013). Following Alice: theories of critical thinking and reflective practice in action at postgraduate level. *Teaching in Higher Education*, *19*(2), 1–14.

Tevenal, S., & Villanueva, M. (2009). Are you getting the message? The effects of SimCom on the message received by deaf, hard of hearing, and hearing students. *Sign Language Studies*, *9*(3), 266–286, 379–380.
Vygotsky, L. S. (1978). *Mind in society: The development of higher psychological processes*. Cambridge, MA: Harvard University Press.
Wenger, E. (1998). Communities of practice: Learning, meaning and identity. Cambridge, MA: Cambridge University Press.
Wilbur, R. B. (2000). The use of ASL to support the development of English and literacy. *Journal of Deaf Studies and Deaf Education*, *5*(1), 81–104. doi: 10.1093/deafed/5.1.81
Wilbur, R. B. (2009). Effects of varying rate of signing on ASL manual signs and nonmanual markers. *Language and Speech*, *52*(2–3), 245–285.
Wood, D., Wood, H., Griffiths, A., & Howarth, I. (1986). *Teaching and talking with deaf children*. London: John Wiley & Sons.

Epilogue

27

Educating Deaf Learners in the 21st Century

What We Know and What We Need to Know

Marc Marschark and Harry Knoors

Where to start, where to start? There can be little doubt that there has never been a better time to be a deaf child—or the parent or teacher of one. We know so much, and knowledge continues to accumulate at a rapid pace, as does the ability of all stakeholders in educating deaf and hard-of-hearing (DHH) learners to access the experts who have helped to acquire that knowledge. Yet, while at the threshold of change, we are confronted with two barriers. First, with each "answer" to a question confronting us as stakeholders, multiple other questions arise. So each time we come to know something, it seems like there is so much more that we need to know. There is at least one thing that is unambiguous, however: There are no unitary, simple answers to complex questions facing deaf education (Knoors & Marschark, 2014). As the chapters in this volume explain and will be discussed further below, sign language, cochlear implants (CIs), and special schools for DHH children seem to be simple answers, but each of them, too, raises a host of other complex questions.

Second, and closely related, it often seems (especially to parents and classroom teachers) that we cannot even agree on what the questions are. For example, to some people, questions about whether deaf children should receive CIs (e.g., Sorkin, 2013) or whether there should be bilingual education for DHH children (e.g., Humphries et al., 2012) are either not questions at all or ones with incredibly obvious, affirmative answers. Yet, as will be described below, such positions largely ignore complicating factors that beg additional questions. Thus, for many deaf children, focusing their and our energies on one language modality or the other early on might be a more effective and efficient strategy than universal bilingualism—or not. Flexibility in language policy is needed to ensure that we are meeting DHH children's needs rather than anyone else's (see Knoors & Marschark, 2012). Similarly, the huge variability among pediatric CI recipients, with significant numbers receiving little or no benefit to spoken language (with other domains yet to be explored), shows that implants are not for everyone (see Niparko et al., 2010). At the very least, the fact that different stakeholders come at the same issues from different directions means that even if we share the same concerns, we often have different priorities in dealing with them (e.g., Swanwick & Marschark, 2010).

Because of the complexity issue and the still-emerging evidence base in deaf education (Easterbrooks & Stephenson, 2006; Knoors & Marschark, 2014; Spencer & Marschark, 2010), parents and teachers of deaf children often are confronted with mixed messages in the literature pertaining to raising and educating DHH children. For example, it is often noted that deaf children who rely on spoken language early on tend to read better than "average," presumably referring to norms showing a median reading level for DHH children far below their hearing peers (see below). In fact, that conclusion and the data on which it is based are far more complex than they would appear, but that is not the point here. Rather, it is often noted that deaf children who rely on sign language early on also tend to read better than "average" (also a far more complex issue than it would appear; see below). Taken together, what these results show is that early access to language leads to better reading, and yet various commentators continue to argue that the research supports one mode of communication over the other. But, just perhaps "[r]ather than engaging in arguments in the literature that one piece of the puzzle is more important than another, a more productive view would be to embrace the fact that reading requires multiple skill sets and that these sets may vary by child" (Easterbrooks & Maiorana-Basas, Chapter 7 in this volume).

The above challenges are not just an academic issue: They affect the everyday lives of DHH children, their families, their teachers, and their peers. This situation brings to mind a quotation attributed to the American educator and philosopher, John Dewey:

> When your fork proves inadequate to the task of eating soup, it makes little sense to argue about whether there is something inherent in the nature of forks or something inherent in the nature of soup that accounts for the failure. You just reach for a spoon.

Fully understanding that science and, indeed, all (or most) of societal gains involve incremental progress, disagreement, and compromise, it does no service to DHH children or other stakeholders in deaf education to devote limited resources to search for (or declare) "the one true path" to improved deaf education. What is essential is to establish an evidence base and work from it in the best interests of those children and their families. That means first recognizing that the large individual differences among DHH children mean that there is no single or simple answer to the complex questions pertaining to their language and learning (Knoors & Marschark, 2014, Chapter 2). Then, there must be a willingness to use the evidence base to adapt home and school environments to the strengths and needs of individual children rather than the generalized beliefs or desires of teachers, researchers, and commentators (Swanwick & Marschark, 2010).

One way to approach these issues is to look for ways to profile the languages and communication modalities used by individual deaf children in particular contexts and at specific moments in time in interaction with their relatives, peers, teachers, and significant others (Swanwick et al., 2014). Another fruitful approach would involve focusing on enhancement of the assets and minimizing the risks for individual deaf students, their families, and their schools, thus bringing an ecological approach to learning and the broader educational endeavor (Antia, Chapter 23 in this volume). Further, rather than being nationally and domain specific, as work in this field has tended to be, it is time to push for more international and interdisciplinary collaboration. As Easterbrooks and Maiorana-Basas (Chapter 7 in this volume) noted, "our debates in the scientific literature have focused on practically anything and everything that took us away from helping teachers understand and engage in the most effective practices that affect positive outcomes in the children under their guidance." If we really want to help teachers deal with the fast-changing complexities of deaf education, the broader and more inclusive our collaborations in terms of being interdisciplinary and international, the better. It's time to reach for a spoon.

WHAT WE KNOW ABOUT EDUCATING DEAF LEARNERS

With an introduction like that, wading into the waters of research in deaf education might seem dangerous. However, the chapters of this volume confirm and extend what we know about educating DHH children who vary in many ways and are learning in different family, social, and academic contexts. Indeed, our focus in this volume on *educating* deaf learners rather than *teaching* them is intended to emphasize that the accumulating global evidence base represented and cited by those chapters is not limited to formal classroom instruction. It also includes the informal "teaching" and learning that happens in the home, on the playground, and throughout DHH children's daily lives. This approach converges nicely with the educational philosophy of John Dewey. He saw learning and education as distinct but interactive processes. Like Jean Piaget and Maria Montessori in Europe, he believed that American children would benefit most from educational settings in which they are active learners. Education, in his view, was not only the acquisition of knowledge and skills required by a curriculum, but the positive application of education in the life of the individual and in society.

In broadening the scope of education for the purposes of this chapter, and considering deaf education, in particular, in its broadest possible terms, there is no way to address all that we know about educating deaf learners, nor is that the intention here. Rather, the goal is to highlight some of the key elements of the evidence base so as to show ways in which they fit together and synergistically may add up to more than the sum of their component parts. In addition, weaving together contributions to the fund of knowledge offered by the contributors to this volume and others will highlight some of the existing gaps in that knowledge and some important things that we still need to know about educating deaf learners. Given the demands of our 21st-century global society and large individual differences among students in increasingly inclusive educational settings, parents, teachers, and researchers need broad cooperation in order to ensure that we provide DHH students with the skills they need for academic, employment, and personal success. As Swanwick (Chapter 26 in this volume) notes, such formal and informal types of education are ecological processes, situated in particular contexts, and those need to be studied where and when they occur and how they influence each other. For the present purposes, therefore, this chapter will touch on six areas of investigation: two involving context (school placement and parents and families) and four involving competencies (language, academic achievement, social-emotional functioning, and cognition). These touches necessarily will be light and selective; the other chapters in this volume are the ones that provide the depth.

School Placement

If there is one point of agreement among all stakeholders involved in educating DHH children, it is that we are dealing with a very heterogeneous group (see, in this volume, Antia, Chapter 23; Caselli, Rinaldi, Onofrio, & Tomasuolo, Chapter 19; De Raeve, Chapter 24; and Hintermair, Chapter 13). For this reason, it seems most reasonable to conclude that there is no single kind of educational setting that will be optimal for all of them. If this is the case, "forcing" a population of children exhibiting such large individual differences into a single mold, whatever it is, seems likely to cause significant harm, or at least inhibit optimal development and learning. As Harry Knoors often notes, "one size fits none."

In contrast to a special educational setting for DHH learners, regular school classrooms have to provide a variety of support services, often for only a single student. Whether this is economical or efficient remains a matter of some debate (e.g., Francis, Koch, Wyatt, & Niparko, 1999). More important for the present purposes is the issue of whether regular schools and teachers, in particular, fully recognize the strengths and needs of deaf students. Herman (Chapter 9 in this volume) points out that "[o]ne consequence of earlier diagnosis and better amplification is that deaf children are increasingly placed in the mainstream [where] clear speech and competent conversational skills ... effectively mask more subtle underlying problems with language comprehension" and impede learning.

Seemingly in contrast to arguments for special education settings for DHH students, a review of more than 20 years of relevant literature by Stinson and Kluwin (2011) showed that only between 1% and 5% of the variance in DHH students' academic achievement could be attributed to school placement. They suggested that 20% to 25% of the total variance in achievement could be attributed to a priori differences among DHH students (e.g., disability status) and that as much as 75% of the unexplained variance could be attributed to instruction factors. More recently, Marschark, Shaver, Nagel, and Newman (in press) examined student, family, communication, and school factors from a nationally representative sample of approximately 500 DHH high school students in the United States, seeking to predict achievement scores in reading, science, mathematics, and social studies. They found that when other factors were controlled, DHH students who attended regular schools, including self-contained classrooms, performed significantly higher across all achievement measures than DHH students who attended only special schools or who had attended both regular and special schools at some point. Consistent with Stinson and Kluwin's review, educational factors, including the type of school attended, accounted for between 1% and 7% added variance beyond the contributions of demographic/disability and hearing/communication factors.

In summary, DHH learners represent a changing population (Archbold, Chapter 2 in this volume) enrolled in changing school environments (Knoors & Marschark, Chapter 1 in this volume). Despite this diversity, or perhaps because of it, the evidence shows that school placement *does* make a statistically significant and independent difference in the academic outcomes of DHH learners, even if it is not large. The true size of that effect is still unclear, but it is real. But, of course, it's complicated. First, regardless of school setting, DHH students typically perform below the levels of their hearing peers (Antia, Chapter 23 in this volume; Marschark et al., in press). The extent to which the observed differing levels of academic performance across settings is the cause (i.e., due to a priori student characteristics) or the result of the placement itself remains unclear, and it is probably some of each. Second, one cannot separate, at least at present, teaching and instruction variables from the school setting. Special schools and programs for DHH students not only occur in different places with smaller classes and perhaps with more appropriate support services and technologies, but they typically include full-time teachers who have been trained specifically to work with DHH students. At the same time, smaller, specialized programs lack the resources to be able to provide for advanced placement and other upper-level courses, one of the best predictors of postsecondary school academic persistence and success. On the other side of the education fence, mainstream teachers, even if they have taken a course in special education, rarely are fully aware of the knowledge, strategies, strengths, and weaknesses of the occasional DHH students who show up in their classes. We know that classroom support from a sign language interpreter, real-time text ("captioning"), or even an itinerant (peripatetic) teacher of the deaf is not sufficient to compensate for being unprepared for school in classes with hearing peers. Beyond academic content, as De Klerk, Fortgens, and Van der Eijk (Chapter 25 in this volume) and Leigh and Crowe (Chapter 4 in this volume) argue, teachers have to be open to diversity and acknowledge the different cultural and practical aspects of deafness. Such openness can be supported by professional development programs (Gervedink Nijhuis & Terpstra, Chapter 22 in this volume), but it also takes a special kind of person.

Finally, let us consider one more type of school placement, co-enrollment. Co-enrollment classrooms, typically placed in regular schools, seek to avoid both the academic segregation of DHH students and their integration into classes with hearing students without appropriate support services or modification of instructional methods and materials. Rather, co-enrollment seeks to give DHH learners the best of both educational worlds by offering both signed and spoken instruction from two teachers (often one of them deaf) and a critical mass of DHH peers (preferably at least 25%, but see Tang, Lam, & Yiu, 2014). The advantages of co-enrollment classrooms thus far largely have been confined to social-emotional functioning (e.g., Yiu & Tang, 2014) and language (e.g., Peréz Martin, Valmaseda, & Martin, 2014; Tang, Lam, & Yiu, Chapter 6 in this volume). They may yet yield significant influences on academic outcomes, but evidence in that regard is just beginning to emerge (Hermans, De Klerk, Wauters, & Knoors, 2014). Outcome data for a Dutch co-enrollment project involving a mainstream primary school where the hearing students achieve well above average national standards still showed significant gaps in reading comprehension, spelling, and mathematics scores between DHH students and their hearing classmates over a five-year period. DHH students scored below their hearing peers overall; the gap was greatest in reading comprehension, less so in spelling and mathematics (Hermans et al., 2014; see Kreimeyer, Crooke, Drye, Egbert, & Klein, 2000; McCain & Antia, 2005). Still, some DHH students performed remarkably well. Depending on the grade, between 22% and 39% of the DHH students scored in the two highest (out of five) levels of achievement on the mathematics assessment. Percentages varied from 16.8% to 30.3% for spelling and from 0% to 12.7% for reading comprehension.

Still to be determined is whether identifying the materials and methods of successful teachers of the deaf will allow their transfer to mainstream teachers in a way that permits DHH students in regular schools to learn as much as hearing peers, acknowledging different starting points and continued gaps in performance relative to hearing peers (Marschark, Sapere, Convertino, & Pelz, 2008). Ultimately, the goal is to determine how we can close those gaps. If decades of underachievement despite new philosophies, methodologies, and educational models tell us anything, they say that sometimes we just need to reach for a spoon.

Parents and Families

We know that approximately 95% of deaf children come from hearing families. Hearing parents of those children most often have no experience with or even exposure to deaf individuals, sign language, CIs, or schools for the deaf. Zaidman-Zait (Chapter 15 in this volume) pointed out that the evidence base clearly shows that "stress among either parents or children is not a direct outcome of child deafness, but rather, stems from differences in the context, child experiences, parent and child characteristics, coping resources, and school and community supports" (see also Gregory, Bishop, & Sheldon, 1995). Bruin (Chapter 5 in this volume) emphasized the importance of soliciting, understanding, and incorporating parents' perspectives in early intervention if we want to empower them and have them be active partners in the programming. Swanwick (Chapter 26 in this volume) added that such involvement helps parents as well as their DHH children adapt to their new situation, giving them control and a better understanding of their children's needs. Indeed, a deaf child changes the dynamics of the whole family.

From the outset, a deaf child's language development, cognitive development, and social development are cumulative, interacting among themselves and with a variety of environmental and contextual factors. Whether children are born deaf or lose all or some of their hearing at later points, their interactions inside and outside the family are going to differ from those of hearing siblings and age-mates. Moreover, given the new social, audiological, medical, and linguistic contingencies facing them and their parents, the cumulative, interactive nature of early development usually will lead to greater individual differences early on and those differences widening at a faster rate than is typical for hearing children.

We know that parents' involvement in their children's language development, learning, and education is perhaps the best predictor of their educational outcomes. The evidence base with regard to the development of hearing children shows that the amount of language that parents use with their children predicts vocabulary development (Hart & Risley, 1995), shared parent–child reading leads to greater reading comprehension skills during the school years (Whitehurst & Lonigan, 1998), and parents' taking on active roles in curricular and co-curricular school activities is strongly associated with academic outcomes (Houtenville & Conway, 2008). Although there is less direct evidence with regard to DHH children, we assume that all of these are also true for them and their parents (e.g., DesJardin & Ambrose, 2010; DesJardin et al., 2014; Dirks & Wauters, Chapter 18 in this volume).

Knowing how best to engage with their DHH children and their children's schools is sometimes a struggle for parents, as they have to make a variety of decisions that they do not have to make for their hearing children. Yet, Leigh and Crowe (Chapter 4 in this volume) emphasized that "[h]ow and when parents make decisions about language use with their DHH children is a relatively unexplored area," and decision making about amplification, school placement, and participation in activities outside of school similarly remain to be elaborated. Organizations supporting families with deaf children, particularly those involving parent-to-parent contact, can be helpful, but there apparently are no metrics available with regard to their impact on parental stress and satisfaction or children's developmental or educational outcomes. Most of those organizations (at least in the United States) are focused on emphasizing a particular communication modality for DHH children, whether or not that is an explicit statement or litmus test for membership.

Dirks and Wauters (Chapter 18 in this volume) and Zaidman-Zait (Chapter 15 in this volume), among others, have noted that the lack of a shared language between deaf children and their hearing parents may impede informal, educational opportunities as well as opportunities to engage with their children's schools. In part, this situation arises simply because there may be less discussion in the home about what is happening (or not) in school. Communication barriers—both lack of discussion and misunderstanding—also result from DHH children and their parents' holding somewhat different ideas of how those children are doing in school, particularly with regard to social-emotional functioning and friendships (Marschark et al., 2012). Dirks and Wauters suggested that deaf children might need or at least benefit from additional support in the home to obtain the same literacy skills as hearing peers; Kritzer (2008) found a similar need with regard to mathematics skills; and Pagliaro (Chapter 8 in this volume) described how such findings link parent–child communication and the acquisition of mathematics skills. She pointed out that parents of DHH children who are relatively low in mathematics ability have been found not to extend and enhance informal communication about everyday activities but rather tend to give short, limited answers to children's questions. By their parents' not elaborating and using quantity-, comparative-, or magnitude-related terms, those children do not have as much opportunity to place core mathematics concepts in richer contexts. The issue thus becomes one of how professionals, educators, and researchers can best inform and empower parents to promote their child's emergent academic skills (Calderon & Greenberg, 2011; Lukomski, 2002).

The most direct means of informing and empowering parents of DHH children is through early intervention programming (Moeller, Carr, Seaver, Stredler-Brown, & Holzinger, 2013). Such programming may emphasize a particular communication modality (e.g., Brown & Nott, 2006; Young, 1997) or be more neutral (e.g., Sass-Lehrer, 2011), but the key is to be family centered rather than focusing solely on the DHH child (Bruin, Chapter 5 in this volume). Moeller and colleagues (2013) provided an international consensus statement on family-centered early intervention, emphasizing that such programming should be evidence based and sensitive and respectful to different preferences, choices, and families. On the basis of existing research, they described comprehensive guidelines for family-centered intervention. Perhaps what was most notable was that the guidelines were accompanied by the listing of more than 150 pertinent research articles, reviews, and position statements. In other words, we *know* these principles are important to effectively supporting young DHH children and their families. Also noteworthy is the fact that none of the guidelines mentioned a particular communication modality but implicitly emphasized that such decisions have to be made by the family after receiving full, objective information.[1]

Research conducted during the 1980s and 1990s found that, on average, DHH children whose early intervention programming involved sign language demonstrated better academic, linguistic, and social functioning than those who relied exclusively on spoken language (see Calderon & Greenberg, 1997, for a review). The proliferation of digital hearing aids and CIs presumably has changed that situation. However, the added complexities (and differences of perspective) associated with age of implantation, the extent and quality of sign language exposure, and the frequent combination of CI use and sign language are such that there does not yet appear to be a current, definitive evidence base with regard to language and communication alternatives during early intervention (but see the next section). More importantly, despite more than 40 years having passed in the "early intervention movement," we still do not know about the long-term impact of such programming on academic outcomes, whatever its approach. As Bruin (Chapter 5 in this volume) argued, we need more long-term studies addressing changing family perspectives (and teacher perspectives; see De Klerk et al., Chapter 25 in this volume; Gervedink Nijhuis & Terpstra, Chapter 22 in this volume) on language and education to ensure that support services in this technological era change to meet the families' changing needs. These are not one-time decisions (e.g., Watson, Hardie, Archbold, & Wheeler, 2007). Such studies would benefit greatly from interdisciplinary cross-talk rather than being limited to the research area of one or two investigators. Only then can we be sure that we are providing young DHH children with the tools they need to be lifelong learners and leave school with the knowledge and skills they need to function in today's society. That is going to require a lot of people reaching for spoons, and it is unclear if we are ready for that (Swanwick & Marschark, 2010).

Language

One can find published research to support almost any position on the language of instruction for DHH learners. In part, this situation and the resulting confusion derive from the general issues alluded to earlier: The language question is a very complex and multifaceted issue (see Caselli et al., Chapter 19 in this volume), there are variety of perspectives from different quarters on the rationale and goals of alternative language approaches (Tang et al., Chapter 6 in this volume), and there are differing interpretations of the available evidence (Knoors & Marschark, 2012). Because the focus of this volume is on education, developmental and linguistic issues associated with language and deaf learners essentially will be ignored in this chapter. As Swanwick (Chapter 26 in this volume) noted, "issues of learning can become separated or omitted from discussions around language in deaf education, sometimes inhibiting fruitful transactions between research and practice." The goal here is to encourage such fruitful transactions. With that educational focus in mind, let us describe what seem like the three most well-established things we know about language in (formally and informally) educating deaf learners.

First is the practical issue raised by Swanwick (Chapter 26 in this volume) that if we are going to optimize the academic (and personal) outcomes of deaf learners, we need to recognize the increasingly plural use of signed and spoken languages in their daily lives. As noted earlier, CIs and digital hearing aids, as well as improved speech-language and educational methods, have created a situation in which (better) spoken language is now available to many more deaf children than ever before. Swanwick and colleagues (2014) described the waning of interest in bilingual education in the United Kingdom and Scandinavian countries, the latter being in many ways the birthplace of bilingual deaf education in the 1980s. They attributed this shift in policy and practice, to a large extent, to the marginalization of spoken language within bilingual programs, leading to "pushback" from parents. Marschark and Lee (2014) argued further that the evidence for bilingual deaf education, per se, contributing to better academic outcomes for deaf learners is thin to nonexistent, an issue to be addressed later.

Whether one mode of communication or another might be better or in some sense easier for teaching/learning particular kinds of material for DHH learners is an empirical question that remains to be explored. Bauman and Murray (2010), for example, suggested that a sign language-fluent biology professor could describe the splitting of chromosomes and cell wall division in mitosis using sign language classifiers in a way that would enhance deaf students' understanding. Dowaliby and Lang (1999), however, found that offering a sign language version of a description of the working of the human eye did not enhance deaf students' learning over reading a text version. In a number of studies, Marschark and his colleagues (e.g., Borgna, Convertino, Marschark, Morrison, & Rizzolo, 2011; Marschark et al., 2006) also failed to find an expected advantage of sign language over reading in deaf students' learning in STEM content areas or even in content more familiar to deaf than hearing students. Clearly, more research is needed, but it's complicated (and culturally sensitive; see Leigh & Crowe, Chapter 4 in this volume).

A second well-established finding concerning language and learning pertains to reading comprehension. As noted earlier, at least by secondary school, deaf learners who rely on spoken language have been found to read better than those who rely on sign language (e.g., Geers, 2002), even when CI use is controlled (Marschark et al., in press). There are several caveats associated with this finding because, as already noted, it's complicated. One is the finding mentioned earlier from Calderon and Greenberg's (1997) review that deaf children in preschool programs that included sign language demonstrated better early literacy skills than those in programs exclusively using spoken language. Likely explanations for this apparent contradiction rest in the changing population of deaf children or differences between emergent and later literacy (see Archbold, Chapter 2 in this volume; Dirks & Wauters, Chapter 18 in this volume). The second complicating finding is that although primary school children who are using spoken language by virtue of having received CIs have been found to be reading at grade level, they fall behind hearing peers, on average, by the time they are in secondary school (e.g., Geers, Tobey, Moog, & Brenner, 2008; Marschark et al., in press). Possible explanations for this situation include that we have not yet learned how best to educate deaf children with CIs (Marschark, Sarchet, Rhoten, & Zupan, 2010); the fact that reading materials at the secondary school level are more complex and abstract and require far more world knowledge than those at the primary school level (Archbold, Chapter 2 in this volume); and, again, that the heterogeneity among deaf children leaves us with no simple solutions to their academic needs—that we just need to get a spoon.

Meanwhile, there also is research showing that early sign language skills are associated with better reading comprehension (e.g., Lange,

Lane-Outlaw, Lange, & Sherwood, 2013; Padden & Ramsey, 2000; Strong & Prinz, 2000). This finding, too, has its caveats, including the extent to which the children in those studies have been representative of the larger population of deaf learners (Lange et al., 2013) and whether it was the use of sign language or some other mediating factor that explains the relation (Hermans, Knoors, Ormel, & Verhoeven, 2008). And therein lies the finding of real importance: The issue is not so much language modality as early and consistent access to language, whatever its form. Whether we are talking about having deaf parents or CIs, intensive speech and hearing intervention, or immersion in a sign language setting, when it comes to language, more and earlier is always going to be better. Yet, the emotional arguments associated with exclusive views of the necessity of one language modality or another are such that we continue to argue about soup and forks.

A third well-established finding with regard to language in educating deaf learners is that whichever modality or modalities they might be using, it apparently is not sufficient to provide them with all of the academic knowledge and tools possessed by their hearing peers. This is neither an easy nor a simple claim to make. From an optimistic perspective, the statement can be read as saying simply that deaf children are not hearing children who can't hear, and thus to achieve academic outcomes comparable to hearing peers they need more than *just* the access to sign language or spoken language currently possible in the real world (Knoors & Marschark, 2012; Marschark & Knoors, 2012; cf. Humphries et al., 2014). Here, again, the issues of complexity and identifying the challenges/questions that so often result in underachievement come into play.

Setting aside for the moment (as researchers often do) the large minority of perhaps 40% of deaf children who have physiologically-based challenges associated with the etiologies of their hearing losses, there well may be specific, academically-related language challenges, as well as others associated with language learning itself, that result from significant hearing loss. This is not just a matter of the frequently-cited suggestion that because deaf children cannot passively overhear the conversations of others (a situation not resolved by sign language immersion, which requires active visual attention); they also show lags in the acquisition of Theory of Mind, executive functioning, age-appropriate social-emotional functioning, and world knowledge (see, all in this volume, De Raeve, Chapter 24; Hermans, Vugs, van Berkel-van Hoof, & Knoors, Chapter 9; Morgan, Chapter 12). Convertino, Borgna, Marschark, and Durkin (2014) found that deaf college students' greater ability to overhear others via CIs was not associated with either vocabulary or knowledge of the world significantly greater than peers without CIs. Neither age of implantation nor the length of CI use predicted word or world knowledge. Meanwhile, numerous studies in both education and cognitive psychology have shown that simultaneous auditory and visual presentation of information leads to better learning and memory than presentation in either modality alone (e.g., Goolkasian & Fools, 2005; Mayer & Morena, 1998; Paivio, 1986). The integration of the two forms by hearing infants also may carry advantages later with regard to relational processing in language, problem solving, and executive functioning (see Bahrick & Lickliter, 2000; Hermans et al., Chapter 11 in this volume; Marschark & Wauters, 2011).

The foregoing should not be taken to imply that deaf learners are doomed to academic mediocrity. The point is that neither spoken language skill (e.g., among those with CIs, see Archbold, Chapter 2 in this volume; De Raeve, Chapter 24 in this volume) nor sign language (e.g., among those in bilingual programs, see Tang et al., Chapter 6 in this volume; Tijsseling, Chapter 3 in this volume) should be taken to mean that those learners do not need any other, specific cognitive-academic interventions. Easterbrooks and Maiorana-Basas (Chapter 7 in this volume) pointed out that "DHH children have fewer experiences with words and do not overlearn their meanings through conversations with others," and thus there is less automaticity in learning new words from old. Archbold (Chapter 2 in this volume), Herman (Chapter 9 in this volume), and Morgan (Chapter 12 in this volume) all noted that the demonstration of competent conversational skills by deaf children may mask more subtle underlying problems with language comprehension, social functioning, and learning. And this is not just an issue for parents and teachers. Antia (Chapter 23 in this volume) described the deaf learners in the mainstream classrooms she studied as, on average, reporting that they almost always understand the language of teachers and classmates. The evidence base, however, shows that DHH students regularly overestimate their comprehension of through-the-air communication (e.g., Borgna et al., 2011) as well as print (e.g., Banner & Wang, 2011; Kelly, Albertini, & Shannon, 2001) to a greater extent than hearing students. This means that a nod of the head should not be taken as confirmation that a deaf learner understands a statement; both student and teacher/parent will benefit from frequent comprehension checking (e.g., "Explain what I just said in different words") and questioning (Dowaliby & Lang, 1999). Cawthon (Chapter 10 in this volume) made a similar point in noting that deaf learners would rather take tests in their preferred mode of communication and may be "more engaged and less stressed about performing up to their potential when the language of the test is the same as the language of instruction." But that does not mean that mean that they necessarily are correct in the belief that they will do better. Cultural sensitivity aside (in deference to academic success), what matters is the reality, not the perception.

So, what can we do about it? Leigh and Crowe (Chapter 4 in this volume) raised the issue of the need for cross-cultural work in this area. Working across multiple languages admittedly is difficult, but there are cross-cultural differences in perspectives on education, disability, and language use that enter into (and complicate) the language-education mix for deaf learners. While there currently are a number of international efforts to explore the linguistics of various sign languages, and research in deaf education is happening in a number of countries, possible interactions of language and academic outcomes are rare and appear largely to be limited to English-speaking countries and the Netherlands.

Another front for language action, evident in several (mainly Dutch-authored) chapters of this volume, is technology. Knoors and Marschark (2014, p. 195) suggested that "[t]he possible contributions of multimedia-enhanced instruction and practice to learning by deaf children and adolescents are an exciting development in deaf education that appear to hold considerable promise," including the availability and accessibility of signed and spoken/written languages, in parallel. Chapters in this volume by Knoors and Marschark (Chapter 1), Caselli and colleagues (Chapter 19), Cawthon (Chapter 10), Dirks and Wauters (Chapter 18), Hermans and colleagues (Chapter 11), and Segers and Verhoeven (Chapter 21) all have looked to the future of computer-based accommodations for information and test delivery, teaching, and self-teaching tools. Several of those authors tied such tools to reducing unnecessary cognitive load and offering deaf learners augmented materials that could build on their strengths and accommodate their unique needs. Preliminary reports reported in those chapters are encouraging, but much more needs to be done. Meanwhile, the horizon does look bright for technology to be able to adjust to the individual differences among deaf learners through student control, parent/teacher control, or self-adapting systems (e.g., Di Mascio et al., 2012). Such tools would be invaluable in regular schools, in schools and programs designed for DHH learners, and for home use. At present, unlike arguing about soup and forks, technology appears at the threshold of significantly improving academic achievement and outcomes for DHH learners across a variety of formal and informal settings. While waiting for the future, we turn to what we know about academic achievement and outcomes in this population.

Academic Outcomes in Deaf Education: A Never-Ending Struggle?

Academic underachievement among DHH students has been documented in a variety of countries (e.g., Bagga-Gupta, 2004; Hendar, 2009, 2012 cited in Swanwick et al., 2014; Hermans et al. , 2014; Powers, 1999, 2003; Qi & Mitchell, 2012; Thoutenhoofd, 2006). There are occasional claims that the locus of that situation (read: "blame") lies in school placement and language policies by oppressive or ignorant school systems (e.g., Bauman & Murray, 2010; Lane, 1992), but those claims do not have evidence to support them. Indeed, as noted earlier, school placement appears to have a relatively small, if significant, impact on DHH students' academic achievement (and not in the direction hoped for by Bauman and Murray or Lane). Complicating that issue is the fact that most conclusions about DHH students' academic challenges, at least in the United States, are based on data from the Gallaudet Annual Survey, which involves a sample weighted heavily toward schools for the deaf. Recent U.S. research based on nationally representative samples of primary school children, the Special Education Elementary Longitudinal Study (www.seels.net), and secondary school students, the National Longitudinal Transition Study 2 (NLTS2; www.NLTS2.org), show that DHH students have rather better academic outcomes than are suggested by Annual Survey data (e.g., Blackorby, Knokey, Wagner, Levine, Schiller, & Sumi, 2007; Marschark et al., in press). NLTS2 data also show that secondary school DHH students who speak better also read better, although there may be a mutual benefit between those two variables. This is one of those points where a spoon is very much needed, and two potential spoons, in particular, will be considered here: bilingual education and CIs.

Bilingual Deaf Education and Academic Achievement

At an intuitive level, bilingual education for deaf learners seems an obvious route to facilitating academic outcomes. If they are to succeed academically, in employment, and in daily living, deaf learners clearly are going to need facility in the written, if not the spoken, vernacular of their home country or region. Rather than sign language necessarily interfering with the acquisition of spoken language, there is now evidence that, at least in some cases, early sign language can provide a foundation for later learning of spoken language for children with or without CIs (e.g., Giezen, Baker, & Escudero, 2014; Yoshinaga-Itano & Sedey, 2000). However, the theoretical and practical paths from sign language to literacy remain obscure and confounded (Mayer & Akamatsu, 1999). The broader impact of sign language on academic learning is even less clear. There is little doubt that the 100 years of oral education placed on the shoulders of deaf children left most of them linguistically and academically disadvantaged (Lang, 2011). While an emotional response to that history is understandable, the question at issue here is whether the empirical case has been made for bilingual deaf education leading to better academic outcomes.

This discussion is not about bilingualism in language development (a topic for another time and place) or even what language or language modality might be best for educating particular subgroups of deaf students, a topic superficially considered in the previous section. It also is not about the impact of bilingual education on nonacademic domains such as social-emotional functioning, cognition, or various aspects of linguistic competence. These domains and others have been considered at length in a variety of research articles and the chapters of the 2014 book by Marschark, Tang, and Knoors, *Bilingualism and Bilingual Deaf Education*. In the context of this volume the issue is whether bilingual education has a significant impact on deaf students' academic outcomes (see also Marschark & Lee, 2014).[2]

Ormel and Giezen (2014) and Marschark and Lee (2014) described ways in which bilingualism could affect the language and cognitive abilities of DHH children and, in turn, might affect academic outcomes. At least among hearing children with approximately equal facility in their two (or more) languages, bilingualism has been found to be associated with greater verbal and nonverbal IQ scores and problem-solving skills, attention, executive functioning, and working memory. In a study involving deaf children in programs using either Sign Language of the Netherlands or Sign Supported Dutch, Hermans, Knoors, Ormel, and Verhoeven (2008) found that written words were more easily learned when children already knew the signs for the concepts. Ormel and Giezen suggested that such cross-linguistic activation might help to avoid one of the cognitive disadvantages of spoken language (unimodal) bilingualism, the slower retrieval of information from long-term memory. However, the empirical question remains.

Studies explicitly examining relations among bilingualism, related cognitive effects, and academic achievement are just beginning. Tang and colleagues (Chapter 6 in this volume) stated that in their co-enrollment program, Hong Kong Sign Language is crucial for the deaf children's comprehension of teachers' presentations, explanations, and clarifications, and when supplemented with manually coded Chinese it is effective for supporting some specific reading and other pedagogical activities.[3] Empirical evidence in that regard and, most importantly, evidence concerning the long-term impact of two languages in the co-enrollment classroom remain to be provided. Antia and Metz (2014) emphasized use of the regular curriculum and the high academic expectations of students in co-enrollment classrooms, as well as their teachers and parents, all of which were expected to enhance academic outcomes. Kreimeyer and colleagues (2000) reported mixed, if early, results from one program, as co-enrolled students did as well as or better than DHH norms on reading and mathematics achievement tests but were still below grade level. A follow-up study by McCain and Antia (2005) showed that although the DHH students gained academically from the co-enrollment program, the achievement gap between them and their hearing classmates remained (Hermans et al., 2014).

In summary, for all of the research into the cognitive, linguistic, and neurobiological aspects of sign language and bimodal bilingualism, there remains little evidence for a direct impact of sign bilingualism on DHH students' achievement (Caselli et al., Chapter 19 in this volume; Tang et al., Chapter 6 in this volume). It may be that it is still too early in our understanding of how to teach bilingually to take advantage of the benefits of the two modalities while avoiding potential pitfalls (De Klerk et al., Chapter 25 in this volume; Gervedink Nijhuis & Terpstra, Chapter 22 in this volume). Whatever its cause(s), if we are going to establish a global evidence base relevant to teaching deaf students, the question of whether bilingual deaf education leads to better educational outcomes is obviously a central one. Even if better sign language skills are correlated with better reading abilities, there are too many confounds in the existing research to know yet whether it is the bilingual programming or some other factor(s) that mediates that relation (see Mayer & Akamatsu, 1999; Mayer & Leigh, 2010).

Cochlear Implants and Academic Achievement

We noted earlier that there is evidence that CIs enhance the early reading comprehension abilities of young deaf children, but evidence with regard to long-term outcomes is unclear. In fact, results to date for secondary and postsecondary students have largely yielded null results (e.g., Convertino et al., 2014; Convertino, Marschark, Sapere, Sarchet, & Zupan, 2009; Harris & Terlektsi, 2010; Marschark et al., in press; Thoutenhoofd, 2006). But, as with other issues addressed thus far, the situation is not quite that simple. Among other complicating factors are wide variability in spoken language outcomes following pediatric implantation (e.g., Niparko et al., 2010) and the use of sign language by many deaf learners, before and/or after implantation (e.g., De Raeve, Chapter 24 in this volume; Spencer, Gantz, & Knutson, 2004). Archbold (Chapter 2 in this volume) questioned whether the early encouraging results with regard to reading among children with CIs will continue as they move into adolescence, "with the more demanding and subtle skills required to achieve age-appropriate reading levels (e.g., inferencing)." As noted earlier, Geers and colleagues (2008) found that CI recipients who had been reading at grade level when they were eight to nine years old had fallen an average of two years behind hearing peers seven years later. However, many of those children had received their CIs relatively late by current standards. Yet the sample studied by Spencer and colleagues (2004), in apparently the only study to find secondary school CI users reading at grade level, had received their CIs even later on average. Confounding those findings, however, the students with CIs also had support from a sign language interpreter throughout their school years.

Archbold and colleagues (2008) found a significant relation between age of implantation and reading ability seven years after implantation among children who had received their CIs between one and seven years of age. However, even among the children who had received their CIs between one and three years of age, over 40% were reading at least one year behind grade level. Similar findings were reported by Thoutenhoofd (2006) with regard to mathematics. The hope has been that we will see even better outcomes from the cohort of children who receive CIs earliest, at around one year of age. There appears little benefit to spoken language development among children who receive CIs in their first year compared to those who receive them in their second year (Duchesne, in press), but long-term implications for other domains remain to be explored. At the same time, we need to expand consideration of educationally relevant variables beyond those related to hearing, speech, and language modalities (i.e., soup and forks). Morgan (Chapter 12 in this volume), for example, alluded to the interaction with cognitive abilities, pointing out that CIs may support enhanced language comprehension in quiet classrooms, but "as conversation partners, ambient noise, and distances between speakers increase more complex pragmatic skills may be required for academic learning."

In short, simple correlations between CI-related variables and academic achievement are unlikely to give a full understanding of the complex interplay of hearing, language, and learning. CIs clearly influence children's cognitive, social, and linguistic interactions in the world in many ways that also will influence academic outcomes (Marschark et al., 2010). The interactive, cumulative nature of development in various domains is such that focusing solely on age of implantation, the language of instruction/socialization, and reading will be insufficient to fully close the achievement gap if for no other reason than children with CIs do not hear everything that hearing children hear. Given the large, and largely unexplained, individual differences in spoken language outcomes following implantation, the establishment of a global evidence base in this domain is going to require greater interdisciplinary cooperation and less internecine argument. That's right, we need more spoons.

Social-Emotional Functioning

It is interesting to note that although investigators and commentators in North America frequently talk about social and emotional functioning among deaf learners, they conduct relatively few relevant investigations beyond asking about peer relations in different school settings. The vast majority of studies concerning social-emotional functioning among deaf children has come from Europe (but see Yiu & Tang, 2014). Within North America, there was a widespread belief in the 1990s that CIs would leave deaf children "stuck" between deaf and hearing worlds and members of neither. As far as one can tell, that never came to pass. Bat-Chava and Deignan (2001) found that CIs improved social interactions with hearing peers, at least for those children who had better speech and hearing outcomes. Knutson, Boyd, Reid, Mayne, and Fetrow (1997) and Jambor and Elliot (2005), however, found that CIs rarely provided children with sufficient speech and hearing to achieve full social acceptance with hearing peers. But were those children any less socially integrated than deaf peers without CIs? In the 1990s, deaf children in U.S. regular schools reported feeling lonely and isolated more than their peers in special programs (e.g., Capelli, Daniels, Durieux-Smith, McGrath, & Neuss, 1995; Mertens, 1989; Stinson & Antia, 1999; Stinson, Whitmire, & Kluwin, 1996). It is unclear whether that situation has persisted now that over 85% of DHH learners are in regular school programs for all or part of the school day.

Knoors and Marschark (2014, Chapter 7) described a strong evidence base showing a broad impact of hearing children's social-emotional functioning on academic performance. They described the parallel, emerging evidence base with regard to deaf children. Internationally, as reflected in the chapters of this volume, there has been increasing concern about the social-emotional functioning of deaf learners, relationships with teachers, and how these might affect achievement in school (e.g., Hermans et al., 2014; Wauters & Knoors, 2008; Wolters, Knoors, Cillessen, & Verhoeven, 2011). A review by Batten, Oakes, and Alexander (2013) echoed the findings from studies involving children with CIs, concluding that while there is a strong link between communication/language abilities and peer social interactions, the link between social interaction and academic outcomes is rather tenuous. Wolters and Isarin (Chapter 14 in this volume), however, noted that, as was the case with language and reading outcomes, young deaf children might do quite well on the social front using relatively simple language, "but early adolescents need to be equipped with much more complex language to function in social interactions with peers. Communication with hearing peers not only requires (speech) perception and production, but also the ability to participate actively and incidentally, whether in spoken or signed language." Morgan (Chapter 12 in this volume) went farther, arguing that successful language comprehension in the classroom and the ability to assimilate new information relies on "an intertwined set of cognitive and social skills." He therefore suggested that "[t]he take-home message is for professionals to devote time in the school to social-cognitive as well as speech and language interventions."

Going beyond the classroom, if ultimately feeding back into it, Herman (Chapter 9 in this volume) noted that poor interpersonal communication skills are associated with greater emotional and behavioral difficulties in childhood and, eventually, more mental health problems as adults. Tijsseling (Chapter 3 in this volume) and Wolters and Isarin (Chapter 14 in this volume) thus argued that we need studies examining deaf learners' empowerment, not simply viewing them as victims of societal barriers. Wiefferink and colleagues (Chapter 20 in this volume) similarly emphasized the importance of children recognizing and understanding their own emotions in order to have healthy social-emotional development, although they also are intimately tied to executive function and Theory of Mind (Morgan, Chapter 12 in this volume). Other investigators have emphasized successful social-emotional functioning in various contexts as important to mental health. Hintermair (2014, and Chapter 13 in this volume) noted that social relationships can provide emotional stability that serves as a protective factor in development, and Rieffe, Netten, Broekhof, and Veiga (Chapter 16 in this volume) argued that such protective factors may be more important to deaf individuals, who are more likely at risk than hearing individuals. Fellinger and Holzinger (Chapter 17 in this volume) and Wiefferink and colleagues (Chapter 20 in this volume) even provided examples of how research outcomes in this area can be applied to intervention programs addressing social functioning, emotional stability, and mental health to create real change.

Still to be determined are how the complex factors associated with deaf learners' home and peer interactions interact with their social-emotional stability and academic performance. No doubt these will be mediated by language and cognitive factors. Such studies thus will require interdisciplinary cooperation and, because of the large individual differences among deaf learners, collaboration across age groups, academic settings, and even countries. The return on such an investment would be significant, clarifying some of the frequently misinterpreted findings related to school placement, communication modality, and predictors of academic achievement and filling in gaps that remain—as well as some we have not yet even discovered.

Cognition and Learning

Numerous studies have examined aspects of cognitive functioning among DHH children and adults. Early studies were aimed at understanding the relation of language and thought (i.e., which comes first), frequently on the assumption that deaf individuals had no language. Over the past 50 years, with recognition of sign languages as true languages, with advances in cognitive psychology, and now with the advent of CIs, cognitive investigators have been interested in the performance of DHH children and adults, with and without CIs, in a variety of verbal (signed, spoken, or print) and nonverbal tasks. These have included concept learning, short-term and working memory, long-term memory, visual-spatial functioning, attention (see Marschark & Wauters, 2011, for a review), and, more recently, executive functioning (e.g., Hermans et al., Chapter 11 in this volume; Ormel & Geizen, 2014) and Theory of Mind (e.g., Morgan, Chapter 12 in this volume). Noticeably absent from all except the most recent work have been ways in which such cognitive abilities among DHH individuals affect (formal and informal) learning and academic outcomes. De Raeve (Chapter 24 in this volume), however, pointed out that "Success at capturing information in the classroom and assimilating it into learning relies on an intertwined set of language, cognitive and social skills. These include joint attention, working memory, executive function, Theory of Mind, and pragmatics."

To a large extent, the history of research concerning cognition among deaf individuals has found delays and/or deficits relative to hearing peers in tasks involving both verbal and nonverbal materials. A number of relevant studies now can be seen to be biased against DHH individuals by virtue of language demands or world knowledge, although such factors still influence cognitive functioning and learning (see Knoors & Marschark, 2014, Chapter 6, and Maller & Braden, 2011, for reviews). Inconsistent and contradictory findings in other studies have now been clarified by consideration of subgroups of DHH individuals (e.g., native signers, CI users) and more carefully crafted experimental designs. For example, recent research has demonstrated several domains of visual-spatial functioning in which deaf individuals, or at least those who use sign language, seem to have memory and mental manipulation abilities comparable to or even superior to hearing individuals (e.g., Wilson, Bettger, Niculae, & Klima, 1997; see Marschark & Wauters, 2011, for a review). Although deaf adults and children frequently score lower on recall tasks than hearing peers, we now know that working memory capacities in deaf and hearing populations are essentially the same (Boutla, Supalla, Newport, & Bavelier, 2004). Deaf individuals also demonstrate better visual-spatial memory than verbal memory and, in some tasks, demonstrate better visual-spatial memory than hearing nonsigners (Hall & Bavelier, 2010; Wilson et al., 1997).

Hermans and colleagues (Chapter 11 in this volume) and Pagliaro (Chapter 8 in this volume) describe several ways in which DHH children's visual-spatial skills can support learning and even surpass their hearing age-mates. Pagliaro, for example, noted that while understanding of number is generally assumed to be a critical skill for hearing preschoolers, deaf preschoolers show greater understanding of concepts related to geometry and space rather than number. Zarfety, Nunes, and Bryant's (2004) finding that deaf preschoolers could remember and reproduce spatial arrays better than hearing peers led Pagliaro to suggest "that for DHH learners, the geometry concepts and skills are developed sooner and/or more quickly than those of other areas, perhaps influenced by their visual access to information." Other studies involving mathematics, in contrast, have found that DHH students may fail to use the visual-spatial processing that is assumed to be their strength. Blatto-Vallee, Kelly, Gaustad, Porter, and Fonzi (2007), for example, found that hearing students outperformed DHH students on visual-spatial tasks involving mental paper folding and puzzle assembly. The DHH students, in middle school through college, also were less likely than hearing peers to use visual-spatial processing to represent conceptual aspects of mathematics problems. Instead, the DHH students took diagrams essentially as pictures, without appreciating or at least using the quantitative and conceptual relations depicted to help with problem solution. Pagliaro (Chapter 8 in this volume) suggested that in such situations, "Subsequent instruction, then, might focus on explaining the concept at the concrete and pictorial levels, thereby building in the student a deeper, comprehensive, *conceptual* understanding."

Marschark, Morrison, Lukomski, Borgna, and Convertino (2013) replicated the results of Blatto-Vallee and colleagues, finding hearing college students to equal or surpass the performance of DHH students on seven standardized visual-spatial tasks (see also Cockcroft & Dhana-Dullabh, 2013). They also found that DHH students' scores on the visual-spatial tasks were more strongly related to performance on mathematics problems involving diagrams than were those of the hearing students, suggesting that the two groups might have been bringing different cognitive abilities to bear on the problems. Most generally, Marschark and colleagues argued that there is no evidence that DHH students are either more likely to be "visual learners" than verbal learners or more likely than hearing students to be visual learners. Such comparisons would be of both practical and theoretical interest but remain to be done using appropriate instruments. Meanwhile, it is important to note that these findings with regard to both memory and visual-spatial processing reflect more than visual-spatial abilities; in particular, performance on such tasks also involves executive functioning, a domain in which DHH children frequently demonstrate lags relative to hearing peers (e.g., Beer, Kronenberger, & Pisoni, 2011; Hintermair, 2013; Kronenberger, Colson, Henning, & Pisoni, 2014).

Executive function is considered the highest level of cognition, controlling lower-level cognitive activities such as attention, inhibition, learning, and memory. The executive functions of metacognition and behavioral regulation are two areas that have been of particular interest with regard to DHH children insofar as DHH students through college age have been found to have difficulties in these domains (e.g., in monitoring their language comprehension, using prior knowledge in problem solving, and social-emotional functioning) (Borgna et al., 2011; Hintermair, 2013; Morgan, Chapter 12 in this volume). DHH students' not using the representational properties of mathematics diagrams in the study by Blatto-Vallee and colleagues is another example.

Apparent cognitive challenges of DHH learners notwithstanding, Marschark (2000) and colleagues have argued that deaf children are not just hearing children who can't hear, and that cognitive differences between the two may not be indicative of deficits. With the increasing emphasis on inclusive education, those differences may get in the way of teaching in regular classrooms, and the greater heterogeneity in cognitive skills among DHH learners can create challenges even in schools and programs for the deaf. At the same time, Marschark and colleagues (2008) showed that when taught by skilled teachers of the deaf, DHH students can learn as much as hearing peers in the same classroom. Because we know that DHH learners typically come into the classroom with less content knowledge than their hearing peers, this only means that the DHH students learn proportionally the same amount as hearing classmates, given their own starting points. Their learning trajectory may be the same as their hearing peers in such situations, but targeted interventions appear to be necessary if they are to catch up. This means that teachers (and parents) first will have to know the ways in which DHH children are different from hearing children. Then, we should be able to adjust instructional materials and methods appropriately (Marschark & Knoors, 2012; see Herman, Chapter 9 in this volume, and Hintermair, Chapter 13 in this volume).

WHERE DO WE GO FROM HERE?

The preceding discussion provided a brief overview of some of what we know and what we need to know about educating deaf learners in several domains. Because of the complexity of the issues involved as well as differing views on what the significant questions are and what the existing data say about them, it is not expected that everyone will agree with the "knowns" and "unknowns" described. That's okay. The point is that rather than arguing about them—about soup and forks—this chapter and this book are intended to be calls for action, for finding and sharing spoons.

Unlike other research-oriented volumes, at least in deaf education, this one includes contributors who are parents and teachers of deaf children as well as researchers involved in deaf education, including a number of individuals who fit into more than one of those categories. All understand the challenges we face, even if we do not always agree on the solutions. By the same token, the larger field of deaf education and the even larger field of general education now dealing with the majority of DHH students both recognize the need for change. At present, however, our evidence base is limited, and at least partly as a result, the directions we need to move for change remain unclear, at least to some of us. It was recognition of this unacceptable situation that led to this volume in the first place as one step in creating an agenda for interdisciplinary cooperation in establishing a global evidence base in deaf education.

Of course, there already is a huge literature on virtually every aspect of educating deaf children. As Knoors and Marschark (Chapter 1 in this volume) argued, our goals, therefore, need to include not only the generation of new data but also the organization and making some sense out of what we already have. This will require the replication of previous studies with new subpopulations of DHH learners who use various modes of communication in various settings. It will require international replications and multicenter studies across countries to determine which findings are related directly to being deaf, which follow from specific local or national contexts/factors, and where interactions occur between the two. And it will require literature reviews that are not selective and intended to support one point of view or another but that aim to explain seemingly contradictory or ambiguous results from existing studies. All of this likely will reveal flaws in methodology or interpretation in some previous studies, overlooked but revealing findings from others, and important questions that we never thought to ask. That's okay too. This is the nature of science; this is the nature of progress. The key is to keep moving forward.

NOTES

1 Yoshinaga-Itano (2014) provided guidelines for early intervention from the Joint Committee on Infant Hearing in the United States that make recommendations with regard to both sign language and spoken language.

2 Issues associated with bilingual-bicultural deaf education programming, and the bicultural aspect in particular, are beyond the scope of this discussion but are considered by L eigh and Crowe (Chapter 4 in this volume) and Marschark and Lee (2014).

3 See Marschark and Lee (2014) regarding the use of simultaneous speech and sign in the classroom.

REFERENCES

Antia, S., & Metz, K. K. (2014). Co-enrollment in the United States: A critical analysis of benefits and challenges. In M. Marschark, G. Tang, & H. Knoors (Eds.), *Bilingualism and bilingual deaf education* (pp. 424–441). New York: Oxford University Press.

Archbold, S. M., Harris, M., O'Donoghue, G. M., Nikolopoulos, T. P., White, A., & Richmond, H. L. (2008). Reading abilities after cochlear implantation: The effect of age at implantation on outcomes at five on seven years after implantation. *International Journal of Pediatric Otorhinolaryngology*, *72*, 1471–1478.

Bagga-Gupta, S. (2004). *Literacies and deaf education: A theoretical analysis of the international and Swedish literature*. Stockholm: The Swedish National Agency for School Improvement.

Bahrick, L. E., & Lickliter, R. (2000). Intersensory redundancy guides attentional selectivity and perceptual learning in infancy. *Developmental Psychology*, *36*, 190–201.

Banner, A., & Wang, Y. (2011). An analysis of the reading strategies used by adult and student deaf readers *Journal of Deaf Studies Education, 16*, 2–23.
Bat-Chava, Y., & Deignan, E. (2001). Peer relationships of children with cochlear implants. *Journal of Deaf Studies and Deaf Education, 6*, 186–199.
Batten, G., Oakes, P. M., & Alexander, T. (2014). Factors associated with social interactions between deaf children and their hearing peers: A systematic literature review. *Journal of Deaf Studies and Deaf Education, 19*, 285-302.
Bauman, H.-D., & Murray, J. J. (2010). Deaf studies in the twenty-first century: "Deaf-gain" and the future of human diversity. In M. Marschark & P. Spencer (Eds.), *The Oxford handbook of deaf studies, language, and education* (Vol. 2, pp. 210–225). New York: Oxford University Press.
Beer, J., Kronenberger, W. G., & Pisoni, D. B. (2011). Executive function in everyday life: Implications for young cochlear implant users. *Cochlear Implants International Supplement, 12*, S89–S91.
Blackorby, J., Knokey, A.-M., Wagner, M., Levine, P., Schiller, E., & Sumi, C. (2007). *What makes a difference? Influences on outcomes for students with disabilities*. Menlo Park, CA: SRI International.
Blatto-Vallee, Kelly, R., Gaustad, M., Porter, J., & Fonzi, J. (2007). Visual-spatial representation in mathematical problem solving by deaf and hearing students. *Journal of Deaf Studies and Deaf Education, 12*, 432–448.
Borgna, G., Convertino, C., Marschark, M., Morrison, C., & Rizzolo, K. (2011). Enhancing deaf students' learning from sign language and text: Metacognition, modality, and the effectiveness of content scaffolding. *Journal of Deaf Studies and Deaf Education, 16*, 79–100.
Boutla, M., Supalla, T., Newport, E. L., & Bavelier, D. (2004). Short-term memory span: Insights from sign language. *Nature Neuroscience, 7*, 997–1002.
Brown, P. M., & Nott, P. (2006). Family-centered practice in early intervention for oral language development: Philosophy, methods, and results. In P. E. Spencer & M. Marschark (Eds.), *Advances in the spoken language development of deaf and hard-of-hearing children* (pp. 136–165). New York: Oxford University Press.
Calderon, R., & Greenberg, M. (1997). The effectiveness of early intervention for deaf children and children with hearing loss. In M. J. Guralnik (Ed.), *The effectiveness of early intervention* (pp. 455–482). Baltimore, MD: Paul H. Brookes.
Calderon, R., & Greenberg, M. (2011). Social and emotional development of deaf children: Family, school, and program effects. In M. Marschark & P. Spencer (Eds.), *The Oxford handbook of deaf studies, language, and education* (Vol. 1, 2nd ed., pp. 188–199). New York: Oxford University Press.
Cappelli, M., Daniels, T., Durieux-Smith, A., McGrath, P. J., & Neuss, D. (1995). Social development of children with hearing impairments who are integrated into general education classrooms. *Volta Review, 97*, 197–208.
Cockcroft, K., & Dhana-Dullabh, H. (2013). Deaf children and children with ADHD in the inclusive classroom: working memory matters. *International Journal of Inclusive Education, 17*, 1023–1039.
Convertino, C. M., Borgna, G., Marschark, M., & Durkin, A. (2014). Word and world knowledge among deaf students with and without cochlear implants. *Journal of Deaf Studies and Deaf Education, 19*, 471–483.
Convertino, C. M., Marschark, M., Sapere, P., Sarchet, T., & Zupan, M. (2009). Predicting academic success among deaf college students. *Journal of Deaf Studies and Deaf Education, 14*, 324–343.

DesJardin, J. L., & Ambrose, S. E. (2010). The importance of the home literacy environment for developing literacy skills in young children who are deaf or hard of hearing. *Young Exceptional Children, 13*, 28–44.

DesJardin, J. L., Doll, E. R., Stika, C. J., Eisenberg, L. S., Johnson, K. J., Ganguly, D. H., . . . & Henning, S. C. (2014). Parental support for language development during joint book reading for young children with hearing loss. *Communication Disorders Quarterly, 35*(3), 167–181.

Di Mascio, T., Vittorini, P., Gennari, R., Melonio, A., De la Prieta, F., & Alrifai, M. (2012). The learners' user classes in the TERENCE adaptive learning system. *Proceedings of the 12th IEEE International Conference on Advanced Learning Technologies* (pp. 572–576). Taiwan: IEEE.

Dowaliby, F., & Lang, H. (1999). Adjunct aids in instructional prose: A multimedia study with deaf college students. *Journal of Deaf Studies and Deaf Education, 4*, 270–282.

Duchesne, L. (in press). Language abilities following early cochlear implantation. In M. Marschark & P. E. Spencer (Eds.), *The Oxford handbook of deaf studies in language: Research, policy, and practice*. New York: Oxford University Press.

Easterbrooks, S., & Stephenson, B. (2006). An examination of twenty literacy, science, and mathematics practices used to educate students who are deaf or hard of hearing. *American Annals of the Deaf, 151*, 385–399.

Francis, H., Koch, M., Wyatt, R., & Niparko, J. (1999). Trends in educational placement and cost-benefit considerations in children with cochlear implants. *Archives of Otolaryngology Head and Neck Surgery, 125*, 499–505 [see erratum in *Archives of Otolaryngology Head and Neck Surgery, 126*, 1088].

Gallaudet Research Institute. (April 2011). *Regional and National Summary Report of Data from the 2009-10 Annual Survey of Deaf and Hard of Hearing Children and Youth*. Washington, DC: GRI, Gallaudet University.

Geers, A. (2002). Factors affecting the development of speech, language, and literacy in children with early cochlear implantation. *Language, Speech, and Hearing Services in Schools, 33*, 172–183.

Geers, A., Tobey, E., Moog, J., & Brenner, C. (2008). Long-term outcomes of cochlear implantation in the preschool years: From elementary grades to high school. *International Journal of Audiology, 47*(Suppl. 2), S21–S30.

Giezen, M., Baker, A., & Escudero, P. (2014). Relationships between spoken word and sign processing in deaf children with cochlear implants. *Journal of Deaf Studies and Deaf, 19*, 107–125.

Goolkasian, P., & Foos, P.W. (2005). Bimodal format effects in working memory. *American Journal of Psychology, 118*, 61–78.

Gregory, S., Bishop, J., & Sheldon, L., (1995). *Deaf young people and their families*. Cambridge: Cambridge University Press.

Hall, M. L., & Bavelier, D. (2010). Working memory, deafness, and sign language. In M. Marschark & P. E. Spencer, *The Oxford handbook of deaf studies, language, and education* (Vol. 2, pp. 458–471). New York: Oxford University Press.

Harris, M., & Terlektsi, E. (2010). Reading and spelling abilities of deaf adolescents with cochlear implants and hearing aids. *Journal of Deaf Studies and Deaf Education 16*, 24–34.

Hart, B., & Risley, T. R. (1995). *Meaningful differences in the everyday experience of young American children*. Baltimore, MD: P. H. Brookes.

Hendar, O. (2009). *Goal fulfillment in school for the deaf and hearing impaired.* Härnösand, Sweden: The National Agency for Special Needs Education and Schools.

Hendar, O. (2012). *Elever med hørselshemming i skolen. En kartleggingsundersøkelse om læringsutbytte [Pupils with hearing impairment in school. A study on learning outcomes].* Skådalen Publication series No. 32. Oslo: The Research and Development Unit, Skådalen Resource Centre.

Hermans, D., De Klerk, A., Wauters, L., & Knoors, H. (2014). The Twinschool: A co-enrollment program in the Netherlands. In H. Knoors & M. Marschark (Eds.), *Educating deaf learners: Creating a global evidence base* (pp. 396–423). New York, NY: Oxford University Press.

Hermans, D., Knoors, H., Ormel, E., & Verhoeven, L. (2008). The relationship between the reading and signing skills of deaf children in bilingual education programs. *Journal of Deaf Studies and Deaf Education, 13,* 518–530.

Hintermair, M. (2013). Executive functions and behavioral problems in deaf and hard-of-hearing students at general and special schools. *Journal of Deaf Studies and Deaf Education, 18,* 344–359.

Houtenville, A. J., & Conway, K. S. (2008). Parental effort, school resources, and student achievement. *Journal of Human Resources, 43,* 437–445.

Humphries, T., Kushalnagar, P., Mathur, G., Napoli, D.J., Padden, C., Rathmann, C. & Smith, C.R. (2012). Language acquisition for deaf children: Reducing the harms of zero tolerance to the use of alternative approaches. *Harm Reduction Journal, 2012,* 9–16.

Jambor, E., & Elliott, M. (2005). Self-esteem and coping strategies among deaf students. *Journal of Deaf Studies and Deaf Education, 10,* 63–81.

Kelly, R. R., Albertini, J. A., & Shannon, N. B. (2001). Deaf college students' reading comprehension and strategy use. *American Annals of the Deaf, 146,* 385–400.

Knoors, H., & Marschark, M. (2012). Language planning for the 21st century: Revisiting bilingual language policy for deaf children. *Journal of Deaf Studies and Deaf Education, 17,* 291–305.

Knoors, H., & Marschark, M. (2014). *Teaching deaf learners: Psychological and developmental foundations.* New York: Oxford University Press.

Knutson, J. R., Boyd, R. C., Reid, J. B., Mayne, R., & Fetrow, R. (1997). Observational assessments of the interaction of implant recipients with family and peers: Preliminary findings. *Otolaryngology-Head and Neck Surgery, 117,* 196–207.

Kreimeyer, K. H., Crooke, P., Drye, C., Egbert, V., & Klein, B. (2000). Academic and social benefits of a coenrollment model of inclusive education for deaf and hard-of-hearing children. *Journal of Deaf Studies and Deaf Education, 5,* 174–185.

Kritzer, K. (2008). Family mediation of mathematically based concepts while engaged in a problem-solving activity with their young deaf children. *Journal of Deaf Studies and Deaf Education, 13,* 503–517.

Kronenberger, W. G., Colson, B. G., Henning, S. C., & Pisoni, D. B. (2014). Executive functioning and speech-language skills following long-term use of cochlear implants. *Journal of Deaf Studies and Deaf Education, 19,* 456–470.

Lane, H. L. (1992). *The mask of benevolence: Disabling the deaf community.* New York: Knopf.

Lang, H. (2011). Perspectives on the history of deaf education. In M. Marschark & P. Spencer (Eds.), *The Oxford handbook of deaf studies, language, and education* (Vol. 1, 2nd ed., pp. 7–17). New York: Oxford University Press.

Lange, C. M., Lane-Outlaw, S., Lange, W. E., & Sherwood, D. L. (2013). American Sign Language/English bilingual model: A longitudinal study of academic growth. *Journal of Deaf Studies and Deaf Education, 18*, 532–544.

Lukomski, J. A. (2002). Best practices in program planning for children who are deaf and hard-of-hearing. In A. Thomas & J. Grimes (Eds.), *Best practices in school psychology IV* (Vol. 2, pp. 1393–1403). Bethesda, MD: National Association of School Psychologists.

Maller, S. J., & Braden, J. P. (2011). Intellectual assessment of deaf people: A critical review of core concepts and issues. In M. Marschark & P. Spencer (Eds.), *The Oxford handbook of deaf studies, language, and education* (Vol. 2, pp. 473–485). New York: Oxford University Press.

Marschark, M. (July, 2000). *Understanding language and cognition among deaf learners*. Presentation to the International Symposium on Mental Health: Deaf Children and Youths, Sydney, Australia.

Marschark, M., Bull, R., Sapere, P., Nordmann, E., Skene, W., Lukomski, J., & Lumsden, S. (2012). Do you see what I see? School perspectives of deaf children, hearing children, and their parents. *European Journal of Special Needs Education, 14*, 483–497.

Marschark, M., & Knoors, H. (2012). Educating deaf children: Language, cognition, and learning. *Deafness and Education International, 14*, 137–161.

Marschark, M., & Lee, C. (2014). Navigating two languages in the classroom: Goals, evidence, and outcomes. In M. Marschark, G. Tang, & H. Knoors (Eds.), *Bilingualism and bilingual deaf education* (pp. 211–241). New York: Oxford University Press.

Marschark, M., Leigh, G., Sapere, P., Burnham, D., Convertino, C., Stinson, M., . . . & Noble, W. (2006). Benefits of sign language interpreting and text alternatives to classroom learning by deaf students. *Journal of Deaf Studies and Deaf Education, 11*, 421–437.

Marschark, M., Morrison, C., Lukomski, J., Borgna, G., & Convertino, C. (2013). Are deaf students visual learners? *Learning and Individual Differences, 25*, 156–162.

Marschark, M., Sapere, P., Convertino, C. M., & Pelz, J. (2008). Learning via direct and mediated instruction by deaf students. *Journal of Deaf Studies and Deaf Education, 13*, 446–461.

Marschark, M., Sarchet, T., Rhoten, C., & Zupan, M. (2010). Will cochlear implants close the gap in reading achievement for deaf students? In M. Marschark & P. Spencer (Eds.), *The Oxford handbook of deaf studies, language, and education* (Vol. 2, pp. 127–143). New York: Oxford University Press.

Marschark, M., Shaver, D.M., Nagel, K., & Newman, L. (in press). Predicting the academic achievement of deaf and hard-of-hearing students from individual, household, communication, and educational factors. *Exceptional Children*.

Marschark, M., Tang, G. & Knoors, H. (Eds). (2014). *Bilingualism and bilingual deaf education*. New York: Oxford University Press.

Marschark, M., & Wauters, L. (2011). Cognitive functioning in deaf adults and children. In M. Marschark & P. E. Spencer (Eds.), *The Oxford handbook of deaf studies, language, and education* (Vol. 1, 2nd ed., pp. 486–499). New York: Oxford University Press.

Mayer, C., & Akamatsu, C. T. (1999). Bilingual-bicultural models of literacy education for deaf students: Considering the claims. *Journal of Deaf Studies and Deaf Education, 4*, 1–8.

Mayer, C., & Leigh, G. (2010). The changing context for sign bilingual education programs: Issues in language and the development of literacy. *International Journal of Bilingual Education and Bilingualism, 13*, 175–186.

Mayer, R. E., & Moreno, R. (1998). A split-attention effect in multimedia learning: Evidence for dual processing systems in working memory. *Journal of Educational Psychology, 90*(2), 312–320.

McCain, K., & Antia, S. D. (2005). Academic and social status of hearing, deaf, and hard-of-hearing students participating in a co-enrolled classroom. *Communication Disorders Quarterly, 27*, 20–32.

Mertens, D. (1989). Social experiences of hearing-impaired high school youth. *American Annals of the Deaf, 134*, 15–19.

Moeller, M. P., Carr, G., Seaver, L., Stredler-Brown, A., & Holzinger, D. (2013). Best practices in family-centered early intervention for children who are deaf or hard of hearing: An international consensus statement. *Journal of Deaf Studies and Deaf Education, 18*, 429–445.

Niparko, J. K., Tobey, E. A., Thal, D. J., Eisenberg, L. S., Wang, N.-Y., Quittner, A. L., & Fink, N. E. (2010). Spoken language development in children following cochlear implantation. *Journal of the American Medical Association, 303*(15), 1498–1506.

Ormel, E., & Giezen, M. (2014). Bimodal bilingual cross-language interaction: Pieces of the puzzle. In M. Marschark, G. Tang, & H. Knoors (Eds.). *Bilingualism and bilingual deaf education* (pp. 74–101). New York: Oxford University Press.

Padden, C., & Ramsey, C. (2000). American Sign Language and reading ability in deaf children. In C. Chamberlain, J. Morford, & R. Mayberry (Eds.), *Language acquisition by eye* (pp. 165–189). Mahwah, NJ: Lawrence Erlbaum.

Paivio, A. (1986). *Mental representations: A dual coding approach*. New York: Oxford University Press.

Pérez Martin, M., Valmaseda, M., & Morgan, G. (2014). Sign bilingual and co-enrollment education for children with cochlear implants in Madrid, Spain. In M. Marschark, G. Tang, & H. Knoors (Eds.), *Bilingualism and bilingual deaf education* (pp. 368–395). New York: Oxford University Press.

Powers, S. (1999). The educational attainment of deaf students in mainstream programmes in England: Examination results and influencing factors. *American Annals of the Deaf, 144*, 261–269.

Powers, S. (2003). Influences of student and family factors on academic outcomes of mainstream secondary school students. *Journal of Deaf Studies and Deaf Education, 8*, 57–78.

Qi, S., & Mitchell, R. E. (2012). Large-scale academic achievement testing of deaf and hard-of-hearing students: Past, present, and future. *Journal of Deaf Studies and Deaf Education, 17*, 1–18.

Sass-Lehrer, M. (2011). Early intervention: Birth to three. In M. Marschark & P. Spencer (Eds.), *The Oxford handbook of deaf studies, language, and education* (Vol. 1, 2nd ed., pp. 63–81). New York: Oxford University Press.

Sorkin, D. L. (2013). Cochlear implantation in the world's largest medical device market: Utilization and awareness of cochlear implants in the United States. *Cochlear Implants International, 14*, S1–S12.

Spencer, L. J., Gantz, B. J., & Knutson, J. F. (2004). Outcomes and achievement of students who grew up with access to cochlear implants. *Laryngoscope, 114,* 1576–1581.

Spencer, P. E., & Marschark, M. (2010). *Evidence-based practice in educating deaf and hard-of-hearing students.* New York: Oxford University Press.

Stinson, M., & Antia, S. (1999). Considerations in educating deaf and hard-of-hearing students in inclusive settings. *Journal of Deaf Studies and Deaf Education, 4,* 163–175.

Stinson, M. S., & Kluwin, T. N. (2011). Educational consequences of alternative school placements. In M. Marschark & P. Spencer (Eds.), *The Oxford handbook of deaf studies, language, and education* (Vol. 1, 2nd ed., pp. 47–62). New York: Oxford University Press.

Stinson, M., Whitmire, K., & Kluwin, T. (1996). Self-perceptions of social relationships in hearing-impaired adolescents. *Journal of Educational Psychology, 88,* 132–143.

Strong, M., & Prinz, P. (2000). Is American Sign Language skill related to English literacy? In C. Chamberlain, J. Morford, & R. Mayberry (Eds.), *Language acquisition by eye* (pp. 131–141). Mahwah, NJ: Lawrence Erlbaum.

Swanwick, R., Hendar, O., Dammeyer, J., Kristoffersen, A.-E., Salter, J., & Simonsen, E. (2014). Shifting contexts and practices in sign bilingual education in northern Europe: Implications for professional development and training. In M. Marschark, G. Tang, & H. Knoors (Eds.), *Bilingualism and bilingual deaf education* (pp. 292–310). New York: Oxford University Press.

Swanwick, R., & Marschark, M. (2010). Enhancing education for deaf children: Research into practice and back again. *Deafness and Education International, 12,* 217–235.

Tang, G., Lam, S., & Yiu, K. C. (2014). Language development of deaf children in a sign bilingual and co-enrollment environment. In M. Marschark, G. Tang, & H. Knoors (Eds.), *Bilingualism and bilingual deaf education* (pp. 313–341). New York: Oxford University Press.

Thoutenhoofd, E. (2006). Cochlear Implanted pupils in Scottish schools: 4-year school attainment data (2000–2004). *Journal of Deaf Studies and Deaf Education, 11,* 171–188.

Watson, L., Hardie, T., Archbold, S., & Wheeler, A. (2007). Parents' views on changing communication after cochlear implantation. *Journal of Deaf Studies and Deaf Education, 13,* 104–116.

Wauters, L., & Knoors, H. (2008). Social integration of deaf children in inclusive settings. *Journal of Deaf Studies and Deaf Education, 13,* 21–36.

Whitehurst, G. J., & Lonigan, C. J. (1998). Child development and emergent literacy. *Child Development, 69,* 848–872.

Wilson, M., Bettger, J. G., Niculae, I., & Klima, E. S. (1997). Modality of language shapes working memory: Evidence from digit span and spatial span in ASL signers. *Journal of Deaf Studies and Deaf Education, 2,* 150–160.

Wolters, N., Knoors, H. E. T., Cillessen, A. H. N., & Verhoeven, L. (2011). Predicting acceptance and popularity in early adolescence as a function of hearing status, gender, and educational setting. *Research in Developmental Disabilities, 32,* 2553–2565.

Yiu, K.-M., & Tang, G. (2014). Social integration of deaf and hard-of-hearing children in a sign bilingual and co-enrollment environment. In M. Marschark,

G. Tang, & H. Knoors (Eds.), *Bilingualism and bilingual deaf education* (pp. 342–367). New York: Oxford University Press.

Yoshinaga-Itano, C. (2014). Principles and guidelines for early intervention after confirmation that a child is deaf or hard of hearing. *Journal of Deaf Studies and Deaf Education, 19*, 429–445.

Yoshinaga-Itano, C., & Sedey, A. (2000). Speech development of deaf and hard-of-hearing children in early childhood: Interrelationships with language and hearing. *Volta Review, 100*, 181–212.

Young, A. M. (1997). Conceptualizing parents' sign language use in bilingual early intervention. *Journal of Deaf Studies and Deaf Education, 2*, 264–276.

Zarfaty, Y., Nunes, T., & Bryant, P. (2004). The performance of young deaf children in spatial and temporal number tasks. *Journal of Deaf Studies and Deaf Education, 9*, 315–326.

Index